W9-AFS-696

The Foundations of Educational Curriculum and Diversity

1565 to the Present

Joseph Watras
University of Dayton

Allyn and Bacon
Boston ■ London ■ Toronto ■ Sydney ■ Tokyo ■ Singapore

Executive Editor and Publisher: *Stephen D. Dragin*
Editorial Assistant: *Barbara Strickland*
Marketing Manager: *Kathleen Morgan*
Editorial-Production Service: *Omegatype Typography, Inc.*
Composition and Prepress Buyer: *Linda Cox*
Manufacturing Buyer: *Chris Marson*
Cover Administrator: *Kristina Mose-Libon*
Electronic Composition: *Omegatype Typography, Inc.*
Photo Research: *Katharine Cook*

A Pearson Education Company
75 Arlington Street
Boston, MA 02116

Internet: www.ablongman.com

Library of Congress Cataloging-in-Publication Data

Watras, Joseph
The foundations of educational curriculum and diversity, 1565 to the present / Joseph Watras.
p. cm.
Includes bibliographial references (p.) and index.
ISBN 0-321-05400-8
1. Education—United States—Curricula—History. 2. Education—Aims and objectives—United States—History. 3. Multicultural education—United States—History. I. Title.

LB1570. W38 2002
375'.001'0973—dc21

00-140228

Credits
p. 1: North Wind Picture Archives; p. 21: Corbis Digital Stock; p. 51: The Schlesinger Library, Radcliffe Institute, Harvard University; p. 79: North Wind Picture Archives; p. 110: National Archives; p. 145: National Archives; p. 177: AP/Wide World Photos; p. 210: AP/Wide World Photos; p. 241: Library of Congress; p. 270: AP/Wide World Photos; p. 297: UNICEF; p. 327: Pearson Education; p. 359: AP/Wide World Photos.

Printed in the United States of America

10 9 8 7 6 5 4 3 2 1 06 05 04 03 02 01

CONTENTS

Introduction xi

1 Culture, Religion, and Colonial Education: 1565–1776 1

Did Missionaries Adapt Their Instruction to Native American Practices? 2

What Enabled Spanish Catholic Missionaries in the South and the Southwest to Succeed? 3

Did the French Missionaries Introduce New Educational Ideas? 7

Why Did the Dutch Colonists on the Atlantic Seaboard Establish Schools? 8

Did the Puritans Bring a Faith in Education to the Massachusetts Bay Colony? 10

Was Religious Tolerance Taught in Colonial Schools? 12

Did Any Colonies Resist Education? 14

Did Colonial Education Set the Pattern for Twentieth-Century Education? 16

Did Education in the Colonial Period Encourage Assimilation, Integration, or Separation? 18

2 Moral Training, Women's Seminaries, and Leadership in the New Republic: 1776–1830 21

How Could the Republic Be Preserved? 23

Could Education Change People's Morals? 24

Did Franklin Think Schools Could Shape Children's Morals? 26

Franklin Believed That Schools Liberated Students in What Way? 28

How Did Benjamin Rush Think a System of Schools Should Inculcate Correct Virtues in Children? 29

How Did Noah Webster Want to Teach Children the Virtues Needed to Preserve the Republic? 30

Could a Teaching Technique Impart Republican Virtues? 34

Could a System of Schools Select and Train Leaders? 37

Could Students Preserve Their Cultural Perspectives When They Studied the Same Subjects? 39

Were the Classical Languages of Latin and Greek Essential to Higher Education? 41

What Did Men Think Women Should Learn? 45

What Did Women Think Women Should Learn? 46

What Was Wrong with People's Views of Education during the Early National Period? 49

3 Common Schools, Teacher Training, and the Bible: 1830–1860 51

In the 1830s, Why Did Reformers Want to Change Schools? 52

Did the Popular Press Play a Role in the Common School Movement? 57

Did Common School Advocates Improve the Training of Teachers and the Status of Women? 58

Did the Advocates for Common Schools Change the Curricula? 63

How Did Common School Reformers Change the Curriculum for Women? 66

Did Common School Advocates Share an Ideology? 67

Did Common Schools Face Opposition from Religious Groups? 70

Did Common School Advocates Overcome Opposition from Wealthy People and from Poor People? 72

What Happened to the Common School Movement? 75

What Did the Common School Movement Show about Schools and Diversity? 77

4 Reconstruction, Kindergartens, and Religious Schools: 1861–1890 79

What Did Northerners Do to Help the Newly Freed Slaves? 80

Did Education Help African Americans in the South? 82

Did Education Change Southern Society? 84

Did People Want New Forms of School Governance after the U.S. Civil War? 87

Did Educators Think Schools Could Heal the Wounds Caused by the Civil War? 88

Could Textbooks Liberate People? 90

What Role Did Science and Psychology Play in the Development of the Curriculum? 93

Did the Kindergarten Strengthen the Role of Textbooks? 95

Did the Manual Training Movement Challenge Harris's Textbook Method? 98

Why Did Catholics Form Their Own Schools? 102

Did Other Religious Denominations Create Their Own Schools? 106

Could Public Schools Reinforce the Values People Should Share? 107

5 Industrialism, Immigration, and the New Psychology: 1890–1915 110

How Did Educators Want to Consolidate School Curricula? 112

How Did Industrial Progress Change the United States? 114

How Did Journalists Encourage Educational Reform? 116

Was School Governance Improved? 120

How Were Schools Changed to Meet the Needs of the Students? 122

How Did Booker T. Washington Use Industrial Education at Tuskegee Institute? 123

How Successful Was Washington? 125

Did Industrial Education Have to Separate Students? 127

How Did Dewey Use the Ideal of Democracy to Construct a Curriculum? 129

Were Addams's and Dewey's Proposals Appropriate? 132

Did the Efforts to Enhance School Success Encourage Diversified Curricula? 133

How Did Psychologists Encourage the Development of a Diversified Curriculum? 136

Did Studies of the Transfer of Training Weaken the Rationale for the Liberal Studies? 139

Did Diversified Curricula Reinforce Social Biases? 142

6 Science, Sexism, and Theology: 1918–1930 145

Why Did Educators Seek to Reorganize Secondary Education? 147

Did Educators Create Improved Curricula by Analyzing the Activities of Individuals? 149

Did Educators Offer Separate Studies for Women? 150

Did the Home Economics Movement Reinforce Gender Inequalities? 151

Did Business Education Segregate Women? 154

Did Educators Use Science to Reinforce Gender Distinctions? 156

Did the Social Studies Reinforce Social Prejudices? 158

What Was the Source of the Biases in the Social Studies? 160

Did Educators Use Scientific Surveys to Justify Their Own Preconceptions? 162

Was It Beneficial to Separate Children according to Ability Levels? 164

Could Science Liberate Students? 165

Was the Project Method a Good Method of Instruction? 168

Did Catholic Schools Avoid Sexism? 171

Did Science Cause School Curricula to Become Biased? 175

7 The Great Depression, Critical Thinking, and Hispanic and Native Americans: 1930–1940 177

How Did the Depression Affect Schools? 178

Did Teachers Try to Reshape Society? 180

Did Historians Accept the Integrated Social Studies as a Replacement for History? 182

How Did the Depression Influence Historians? 184

What Methods of Curriculum Planning Did Historians Recommend? 186

How Did Other Historians React to the *Charter for the Social Studies*? 188

How Did Historians and Social Studies Teachers React to the CEEB Report? 189

Did Educators Think the Reorganization of Schools Would Lead to Social Reform? 190

Did the Interesting Lessons Lead to Social Reform? 192

Did Educators Combine Opposing Theories of Students' Needs? 194

Why Did Planners Want to Include Community Members in Curriculum Planning? 197

Did Organized Curriculum Making Lead to Social Reform? 199

Did Hispanic Education Lead to Social Reform during the Depression? 201

Did the Curriculum for Native Americans Improve during the Depression? 203

How Did the Depression Influence Teachers and the Education of Minorities? 207

8 War, Democracy, and Isolation within Minority Groups: 1940–1954 210

How Did Educators Try to Rebuild Elementary and Secondary Schools after the Depression? 211

How Did the Need for Correct English Affect Chinese Students? 215

How Did Concerns about English Influence Schools in Hawaii? 217

Were Japanese Students Encouraged to Study Their Native Language? 220

Did the Language Question Advance Democracy in Puerto Rico? 222

How Did World War II Influence U.S. Elementary and Secondary Schools? 226

Did the Federal Government Influence Education during World War II More Than It Had during World War I? 229

How Did Educators Want Schools to Serve Democracy after the War? 230

In the 1950s, Did Educators Think It Was Important to Meet the Students' Needs? 232

Did Educators Criticize the Ideal of Meeting the Needs of Youth? 236

Did Educators Try to Serve the Students' Needs or the National Labor Force? 238

9 Desegregation, Academics, and the Comprehensive High School: 1954–1964 241

What Caused School People to Racially Integrate the Schools? 242

What Caused People to Improve the Instruction of Academics? 245

How Did Prominent Scientists Try to Change the Teaching of Science in Elementary and Secondary Schools? 249

How Did Specialists Change Subject Matters Such as Mathematics? 250

How Successful Were the Efforts to Revise the Subject Matters? 253

Could the Structure of a Discipline Capture the Students' Interest? 256

Why Did Educators Turn to James Conant to Resolve Contradictions among Different Educational Aims? 260

Did the High Schools Offer Equal Opportunity? 262

Did the Differentiated Curriculum Increase Opportunities for Different Students? 264

Why Did High Schools Sort Students into Ability Groups? 266

10 The Civil Rights Movement, Christian Day Schools, and Multiculturalism: 1964–1980 270

How Did the Pursuit of Civil Rights Change in the 1960s? 272

What Curricular Changes Enhanced Racial Integration? 273

Was the Effort to Racially Desegregate Schools Successful? 275

Why Was Cross-District Busing for Racial Desegregation of Schools Controversial? 277

Did Minority Groups Resist the Racial Integration of Schools? 279

How Did Christian Day Schools Respond to the Civil Rights Movement? 281

How Did Catholic Schools Respond to the Civil Rights Movement? 282

What Curriculum Models Were Popular in Public and Catholic Schools during Desegregation? 284

Did Magnet Schools Encourage Racial Integration? 285

Did Multicultural Studies Enhance Racial Integration? 287

Did Any Groups Disagree with the Aims or the Methods of Multicultural Education? 289

How Did Educators React to the Complaint That Multicultural Texts Undermined Traditional Values? 290

Was the Kanawha County Dispute a Clash of Cultures? 291

Did Educators Abandon Integration? 293

How Did the Civil Rights Movement Change Educational Aims? 294

11 The Culture of Poverty, Compensatory Curricula, and Federal Funding: 1964–1998 297

Did Urban Schools Face Unique Problems in the 1960s? 299

Was There a Slum Culture? 300

Was the Culture of Poverty a New Phenomenon? 301

How Did the Federal Government Begin the War against Poverty? 302

What Types of Curriculum Innovations Did the ESEA Sponsor? 304

What Was an Example of a Curriculum That Followed an Acceptable Model? 305

Did Classroom Materials Reinforce a Coherent Approach to Compensatory Education? 307

Did Project Head Start Offer a Reasonable Curriculum? 307

Did the Compensatory Education Programs Succeed? 309

Why Did the Programs Fail? 311

Did the Failure of Compensatory Education Influence National Politics? 314

Did New Measures or a Different Label Change the Curriculum? 315

How Did Failure Indicate the Need for Extended Efforts? 316

How Did Reformers Try to Redesign Schools or Districts? 317

Did Anthropologists Think That Poor People Formed Unique Cultures? 319

Were the Anthropologists Wrong? 322

Did Compensatory Education Increase Racial or Social Segregration? 324

12 The Advocates—Feminism and Special Needs: 1964–1998 327

How Did Advocacy Groups for Children with Disabilities Originate? 328

How Did Local Advocacy Groups Advance Special Education? 331

How Did Advocacy Groups Establish Children's Right to an Appropriate Education? 332

How Did Federal Litigation Determine the Process of Planning a Child's Curriculum? 334

What Was the Model of Curriculum Mandated by PL 94-142? 335

How Successful Were the Advocacy Groups for Special Education? 336

How Did Advocacy Groups Encourage the Adoption of Bilingual Education? 337

How Did Advocacy Groups Use the Federal Courts to Support Bilingual Education? 341

Was Bilingual Education Effective? 344

Did Bilingual Education Spread? 345

Why Did Some People Disagree with the Aims of Bilingual Education? 346

Why Were Special Education Advocates More Successful Than Bilingual Education Advocates? 347

How Did Advocates for Women Advance Their Cause? 348

What Kind of Curriculum Offered a Feminine Approach to Morals? 350

What Criticisms Did the Curriculum for Caring Suffer? 351

Was There an Appropriate Method to Teach Women? 352

Did Freire Present an Appropriate Model for Women's Education? 353

Do Women Think Differently Than Men? 354

Did Advocates for Women Seek Separate Schools? 355

What Was the Effect of Advocates' Efforts to Legislate the Curriculum? 356

13 Technology, Diversity, and Iconoclasm: 1980–2000 359

What Pattern of Changes Did Social Critics Find in the Wider Society? 360

How Did the Federal Government Try to Reform Education in the 1980s? 361

Was NCEE Correct in Assuming That Public Schools Failed? 366

Did the Excellence Movement Achieve Its Objectives? 368

Did Competency Tests Improve the Education of Minority Groups? 371

Could Choice Improve Schools? 373

How Did States Allow for Choice in Education? 375

Did the Charter Schools Use Educational Innovations? 376

Did Schools Encourage Freedom and Tolerance? 379

Was the Pursuit of Competence and Freedom Related to the Problems of a Technological Society? 381

Conclusion: What Should School People Do? 384

Appendix 388

Works Cited 390

Index 407

INTRODUCTION

This book is about curriculum and diversity. In general, educators use the word *curriculum* to mean a course of study and the word *diversity* to refer to the different types of students who enroll in a school. However, because these words are popular, they have several different meanings. For example, some curriculum texts refer to things such as the organization of the school, student attendance patterns, schedules, and teaching methods as essential parts of the course of study. In a similar fashion, educators use the word *diversity* to refer to people from different racial or ethnic groups, to students with linguistic differences, or to children from various social classes. In addition, diversity can refer to differences in gender, physical or mental abilities, and sexual orientation among students or faculty. In this text, I use most of these different meanings for *curriculum* and *diversity* in one place or another. However, I trust that the context enables the reader to understand the appropriate definition.

My aim in *The Foundations of Educational Curriculum and Diversity: 1565 to the Present* is to offer a description of the ways that policymakers from the colonial period to the present sought to resolve the conflict between the need for social unity and the desire to preserve minority values. Consequently, the book offers a considerable amount of information about curricula and the effect they have had on different peoples. I have organized this information into patterns that should help students, prospective teachers, and faculty members think more deeply about the role that education plays in the society. In this way, I designed the text for courses or activities that explore the social foundations of education. As a result, I did not try to offer a definitive view of the different ways to construct the curriculum, nor did I offer new information culled from archives about the events that led to certain curricular arrangements.

Social foundations of education is a broadly conceived field of study that combines several academic disciplines such as history, philosophy, economics, and political science. According to the Council of Learned Societies in Education (CLSE), which sets the standards for such instruction, the aim of subjects in the social foundations of education is to help students develop interpretive, normative, and critical perspectives on education (CLSE 7).

Although different, these perspectives complement each other and enable people to understand how schools work and to consider how they should function. Using the interpretive perspective, students analyze the effects of schools in different contexts. With the normative perspective, students consider value orientations as they probe assumptions about schools. Using the normative perspective as the basis of comparison, students employ the critical perspective to develop inquiry skills, identify contradictions, and assess the influence of educational practices. This combination of perspectives is important for educators because they must exercise judgment amidst competing cultural and educational beliefs (CLSE 5–8).

I wrote this text to inculcate in readers the interpretive, normative, and critical perspectives that the CLSE deems essential to foundations courses. To achieve the interpretive perspective, I considered the effects of schools in different parts of the United States

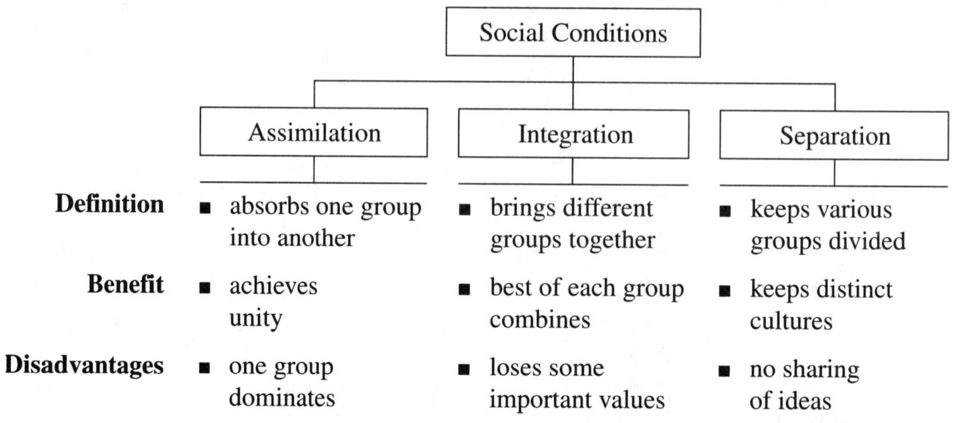

at different times. Seeking to bring about the normative perspective, I considered the value orientations that educators held as they sought to reform schools. Finally, using the normative perspective as the basis of comparison, I sought to enhance the critical perspective by assessing the influence of educational practices.

Social Conditions
Assimilation
Integration
Separation
Definition
absorbs one group into another
brings different groups together
keeps various groups divided
Benefit
achieves unity
best of each group combines
keeps distinct cultures
Disadvantages
one group dominates
loses some important values
no sharing of ideas

Because foundations courses enable educators to think interpretively, normatively, and critically about their profession, they are part of programs to prepare teachers, counselors, and administrators who are accredited by such organizations as the National Council for the Accreditation of Teacher Education (NCATE). The standards for NCATE accreditation state that candidates preparing to work in schools as teachers or other personnel should understand and be able to apply knowledge related to the social, historical, and philosophical foundations of education. Further, the NCATE standards refer to CLSE as the organization that defines the content of those fields.

In this text, I hope to serve the NCATE requirement for studies in the social, historical, and philosophical foundations of education by offering a history of ideas about schooling. This history describes the relationship of those conceptions of education and the type of schooling received by different groups of people. Sometimes, thoughts led to programs. At other times, the social settings made some notions appear more reasonable than others. Although the question of cause and effect is complicated, I want to introduce this text as a history of curriculum that describes the relationship between those ideas and social circumstances. Such a process should satisfy the NCATE requirement to understand and apply the knowledge from the social, historical, and philosophical foundations of education.

At this point, I offer a word of caution. The aim of foundations texts is to examine and evaluate educational plans; social foundations texts that are true to the interpretive, normative, and critical perspectives neither propose nor advance such plans. This fits my personal feelings about what is called multiculturalism. That is, unlike many proponents in the field, I do not believe that any model of curriculum or method of teaching can solve the problems that exist between people. My view is that when any group of people enters a new and already populated land, the members can separate, assimilate, or integrate with the group already present. These same choices exist for people who differ from those considered the majority for other reasons such as gender, social class, or physical abilities. Most important, there are flaws in each alternative. As a result, I do not advocate a particular approach to multiculturalism, nor do I claim that progress in overcoming social difficulties is either possible or essential. Instead, I contend that the best thing people can do is avoid following any idea beyond the point at which it begins to break down. Albert Camus described such an approach in his book *The Rebel,* claiming that reforms should correct one another, and some limit must curb them all (306). My hope is that the search for those limits can grow out of an appreciation of the complexity of life and of schools.

Perhaps it will be clearer why I say that each alternative is flawed if I place separation on one end of a continuum and assimilation on another, with integration in the middle. In the case of separation, the groups keep their distinct cultures and language. However, an isolated group may languish while a neighbor develops improvements in medicine, food production, or transportation. Furthermore, the wealthier group may not enjoy all the progress it could because the members overlook the ways in which the other groups could help. Within the model of separation, progress from the sharing of ideas does not take place. Under assimilation, the same problem appears but in a different way. That is, one group gives up its particular approach to life and takes on the ways of another group. In this case, there is no cross-fertilization of ideas because one group surrenders completely to the other. On the other hand, within integration the best elements of each perspective should mix or combine into a new and better form. In real situations, most frequently some form of integration occurs because total separation or assimilation is almost impossible to achieve. However, integration is not always optimal because even under benign examples of integration some important values are lost in the blending.

The point is that problems facing immigrants, for example, derive from the inability of any minority group to maintain its own identity and at the same time belong to a larger whole. Members of most groups cherish long-standing traditions that gave sense to their lives. However, they see the need for members of a nation to share common understandings. As a result, they often express the ambivalent feelings found in such stories as Anzia Yezierska's "Children of Loneliness."

Many people have believed they could solve the problems inherent in ethnic diversity and differences of social class and occupation. For example, Thomas Jefferson thought that some form of a public school system would help people to maintain their separate communities while teaching them to cooperate in making a strong republic. Jefferson's plan was to have the children from each geographic area receive a state-supported basic education from which the best and brightest males would go on to college training. Assuming that distinct types of groups lived in different regions, Jefferson hoped that some people from each social group would learn to become representatives, senators, or other leaders serving the interests of their communities.

If each option to the problems of diversity has some disadvantage, what is wrong with Jefferson's idea? The problem was that the content of Jefferson's college training—liberal arts—was not as neutral as Jefferson hoped. Andrew Jackson seemed to recognize this bias, fearing that when a person was schooled in the ways of the wealthy and the powerful, that individual would forget the interests of his or her original community. Consequently, Jackson is often quoted as saying that he could not trust a man who knew only one way to spell a word.

At this point, we must take care to avoid two logical fallacies. First, I do not want to imply that since every strategy will fail, teachers can remain ignorant. Instead, my point is that unless people recognize the problems inherent in each view, they will not understand fully the available models. Second, although I think that assimilation, separation, and integration are the only options available, I do not want to force on the reader a false dilemma. That is, I do not want to imply that there are few things people can do. In fact, because people have combined alternatives there are a multitude of curriculum proposals. For example, Booker T. Washington established a separate school to help African Americans learn the values and attitudes of the majority group. Although he advocated a form of accommodation to racism, he implied that it would eventually disappear and that African Americans would assimilate into the wider culture. However, Washington may not have mixed perspectives so much as he expressed what he considered a reasonable approach to the social conditions African Americans faced.

In similar ways, other educators changed their curriculum proposals as the social conditions brought about different styles of thinking. However, no perspective dominated. As a perspective became popular, old ideas blended with new forms, giving rise to a range of conceptions of what was needed in society or in schools. For example, after World War I, the ideal of efficiency seemed to dominate U.S. culture, and some educators argued that it was wasteful not to identify students' abilities in order to place them in appropriate vocational educational programs, even if these placements reflected a bias against women and certain groups of immigrants. At the same time, however, and recalling the ideal of integration, other educators tried to use the social studies to advance underprivileged children by having them investigate problems facing their communities.

My point, again, is that each alternative had a flaw. The efficiency movement with its dependence on the testing of children encouraged the separation of different groups in ways that were artificial and sometimes harmful. Furthermore, in the hands of some educators, such as Thomas Jesse Jones, the social studies movement turned into activities designed to teach students to accept the form of civilization favored by the majority. Again, however, this does not mean that the efficiency movement was concerned only with profit or that the social studies movement sought to destroy various cultures. These are the tendencies in each strategy that must be understood if they are to be controlled.

In addition to my basic interpretation, I would like to point out four important limitations to the text. First, I cover the main types of curricula that are found in most histories of education or collections of documents. Further, I place these models in the time periods when they were most popular, with some description of the prevailing social conditions. Generally, I quote the foremost spokespersons of the curriculum movements, and I try to list the objections made by the major critics. However, I do not offer a detailed survey of the field. Instead, the material provides an overview that should enable students and teachers to think more about the social contexts in which these curricula functioned. From here, they can go on to texts that describe specific curriculum plans in more detail.

Second, although I discuss the ways that educators responded to many different minority groups, I do not cover each minority group that appeared in the United States. In general, I use a minority group when its experiences best illustrate the then-popular views of educators. This leads to some problems. For example, critics may feel that some groups are overrepresented or overlooked. Other critics may feel that the text jumps around from one group to another. The only defense I can make to these criticisms is that I do not offer a complete record. Instead, I hope that the historical examples of how teachers tried to reduce intergroup conflicts will help students develop the interpretative, normative, and evaluative perspectives that the foundations of education should instill.

Third, while many of the problems experienced by minority groups are the result of prejudice, I do not provide any explanation for the sources of such prejudice. Such questions lie in the area of the psychological foundations of education, which, unlike the social foundations, draw on the behavioral sciences (CLSE 5).

Fourth, although I try to place the descriptions of the curricula and their social settings in chronological order, I cannot follow this scheme in all cases. The reader will find the chapters separated into thirteen general periods marked by dates. However, these divisions are flexible. Because the aim is to show how ideas about education change, the discussion in a particular section may cover events that took place before or after the chapter's time frame.

Finally, I would like to offer a brief explanation of the way that I constructed each chapter. The reader will find each chapter to be a complete unit. That is, each chapter has a particular theme that is related to the topic of the book. Generally, each chapter builds on previous chapters and leads to the next. However, each one should make sense if read separately. As a result, if the teacher or a class of students is pressed for time, they need not read everything. The overview in each chapter gives a brief summary of the way that chapter is constructed and the main ideas it presents. As a result, they can select the chapters they wish to pursue by reading the overviews.

In addition, I broke the chapters into short sections introduced by questions. While the questions serve as markers that signal the transition to a different point, I tried not to rely on the questions to make the transitions among the sections. They should reinforce shifts that are integral to the content.

Within chapters, the material should follow the same general pattern. That is, there should be some discussion of the social conditions followed by a description of the popular educational theories and a consideration of the resulting educational practices. However, such divisions are not clearly set apart nor do they always appear, because this order is more logical than realistic. In real life, educators did not survey social conditions, construct theories, and devise practices. Instead, they may have constructed a theory that led to a practical change. And once people tried their ideas, they may have revised their theories, thus leading to another change in practice. Other times they may have tried something and constructed a theory later to explain its success or failure. At any rate, I try to show the close relationships among such categories as social conditions, educational theories, and classroom practices.

It is my hope that the headings or questions will facilitate instruction in courses that use this text. My classes are part of a teacher training program. When I use a book, I prepare lists of such questions in advance for the students. I tell them that I will use the same questions on tests or on essay assignments. Of course, some students spend their time looking for what they think is the right answer. They want to know which facts are important to recall. These students do not develop the interpretative, normative, and evaluative perspectives that are essential for foundations courses. All I can do to reduce this tendency is to ask as many questions as I can that require the students to make difficult choices and to defend them. I hope that the questions in each section of this book give the readers a sense of the material in each section. For students, this organization can become a guide in preparing for class discussions or tests. Above all, I hope readers will see the questions as invitations to analyze the contradictory factors that make up the problems under discussion. In this way, they might engage the subject without being dismayed by descriptions of complex situations.

Acknowledgments

I would like to acknowledge the following reviewers: Donald Blumenfeld-Jones, Arizona State University; Richard Thomas Bothel, Troy State University; Rick Breault, University of Indianapolis; Samuel M. Craver, Virginia Commonwealth University; Roberta L. Derlin, New Mexico State University; Mary Ann Doyle, Loyola University; Amy Gratch, University of South Carolina Aiken; Robert Gustafson, University of Central Florida; Dennis R. Herschbach, University of Maryland; Shane Martin, Loyola Marymount University; B. Edward McClellan, Indiana University; Maike Philipsen, Virginia Commonwealth University; and David B. Ripley, Northern Illinois University.

CHAPTER

1 Culture, Religion, and Colonial Education: 1565–1776

A Spanish mission in California

OVERVIEW

More than other colonial powers, Spanish and French Catholics came to the New World to spread their faith to Native Americans. And the missionaries succeeded when they could fit their process to the religious or spiritual patterns Native Americans followed on their own. Other European groups such as the Dutch and the English used schools to reinforce the spiritual aims of their churches among their own settlers. Thus, schools in the colony of New Netherland reinforced the Dutch Reform Church. The Puritan theocracy in the Massachusetts Bay colony used schools to spread its ideals throughout the community. Pennsylvania schoolmasters taught morality to members of different sects using the Bible. They succeeded because all the sects involved expected their members to base moral decisions on scriptural passages, not on the teachings of church leaders. In Virginia, where the Church of England held sway, people felt little need to set up schools, although they enacted charity schools

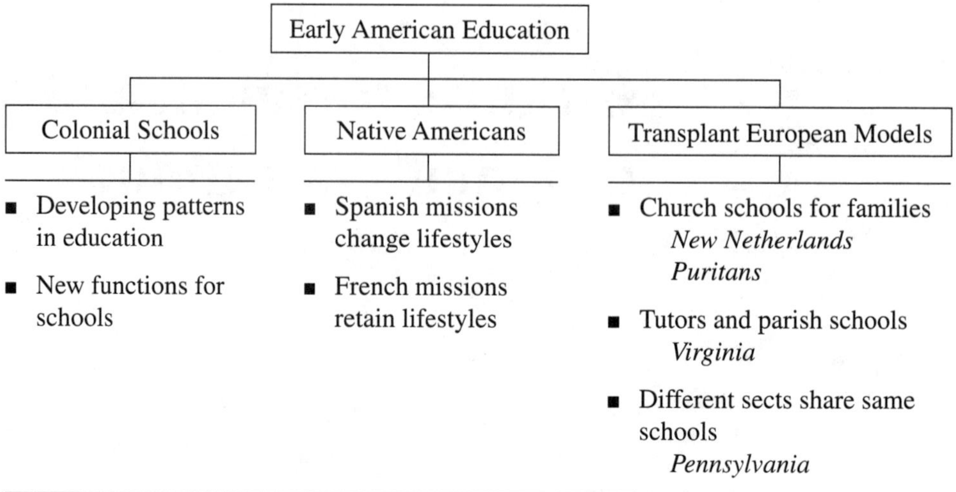

for the poor and engaged in informal efforts such as old field schools for tradespeople. The point is that among the Spanish and French missionaries a process of integration took place that mixed the Christian message with the practices of the Native Americans. Although other colonists tried to use schools to reinforce the ideals held by the family and the church, they could not maintain this effort. As a result of constantly changing situations, the colonists had to accommodate the ideals of other groups. By the nineteenth century, people thought of schools as having distinct purposes such as building a new republic.

Did Missionaries Adapt Their Instruction to Native American Practices?

Scholars who wish to understand the relation between curriculum and diversity might begin by considering the ways in which the encounter between the Europeans and the Native Americans changed both parties. The Native Americans followed an organized culture and used complex methods of raising their children. At the same time, the Europeans possessed a fully developed religion and an advanced technology. As a result, the two societies influenced each other when the colonists tried to transplant their systems from the old world to the new. For example, the Spanish and the French missionaries blended European cultures with those of the Native Americans by turning Native American ways of life toward Christian goals.

Most Native American groups incorporated three processes in their education that coincided with the aims the missionaries strove to achieve. First, before Columbus landed, indigenous peoples in the New World held to complex systems of cosmology and spiritual understandings. They surrounded their children with adults who acted as teachers explaining the traditions and the beliefs of the tribe. Oftentimes, storytelling by cultural leaders served as an important means of communicating to the younger members some explanation of the mysteries of creation, growth, and death. Within most tribes, rites of passage marked the entrance of children into the world of adults and opened opportunities for them to understand the spiritual insights of the older members. Second, the children within most of the tribes participated directly with adults as they hunted game and gathered food. Frequently, adults monitored these activities so that the children immersed themselves slowly in the procedures. In most cases, the children's games re-created many of the adult activities. Taken together, such activities helped these new members of the society understand how the adults provided food and shelter for themselves and their families. Third, the children had to learn to defend the community from attacks by hostile neighboring tribes. In doing all these things, the adults motivated the children by offering them public praise and rewards. They might hold feasts in honor of a child's exploits or they passed stories of triumphs from family to family. At the same time, some tribes subjected the children who failed at various tasks to public ridicule (Urban and Wagoner 3–5).

The Catholic missionaries pursued these three activities using comparable methods, but they directed the Native Americans to accept the faith that the missionaries believed God offered all people as a gift. First, the missionaries learned the languages of the people and constructed ways of communicating the understandings of Christianity through stories and rituals. Second, to attract more converts the missionaries offered improved agricultural techniques that produced more food and other skills that made life more comfortable, such as blacksmithing, spinning, and weaving. Third, the missionaries traveled with military men who defended them and their converts from hostile attacks. If the missionaries traveled alone, they built palisades to offer some protection.

Although the missionaries pursued the same general goals the Native Americans had followed on their own, members of various religious groups used different techniques to fulfill the biblical injunction to spread the good news of the Gospel. For example, the Spanish missionaries in Florida pulled the Native American converts into villages near Spanish settlements. Although the Native Americans mingled with the Spanish, the missionaries exerted spiritual authority over the settlement and the villages but allowed the converts to remain under their own tribal government. On the other hand, the French Catholic missionaries in Maine, New York, and Illinois went into the wilderness, won the converts they could, tried to form distinct villages, and built forts to protect them. In this model, however, the tribes remained separate from the colonies. A third type of arrangement developed when the Spanish missionaries moved into the southwest areas of New Mexico, Texas, and California and adopted a different version of the mission system. Frequently, one or two missionaries, a few converted families of Native Americans, and a soldier took possession of some land and endeavored to draw members of surrounding tribes into the mission. Although the members of different tribes remained in separate sections of the mission governed by their own leaders, they submitted to a new routine that met the spiritual, material, and defensive goals the tribes traditionally pursued (Shea 115–116, 128).

What Enabled Spanish Catholic Missionaries in the South and the Southwest to Succeed?

The Spanish missionary efforts can be divided into two parts. The first took place in the years before 1700 when the missionaries spread through the southern parts of the United States east of the Mississippi River. Those settlements declined after 1700, when Spanish missionaries spread through the area west of the Mississippi and to the south. In these efforts, the missions provided the most effective institution of the Spanish movement. A mission might begin when a missionary, a soldier, and a couple of families of converted Native Americans moved into an area. They built a wall around a chapel, living quarters, wood and metal shops, and garden spaces. Such settlements provided discipline that was religious, moral, social, and industrial. The system succeeded among Native Americans who lived in settled communities, such as the Pueblo of New Mexico. However, the missionaries tended to fail when they worked with tribes that followed more nomadic lifestyles (Bolton 53–54).

The Spanish colonial effort began, at least in part, as a religious exercise. In 1492 the armies of Aragon and Castille drove the last of the Moors from Granada and united the Iberian Peninsula under the Catholic faith. Christopher Columbus took advantage of King Ferdinand and Queen Isabella's desire to spread Catholicism around the world when he petitioned their support for a voyage to what he thought was India. He suggested that one of the reasons he should take the voyage was to convert the native peoples to the Catholic religion. As a result, among the expeditions of soldiers and explorers searching for gold and wealth were missionaries, who came to plant the Christian faith in the hearts of untutored peoples. At times the missionaries went in advance of the soldiers. When a group tried to settle in Florida without armed protection, however, the Native Americans killed them. After this, the missions advanced under the protection of the Spanish military (Ellis 27–33).

Spanish settlement in Florida proved so difficult that in 1561 Philip II forbade colonizing efforts on the peninsula. Nonetheless, in 1565 Pedro Menéndez de Avilés established the first permanent settlement of St. Augustine. Missionary work began in earnest in 1595 when eleven Franciscans arrived in the colony. By 1618 thirty-eight Franciscan missionaries were settled in Florida. They estimated that they converted 26,000 Native Americans to the Catholic faith. In 1661, however, the English in Carolina incited the Westoe tribe to attack the Florida settlements. As a result, more Spanish military had to come to protect them. But the soldiers did more than protect the missions against attacks from the outside. Within the settlements and the missions, the soldiers ensured that renegades did not murder the missionaries, prevented fights, and settled arguments (Ellis 34, 38–41; Bolton 54).

Unfortunately, some of the soldiers who accompanied the missionaries on their evangelistic efforts felt no sympathy for the Native Americans. The soldiers forced them to labor and otherwise degraded them. However, church authorities tried to impose moral and religious discipline on the Spanish citizens and the military. At the urging of Franciscan Cardinal Ximenes, Pope Paul III set out the bull *Sublimis Deus* in 1537 that urged Spanish settlers to recognize Native Americans as free persons open to conversion to Christianity. This meant that Native Americans should not be enslaved, they should be allowed to possess private property, they should mingle with Spanish settlers, and they should receive an education. Following the pope's statement, some Spanish missionaries imposed ecclesiastical penalties on Spaniards who mistreated Native Americans. Charles V pressured the pope to nullify these punishments, however. Thus, although the pope did not enforce his message, he made it clear that Spain's conquest of the New World was an evangelical effort. Spanish church authorities expressed this view by requiring that each mission have its own school and church (Ellis 50–51).

The laws of the Indies enjoined Spanish missionaries to offer religious instruction in the language of the Native Americans. In this way, the missionaries tried to take the place of the traditional storytellers who passed on the spiritual understandings of the tribe. Priests set about learning the native languages and writing catechisms in those languages. As the colonial period progressed, Spanish colleges and seminaries established professorships to teach prospective missionaries those languages. But both teachers and students faced two problems. One was that the Native American languages lacked terms to convey many Christian ideas and meanings. The other was that in some areas, such as around the Rio Grande, the Native Americans spoke more than two hundred dialects. Because this was more than any friar could learn, they offered religious instruction in Spanish through interpreters. Later, as the Native Americans learned Spanish, they offered religious instruction directly. Children learned Spanish quickly, so the missionaries devoted extensive religious instruction to them (Bolton 55–56).

The missionaries were not discouraged when they found that Native Americans lacked a written language. For example, when the Spanish missionaries established in 1598 the first colony of the American Southwest, Real de San Juan, they imported the methods of Brother Peter of Ghent from Mexico. These included a catechism written in a type of hieroglyphics that illiterate Native Americans could understand. In addition, they adapted Native American music and arts to enhance the liturgy. These techniques helped the missionaries meet with such success that by 1616, twenty-five Franciscan friars ministered to around 10,000 Native Americans in eleven missions in New Mexico (Buetow 6–8; Ellis 54).

Most missionaries trained Native Americans to become teachers and clerics. The Jesuits refined this system in southern California. In 1697 they established the main mission at Loreto, which served as a central school. Jesuit teachers in outlying areas selected the most talented Native American boys and brought these gifted children to Loreto, where they learned Spanish, reading, writing, and ecclesiastical singing. The graduates went on to become teachers in Jesuit schools and assistants to the missionaries. In 1767, however, these efforts in California ended when Charles III expelled the Jesuits from all parts of the Spanish empire (Buetow 11–12).

While the religious instruction offered one form of discipline, the liturgies offered another for the Native Americans on the mission. The daily ritual required them to rise at dawn, clean the mission rooms, and celebrate Mass. The missionaries chose two or three Native Americans to usher the people on the mission to the morning Mass. At sunset these Native Americans conducted everyone to the chapel for prayers and devotions. On Sundays they made sure that all men, women, and children dressed properly and attended Mass (Bolton 56).

The missionaries chose Native Americans to lead their followers because they wanted to extend discipline throughout the mission through social means. Spanish authorities required that the missions be self-governing and appoint indigenous people to serve as governors, captains, and council members. Thus, Native Americans controlled Native Americans. Without such mechanisms, two missionaries and three soldiers could not supervise two thousand Native Americans assembled from formerly hostile tribes. Missionaries made self-government easier by bringing approximately three Native American families from old missions to serve as examples for the families of Native Americans who joined the new missions (Bolton 54, 59–61).

At the same time, the Spanish Catholic missionaries used the manual arts to discipline the Native Americans. Within the settlements and the missions, friars taught Native

Americans to grow large and varied crops. From imported trees, they grew figs, quinces, oranges, and peaches. They also raised cattle, sheep, and goats. By 1767, when Fray Gaspar Jose de Solis visited some missions in Texas, he found workshops where Native Americans learned pottery, carpentry, masonry, blacksmithing, and spinning. Women learned spinning, sewing, and cooking. Although these activities uprooted the Native Americans from previous cultural practices, the missionaries in Texas did not boldly impose their culture. The fruitful, secure life they created attracted the Native Americans away from the sparse and often insecure lifestyle of hunting and gathering (Bolton 57–61; Buetow 8–10).

Some Native Americans resisted the missionary training. For example, in New Mexico, although the improved agriculture of the missions brought increased harvests, Native American men had to labor constantly at what they considered to be women's work. They reacted to the constant supervision of friars with armed revolts from 1645 to 1675, but the Spanish military subdued them. In 1680 the Apache joined with other tribes in a successful effort to remove the Spanish presence from New Mexico. The rebels killed more than four hundred Spaniards and many converted Indians, and destroyed the missions. Although the Spanish military ended the revolt by 1697, the Spanish missionary effort never regained its former vigor (Ellis 47–59; Buetow 6–9).

Some nineteenth-century historians argued that the Spanish missionaries introduced Christianity through tyrannical methods. They claimed that the mission friars in the Southwest deprived Native Americans of their rights and liberties in order to introduce them to the benefits of civilization. The historians added that the friars degraded a once noble race of people and turned them from independent beings into a herd of slaves. In 1993 George E. Tinker revived these arguments. Describing the efforts of Junípero Serra, a Spanish Franciscan missionary in California, Tinker argues that the mission system participated in the political and economic conquest of the native peoples, calling it cultural genocide (Shea 116–120; Tinker 67–68). Some historians, however, counter this belief, insisting that the benefits of the missions outweighed the problems. These historians assert that the missions introduced Native Americans to advanced agriculture and many manufacturing techniques. The best proof of their benefits, they add, was the affection the Native Americans expressed toward the friars who ran the missions. Further, Spanish missionaries convinced the Mexican government to give citizenship to the members of the Pueblo nation of New Mexico. Years later, by treaty the Pueblo became citizens of the United States. The advocates for the missionaries claim that the degradation and poverty among Native Americans began after settlers from the United States took away the land from the missions (Shea 116–120).

To some extent, the argument about the effect of the missionaries' efforts unfairly ignores their religious impulses. Although they sought to improve the material lives of the Native Americans, they did not consider the spread of advanced agricultural techniques their ultimate aim. The missionaries centered their concerns on the spiritual gifts they sought to share with the Native Americans. Interestingly, the missionaries may have started a process that later spiritual leaders condemned. In the eighteenth century, missionaries adapted the Christian message to the ways of the Native Americans. As the nineteenth century advanced, American Catholics urged church leaders to adapt the absolute character of Christian teaching to fit the characteristics of a changing time. In 1899, however, Pope Leo XIII condemned this tendency to compromise the truth under what he called Americanism.

Did the French Missionaries Introduce New Educational Ideas?

The French missionaries tried to imitate the Spanish and utilize missions. However, they were unable to do so because the tribes they encountered were more nomadic and because French officials interfered with their spiritual aims. To some extent, they were more successful in educating their own settlers. For example, the Ursuline Sisters from France introduced models of instruction in the education of women that anticipated many innovations popular in the nineteenth century.

When Jacques Cartier returned to France to tell Francis I about the New World, he brought back two Native Americans to show that these people deserved the opportunity to convert to Christianity. The king accepted the idea enthusiastically. Thus, religion joined the economic and political motives that spurred the Catholic nation of France to explore and to claim those lands (Ellis 126).

Whereas Spanish missionaries entered the area of the United States from Mexico and the West Indies, French explorers and missionaries came into what would become Maine, New York, Illinois, and Louisiana from Canada. Although several French religious societies took part in these missionary works, the Jesuits sought to dominate the effort. They wanted to imitate the Spanish method of concentrating the Native Americans into separate villages where they could be free from contamination from traders. Unfortunately, the military commanders of the areas in which the Jesuits worked often looked on these evangelistic endeavors as instruments of their own economic policies. For example, in 1694, when Antoine de la Mothe Cadillac took control of the area around Detroit, he urged that the northern tribes come to live in the settlement, mingle with the French settlers, learn the language, and intermarry. His hope was that a mixed force of Whites and Native Americans could defend the fort against the English, the Iroquois, and the Sioux. However, the Jesuits complained that the French gave the Native Americans brandy and turned the women into prostitutes. As a result, the Jesuits called the commanders and their garrisons the greatest scourge of their missions (Ellis 132, 136, 219–221).

The Black Robes, as the Jesuits were called, went among the Native Americans, often at great peril, and won many people to the Christian faith. Unlike the Spanish missionaries, the French did not interfere with the Native American cultures. When the French missionaries could build forts against hostile attacks, they did. The converted Native Americans lived outside these forts and followed their own ways of life, entering the palisade in times of danger. The Jesuits considered their work in the New World important and successful. In New York, for example, from 1668 to 1678 about two thousand Native Americans converted to the Catholic faith, including Blessed Kateri Tekakwitha, whom the Catholic church beatified in 1980 (Shea 128; Buetow 16).

In addition to missionary work among Native Americans, French women religious sought to meet the spiritual needs of the families in the territories. In 1727 the French Ursuline Sisters founded a school for young women in New Orleans. This school set a model of women's education that remained unchanged into the nineteenth century. The eleven religious women who opened the school admitted rich and poor alike. For those students whose families could pay tuition, they offered a boarding school and an academy. For the students from impoverished families, they began a day school. In the first year, they enrolled twenty-four boarders and forty day school students. In New Orleans, the sisters applied the program of studies they had used in their schools in Paris. This required that students begin with morning prayers, then reading, some form of manual training, arithmetic, and writing for about one and a half hours. In the afternoon session, which took about two and a half hours, they repeated the same schedule, adding religious instruction. By 1860 the schools followed essentially the same schedule (Burns 68–76).

In France the Ursuline system of teaching depended on pupil-teachers called *dizainières*. Later, in the nineteenth century, Joseph Lancaster, an Englishman, claimed that he invented a similar model by which to instruct poor children in charity schools. Among the Ursulines, the system worked as follows: Assigned a group of ten younger students, these pupil-teachers distributed texts and watched over the books. They helped during recitation by standing near the teacher and asking questions of the students in their groups. One teacher devoted herself to writing, another to arithmetic, and a third to manual training such as sewing or embroidery. Although the limited number of teachers in New Orleans prevented the religious women from adopting such specialization immediately, they moved in this direction (Burns 77–79).

By 1740 the Ursuline convent in New Orleans educated most of the ladies of the colony, but the numbers remained small. In 1803, when the convent was a center of education for girls in the territory, the teachers numbered eleven and the boarding students reached 170. In 1804, after the United States bought the Louisiana Territory, U.S. President Thomas Jefferson wrote the Ursuline convent to assure the religious women that he applauded their work and would do all he could to help them continue (Woody, *A History of Women's Education* 329–330; Burns 82–83).

Why Did the Dutch Colonists on the Atlantic Seaboard Establish Schools?

The Dutch explorers did not seek to convert the Native Americans to Christianity as did the Spanish and French Catholic missionaries. They established settlements to advance such industries as the fur trade. For them, schools in the New World attracted families of settlers. In New Netherland, the schools reinforced the families' religion. In fact, the colonists retained the interlocking nature of the home, school, and church after the English took over the colony, changed its name to New York, and sought to change the colony's religion to Anglicanism.

In 1621 the States General of the United Netherlands granted a charter to the West India Company allowing the corporation to control trade with the countries in America and to promote settlements in those areas that would increase trade. Within two years, the company sent about thirty families to the area that is now Delaware, Connecticut, and New York. In 1626 the company bought Manhattan Island and concentrated settlements there. In an effort to attract settlers, the West India Company established the first town school in 1638 and paid the schoolmaster's salary. Although the company encouraged the spread of schools throughout its colony, the church selected the teachers. In New Netherland, the official religion, the Reformed Dutch Church, allowed local parishes some independence but required that an executive body oversee them. As a result, several ministers of churches in Amsterdam, Holland, formed a classis—or a governing body—to examine and license ministers for New Netherland. Because schools were part of the church, the classis selected the teachers as well (Kilpatrick, *Dutch Schools* 11–15; Cremin, *American Education, 1607–1783* 178–180).

The first elementary school in New Netherland opened around 1638. Because passage to and from the colony was difficult, the teachers contracted for a period of three or four years. Although they were not always successful, the directors sought God-fearing men of good character to teach in the elementary schools. Sometimes the teacher served as the church sexton as well (Kilpatrick, *Dutch Schools* 50, 63).

In 1650 the director general in New Netherland, Peter Stuyvesant, recommended appointing a teacher to start a Latin academy. The Lords Directors in Holland approved the appointment and the idea of such a school, which would meet in the city tavern. Although the parents paid some tuition, the West India Company paid the teacher's salary. With income from two sources, the teacher was able to earn a considerable sum for the period. However, the school remained small. At its peak, the academy enrolled about twenty-five students. Once the Dutch lost control of the colony, the academy closed (Kilpatrick, *Dutch Schools* 95–109).

The Dutch failed to attract many people to New Netherland. Population grew slowly so that by 1660 New Netherland, which included Manhattan, contained only 6,000 people. At this time, Massachusetts had 25,000 settlers and Virginia had 33,000. In 1664 the English took control of the colony, although they allowed the Dutch to retain the same schoolmasters and to continue using the Dutch language. The English strengthened their control in 1674, giving the Church of England equal status in the colony with the Reformed Dutch Church. Although they required that the Archbishop of Canterbury license schoolmasters, officials did not enforce this regulation, nor did they encourage communities to establish schools. Consequently, local residents started and maintained their own schools (Kilpatrick, *Dutch Schools* 13–18).

After 1664 the typical elementary school in a Dutch village served as the living quarters of the schoolmaster. Most of the buildings were about twenty feet long and twenty feet wide. One part of the building served as the master's living quarters, and another part served as the room for instruction. The teacher had a desk, and the boys and girls, separated by age and sex, sat on benches. School met six days each week, summer and winter, from eight to eleven in the morning and from one to four in the afternoon. The instruction began with reading in an alphabet book that led from letters, to syllables, to the Ten Commandments. All of the boys entered a writing class; most of the girls left school after they learned to write their names. Many boys stopped attending by age twelve, and most students attended irregularly. Some teachers offered a little instruction in arithmetic, but many ignored it. The bulk of the instruction concentrated on denominational religious training. For example, in their first book the students read the creed of the church and descriptions of the rituals for baptism and communion. As part of the schoolwork, student learned the Heidelberg catechism. They demonstrated their abilities to answer the questions in the catechism once a week in church. On Saturday morning at school, the students learned the psalms for the next day's church service (Kilpatrick, *Dutch Schools* 216–227).

Thus, even after the Dutch lost control of the colony, the ties between the school, the Dutch church, and the families remained close. Some Dutch settlers in New York retained those traditional ties into the nineteenth century. Authors such as Washington Irving ridiculed them for isolating themselves from their neighbors.

Did the Puritans Bring a Faith in Education to the Massachusetts Bay Colony?

Some historians credit the Puritans with setting the model of education that people adopted in the United States. Others claim that the Puritans represented only one part of the combination of ideas that became the contemporary model of schools. The lasting part was the Puritan faith in education to pass on conceptions of morality and religion.

The Puritans who sailed from England to Massachusetts in 1630 enjoyed wealth, prestige, and good educations in their former homes. They hoped that their sacrifices would make others realize that they considered their mission a holy crusade. Although the Puritans worried that they would deprive Native Americans of their land, they decided to seek the Native Americans' permission to settle. Most of all, they worried that they were deserting England in its time of need (Schweninger 36–38).

The Puritans opposed what they saw as corruption in the Church of England, also known as the Anglican Church, and in the monarchy because those institutions supported what they considered heresies, such as Arminianism, a belief that people could achieve salvation by their own efforts. Nonetheless, the Puritans retained their allegiances to their king, their country, and their church. Consequently, they desired to leave England with the King's blessing and without repudiating the church. This became possible when, in March 1629, Charles I granted a charter to the Massachusetts Bay Company to establish colonies in New England. Typically, the owners of such companies remained in England while settlers went to the specified region. For some reason, Charles neglected to make such a stipulation in this charter. As a result, John Winthrop and his colleagues sailed to Massachusetts and governed the colony while living in it. Their success in Massachusetts, they hoped, would show the truth of their convictions (Morgan 28–33, 36).

Although the Puritans thought they had a Christian or theocratic state, they constructed it in ways that resembled the four prescriptions Plato outlined in his *Republic* to maintain justice. First, Plato felt that the concept of the good had to permeate every part of society. In Massachusetts the courts tried religious as well as civil cases and punished people who committed moral offenses with fines or imprisonment. Second, Plato wanted the social classes divided according to assigned tasks. In the Puritans' case, they turned the command of the state over to individuals trained in statecraft who were also known to be members of the elect—a special category of worldly saints who attained success while adhering to the tenets of the faith. Third, Plato demanded that no false views enter the minds of the citizens. In a similar fashion, the Puritans excluded alien faiths and heresies from their colony. Fourth, Plato believed that the people should not try to acquire new territory or to increase wealth. The Puritans sought to reduce people's avarice by delimiting where the colony ended and the frontier began. They wanted all good citizens to remain in the community and flourish there (Mehl, "Education" 4–5).

For the Puritans, education depended on the family. Parents devoted some time in each day to instruction such as teaching the children to read and write. Further, they watched over the children's behavior, urged them to fulfill God's mandates, and drilled them in catechism. In religious instruction, most Puritans followed a version of the Westminster Catechism, a series of question and answers that provided the tenets of faith. For example, one question asked, What is the chief end of human beings? The answer: We should glorify God and enjoy Him forever. Families also might begin the day with devotions in which the children read portions from the Bible and perhaps sang psalms. As a result of the catechism and Bible readings, literacy took on a religious purpose among the Puritans. Most important, all members of the community shared the same values, so boys and girls learned the same material (McClellan 2–4).

In 1642 Puritan leaders demonstrated their views about the importance of education. The general court gave town officials the authority to fine parents who failed to properly educate their children and to place the children in apprenticeships in which they could obtain proper education. The general court expressed dismay that parents and masters continued to fail in their educational tasks. As a result, in 1647 the court required every town of fifty families to hire a teacher to instruct in elementary subjects and every town of one hundred families to establish a secondary or grammar school. These laws revealed the Puritans' determination to not let people educate themselves. Because the Puritans' conception of the good had to permeate all aspects of society, they could not leave the destiny of the state to chance; the old deluder, Satan, would turn things to evil (Mehl, "Education" 7).

In the schools, teachers reinforced the home instruction, also using materials that taught literacy skills through religious lessons. Hornbooks, sheets of wood covered with translucent horn, and primers carried scriptural verses or poems expressing Christian virtues. Although some ministers gave lessons, they did not interfere directly in school matters. Instead, the church governed the school, as it directed the family, through the guidance ministers offered in their sermons (McClellan 5–6).

While some Puritans were strict and harsh parents, many treated their children with tenderness and permissiveness. Cotton Mather, for example, imitated the kindness his father showed him when he was a child. Mather took such pleasure in his children that when he spoke to them he used a term of endearment such as "lovely" or "my dear." When they disobeyed, Mather punished them by banishing them temporarily from his presence or by refusing to teach them a lesson. Mather considered the latter a severe punishment because he held learning to be the noblest aim of life. The family said many prayers together even during days of sickness. The children recited their catechisms regularly and read the Bible together (Levy 20–21).

In 1686 in England, James II, a Catholic king, consolidated all the New England colonies, New York, and New Jersey under the control of the appointed governor, Sir Edmund Andros. Andros abolished the colonial assemblies such as the general court and tried to force the Puritan colonists to attend the Anglican Church. In 1687 the leaders of the Massachusetts colony sent Increase Mather, their foremost preacher, to plead for a renewal of the former charter to restore control to the Puritans. But though the citizens of Boston forced Andros out of office, they failed to regain control of the colony. Despite Mather's efforts, the king extended a new Royal Charter in 1691 that placed the colony under the control of a governor appointed by the Crown and opened liberties and privileges to people who did not belong to the Puritan church (Hofstadter, Miller, and Aaron 68–70; Wertenbaker 338).

Not only did the Puritans lose political control, but they also fought a losing battle with prosperity. As traders from Boston sailed to different ports, they learned that Catholics in Spanish colonies and Quakers in Pennsylvania had many good qualities such as honesty, diligence, and industriousness. As a result, they lost their belief that God had damned these outsiders. Further, many merchants came to the Boston colony lured by opportunities to prosper through trade. As early as 1645, these merchants petitioned the general court to accept strangers into the colony and to end the ban on Anabaptists. As the economic growth continued, different types of people flowed into the formerly restricted colony. By 1750 Boston had a population of fifteen thousand. The major industries were whaling and cod fishing, but supporting businesses such as rope and sail making, home construction, and agriculture expanded. In keeping with Puritan fears, the families became affluent and joined the more lenient Anglican Church. They decorated their bodies with satins, and they built fine colonial homes. Not surprisingly, the demands that parents educate the children declined (Wertenbaker 206–207; Hofstadter, Miller, and Aaron 87–88).

While some historians contend that these political and social changes ended the theocracy, Bernard Mehl claims that a more philosophic reason weakened the Puritan mission. He contends that the Puritans could not withstand external pressures because the members of the elect located morality in education instead of in piety. Under pietistic models, Mehl claims, morality depended on intrinsic feelings that were not subject to external rules. In this way, a person might be able to live beside people who ignored those inspirations without noticing or caring. But the Puritans tried to live in the world and to command children to follow moral edicts, thus making morality a function of reason. Although this enabled the Puritans to spread civilization, it meant that a new secular order could replace the church as the moral force holding sway in the colony. However, Mehl adds, the Puritans' view of education as the means to combat lust, crime, and emotionalism continued after their theocracy faded. It was this idea that combined with others to form contemporary notions of schools. Although Mehl acknowledges that these contemporary ideas resemble the Puritan notion of education, they differ in an important respect: They do not contain the religious message the Puritans believed to be central (Mehl, "Education" 5–6).

Was Religious Tolerance Taught in Colonial Schools?

To the Puritans, tolerance could break the ties that existed between family, school, and church. However, religious tolerance was one of the virtues in Pennsylvania. Tolerance could prevail in Pennsylvania but not in Massachusetts for a simple reason: Among the Puritans, the teachings of particular church leaders revealed the important aspects of the faith. Among the denominations in Pennsylvania, a consensus maintained that the Scriptures held the source of true morality. As a result, Pennsylvania schoolmasters reinforced the various sects by staying close to scriptural messages and avoiding denominational differences.

In 1681 Charles II granted William Penn a charter to the Pennsylvania colony. Penn, a Quaker, recruited settlers to his colony from various Protestant sects such as Mennonites,

Amish, Dunkers, and Schwenfelders. As governor, Penn affirmed that education would maintain public order in the colonies. Although the members of each group thought their schools, homes, and meetinghouses should reinforce their sects' moral messages, Penn urged toleration among the different denominations that were practiced in his colony. Ironically, Penn's dislike of universities and advanced learning resolved the difficulty. He believed that learned men might cause theological controversies and therefore should not become teachers. Instead, inspired brethren who knew the Scripture well could teach the children useful knowledge consistent with godliness. Consequently, most of the sects living in Pennsylvania sought simple, kind men to be teachers who could win their students' hearts and direct their attention to the Bible. All the groups saw love and the Bible as the foundation of moral training (Cremin, *American Education: The Colonial Experience* 305–309).

Christopher Dock, a Mennonite farmer who had emigrated from Germany, illustrated the type of teacher whom Penn thought could create a moral community out of the different Protestant sects. Around 1714 Dock opened a school in Pennsylvania. He conducted classes for ten years. Because he made little money teaching school, he turned to farming while teaching in the summers. In 1750 Dock wrote *Schul-ordnung,* which described how to conduct classes. Although the manuscript was not published until 1770, it explained how Dock brought different students together (Brumbaugh 11–16).

In his treatise, Dock explains that he began his school because he noticed that some parents appeared unable to raise their children properly. In his classroom, boys and girls worked separately. When children entered his school, Dock asked them if they would be diligent and obedient. When they responded that they would, he asked the other boys or girls to watch over them. Dock's school was in a rural area, requiring the children to walk different distances. Consequently, they did not arrive together. While Dock waited for the other students to arrive, he placed the students who were present together on a bench and asked them to read a passage of Scripture. As they demonstrated that they could recite it flawlessly, each moved to a table until the bench was empty. When all students arrived in class, Dock began the day with a prayer. Although he did not hit poor students to make them work harder, he did write their names on slates with the word *Lazy.* When those students succeeded at their lessons, the class called them diligent and erased their names. In spelling instruction, Dock pronounced a word and students spelled it (Dock 105–108).

To prevent confusion when the students left the room for personal hygiene, Dock hung a wooden tag on the doorpost. A student who wanted to leave had to take the tag. If another child wished to leave, he or she waited until the tag was returned to the doorpost. Thus, Dock tried to establish routines that enabled students to manage their affairs in orderly ways. If they stole, swore, or lied, Dock beat them with a rod for the benefit of their souls. But he preferred that the students act correctly because they wanted to conform rather than because they feared him. In this effort, he was aided by his love for the children, which he claimed was a gift from God (Dock 115–124).

To convey to the children the proper fear and respect for God, Dock wrote a set of sixty-eight questions and provided the places in the Scriptures where those answers could be found. For example, one question asked, From where does faith come? The answer, from Romans 10:17, was that faith came from hearing the word of God. Dock's catechism differed from the Westminster Catechism the Puritans used in that the answers came directly from Scripture rather than from interpretations written by church leaders. Such an orientation to the Scriptures suited the pietism that separated the Mennonite and Quaker sects from the Anglican Church (Dock 136–137).

Thus, Dock developed a model of integration, bringing together different sects with a moral training based on biblical training. However, this tolerance required that no one think deeply about the denominational teachings that separated the groups. In the early nineteenth century, Joseph Lancaster attempted a similar compromise with a Quaker catechism. Anglicans, less willing to ignore the views of their church leaders, rejected his approach.

Did Any Colonies Resist Education?

Although some colonies, such as Virginia, made limited efforts to establish public schools, the colonists established charity schools for the poor, wealthy citizens hired tutors who reinforced the values of the family and the church, and some teachers held informal but practical schools for tradespeople and their children. The result was that, even in these less organized situations, children attended schools, although the aims of that instruction varied among social classes.

Although Virginians followed the English model of encouraging parishes to establish charity schools, they depended on informal arrangements such as tutors or part-time instruction. If parents refused to educate their children, the colony required them to apprentice their children to tradespeople who would provide vocational training. However, the parish vestries rarely enforced this law. Part of the reason Virginia colonists did not establish schools was that the population lived in frontier conditions; settlements were widely separated from each other, preventing children from traveling to and from schools. Another reason few Virginians wanted to establish schools was that most of the colonists agreed with the doctrines of the Anglican Church. As a result, they did not need schools to reinforce the perspective of their sect (Wells 90–91).

In Virginia the local parish of the Church of England served as the local governmental institution, administering church and civil affairs as it did in England. According to the Virginia code of 1661–1662, members of the vestry engaged in such unrelated acts as the control of church business, care for the poor, inspection of morals, and counting of tobacco plants. The twelve most able men of each parish made up the members of the vestry. Such vestries were self-perpetuating and oligarchic. When a vestryman left his position, the vestry and the minister appointed a replacement. As a result, few members of the lower or middle classes found their way into the vestries (Wells 3–6).

Although Virginia colonists adopted an English style of government, they neglected several English practices to encourage the spread of schools. First, whereas English churches established parish schools taught by the parish clerk or other person, Virginia churches chose not to pay teachers. Second, although clerks and ministers opened their own private schools in Virginia, they were not paid from parish funds. Third, the parish in Virginia did not pay to send poor children to private schools as did England parishes. Fourth, Virginia parishes did not follow the English practice of constructing school buildings to induce the ministers to become schoolmasters (Wells 17–29).

In England many parishes established schools because wealthy patrons donated money to support them. From 1660 to 1730, more than nine hundred endowed schools in

England began to teach children to write, read, and keep accounts. These schools lacked a classical curriculum, and mostly economically impoverished students attended. In Virginia, from 1634 to 1775, out of a total of ninety parishes only seven had endowed schools. Therefore, free schools were not available to many students in Virginia (Wells 30–49).

The English poor law of 1601 gave church officials the responsibility of finding apprenticeships for children whose parents could not afford to raise them. The English parish officials paid the masters for taking charge of the children. In Virginia, vestries took on this responsibility, although the law did not specify it. At first, the law of Virginia required the masters to provide training in such trades as weaving, tanning, tailoring, or bricklaying. Girls learned to sew, spin, and knit. By the early 1700s, the law required masters to ensure that children learned to read and write. Despite the law's detailed requirements, however, record books of the different vestries in Virginia indicated that they sent few children to become apprentices. In some cases, the parents may have objected. In many cases, tradespeople may have had such small businesses that they could not take on apprentices (Wells 70–86).

Wealthy Virginians, especially those of the planter class, hired private tutors to teach their children. Tutors were often young men who had trained for a position such as the ministry. They advertised their availability in local papers. Many tutors took the job of teaching the children of a wealthy family as temporary employment until they found an opening in their chosen field. Occasionally, the local minister served as a tutor. At other times, men indentured themselves to a family as a tutor to earn transportation from Scotland or England and room and board in Virginia (Gordon with Gordon 252–254).

Although tutors devoted their attention to the children of wealthy families, children of relatives or neighbors often boarded at the same estate and shared the tutor. In some cases, the owners built a house on the plantation where the tutor could sleep on the second floor and hold classes on the first. Because the owners constructed these buildings on exhausted land, they called them old field schools. The tutors also used these buildings to teach local tradespeople or poor children during their leisure time (Gordon with Gordon 252–253).

Most tutors used one-to-one instruction even when they worked with groups of children. This required some ingenuity, but tutors could manage if they knew the capacities and the interests of the students. With the children of the wealthy farmers, they followed a classical curriculum of French, Latin, Greek, and arithmetic. They taught more practical subjects such as writing and arithmetic to tradespeople and their children (Gordon with Gordon 253, 258).

Although one person could not offer extensive training in a variety of subjects, a tutor offered sufficient education for most Virginia gentlemen. Wealthy plantation owners wanted their sons to acquire a knowledge of books to prepare them for social conversation and of arithmetic so they could manage their own affairs. However, most planters believed that gentlemen did not need to become scholars. Thus, they preferred to hire tutors rather than send their children to the College of William and Mary in Williamsburg, Virginia, or to Europe for an education (Gordon with Gordon 254–255).

Tutors often developed ties of affection with the families they served. This was true of Phillip Vickers Fithian, even though he remained with his students for less than one year. However, some tutors stayed with the same family for years, and here the ties between family and tutor grew stronger. One of Fithian's replacements, John Peck, married one of the daughters who had been his student. Another Virginia planter, William C. Preston, recorded in his diary that his tutor, Peter Byrnes, taught successive generations of his family from 1780 to 1820. When Byrnes died at age eighty-two, the family buried him in their cemetery plot (Gordon with Gordon 251–255).

Did Colonial Education Set the Pattern for Twentieth-Century Education?

Historians question the extent to which educators integrated the ideas of different groups into their schools. For example, some historians claim that the colonists transplanted their schools from Europe to America and spread them across the land, where they endured for many years. They argue that the colonial schools served as models for later educational efforts. Other historians contend that new conditions brought forth new schools. For example, after the revolution, Americans created schools that served different purposes from those of the colonial models.

At the beginning of the twentieth century, most historians of education treated the colonial period as an introduction to the development of later schools. They described some materials used in instruction and some differences among the schools in various colonies. They aimed to show how methods and content of instruction had continually improved in the United States. In 1919, Ellwood P. Cubberly offered an example of this interpretation in *Public Education in the United States.* Describing his text as a history of administrative progress and curriculum change and expansion, Cubberly compared what he called the compulsory maintenance attitude of the Puritans in New England, the parochial school attitude in Pennsylvania, and the lack of state interference in Virginia. Within these frameworks, he discussed three types of schools: the dame school, the school of the 3-Rs, and the Latin grammar school. In each, he contended, religious aims dominated. He described some textbooks and materials used in those schools and the type of teachers. Cubberly claimed that the religious influences waned in colonial schools and that various colonies developed district control of the schools. He thought that these aspects led to the development of contemporary schools. He concluded, however, that after the revolution, Americans stopped transplanting educational ideas from England and evolved distinctive American types of schools suited to the needs of the country (Cubberly, *Public Education* 13–46).

Cubberly's view became the traditional orientation in curriculum studies. In the 1960s, however, historians complained that Cubberly and others distorted the past in an effort to serve teacher training programs. That is, Cubberly wrote his book as a text for courses in institutions for the training of teachers. These normal schools required students to study the history of education so they could gain some sense of the nature and purpose of education. Without this appreciation, the new teachers might be discouraged by their first failures. Historians argued that Cubberly's effort to show the origins of present educational practices led him to assume the past was more like the present than it was (Bailyn 7–13).

Such criticisms did not dispel the notion that colonial education set the pattern for contemporary schools. In 1976, Lawrence A. Cremin offered a more sophisticated view of the idea that a close connection existed between colonial schools and later educational efforts. Cremin claims that in the United States, English culture triumphed. With it came English law, English custom, and English language. As a result, the English model of education spread across the country as the country grew and prospered. Cremin offers four reasons for this success. First, in the Tudor and early Stuart periods in England, a system of universal compulsory education developed that centered around parish churches. Second, most English colonists were educated and knew its value for a variety of purposes. Third, with the conception of colonies as self-sustaining communities, the English spread their culture more easily than other nationalities whose colonists exploited the land in the search for riches they could take back to Europe. Finally, the English colonists saw themselves as agents of God's design for the world, motivating them to spread their views (Cremin, *Traditions* 6–10).

Although Cremin argues that English culture swept over the United States, he acknowledges that there were a considerable number of local variations in the way people set up schools. These included changes required to fit local conditions, differences that arose from different religious groups in different colonies, adjustments that resulted from the distinct nationalities in some colonies, and forms of what Cremin calls "guardedness" in offering education to Native Americans and African Americans (Cremin, *Traditions* 11–22).

Alternately, some historians claim that the English colonial schools did not set a pattern for later educational efforts; they view the development of education in the United States as less the triumph of English culture and more the result of the rise of modern society. In 1960 Bernard Bailyn offered one version of this perspective. Concentrating his studies on the Atlantic coast colonies, Bailyn observes that seventeenth-century education in the United States differed dramatically from nineteenth-century education, and that in later years conceptions and methods of schooling underwent similar changes in other parts of the world. According to Bailyn, educators in the United States suffered the effects of the forces of the modern world earlier than people in other societies because the wilderness setting conflicted with the traditional European society the colonists brought to the New World. Bailyn acknowledges that the first generation of settlers tried to transplant the forms of education from the medieval period. They depended on a tightly connected community in which the family, the church, and the school shared many tasks and reinforced each other. Families taught the children morals and vocational skills; the church introduced children to the values and methods of thought that framed the culture; and schools reinforced the lessons from the family and the church by providing literacy skills that served useful and cultural ends. Yet, Bailyn adds, by the end of the colonial period, people thought about schools as playing separate, new, and isolated roles such as building a new republic (Bailyn 14–23).

According to Bailyn, the colonists broke tradition because of the frontier conditions in the New World. The distances colonists traveled disrupted the extended family, reducing it to a wife, a husband, and children. Without aunts, uncles, cousins, and grandparents to tie people together, the family's ability to socialize the children declined. Further, both parents and children confronted new experiences in the colonies. The young people accepted these changes more easily than their elders. As a result, the family lost its ability to guide its members. At the same time, the institution of apprenticeship changed. Under the medieval conception, a master exercised moral leadership over his charges. But with few available workers in the New World, shopowners looked on apprenticeship as a way to solve a labor shortage rather than a means of passing on a way of life. In this setting, people turned to schools as separate agencies charged with passing on the culture. Once in such a position, schools could conserve tradition. However, schools could also break tradition by introducing new ideas that contradicted the views of family members or church people (Bailyn 20–22, 30–31, 48).

Bailyn's idea of the corrosive influence of the frontier grew out of Frederick Jackson Turner's view that the existence of a physical limit to civilization caused the settlers to break the bonds of custom, create new institutions, and adopt new ways of acting. Turner noted that, in 1690, the General Court of the Massachusetts Bay colony declared a line separating the territory of the Native Americans from the settlers' land. Although authorities sought to restrain colonists from going beyond it, this frontier helped Americans become individualistic and democratic. More important, according to Turner, these tendencies increased as the country grew. As a result, when the settlers in Massachusetts pushed westward to occupy the prairie zone of the Midwest and parts of California, they took on the character traits that enabled them to become captains of industry, political leaders, and founders of educational systems in the nineteenth century (Turner 38–39, 65–66).

Turner proposed his hypothesis to the American Historical Association in 1893, and within a decade, his idea enjoyed wide popularity. However, critics soon attacked it. The biggest difficulty was that although other countries had frontiers, their citizens did not develop the democratic or individualistic tendencies Turner attributed to Americans (Hartz 95). For example, Richard Pipes argues that Russians under the old regime pushed into the steppes, occupying and claiming more and more unsettled territory. But instead of developing democratic and individualistic characteristics, they imitated their Mongol conquerors and created a rigid, authoritarian society in which people tended to adopt bureaucratic, status-oriented attitudes (Pipes xxi–xii, 281–286).

Despite the problems with Bailyn's and Turner's theses, it is clear that some sort of integration took place. Schools in modern society became separated from the families, churches, and communities they served initially. Instead of reinforcing those institutions, schools took on goals of their own. In the United States, this meant that schools tried to integrate the children from different groups into the larger social whole. Specific groups, such as Catholics, found that creating schools to serve their own ends became increasingly difficult.

Did Education in the Colonial Period Encourage Assimilation, Integration, or Separation?

In the different periods described in this chapter, some form of integration of various forms of schooling took place. Although this blending strengthened educational practices, it also led to difficulties. For example, the Spanish and French missionaries sought to transform Native American practices in order to reinforce the principles of the Christian faith. In many areas, they succeeded, although some historians contend that they also destroyed viable indigenous cultures. The Dutch settlers managed to transplant a strong system of churches and schools. Although they resisted the influence of dominant groups such as the English, nineteenth-century critics portrayed them as simple, gullible, and backward. The Puritans sought to establish a pure and moral state based on reasonable but theological principles that could be taught by schools. When their children had experiences with different groups, however, they began to question their faith. The Pennsylvania colonies appeared to be models of toleration and acceptance, but the work of schoolmasters such as Christopher Dock implied that this tolerance depended on people's abilities to avoid thinking deeply about religious principles. Instead of building a community on shared understandings, Dock based his school on his personal kindness. Finally, Virginia colonists relied on more informal methods of education. Although this allowed tutors to reinforce the values of the family and the church, the children from different social classes had different educational experiences.

Finally, historians provide a measure of the integration that took place in schools during the colonial period, disagreeing about whether the colonial schools served as models for later educational efforts. Those historians who felt they did imply that education encouraged assimilation as a model of social change. But because modern schools broke from the religious purposes that colonial teachers pursued, it is apparent that integration did take place, at least to some extent.

TIMELINE
1565–1776

1565 Pedro Menéndez de Avilés established the first permanent settlement, called St. Augustine

1595 Eleven Franciscan missionaries arrived in St. Augustine

1598 Spanish missionaries founded Real de San Juan, the first colony in the Southwest

1616 New Mexico had eleven different missions

1618 Thirty-eight Franciscan missionaries settled in the land that now makes up Florida

1621 The States General of the United Netherlands granted a charter to the West India Company

1629 Charles I allowed the Massachusetts Bay Company to establish New England colonies

1630 A group of Puritans sailed from England to Massachusetts

1638 The West India Company established the first school on Manhattan Island

1642 Puritan town officials used their authority to fine parents who neglected to educate their children properly

1647 Puritan towns were required to hire a teacher to provide instruction in certain subjects

1650 Peter Stuyvesant recommended appointing a teacher to start a Latin academy on Manhattan Island

1661 The Westoe Native Americans attacked the Florida settlements at the English colonists' encouragement

1664 The English took control of the colony on Manhattan Island

1674 The Church of England acquired equal status with the Reformed Dutch Church in the colony of Manhattan Island

1680 The Apache and other Native American peoples fought together against the Spanish in New Mexico

1681 William Penn received the approval of Charles II to form a colony

(continued)

TIMELINE Continued

1686 James II appointed Sir Edmund Andros governor of the New England colonies

1687 Increase Mather tried to persuade King James to return control over their settlements to the Puritans

1690 The General Court of the Massachusetts Bay colony designated different land for the Native Americans and the settlers

1691 James created a new Royal charter that gave non-Puritans special privileges

1694 Antoine de la Mothe Cadillac took control of the Detroit area and encouraged the Native Americans to mix with the French settlements

1697 The Spanish military ended the Apache revolt

1697 The Jesuits built the main mission in Lorento, California

1727 The French Ursuline Sisters founded a school for young women in New Orleans

1750 Christopher Dock wrote *Schul-ordnung,* on teaching children

1767 Charles III expelled the Jesuits from the Spanish empire

CHAPTER

2 Moral Training, Women's Seminaries, and Leadership in the New Republic: 1776–1830

Thomas Jefferson

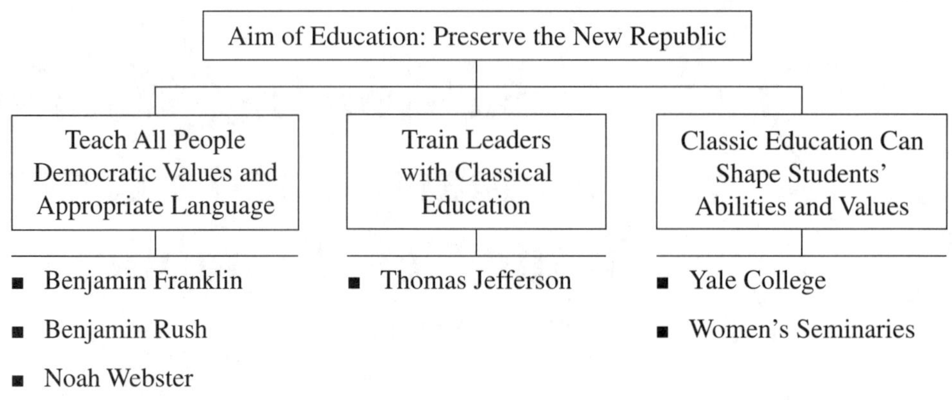

OVERVIEW

In 1787 the framers of the U.S. Constitution disagreed about how they should construct and preserve the new democracy. Some believed that a republic would fail unless the citizens maintained their personal virtues. Others held the contrary view that the government had to be structured to prevent people's evil tendencies from corrupting the republic. These two perspectives also permeated contemporary educational theories. Benjamin Franklin thought that people's morals had to change, and he proposed a type of self-education that would enable young men to become diligent, independent, civic-minded citizens. His friend Benjamin Rush proposed a system of schools that would mold all boys and girls into loyal citizens. To spread the proper virtues, educators turned to two techniques. Noah Webster wrote spellers and textbooks to enable teachers to create a national language. To help urban dwellers, educators imported from England the monitorial system developed by Joseph Lancaster. In all these cases, the standards that educators set seemed to reinforce the ideals of people from the New England states. However, some people thought the schools themselves should structure government so no one could corrupt it. Taking this view, Thomas Jefferson called for a system of schools that would select able young men from all social groups in the state and train them to become leaders. Once elected to office, these specially trained people would serve the interests of their constituencies and prevent any one individual's selfish aims from distorting the republic. For Jefferson, the basis of such training was the classical liberal arts. In 1828 the faculty of Yale College extended Jefferson's view, arguing that the best way to prepare for any vocation was to study the classical languages. Many educators adopted similar ideas for women's education. Part because many people ignored the women's seminaries, reformers such as Emma Willard focused their efforts on obtaining state financing for women's schools. They accepted the segregated and dependent status in which women lived. Consequently, though educators proposed a variety of ways to consolidate the progress they thought the War for Independence represented, those approaches favored some groups more than others.

How Could the Republic Be Preserved?

When the framers of the U.S. Constitution met in 1787, they reconsidered potential ways to hold the various states together. They were confronting a problem different from the one that caused them to revolt against British rule. During the revolution, the members of the thirteen colonies opposed the tyranny of a monarch. During the convention to consolidate the union, the fifty-five delegates from those states sought to create a system that would protect the community from the licentiousness of its citizens (McDonald 1–3).

Most citizens of the former colonies believed that a republic was the best form of government, but they did not agree about what they meant by the terms "republic" or "republicanism." First, many politicians used the term "republic" to refer to something they liked. To them, it referred to a form of government with some type of elected representatives rather than hereditary status. Second, although a few Americans had read the ancient works of Cicero, Livy, and Tacitus, these intellectuals disagreed about whether republicanism represented an affection for the common person or if it was a form of government that prevented mobs from acting badly. Third, because most Americans picked up classical ideas about republicanism in a secondhand fashion from plays, newspapers, and orations, they took republicanism as a combination of stilted views that suited their local prejudices (McDonald 67–69).

Because people had difficulty deciding what constituted a republic, they disagreed about the ways to run it effectively. For example, after analyzing the debates during the Constitutional Convention, Forrest McDonald has noted that the delegates' ideas of how to preserve a republic fell into two categories. One category contained delegates who thought that unless people could be courageous, hardworking, and frugal, the republic would fail. Many of New England's delegates to the Constitutional Convention believed this. They demanded that citizens dedicate themselves to the public good, and they expected each person to be self-reliant. They doubted that people could be virtuous if their livelihoods depended on other, richer people (McDonald 70–71).

The second category consisted of approaches that were based on the view that government should not try to change the entire moral fabric of the people but should take their manners into account. As a result, they approved of a system of checks and balances in government to prevent a wicked minority or an unruly majority from overwhelming the needs of the citizens. The farmers from the South took this more modest view and disagreed with the puritanical conception that the success of a republic depended on the virtues of its citizens (McDonald 71–82).

By extension, the views the founders took toward education fit these differing ideologies about republicanism. For example, Benjamin Franklin took the view that children had to learn to be virtuous, diligent, and independent. His friend Benjamin Rush expressed this perspective even more strongly. Noah Webster agreed with them. On the other hand, the delegates who thought that government should be structured to restrain the citizenry usually believed that the role of education was to provide leaders for society. Thus, Thomas Jefferson proposed the creation of a system of schools that would select and train students from all social groups to become leaders.

The final draft of the Constitution arranged the two houses of Congress and placed the legislative, administrative, and judicial branches of government in opposition to one another to prevent majority rule from dominating minority concerns. This seemed tailored to the second ideal that compensated for people's morals more than it sought to change them. Despite the controversies it caused during ratification, however, the model was not overly restrictive, and it changed as the country developed (McDonald 291–293).

In a similar fashion, the ideas of the proper arrangement of schools and the correct subject matter that developed at the same time seemed designed to select leaders rather than shape the morals of all people. But as controversies arose about the proper arrangement of schools and curriculums, educators blended the different aims of education to fit the growing and changing society.

Could Education Change People's Morals?

Benjamin Franklin was an exponent of the view that education helped children develop the virtues needed to preserve a republic. Furthermore, he felt that these virtues were the morals and behaviors that were proper for all times and all places. However, the values he chose to set up as standards were those personal characteristics approved of by people of his own social class. In line with his middle-class affiliation, Franklin disliked anything that appeared aristocratic. To him, the manners and the abilities of the aristocracy were artificial talents that nobles cultivated to earn status among themselves. Therefore, he sought to teach children the skills he believed they needed in life and that would prepare them to serve the public and their country. The best way to achieve this, Franklin proclaimed, was self-education (Curti 34–38).

To help young men undertake self-education, Franklin wrote his autobiography. In that text, he described his efforts to arrive at what he called moral perfection. He began by making a list of the thirteen virtues he believed were most important for him to acquire. Among these thirteen virtues were such things as resolution, or the courage to face adversity; diligence, or the tendency to work hard; and frugality, or the ability to save money (Franklin, *Autobiography* 79–81). Forrest McDonald has found that the delegates to the Constitutional Convention thought citizens needed these same virtues for the republic to survive (McDonald 291–293).

To acquire these virtues, Franklin wrote the name of each virtue on a separate page of a little book with seven columns labeled for the days of the week. Thinking he could not develop every virtue at once, Franklin resolved to concentrate on one virtue each week. Thus, he began with temperance, which he defined as eating and drinking in moderation. At the end of each day, he made a mark in one of the seven columns to indicate whether he had been temperate in his eating and drinking. After the week ended, he turned to another virtue for the next week. In this way, he practiced each virtue every thirteen weeks, and he repeated the cycles four times a year in order to acquire each virtue gradually (*Autobiography* 81–84).

Franklin did not design this project to aid his spiritual development. Instead, he admitted that he wanted to acquire these virtues to help himself advance socially. For example, he acknowledged that although he did not become humble, he was able to maintain the appearance of humility, and this helped him with other people. By avoiding words such as *undoubtedly,* for instance, he could more frequently convince people of the truth of his ideas, and when he was wrong, he could easily change his views (*Autobiography* 88).

Likewise, by appearing industrious and orderly, which he defined as working steadily and keeping regular hours, he succeeded in business. When Franklin first married and set up his printing house, he took care to avoid any appearance of being lazy or irregular. He never wasted time in idle chatter in public houses nor went hunting or fishing, although he loafed in private with a book. Further, when he bought paper from the stationery importers, he carted it at midday through the streets in a wheelbarrow to his shop. Other businesspeople saw him doing this manual labor and decided he was a hard worker. As a result, of developing the reputation for being dependable, shopkeepers gave him work. Franklin boasted that because his competitor did not take such care with his reputation, he lost his business (*Autobiography* 70–71).

To help young, single men follow his plan for moral perfection, Franklin devised the idea of starting a secret organization whose members would devote themselves to avoiding vice, practicing industry, and living frugally. Although he never established this organization, Franklin spread his ideas of self-improvement through *Poor Richard's Almanac,* published under the name Richard Saunders. Franklin thought that if it was useful and entertaining the almanac could educate people who did not buy other books. Consequently, he filled the spaces between the days in the calendar with sayings that carried moral messages such as, "An empty sack cannot stand upright." Franklin claimed he brought the wisdom of the ages to semiliterate people because he had gathered these proverbs from many different countries and historical epochs. *Poor Richard's Almanac* sold widely for about twenty-five years, and it made Franklin wealthy. The sayings were republished in other forms, translated into French, and circulated throughout Europe as well as the American continent (*Autobiography* 90–92).

Franklin realized that for young people to instruct themselves, they needed access to books. Therfore, his first public project was to establish a subscription library. In 1724 Franklin set off on his first visit to England. While there, he joined literary club conversations that took place in coffeehouses. When he returned to Philadelphia, he proposed to several friends that they set up a club, the Junto, dedicated to mutual improvement. In 1728 the members drew up rules for themselves that included promises to love humankind, respect one another, believe in freedom of speech and worship, and love truth. As the meetings progressed, they found they needed more books to fuel their discussions. Consequently, the members put their personal copies of books in a common reading room to offer the individual members a wider selection. In 1731 the Junto disbanded its reading room, and the members drew up plans to convert it to a subscription library. At first Franklin could not find enough people willing to subscribe to form the library. But when he disguised his interest in the plan and told shopkeepers that a group of friends had asked him to solicit contributions, many people were willing to contribute (Korty 6–8).

In 1742, as the collection increased, the Library Company received a charter and became a formal institution. Franklin himself took advantage of the collection. Among the library's texts was a book describing how to improve fires that Franklin probably consulted when he designed his stove in 1744. In addition to keeping books, the library provided space for scientific experiments, and it displayed mementos that ship captains had gathered on their voyages. Thus, the library became both a research center sponsoring experiments about such things as electricity and a type of museum with exhibits of fossils, collections of ancient pottery, and an Egyptian mummy (Korty 10–12).

Franklin claimed that he started the first subscription library and that its success caused other communities to establish similar institutions. To some extent, his claim was true. After the Library Company in Philadelphia received its charter, subscription libraries sprang up in Trenton and Burlington, New Jersey; Charleston, South Carolina; New York; and some towns in Pennsylvania. However, there were other libraries in America that had no connection with Franklin's. For example, in 1733, before Franklin's Library Company received its charter, other communities such as Durham, Connecticut, began libraries. In addition, in that same year Franklin reported that the libraries at Harvard and Yale had acquired large collections (Korty 21).

In the 1770s, Franklin claimed that as libraries spread across the land, they enabled all citizens to improve their conversation to the point where farmers were as intelligent as the wealthy people. He added that the libraries diffused knowledge and thereby contributed to the willingness of citizens from every social class to pursue independence from England (Crane 33).

Did Franklin Think Schools Could Shape Children's Morals?

Franklin's devotion to self-education has obscured his concern for schools. That is, in the nineteenth century, conservative politicians pointed to Franklin's works on self-education to show that citizens should not have to pay taxes for public schools because children could learn on their own. In making these arguments, the conservative politicians twisted Franklin's ideas. Franklin did not counsel people to ignore schools. He offered self-education as a means of learning when schools were not available. However, his ideas of the proper curriculum were more practical than those found in most schools (Curti 38).

Franklin took an active part in establishing schools in Pennsylvania. When he was forty-two, he retired from business and turned his attention to civic and scientific matters. In 1749 he wrote a proposal about the education of the youth of Pennsylvania as part of a series of papers that included a suggestion for regulating the city watch and another for organizing the fire department (Crane 30–31).

In his proposal for an academy, Franklin noted that the colonial settlers were educated people who used their learning to create prosperous settlements. Building these communities took all their time, he noted, and they could not devote adequate attention to training their children. To ensure that children grew into capable adults, Franklin proposed that individuals of wealth and leisure establish an academy. He suggested that the joy of seeing the children learn and grow would be adequate reward for their pains ("Proposals" 20–21).

He wanted the academy to have a house located near a river and that included a garden, an orchard, a meadow, and at least one field. This location and these surroundings would enable the students to maintain their health by running, swimming, leaping, and wrestling. The house had to contain a library, maps, globes, mathematical instruments, apparatus for experiments in natural science, and machinery for printing ("Proposals" 21).

The principle by which Franklin selected the curriculum was simple. He thought students should learn those things that were most useful and most ornamental, especially subjects that would help them in their future professions. Interestingly, Franklin did not separate the qualities of being useful and being ornamental. The students had to learn penmanship that was easily read and attractive. Although Franklin pointed out that this was a useful skill, it was also ornamental. Likewise, drawing was both ornamental and useful. It offered students the chance to experiment with beauty while simultaneously giving them some understanding of perspective. Of all subjects, Franklin paid the most attention to history, possibly because he thought that historical studies would inspire students to serve humankind, their country, and their friends and families. He claimed this desire was the aim of all true learning ("Proposals" 21, 23).

Among the benefits of historical studies, Franklin listed an awareness of the order of past events and an understanding of the customs of previous generations. He added that historical readings could impress on students the beauty and usefulness of virtue and demonstrate the usefulness of well-crafted and attractive speech. In addition, history could show that religion helped regulate people's behavior. Further, Franklin thought that historical studies would show students how to design their own society. They could compare different forms of government or constitutions and learn how people formed governments to protect property and reward diligence. The study of contemporary history would also show how the colonies were connected to other countries including England. Finally, Franklin noted that historical studies were pleasant. They made people aware of things going on in the world and improved the level of their conversations ("Proposals" 22–23).

Although Franklin favored the study of history, he disapproved of training in classical languages. To learn about ancient Greece and Rome, students could use translations of the original authors. Learning Latin and Greek might help prospective clerics, he added, but students who wanted to become lawyers should study Latin and French, whereas those who would become merchants would profit more from the modern languages of French, German, or Spanish ("Proposals" 22).

Franklin's academy opened the same year he made his proposal. From among the group of subscribers willing to contribute to the project, they chose twenty-four trustees. To keep the school from falling under church control, they ruled that only one member from each of the several religious sects found in Philadelphia could be a trustee. Thus, among the trustees there was one Anglican, one Presbyterian, one Baptist, and one Moravian. Franklin believed that such democratic procedures enabled the academy to grow (*Autobiography* 113–115).

In 1751 Franklin amplified his views in "The Idea of the English School Sketch'd Out for the Consideration of the Trustees of the Philadelphia Academy." Although he did not specify how old the students should be, he suggested that the students, all boys, should range from eight to sixteen years of age. Before entering, they should be able to read and write. The school was divided into six grades or classes. In the first class, students would learn correct spelling and increase their vocabulary by reading short stories or fables. The second class would read similar stories, giving brief descriptions of how the authors constructed them. After students analyzed a story, the master would read it aloud for them in the proper way. The third class would concentrate on proper grammar and begin the study of history, mechanics, and natural sciences. In the fourth class, students would study composition by writing such things as accounts of their readings and letters to each other. They would begin the study of ethics to lay the foundation of virtue and the study of geography to learn where the places about which they read were located. The fifth class would write essays and some verse, and begin the study of logic and reasoning. Finally, the sixth class would add English translations of the classics such as Homer, Virgil, and Horace.

It is not clear how successful Franklin was in establishing the academy he had envisioned. He gave two different reports of its success. In his autobiography, Franklin proudly noted that the academy grew to become the University of Philadelphia. However, in the last year of his life, he wrote a letter criticizing the trustees for erecting a Latin academy instead of an English school as he had recommended. In his letter to the trustees, Franklin complained that, contrary to his proposal, the original constitution stated that students would learn Latin and Greek as well as English. The trustees added the study of Latin and Greek to satisfy people who wanted classical training for their children. However, Franklin accused the trustees of violating this compromise and weakening the idea of an English school. For example, they gave the head of the Latin school the title of rector while offering the master of the English school none, and the Latin rector received twice the salary of the English master. Second, when purchasing books for the library, the trustees bought Latin and Greek texts but no books in English. Among the other discrepancies Franklin noted was the replacement of an excellent first master of the English school with a less competent individual, which caused the reputation of the English school to decline. In his protest of the unfair treatment of the English instruction, Franklin contended that the ability to speak good English was much more important than the ability to speak or read Latin. He thought that the prejudice in favor of learning Latin was similar to the ideas of fashion he had found in France. Members of the French nobility believed they had to have fine hats whenever they appeared in public even though these beautiful and expensive hats disturbed their wigs. To preserve their hair, they carried these hats under their arms as elegant but useless decorations ("Observations" 83–87, 103–104).

Franklin Believed That Schools Liberated Students in What Way?

For eighteenth-century patriots such as Benjamin Franklin, personal freedom meant having the opportunity to choose the proper course of action. Freedom was not the chance for people to do as they pleased. Although Franklin valued the freedom to choose, he believed that people would act properly once they realized that those actions brought them success. Thus, according to Franklin, when students thought properly, they were liberated. In his autobiography, Franklin showed his readers how his business flourished when he appeared diligent, and how he designed *Poor Richard's Almanac* to elevate the public wisdom that made it popular.

Although Franklin thought of such virtues as diligence and social concern as universal, critics have complained that they only served a particular type of person. According to D. H. Lawrence, the famed British author, Franklin was a calculating individual who ignored higher, more spiritual truths while pursuing material gain. For Max Weber, an important sociologist, Franklin's autobiography illustrates the spirit of capitalism, wherein acquisition is the ultimate purpose of life. Weber argues that Franklin turned the earning of money into a principle of living. However, Weber is careful to point out that Franklin wanted people to demonstrate proficiency in a calling by pursuing material success legally and by governing their actions virtuously. This was important to Franklin, Weber notes, because he believed the biblical prediction that a man diligent in business shall stand before kings. Consequently, Weber concludes, Franklin laid the ethical foundation for the capitalistic order that took place in the nineteenth century because he invested business with a spiritual sense deeper than that of satisfying people's greed (47–57).

If Franklin lent respectability to the spirit of capitalism, it was because his notion of freedom or liberty coincided with a then popular conception of natural law. In his case, this meant that the rules for proper behavior existed in the world. It was the duty of all people to determine what those rules were and to follow them. If they did this, they would be rewarded because they lived in harmony with nature. Returning to the example of his triumph with the almanac, Franklin might say that his success demonstrated that it was natural for people to serve humankind. When he created an almanac to enlighten people, he benefited from that action.

In a similar way, Franklin extended his views of freedom and natural law to his conceptions of authority. Like other American authors, Franklin compared authority to a form of paternity wherein the father helps the children to correct mistakes that the children would have corrected on their own if they had had the necessary experience. This conception of paternity differed from the earlier puritanical notions that the father epitomized the standard of acceptability.

Imitating many other authors, Franklin extended this view of paternity to international relations. In "Observations of the Increase of Mankind," Franklin wrote that the role of the mother country was to encourage the natural development of the colonists' capacities. Consequently, he complained that when rulers tried to achieve their own ideas and restrained colonial trade or reduced colonial manufacturing, they weakened the potential for the growth of all parties. Franklin applied the same idea to his proposal for the academy by implying that a teacher should help the students recognize how a lesson would help them achieve their goals. In adopting this model, Franklin suggested that a teacher acquired authority over students by recognizing the legitimacy of their desires (Breitwieser 180–181).

How Did Benjamin Rush Think a System of Schools Should Inculcate Correct Virtues in Children?

Franklin did not advocate the development of a *system* of schools. This task fell to a friend of his, Benjamin Rush. Like Franklin, Rush thought of personal and social freedom as the opportunity for all people to desire the things that would make everyone better. These two men disagreed about the role of religion in the new republic. Another difference was that Rush owned slaves. However, he argued strongly in 1773 against maintaining slavery in the colonies because it fostered idleness, theft, and treachery. He thought that the slave trade should stop and that young African Americans already in the colonies should be taught to read and write and to practice virtue and religion. With these lessons, the slaves could profit from freedom. As a result, Rush thought that laws should be passed limiting their time of servitude (Hawke 104–105).

Rush's ideas of a proper education came from his own experiences. He had grown up under the influence of two leaders of the Great Awakening, a religious revival that swept the colonies in 1740. The participants in this movement believed that the millennium would arrive immediately and holiness would spread justice and happiness throughout the world. Under the direction of his teachers, Rush learned to obey authority and to live a strictly moral life. Although he grew to regret the time that he spent studying Latin and Greek under their care, he praised the moral lessons his teachers conveyed about the need to study and to serve the people in society. Rush's belief in the importance of serving people led him to become a physician. In this occupation, he thought he would earn a good living and have many opportunities to improve the lives of the people around him (Hawke 13–24).

When Rush proposed a plan for the establishment of public schools in Pennsylvania in 1786, he sought to imbue children with principles similar to those he had learned in school. Basing his proposal on the view that unless people acquire some education they devolve into savages, he urged the state to construct a system of schools to preserve civilization. Such a system would tie together the different regions, he added, because they would teach all citizens the same sorts of grammar, literature, and philosophy. He recommended that the system have four levels. At the base, each township would open a school where children could learn to use numbers and to read and write English and German, the two main languages spoken in Pennsylvania. At the second level, each county in the state would open an academy to prepare youth to enter college. For the third level, Rush wanted four colleges, each in a different part of the state, where young men could learn mathematics and science. Capable graduates of the colleges would go on to the university, which was at the top of the system. At the university in Philadelphia, the subjects of instruction could include law, divinity, science, and political theory ("A Plan" 4–5).

Most important, Rush thought that the different schools should inspire young people to be patriotic. First, students would learn to hold the Christian faith because a Christian had to be a republican. In Rush's view, the values of the Gospel pointed toward democracy and away from aristocracy. Consequently, he wanted the students to read the Bible along with other books of history, poetry, and fables. However, Rush allowed students to adopt any sect of Christianity that suited them and their parents. Second, he wanted students to learn that they were public property and must forsake their families when the welfare of the country demanded it. Thus, although students would learn to gain wealth, they would do so to improve their state. Third, students had to learn that liberty was possible only in a republic. In Europe, Rush claimed, aristocracies stifled scientific investigations, but in the republic of the United States science flourished. Fourth, youth should learn to work and to avoid drinking liquors. Fifth, Rush recommended that teachers rule by arbitrary authority so that students never learned that they had their own wills. Sixth, he urged that the youth be allowed to engage in amusements, such as appropriate theater productions, that would reinforce Gospel messages. In these ways, Rush claimed, the schools would turn the students into republican machines ("A Plan" 9–17).

How Did Noah Webster Want to Teach Children the Virtues Needed to Preserve the Republic?

Among the different techniques educators used to infuse students with the virtues needed to build a strong republic, textbooks represented an important contribution. Recognizing that many teachers lacked sufficient training, Noah Webster began to write and publish textbooks, spellers, and dictionaries to increase students' feelings of patriotism, strengthen schoolchildren's morals, and build a uniform national language.

Like Rush, Noah Webster wanted schools to implant in children principles of virtue, inspire them to secure justice, and teach them to have a profound love for their country. He opposed the study of the classical languages of Greek and Latin, and he complained that students often spent more time learning these dead languages than they took to learn English. Webster believed that university training with its emphasis on classical tongues made the students lazy and afraid of hard work. Instead of classical training, Webster thought that students should study those things that would help them in an occupation. When they were fifteen or sixteen, they should go to work ("On the Education" 45, 51, 54–56).

Webster urged the legislature to set up a system of schools moving from lower levels to higher ones, as Rush had done. In these schools, teachers should emphasize moral lessons rather than intellectual ones. Webster thought teachers should impart these morals by supervising the children closely and keeping strict discipline. For Webster, firm classroom control meant the teacher governed absolutely while the students obeyed without question, and should students misbehave, the teachers chastised students with rods. To encourage patriotism, classroom books should teach about the development of the U.S. government and the ways it differed from other countries ("On the Education" 57–64).

On one point, Webster disagreed with Rush: Webster warned against using the Bible in classrooms. However, this was more a disagreement about the proper method of teaching than about the purpose of the training. Both men wanted children to adopt a religion. Webster feared that if the students read the Bible in schools, it would appear commonplace to them. He thought that students might take the biblical lessons to heart if its use was guarded ("On the Education" 50–51).

But Webster's ideas about education were not as important as his sustained effort to build a national language. He offered two reasons why language development was an important part of nation building. First, although the descendants of the immigrants who settled the United States spoke English, they corrupted it with localisms and inaccuracies. As a result, people in one region harbored prejudices against people in other regions who spoke differently. A common language would reduce these ill feelings. Second, because the United States was an independent nation, it should have its own language in the same way that it had its own system of government. For Webster, the best way to create this language was for the states to establish schools and to require teachers to use books that held to uniform standards of spelling and pronunciation (*English Language* 19–22).

In his effort to create this democratic language, Webster followed what he thought were the universal rules of languages. Just as Franklin determined the universal virtues, Webster described what he thought to be the proper language. Webster believed those standards of pronunciation and spelling came from natural laws rather than people's opinions. For example, Webster cited what he called the principle of analogy. This rule held that similar combinations of letters represented the same sound and that words terminating in the same syllable received the accent the same distance from the end of the word. Webster acknowledged, however, that if an entire nation violated any rule, the accepted practice should take its place. In such extreme cases, he accepted the subjective habits of people over the objective laws of speech (*English Language* 27–28).

Webster claimed to have discovered the idea of building a dictionary on the universal rules of language. He believed that English authors took their words, meanings, and pronunciations from literature, the theater, and the royal court. The problem he found with this approach was that the habits of a restricted group of people became the standard of the language (*English Language* 24–27). According to Webster, by following the universal rules of language, an able compiler could collect a language that was free from the caprices of an elite group or the ignorance of the masses. He believed that the American Revolution offered an opportunity for people to change the language, especially because national languages often change after military conquests. Therefore, he proposed to look at current practices in pronunciation, spelling, and grammar to determine whether they fit the universal rules (*English Language* 28–36).

Although Webster thought he was following the universal laws of languages, some biographers such as Richard J. Moss accuse Webster of selecting the speech of people in isolated villages of New England to be the national standard because he had grown up on a farm in what became Hartford, Connecticut (Moss 94–96). Webster thought that he had avoided this tendency and instead had found the benefits and liabilities in everyone's speech. For example, Webster believed that the way in which members of a group governed themselves and distributed property influenced their speech patterns. He noted that wealthy people and slaveholders spoke with a boldness and authority that came from their habit of giving orders. On the other hand, New Englanders, who lacked family distinctions and slaves, expressed themselves with an air of inquiry or doubt. Further, he noted that some of these New England townsfolk preserved an original English style of speech because their isolation prevented them from acquiring the corruptions that had crept into the language in more populated areas. But he also criticized these New Englanders for making many errors in their pronunciation because they were too lazy to speak correctly (Webster, "Influence of Language" 106–109).

Of course, Webster was not the first to offer suggestions about changing the American language. Years earlier Benjamin Franklin had tried to make the skill of writing proper English easier by having the sounds match the letters used to represent them. In the 1760s, Franklin devised a new alphabet that prevented different words from being spelled alike, such as the present and the past tenses of *read*. When he published this system in 1779, people complained that the new spelling confused words because it obscured their etymologies. At any rate, Franklin's system did not catch on (Van Doren 425–428).

Webster was also not the first person to produce a dictionary. In 1755 Samuel Johnson had published a highly acclaimed European English dictionary. Before 1880, when Webster announced his intent to publish a dictionary, other Americans had published three dictionaries of English. Webster's contribution was that he combined his efforts to simplify spelling with his desire to compile dictionaries with useful listings of words. In addition, he claimed his dictionaries served the social function of enabling Americans to better understand each other and thereby cooperate more easily. Convinced of the value of his effort, he worked persistently on his dictionaries and other books throughout his long life.

As a young man, Webster was not overly concerned with the subject of language. He attended Yale College in hopes of becoming a lawyer. In 1779 he left Yale for want of money and took the job of schoolmaster in Hartford, Connecticut. Always diligent, he continued his studies in law while he taught. In 1781 he was admitted to the bar and graduated with a master's degree from Yale. Because lawyers had few prospects in early America, he continued to teach school. It was his work as a teacher that led him to seek a system of instruction that would produce what he called a federal language. He hoped that such a common tongue would unite the disparate states and ensure the feelings of fraternity needed for self-government (Unger 33–44).

In 1783 Webster published *A Grammatical Institute of the English Language,* later known as the *American Spelling Book* and commonly referred to as the Blue-Backed Speller. In the introduction to the book, he explained that after Americans broke political ties with Britain, they created a new political system. The job that lay ahead was to create a new educational plan. Such a project had to begin with the improvement of the language. People in different regions pronounced words differently, spelled them in various ways, and followed different grammatical rules. These peculiarities had to give way to uniformity. Part of the problem lay with the teachers who were ill trained and required some standard. By offering a guide to standardize the spelling of words, Webster hoped to promote the honor and prosperity of his country ("American Glory" 20–26).

The speller became widely popular. Within the first year, his publisher sold five thousand copies. In 1807 annual sales reached about 200,000 copies, and by 1837 the total sales to that date exceeded fifteen million copies. In 1880 Webster's speller sold more copies than any book except the Bible, with annual sales exceeding a million copies. In 1908 Webster's *Elementary Spelling Book* carried a heading describing it as the acknowledged standard of the English Language (Cremin, Preface np).

The popularity of Webster's speller endured because it defined American education. In the early nineteenth century, an important measure of people's education was their ability to spell. Webster arranged the speller so that it began with short words and moved on to longer, more difficult ones. Thus, people could rank their progress by the number of pages of the speller they had mastered. Spelling bees were public tests of individual ability and of community status. These contests grew into major social events that people held to demonstrate and reinforce the democratic character of America. The view was that in an aristocracy, people from different social classes wrote and spoke differently. But because American schools followed Webster's rules, anyone could win a spelling bee, and rich people and poor people learned to speak and write alike (Church and Sedlak 16–21).

In 1784 Webster published the second part of his series, *A Grammatical Institute of the English Language.* This part was a grammar. In the introduction, Webster claimed that his innovation was to frame the language on its own principles. Up to that time, Webster claimed, authors had constructed such texts by superimposing Latin grammar onto English. As a result, they made mistakes, did not adapt their texts to the abilities of youth, and made them more complicated than necessary (*Grammatical* 3–6).

A year later, Webster published the third volume of his *Grammatical Institute,* a collection of essays and dialogues. It was the first anthology to include works by American authors. To foster nationalism, Webster included speeches by leaders such as George Washington and exhortations by patriots such as Thomas Paine. At the same time, he incorporated works by eminent authors such as Shakespeare and Swift. One interesting addition was an essay by Thomas Day warning that Americans had to consider the rights of African Americans if they were to build a republic worthy of the name (Unger 80–81). In order to protect his work, Webster traveled from state to state urging the legislatures to adopt laws that would prevent other people from copying his books and selling them as their own. As a result, one historian calls Webster the father of the copyright (Commager 3).

In 1800 Webster took out an ad in a newspaper to announce his plans to compile a dictionary. He claimed that this contribution would complete his system for the instruction of youth. In it he proposed to remove those words that applied only to the lives people led years ago in England, and he wanted to add those new words that reflected changes in the way people lived in America. At Webster's announcement, critics attacked the project as a misguided effort to make money. They predicted that the dictionary would confuse people because Webster would pollute the language with slang and spread the capricious spellings of words (Moss 97–99).

Despite the criticisms, Webster set to work by himself. He approached the task in stages. In 1806 he published his first dictionary, *Compendious.* In 1807 and 1817, he offered abridgments for school use. His large work, *An American Dictionary of the English Language,* appeared in 1828.

The amount of labor involved in writing the dictionary was enormous. Webster compiled and wrote out in his own hand more than 70,000 listings, a preface that constituted a textbook for the study of the language, and a considerable amount of supplementary material. He gathered the citations for each word, traced its etymology, established its usage, determined the order of precedence of the multiple meanings of many words, and confirmed the definitions. In addition, he edited the manuscript, alphabetized the words, and read the printer's proofs for errors. All these jobs Webster did himself while he supported himself with other work that brought in money (Leavitt 21–22).

The dictionary was as popular as his speller. In 1829 Webster offered an abridgment, and in 1841 he published a business version. In that same year, he began a series of revisions to the corrected and enlarged edition. These revisions continue today as Webster's literary heirs carry on his work (Leavitt 23).

Although Webster wanted to build a national language, he also hoped his efforts would improve humankind. In 1788 he wrote that people considered grammatical searches to be the work of schoolboys. But because the incorrect use of words could lead nations into war, he insisted that grammatical questions were of importance to adults. To illustrate how ideas came into being from language, Webster traced how ideas originated from the way words were used. For example, Webster held that the word *devil* was a corruption of the phrase "the evil." Because the first two letters of *the* were often written and spoken as the letter "d," Webster imagined that people came to think of an entity that caused the problems that the word described ("Dissertation Concerning" 222–224).

Although more sophisticated theories of language have replaced Webster's contributions, his spellers and dictionaries facilitated those efforts. In writing them, Webster thought that he followed universal principles of language. Yet critics saw his efforts as serving specific social classes. Elite groups disliked the fact that Webster included words commonly used in industry and agriculture. Western agriculturalists complained that he imposed on them the speech of eastern bankers. Agreeing with these complaints, a spokesperson for western farmers, Andrew Jackson, reportedly said that he could not trust anybody who knew only one way to spell a word.

Could a Teaching Technique Impart Republican Virtues?

While Webster tried to use spellers and dictionaries to teach republican virtues, other educators sought a way to conduct classes that would teach large numbers of children obedience, diligence, and independence. In 1807, thinking they had found such a method, the members of the Free School Society in New York published *Improvements in Education as It Respects the Industrious Classes of the Community,* a book by Joseph Lancaster. It had appeared in England in 1803, attracting widespread attention and praise because it described how a single teacher could conduct a school for as many as eight hundred students. Most important, the teacher did not use corporal punishment to force students to work because a system of rewards and competition inspired them to work (Kaestle, Introduction 36–37).

An important reason the Free School Society chose to support the Lancaster method was that urban life presented new problems for the republic. From 1789 until 1830, most Americans lived in small communities. In 1830, for example, 91 percent of the population lived in towns with less than 2,500 inhabitants. The school in such communities was usually a small, crude structure constructed and controlled by the local citizens. Residents selected the teacher and to some extent determined the curriculum, usually requiring only the basic skills. In urban schools, however, the parents of the students did not exert the same control. Before 1830 most of the lower-class inhabitants of the few cities that existed were native born. Because many Americans feared these people would fall into vice and crime if they lacked education, charity schools spread throughout these cities during the 1790s and early 1800s. People turned to the Lancaster method to solve the problems represented by the instruction of these lower-class children (Kaestle, *Pillars* 13, 30, 36, 40).

Although Lancaster claimed to have devised his method entirely alone, it was not a new approach. He had trained students to teach other students, a strategy many other instructors had used before him. Lancaster's innovation was to delegate the instruction in a thorough and complete manner. He divided the classes into groups of ten to twenty students who had approximately similar abilities to learn certain tasks. He assigned students who knew the skill and could instruct the others to act as monitors. In spelling lessons, for example, words were written in lists on posters large enough for the group to read. As the group of students gathered around the poster, the monitor pointed to a column of words and one of the students attempted to read the first six words and spell each word by syllables. If the student made any mistake, the monitor asked the second student to correct the first. Throughout this process, the monitor did not provide any information unless none of the students knew the correct answer (Lancaster, "Improvements" 68–70).

The students changed groups frequently during the school day. Each group consisted of students who were to learn the same set of skills. Thus, in arithmetic the students who had to learn to make figures assembled with a monitor. However, some of them may have been in different groups for reading if they had acquired different skills in that subject. According to Lancaster, when students moved up the levels of the groups, they inspired the other students to work harder and follow them. He thought such emulation was an important stimulus to learning, and he used it along with competition and rewards for excellence. The highest award was to be a monitor. To make his system accessible, Lancaster claimed that anyone could become a tutor because the monitor's job was to ensure that the students taught each other (Lancaster, "Improvements" 71–74).

According to Lancaster, his system taught students to be obedient. They had to perform simple actions throughout the day, and they did them with other students. Because students knew the correct actions, they did not suffer under a teacher who acted arbitrarily. Oftentimes, the monitors gave short commands such as "front," "show slates," or "clean slates," and the group responded quickly. Some of these commands appeared on cards in abbreviated form. For example, T.S. meant "turn slates." When these appeared, the students responded; no one had to speak and the work went quickly. After giving a signal to "extend hands," the monitors took only a few moments to walk through the groups sitting in their rows and look at every student's hands to ensure they were well scrubbed (Lancaster, "Lancasterian System" 94–95).

Within the small groups, students learned to be diligent when they worked beside their fellows trying to master the material. They learned obedience when they learned to follow the short instructions and made the motions the monitors requested. Most important, since neither the teacher nor the monitors imposed their personalities during instruction, Lancaster thought that any group should be able to use his method. This belief was manifested most clearly in his efforts to teach religion.

The method commonly used to teach religion was to have children memorize passages from the Bible. Lancaster disliked this technique because he thought the tasks were difficult and the children might begin to hate the Scriptures as they repeated them again and again. To his delight, Lancaster found a catechism written by an eighteenth-century Quaker in which the answers were taken directly from the Bible. The catechism approach, wherein students repeated a series of short questions and answers, suited Lancaster's monitorial method. For example, one question was as follows: What will be the end or the reward of the perfect and upright man? The answer came from the Book of Psalms: The end of that man is peace. Lancaster reproduced the questions and answers and had the monitors lead the students through them. He proclaimed this method superior to all others because the answers were biblical passages and therefore acceptable to people of all denominations (Lancaster, "Improvements" 85–86).

Although Lancaster thought that using words from the Bible did not favor any particular denomination, critics complained that it did. Lancaster had joined the Society of Friends, known as the Quakers, and brought that Quaker influence to his method. As a result, in 1805 English critic Sarah Trimmer argued that he was using a catechism that supported the views of his religious denomination and ignored the catechisms written and approved for her denomination, the Church of England (Trimmer 103–104).

To strengthen her criticism, Trimmer turned to Andrew Bell, who had developed a similar monitorial system in India, to begin a controversy over the Lancaster method that lasted more than twenty years. Bell wrote a three-volume work, *The Elements of Tuition,* to explain his system, which was similar to Lancaster's except that he incorporated Anglican catechisms and liturgies. A group of philanthropists supported Bell and opened a model school in London to train monitors in Bell's method. As a result of the controversy, Lancaster could not create the national system in England to which he aspired. Instead, in 1818 Lancaster came to the United States to spread his ideas (Kaestle, Introduction 19–24, 29).

Some religious denominations, such as Catholics, resisted the monitorial method in the United States. In 1824 manuals of pedagogy written for Catholic teachers and brought to the United States recommended that teachers be the soul of their classes. According to these manuals, Catholic educators inspired the students to become more perfect Christians by providing competent instruction, instituting proper discipline, creating a comfortable environment, and setting a good example. Manuals published somewhat later criticized the Lancaster method for lacking denominational teachings and restricting the contact between teachers and students. Although these manuals did not prohibit the use of student monitors, they recommended that teachers mix a variety of methods. In Catholic schools, the manuals pointed out, the teacher should perform the instruction and maintain personal contact with all students (Panzer 116, 156–157).

Despite these criticisms, the supposed neutrality of Lancaster's method offered a rationale for charity schools to serve the urban poor in different settings. As a result, Lancaster schools spread quickly beyond their beginnings in New York City and Philadelphia. By 1825 Lancaster schools opened in such New York cities as Poughkeepsie, Hudson, Troy, Schenectady, and Utica. The Pennsylvania cities of Harrisburg, Pittsburgh, Erie, Lancaster, and New Castle opened monitorial schools. In Connecticut, Lancaster schools flourished in New Haven, Hartford, and Guilford. Other cities such as Detroit, Cincinnati, Lexington, and Louisville joined the movement (Kaestle, *Pillars* 42).

The Lancaster schools spread because they turned students into teachers who founded their own schools and followed the same method. During the day, students moved through the groups until they became monitors. Out of all the monitors, some became supervisors or monitor-generals. Often, these older monitors broke away from the school and started their own Lancaster school. However, by 1838, when Lancaster was killed in an accident in New York City, the movement fell into decline. There were two reasons why the movement failed. One was that Lancaster schools advertised themselves as an inexpensive way to educate the children of poor families. As the schools spread, communities decided they could afford something better for their local children. The other problem was that the system was built on the idea of poorly trained youth directing other children. As other schools produced more professionally trained teachers, monitorial systems fell into disrepute (Kaestle, Introduction 38, 44).

Could a System of Schools Select and Train Leaders?

At the same time that educators tried to use techniques such as the monitorial method to inculcate in students the virtues they thought people needed in order to preserve the republic, other educators sought to use the schools to select and train leaders who would protect the government from corruption. Thomas Jefferson represented this aim. Jefferson's ideas were complex. As noted earlier, the U.S. Constitution was drafted so as to prevent any group from corrupting the government. Although Jefferson disapproved of the Constitution when it was written, his conception of political reform fit this approach. In his efforts to reform Virginia's legal system, Jefferson recommended a system of checks and balances that restrained any leader or group from gaining excessive control. At the same time, he advocated freedom of the press and regular elections to make government accountable to the electorate (Howe 62–66).

Jefferson concentrated his efforts in education on building a set of institutions capped by a university that would select those geniuses who could best determine what was in everybody's interest. The schools would train these gifted students to exercise intelligent leadership. As he matured, Jefferson concentrated his efforts on the university. In fact, when political circumstances forced him to make a decision whether to distribute money to the primary schools or to the university, Jefferson chose to spend the money on the university where knowledge would be tested and sciences would flourish (Kett 242–246).

To some extent, Jefferson shared the notion that the republic depended on the virtue of the people, and that elementary schools could teach people to consider the needs of society before their personal desires. Jefferson sought to teach children to act morally by encouraging them to reflect on the consequences of their decisions. Instead of indoctrinating the students as Rush suggested, Jefferson wanted students to arrive at virtue through clear thinking. Although Jefferson thought most fiction would harm children, he acknowledged that judicious reading of some novels might be useful. These books could help students realize how beneficial an act of charity was and how disgusting an act of atrocity was. By appeals to their intelligence, Jefferson contended, children might be encouraged to act kindly and to avoid meanness (Wagoner, "That Knowledge" 122).

In 1779 Jefferson submitted the bill "For the More General Diffusion of Knowledge" to the Virginia legislature. The bill called for the division of every county into small districts of about six square miles. In each district, a school would be established to teach reading, writing, and arithmetic. This would total about one hundred schools in each county. Both boys and girls would attend these schools. From each district school, the smartest and ablest boy would proceed to one of the twenty grammar schools Jefferson proposed for the state. Girls would not be eligible for further education. In the grammar schools, the boys would learn Greek, Latin, geography, and the higher branches of arithmetic. At the end of six years, the top half of the students in the grammar schools would proceed to the College of William and Mary. Members of this college would act as overseers to ensure that the curricula in the lower schools fit the needed preparation for college (Jefferson, *Notes* 146–149).

Jefferson claimed this legislation had two aims. One benefit was that it would provide an education adapted to the age, abilities, and condition of every student because those who could not afford the school would be sent free of charge. Children from wealthier families would pay tuition. Another benefit was that the plan would select the best and brightest boys from each social class and each geographic region of the state and train him so that he could return his talents to the state. Jefferson believed that his plan would ensure that all people had sufficient education to make intelligent choices when they voted for their leaders. At the same time, it encouraged people to select leaders from all social classes and be assured that they were well qualified for the positions they were to occupy (*Notes* 146–149).

Jefferson submitted this bill as part of the revised general code a few days after he had been elected governor of Virginia. At the same time, to broaden the College of William and Mary's curriculum to include more than theological studies, Jefferson sought to amend the charter of that college to free it from control of the church. He also offered another bill to build a public library in Richmond that was open to all people. Although the legislature rejected Jefferson's plans, he and his supporters repeatedly introduced them in various forms. In 1786 James Madison wrote to Jefferson that his bills had undergone another and indulgent consideration. However, the legislature's chief objection was the expense of instating his ideas. Although parts of the bill calling for the establishment of elementary schools passed in 1796, the legislature did not require county courts to begin building them. As a result, Jefferson considered this a defeat. In 1810, however, the legislature created a literary fund to establish public schools. This rejuvenated Jefferson's ideas. Finally, in 1817 the legislature passed a less extensive version of Jefferson's school bill (Honeywell 10–21).

In an 1814 letter to his nephew, Peter Carr, president of the board of trustees of Albemarle Academy, Jefferson explained why he maintained his campaign for public education.

Specifically, the letter explained how to set up the academy. To describe what the school should become, Jefferson outlined his views on education, asserting that all citizens should have educations proportionate to their conditions and pursuits in life. According to Jefferson, most citizens fell into two classes of people. One was a laboring class that should enter into agriculture or apprenticeships after three years of rudimentary training in reading, writing, and arithmetic. The second class was a learned group that should go into the sciences and on to college. This group would attend general schools where they would study language, mathematics, and philosophy ("Letter to Peter Carr" 222–223).

This learned group could be subdivided into two more groups. One group consisted of students who were wealthy and wanted to prepare for government service or usefulness in a private branch of life. They would leave after attending the general school to pursue more specified studies. The other group of learned students had to obtain a livelihood, and they would prepare for the learned professions. These students would move from the general schools to professional schools, where they would pursue one of three courses: the fine arts such as civil architecture, gardening, painting, sculpture, and music; rural economy and technical philosophy such as horticulture, veterinary medicine, human medicine, surgery, and pharmacy; or, finally, theology and law ("Letter to Peter Carr" 224–225).

Within this overview, Jefferson described the role that Albemarle Academy would play. The academy should serve as a general school that would prepare students for further training. Thus, he recommended that the school set up four departments and that each department have one professor. These departments included languages and history; mathematics, medicine, and anatomy; chemistry, zoology, botany, and mineralogy; and philosophy ("Letter to Peter Carr" 226–227).

To Jefferson, this division of subject areas was merely a reasonable beginning; the curriculum should change when circumstances allowed. However, he outlined three points about education in this letter and in most of his other writings that he felt were appropriate for all schools at all times: (1) students should be separated into groups by their abilities; (2) some students should receive vocational training; and (3) gifted students should undertake theoretical studies and the classical languages that were the foundation of scientific studies.

Could Students Preserve Their Cultural Perspectives When They Studied the Same Subjects?

Although Jefferson wanted students to receive an education suited to their abilities, he thought everyone deserved the same primary education. Had Jefferson been thinking like Benjamin Rush, he might have suggested that this was the opportunity for a teacher to indoctrinate students into Christianity and mold them into republican machines. But in 1818, when Jefferson repeated the aims of primary education, he made those objectives more neutral, including such things as providing students with the information they needed to transact business, enable them to calculate, improve their morals by reading, help them understand their duties to neighbors and the country, teach them about their rights, and equip them to choose with discretion those they select to lead them. To the higher branches of education attainable by the better students, Jefferson relegated the formation of legislators and judges; the instruction about the principles of government; the development of the ability to harmonize the interests of manufacturers, farmers, and businesspeople; and the development of the faculties of reason and the cultivation of morals ("Report" 249–250).

A distinctive element in Jefferson's design of the University of Virginia was the devotion to the principle of intellectual freedom. At a time when most institutions of higher learning were tied to religious denominations, Jefferson wanted to base the university on the idea that the human mind had to be free to explore any subject. To ensure that religious indoctrination did not intrude on the freedom of inquiry, Jefferson did not affiliate the university with any religious organization. He called for no professor of theology, nor did he require students to attend any religious services. In short, Jefferson applied the principles of the Virginia Statute of Religious Freedom to the university (Wagoner, *Thomas Jefferson* 33–35).

Jefferson wanted students at all levels to learn to act decently toward their fellows, to develop the ability to think clearly, but to recognize the limits of their own knowledge and to appreciate those who were more competent. However, even for the students with the least ability and training, this did not mean that they learned to trust an elite group of privileged individuals. Jefferson took pains to ensure that the governing elite would be chosen from every group in the state to receive the training that would qualify them for those positions.

Jefferson's idea was to divide all the counties in the state into wards and to allow each ward to control its school. On the one hand, this meant that every group could offer some members opportunities to prepare for leadership. Equally important to Jefferson, if the lowest level of local schools was controlled by the people who would attend them, they would do everything possible to advance them. He argued that the advantages of such a practice had been gained in New England by the practice of town meetings, which gave all citizens a sense of responsibility for decisions. On the other hand, Jefferson's opponents recommended that the schools should be controlled by a central authority that would hold public meetings. Jefferson replied that this would prevent diligent, honest parents who lived and worked in outlying regions from participating in the governance of the schools. Jefferson claimed that the only citizens who could attend such central meetings were the drunkards and loafers who remained around the capital ("Plan" 228–229).

Under his system, the wards offered three years of rudimentary education. From each of these schools, one student proceeded to the middle level of education, which Jefferson called general schools. In the general schools, which students entered when they were nine or ten years old, students pursued classical languages. According to Jefferson, students should begin studying the classical languages at such an early age because those languages formed the foundation of the study of the sciences. Unfortunately, the schools were scattered over the state in places inaccessible to many students. Because such schools served as entryways to the university, Jefferson proposed that there be one such school every eighty square miles. This would mean that every person in the state could reach such a school in one day on horseback ("Letter to Governor" 231).

Jefferson hoped that his plan for public schools would help people maintain their separate communities and teach them to cooperate. That is, students from each geographic area would receive a state-supported basic education from which the best and brightest males would go on to receive college training. Assuming that distinct types of groups lived in different regions, Jefferson believed that some people from each social group would learn to become representatives, senators, or other leaders who could serve the interests of their former communities.

However, Jefferson did not hold attitudes that would be described today as multicultural. He did not believe that women were qualified to vote intelligently, because they lacked the economic and personal independence essential to making informed judgments. According to him, their emotional nature suited them more to be mothers rather than careful, deliberating citizens. Further, Jefferson was certain that Black people could never live with White people on equal terms. The problem was not the inferiority of either group to the other but that White people held strong feelings of prejudice against Blacks and that African Americans resented the infinite wrongs of slavery. Although Jefferson held that Native Americans were capable of civilized behavior, he did not imagine them to be part of the republic until they gave up their original cultures. Consequently, Jefferson had in mind a republic that was ethnically uniform (Howe 68–70).

In fact, Jefferson's model became controversial because it implied that all citizens had to learn the same material before they could participate in government. That is, small farmers could not participate on an equal footing with landed aristocrats until they developed the intellectual sophistication of the upper classes. Jefferson may have wanted to offer all groups the opportunity to learn the literary and legal traditions that he believed were the basis of governmental actions. Nonetheless, he believed that training in the classical liberal arts provided the prerequisite for leadership. For him, this training not only taught people how to think but it screened out those who were less able. His idea was that if everyone had to pass through such courses in order to occupy positions of authority, only the most talented individuals would become leaders. Further, because those leaders came from all social classes and from all different regions, Jefferson assumed they would take the interests of their original groups into account when they had to make decisions for the common good (Mehl, "Education in American History" 15–16).

Jefferson's ideas suffered from two flaws. First, nothing about the liberal arts warranted their use as a selection device. In fact, many people came to believe that when people used the classical studies to test students' abilities, the testing function distorted those subjects. Instead, they argued that classical works demonstrated their power only when teachers sought ways to enable everyone to learn the material. The second problem was that when children of one social class received schooling in the ways of another social class, they lost the perspectives of their former group and adopted the values and orientations of the new social class. As a result, rather than teach the liberal arts some educators sought materials that reinforced the different values of various groups (Mehl, "Education in American History" 15–16).

Were the Classical Languages of Latin and Greek Essential to Higher Education?

Although Jefferson recommended that the College of William and Mary stop providing instruction in Latin and Greek, he did this because he expected students to learn those languages in middle schools, and he wanted to substitute instruction in other languages at the university. He retained his view that the study of the classical languages of Greek and Latin was the basis of higher education (Honeywell 112–114).

Interestingly, the founders of the republic may not have known Latin and Greek. In fact, some historians claim that the ancient writers did not influence the thinking of the leaders of the American Revolution. Nonetheless, Jefferson acquired considerable ability in the classical languages. According to one historian, Jefferson's favorite language was Greek. He considered Homer the father of Western literature, and he took Livy, Sallust, and Tacitus as models for correct writing. In a similar fashion, John Adams distinguished himself in Latin studies at Harvard and often quoted Latin authors. Many other founders of the U.S. republic had difficulty with Latin and Greek. If they knew the works, they read the classics in translation. In this form, however, they may have read and reread these books. For example, George Washington loved Joseph Addison's play *Cato,* which was based on Plutarch's biography. Washington designed his actions to conform to scenes from this play when he faced difficulties with disgruntled officers in his army. Later, when president, Washington recited several lines from the play at various times. Although he never owned a copy of the play, he had seen it several times and memorized some of the words (Richard 1–2, 28–32, 57–60).

Although many American leaders may not have been able to read Greek or Latin, classical authors held a position of prominence during the early republican period. When the former colonists thought about how to construct a republic, their discussions were filled with references to history and to the ancient societies of Greece and Rome. Most of the founders would have agreed with Benjamin Franklin that people could understand the historical references without personal knowledge of Latin or Greek. However, the fact that the words and the names of ancient authors appeared in everyday life made the ability to speak Latin appear to be a sign of greater understanding. As a result, it was not surprising that many people who lacked any knowledge of Greek or Latin would see training in these classical languages as essential to a complete education.

By 1828, despite the prestige that training in the classical languages might afford, reformers complained that they were meaningless and useless. But the greatest shortcoming in the study of classical languages may have been the teaching methods. For example, at Yale College, recent graduates served as tutors who carried out most of the instruction. As a result, they could do no more than drill students on the assigned passages from the textbooks. Furthermore, at the smaller, less prestigious colleges, the quality of instruction may have been worse, especially if they imitated the Yale curriculum (Kelley 160–161).

Despite the problems in instruction, critics looked for changes in the curriculum. In 1827, Noyes Darling, who had graduated from Yale in 1801, recommended to the Yale Corporation that the college drop instruction in the ancient languages of Greek and Latin and substitute other subjects more relevant to modern life. Because Darling was a state senator and his feelings represented the thoughts of many members of the General Assembly, the corporation appointed a committee to study the issue that included the state governor, Darling, and the president of Yale. Their investigation led to a report in 1828 in which the faculty of Yale College attempted to explain why they should retain these dead languages in the curriculum (Kelley 161–162).

In the report, the faculty acknowledged that some of the subjects taught at the college appeared to be irrelevant to modern life. However, the report contended that when those subjects were joined together, they formed a balanced curriculum that enabled the college to lay the foundations of superior education. The curriculum taught students how to learn.

According to the faculty report, the students' minds were made up of various powers such as reasoning, imagination, taste, eloquence, judgment, and memory. The curriculum trained all of these powers, thereby enabling students' minds to develop harmoniously and naturally. For example, mathematics developed demonstrative reasoning. Physical science taught students how to gather facts, determine principles from particular evidence, and consider probabilities. Ancient literature offered models of taste, and philosophy taught the art of thinking (Faculty 297–301).

To profit from the instruction at the college, the report continued, the students had to work by themselves to acquire a grasp of the subject matter. They were not left completely on their own, however. Professors headed the departments, arranged the plan of instruction, and taught the more difficult aspects of the subjects. After a professor assigned a particular portion of the text to the students, the tutors administered frequent examinations that came from textbooks to ensure that students mastered the material. The report justified using recent graduates as tutors on the grounds that such young men had the most enthusiasm in communicating common principles. Consequently, according to the report, they made better teachers of fundamental ideas than did the more advanced professors (Faculty 302–307).

To further justify using young, inexperienced tutors, the faculty report held that the daily examinations in the recitation room were the most important part of the college activities. Every year the college held public examinations of the seniors. Prominent persons attended these oral tests that took up to twelve to fourteen days. However, the faculty report asserted that these tests were for public display. In the examination room, the report noted, true education took place. The students showed the extent of their mastery, and the tutor could make corrections or introduce information in an informal lecture (Faculty 304–305).

Yale's curriculum omitted professional studies. The faculty report explained that this was to encourage students to pursue literary and scientific understandings that they would not develop in the bustle of earning a living. In fact, the report argued that Benjamin Franklin could not have developed his wide interests if there had been no colleges, because these institutions set an example that stimulated him to aim at a similar goal (Faculty 308–309).

The faculty report also admitted that college training did not fit young men for practical affairs in the world. The college began a process of education rather than completed it. However, the report noted that a college education prepared the students' minds to learn the practical steps needed in any pursuit such as business or manufacturing, and to apply them in enlightened, comprehensive ways. This happened, the report asserted, because in the various subjects the college taught students the relation between theory and practice (Faculty 310–312).

The faculty report gave two reasons why all students should pursue the same course of studies. First, if students selected those branches they found most important, they would avoid other subjects from the curriculum and upset the balance it provided. Second, students might find they had an interest and a capacity for classical subjects if they tried to learn them. At any rate, the faculty report suggested that students should pursue their particular interests after they learned the common elements of the several sciences. In this way, they could acquire the foundation of learning that the faculty believed to be important (Faculty 313).

Although the faculty report asserted that the college should require all students to learn the same subjects, it did not ask that all students attend colleges. Instead, the report noted that other schools such as commercial high schools or agricultural seminaries served proper and distinct functions. Students who disagreed with the aims of the college could go to these schools. Even if the college could increase its enrollment and its income by diversifying, the faculty report recommended against it (Faculty 318–319).

As far as the particular value of the classical languages of Greek and Latin, the faculty report listed three advantages. First, such learning was essential to the study of all European literatures because they derived from classical sources. Similarly, the standards of taste and beauty in fields such as architecture and sculpture came from Greece. Second, a study of those languages exercised every faculty of the mind including memory, judgment, reasoning, taste, and imagination. According to the report, the classical languages were more helpful in exercising these faculties than was a study of modern languages. Third, ancient Greek and Latin appeared in several professions such as theology, law, and medicine, and an understanding of those languages aided practitioners. Although the faculty report acknowledged that a mastery of French or German appeared more practical, it contended that those languages did not reveal the elements of modern cultures, discipline the faculties of the students' minds, nor prepare for professional studies. For these skills, the students should pursue ancient Greek and Latin (Faculty 328–330).

The Yale report was important because the college enjoyed the largest enrollment of the colleges in the country, and its graduates started other smaller schools throughout the South and West. In 1829, Yale had 359 students. In the same year, Harvard had the second largest enrollment with 247 students, while Union was third with 227. By 1839, Yale's enrollment grew to 411 students. Union was second with 286 students and the University of Virginia was third with 247 (Schmidt 53). In addition, of the 75 colleges operating in 1840, graduates of Yale were the presidents of 36. Twenty-two of those colleges had presidents from Princeton, which followed a similar curriculum. In part, Yale's graduates became presidents of other colleges because the college was a center of evangelical groups that sought to save the western regions from infidelity and Catholicism. These groups established small frontier colleges to further their aims. In addition, former students of Yale, such as Frederick A. P. Barnard, carried the principles of the report to many southern institutions such as the University of Alabama, the University of Virginia, and the University of Mississippi (Urofsky 62–63; Butts 125–128).

The report had two clear effects on higher education up to the U.S. Civil War. First, because the report defended the humanist tradition that Jefferson supported, it reduced the role religion could play in forming the college curriculum. At the same time, however, people accorded the report such respect that colleges did not attempt other reforms. Thus, the report encouraged Yale and many other schools to retain only literary and scientific curricula (Rudolph 134–135).

According to historians such as Herbert Kliebard, the report had an unfortunate effect on elementary and secondary schools. Because the Yale report compared the mind to a group of muscles and explained how each subject in the curriculum exercised these various muscles, teachers used this metaphor to justify monotonous drill and mindless recitation in their classrooms (Kliebard 5–7). However, if nineteenth-century teachers used the Yale report as Kliebard claims, they distorted the ideas the faculty presented. The report did not justify boring classrooms nor outdated subject matters, although such things may have resulted even at Yale. Instead, the report was a plea that all students from all social groups study a balanced literary and scientific curriculum as the faculty understood those terms.

What Did Men Think Women Should Learn?

In the new republic, people's views about women's education were often consistent with those they held about men's education. Patriots such as Franklin, Rush, Webster, and Jefferson agreed that women should learn the correct virtues to be wives and the knowledge needed as mothers to instruct the boys. According to historians such as Thomas Woody, these suggestions represented a new concept of women's education because they urged women to pursue higher studies than were available during the colonial period (*History* 301).

The struggle for independence seemed to make people think more liberally about the education of women. Although they did not challenge the role of women as subordinate to men, Franklin came close to taking such a view. He contended that women had the same capacity as men to be reasonable if they had the same advantages. He did not think that men should be the head of their households unless they were the more intelligent of the partners (Van Doren 152–153).

Franklin further warned against women being trained only in what might be called the decorative arts such as music and dancing. Although such skills might enable them to attract fiancés, he thought these young girls should receive some sort of business training to prevent them from having difficulty later in life should their husbands die. One problem Franklin foresaw was that many widows would have restricted estates and therefore difficulty providing for their children. In these circumstances, widows would be easy prey for crafty men who wanted to take their meager inheritance (Franklin, *Autobiography* 93–94).

Benjamin Rush urged the state of Pennsylvania to attend to the education of women. He approved of coeducation, which Philadelphia had proved to be successful when it admitted women into its academy. Further, Rush criticized men who wanted to prevent women from learning philosophy, science, and religion on the grounds that these studies would make them unfit for domestic life. According to Rush, these men thought they could more easily control ignorant women. To show the error of this view, Rush warned that weak-minded women would resist the most reasonable controls. Rush also argued that women in America needed an education because they cared for their husbands' properties, educated the children, participated in social affairs, and directed poorly trained servants. This meant that women should learn English, handwriting, bookkeeping, geography, history, vocal music, dancing, poetry, and moral essays. Rush thought it was most important for girls to learn about the different sects of the Christian religion. Unfortunately, women married when they were young, leaving them little time for education. Hence, Rush excluded subjects that took substantial time such as instrumental music and French. He suggested it would be more advantageous for girls to read French literature in translation ("Thoughts" 27–39).

In a similar manner, Webster complained about what he saw as the prevailing tendency for families to spend money they could ill afford to send their young girls to boarding schools for two or three years, where they learned to play the harpsichord, to dance, and to draw. The problem was that this education unfit them for daily life that required them to work with their husbands. Instead of providing practical skills and solid virtues, these boarding schools gave girls dreams of fine dresses, beautiful coaches, and extravagant living that they could never acquire or achieve. According to Webster, a better solution was for women to undertake an education to fit them for the duties of their station. This meant they should learn to speak English properly and to write it beautifully. He did not think it was important for them to learn French, but arithmetic and geography were essential ("On the Education of Youth" 70–72).

For his part, Jefferson demurred that he never systematically worked out a plan of education for women. Yet he offered several clues to indicate that, had he devoted the time to the project, it would not have differed from the education he proposed for boys. In his original plan to create a system of public schools, he included both girls and boys among the students in the elementary schools. Although Jefferson made no recommendations for public training of girls beyond that level, he devoted considerable care to educating his daughters, whom he raised after his wife died. He wrote to Martha and Mary urging them to practice domestic skills and asking how they could direct plantation work when they were married if they could not perform the functions themselves. At the same time, he thought they should have an education similar to the training given to boys because they might have to direct the family should their husbands be unable or unwilling to carry out their responsibilities. He feared they might marry what he called "blockheads." Therefore, Jefferson encouraged his daughters to study languages such as Latin, French, and Spanish, as well as English. He directed their reading in literature and history. For young women, he recommended dancing although he believed that married women did not use the skill. In addition, he thought that drawing was a useful amusement. Except for asking his daughters to learn how to run a household, he thought they should understand those subjects men were to study (Wagoner, "That Knowledge" 123–125).

What Did Women Think Women Should Learn?

Rush, Webster, and Jefferson thought that women should study the courses available to men, and women joined in the effort to expand those opportunities. The colonial schools had offered women little more than basic instruction. As cities grew, however, private masters offered higher studies to some women students. These masters and their students campaigned to extend schools for young women. An example of such a woman reformer was Emma Willard (Woody, *History* 301). Born in 1787, Willard studied at the public school in Berlin, Connecticut. When she was fifteen, she entered the town academy and studied for two years under the able guidance of Thomas Miner, a Yale graduate. Married in 1809, Willard opened a boarding school in 1814 when her husband suffered financial problems. In 1819 she sought to move her school to New York and with the support of Governor De Witt Clinton petitioned the state legislature for support for her school (W. Goodsell, *Pioneers* 16–23).

In her petition, Willard argued that an enlightened government should provide education for females because this would elevate the character of the community. For example, women needed a proper education in order to raise their children appropriately. The problem Willard noted was that private teachers ran the schools for women, whereas the schools for men received public support. According to the law, any woman could open a school. Usually, these facilities were crowded and unattractive. Although some teachers were well trained, many were not. In some cases, to save money one teacher conducted ten different classes at the same time. Further, all of these female teachers depended on their students for support. Therefore, it was in the teachers' interest to offer lessons that were easily learned and fancy enough to attract more students. They tended not to undertake the rigorous training that would slowly cultivate students' minds ("Plan" 45–53).

Willard complained that many of the female seminaries taught female students to be pleasing to men. Although she acknowledged that women should retain feelings of submission and obedience to men, she thought it was better for them to strive to perfect their moral characters and to learn to be companions to men. In this way, she argued, women could influence men to keep their proper course ("Plan" 56–57).

In explaining the curriculum of an institution for women's education, Willard offered a sketch of what a public seminary for women should offer. The building should be large and comfortable with a library containing an adequate number of books on different subjects and some good paintings to offer models of taste. Instruction would fall under four headings. Religious and moral instruction would be conducted in all classes by the example of the teachers, and religious observance on campus would be required. Literary studies included the sciences and philosophy. Domestic classes would provide exercise and offer the chance for women to improve their own homes when they left school. The ornamental branches included drawing, painting, penmanship, and dancing. Although Willard suggested that women not be trained for public speaking, she thought they gained some opportunity in preparing for public examinations ("Plan" 59–69).

Willard offered a new argument to the New York legislature by asserting that a systematic course of study in science and philosophy could not exist without state control and support. Willard appealed to the reasons the legislators supported men's colleges. In the early nineteenth century, colleges teaching liberal arts curricula did not attract enough male students and garner enough tuition to support themselves. Because legislators thought the programs were valuable for students, they extended state financial support to these colleges. Willard asked for similar treatment for women's seminaries that chose to offer equally unpopular but beneficial courses (Beadie 189).

The legislature did not approve the support Willard requested. However, the people in the city of Troy, New York, raised $4,000 through taxes and erected a three-story brick building that met her requirements for a seminary. This allowed Willard to open the seminary in Troy in 1821. One of her hopes in moving there was that it would inspire the legislature to change its policy about offering financial aid to women's educational institutions. She believed one of the reasons her first petition was not granted was that the town where she had her school, Waterford, offered no support. According to one of Willard's biographers, however, the New York legislature did not change its policies (Lord 92–95).

Despite the report of Willard's biographer, the New York legislature did provide aid to women's seminaries, but it did so in increments. In 1819 the New York legislature incorporated Waterford Female Academy, and by 1826 it extended five more charters to female seminaries. Although this process did not extend financial state support, it provided the schools a permanent status and allowed them to accumulate endowments. In 1828 New York began awarding regents status and extending monies from a literature fund to academies for higher branches of English education and classical studies. This made female seminaries eligible, and twenty-four female academies won regents status by 1860. Unfortunately, after 1875 state support for female education in New York rapidly diminished as coeducational high schools replaced women's academies (Beadie 191, 200).

In addition to petitioning for state aid for women's academies, Willard published textbooks. Some of these, such as her textbooks on geography and history, sought to improve the education of all children. For example, in her book *Geography for Beginners,* she wrote that she tried to make the subject comprehensible to young children by asking them to begin with maps of their own towns. From there they proceeded to construct a map of the United States and then a map of the world. This strategy was contrary to the procedure common in texts in which the authors presented maps of the world immediately to young children. Willard acknowledged that these authors tried to make things simple by reducing the ideas to general statements. But Willard found that the most general statement, a map of the world, was hardest for children to understand ("Geography" 91–93).

Although some of her aids were helpful, others must have been difficult to use. For example, in her history book Willard produced chronological plans in the form of trees. The chart marked eras in time chronologically from left to right over the top of the tree. The branches that reached to these eras represented events. Thus, from a central trunk marked "History of the United States," a branch reached to the extreme left marked "Columbus' Discovery of America, 1492," and a similar branch extended to the extreme right marked "Florida Ceded, 1820." Despite this graph's complexity, Willard was convinced it would help children associate dates and events (W. Goodsell, *Pioneers* 83–87).

Willard seemed trapped in a paradox about political activity for women. Although she petitioned the New York state legislature for financial assistance for women's seminaries, she discouraged her female students from taking any interest in elections, and she urged her friends to have little to do with political struggles. For example, in 1832 a group of women founded the Female Anti-slavery Society. As members attempted to speak out in favor of abolition, they also confronted the fact that they could not hold property or retain their own earnings. As a result, they began to join together to change their own legal status. However, Willard was careful to stay away from this movement. She wrote to her friend Catharine Beecher, pointing out that the family with the father at its head was the natural government. Should a woman take a position on political affairs, she added, the father might contend that academic studies inflated her ideas. Therefore, she concluded, they should not become involved with such political causes as abolition or temperance because it would hurt their efforts to advance women's education (Lutz 61–63).

Willard was convinced that rigorous academic training was essential if young women were to contribute to their families and their communities, but she did not believe that such training enabled them to compete with men or perform tasks usually carried out by men. This attitude seemed to be shared by many Americans. In 1831, when Alexis de Tocqueville arrived in the United States to survey the effects of democracy on a nation, he was struck by the general equality of condition among the people. In one sense, this extended to the sexes, he added, because young women guided themselves more completely than he had seen in any other society. However, young women followed quite different lines of action than did men. Tocqueville concluded that the members of each sex kept pace with the members of the other, but they remained in different pathways (26, 234, 244).

Tocqueville found that women in the United States were confined to a narrow circle of domestic life and that their position made them dependent. Nonetheless, he was surprised to find women occupying positions of moral and intellectual equality with men. In fact, he noted, in the United States men were more likely to treat women as virtuous and refined than men were in Europe. He noticed that young, unmarried women could travel alone in the United States in safety whereas they could not in Europe. This happened, he thought, because Americans believed that women and men deserved the same respect even though they performed different functions in society. While Americans did not believe women had the same type of courage or intellect as men, they did not doubt that they had courage and intellect. Such views would provide the basis for an intelligent and stable democracy, Tocqueville concluded with approval (246). Willard appeared to concur.

What Was Wrong with People's Views of Education during the Early National Period?

During the early national period, social leaders sought to reinforce the goals they believed they had won during the War for Independence. For this reason, no matter which direction they took, the resulting educational plan suffered from the same problem. When educators sought to inculcate the students with the virtues they believed supported the republic, they chose those virtues from a restricted group. Likewise, when educators sought to use the schools to select and train leaders for the republic, they designed a program that fit the backgrounds of a specific group.

Naturally, these two approaches did not remain distinct. As controversies arose about the proper arrangement of schools and curricula, educators blended the different aims of education to fit the growing and changing society. That is, while they sought to implant in all students republican values, they also selected and trained prospective leaders. Again, however, one group seemed to provide the standard for the others to emulate.

Politicians and educators recognized this danger. When Webster sought to form a national language, he claimed that he did not affirm the tendencies of any one group. He thought he chose the standard according to universal laws of language. Nevertheless, critics complained that he took his standard from the speech found in New England villages. The same problem arose for Jefferson. When he presumed that the liberal arts were the basis of further learning, he thought he had a neutral device with which to select and train prospective politicians. However, even here the course of study served one group more than others.

There may be no solution to these problems. But if people realize the dangers, they may reduce their effects. Although teachers must approach their work as if a particular subject matter is universally important, they must also realize that, after a certain point, any knowledge or any particular way of behaving or speaking cannot be imposed on all peoples. However, if teachers surrender easily and decide they will not impose some behavior pattern or learning on recalcitrant children, students may lose the chance to profit from a new way of acting or thinking. If teachers refuse to acknowledge that some learning is not essential, they may become hollow imitations of educated human beings.

Most important, educators cannot determine where necessary instruction stops and excessive imposition begins. But knowing that the point exists can help teachers avoid the problems that confronted Rush and Webster. Because they considered selflessness an essential virtue for people living in a democracy, these men suggested that students should have no control in classrooms so that they avoided selfishness. Unfortunately, in following this suggestion, teachers may have acted in ways that contradicted the ideal of democracy.

TIMELINE
1776–1830

1779 Noah Webster left Yale and became a schoolmaster in Hartford, Connecticut

1779 Thomas Jefferson submitted an education bill to the Virginia legislature

1781 Webster graduated with a master's degree from Yale and passed the bar

1783 Webster's *A Grammatical Institute of the English Language* became a success

1784 Webster published a second part to *A Grammatical Institute*

1786 Benjamin Rush proposed a public school system for Pennsylvania

1787 The U.S. Constitutional Convention sought to keep the country united

1796 Virginia passed parts of Jefferson's school bill

1805 Sarah Trimmer argued that Lancaster's religious teaching methods influenced students in a way instruction should not

1806 Webster published his first dictionary, *Compendious*

1810 Virginia's legislature established a literary fund for its public schools

1814 Emma Willard opened a boarding school

1817 The state of Virginia passed a larger part of Jefferson's school bill

1818 Joseph Lancaster came to the United States to spread his education ideas

1821 Willard opened a seminary in Troy, New York

1824 Catholic teachers received pedagogy manuals

1827 Noyles Darling suggested to the Yale Corporation that Yale College drop its Greek and Latin studies

1828 Webster released *An American Dictionary of the English Language*

1828 Yale College faculty defended classical languages as part of their curriculum

CHAPTER

3 Common Schools, Teacher Training, and the Bible: 1830–1860

Catherine Esther Beecher

OVERVIEW

From 1830 until 1860, advocates of the common school movement campaigned to create systems of state schools. They believed that the country's population growth, increased immigration, and economic development made the state support and control of schools essential. Several individuals in different parts of the United States took prominent positions in

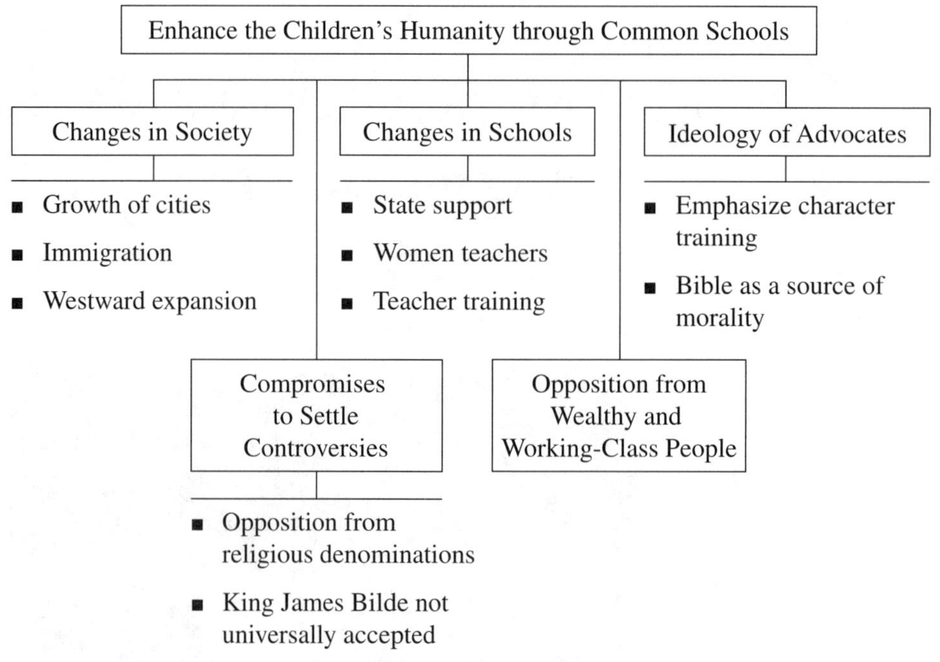

this movement. The popular press helped by publishing articles in educational journals and women's magazines that called for the advancement of education. In these articles, the authors combined into one issue the development of normal schools, the education of women, and the replacement of male teachers with women. Common school advocates shared an ideology, which they expressed in speeches, reports, textbooks, popular magazines, and curriculum proposals, that might be considered a Protestant, middle-class view. These common school advocates asserted that republican government depended on the individual character of its citizens, and they also believed that people fell into poverty because of flaws in their own characters. They thought that moral reform and social progress were best aided by Protestant Christianity. However, these advocates avoided most political controversies and offered compromises to win support from groups such as religious denominations that feared their children would be forced to learn another faith, poor people who thought their children would not be able to attend school, and wealthy people who opposed paying taxes for the education of other people's children. These compromises were not entirely successful, and they resulted in educational controversies throughout the twentieth century.

In the 1830s, Why Did Reformers Want to Change Schools?

In 1830 most White Americans had attended schools near their homes. Although few people kept careful records, most residents in rural, northern districts attended an elementary school for some period. In cities, philanthropists established charity schools for the children of poor families. Southern states appeared to have lower rates of school attendance. In all these cases, school sessions were brief, buildings were primitive, and teachers knew only a little more than their students. For adult education, there were lyceums, mechanics' institutes, and libraries. Printing businesses flourished because most people were literate (Kaestle, *Pillars* 62–63).

One advantage to this pattern was that every group could have schools serving their interests. But a serious shortcoming remained. Groups with wealth could afford more schooling for their children, whereas impoverished groups could not. States lacked ways to spread the costs among all citizens. Although states had had many opportunities to support schools before 1830, none of these proposals provided an adequate basis to develop schools. For example, in a series of ordinances in 1785 and 1787, the federal government set aside land in the Northwest territories to be used to support schools. When the lands were leased, they failed to raise sufficient funds. When the lands were sold, as they were in Ohio, Indiana, and Illinois, they did not produce adequate revenue. In Wisconsin the lands were sold at very low rates to attract people to the state. When the sales did make money, state officials lost or squandered it (Taylor 114–120).

People may have ignored such opportunities because the voluntary arrangements for education appeared adequate. However, from 1830 to 1860, three changes in the United States made people think that state governments should enact legislation to provide financial assistance to local community schools. First, when the population increased, it drew more immigration to the United States, attracted people from farms to cities, and caused western expansion. Second, the industrial changes that inspired the growth of cities required that people learn to live differently than they had on farms. Third, with western expansion, a political party serving agrarian interests replaced the party that served industry and commerce. Because the new political leaders came from rural areas, members of the older social groups feared that the new political leaders would destroy the republic unless they acquired the virtues needed in a democratic society.

The first change, the expansion of the population, was rapid and universal. In 1750 the population in Europe totaled about 140,000,000 people. By 1850 it had grown to about 260,000,000. Similar gains appeared in eastern countries such as Russia. The United States shared in this growth. In 1800 the United States had a total population of 864,746. This increased to 2,969,640 by 1860. This growth within the United States took place at a rate of about 35 percent per year (Handlin 25; U.S. Bureau of Census 8).

A high birthrate of about 55 births per 1,000 people in 1800 contributed to the increase in population in the United States. However, from 1820 to 1854, immigration added increasing numbers of residents. Rough figures, which include returning Americans as well as immigrants, estimate that 8,000 immigrants entered the United States in 1820. By 1830 the number rose to 23,000. In 1831 the number of immigrants doubled. Around 430,000 immigrants entered the United States in 1854. Ninety percent of these immigrants came from England, Germany, and most of all from Ireland. In 1820 and again in 1853, almost one-half of the immigrants were Irish (North 23, 96–97).

According to Oscar Handlin, Europe's population growth caused the increased immigration to the United States. The European population expanded because the death rate of infants under the age of two declined. Although Handlin cannot say why more children survived infancy, he notes that this increase pushed young people to leave their homes. In

European villages, for example, under this new situation a young man could no longer be sure that he would be able to live at the status his father enjoyed. With more children in the family, some young men had to find work outside the home or each son had to accept a part of the farm his father owned. As more people sought land, prices rose and the margin left for living expenses shrank. In addition, from 1750 to 1860, landlords in England removed the peasants, consolidated farms, and turned to more efficient means of agriculture. By the middle of the nineteenth century, landlords in other countries such as Germany, France, Russia, Poland, and Czechoslovakia did the same (Handlin 25–30).

Other pressures forced Europeans to the United States such as the Irish potato famine of 1845 to 1849. However, the United States also offered several attractions. The growth of industry created an increasing need for workers. At the same time, the cost of passage to the New World declined. Partly empty boats had sailed from Europe to the United States in search of raw materials to bring back for manufacture. Shipowners realized they could charge immigrant fares to make money on the westward voyage and to provide ballast for the boats (North 96).

The population growth in the United States reinforced economic development, which was the second social change that made the common school campaign appear reasonable. According to some historians, the United States' version of the industrial revolution began in 1813, fueled by cotton. In 1793 Eli Whitney invented the cotton gin, which extracted seeds from the hardy varieties of cotton plants. As a result, cotton production spread over any land where the warm growing season was long enough. When cotton crops wore out the soil, farmers turned westward into Alabama and Mississippi. Canals and railways transported the cotton to cities in the Northeast, where it was manufactured into textiles or exported to Europe. Although thousands of miles of roads were available, these were little more than country paths. From 1811 to 1818, the federal government built the National Highway from Cumberland, Maryland, to Wheeling, West Virginia, and some private companies built toll roads. In 1840 canals were the best form of commercial transportation between the East and the West. There were about 3,326 miles of canals, most of them in the North and the West. Although railroads covered as many miles, only 200 miles of them extended into the West (Hofstadter 247–252).

As trade increased, cities grew. In 1800 there were 33 cities with populations of more than 2,500, but only one of them exceeded 50,000 residents. By 1860 the number of cities with populations of more than 2,500 grew to 236. Sixteen of those cities exceeded 50,000 residents (U.S. Bureau of Census 11). New York City experienced phenomenal growth because its location was ideal for sea trade. Ships from New York sailed along the coast to New Orleans, where they exchanged European manufactured goods for cotton. This trade was so successful that by 1830, forty cents of every dollar paid for cotton went to New York for costs associated with its transportation (Hofstadter 252–253).

Although New York City became a center of trade, the United States' version of the industrial revolution began in 1813 in Waltham, Massachusetts, where four wealthy businessmen formed a corporation, the Boston Manufacturing Company, to manufacture textiles. The success of their venture led others to try this new form of financing. This style of ownership turned factories into self-perpetuating entities. Businessmen could reside in a distant city and serve as directors. Factories opened in distant mill towns supervised by professional managers. Because the stocks could be transferred easily, the factories did not depend on any particular owner. The directors hired the managers and could replace them easily. Further, because the work was done by machines, it did not depend on individual craftspeople (Hofstadter 254–255).

The rise of industry in the United States caused two different groups of people to seek the state support of schools for contradictory reasons. On the one hand, the development of corporate systems for production caused factory owners to want public schools in order to instill a sense of self-discipline and obedience to authority among the workers. According to these factory owners, the immigrants who came to the cities to work in the factories lacked the judgment to work diligently. Worse, they were prone to strikes over grievances. Therefore, the owners of manufacturing plants argued that communities should provide regular public schooling that would train workers. This would keep the factories running, help the community, and maintain high profits (Bowles and Gintis 161–163). On the other hand, workingmen saw schools as a means to weaken the aristocracy of capital that the corporate system produced. In the late 1820s and early 1830s, skilled craftsmen and small businessmen recognized the rise of factories as a threat to their occupations. In cities such as New York, Boston, and Philadelphia, they formed workingmen's parties that published papers claiming that the most important safeguard for liberty was public education. For them, the schools would do two things. First, public schools would alert the children of all social classes of the problems facing society. Second, the schools would train the children of the lower classes and enable those with talent to become leaders of society who would produce policies favoring the continued existence of their social groups. This faith in education led the early unions to establish mechanics' institutes, reading rooms, and libraries where young men could expand their horizons. By the late 1830s, these unions adopted a new view of the role of education. Instead of hoping that common schools could educate voters, they decided that universal education was the aim of their political reforms. That is, instead of looking to schools as a first step in political liberation, the candidates for the workingmen's party campaigned for votes with promises to open schools for all children, allowing them to expand their human capacities (Welter 45–54).

The third social change that encouraged people to take an interest in the education of other people's children was a shift in national politics. The country's growth brought a new group into power, and many people thought these newcomers should learn to govern properly. Here, the common school advocates altered Thomas Jefferson's idea that schools could teach children to participate in a democratic government. Whereas Jefferson wanted schools to select and train potential leaders from all social groups, common school advocates suggested that public education would teach immigrants to adopt American ideas.

National politics changed in the 1830s because the country had grown so rapidly. In 1803 the Louisiana Purchase added about 828,000 square miles, almost doubling the size of the country. The U.S. Congress promised that as people moved into those areas, they would receive the rights of citizens, and their states would be admitted into the union. Thus, as the country grew in size, populations relocated and political alignments changed. In 1789, when George Washington took office as president, there were thirteen states in the union. By 1821 eleven new commonwealths had joined the union in the following order: Vermont, Kentucky, Tennessee, Ohio, Louisiana, Indiana, Mississippi, Illinois, Alabama, Maine, and Missouri. In the same period, the population nearly tripled and moved west. As a result, the population of Kentucky and Tennessee exceeded the combined populations of Massachusetts, Rhode

Island, Connecticut, and Vermont. This altered the political balance of power. In 1824 John Quincy Adams of Massachusetts retained the presidency for the Democratic-Republican Party. However, in 1828 Andrew Jackson of Tennessee reinforced the political forces of agriculture as he swept aside the party of commerce, industry, and finance. In 1832 politicians opposed to Jackson united in the Whig party (Beard and Beard 507–508).

In part, the Whig opposition to the Jacksonian Democrats was based on the fact that the politics of the frontier was the politics of backwoodsmen. According to Charles and Mary Beard, the frontiersman known as Davy Crockett was fairly typical of the spokespeople who entered state capitals and advanced to Washington with Jackson to govern the country. When he was a young man, Crockett became a local magistrate even though he boasted that he lacked formal education, never read a law book, and decided cases according to his sense of fair play. Shortly afterward, he campaigned for a seat in the state legislature of Tennessee as a supporter of Jackson. In his campaign speeches, Crockett told amusing stories and bought whiskey for all the voters who came to hear him. He was elected, although he claimed that he had never read a newspaper. In fact, he was so ignorant of the structure of government that he did not know the meaning of the word *judiciary,* and he thought that Jackson ruled alone. When Crockett ran for Congress, he won again. To the Whigs, the most distressful fact about Crockett was that his ignorance did not harm his political career but that his disloyalty to the Jacksonian Democrats did. He lost at the polls when he turned against Jackson. Insulted by this rejection, Crockett fled to the Southwest and died fighting at the Alamo (Beard and Beard 538–540).

To many people in the learned professions, politicians such as Crockett forecast the threat of demagoguery. These ministers, engineers, college teachers, and successful merchants considered the uneducated people a rabble who would form mobs under the leadership of illiterate people such as Crockett. They feared that these bands would twist the government to serve their narrow interests. Interestingly, in the 1830s several foreign visitors to the United States noted that the terms "mob" and "rabble" did not apply to any of the country's citizens. Nonetheless, newspaper editors applied these terms readily to lower-class individuals or settlers on the frontier, and their readers agreed that the labels were appropriate. Consequently, many conservatives developed such a fear of Jacksonian democracy that they agreed to tax themselves so that state governments could support schools (Jackson 17–18, 29–31).

The prevalent view among supporters of common schools was that the public must educate the citizens of the state or else the devil would educate them for his evil purposes (MacMullen 157). During his twelfth and final report to the Massachusetts Board of Education in 1848, Horace Mann offered an example of this belief. He warned that wisdom would not preside over the halls of legislation until common schools spread more intelligence and purer morality throughout communities. Mann claimed that if there were no intelligence and self-restraint among citizens, a republic would become similar to a madhouse without a supervisor. He noted that a republic is easier to construct than to maintain because ignorance, selfishness, and passion had to be rooted out of people for the republic to survive (Cremin, "Horace Mann's Legacy" 7; Mann, "Twelfth" 92).

Although Mann claimed that common schools would improve all people, make cooperation possible, and thereby strengthen the entire republic, some advocates declared that common schools would improve a specific state and solve the specific problems that the state faced. For example, in 1851 in North Carolina, Calvin Wiley asserted that common schools would strengthen his state and relieve it from competition from western and northern states. In his *North Carolina Reader,* Wiley predicted that common schools would develop a noble type of citizen who would have a new public spirit and a profound love for North Carolina. As North Carolina citizens moved to new lands seeking wealth, Wiley wrote an article describing the resources of the state and suggested that common schools could help people to develop these assets so that everybody would prosper. When it appeared that civil war might begin in 1856, Wiley used the threat to reinforce his pleas for state support of education. He promised that such schools would bring the people of the state together and enable the different people within North Carolina to cooperate with each other and prepare for the conflict (Curti 71, 74).

Did the Popular Press Play a Role in the Common School Movement?

Between 1827 and 1842, metropolitan journalism increased, the penny press appeared, and almost every county seat had one or two newspapers. Although newspapers carried some stories about issues or events that took place outside the local area, book publishers offered the stablest source of such information. Centered in larger towns, publishers expanded by offering collections of famous authors' works at low prices. This popular press became an important means for common school advocates to garner support for the creation of a system of public schools. Ironically, however, the books, magazines, and almanacs of the 1830s nurtured a contradictory set of attitudes toward education. On the one hand, they described general learning, including the ability to read, as essential for human life. On the other hand, the almanacs ridiculed colleges as places that damaged people's intelligence, and described higher education as a pastime for the wealthy who did not need to work. This paradoxical set of opinions may explain why common school advocates urged the states to support elementary and secondary schools and teacher training institutions. These last were called "model" or "normal schools" because they modeled a norm for good teaching practices. They did not advocate the maintenance of colleges and universities (Jackson 10–13).

The popular press did not influence the legislature directly. Its effect was more indirect in that the articles caused readers to think about certain issues. They formed associations whose members sought more information, wrote more articles, and petitioned the legislature to reduce the obstacles to the establishment of public schools. Some organizations that spread information about education and petitioned the legislature also educated teachers. For example, the Western Literary Institute and College of Professional Teachers in Cincinnati, Ohio, became the first regional educational association in the United States, with affiliated societies in eighteen states throughout the Mississippi Basin. Its members lobbied for the creation of the office of a superintendent of schools for the state, and in 1838 succeeded in persuading the Ohio legislature to pass the Ohio School Law (Rich 2).

At the time, Ohio was an important state. From 1800 to 1826, Ohio grew from about 42,000 people to more than 800,000. By 1840 Ohio had a population of 1.5 million and was the third most populated state in the union. Most of the cities in the state were surrounded by a vast forest, but Cincinnati was a center of culture and trade that attracted people from

New York and New England. In 1830 Cincinnati had a population of about 24,000, but it grew to 115,400 by 1850. As a result, people such as Albert Picket, who had moved to Cincinnati from New York to start a female seminary in 1822, found themselves at the forefront of educational movements. In 1829 Picket called a meeting of teachers to discuss and promote ideas about education. At the same time, he published his own spelling book and an educational journal, *The Academician.* After two years, Picket declared the organization limited and proposed a general meeting of all teachers in the western region to discuss subjects of education and to spread information. Called the Western Literary Institute and College of Professional Teachers, the organization created a fact-finding committee to gather information for petitioning the legislature. The majority of the association members were clergymen who believed that the public would agree and support their cause if they presented their arguments and supported them with facts (Rich 12, 16, 45–47).

The Western Literary Institute and College of Professional Teachers appointed a committee of three men who lobbied the legislature for changes in the law. At the beginning of each legislative session, this committee called a general educational meeting and invited the governor of the state to preside at the convention. Each year committee members petitioned the legislature to pass measures such as the one creating an institute to train teachers. They also appointed traveling agents who collected information about schools that the members could use in publications to alert the public about the condition of schools and in their petitions. The high point of their influence came in 1837. At the insistence of the Western Literary Institute and College of Professional Teachers, the Ohio legislature established the position of state superintendent of common schools and appointed Samuel Lewis to the position. In his first report, Lewis made several recommendations to the legislature such as reducing the number of school officials, creating county superintendents of schools, building township libraries, and preventing corrupt administrators from misusing the funds derived from the sale of public lands that should have supported schools. In 1838 the Ohio legislature passed a school law that incorporated most of his suggestions and created a common school fund of $200,000 (Rich 96–100; Petit 84–89).

The Western Literary Institute and College of Professional Teachers did more than engage in political efforts. This institute offered teachers the chance to hear informative speeches about teaching and to talk with each other about professional concerns. For many teachers, this was the only training they received. The sessions were held during the first full week in October, beginning on Monday and ending on Saturday. After each meeting, the members printed the transactions, which included copies of the speeches that they sold for one dollar. These meetings became popular, and the organization spread through western and southern states. It disbanded in 1845 (Rich 50–52).

Did Common School Advocates Improve the Training of Teachers and the Status of Women?

During the 1830s and 1840s, the campaign for state support of common schools and normal schools mixed with concerns for the status of women. For example, Catharine Beecher wrote in 1851 that since popular education was a topic of rising public concern, she thought the best way to improve the position of women in society was to work for the education of deprived children. In that way, she reasoned, she would avoid the potential embarrassment of fighting about women's roles and have the many advantages of pursuing a philanthropic end (Woody, *History* 465).

Articles in magazines mixed the issues of women's rights and common schools. Eleanor Wolf Thompson looked at articles in forty magazines published between 1830 and 1860 written specifically for women. These included thirty-seven general magazines, two magazines published in French for Americans, and two written in German. In addition, she researched ten educational journals to compare the views of educators with those of the general public. Thompson found the questions about common schools, normal schools, and the education of women so entwined that the journals and magazines treated them as if they were the same (Thompson vi, 97).

According to Thompson, the editors of women's magazines wanted to promote teaching as desirable employment for young women. Consequently, they published stories that explained why women made natural teachers. In many fictional stories, for example, the heroine was a young woman teacher who triumphed through patience, self-sacrifice, and diligence. Some articles demonstrated that communities could not find sufficient numbers of men to fill the teaching positions in the new schools. Trained women could meet those needs, the articles added. Other articles claimed that women had talents that men lacked. For example, Harriet Beecher Stowe wrote that men might have more knowledge than women, but they lacked the patience and gentleness needed to teach. The editors also campaigned for state support of normal schools to train women. As a result, they joined the educational magazines in a campaign for state-funded normal schools (Thompson 91–97; Woody, *History* 462–463).

As part of the magazines' effort to highlight the campaign to train the teachers in common schools and to replace the men who dominated teaching positions with women, women's magazines published stories about the schools of reformers such as Emma Hart Willard, Catharine Esther Beecher, and Mary Lyon. These three women considered teaching an honorable profession for women. They believed that the Creator had endowed women with talents suited to nurturing young children, and that women had the intellectual capacity to master the subjects teachers taught. As a result, the graduates of their schools ventured into many different parts of the country to start schools and apply the knowledge and skills they had learned from their teachers (MacMullen 159–160; Thompson 97).

In the 1830s, the little teacher training that existed took place in the female seminaries or in academies, and schools such as Andover Theological Academy and Princeton sent out young men to be preachers or teachers. There were also private institutions of teacher training. For example, in 1823 Samuel Reed Hall established the Model School at Concord, Vermont, where he enrolled young children to serve as demonstration and practice for prospective teachers. He carried his plans of teacher training further when he became the principal of Holmes Plymouth Academy in 1837. Although the school had previously prepared young men for the ministry, Hall changed the academy's aim to the training of men and women as teachers. Many other schools set up departments for the instruction of teachers (Woody, *History* 457, 469).

Massachusetts established the first state-supported normal school in 1839 in Lexington and dedicated its efforts to training female teachers. The course of study was for one year. Although tuition was free, the twenty-one women who enrolled during the first year paid their room and board. The principal, a man named Cyrus Pierce, was the only teacher of the normal school. The prospective teachers studied subjects such as composition, algebra, natural history, and moral philosophy. Attached to the normal school was a model school where thirty children from ages six to ten attended tuition free. The pupils of the normal school served as the teachers, applying the principles and methods they learned in their own classes. According to most observers, the normal school in Lexington was a success, and other states began supporting normal schools (Woody, *History* 474–476).

A report of the Prussian school system written by Calvin Stowe played an important role in the campaign for state-supported normal schools. In 1836 Stowe went to Europe to purchase a library for Lane Seminary in Cincinnati, where he taught. The Ohio governor and legislature asked Stowe to survey the condition of schools while he was there. On his return in 1837, he delivered his report urging the people of Ohio to imitate the Prussians and use public schools to develop the moral and intellectual powers of all children throughout the state. The legislatures of Pennsylvania, Michigan, Massachusetts, North Carolina, and Virginia ordered reprints of Stowe's report (Knight 244–247).

Stowe praised the Prussian ruler, Frederick William, for being as simple and practical as an Ohio farmer. Stowe noted that the system of instruction in Prussia fostered a warm attachment in students for their native land and its institutions. He urged the legislature in Ohio to do the same because republics depended even more on the character of its citizens than did monarchies. In the common schools in Prussia, Stowe found a course of instruction that lasted eight years, educating children from age six through fourteen. The curriculum included studies in reading, arithmetic, language, and moral instruction. Stowe was impressed at the way many lessons moved toward moral instruction. With young children, for example, an opportunity to draw flowers in the garden led to questions about the ways that flowers grow. After a short period, the teacher read the story in Genesis of the garden of Eden to tell of the God who made such wonders possible. In future lessons, the teacher introduced some Psalms to show the children how the glory of God in creation was tied to the love their parents had for them. Thus, students began by drawing flowers but undertook different activities that led them to think about their duties within their families (Stowe, "Report" 255, 278–279).

Stowe was most impressed with the practical nature of this system. He thought the lessons developed all the intellectual faculties or qualities of the children's minds. Students learned to speak their own language well and to acquire skills such as arithmetic that they needed in everyday life. Stowe liked the fact that the teacher began with practical lessons and then moved to theoretical and moral ones. Although this represented religious instruction, he admitted it was not sectarian. That is, the teachers did not advance any particular denomination. Instead, Stowe believed that they reinforced the universal morality found in the Bible (Stowe, "Report" 305–306).

Finally, Stowe explained six things the Prussians did that the Ohio legislature and the governor could do to create a similar system. First, there should be model schools available in all large towns for teachers to learn how to conduct classes. Second, the teachers had to earn a wage adequate for them to support themselves by their labors. Third, women should be employed in the elementary schools because this was the area in which they distinguished themselves. Fourth, the buildings and facilities had to be clean and comfortable. Fifth, parents had to trust the teacher and resist the temptation to interfere with his or her control of the classroom. Sixth, the government should not try to introduce the system all at once. Instead, it should support various features that would allow people in the state to do the work themselves. Finally, all instruction, even to immigrants, should aim for command of the English language. Although Stowe approved of hiring teachers who spoke more than one language, he believed examinations should be in English (Stowe, "Report" 308–315).

Because Stowe's remarks centered on his observation that the teacher had to be well trained, his report stimulated the growth of state-supported normal schools. Common school advocates asked the U.S. Congress to open federally supported normal schools, but this never happened. Nonetheless, by 1872 almost 12,000 pupils attended 101 normal schools in the United States. Of these schools, states supported 48, counties or cities ran 9, and other institutions controlled the rest (Woody, *History* 476–483).

Many common school advocates hoped that normal school training would teach ways to maintain order and discipline classes other than beating misbehaving students. In his second annual report, Horace Mann listed the qualities of good teachers. One was the aptness to teach that included the ability to manage students. Normal schools should suggest a variety of ways to teach material so that teachers did not have to rely on punishments. Mann repeated his distaste for corporal punishment in his seventh lecture, complaining that beatings and the fear they instilled in children caused them to dislike school and to become cowardly adults. Such cruelty by teachers harmed the moral development of students (Mann, "Second" 47–48, "Lecture" 312–314).

While Mann urged teachers to learn new ways of managing children, articles in women's magazines offered articles about raising children. Most of these articles focused on molding the children's character and ignored more practical concerns about proper dress or diet. The authors uniformly disapproved of corporal punishment in the raising of children and agreed that discipline should come from reason, kindness, and love. The authors recommended that instead of beating children mothers should help them understand what they did wrong and why it was wrong. The articles further noted that parents had to set good examples (Thompson 110–113).

When Mann criticized corporal punishment, Boston schoolmasters accused him of being unrealistic. In the 1840s, most teachers believed that students who failed to learn a lesson had been lazy or inattentive. To make them work harder, teachers struck students while wearing thimbles on their fingers, spanked them on the bottom, or whipped them with sticks. Although Mann may have thought that women would bring gentleness and patience to the teaching profession, they also relied on corporal punishment, combining these practices with humiliation such as dunce caps to encourage the other students to work harder. Over time, however, the criticism of corporal punishment had an effect. By the 1850s, teachers used less physical discipline. They introduced other means to inspire students, such as report cards, and encouraged competition among the students for honors. However, some women worried that this trend led teachers to tolerate laziness and caused students to learn less (Urban and Wagoner 108; Finkelstein 97, 103–105).

Some school committees arranged classes so that women taught the younger, less disobedient students. However, some common school advocates wanted women to undertake hazardous assignments. For example, Catharine Beecher wanted women to immigrate to frontier towns to open schools. She thought such a campaign would help establish normal schools for women and elevate the status of women. Her effort began in 1833, when the *American Annals of Education* published an article claiming almost 1.5 million children could not attend schools in the United States because there were not enough teachers. The Western Literary Institute and College of Professional Teachers in Cincinnati took up this call, and Catharine Beecher took part in several of the sessions describing the problems. However, it was not until 1843 that Beecher began her own campaign to seek women who would travel the western frontier settlements to teach. Beecher had conducted women's seminaries, and she saw this as an opportunity for women to assert their rights to professional training and at the same time enhance the education of destitute children. Her efforts picked up momentum in 1845, when she wrote a paper claiming that American women had a responsibility to their country to organize institutions and recruit young women able to leave comfortable surroundings to go into the frontier and teach. In 1846 a group of women in Mount Vernon Church in Boston heard Beecher's plea. They wrote to Calvin Stowe, Beecher's brother-in-law, and asked what they should do. On his recommendation, they formed the Ladies Society for the Promotion of Education in the West to recruit women teachers. This society did not satisfy Beecher, however, because it only considered women who belonged to the Congregationalist faith, and it selected women who had no training in education. That same year, though, William Slade, former governor of Vermont, agreed to join Beecher to form the Central Committee at Cincinnati for Promoting National Education. Unfortunately, Slade did not want to establish institutions for training women to be teachers; he wanted to transfer already trained teachers to the West (Harveson 81–99).

In the first year, thirty-five women gathered in Albany, New York, for a one-month training session. At the end of that year, newspapers ridiculed the project. Labeling it "Wives for the West," newspaper stories reported that the women Slade and Beecher sent to the Mississippi Valley met men and married soon after they arrived. As a result, the stories claimed, the women did not help the schools. In the meantime, Slade formed the Board of National Popular Education in Cleveland without consulting Beecher. When Beecher heard that some of the teachers in Iowa faced difficulty getting through the winter, she made a quick tour to solicit funds; traveled to Burlington, Iowa; rented a house; and invited the teachers to live with her until the winter passed. Slade was furious and expelled Beecher from the organization (Harveson 99–104).

From 1845 to 1848, the plan of sending teachers to the West took on even more urgency when the United States added more than 1.2 million square acres including Texas and California. Even so, in 1858 the Board of National Popular Education disbanded and ceased its efforts. Lawrence Cremin claims the effort had been a failure (*American Education 1783–1876,*146). However, Polly Welts Kaufman argues that the board made an important mark on the frontier. In its short existence, the board recruited and sent nearly six hundred women from New England and New York to teach in the West. Many of these women remained to marry and thereby became early settlers in these communities. Their motives varied. Some women went because they loved the idea of the West, others went because their husbands died and they wanted to pursue a useful career. In all cases, however, the women felt a missionary fervor. Most of the women went through the second Great Awakening and accepted the evangelical Protestant religion. They went West in the belief that this was the way to serve God (Kaufman xvii–xxii).

In part, the women missionaries to the West chose to teach in common schools because the moral development of the children played an important part in the curriculum. Common school advocates turned the curriculum away from the intellectual goals that marked the notions of leaders such as Thomas Jefferson and instead, in accordance with the intellectual prejudices of their day, sought to make the curriculum as practical as possible without being purely vocational. Moral training fit these requirements.

Did the Advocates for Common Schools Change the Curricula?

Primarily, advocates for common schools sought state support of education. Nonetheless, they agreed on three important changes in the curriculum that they thought would improve the students' morals. These included teaching about health, using the Bible as an instructional book, and dividing the courses of study into graded school plans. Common school advocates believed that these strategies represented practical changes without adopting vocational education. They hoped this training would prepare students for vocational, cultural, and political affairs. For example, to describe what subjects students should pursue, Horace Mann, in his third annual report to the Massachusetts Board of Education in 1839, compared human beings to the trunk of trees and equated occupations and professions with the fruits those trees should yield. Through this metaphor, Mann explained that the common school should devote itself to improving those qualities common to all people (Cremin, "Horace Mann's Legacy" 12).

In 1842, in his sixth report to the Massachusetts Board of Education, Mann complained about the courses many schools taught. He began by noting that state law required all schools to teach such basic subjects as reading, writing, English grammar, geography, and arithmetic. As a result, all schools employed teachers who could teach these things. However, Mann added, the law did not specify any other subjects that should be taught. When Mann looked at the reports the schools had turned into his office, he could not find a pattern in the courses students covered. While 2,333 students took algebra, 1,472 students had bookkeeping. At the same time, 463 studied geometry, while only 249 took up surveying. This puzzled Mann because the more practical courses had the lowest enrollments (Mann, "Selection" 45–47).

Mann's greatest concern was that only 416 students studied human physiology, which he considered the most important course. It taught the laws of health, which were few and simple but vital. Noting that God wanted people to improve their lives, Mann believed that the common schools were the best means to spread this knowledge. To illustrate the benefits, Mann described the children living in rural areas as robust but mentally slow and the children in cities as physically weaker but more observant. He thought that schools should develop both sets of strengths and thereby create a new human race (Mann, "Selection" 49–51).

Unfortunately, Mann found teachers ignoring simple things such as children's need to exercise. Instead of encouraging all children to play outdoors during recess, they praised the children who stayed inside to read. Further, most schools offered children below seven years of age one short recess after three hours' study, but Mann claimed they needed ten minutes of exercise in open air every hour. Worse yet, he claimed, people built schools in ways that prevented adequate ventilation. As a result, children rarely breathed pure air. If people would pay attention to these simple points, children would be healthier and happier (Mann, "Selection" 51–52).

In taking the position that schools could change human beings, Mann was reacting against the New Light or strict Calvinism branch of the Protestant religion within which he had been raised. This sect believed that God had selected a few people arbitrarily, called the elect, to receive the grace of salvation. The rest of humankind was destined for damnation. According to one of Mann's biographers, Mann decided, at the age of twelve, to rebel against Calvinism when his brother drowned. Nathaniel Emmons, a prominent New Light preacher presiding at the funeral, warned young people about the evils of dying unconverted. At his words, Mann's mother groaned, and Mann began a lifelong rebellion against the Calvinist doctrine of predestination (Hinsdale 82–83).

In 1837, when Mann was appointed secretary of the Massachusetts State Board of Education, he found in George Combe's book *The Constitution of Man Considered in Relation to External Objects* a set of ideas that repudiated Calvinist doctrine. According to Combe's explanation of phrenology, the human mind was composed of thirty-seven faculties such as aggressiveness, benevolence, and veneration that governed the attitudes and actions of the individual. Phrenologists thought these faculties resided in particular sections of the head so that a certain shape of the skull indicated a particularly well-developed faculty. Some bumps indicated particular temperaments. Other bumps denoted specific levels of intelligence. Unlike the Calvinist doctrine that suggested a person's character was ordained by God in ways that determined a child's future, this theory held that children could cultivate some faculties that benefited them and society by exercising those traits and they could weaken other faculties by ignoring them (McCluskey, *Public Schools* 23–28).

In the 1840s, many physicians advocated phrenology as a method of treating insanity in mental institutions and rehabilitating criminals in prisons. They argued that the mind required the brain, and the brain was part of the body. Therefore, a healthy body was a necessity for a healthy mind. In education, phrenology dictated that children have plenty of exercise and avoid excessive mental fatigue. This meant a short school day and lots of play outdoors. Further, the theory discouraged punishing children, but advocated rewarding them for good behavior. Phrenologists added that children learned best by objects, not by words; studies should be practical; and children should ask questions (Davies 80–81, 89–90, 99–100).

Common school advocates such as Mann also thought the Bible could teach morals. These advocates claimed that the Bible was accepted by all people as a source of morality and that students should read it so they would take on Christian virtues. Mann believed that the Bible should appear in all schools because it contained all the different forms of Christianity. Even Judaism appeared in the Old Testament. Because the Bible would reinforce these faiths, he argued, it enabled the common school to impress on children principles such as piety, justice, and love of country (Mann, "Twelfth" 106).

Other common school advocates argued that, in addition to providing moral lessons, the Bible encouraged intellectual development. In 1838 Calvin Stowe gave a speech to the Western Literary Institute and College of Professional Teachers entitled "The Bible as a Means of Moral and Intellectual Improvement." Noting that the members of the institute agreed that reading the Bible was the best means to develop the intellectual powers of young children, Stowe described ten characteristics of the Bible that he thought made it the most important educational tool. For example, he noted that the Bible explained why God let things happen and therefore demonstrated how progress took place. On the other hand, most histories could do no more than inform people about empires or cities. Stowe thought the Bible explained the different types of human beings that existed and why they acted as they did. Stowe also argued that the Bible offered a view of human destiny that encouraged people to concentrate on academic studies. Finally, Stowe believed that the Bible could exhilarate students as they read it because the spirit of the living God moved into their souls through the words (Stowe, "Bible" 43–52).

Stowe acknowledged that some people read the Bible regularly without enhancing their intellectual abilities. He offered eight reasons why some people did not benefit from regular reading of the Bible. For example, he thought such people read the Bible in disconnected sections, taking a small part and extracting a message from it without considering the context within which the section appeared. Some of these people read without thinking. However, Stowe assured his listeners that if students avoided such errors, they could read the Bible with pleasure and profit (Stowe, "Bible" 52–59).

Although common school advocates recommended some form of a graded school plan, rural schools resisted change. In rural settings, usually a woman teacher worked in a summer school with younger students who ranged in age from four to twelve. They studied reading, writing, and basic arithmetic. Often, a male teacher worked in a winter school with the older students, who ranged in age from ten to twenty. The older students covered more advanced subjects such as history and geography. During the day, most students worked alone at their desks. Groups of students gathered around the teacher to work on a subject at the same level and recite. When they finished, another group working at another level took their place (Vinovskis, Angus, and Mirel 176).

In urban schools with more students and more teachers, more elaborate plans evolved. Cities such as New York, Boston, and Philadelphia adopted partially graded systems. In Boston, for example, at the first level children ages four to eight attended primary schools. In the second level, boys ages eight to fourteen and girls ages eight to sixteen enrolled in grammar schools or writing schools. Although boys and girls enrolled in each of these schools, they attended separate departments. For the third level, students attended Latin grammar schools or the English high school. But in 1840, Albert Picket and other members of the Cincinnati school board recommended a more careful separation of the studies for elementary schools in Cincinnati. They broke down the teaching of the basic skills of spelling, reading, and arithmetic into stages of increasing difficulty from grades 1 to 5. In grades 4 and 5, subjects included history, geography, botany, geology, and natural philosophy (Ohio Education Association 108–111).

Cincinnati did not adopt Picket's system for several years. Therefore, early historians gave credit to John D. Philbrick of Quincy, Massachusetts, for organizing courses of study in 1847. Philbrick arranged subject matters into sequences of increasing complexity and assigned teachers particular segments of the material. In this system, a school might have eight different levels and each one would take a year to complete. Because most students could not advance easily, students of several different ages made up each level. Thus, the grade level depended on the complexity of the material, not on the age of the students. Such a system made discipline easy, and women could control classes. Further, teachers could be assigned levels that matched their level of preparation. As a result, by 1860 most cities had schools that followed this system. Because it worked smoothly, schools grew in size. In the 1830s, most buildings had four classrooms; thirty years later, the buildings had eight to ten rooms (Vinovskis, Angus, and Mirel 176).

Besides making education more efficient, the reformers thought that the graded school plan helped students develop moral behaviors. Because children of similar abilities and roughly similar ages worked together on the same lessons, they could compete with each other. Reformers believed this competition better stimulated students to do their work than did threats of punishment. More important, under the graded school plan students could advance on the basis of their accomplishments. As a result, reformers believed that the plan provided moral lessons expressing the ideal that diligent people became social leaders in a democracy (Kaestle, *Pillars* 133).

How Did Common School Reformers Change the Curriculum for Women?

The campaign for changing the curriculum of common schools extended to making the curricula of women's seminaries more practical and reasonable. During the 1830s and 1840s, women's magazines devoted attention to the popular boarding or finishing schools of the day. These schools taught painting, music, dancing, deportment, some French and Spanish, a little Latin and grammar, philosophy, logic, and, if time allowed, English and mathematics. However, students skimmed through the materials because these programs lasted only six months. Although the women's magazines promoted these superficial schools, they also informed readers about efforts to build more substantial institutions. Such stories included descriptions of Emma Willard's campaign for state support for a female seminary in Troy, New York. At the same time, the magazines complimented Mary Lyon and Catharine Beecher for trying to include domestic economy or what became known as home economics and calisthenics or physical education in women's seminaries (Thompson 46–47).

The women's magazines carried editorials supporting the inclusion of domestic economy and physical education in female seminaries and quoted authorities about the need for these subjects. Finally, in descriptions of schools the authors of the articles complimented the school when the subjects were present and complained when they were not. For example, in a description of Emma Willard's Troy Female Seminary, the author noted that Catholic schools had departments of home economics but Willard's did not. The author urged Willard to imitate the Catholic schools (Thompson 47–49).

As a result of such pressures, some common school advocates began departments of domestic science in their female seminaries. In 1834 Mary Lyon suggested that the women students could do all the domestic work in a school. She hoped this would demonstrate to the public that female seminaries did not threaten home life by making women unfit for domestic chores, and also bring success to her campaign for state support. However, Lyon warned against engaging in domestic work such as producing silk to support a school. These manual training projects would not bring in money, she feared, but instead become expenses. In 1837 she had an opportunity to put her ideas of domestic work into practice. When Lyon opened Mount Holyoke, she adopted the model of a female seminary, with its concentration on academic subjects, that she had learned from Zilpah Grant. However, she made an important addition. Lyon hired a superintendent of the domestic department to ensure that students adequately performed the work of cleaning, cooking, and serving meals for the school. Although Lyon called her innovation a success, her department of domestic economy did not convince state legislators or leaders of other organizations to financially support her school. However, Lyon's innovation might have helped her as she solicited contributions for her school from individuals. Looking back on her innovation, Lyon listed three advantages the school gained from the domestic department. She claimed that the work of domestic economy provided the students with exercise, with opportunities for sociability, and with the chance to feel concern for the welfare of all students (Green 115, 180–181, 344).

At the same time that antebellum women's magazines recommended including domestic economy in schools for girls, they complained of the greater need for physical education. To some women's magazine writers, physical education represented plans for healthful living. Therefore, they criticized the schedule and the diets offered at female seminaries, claiming that female students lacked adequate sleep, remained inactive, and ate sparsely. The authors recommended that the girls run in the open air or plant gardens. Some articles suggested calisthenics, swimming, or horseback riding (Thompson 50–52).

Catharine Beecher approved strongly of engaging young women in calisthenics. In 1827, when Beecher conducted the Hartford Female Seminary, she hired a teacher from England to conduct calisthenics. The entire school took lessons and had daily practice sessions in physical exercise. Beecher thought these activities would cure any physical defects. In fact, Beecher was so impressed with these activities that in 1856 she incorporated many of the exercises in her book *Physiology and Calisthenics* (Harveson 50).

Did Common School Advocates Share an Ideology?

The strong, independent women who started their own schools accepted the view that women should submit to men's authority. When Catharine Beecher wanted to create a society to recruit and train women to teach in the West, she refused to lead the project herself. She asked seven different men to take over the direction of the project. Although Beecher did not think the man who accepted her offer understood the plan, she adopted the subordinate role because, in the 1830s, most Americans felt that women had different talents than men. This did not necessarily mean they held women to be inferior. They wanted the members of each sex to use their abilities to contribute to the good of society. Thus, the ideal relationship was similar to the one Mary Lyon found in the home of a male teacher she admired. She wrote that her teachers considered it the universal duty of a wife to obey, but he did not think a husband should command. Instead, he wanted mutual respect and esteem to determine each party's actions (Harveson 96; Green 25).

The view that women should take a subordinate role to men represented one aspect of an ideology shared by the advocates of common schools. Because they came from similar social backgrounds, they shared a set of understandings or an ideology that influenced how they saw schools and social problems. The families of most of the advocates had modest resources, and they rose in the world through hard work. Many of them knew and helped each other. When Carl Kaestle read sermons, political economy texts, educational reports, and social commentaries written from 1830 to 1860 by several different reformers, he found three frequently repeated themes that influenced their ideas of the proper curriculum. First, republican government depended on individual character. Second, people fell into poverty because of flaws in their own characters. Third, Protestant Christianity supported moral reform and social progress (Kaestle, *Pillars* 102, 105).

As with any ideology, the theories of common school advocates meshed in ways that appeared coherent to the people who believed them. For example, the view that republican government depended on individual character had two sides. One side promulgated the idealistic notion that good citizens possessed the qualities of diligence and honesty. The other side espoused the individualistic belief that people with those character traits succeeded in life and that people fell into poverty because of flaws in their own characters. These perspectives appeared in texts such as the McGuffey readers that advocates wrote for classrooms.

From 1835 to 1857, William Holmes McGuffey wrote and compiled six graded collections of moralistic tales and excerpts from great literature. These texts became so popular that when they ceased publication in 1922, they had reputed sales of about 122 million copies. In fairness to the McGuffey readers, they changed as they went through revisions that continued after McGuffey's death in 1873. In the editions published around 1836, Calvinist theology dominated. These readers contained Psalms from the Bible and sermons from McGuffey's friend, Presbyterian minister Lyman Beecher, that appeared beside selections from Shakespeare and Longfellow. In the versions published in 1879, a civic morality replaced the theological view. Thus, the readers published after McGuffey's death reinforced an individualistic view of morality that overemphasized the work ethic. McGuffey wanted children to learn to be diligent and honest, but he thought such traits were more important in forging the republican community than in bringing personal success (Fraser 40–43).

The distinction between the various editions was important. When Richard D. Mosier sought the social values found in the McGuffey readers for his book *Making the American Mind,* he concentrated on the editions published after 1850. Yet it was Mosier's interpretation that most people in the late twentieth century adopted. Mosier found that McGuffey's readers insisted that God blessed industrious people and punished lazy ones. For example, one story entitled "The Advantages of Industry" traced the lives of two boys, Charles Bullard and George Jones, through their school days and into adulthood. George idled away his time, while Charles studied and worked assiduously. At the conclusion of the story, the narrator questioned why any person would want to live in idleness when it made him poor and miserable while industrious children grew and prospered. At the same time, Mosier found that the McGuffey readers warned against those evils that could keep people from working hard. The drinking of alcohol stood foremost among such evils. A story entitled "Whiskey Boy" described how a father taught his child to drink whiskey by mixing it with sugar. Soon the boy drank whiskey straight. He grew ugly and ended up alone in the poorhouse. Following this theme, aphorisms in the readers repeated the message not to drink rum or whiskey. The readers warned the children that the Bible says no drunkard will inherit the kingdom of heaven (Mosier 107, 118).

The McGuffey readers published before 1850 to which Mosier paid little attention did remind children to work hard and avoid alcohol, but they did not focus on these issues. Instead, they presented children with stories, essays, and poems about the character of God and his relationship with people and the world. Thus, these earlier readers showed how the attributes of diligence and temperance played into the natural scheme God created. The moral lessons demonstrated that the natural world was as orderly as God. That is, people reaped what they sowed. One story told of a child who tied grass together, making a rope that he placed across a path. He took delight in watching people trip and fall. One of his victims was an older man who was seriously hurt. Unfortunately, this fellow was hurrying to fetch a doctor to save the boy's sick father. The story did not reveal whether the father died as a result of the delay but it pointed out that the boy learned never to do mischief again. However, McGuffey did not want children to be afraid that God would punish their every misdeed. The early readers informed children that all the people and creatures who helped them were sent by God. God made the lambs bring forth wool so that the children could have clothes to keep warm (Westerhoff 26, 75–76, 82–83).

The versions of the reader that McGuffey wrote before 1850 affirmed piety, kindness, and patriotism as the central values children should learn. In these readers, piety served an instrumental purpose. The stories or prayers admonished children to thank God for His blessings so that God would take them to heaven when they died. The other virtues derived from this desire for eternal life. For example, love of God led to love of neighbor, and God rewarded such kindness. In one story, a Russian peasant farmer was blessed with good crops for his hard work and pious ways. When he learned his neighbors suffered poor fortune, he offered them food. This impressed the neighbors, who began working and praying in earnest. The next year everyone had excellent crops. In a similar fashion, the readers portrayed love of country as a religious act. The essay "The Happy Consequences of American Independence" stated that people in the United States enjoyed more happiness than other people did. The readers told children to thank God for their birth in America and to remember the sacrifices that patriots made while fighting for their country's freedom (Westerhoff 94–103).

Without doubt, the McGuffey readers derived a great deal of their popularity from the social values they advanced. However, they offered several innovations to increase sales. First, the beginning readers used stories written in simple sentences arranged with some elegance. This allowed children to master literary skills while doing something that captured their interest. Previously, beginning texts lacked such amusements. The students and teachers repeated words and sentences that were chosen only to develop reading skills. Second, McGuffey included pictures to illustrate the stories. Third, as the readers advanced in difficulty, they included the classics of Western literature. For example, the *Fifth Eclectic Reader* of 1844 included twenty-six English and thirteen American authors whose works remained famous throughout the twentieth century (Minnich 59–72).

Most common school advocates shared McGuffey's concern for piety and the belief that Protestant Christianity brought about moral and social progress. In 1835 Calvin Stowe clearly expressed this ideal in an address entitled "The Education of Immigrants" that he gave in Cincinnati, Ohio, to the Western Literary Institute and College for Professional Teachers. In his speech, Stowe warned that immigrants would ruin the country unless Americans educated them. In Cincinnati, he added, there were 10,000 immigrants, about 3,000 of which were Protestant and the rest Catholic. Although most were German, they came from different kingdoms and spoke a variety of dialects. Less than 2,500 of the immigrants spoke English. He added that these immigrants held strong hopes of educating their children, but they lacked the money to pay for it. Stowe, a professor of biblical literature at Lane Seminary, complimented his students for starting a Sunday school to teach

English and biblical virtues. These students collected books for the children to read, started a library, opened an evening school for adults, and two years later began a day school for children. According to Stowe, the day school enjoyed an average attendance of eighty children. Such efforts could not educate the 100,000 immigrants that Stowe estimated entered the United States each year. To make the country safe and secure, Stowe asserted, these immigrants had to become Americans. They had to learn English, acquire new habits, and recognize new laws. Stowe believed that elementary schools could accomplish this by teaching the same material to everybody everywhere in the United States. Such a common education would encourage openness and cooperation among the different groups that came to the United States, he concluded. Such schools could also prevent crime if they were Christian. This meant to him that they should be founded on the principles of the Bible. If students from the primary school to the university or seminary read the Bible, he asserted, those teachings would be cornerstones onto which could be built a common culture that would purify everyone (Stowe, "Education" 3–12).

Although Stowe thought all religious groups could accept his plan, minority religious groups argued that he represented a biased view of the curriculum. The members of minority religious groups feared that the most powerful denomination would control the schools and impose its views on all the others.

Did Common Schools Face Opposition from Religious Groups?

Because many of the advocates of the common school were Protestant clergy, they tended to see their religion as something all people would accept. For example, in Cincinnati the majority of the members of the Western Literary Institute and College of Teachers were Protestant clergymen who agreed that the common school should be Christian. Consequently, each year that the institute published the record of its meetings, entitled *Transactions,* it carried a recommendation that teachers use the Bible as a text. Although most insisted that the Bible was nonsectarian, not everyone agreed. At one meeting, Rev. Benjamin P. Aydelott, president of Woodward College in Cincinnati, contended that using the Bible as a textbook in common schools would not abridge anyone's religious liberties. He claimed instead that it would teach every person to respect the rights of other people, to live in peace, and to oppose oppression of any type. At the same meeting, however, Bishop John Baptist Purcell of Cincinnati replied that all people did not accept the Bible as a neutral text. Instead of placing the Protestant Bible in students' hands, Purcell suggested that students of different religious backgrounds be separated for one or two days a week and receive instruction in their specific denomination. Other commentators tried to mediate between Aydelott and Purcell by suggesting that passages from the Bible be included as McGuffey had done in his readers. However, members wanted to do more, and Aydelott's view dominated the organization until it disbanded (Rich 58).

In New York City, the issue of reading the Bible in common schools erupted in a way that set the pattern for separate Catholic elementary and secondary schools across the nation. Worse, it contributed to what Timothy Walch calls the siege mentality among Catholics. The controversy began in 1840 when Governor William Seward called attention to the increasing number of immigrant children in New York City. He asked the legislature to establish schools where these children could learn from teachers who spoke their language and shared their religious faith. He hoped to make the schools more attractive to the children. Although he retreated on the question of language in the face of the resulting controversy, he maintained his view about religion. The Catholic clergy petitioned for a share of the state school funds allocated to the city to support their parish schools. The Public School Society rejected this petition, but the members were willing to compromise with the Catholic clergy in New York City about passages in books. Because they refused to remove the King James version of the Bible from schools, John Hughes, the archbishop of New York, repeated the demand to share the school funds. Hughes and the clergy asserted this was essential for Catholic schools to teach the morals needed to live in the United States (Church and Sedlak 161–162; Walch 41–42).

Hughes engaged opponents in a debate in front of the New York City Common School Council over questions such as which Bible should be used in schools. Because the discussants did not come to any compromise, the council did not either. As a result, the issue became central to the state's legislative election of 1841. Bishop Hughes urged all Catholics to vote for ten Democrats, and with his support they won. Once in office, those congressmen supported a bill that allowed school districts in New York City to control the curriculum in their schools. However, the state senate rescinded important parts of the bill and allowed the Public School Society to require that the King James version of the Bible be used in all schools receiving state money. In response, Hughes set out to build separate Catholic schools (Church and Sedlak 167–169).

In his memoirs, Hughes recalled that he used this controversy to unite the different groups in his diocese to a common cause. The Catholics in his diocese came from many different countries, and they had difficulties cooperating in the strange, new land. Unfortunately, although Hughes used the Catholic school controversy to unite his congregation, he raised the issue in ways that forced Catholics to choose between being loyal to their religion and seeking acceptance in U.S. society. For many years, this caused difficulties for Catholics who wanted to remain faithful to the church yet be accepted by the wider community (Walch 42).

In 1848, after the controversy in New York, Horace Mann noted that some towns in Massachusetts had removed the reading of the Bible from their school curricula about twelve years earlier. The members of the community did this, he added, because they feared the practice imposed a double wrong on minority religious groups. That is, the members of this minority religion paid taxes to support a school that taught a religious doctrine they did not believe. Also, to educate their own children in their own faith, these people had to send their children to schools of their own, thus paying twice for education. However, Mann felt that the schools in which no person read the Bible taught the students to ignore religion. So, he was pleased to note that the members of most local communities in Massachusetts had restored regular Bible reading when the citizens decided it was a neutral practice (Mann, "Twelfth" 104–105).

Mann's statements about changes in the educational practices in local districts revealed what one historian calls the center of the common school ideal—the concept of public control of schools. The public controlled the school by electing legislators who instituted state laws, such as creating a board of education, that supported education.

Through elections within local districts, citizens elected school committees that controlled the schools in the district. They could decide how and where to build the schools; they could hire the teachers and select the curriculum. Common school advocates hoped two things would result from this local control: (1) the public would be willing to pay for the schools, and (2) this public support would prevent any partisan group from taking control of the schools (Cremin, "Horace Mann" 19–20).

Unfortunately for common school advocates, the ideal of local control could not overcome all partisan biases. In several cases, the legislators set limits on how much control a school committee could have, and as the case with the reading of the King James version of the Bible in New York demonstrated, these limits could be set by partisan politics rather than by rational investigation and discussion. And because the community controlled the schools, it was even more difficult to prevent the majority of the members of a community from creating institutions that suited their biases. Usually, this meant the schools were Protestant. Naturally, however, when the majority of the members of a community were Catholic, the schools were Catholic. In 1833, when Purcell was installed as the second bishop of Cincinnati, he opened churches and schools to serve the several thousand German Catholic immigrants who settled in the Cincinnati area. Purcell established the pattern of opening a school in the basement of any church the German Catholics built when they arrived in the area. Driven from their native land by struggles over the control of their church, the rate of German Catholic immigration to the United States grew steadily so that by 1865, it equaled the level of Irish immigration. Most of these German Catholics were farmers who settled in an area known as the German belt that extended through the Ohio River basin. As a result, German Catholics dominated the rural areas north of Cincinnati, where they followed Purcell's pattern of building a church and a school. Unlike the Catholics in New York City who had to pay for their own schools, these German Catholics turned the common schools into Catholic ones. That is, they built public schools near the churches, hired parish priests to serve as schoolmasters, and paid their salaries from common school funds. Until 1880 most of the teachers in the public schools in the rural, northern sections of the Cincinnati diocese were Catholic, sometimes religious women who taught catechism, Bible history, and secular subjects (Buetow 113; Perko, "By the Bowels of God's Mercy" 19).

Did Common School Advocates Overcome Opposition from Wealthy People and from Poor People?

Although common school advocates hoped that citizens would be willing to pay for schools they could control through local elections, this was not the case. Advocates faced opposition from wealthy individuals who believed they should not have to pay to support schools for other people's children. In 1850, during a session of the New York legislature devoted to determining details of the common school law adopted four months earlier, critics complained about using property taxes to pay for schools. These people argued that they paid their own children's education and should not have to pay to educate other people's children. If the state adopted a law for free schools, their argument ran, it should do so without taxing individuals. Supporters of common school law replied that these critics were paying to support people who had been denied an education and were sent to poorhouses and penitentiaries. Supporters adopted a resolution stating that the welfare of the state came from free schools and that schools should be supported by property taxes because they protected the property of the state. When a critic complained that the state did not have any authority to build schools, a supporter claimed that because the state had the right to build prisons, it had the right to build schools that could remove the need for those prisons (Randall 263–267).

To explain why all people should pay for common schools, a committee headed by Horace Greeley presented a letter to the New York legislature. Reading from the letter, Greeley pointed out that the legislature should tax all people's property because their farms, banks, and mills profited from the maintenance of schools. For example, an educated citizenry would keep the community out of needless wars. It also prevented robberies and riots. In fact, Greeley added, because the legislature refused to support a public religion, schools were the only means by which the state could direct the morals of its citizens. Although he acknowledged that some of the money went to educate children of drunkards, it helped to prevent the children from becoming drunkards themselves. Finally, he warned that wealthy families could lose their riches someday and need the free schools to provide opportunities for their children (Randall 268–272).

Although Horace Mann agreed that schools taught the poor the moral lessons that restrained their desires to loot the property of rich people, he thought schools offered more than this narrow function. In 1848 he claimed that education equalized the social conditions between people and therefore acted as the balance of society. Schools might prevent the poor from stealing the wealth of richer people. More important, they gave people a reason to resist selfishness. This happened in two ways, he thought. First, schools cultivated feelings of sympathy among the students and spread students among as many groups in society as possible. He predicted that this would reduce the feelings of antagonism between social classes. Second, schools expanded the available wealth in society. Mann believed that this second function prevented poor people from stealing from rich people to improve their own status. He asserted that schools taught people to be creative and to determine new and better ways of doing things. Working together, these intelligent workers could increase the productivity of farms and factories. As a result, there would be enough wealth for all people to share and live comfortably (Mann, "Twelfth" 86–89).

In such statements as these, Greeley and Mann promised that schools would spread conventional morals, provide a ladder on which an aspiring child could climb, and protect the wealth of established classes. According to some commentators, this demonstrates that common school advocates retained a conservative view about private property even while they campaigned for a socialistic model of free schools for all citizens. However, other historians complain that these goals were too grandiose, that they favored the upper classes, and that common school advocates imposed their plans on the lower classes with the result that the more numerous working people rejected the campaign (Burgess and Borrowman 35; M. Katz, *Irony* 19–20, 112).

In order to prove that the lower classes rejected the common school movement, Michael B. Katz published a study of an election in Beverly, Massachusetts, that took place in March 1860 to abolish a high school built two years earlier and redistribute the money among the school districts. Town leaders built the high school because a state law required one. If the citizens voted to abolish the school, they would challenge the law in the state supreme court. Although many citizens refused to vote, 143 voted to retain the school and 249 voted to remove it. Katz discovered that the town clerk had recorded the names of each individual who voted. From tax records and census data, Katz determined the social class of voters. He concluded that social and financial leaders of the community supported the high school, while the lower income people did not (M. Katz, *Irony* 19–20, 112).

From this record, Katz concludes that people voted against the high school in Beverly for three reasons. First, people without children did not want to pay taxes to educate other people's children. Second, the least affluent parents were convinced that the high school would not help their children. Finally, social change had increased social antagonisms so that many people wanted to reject any plan favored by the community leaders. As Katz explains, in 1840 the railroad had come to Beverly and changed it from a small homogeneous community into one that housed a large shoe factory that employed many local residents. However, as a result of technological change, these shoemakers were losing their jobs and taking pay cuts. They went on strike just before the vote, Katz notes, and this conflict exacerbated the class conflict that already existed (M. Katz, *Irony* 80–85).

In 1985 Maris Vinovskis went to Beverly to research the records Katz had studied. He notes that the battle over the high school had begun in the early 1840s. At that time, thirteen citizens established a private academy. For several years, they tried to persuade the community to build a high school. In 1857, after repeated failures to convert the community to their point of view, they called attention to a state law passed in 1827 requiring every town of more than five hundred residents to construct an upper-level school offering classes in American history, bookkeeping, geometry, and surveying. Cities of more than five thousand had to employ a master competent to teach Latin, Greek, and rhetoric. Although there was no definition of a high school and officials rarely enforced the law, these supporters claimed that the town would have to pay a fine to the state if the high school was not built. By a narrow margin, the measure to build the high school passed. Seeking revenge, the majority voted to place the high school in an obscure location. Finally, in 1860 the town voted to abolish it (Vinovskis 60–65).

Vinovskis suggests that the controversy went on longer than Katz described, and it involved more than social class antagonism over factory jobs. Further, Vinovskis suggests that the votes against the high school did not mean that people disapproved of the common school movement. They may have disliked that particular proposal but later supported similar legislature. For example, they wanted to spend on the common schools the same amount of money that went to the high school. Vinovskis used more sophisticated statistical measures than the calculations Katz employed and finds that the results support Katz's contention that social classes voted differently. However, the influences were less marked than Katz made them appear. Instead, he finds a connection between religion and voting patterns. The local Protestant clergy were the members of the school committee who recommended building the high school. Interestingly, people who belonged to their churches were more likely to vote against the committee than were people who were not church members.

Yet, at the same meeting, after abolishing the high school residents elected the clergy who supported the high school to subsequent terms on the school committee. Vinovskis concludes that it is not easy to determine why people opposed such innovations as a high school (Vinovskis 90, 109–113).

What Happened to the Common School Movement?

By 1860 common school advocates claimed a victory. Most states had laws that instituted some form of state support and statewide control of schools. Teachers were better paid. From 1840 to 1860 in Massachusetts, the average salary of male teachers increased about 65 percent, while the salary of women teachers increased about 71 percent. The teaching force changed in Massachusetts, as well. In 1840, 61 percent of the teachers were men; by 1865, only 14 percent were men (Kaestle, *Pillars* 134–135; M. Katz, *Irony* 12–13).

Some school committee members admitted that they hired women because they could pay them less than they paid men. For example, in 1840 in Connecticut, men received an average wage of $14.96 per month while women received on average $6.50 per month. These were meager wages for both sexes. Therefore, people such as Horace Mann urged school committees to pay teachers more and to equalize salaries. By 1878 the city of St. Louis, some southern states, California, Idaho, and Nebraska offered the same pay to women as to men for the same work. Nonetheless, as late as 1911 some educators, including women, felt that women should be paid less because a woman's primary occupation should not be education but marriage (Woody, *History* 492–496, 504).

Another reason for the difference in pay was that some educators believed that men were better teachers than women. The extra pay was to induce men to become schoolteachers. These people feared that a woman could not influence the older boys as well as a man could and that men were less mechanical in their teaching than women. When it appeared that students in classes taught by women learned more information, these educators asserted that male teachers made more of a difference in the students' characters, which they held to be more important than immediate intellectual results (Tyack 61–63; Woody, *History* 505–511).

Even though common school advocates made some advancements, their main goal of constructing a system of education eluded them. They established few high schools. In 1820 Boston opened the first high school, the English Classical School, on the second floor of a grammar school building for 102 students. This school differed from classical academies such as Boston's Latin Grammar School because it did not offer instruction in ancient languages and was open only to men. In other villages and towns, high schools opened after elementary or grammar school enrollments grew, and they enrolled both men and women. However, in the 1820s and 1830s, academies, seminaries, and colleges, with their mix of public and private support, remained the chief sources of higher education. In fact, Horace Mann recommended to his supporters that they avoid using the phrase "high school." He thought it was easy for critics to attack the concept. Anything can be considered high, he added, and critics could claim that these schools caused class distinctions (Reese, *Origins* 1–2, 36–37).

Despite these problems, common school advocates thought of high schools as an important part of the democratic ethos. In the 1820s and 1830s, advocates argued that high schools rewarded individual merit and enabled talented youth from all social classes to advance. As a result, they called them "people's colleges." However, critics complained that high schools served only rich people, and they called them "palaces of privilege." Critics feared that at their best, high schools would drain the money from common schools, which enrolled the middle-class and working-class children. Critics also feared the loss of local control. In order to stimulate the growth of high schools, state legislatures permitted townships to join together to build a school for the combined district. But the educators who controlled these new schools wanted to teach more academic subjects such as foreign languages than the residents thought reasonable (Reese, *Origins* 46–49, 64–70).

As a result of these controversies, the spread of high schools was slow until the end of the nineteenth century. In 1850, W. T. Harris counted 11 high schools in the United States. This number grew to 44 in 1860, 160 in 1870, 800 in 1880, and 2,526 by 1890. Other experts counted differently than Harris. In Maine the state superintendent counted 143 high schools in his state alone in 1874. These educators made different estimates because they used different definitions of a high school. For Harris, a high school offered a two- or four-year curriculum, whereas the superintendent in Maine considered small ungraded schools where a few scholars studied some algebra, astronomy, or natural philosophy to be high schools (Reese, *Origins* 209–212).

In part, the common school movement lost momentum in the middle of the nineteenth century because many powerful advocates moved on to other activities. They did so for a variety of personal and political reasons. In 1848 Horace Mann left his position with the Massachusetts Board of Education. A year earlier, he had complained in a private letter about the war with Mexico, asking how a republican nation that proclaimed itself to be a champion of freedom and peace could raise $10 million, call up 50,000 soldiers, and carry out an attack on a neighboring country in order to spread slavery. However, Mann made no public comments about his feelings because he worried such overt opposition would hurt his campaign for education. When the Whig party asked if he would accept the nomination to the U.S. House of Representatives, he accepted on the belief that from this position he could stand against military aggression and slavery (Messerli 448–452).

Other leaders of the common school movement drifted into other ventures because of political difficulties. In Ohio in 1839, Samuel Lewis fell into disfavor with the Ohio legislature and resigned his duties as superintendent of schools on the grounds of ill health. In 1840 the Ohio legislature merged the position of superintendent into the duties of the secretary of state. This ended Lewis's efforts to collect information about schools that could be included in reports and used to advance education. In fact, one historian suggests that the legislators removed the job of superintendent because Lewis uncovered and broadcast corruption in the selling and leasing of school lands (Petit 100–101; Carr 130–133).

When the Ohio legislature dissolved the independent office of the state superintendent, the action disheartened members of the Western Literary Institute and College of Professional Teachers. However, the founders of the institute took more passive roles than they had in the past. Albert Picket was nearly seventy, and several others had died. At best, most of the former energetic leaders drifted into other activities. Only Samuel Lewis had made his living in education, and he did so at great personal hardship. The other members practiced other occupations, such as college president and lawyer. Although the original leaders of the institute participated actively in the campaigns for state support of schools, they saw education as an avocation rather than an occupation. When they gave up their active roles, leadership fell to teachers. Unfortunately, they were not as popular and attendance at the annual meetings declined. Furthermore, many of the Northern members held abolitionist views that alienated the Southern delegates who supported slavery. To mollify the Southerners, the institute moved its annual meetings to Louisville, Kentucky, in 1842. Unfortunately, few delegates wanted to go to the smaller city. Although the institute moved the meeting back to Cincinnati in 1845, few people attended. Because sales of the annual publication *Transactions* had declined, the organization faced financial problems. It passed out of existence without any announcement that it was disbanding (Rich 162–170).

Although common school advocates achieved modest success in their own lifetimes, they set the stage for later changes. After the Civil War, people thought differently about their nation. Reconstruction demonstrated that they were willing to accord a strong role to the federal government. As large cities with factories replaced villages surrounded by farms, citizens of the United States dropped their resistance to the centralization of school financing and standardization of curricula. They no longer believed that local control of schools was more important than the coordinated planning of education. The growing public acceptance of a national identity that superceded local or ethnic ties made it possible for educators to create a system of schools that would Americanize immigrants (Kaestle, *Pillars* 218–219; Urban and Wagoner 162–164).

What Did the Common School Movement Show about Schools and Diversity?

Advocates for common schools organized their campaign to meet the social changes caused by the expansion of the United States and the rising political power of different groups. To achieve their ends, advocates forged compromises with their opponents. Unfortunately, the compromises could not satisfy any one of these groups. When advocates recommended that the Bible represented a neutral source of values for all ethnic and religious groups, some denominations complained that different sects used different Bibles. Most important, the controversies about whose values the schools should teach, which group's interests the schools should meet, and who should pay for schools continued throughout the twentieth century (Mehl, "Education" 19–25).

Common school advocates wanted teachers to impart those skills and information that should be shared by all people. Therefore, the common aspect of schools was that the subjects or courses enhanced each student's essential humanity. If schools could achieve such an end, they would represent integration and social progress. Although advocates failed in many ways, U.S. citizens came to believe that such a set of values existed and could be spread among different peoples as the nineteenth century proceeded. However, critics pointed out that these compromises never satisfied everyone.

TIMELINE
1830–1860

1832	The Whig party was established
1833	The *American Annals of Education* reported that the United States did not have enough teachers to educate large numbers of children
1833	Purcell became the second bishop of Cincinnati and opened new churches and schools for German Catholics
1836	Calvin Stowe purchased a library from Europe for Cincinnati's Lane Seminary
1837	Samuel Reed Hall became the principal of Holmes Plymouth Academy
1837	The Ohio state legislature appointed Samuel Lewis as the first state superintendent of common schools
1837	Horace Mann became secretary of the Massachusetts State Board of Education
1837	Mary Lyon opened a female seminary called Mount Holyoke
1838	Samuel Lewis convinced the Ohio legislature to pass a school law and to create a common school fund
1839	Massachusetts established the first state-supported normal school
1839	The Ohio legislature disagreed with Samuel Lewis on many issues, and he resigned as superintendent of schools on grounds of bad health
1840	The position of Ohio's superintendent combined with the duties of secretary of state
1840	Albert Picket and other members of the Cincinnati school board recommended separation of subjects and stages of learning in elementary schools
1842	The Western Literary Institute and College of Professional Teachers moved its annual meetings from Cincinnati to Louisville, Kentucky
1843	Catharine Beecher campaigned for women to go teach in the West
1845	The Irish potato famine began
1845	The Western Literary Institute and College of Professional Teachers disbanded
1847	John D. Philbrick organized courses of study in Massachusetts
1848	Horace Mann wrote his final report to the Massachusetts State Board of Education and supported common schools
1849	The famine in Ireland ended
1850	New York critics complained about property taxes going toward schools
1850	The United States had eleven high schools, as counted by W. T. Harris
1851	Calvin Wiley supported common schools in North Carolina
1856	Beecher published *Physiology and Calisthenics*
1860	Beverly, Massachusetts, voted to abolish one of its high schools

CHAPTER

4 Reconstruction, Kindergartens, and Religious Schools: 1861–1890

A public kindergarten class models with clay.

OVERVIEW

After the United States Civil War, people sought to unite Americans as the country and its industries grew. Unfortunately, some of the educational reforms exacerbated the differences among groups. For example, during the Southern Reconstruction, reformers opened

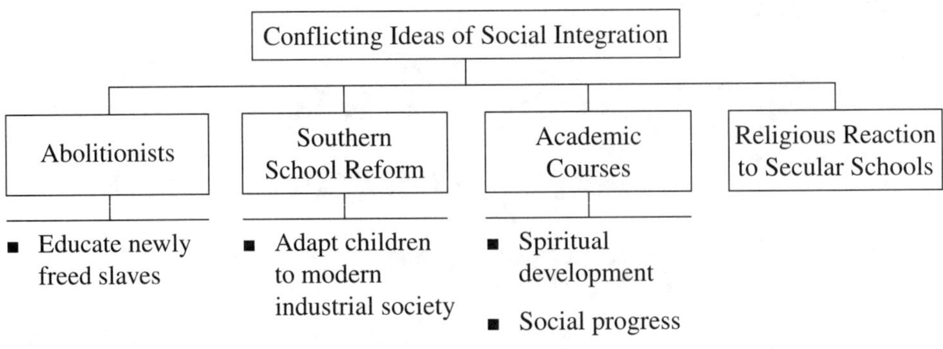

schools to educate the newly freed slaves, but some of the educational materials suggested that African Americans should accept subservient positions in a capitalistic society. In schools for Southern White children, educators introduced graded school plans in the hope that this system would prepare students for the market system that replaced the rural aristocracy. In the North, educators such as W. T. Harris believed that innovations such as the textbook method of instruction and the kindergarten movement would enable those graded schools to improve the entire society. According to Harris, both innovations began a process of instruction that he called self-determination. He hoped that improved schools would bring people together, enable the students to learn how to participate in society, and teach them to use social institutions to advance themselves. Another approach, called manual training, complemented academic training in the same ways the kindergarten movement did. However, manual training did not become as popular as kindergartens. Most important for this discussion, educators thought that if schools were to bring people together there should be no instruction in denominational religion. In accord with this compromise, some people sent their children to public schools for secular instruction and sought religious teaching outside of school hours. Fearing that strictly secular schools were godless, Catholic leaders and some other religious groups built private, religious schools in which the students learned about their denominations while they studied academics.

What Did Northerners Do to Help the Newly Freed Slaves?

On November 7, 1861, following a brief attack on the Confederate Army's fortresses on Hilton Head Island and Bay Point, the U.S. Navy seized the islands in Port Royal Sound, which lay off the South Carolina coast. In this region, plantations had prospered because the level, sandy land produced the finest quality cotton. By 1861 these plantations were large, and about 83 percent of the islands' population consisted of African American slaves. Many of them remained on the island when the White families fled from the Union soldiers. Following a practice that the Union Army and the U.S. War Department had set, all the property on the islands, including the slaves, became contraband of war. The task of collecting this property fell to Secretary Salmon P. Chase of the U.S. Treasury Department.

Because he held abolitionist sentiments, he decided to use this opportunity to test the notion that former slaves could become free laborers. He was aided in this decision by Edward L. Pierce, who went to Port Royal at Chase's request. Pierce found that the former slaves knew everything necessary to produce cotton. Further, Pierce believed the former slaves would perform the work if given proper inducements. At the same time, Pierce contacted missionary societies and religious leaders in Boston, seeking teachers for the more than ten thousand former slaves on the islands (Rose 3–31).

When Pierce returned to Boston, many supporters rallied to his cause. Several of the abolitionists argued that free labor was more efficient than slavery, and they believed that Port Royal represented an opportunity to test this view. Other abolitionists were sympathetic to the former African American slaves who faced difficult situations. Pierce recruited fifty-three missionaries from New York and Boston, who arrived in the Sea Islands in March 1862. These evangels of civilization, as they called themselves, included men and women who were teachers, clerks, doctors, divinity students, and socialists. Among the members were Unitarians, freethinkers, Methodists, and members of other, more conservative religious sects (Rose 32–61).

For the agricultural component of the experiment, the missionaries tried to organize the abandoned cotton plantations and encourage the former slaves to continue production. In 1862, after the first year, the cotton crop was dismal. Although they planted about 3,384 acres of cotton, the yield reached only about 26 pounds per acre, considerably lower than the previous yields of about 137 pounds per acre. The results were more favorable in food production because the former slaves grew sufficient corn and potatoes to feed the population on the islands. Part of the problem was that federal troops stole livestock, crops, and farm materials from the former slaves. Further, in May 1862, the U.S. Army drafted hundreds of former slaves who were tending the cotton crops to form the First Regiment of South Carolina Volunteers (Rose 177–241).

The missionary teachers enjoyed greater success. Although many of the teachers doubted that all races had equal capacities to learn, they attributed these differences to the institution of slavery. Therefore, they set about the business of instruction. In 1862 more than 1,700 children attended schools on St. Helena, Ladies, and Port Royal Islands. Most important, the missionaries noted that the newly freed slaves expressed a genuine desire to learn (Rose 230–231).

As a result of the African Americans' desire to learn, missionary societies provided increasingly large numbers of teachers. Consequently, by the end of the war the New York National Freedmen's Aid Society maintained 206 teachers throughout the South. The New England Freedmen's Aid Society sent 180 teachers. Similar societies in Philadelphia, Baltimore, Cincinnati, and Chicago supported 240 teachers. The American Missionary Society provided about 330 teachers (Rose 333).

By 1866 nearly every major religious denomination set up an aid society for what were called the freedmen. However, their interest was not entirely philanthropic. These societies competed with each other and used their schools to convert the students to their denominational creeds. Although the societies desired to advance themselves, their members did not ignore the enormity of the educational problems. As early as 1863, recognizing their efforts to be inadequate, they called for federal intervention. In March 1865 the U.S. Congress passed a bill to establish the Freedmen's Bureau, which assisted the aid societies by offering transportation to teachers, helping to pay for buildings, and aiding in the creation of normal schools and colleges throughout the Southern states (Butchart 8–9).

The official name of the Freedmen's Bureau was the Bureau of Refugees, Freedmen, and Abandoned Lands. This indicated the wide range of the bureau's duties. The word *refugee* suggested that the bureau was not solely concerned with African Americans. The phrase "abandoned lands" implied that the bureau would supervise and distribute lands to destitute refugees and former slaves. In fact, an early version of the Congressional bill to establish the Freedman's Bureau suggested that the bureau would oversee large plantations with many workers. In practice, though, the situation was chaotic. The various state agencies of the bureau had to provide aid for the destitute, the aged, and the insane. They had to adjudicate disputes among people belonging to every race. Further, they were expected to establish schools throughout the South. To some degree, these scattered efforts were united by bureau's aim to lay the foundation of a free labor society in which African Americans worked voluntarily. The bureau wanted African Americans to adopt the values of capitalism and to receive the rights enjoyed by Northern workers. According to the first commissioner, General Oliver Otis Howard, education was the basis on which all other efforts rested. However, the bureau could not establish the schools itself. Consequently, it sought to coordinate the activities of the aid societies (Foner 68–70, 142–145).

Did Education Help African Americans in the South?

Historians disagree about whether education helped African Americans in the South. Writing in 1903, W. E. B. Du Bois declared that "the greatest success of the Freedmen's Bureau lay in the planting of the free school among Negroes, and the idea of free elementary education among all classes in the South." Du Bois added that "six million dollars were expended for educational work, seven hundred and fifty thousand dollars of which the Freedmen themselves gave of their poverty" (71). On the other hand, Henry Lee Swint contends that the Northern missionaries caused the White Southerners to oppose education for African Americans. He claims that these teachers descended on the South in an effort to teach the newly freed slaves and win their support in elections for programs favorable to the North. To prove his point, Swint quotes letters from teachers who described their work as a continuation of the hostilities. He repeats descriptions of lessons in which African American children recited prepared answers to set questions. For example, when the teacher asked who gave them their freedom, the African American students stated that God did, but U.S. President Lincoln was His agent. In another exercise, the students repeated sentences that indicated they were equal to White people and that attributed the superior wealth of White people to the exploitation of African Americans. However, Swint claims that the strongest reason White Southerners had for resisting African American education was that they feared Northern teachers would introduce racially mixed schools (88–90, 137–140).

In part, of course, both Du Bois and Swint were correct. Although schools were beneficial to African Americans, there was a limit to the extent to which education could overcome serious social problems. For example, most members of the freedmen's aid societies recognized that the newly freed slaves could not thrive unless they developed economic power. Without land, they frequently remarked, the former slaves would not profit from their freedom. Further, with the creation of the Freedmen's Bureau, the federal government appeared to promise that the land would be redistributed in ways that aided African Americans. When this promise was not fulfilled, members of the aid societies did not help African Americans gain land. Instead, they asserted that with an adequate education, the former slaves would eventually reach equality (Butchart 198–199).

Furthermore, although Swint portrays Northern teachers as demanding equality for African Americans, many missionary teachers believed that African Americans should accept a subservient place in a hierarchical society. This bias appears in their educational materials. For example, when Ronald Butchart analyzed the primers, spellers, and readers the American Tract Society (ATS) published inexpensively for use in the freedmen's schools, he found they carried lessons aimed almost exclusively at the character of the students. Within this *Freedmen's Reader* series, Butchart discovered the important themes to be the need for piety, the importance of stable domestic relations, the virtue of hard work, and the benefits of avoiding alcoholic drinks. The texts avoid any mention of the right to vote or of freedom. Instead, they emphasize the need to accept one's role in life and the importance of proper behavior. In addition, they often portray African Americans as inferior to White people. Thus, Butchart argues, the ATS texts sought to replace the slave driver with a self-imposed tendency for African Americans to restrain themselves and to accept a hierarchical society (136–150).

On the other hand, some aid societies disagreed with this conservative perspective. Butchart notes that the American Freedmen's Union Commission (AFUC) criticized the *Freedmen's Reader* series because it was prepared specifically for the Freedmen schools. Claiming that African Americans were human beings similar to everyone else, the AFUC argued that the newly freed slaves deserved the best literature available and the opportunities to learn from the same texts other students used (138–139).

Other organizations thought the former slaves needed texts designed specifically for them and that presented African Americans in positive ways. Following this idea, Lydia Maria Child of the New England Freedmen's Aid Society published *The Freedmen's Book,* which described the accomplishments of African American men and women. Child's book sought to instill in the students a sense of self-worth and pride through biographies of people such as Benjamin Banneker, Toussaint-Louverture, and Phillis Wheatley. In these works, Child showed that Black people were the moral equals of White people (Butchart 151–152).

In another effort to introduce equality, the aid societies and the Freedmen's Bureau employed African American teachers as much as possible. For example, in 1865 the superintendent of schools for the bureau, Rev. John W. Alford, visited a school in New Orleans with three hundred African American students that was entirely supported by the Black residents of the city and staffed entirely by what he called "colored men." The standards in this school were comparable to any Northern institution, Alford noted. The pupils advanced through the basic studies, and the students in the higher grades had mastered French as well as English (Morris 85–86).

In some states, such as South Carolina, there was an ample supply of Black teachers because free African Americans had maintained schools in those places since the early nineteenth century. In general, however, the aid societies had difficulty finding competent

African American instructors. Although they appealed to many Northern institutions, such as Oberlin College in Ohio, for qualified Black recruits, the shortage persisted. As a result, by 1866 many school officials were turning their own African American pupils into teachers as soon as possible. In 1867 the Freedmen's Bureau stepped up its efforts to provide teacher training. At that time, about one-third of the teachers the bureau employed were African American. By 1869 the number grew to 53 percent. In addition, in 1869 several newly created Black colleges began teacher training programs and opened model schools where the prospective teachers could practice their skills. For example, Howard University enrolled 139 students in its normal school. Fisk University took on 41 in its normal school and 248 in its model school (Morris 90–92, 101–102, 114–115).

To some extent, competition between White and Black churches increased the supply of African American teachers. As early as 1865, Black American Methodist Episcopal church leaders urged local ministers to set up their own schools and draw students away from White preachers and White teachers. However, this competition was not heated (Morris 113–114).

As Reconstruction ended, many aid societies stopped supporting schools, and federal control of Southern education ended. In 1871 the Freedmen's Aid Society limited itself to supporting a few teacher training institutions. The organization decided its efforts were unnecessary because public schools were rising throughout the South and more African American self-help efforts were under way. In 1872 the U.S. Congress decided to discontinue the Freedmen's Bureau. Most of the officials had already resigned because Congress had denied the bureau appropriations. In 1874, after some accusations of misappropriation of funds, the bureau closed its doors. In what was called the Compromise of 1877, the newly created Electoral Commission elevated Rutherford B. Hayes to the office of United States president. He ended what was left of Reconstruction (Morris 245–246; Bentley 213–214; Foner 581–582).

Although the freedmen's societies and the missionary teachers spread literacy, they left some unfortunate legacies. Some missionaries considered Blacks to be inferior to Whites. Consequently, instead of teaching African Americans to achieve independence, they taught them to accept the roles they had. Further, the missionaries' desire to make converts for particular creeds sometimes overshadowed other concerns. Although some missionaries sought to help African Americans achieve equality, they could not bring about the racial integration of schools. In the face of such efforts, Whites sought to eliminate public schooling.

Did Education Change Southern Society?

Education did not alter Southern society, but it encouraged changes already taking place. Within the schools for African Americans, the freedmen's aid societies and the agents of the Peabody Fund, a northern philanthropic organization, advanced racial segregation. Although they capitulated to racism, these educators sought to improve the conditions of African Americans. Once they settled the issue of segregated schools, White Southerners used the graded schools and the object method of instruction to speed the introduction of modern systems of business and transportation. They thought schools could aid in the effort to replace the aristocracy with capitalism and thereby usher in what they called the New South.

Frequently, people conceive of Southern race relations as marked by segregation. However, in 1955 C. Vann Woodward published *The Strange Career of Jim Crow* in which he argues that racial segregation did not begin immediately after 1877 when Reconstruction ended. Woodward claims that the laws requiring civil rights and equality remained, and many African Americans maintained the hopes inspired by such institutions as the Freedmen's Bureau. At the same time, he notes, Southern White conservatives saw themselves as custodians of African Americans, and they felt an obligation to protect and educate the former slaves. A third alternative to segregation Woodward describes was the movement of Southern radicals, such as the Populists, who thought that African American farmers and White farmers faced the same problems and had to work together. However, Woodward claims that by the end of the nineteenth century, these forces lost their effectiveness, and many Southern states passed laws requiring extreme segregation.

Woodward's book sparked a controversy as historians tried to find out when segregation began. According to Howard Rabinowitz, segregation was an improvement for African Americans over the exclusion they otherwise experienced. He contends that from 1865 to 1867, White people excluded Black people from orphanages, insane asylums, and schools. During Reconstruction the U.S. Army and the Freedmen's Bureau forced several states to set up segregated poorhouses in order to offer this service to African Americans. Some states chose to build segregated schools out of fear that they would otherwise have to offer integrated schools. Although Rabinowitz finds instances during the 1870s when African Americans challenged segregation, he also finds several cases in which Blacks accepted it. Segregation offered peace, economic opportunity, and a general improvement over exclusion. At times, African Americans created segregated hospitals, hotels, and ice cream parlors when White prejudice seemed inexorable.

In the matter of racially integrated schools, the role of state legislators, the federal government, and Northern liberals was complicated. In 1868 seven former Confederate states crafted new state constitutions to gain readmission to the Union. Of these, only Louisiana and South Carolina specified that all schools would be open to all children regardless of race. Alabama, Arkansas, Florida, Georgia, and North Carolina offered equality of education, not racial integration. Later, Virginia, Texas, and Mississippi drafted constitutions that promised similar equality without racial integration (Urban and Wagoner 146).

In states such as Mississippi and Tennessee, many African American legislators claimed that racial integration was essential for equal educational advantages. Some African Americans complained that separate schools promoted racial prejudice. Further, in 1875 in Louisiana a former Confederate general, P. G. T. Beauregard, advocated the spread of racially integrated schools in the hope that such institutions would win the loyalty of African Americans to Southern institutions. Some mixed schools existed in the South, but these were maintained by Northern philanthropic societies (J. Franklin 119–120).

On the other hand, some Northern philanthropists urged the spread of racially segregated schools. One influential advocate of public education in the South was Barnas Sears, who left the presidency of Brown University to become general agent of the Peabody Fund. This fund began in 1867 when George Peabody, a banker who was born in Danvers, Massachusetts, but made his fortune in England, set aside about $2 million to promote education in the South. The annual grants never exceeded $150,000. The grants went to established schools that were supposed to become models for other efforts. To ensure local support,

Sears required that communities provide twice what they received from the fund to maintain the school. Yet he proposed that grants to Black schools be for one-third less than those for White schools on the grounds that it cost less to maintain African American schools. When Louisiana adopted racially integrated schools, the Peabody Fund's Louisiana agent would provide funds only to private, White schools. Later, Sears defended this policy by noting that White students would not attend racially integrated schools. Therefore, the public schools in Louisiana became Black schools and thus received all the state funds. The Peabody Fund retained this policy until the conservatives returned to power and reinstalled racially segregated schools in Louisiana (Vaughn 141–152).

Sears claimed that he did not want the fund involved in political controversies, yet he entered at least one such controversy to protect racial segregation. In 1874 Charles Sumner introduced a civil rights bill to the U.S. Congress. Complaining that the bill required racially integrated schools, Sears argued that this would wreck public schools. He successfully lobbied members of Congress and President Grant to remove that requirement (Vaughn 153–157).

In practice, the Civil Rights Act of 1875 made little difference in the education of African Americans. Once the racially mixed school question had been removed, African Americans paid little attention to the legislation. Journals such as *Harper's Weekly* complained that Congress emasculated the bill by removing the section on racial mixing in schools. In 1883 the U.S. Supreme Court ruled the Civil Rights Act of 1875 to be unconstitutional. Despite this reversal, the act changed the federal government's approach to the racial segregation of schools. In the 1870s, most of the bills that sought to establish a national subsidy for public education carried some sort of requirement for racially integrated schools. With the Civil Rights Act of 1875, Congress affirmed that the question of segregated schools should be decided by state governments. The U.S. Supreme Court reaffirmed this position in 1896 with the *Plessy v. Ferguson* decision. The justices allowed states to create and maintain facilities for African Americans that were separate but equal if they chose to do so (A. Kelly 174–175, 194–195).

Once the segregated school issue was resolved, agents of the Peabody Fund continued the campaign for free public schools throughout the South. Sears died in 1880 and was succeeded by Jabez L. M. Curry as general agent of the Peabody Education Fund. In 1888 Curry addressed the general assembly of Georgia, telling senators and representatives that tax-supported schools for the masses to which industrial training could be attached were more important than universities, technological schools, and high schools. If public schools offered well-conceived training to White and Black students, Curry concluded, they would usher in Southern prosperity by multiplying factories, telegraphs, and railroads.

Curry's speech reflected the sentiments of an increasing number of Southerners. After Reconstruction, coalitions of merchants and owners of large properties championed the construction of railroads, towns, and factories. This was to become the New South, a South less tied to tradition and more anxious to become modern. In some areas, the changes were dramatic. For example, in North Carolina in 1880 there were 1,500 miles of railroad track. By 1900 this had increased by 250 percent. With greater access to rail transportation, farmers tried to make money, the old ways of subsistence farming declined, and cities grew. In 1870 the only city in North Carolina to have a population over ten thousand was Wilmington; by 1900 five other cities exceeded that size. Most important, when civic leaders looked for an institution that could help children make the adjustment to this new society dominated by business, they chose graded schools. These graded schools divided the students by chronological age. As a result, students of roughly similar ages and abilities studied together. Teachers believed that in such settings student progress was clearer, emulation more possible, and unruliness less of a problem (Leloudis 18–20).

The first graded schools were established in North Carolina in 1868. After 1881 they spread across the state, and by the late 1890s more than two thousand communities in North Carolina had graded schools for Black and for White students. Advocates expected these schools to prepare children for the new marketplace economy because the teachers would judge the students' abilities by a uniform standard. This was supposed to teach the pupils that success came from work, not from family status or patronage as may have been the case in the Old South (Leloudis 23–24).

According to James Leloudis, educators in North Carolina who favored the creation of the New South believed that the graded schools could change the attitudes and orientations of all students. In these schools, teachers and administrators kept careful records of attendance, honoring students with the best records of punctuality and publishing their names in the newspapers. Teachers used standard textbooks, students took written examinations, and each student received individual grades. Teachers used methods such as object teaching thinking this helped students observe the world rather than accept information from an authority. In object teaching, the teacher showed something to the students and, later, asked them to recall its characteristics. Educators hoped these innovations would teach students that success depended on the abilities they had acquired in school. As a result, they would not accept a traditional system bound by elders (Leloudis 29–34).

Did People Want New Forms of School Governance after the U.S. Civil War?

Although Northern victory restored the Union, it was no longer the same country. After the Civil War, people approved more than they had earlier of the central government influencing local affairs. During the war, the federal government instituted a federal income tax, authorized the creation of paper currency not redeemable in gold or silver, extended citizenship to the slaves, and enacted laws requiring men to serve in the military. Later, during Reconstruction, Northern states dictated to the Southern states the essential reforms. These intrusions into local affairs extended the power of the centralized government. For example, people came to approve of the central government imposing majority thinking on minority groups. When Utah sought statehood, Congress forced the territory to renounce Mormonism as a state religion and polygamy as an acceptable marital practice. Educators tried to use this majoritarian consciousness to create a modern school (Urban and Wagoner 162–164).

In 1867 Congress and President Andrew Johnson took an important step to enforce a system of education by creating a federal department of education. In Congress, discussions about the bill to create the federal agency took up little time: Republicans supported the measure and Democrats opposed it. However, both parties supported the creation of the Freedmen's Bureau and the Reconstruction Act more strongly. In fact, it was not clear what the agency would do. Some advocates wanted the agency to produce statistical reports about schooling in the different states. Other advocates thought the office should provide direction to improve those schools, enabling them to provide effective academic, political, and moral instruction (Warren 87–91).

The Senate confirmed unanimously Henry Barnard as the first U.S. commissioner of education. When Barnard met with Johnson, the president made it clear that the purpose of the office was to help states in their efforts to improve schools. Johnson did not want to create a federal system of education. Unfortunately, Congress appropriated little money for the office, and the president imposed on Barnard a clerk he did not want. Consequently, Barnard warned his colleagues not to expect a great deal. At best, he thought he could collect information to show the progress of education in the United States. With this aim, he opened a temporary office with three clerks, described the type of information he wanted to collect, and delegated assignments to his clerks (MacMullen 259–261; Warren 124–125).

During his first year, Barnard spent most of his time putting together his own *American Journal of Education.* Each issue consisted of about eight hundred pages and contained a wide range of information, from statistical reports to selections from Pestalozzi's classic, *Leonard and Gertrude.* Barnard had begun publication in 1855. By the time he ceased publication in 1881, he had produced a total of thirty-one volumes. Whereas he considered the *Journal* to be part of the U.S. commissioner of education's job, his enemies used this against him, contending that he failed to use his office to gather information. They complained that in 1868 Barnard presented papers previously published in the *Journal* as his first report to Congress. As a result of this and similar complaints, Congress refused to build a strong department of education (Warren 98–99, 121, 131).

The department's greatest weakness was that Barnard had to rely on teachers, school officials, and friends to voluntarily submit information. He lacked the power to require local or state authorities to send him the information he needed, and he could not employ researchers to gather it for him. Worse, in those areas where he should have documented even the smallest efforts to provide schools, he was least able to secure the information. For example, in 1868 an official wrote to Barnard explaining that in Texas citizens did not support public schools and would not tell him anything about what sort of schools existed in the state (Warren 146).

In 1870 Congress appointed John Eaton to replace Barnard as commissioner of education. Eaton was more successful in developing the office. Although unable to require schools to send him information, he built a network of editors and superintendents with whom he shared information. He developed close ties with the National Teachers Association, which in 1870 became the National Education Association (NEA). In fact, he used his office's mailing privileges to distribute NEA publications. In this way, Eaton organized the office so that it worked closely with the nation's educators, trained them to keep and collect statistical information, and encouraged them to use that information to improve their schools (Warren 152–165).

Did Educators Think Schools Could Heal the Wounds Caused by the Civil War?

In 1861 William Torrey Harris decided that the Civil War was the result of a dialectical process that often took place between nations. In this case, Harris contended that the industrial system of the North had resisted the slave methods of the South. Writing a letter to the *Missouri Republican,* Harris asserted that the North required everyone to be self-determining, whereas the South favored an aristocracy and forbade the majority to rule. In that letter, Harris predicted that the hope of the country rested with the patient, conservative people who would continue to work while the controversies increased. After the North had won the war, Harris concluded that both sides had been in the same stage of humanitarianism. However, the North's reliance on free labor was the proper instrument for the realization of human development. Because the democracy of the North could not coexist with the aristocracy of the South, the war was inevitable. Harris concluded that although wars were cruel, God used them to lead humankind into a higher consciousness. He predicted that wars would not disappear until people found other ways to recognize such essential distinctions as the difference between democracy and aristocracy (Leidecker 204–210).

Harris spent his life trying to show how schools could provide a peaceful means by which people could develop this higher consciousness. He believed that if people thought in this way the wounds of the Civil War would heal and the country could avoid future conflicts. Harris's faith stemmed from his work and thought in a dialectic process, which meant he believed that ideas or institutions sparked their opposites. In time, these contradictory ways of thinking or being came together in a new form that contained elements of the former conceptions but in unrecognizable forms.

As a long time devotee of Hegel, Harris took the view that a person had to immerse himself or herself in collectivity to achieve individuality. Education proceeded through what Harris called the five cardinal institutions: family, school, civil society, state, and church. For example, when a child outgrew the family, the school took over. After schooling, the individual pursued an occupation and fulfilled the duties of citizenship (Cremin, *American Education 1876–1980,* 161).

Harris borrowed from Hegel the description of the stages a person should go through to achieve self-determination, but, the list of stages mirrored the experiences Harris went through as he matured. He was born in 1835 in Connecticut. His father was a prosperous farmer. Harris attended rural schools and Phillips Academy, where he learned how to discipline himself and focus his efforts. In 1854 he entered Yale. After two and a half years, Harris left Yale because he wanted to study nature, not just words and dead languages such as Latin and Greek. Consequently, he went to St. Louis, Missouri, which was on the frontier. In 1857, after being a tutor and giving private lessons in shorthand, he joined the city's public schools. In 1868, at the age of thirty-three, he became the superintendent of schools (Clifton 188–191).

Although he lacked formal training, Harris devoted his spare time to the study of art, music, and science. He was among the founding members of the St. Louis Art Society and the Philharmonic Society. He wrote articles on the motions of gyroscopes and built a laboratory in his house where he studied biology. He founded the St. Louis Philosophical Society and the *Journal of Speculative Philosophy* to spread the ideas of Georg Wilhelm Friedrich Hegel through the United States. As superintendent of schools, he visited schools in his district regularly and kept careful accounts of expenses and schedules of activities in each building. Under his system, principals could use any method they wished to achieve the standards he set. To those principals who succeeded, he gave an increase in rank and salary. This model of administration was consistent with his view of the aim of all government. Calling his idea "Americanism," Harris claimed that every form of supervision should lead the individual to self-determination. For example, Harris took interest in the number of times pupils arrived late for school. He was most pleased when there was a decline in the ratio of tardy cases per one hundred pupils in a school. This illustrated, he explained, that teachers were working to enforce his rules. Harris believed that although these external rules such as the need for punctuality were simple, they were also the foundation of higher ethics (Leidecker 253–255, 286–287, 294–316; McKnight 40).

Harris allowed students to work their way quickly through the grades. He thought this system encouraged students to study independently because they received immediate recognition for their efforts. According to his plan, the capable students could be promoted as many as four times a year and thereby select their own status by their own efforts. He added that such a system also offered teachers the advantage of presenting material to a more homogeneous group of students (Leidecker 262–263).

Harris's plan of self-promotion required coeducation. Although other frontier towns had difficulty mixing boys and girls together in the same classroom, Harris decided that coeducation made his plan for flexible promotion more efficient than it would have been had there been distinct schools for boys and for girls. Further, he thought that by placing the boys and girls together, the boys would act better and the girls would be more serious. Harris also hoped that girls would learn mathematics more quickly in the company of boys, and boys would come to appreciate literature if they studied it with girls (Leidecker 262–263, 265–266).

In general, Harris's ideas of Americanism and self-determination permeated the many documents Harris wrote with other school people. Because many important school officials signed these documents, commentators noted that by the end of the century, Harris represented the establishment (Button 253).

Could Textbooks Liberate People?

Among the first important educational documents Harris wrote was the "Statement of the Theory of Education," which was signed by seventy-five individuals who included state supreme court justices, university presidents, secretaries of state boards of education, and state superintendents. Written by Harris and Duane Doty, superintendent of schools in Detroit, this statement was published by the U.S. Bureau of Education in 1872. Harris and Doty asserted that national and state governments should regard education as part of their responsibilities because it enabled people to obey laws and form policies to improve society. Further, in cities, where children received less family supervision, schools had to provide moral guidance. The frontier lacked police supervision, and Harris and Doty thought schools would help children acquire self-control. Thus, this statement endorsed a course of study to provide students with directive power and enable them to pursue further self-education. In elementary or common schools, the cardinal studies included reading and writing, grammar, arithmetic, and geography. Drawing, music, and science instruction came from oral instruction. In the high schools, instruction was more advanced but tended toward the humanities and the study of classical languages. In all schools, the statement noted, the system of instruction emphasized the textbook to help pupils learn to obtain information from the recorded experience of fellow human beings (11–17).

This idea was an innovation because texts had not been the primary method of instruction. For example, in 1861 N. A. Calkins published his manual for object teaching in elementary schools. This became such a popular text that by 1875 there had been eighteen editions. Calkins claimed that object teaching would teach children to observe, to learn a great deal of information, and to develop the faculties of conception, comparison, imagination, reason, and judgment. Books would never do these things, he wrote. In Calkins's view, such instruction should begin before children learned to read. The first step in education was for students to see things before they used words. They had to learn to observe, do, and tell (frontispiece, 22–23).

According to Calkins, object lessons were a series of opportunities for students to see something and recall it. Calkins attributed his system to observations by two prominent educators: the seventeenth-century Austrian John Amos Comenius, who claimed that instruction must begin with inspection, not with verbal description, and the eighteenth-century Swiss Johann Heinrich Pestalozzi, who claimed that observation was the basis of all knowledge. In applying these two principles, Calkins offered a series of example lessons that teachers might use. These were organized according to the subject of the lessons. To begin, a young child could be led through a room. Afterward, the mother or the teacher could ask the student what was in the room. Calkins offered similar lessons for hearing, taste, smell, and touch. In schools, Calkins added, the first lessons were conversational. For example, if a teacher talked with a students about a cat, the teacher could ask how many feet the cat had or how many ears or what a cat did. Later, lessons could employ a series of charts that Calkins provided. One such chart included a picture of a spiral. The teacher could ask what resembled this shape. Students could answer that it resembled a watch spring, a shell, or a spider web. The teacher could take a piece of string, wrap it around a pencil, and ask what it resembled. Again, the students could respond that a barber pole, a vine on a string, or a spring for a sofa had a similar shape (Calkins iii, 26–29, 54, 69).

Although object lessons were popular in all school districts, Harris and other educators tried to minimize their importance. In 1871 Harris noted in his annual report on St. Louis schools that object lessons in subjects such as physiology had been present in all grades. However, he claimed that after he introduced a course of study, such lessons diminished. In that report, Harris quoted other educators who complained that object teaching was dangerous. Although teachers using it could produce immediate and showy results, they did not seem to seek more long-lasting and valuable accomplishments. Harris claimed that textbooks enabled students to learn by themselves, at their own pace, and when they chose. Acknowledging that some students might memorize texts without thinking, Harris felt that even these students could learn from books. In other documents, Harris worried that teachers could unduly influence students by the force of their personalities. However, Harris retained the view that the printed page was more objective and therefore superior to classroom lessons. Most important, through reading students could learn independently. That is, once the students could read, they could learn from a range of sources extending from Plato to Benjamin Franklin. Not surprisingly, Harris became the chief editor of *Appleton's School Reader* during the 1880s (Clifton 194–196, 203; Leidecker 288–289).

In 1876 Harris explained how such a textbook method fit into a larger conception of the curriculum. When he was president of the National Education Association, on behalf of a three-person committee charged to consider a course of study from the primary school to the university, Harris presented an extended statement about the proper curriculum. The first step in the program Harris and his committee members recommended was the establishment of a kindergarten. This would serve as an appropriate transition from the family to the school for children as young as four. In these kindergartens, children would learn to recognize and reproduce forms, study number through toys such as blocks, and practice proper manners. During games the children could exercise their imaginations while directing their impulses into rational channels (Harris, Phelps, and Tappan 75–76).

In the report, Harris and his committee members noted that educators wanted children to approach things first and use words later. However, Harris's committee disagreed. They sought a program that was overwhelmingly literary because they believed that in the study of language students could learn about the human mind and thereby learn to perfect themselves. As a result, they contended that words were more important than things because words included the way people thought about things. Thus, they argued that in language studies, students could find what they called the three parts of the human world: the theoretical, the practical, and the aesthetic (Harris, Phelps, and Tappan 80).

In accord with this division of the human world, Harris and his committee members recommended that all students at all levels study five fields of knowledge. The first was inorganic nature, which included mathematics, physics, and chemistry. The second was organic nature, which consisted of botany, zoology, astronomy, meteorology, and geology. The third was what Harris called theoretical man, which covered philology, philosophy, and psychology. The fourth, called practical man, consisted of civil history and political science. Finally, aesthetics was composed of the fine arts and literature (Harris, Phelps, and Tappan 80–82).

When Harris and his committee members claimed that all students at all levels should study these areas, they did not mean that young children should pursue advanced scientific studies. Rather, because children were prone to fantasy, they should learn descriptive phases of science. As they became adolescents, in secondary education students could attend to the proper classifications and relations of things. Finally, in universities studies might become organic wholes, wherein students saw the progress of individuals through the perspective of history (Harris, Phelps, and Tappan 80).

To explain why all students at all levels should study the same academic or literary subjects, Harris and his committee members relied on a way of thinking found in a report of the professors of Yale, written in 1828, urging all college students to pursue a course of studies that included ancient languages. The Yale professors believed such difficult studies would expand the students' faculties and thereby discipline them. Although Harris and his committee members used the term "mental discipline," they changed its meaning from the way the Yale faculty had explained and used it. Whereas the Yale report contended that mental discipline developed from the close study of difficult subjects such as Latin and Greek, Harris and his committee members claimed that mental discipline did not result from perseverance. They defined discipline as the process of controlling appetite or caprice. This was the aim of moral education, they added. In order to help students substitute moral thoughts for impulses, teachers should direct their attention to things that were remote from their personal lives. This would help them develop objectivity. Study of the ancient languages could help in this endeavor because they would teach the origins of contemporary society. That is, contemporary conceptions of art and literature derived from Greece, and contemporary legal forms were based on Roman precedents. Thus, Harris and his committee members concluded, as students learned about these classic peoples, they would see more clearly the institutions in their own society that formed their lives (Harris, Phelps, and Tappan 79–81).

Because such a program would help teachers improve the students' human capacities, Harris and his committee members believed there should not be separate curricula for students who would go to college and students who would become laborers. Therefore, there was no need to have some form of academy or preparatory school leading to high culture apart from some form of technical training leading to arts and trades. However, they acknowledged that many colleges would have to change their entrance requirements from narrow specialization in certain Latin authors to more broadly conceived training in English (Harris, Phelps, and Tappan 77–78).

Harris believed that such a uniform, academic curriculum led students through the bodies of knowledge that served society. Thus, students could function within that society because they recognized how social institutions helped them develop their abilities. For Harris this was the way to freedom and individualism, and textbooks helped in that process.

What Role Did Science and Psychology Play in the Development of the Curriculum?

Although Harris maintained that studies in what might be called the liberal arts or the humanities would enhance students' self-determination, he faced a growing opposition from advocates of science who took their inspiration from an Englishman, Herbert Spencer. For three decades after the Civil War, it was impossible to be active in intellectual work without understanding Spencer's ideas. Not only did distinguished academics such as William James, Josiah Royce, and John Dewey refer to Spencer, but popular authors such as Theodore Dreiser, Jack London, and Hamlin Garland noted his influence in their lives. One measure of Spencer's impact was that from 1860 until 1903, Spencer's books sold many more copies than any other works in philosophy or sociology had up to that time (Hofstadter 33–34).

Spencer's contribution was to adapt the ideas of Charles Darwin to social life. He argued that the life process was evolutionary in that continuous change integrated matter from incoherent homogeneity, such as that found in protozoa, to coherent heterogeneity, such as that found in human beings. Societies evolved the same way, Spencer argued. They began in states in which everyone was similar and independent. As the societies advanced, people developed different abilities but began to work together in a harmonious fashion. Unfortunately, evolution was limited. Spencer believed that at some point the increasing differences among individuals brought about the disintegration of society (Hofstadter 36–37).

In 1854 Spencer delivered an address to the Royal Institution entitled "What Knowledge Is of Most Worth?" The answer he gave to his question, which became widely popular, was that scientific knowledge was of most worth. Spencer argued that in education, science taught students how to do things. He thought that scientific studies disciplined students' minds as the humanities were supposed to do, and this increased the students' moral and religious sentiments. Although Spencer noted that schools tended to dismiss science as unworthy of attention and to concentrate on ancient literature, he predicted that soon the situation would be reversed and that ancient literature would fall into disuse (158–159).

As Spencer's arguments gained popularity in the United States, Harris submitted an article to the *Atlantic Monthly* criticizing Spencer's philosophy. When that magazine rejected his work, Harris established his own *Journal of Speculative Philosophy.* In that article, Harris criticized Spencer's view that people learned first how to preserve themselves and that this knowledge led directly to higher forms of knowledge. Harris rejected this description of such a smooth path of development (McCluskey, *Public Schools,* 117, 132–133).

In 1899 Harris published a complete explanation of the way he believed people learned. In *Psychologic Foundations of Education,* Harris complained that teachers had long believed students could train various faculties, or mental abilities, in the same way that athletes might improve their muscles. There were two problems with this view, Harris noted. First, people thought that some faculties were simple and led to others that were more complex. According to this view, perception was among the lower faculties and conception was among the higher faculties of the mind. That is, the faculty called perception enabled students to notice something. With the faculty called conception, they placed those observations into categories. However, the ability to perceive an object did not lead to the ability to conceive how the object was related to other objects. Instead, the higher faculty, conception, seemed to replace the lower faculty, perception, when it was developed. The second problem was that teachers approached their work as if students had to develop each faculty in a series. They did not recognize how higher faculties replaced lower ones. As a result, teachers retarded students' intellectual growth by trying to bring many abilities into harmony with each other when those faculties existed on different levels or as distinct types. It was an unnecessary effort because students would place their faculties in harmony, when they developed the highest faculty, which placed all the others into the proper arrangement. At any rate, Harris believed that teachers needed a psychology that explained how the various institutions of family, vocation, state, and church provided different educative effects (Harris, *Psychologic* v–x).

Likewise, Harris believed that the different branches of study helped students to understand their relations to humankind. He divided the school studies into five groups: mathematics and physics, biology, art and literature, grammar and logic, and history. Each one of these groups should be included in the curriculum of schools at all times in ways that suited the age and previous training of the students. In the elementary schools, students acquired what Harris called the conventionalities of intelligence. These included reading, writing, arithmetic, and drawing. In secondary school and college, students acquired culture by studying science and communication (Harris, *Psychologic* 321–333).

In Harris's view, these subjects introduced students to human civilization. For example, in elementary school, the studies taught children how to control nature. Students achieved this in mathematics by learning to keep track of things and in science by learning about forces such as heat, light, and electricity. The next study focused on nature. The third, literature, showed human nature by tracing the growth of a feeling into a deed or by revealing how people were parts of social institutions. Harris thought that grammar had a natural and a spiritual phase. The natural aspect concerned the form of a word or the peculiarity of a spoken message. The spiritual aspect was the way the study of grammar revealed the structure of the intellect that formed the words. In this way, a study of grammar led to a study of logic. In history lessons, Harris wanted students to recognize that the state was the highest human institution. As a result, historical study considered the ways in which states developed, how they had conflicts with other states, and how individuals collided with the states (Harris, *Psychologic* 325–331).

In secondary school, the curriculum followed the same five subject areas. In addition, Harris recommended the extensive study of Latin and Greek, contending that U.S. civilization derived from the cultures of Greece and Rome. He believed that once students knew the origins of their society, they would understand the network of customs within which they lived. If they did not develop such sensibilities, he warned, they might obey those requirements blindly. Once students understood the customs, their obedience would be rational (Harris, *Psychologic* 332–334).

In his description of the psychological foundations of learning, Harris acknowledged the ideas of science and suggested that students should learn about the evolution of society. However, he claimed that these lessons were best conveyed through an academic curriculum. Thus, he turned Spencer's question around: The knowledge that is of most worth, Harris argued, is that knowledge that informs students about the origins of their abilities and of their society. For Harris, this was the literary curriculum that Spencer deplored.

Did the Kindergarten Strengthen the Role of Textbooks?

Although Harris advocated a literary curriculum, he became an advocate of kindergartens. During the 1830s, Swiss educator Friedrich Froebel designed a series of toys he called "gifts" to teach specific concepts or spiritual ideas. The gifts and the idea of the kindergarten spread throughout western Europe and came to the United States in the 1850s as German immigrants established kindergartens in midwestern cities. In 1873 Harris and Susan Blow introduced the first kindergarten into the public schools in St. Louis (Troen 213).

Harris turned to kindergartens when he tried to determine the educational needs of St. Louis. In 1868, soon after becoming superintendent, Harris ordered a series of studies of the different blocks in the city. These studies revealed that children in the poorer districts of town, on the levee and near the factories, left school before they were ten years old. In 1870, seeking a way to lift these children out of an environment where he claimed they were surrounded by vice and iniquity, Harris asked the school board to admit children to school who were less than six years old. Unfortunately, several buildings were overcrowded, and the school board raised the age of admission to seven years. Not to be discouraged, the next year Harris recommended that kindergartens be added to the schools to serve children starting from the age of three (Troen 213–215).

One reason Harris settled on the kindergarten as a means to improve schools for impoverished children was that he met Susan Blow in 1871. After returning from Germany where she had visited several kindergartens, Blow engaged in lengthy discussions with Harris about Froebel's ideas. Blow went to New York in 1872 for one year to study kindergarten methods. When she returned to St. Louis, she found that some people complained about using an imported method of instruction. In part, these complaints may have been aggravated by the fact that the city had a sizable German population. However, Harris remained impressed by the kindergarten's ability to serve as a beneficial alternative to free play in the streets (Beatty 64–65).

Blow and Harris designed a curriculum that would train the virtues emphasized in most school curricula such as regularity, punctuality, silence, and self-control. These habits were supposed to enable the students to join with other citizens in civil society. Blow and Harris borrowed many of Froebel's games. One such game called for students to sit in a circle, use appropriate gestures, and recite a verse describing such things as how much better it is for people to be with other people than to be alone. Instead of encouraging free play, the games were opportunities for students to learn skills and attitudes that would be of value to them and to their city. Some of the twenty kindergarten "gifts" enhanced students' manual dexterity. For example, one gift was a collection of thin blocks the child manipulated. As a result of these activities, once the kindergartens were firmly established, the St. Louis school board decided it did not need to add manual training to the curriculum (Troen 218–222).

The kindergartens were a success. In 1873 the kindergarten began with Susan Blow, 3 assistants, and 68 students. In 1878 the board made the kindergartens part of the school district. By 1880 there were 7,828 children, 166 teachers, and 60 assistants. According to Harris, the kindergartens spread because they helped both children and teachers. They helped the children learn and they served as finishing schools for young women from families wealthy enough to postpone marriage or work (Troen 223–225).

According to Blow, Harris began the national kindergarten movement by doing four things. First, he reduced the cost to five dollars per child per year. Second, he demonstrated that the children who attended kindergartens did better on entering school than did those who had received no such training. Third, he proved that young women of average ability could be trained to teach kindergarten. Finally, Harris gave the movement an acceptable rationale that encouraged other public school people to open kindergartens (Blow 6–7).

Harris's rationale for the kindergarten extended beyond the philanthropic impulses he felt when confronted by lower-class children dropping out of school after two or three years. He claimed that by playing with the kindergarten toys—called Froebel's gifts—the children learned important skills such as manual dexterity and the habit of judging distances and spaces. Most important, Harris added, the children had the opportunity in kindergarten to practice such skills frequently. It was not the job of the kindergarten to teach children to read because they entered school around the age of four. However, when the children were older, the primary school had too many other important lessons to communicate to develop these manual skills. Further, Harris thought that children from all social classes benefited from kindergartens. The children from poor families were kept from associating with criminals in their neighborhoods, and children from wealthy families were spared the experience of being raised by servants with no training in child care (Blow 7–9).

Harris's contention that kindergartens taught manual dexterity, good manners, and diligence antagonized some kindergarten supporters. In 1877 Elizabeth Peabody wrote to Harris complaining that Froebel's principles did much more. For example, she noted that kindergartens developed religious feelings. For her, the kindergarten would open children to religious and moral influences that she termed "joy." In 1879 and 1888, Peabody and Harris attended the Concord Summer School of Philosophy where they talked of such issues (Ross 15–16).

Evidently, Peabody influenced Harris because in 1889 Harris presented an account of the value of kindergartens in a speech that included Peabody's ideas. Harris noted that the home, the kindergarten, and the primary school should complement each other. According to Harris, children learned language in the home. With Froebel's gifts and occupations, kindergarten students learned how to transform material things into symbols for their ideals. In the kindergarten games, children learned that they had social selves to be realized in institutions. This was a new idea to them, he claimed, and it contrasted with their previous individualistic conceptions. At the same time, within the kindergarten games children learned how to shape things to fit their own desires. Harris claimed that the games were humane and offered in symbolic form the treasures of the experience of the human race. As a result, the kindergarten games directed the children while allowing them to preserve their own creativity. Harris believed that children between the ages of four and six should not be forced to follow instructions in accomplishing their work. The kindergarten maintained a proper balance between control and freedom, he concluded. At the age of seven, children should go to primary school. At this age, they were tired of games and ready to begin rational activity or work prescribed by established authority (Harris, "Kindergarten" 7–12).

Although Harris's and Blow's work represented the first kindergarten in a public school, it may not have sparked nationwide reform. According to Barbara Beatty, St. Louis represented a special case rather than the beginning of a widespread movement. Beatty contends that although private kindergartens proliferated, Harris's state of Missouri refused to accept kindergartens as legal. In 1878 legal actions challenged the authority of school boards in Missouri to use public monies to support kindergartens. In 1883 the Missouri Supreme Court upheld these complaints, and in 1884 Susan Blow withdrew from active kindergarten work (Beatty 67).

Beatty believes that kindergartens received a push in 1876 from the Centennial Exposition in Philadelphia where a variety of exhibits appeared, including Susan Blow's kindergarten exhibit. However, other kindergarten advocates criticized Blow for displaying too-perfect examples of children's work. At the exposition, commercial suppliers featured toys that mothers could use at home for kindergarten training. Although the manufacturers spread the idea of kindergartens, the toys were not made to be used according to Froebel's principles; they were designed to sell. For example, one company added alphabet letters to blocks. This turned the cubes Froebel had designed to illustrate complex ideas such as the law of equilibrium and balance into literacy devices (Beatty 43, 67–70).

Nonetheless, kindergartens became more popular as the nineteenth century closed. By 1897 kindergartens appeared in 189 cities. This growth continued at a rapid rate. By 1920 about 510,000 children attended kindergarten programs, and in 1980 more than 75 percent of the nation's children enrolled in kindergartens voluntarily (Feinstein 28).

Some states, however, were slow to establish kindergartens in their public schools. For example, in North Carolina some state normal schools offered courses in kindergarten work in the 1890s, and private kindergartens operated in some cities. However, not until 1945 did the general assembly of North Carolina enact legislation instituting kindergartens for young children in public schools (Murray 28–31).

In part, the rapid growth of kindergartens was possible because the kindergarten movement took advantage of social changes while simultaneously maintaining the social order. For example, Froebel had glorified motherhood. In the United States, his advocates contended that women were essential to educational reform, an idea that appealed to a growing feminism among middle-class women. They urged that these women attend institutions of higher learning, learn the principles of child care, and move from the nursery to the political arena championing their ideas. Most important, women could do all this without challenging the cult of domesticity (Feinstein 29–30).

However, as kindergartens spread, supporters of the movement encouraged changing Froebel's traditional goals. For example, in 1892 G. Stanley Hall began a series of summer sessions offering lectures on experimental psychology, pedagogy, and anthropology. Pronouncing himself an ardent supporter of kindergartens, he praised them for giving children who had been raised in cities the opportunity to become acquainted with natural objects found in the countryside. However, Hall criticized the traditional Froebelian gifts teachers used, claiming that the toys forced children to use delicate muscles they had not yet developed. These criticisms and many teachers' resistance to change made the kindergarten movement appear rigid, inappropriate, and dangerous. Thus, reform seemed essential (Beatty 75–80).

As disagreements about the goals of the kindergartens persisted, educators co-opted kindergartens to serve institutional purposes. For example, by 1905 New York City had adopted syllabi directing kindergarten teachers to assign silent reading. In Denver, Colorado, kindergarten teachers spent up to thirty minutes a day reading and using large charts with advanced students. As the psychological ideas of behaviorism spread throughout the early years of the twentieth century, kindergarten teachers moved away from Froebel's spiritual ideals. They began to help children develop those attitudes, such as satisfaction in using the entire body, or practices, such as proper health habits, that would lead to success in primary school and in later life. Thus, instead of meeting essential but contrasting ideals, kindergartens changed into places where children prepared for the tasks they would meet in primary schools. Although the originators of the kindergartens would have disapproved of these changes, the flexibility ensured the continued success of the movement (Cuban 181–185).

The kindergarten movement was not a threat to the textbook method of instruction. In Harris's view, it provided an opportunity for children to move from home to school. This role ensured that kindergartens would remain in their changed form after Harris's spiritual aims lost their popularity. Another curricular movement—the manual training movement—sought to serve as a complement to the textbook method of instruction. Like the kindergarten movement, manual training gained national attention from innovations in St. Louis. Manual training was also linked to the kindergarten crusade.

Did the Manual Training Movement Challenge Harris's Textbook Method?

The manual training movement required children to use their hands and eyes. Because it required students to do things, it seemed to differ from Harris's textbook method. However, manual training had several elements in common with Harris's ideas. For example, it was not aimed at teaching children a trade, but at teaching them to think abstractly through manual activities. Several commentators contended that manual training shared the style and the aims of the kindergarten. Its supporters often quoted Froebel, who was credited with starting the kindergarten, about the importance of children learning through their hands. But the manual training movement did not seek the spiritual development of students as did Harris and the kindergarten movement.

Some form of industrial activity took place in many schools before the manual training movement began. For example, in 1874 Charles H. Allen, principal of the San Jose Normal School in California, dedicated a large room in the basement of the newly constructed building as a workshop. From his home, he brought in a lathe and wood-turning tools. He bought an anvil and ironworking tools from a blacksmith, and he purchased a chest of carpenter tools from a retired seaman. However, Allen did not make these tools part of any required program. They were available for any student who wanted to pass the time at an agreeable hobby during spare moments (J. Ryan 10–12).

In the 1880s, manual training became an educational movement. According to one interpretation, the manual training movement began when M. Victor Della-Vos, director of the Imperial Technical School of Moscow, displayed examples of his lessons at the Philadelphia Centennial Exhibition of 1876. Della-Vos had delineated the mechanical arts in a series of graded steps similar to the way music or drawing was taught. Dr. John Runkle of the Massachusetts Institute of Technology took great interest in Della-Vos's exhibit and applied it to his students (Ham 328–333).

In 1879 Washington University in St. Louis appointed Calvin M. Woodward director of the Manual Training School. Woodward promoted the idea of manual training across the country. He noted that the chancellor of the university resisted using the name Manual Training School because it implied army training, disguised the intellectual nature of the work, and could be confused with other schools where students undertook actual manual labor. Despite the chancellor's misgivings, the name remained. The Manual Training School was a high school and the students were older than fourteen. It offered instruction in mathematics, drawing, and English. To these subjects, Woodward added instruction in the use of tools in such crafts as carpentry, wood turning, pattern making, and forge work. The course lasted three years, during which students divided their time between mental and manual activities. During their studies, students did not persist in any work they had learned well. Instead, they moved on to other tasks so that they could develop an appreciation of the value and dignity of intelligent labor. Therefore, Woodward claimed that the school did not train young men to become mechanics or carpenters although their progress in the different programs might indicate whether they could learn such trades (Calvin Woodward 5–9).

The idea spread quickly. In 1883 the Baltimore Manual Training School opened as a public school on the same footing as a high school. In 1884 the Chicago Manual Training School started and others began in Eau Clair, Wisconsin; Toledo, Ohio; and New York City. The next year Philadelphia, Omaha, Cleveland, and Denver added such schools (Calvin Woodward 13–15).

Teachers in other states looked to Woodward when they sought to begin such a school. For example, in 1885 William G. Raymond, a professor at the University of California, presented a paper entitled "The Work of the Manual Training School" to the annual meeting of the California State Teachers Association. The bulk of this speech was a complimentary description of the St. Louis Manual Training School and the way it followed the Russian plan of instruction about tools. Raymond's speech appeared in a monthly newspaper produced for teachers by the California State Normal School in San Jose (J. Ryan 31).

Delivering the opening address for the St. Louis Manual Training School, Woodward said that the best machinists, weavers, and ironworkers came to the United States from abroad. This happened because foreign high schools trained all students to become philosophers or philologists. However, Woodward warned against adopting the European system of technical schools because those were fitted to aristocracies in which people never left the station into which they were born. Consequently, he urged people to modify existing schools by adding to them some technical training (Calvin Woodward 240–250).

In his speech, Woodward disparaged narrow conceptions of education that omitted concern for science. Although he acknowledged the value of Latin and Greek as legitimate courses of college study, he noted that they could not claim a monopoly on wisdom. One could also elect chemistry or natural history as a means to wisdom. Furthermore, in technical schools students not only learned how do things but also how to grasp the theory behind them. As a result, Woodward urged that all students receive some training in using tools. This meant they should enter shops at the youngest age possible, and drawing should be available to them. In addition, Woodward noted, in the 1880s, trade unions were making it difficult for young men to enter apprenticeships to learn a trade. Thus, manual training schools offered an alternative that would provide prosperity to workers and citizens alike (Calvin Woodward 250–259).

Woodward contrasted manual training with the work of trade schools, which he thought offered a narrow training unfit for a rapidly changing and free society. In making this comparison, Woodward claimed that the United States would be better served by broader training that could prepare children to master a trade later in life. To explain how the schools should work, he described the Russian Imperial Technical School of Moscow where students learned the mechanical arts through a graded series of exercises. He noted that the Massachusetts Institute of Technology borrowed this model. To give an example of the lessons, Woodward explained the steps through which students passed in learning how to file a piece of cast iron. He reported that the Industrial School Association in Boston had approved this method, and he offered lists of exercises students might follow to learn about carpentry. These lessons progressed from cutting a board along a line with a crosscut saw to using a jack plane to produce surfaces that intersected at exact angles (Calvin Woodward 269, 277–280, 284).

Although manual training had vocational applications, Woodward refused to separate it from general education. As far as he was concerned, manual training improved schools' academic programs. For example, in 1883 he told the members of the National Teachers Association that any tools would be suitable for manual training as long as they helped students form proper habits or morals. In addition, students enjoyed manual training and did not leave before completing their courses. Most important, Woodward argued, with manual training students improved their intellectual development. They learned to make practical judgments, and they understood some activities more clearly than if they read about them in textbooks. And when students enjoyed success in the wood shop, they carried those habits of good workmanship into their academic courses. According to Woodward, the only vocational aspect of manual training was the opportunity to explore various trades (202–211).

Because the function of manual training activities was to further students' thinking abilities, these activities did not have to be related to trades found in the adult world. For example, in 1897 the Horace Mann School in Boston began a course in cardboard construction for students in the fourth and fifth grades. To explain how this curriculum helped students develop abilities they could use to improve society, J. H. Trybom and his coauthors depended on a psychological explanation similar to Harris's. Quoting *Mental Development* by Baldwin, they explained that children developed effective sets of actions when they concentrated on a task. As they practiced, the students discarded ineffective responses. According to Trybom and his colleagues, the pleasure students felt from their success led them to develop willpower. Consequently, a series of exercises in which students experienced increasing success led to improved self-control. Manual training was better designed than academic subjects for this because the results were immediately felt by the students, and the successes were applicable to a wider range of activities than were successes in academic fields such as mathematics (Trybom, O'Connor, and Wilson 3–6).

Originally planned as activities for boys while girls engaged in sewing, Trybom's cardboard constructions appeared to be successful with all children. Arranged systematically, the lessons began with drawing horizontal and vertical lines about one inch apart on a six-inch piece of cardboard. For the fifth lesson, students cut out the squares with scissors. Eventually, the students made simple objects such as octagons out of the cardboard, and in time the objects became increasingly complex. Out of cardboard, students made replicas of familiar objects such as snow sleds and some practical objects such as a brush-broom holder that could be attached to a shelf. The final project was a model house made out of cardboard. The chimney was painted red to appear as if it was made of brick, and the windows were covered with mica instead of glass (Trybom, O'Connor, and Wilson 12–69).

To expand the movement, educators described successful manual training programs in other countries. In 1889 the Industrial Education Association, under the direction of Nicholas Murray Butler, published A. Sluys's description of manual training in elementary schools for boys in Sweden. According to Sluys, the programs varied. While visiting Gothenburg, Sweden, Sluys noticed that manual training took place under the instruction of craftsmen who directed students to specific trades. In Naas, Sweden, however, he found that manual work was an educational means to teach drawing, writing, and arithmetic. As a result, it was taught at the same time as the other subjects and did not serve as an introduction to the trades. To Sluys, this appeared far superior to the system of trade preparation he saw in Gothenberg. He noted that because manual training was separate from the trades, Swedes had created a word, *Slojd,* to refer to the manual work peculiar to schools. In 1877 the Swedish Chamber voted 15,000 crowns to support *Slojd* in public schools. At first educators resisted. They preferred to teach woodcarving, which was a specific skill. According to Sluys, such trades could not integrate the faculties of the mind and the aptitudes of the hands as did manual training. However, by 1884 the number of schools in Sweden offering *Slojd* increased to more than seven hundred. Therefore, Sluys called the program a success (16–24, 36–37).

Although supporters of manual training justified their programs in the name of science, supporters had changed their rationales for manual training by the beginning of the twentieth century. In general, they depended less on abstract psychology and tended to argue that manual training improved students' efficiency. For example, in 1909 Frank Henry Selden asserted that there was a growing public demand for students to learn about industrial practices because those students would spend their adult lives working in industry. He contended that industrial progress came about when people realized they did not have to imitate what their parents had done; they could test their ideas with the materials at hand. Following the ideals of Woodward, Selden claimed that manual training taught the principles behind the movements that craftspeople made with a variety of tools. It was not designed to teach children to be experts at a specific craft or trade. According to Selden, this meant that highly developed industries with traditions of using tools scientifically were better suited to serve manual training than were those industries in which apprentices imitated the actions of craftspeople. Thus, for Selden the aim of instruction in manual training was to help students work efficiently. For example, in using a wood plane, students should realize that there is a definite way to proceed and that the best results come from using those procedures. When students learn to think in this fashion, Selden concluded, every movement is a victory (5, 15–24).

Selden noted that the manual training movement encountered several problems. People tended to judge the quality of the work by the design instead of by its execution. Because teachers selected the designs, people evaluated their choices instead of the students' performances. Selden discovered that in many schools teachers were unqualified and could not help students understand the principles behind the tools they used. As a result of these problems, Selden believed, many people wanted to replace manual training schools with vocational programs and specific trade schools. To retain the manual training movement, Selden advised superintendents of schools to take manual training shops out of basements, provide them with adequate resources, and hire qualified teachers. Above all, he concluded, teachers had to ensure that students were thinking about their actions in the shop. It was not enough for them to imitate their instructors (59–67).

Although manual training did not compete with academic training, it never took on the spiritual or religious aims that characterized Harris's views of liberal education or Froebel's plans for the kindergarten. This may have been because manual training was tied to vocational training, although its advocates claimed that their courses helped students acquire academic skills by working with their hands. Consequently, manual training came to share a flaw with academic preparation. As illustrated by the cardboard lessons, the activities could be as irrelevant to the adult world as lessons in ancient history. As a result, after World I, when supporters of vocational education complained that academic education and manual training were impractical, the federal government supported vocational training programs.

Why Did Catholics Form Their Own Schools?

Although the kindergarten movement and the manual training movement complemented the ideal of academic education, the effort to unify society through public schools antagonized religious groups such as Catholics. During the 1830s and 1840s, the issue of religion and the public schools caused riots and violence in New York and Philadelphia. In 1852, however, when the Catholic bishops met in a plenary council, they changed the nature of the debate. Instead of calling for campaigns to share state school funds with Catholic schools, they decided to leave that question to politicians. Instead, they urged faithful Catholics to ignore people who argued that secular knowledge could be separated from religious understandings (Walch 53–54).

The bishops' efforts to leave questions of school funds to politicians did not end controversies. In 1869 in Cincinnati, Ohio, a school-related contest took place in state courts and in school board elections. It began when a school board member tried to consolidate the public and the parochial schools. Prominent members of the Catholic clergy agreed. The Catholic priests wanted the schools not to teach religion; instead, they asked that school buildings be open on the weekends for religious instruction. The board accepted these conditions. Unfortunately, one of the city newspapers warned readers that this merger was a Catholic trick to share public school funds. Then twenty-four German Catholic priests sent a letter to the papers complaining that the consolidated schools would lack the unique German Catholic character found in parochial schools. Although the Catholic clerics who championed the merger withdrew their cooperation, the school board tried to continue these efforts, proposing that all religious instruction including the reading of the Bible be prohibited in the city's common schools. After an extensive public controversy, twenty-two school board members voted in favor of the motion and fifteen opposed it (Perko, *Time* 154, 165–177).

The day following the school board's vote a group of local citizens filed a petition claiming that the decision violated state law, which required the teaching of the Christian religion in schools. The state superior court decided in favor of the local citizens. But in 1872, when the case went to the Ohio Supreme Court, the court reversed the decision on the grounds that the school board could not ask for any particular religious work to appear in schools because that would be establishing a state religion (Perko, *Time* 177–191).

Such controversies were common, and W. T. Harris confronted the question when he became a school administrator. In 1869, during his first year as superintendent of St. Louis schools, Harris was faced with a controversy over the value of the public schools. Newspapers in the city published articles charging that students learned to be political radicals and religious infidels in the schools. Methodists asked for the Bible to be taught in public schools, and Catholics asked for a share of public funds so they could start their own schools. Harris responded in a report to the school board that all social institutions should divide the responsibility for education. He added that the separation of church and state was a safeguard of individual liberty because it allowed people to follow their consciences. Therefore, he urged that public schools be free of sectarian biases (McCluskey, *Public Schools* 146–148).

At the same time, parish schools were not widely popular among Catholics. Although the number of Catholic schools grew after the Civil War, many Catholics would not send their children to these schools. Further, many priests found the expense of a school to be excessive. To resolve these matters, in 1874 James A. McMaster, editor of the *Freedman's Journal,* sent a formal request to Rome asking Vatican officials if parents could send their children to schools not under supervision by Catholic clergy. The Vatican responded by asking about the nature of the situation in the United States (Walch 58).

The Catholic Church was organized geographically in the United States. Large areas, called dioceses, were headed by bishops. Large or important dioceses were archdioceses headed by archbishops. Within each diocese were several smaller areas called parishes headed by priests who presided over those churches. The bishops from the different dioceses in the United States met in Cincinnati to respond to the Vatican's questions. They indicated that in the United States public schools were not anti-Catholic but that they handed down secular knowledge stripped of any reference to religion. The U.S. bishops added that they had decided to withhold the sacraments from Catholic parents who sent their children to public schools (Walch 58–59).

In 1875 the officials of the Sacred Congregation of Propaganda in the Vatican responded to the U.S. bishops' information by sending them a set of instructions that declared that public schools prevented Catholic children from learning about their faith. Therefore, they urged the bishops to do everything possible to prevent Catholic children from attending public schools. Further, the Vatican's instructions noted that priests could deny the sacraments to obstinate parents who refused to send their children to Catholic schools (McCluskey, *Catholic* 121–126).

In 1884 the U.S. bishops met in Baltimore, Maryland, to hold what was called the Third Plenary Council. Declaring that true civilization was built on the physical, intellectual, and moral education of all people, the bishops stated that moral training depended on religion. Without religion society would degenerate into a struggle of strength. Hence, they added, schools, homes, and churches must foster religion in order to mold good human beings. If these three institutions cooperated to thoroughly imbue children with religion, students could enter the worlds of business or professional practice as adults with principles that would guide and direct their lives. The bishops urged pastors and parents to spread Catholic schools to all parishes and to elevate all those schools to the highest standards (Nolan 223–225).

Although the U.S. bishops omitted from their pastoral letter of 1884 any threats about what would happen to pastors who failed to build schools or to parents who refused to send their children to Catholic schools, they made several in a series of decrees. First, they ordered that every parish must have a school. Second, they promised to remove any priest who failed to build such schools. Third, they promised spiritual punishment for any parish community that did not help priests build schools. Finally, they required all Catholic parents to send their children to those schools unless they remained at home or in other Catholic schools where they received a Christian education (Walch 61).

These decrees had little practical influence because many Catholic parishes did not have sufficient funds to build new schools. Yet, as a result of the decrees, most dioceses established central school boards from 1885 to 1920. With such boards, diocesan officials could coordinate the efforts of local pastors and reduce some of the differences among the parish schools within each diocese (Walch 62).

The decrees of the Third Plenary Council did not settle the matter of Catholic schools in the United States. In 1890 the National Education Association invited Archbishop John Ireland of St. Paul, Minnesota, to address its convention when it convened in his city. Ireland used that opportunity to offer a compromise to public school people. Claiming that he wished there were no need for private Catholic schools, Ireland asserted that state governments should establish state schools and require children to attend. However, he complained that state-run schools excluded religion. As a result, students learned about the world in their schools but not about heaven. To correct this fault, Ireland offered two options. He borrowed the first from England, where the state paid for the secular instruction given in denominational schools. Because this was less than the full cost of tuition, it satisfied public officials and parents. Second, he offered the example of Poughkeepsie, where the city school board paid the Catholic teachers, rented the parish school buildings until three o'clock in the afternoon, and purchased state textbooks. Religion was taught in the hours after those paid for by the school board (McCluskey, *Catholic* 127–140).

Catholic leaders criticized Ireland for proposing to abandon Catholic schools after the Third Plenary Council of bishops decided they were essential. They complained to the pope, who asked Cardinal Gibbons for his opinion. Ireland wrote a clarification to Gibbons in which he argued that his compromise was reasonable. Public schools were not as bad as many bishops made them appear. Furthermore, all religions could enjoy equal opportunity to benefit from his compromise. This was the only fair course he could see. Finally, what he called the Poughkeepsie plan was already in practice in many communities where priests, teachers, and parents found it satisfactory (McCluskey, *Catholics* 141–150).

Cardinal Gibbons's efforts to have the pope affirm the correctness of Ireland's views enjoyed moderate success. In 1893 Archbishop Francesco Satolli traveled to the United States as the pope's ambassador. He presented the bishops with a document attesting that Catholics supported public education, that they complained only about the lack of religious training, and that they approved of such compromises as Ireland had recommended. After considerable controversy, the bishops accepted this statement when the pope acknowledged that it did not contradict the decrees made by the Third Plenary Council. In addition, problems developed among public school educators. In those cities Ireland had cited as models of compromise, controversy arose over public school boards paying religious women to be teachers in Catholic schools. As a result, the school boards withdrew their cooperation (Walch 94–98).

W. T. Harris remained a spokesperson for the public school people who opposed bringing religion into the curriculum. In his last reports to the St. Louis school board, Harris claimed that the moral responsibility of the school was to provide training in punctuality, regularity, silence, truth, industry, and respect for the rights of others. According to Harris, the danger was that if schools began religious instruction, they would have to favor a specific denomination, which would weaken the spirit of tolerance and charity toward others (McCluskey, *Public Schools* 151, 159).

In 1903, as the U.S. commissioner of education, Harris presented similar views in a speech in Boston. He stated that in public schools students were taught to think independently rather than accept truths on the basis of authority as was necessary in religion. Here, Harris gave the issue of the separation of religious and secular instruction more clarity than other educators had offered. He agreed with the arguments of religious leaders who claimed that the basis of education was moral and that the church was the world's most powerful educational tool. But he added that schools should present only secular knowledge and leave society and the churches their special areas (McCluskey, *Public Schools* 126–127, 146, 163, 173).

Religious educators argued that Harris's view was inadequate. After Harris's speech in Boston, a Jesuit priest, Reverend Timothy Brosnahan, complained that separating the work of the church and the work of the school would split students' personalities because they attended one institution that was hostile to religion—the school—and lived in another that was filled with a spirit of faith—the home. Brosnahan also claimed that religion was not antagonistic to secular knowledge. He pointed out that the principle of authority appeared in both religion and secular education. In religion, authority meant two things: the moral power a person has over another, and the intellectual worth of a witness to a fact.

In secular education, both senses of the term were necessary. First, the teacher marshaled moral authority to direct students. Second, in studying history, students did not dig up original records, and even if they did, they had to decide which to believe (McCluskey, *Public Schools* 171–172).

As a result of the failure of political compromises and the lack of theoretical concessions, Catholics and public school people drifted apart. By the end of the nineteenth century, there was a loosely organized Catholic school system. In 1904 the National Catholic Education Association was established to unite Catholic educators and promote the general interests of Catholic education in the United States. Finally, in 1918 a new code of canon law restated the conservative positions of the Instruction of 1875 and the Third Plenary Council decrees of 1884 (Gabert 68–74).

Did Other Religious Denominations Create Their Own Schools?

For some Protestant denominations, the neutrality of public schools was unimportant. Those groups that relied on the religious revivals that swept the United States during the nineteenth century to sustain their growth directed little attention to the public schools. On the other hand, Lutherans looked on conversion as a gradual process in much the same way that Catholics did. Yet, as among Catholics, not all Lutherans felt that schools had to be organized in the same way. Whereas some Norwegian Lutherans advocated parochial education because the public schools lacked religion, other Lutherans complained that there should be two different spheres. These Lutherans believed that the state's sphere included teaching students about secular matters, and they took the view that such teaching should not include instruction intended for God's sphere (Diefenthaler 35–36).

Among Lutherans, the Missouri Synod was most numerous and active in building schools. In 1839 a group of conservative Lutherans left Germany in protest over liberal religious reforms and arrived in St. Louis. Almost immediately they opened a school. In a short time, most of the members of the congregation left the city and settled in Perry County, Missouri, along the Mississippi River, where they opened a secondary school patterned after the gymnasiums they had known in Saxony. In 1847 this congregation sent delegates to a conference in Chicago to meet with delegates from other Midwestern states. They formed the German Evangelical Lutheran Synod. Not only did their constitution mandate the establishment of a school in each congregation, but sometimes the school also preceded the establishment of a congregation and the building of a church. In 1872 this synod boasted 446 congregations and 472 schools enrolling more than 30,000 children (Diefenthaler 36–41).

In their early years, many Lutheran schools protected students from Americanization. In general, until 1873 the language of instruction was German, as was the language of the worship services. Most of the curriculum focused on religion. In the 1840s, some schools in St. Louis introduced students to English, but these failed to survive. However, after the Civil War, as German immigration increased, the number of schools and students increased. These new families did not want to preserve their culture; they wanted to become Americans. A controversy emerged over whether German should remain the language of instruction. When the synod refused to allow congregations to adopt English in the schools, a split emerged. German-speaking congregations continued to establish schools, while English-speaking ones sent their children to public schools and relied on Sunday schools for religious training. This division continued until World War I when, in the midst of patriotic hysteria, many states forbade teachers and pastors from speaking German. A ruling from the U.S. Supreme Court eventually ended such pressure, however (Diefenthaler 44–49).

As in the case of Lutherans, Jewish people set up private day schools for their children to protect them from the Christian influences found in common schools. As a result, during the 1840s, 1850s, and 1860s a succession of day schools appeared in cities such as New York, Cincinnati, Chicago, and Philadelphia. But these private religious schools were expensive and difficult to maintain. They separated the children from contacts outside the Jewish Community and thus prevented social advancement. Some parents also feared that the parochial schools increased Christian prejudice against Judaism. Consequently, Jewish day schools closed rapidly but others opened to take their places. For example, in the 1860s in New York, Jewish families set up Hebrew schools to resist Christian missionaries determined to convert their children. However, these schools closed within a decade (Rauch 134–135).

From 1881 to 1920, more than 20 million Jews entered the United States from eastern Europe. Some of these immigrants sought to establish the religious schools they had had in Europe. However, the poverty many Jews faced made such private education impossible and impractical. As the Jews turned from strict religious observances, they tended to embrace public schools for their children. In this way, in 1908 a Jewish immigrant, Israel Zangwill, boasted of the benefits of assimilation in his play *The Melting Pot.* Other American-born Jewish rabbis, however, turned to Zionism to keep Jewish consciousness alive during the new century in the United States. The tragedy of World War II created a period of phenomenal growth in Jewish education in U.S. cities and towns (Rauch 135–143).

Could Public Schools Reinforce the Values People Should Share?

After the Civil War, abolitionists, public school reformers in both the North and the South, and many religious leaders thought schools could create a new society by bringing the formerly hostile factions together. However, they disagreed about which values people should hold in this integrated society. Abolitionists faced social and self-imposed obstacles. The external problem was that other White people in the South perceived them as members of a conquering army. Additionally, their personal feelings sometimes interfered with their aims. For example, some teachers cared more about the growth of their religious sect than about their pupils. Other teachers held unconscious racial biases that led them to treat their pupils as social inferiors. Public school reformers in the South wanted to use the graded schools to introduce students to the way of life required in the modern industrial society they called the New South. Many Northerners, such as W. T. Harris, agreed that public schools could advance industrial progress. However, Harris believed that social progress occurred when an individual's growth led to spiritual development. In accord with his dialectical reasoning, Harris wanted to keep religious instruction out of secular schools so that churches could have unique influences. Finally, many religious leaders disagreed with the model of schools that Harris recommended. They created their own schools where students could learn the secular subjects while they acquired academic skills. As these differences illustrated, there was no simple way schools could bring about the social integration of the different groups and enhance respect for the traditions each group valued. No matter how intelligently or carefully these educators approached their work, their plans for integration threatened the values that some groups held dear.

TIMELINE
1861–1890

1861 U.S. Navy seized islands in Port Royal Sound near South Carolina

1862 Fifty-three abolitionist teachers arrive from New York and Boston to begin the Port Royal experiment

1867 George Peabody, a banker, designated $2 million for education in the Southern states, funding mostly the White schools

1868 Seven southern states drafted new state constitutions for readmission into the Union. Only Louisiana and South Carolina mentioned interracial schools.

1868 William Torrey Harris became superintendent of the St. Louis public schools and encouraged separation of church and state to avoid treating any single faith unfairly

1869 The attempt to consolidate the public and parochial schools in Cincinnati, Ohio, failed, and the school board prohibited all religious instruction from the city's common schools

1872 The U.S. Bureau of Education published the "Statement of the Theory of Education"

1873 The first U.S. kindergarten was established in St. Louis

1874 The U.S. Congress discontinued the Freedmen's Bureau

1874 Congress and President Grant rejected Charles Sumner's civil rights bill, which included integrated schools

1874 Charles H. Allen built a workshop in the San Jose Normal School

1874 James A. McMaster formally asked the Vatican if U.S. Catholic children could attend non-Catholic-supervised schools

1875 The Vatican urged U.S. bishops to stop Catholic children from attending public schools

1875 The Civil Rights Act of 1875 passed with no mention of desegregating schools

1875 Congress declared that state governments determine whether schools should be segregated or integrated

1876
- Philadelphia held the Centennial Exposition
- Susan Blow presented an exhibit of the kindergarten
- M. Victor Della-Vos displayed his mechanical arts lessons

1877 Rutherford B. Hayes elected President

1879 Calvin M. Woodward became the director of the Manual Training School of Washington University in St. Louis

TIMELINE Continued

1883	The U.S. Supreme Court ruled the Civil Rights Act of 1875 unconstitutional
1883	Calvin M. Woodward promoted manual training to the National Teachers Association
1883	The Baltimore Manual Training School opened
1884	The Chicago Manual Training School opened
1884	U.S. bishops supported Catholic schools during the Third Plenary Council
1885	William G. Raymond presented his paper "The Work of the Manual Training School" in California and was published
1888	Jabez L. M. Curry succeeded Sears as the general agent of the Peabody Education Fund and supported good schools for African Americans
1890	Archbishop John Ireland proposed a compromise between public and Catholic schools in his speech to the NEA

CHAPTER

5 Industrialism, Immigration, and the New Psychology: 1890–1915

Jane Addams

OVERVIEW

In 1893 the National Education Association (NEA) sponsored the Committee of Ten, which tried to build a system of education for all people based on what it considered to be the best of the traditional liberal education. In 1918, however, the NEA sponsored the Commission on the Reorganization of Secondary Education (CRSE), which undid those efforts. In explaining why a new approach to the curriculum was needed after twenty-five years, the CRSE listed three reasons. This chapter explores each of those reasons. First, society had

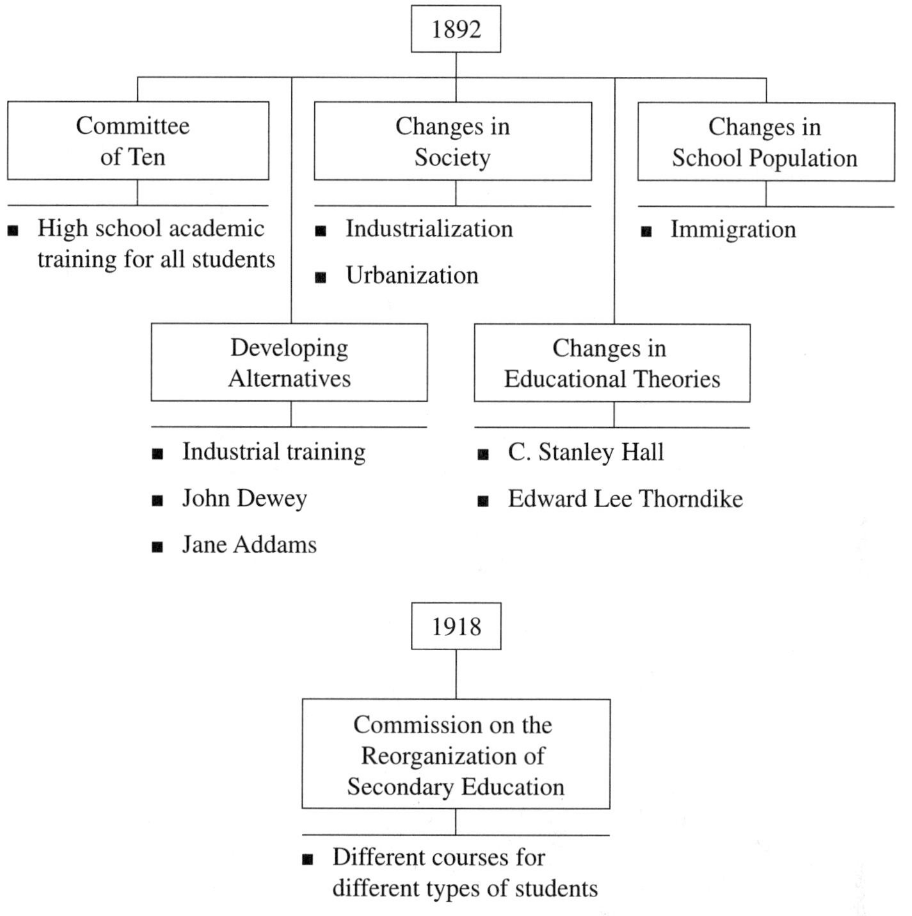

undergone many changes. In a short period of time, the United States had become an industrial and urban nation. Second, as a result of the growth of cities and the subsequent immigration, the population of schools changed. Many journalists argued that the immigrants represented a new and pressing problem. They thought that industrial education could teach the immigrants to become Americans. The idea of industrial education for minority groups turned into a movement in the 1890s led by General Samuel Chapman Armstrong and Booker T. Washington. Third, there had been changes in educational theory. For example, studies revealed the extent to which students withdrew from schools. In response, educators began different types of schools, such as junior highs, to help students adjust to the system. The child-study movement and empirical studies into the ways people learned seemed to weaken the rationale for a liberal education. As a result, educators supported efforts to diversify the curriculum. Unfortunately, when schools offered different programs for different children, they increased the divisions among people. Critics complained that children from wealthy homes studied the liberal subjects that enhanced cultural understandings while children from less affluent families entered vocational programs.

How Did Educators Want to Consolidate School Curricula?

In 1890 Charles W. Eliot, president of Harvard University, complained that no state possessed what could be called a system of education. Acknowledging the common schools to be organized, Eliot noted that a wide gap appeared between those elementary schools and the colleges. This happened for two reasons, according to Eliot. First, few states offered a reasonable number of high schools. Second, in those high schools that did exist, students rarely received instruction that prepared them for further study. As a result, many colleges offered weakened programs into which they could accept students who were unprepared for college work. He concluded that the answer should be sought by states creating more high schools, and those schools should meet reasonable standards to prepare students for higher work ("Gap" 197–219).

In 1892 Eliot returned to the same theme. In a speech to a meeting of the National Education Association (NEA) entitled "Undesirable and Desirable Uniformity in Schools," Eliot suggested a way for the NEA to construct reasonable high school programs. He recommended that the NEA call together a group of experts who would decide which materials students should study, how long they should spend on each topic, and how the materials should be taught ("Undesirable" 299–300).

The NEA accepted Eliot's recommendation. In 1892 it appointed the Committee of Ten to investigate the requirements for admission into college from high school. Eliot served as the chair and William Torrey Harris, U.S. commissioner of education, was among the members. The committee formed ten smaller groups or conferences of experts (each of which had about ten members) that were assigned to examine specific subjects such as Latin, mathematics, and geography. The committee asked each conference to answer eleven questions about issues such as when to teach the subject, for how long, and what topics should be covered. One question was particularly important for future developments: whether the subject should be treated differently for students planning to go on to college than for those who would receive no education beyond high school (NEA, *Report of Committee of Ten* 3–7).

After meeting for three days, the conferences submitted reports to the head committee, which composed an overall report. In general, all conferences wanted their subject matters to be introduced to younger groups of students. Although this meant that all nine high school subjects represented by conferences would be introduced in elementary schools, the committee noted that these could be integrated to prevent a proliferation of elementary school programs (NEA, *Report of Committee of Ten* 16).

The nine conferences unanimously agreed that students who were going on to college should be treated the same as students who would end their education at high school. Thus, according to the committee, every subject taught in a secondary school was to be taught in the same way and to the same extent to all pupils no matter what their future plans. Naturally, this simplified high school programs. However, the committee did not expect all students to study exactly the same materials. The report suggested that schools should offer four different programs, acknowledging that not all schools could teach all subjects nor could all schools offer the same amount of instruction. Instead, the committee recommended four programs that differed in the amount of foreign language students took. For example, in the Classical Programme students concentrated on foreign languages. However, in the English Programme students encountered less foreign language study and spent more time on English and history (NEA, *Report of Committee of Ten* 16–17, 44–45).

The committee acknowledged that most high school students did not proceed on to colleges or scientific schools, yet members believed that the minority of students bound for college was important to the nation. Consequently, committee members asserted that if high schools adopted their recommendations, a graduate of any such program should be able to enter any college or scientific school well prepared for further study. They believed the same college preparatory courses were valuable for those graduates not going on to schools because the courses would improve the students' abilities and thereby help them in the world of work. The report noted that when the main, recommended subjects were taught consecutively and thoroughly, they would train the powers of observation, memory, expression, and reasoning (NEA, *Report of Committee of Ten* 51–52).

In 1895 the NEA released the report of its Committee of Fifteen. Charged with considering the elementary school programs, this committee also included Harris. However, whereas the Committee of Ten was dominated by college and university presidents, most of the members of the Committee of Fifteen were superintendents of large city school districts.

In detailing the courses elementary school students should pursue, the Committee of Fifteen held that language studies were the center of instruction. Arguing that language was the instrument that made social organization possible, members asked that students follow graded steps to learn the meanings of words. They wanted teachers to use fine prose selections as the main aesthetic training, and warned against devoting so much time to formal grammar study that students never learned to appreciate literature ("Report" 99).

In addition to grammar and literature, the committee thought that arithmetic, geography, and history made up the center of the elementary school program. Other courses such as natural science, vocal music, manual training, and physical training had their place, but they were less significant. For example, the report recommended one hour a week of regular exercise in addition to the free play outdoors during recess periods to constitute the suggested periods of physical training ("Report" 99–100).

The report of the Committee of Fifteen justified its conclusions based on an interpretation of psychology that was similar to that used by the Committee of Ten. That is, committee members felt that the topics of study were chosen for three reasons. First, choices were based on what they called the old psychology, meaning that the subjects contributed to the so-called mental faculties, such as memory and observation, because they were difficult. The report suggested that the spiritual training of the mind was analogous to using gymnastics to train muscles. Second, the report noted that a new psychology claimed that the mind did not have faculties but was instead composed of nerves or brain tracts. The studies that require the most brain activity were best, according to this theory. However, committee members believed that both these psychological reasons were less important than the third concern, that of introducing students to the civilization in which they would live ("Report" 98).

When the Committee of Fifteen presented its report at the NEA convention, there were several criticisms. One member of the committee noted that although he agreed with most aspects of the report, he felt that it made traditional school subjects too much the center of a curriculum. He believed that the center of any elementary school program should be the child and his or her natural activities. In another criticism, Francis Parker complained that the report implied that children would spend all their time reading and doing little else. He thought students should have more time to do other things, thus learning through some form of discovery ("Report" 104–106).

The reports of the Committee of Ten and the Committee of Fifteen represented the last popular statements of the need for strict academic preparation for all students in elementary and secondary schools. After less than twenty-five years, the NEA, the same organization that sponsored the Committee of Ten and the Committee of Fifteen, offered a vision that undercut the hopes of a literary curriculum for all students.

In 1918 the NEA established the Commission on the Reorganization of Secondary Education (CRSE). This new committee recommended that schools meet the needs of different students by offering a range of programs in addition to academic courses. The CRSE argued that such diversification was necessary because schools faced changes in society, changes in the secondary school population, and changes in educational theory. The report considered these factors in turn. First, as a result of changes in society, individuals faced more complex social orders. As citizens they had to participate in a bewildering array of local, state, national, and international governments. As workers they had to participate in a more complex economic order. Second, more students and more different types of students enrolled in secondary schools. In 1890 one child out of every 210 in the total U.S. population attended secondary school. However, by 1914 that proportion rose to one child out of every 73. These students represented a wide range of abilities and destinies in life that the schools must consider. Third, educational theory had changed. For example, psychologists urged that more attention be paid to individual differences and noted that the idea of general discipline, such as that called on by the Committee of Ten, was no longer widely accepted. Instead, educators thought it was important to apply knowledge to the activities of daily life (Department of the Interior 7–9).

Although the curriculum innovations the CRSE report encouraged are discussed in Chapter 6, this chapter explores the social and theoretical changes that the CRSE listed as weakening the basis for a unified academic education for all students.

How Did Industrial Progress Change the United States?

The United States changed in a short period of time after the Civil War. First, business enterprises expanded rapidly. In 1860 a total of about $1 billion was invested in manufacturing, and those factories employed about 1,500,000 workers. In less than fifty years, investments in manufacturing totaled almost $12 billion, and the number of industrial workers increased to 5,500,000. During the same period, corporations rather than one person or a small group bought up the manufacturing centers. Consequently, by 1900 about 75 percent of manufactured goods came from factories owned by associations of stockholders. These businesses formed combinations so that monopolies, or huge organizations that acted as monopolies, controlled staples such as oil products, iron, copper, and coal.

Second, as businesses grew, cities expanded. In 1860 more than 15 percent of the population lived in towns or cities with more than eight thousand inhabitants. By 1900 that figure jumped to more than 33 percent of the population. In large cities such as Boston, Fall River, or Jersey City about 80 percent of the families rented their homes or tenements. This percentage was higher in the center of New York City, where almost 90 percent of the inhabitants rented. At the same time, more women engaged in gainful employment. In 1870, 15 percent of women worked for some sort of wage, and by 1900 almost 20 percent were employed in profit-making activities (Beard and Beard 176–207).

One of the ironies of agricultural industrialization was that although people moved off farms into cities, the number of farms increased. In 1860 there were about two million farms. By 1910 there were more than six million, and they produced more food. For example, in 1860 U.S. farmers grew 173,000,000 bushels of wheat. By 1910 wheat production in the United States increased to nearly 700,000,000 bushels, equaling about one-sixth of the world's production. To a large extent, Congress fueled this agricultural growth by giving away land. In 1860 the federal government held 1,048,111,608 acres of land. With the Homestead Act of 1862, Congress distributed this unsettled frontier in lots of 160 acres to people willing to farm them. By 1890 there was no more free land. As a result, untrained, wasteful farmers could no longer abandon exhausted land to start again on virgin soil. On the other hand, the development of mechanical inventions such as corn planters, wheat drills, hay loaders, and tractors made farming more productive, but these machines displaced many human laborers. Furthermore, to pay for the expensive equipment, farmers began to specialize, raising crops such as wheat or corn to sell in distant or foreign markets. As production increased, profits decreased. Consequently, many people moved to the cities searching for better opportunities, leaving the less fortunate to work the soil. Thus, the percentage of people renting the farms on which they worked increased from 25 percent in 1880 to 35 percent in 1900 (Beard and Beard 114, 170, 256–257, 269–277).

At the same time, the U.S. population changed. Since the 1820s, there had been a constant stream of settlers from countries such as Ireland, Germany, and Scandinavia. In the 1880s, the pattern of immigration shifted. Fewer immigrants came to the United States from Germany or Sweden; the new immigrants were from Russia, Poland, Austria-Hungary, the Balkans, and Italy. Many of these immigrants settled in the larger cities of Boston, Chicago, and New York, where some older residents feared that these newcomers threatened their way of life. Immigrants and their children soon accounted for almost half the population. In 1900 the total U.S. population numbered about 76,000,000. However, more than 36,000,000 of these people either had been born in Europe or had parents born there (Johnson 400–402).

As cities grew and newly arrived immigrants became more common, states passed compulsory education laws so that immigrant children could learn about life in their new homeland. By 1890 twenty-seven states had passed such laws, and by 1918 all forty-eight states then in the union had enacted such legislation. In 1852 Massachusetts passed the first compulsory education law. In 1874 the New York legislature required children from the ages of eight to fourteen to attend school for fourteen weeks a year. These laws were ineffective because legislators made little provision for enforcement. Nonetheless, nationwide school attendance increased between 1860 and 1890 (Urban and Wagoner 163–164).

Despite the rise in compulsory education laws and school attendance, there was no apparent decrease in illiteracy from 1870 to 1915. In 1870 U.S. census enumerators began collecting information about illiteracy by asking people if they could read and write. Each year from 1870 until 1915 a greater percentage of children from five to eighteen years old attended school, yet there was little change in the percentage of the population ten years and older who reported that they were illiterate. Although the U.S. surgeon general reported that a larger proportion of men drafted into the army could read and write than the census indicated, teachers may have predicted the apparent failure of compulsory education to reduce illiteracy. In general, educators unwillingly accepted compulsory education laws. In fact, teachers feared that if children who wanted to earn money were forced into their classrooms, they would disturb the routine. As a result, school superintendents declined to enforce the laws. Supporters of Catholic parochial school feared that compulsory education laws would force every child to attend public schools. The groups that exerted the most pressure on legislators to pass compulsory education laws were philanthropic agencies and organized labor. Unlike philanthropists, labor leaders did not concern themselves with education; they wanted the federal and state governments to prevent children from working in factories, where they lowered wages (Ensign 234–249, 251–253).

How Did Journalists Encourage Educational Reform?

In part, the same force that inspired philanthropic agencies to seek compulsory education contributed to many of the political and economic reforms marking the Progressive Era. This force was the stream of stories that appeared in newly popular journals and newspapers exposing corruption. The movement began in 1881 with a series of articles in the *Atlantic Monthly* criticizing trusts such as the Standard Oil Company. In 1906 Theodore Roosevelt labeled these journalists "muckrakers," saying their only interest was to collect noxious facts about business and government. Although Roosevelt meant the term as an insult, it became a tag of distinction (Johnson 550–551).

As the journalistic tradition of muckraking extended into education, authors complained about children's poor living conditions, overly strict classroom discipline, and corrupt school leaders. Almost without exception, reporters contended that the solution was to divorce politics from school life. They hoped that such reform would allow schools to appoint trained leaders who would hire teachers familiar with what they called the modern, scientific advances of education. Journalists also argued that these new administrators would break from the academic curriculum Eliot and Harris had recommended; they believed the new administrators would create curricula more relevant to students' lives. Two popular journalists influenced these educational changes. The first was a newly arrived immigrant, Jacob Riis, and the second was a physician who became interested in schools, Joseph Mayer Rice.

Born in Denmark, Riis came to the United States in 1870 when the woman he loved would not marry him. Once in his new home, he endured at least three years of grinding poverty. By good fortune, however, he became a police reporter for the New York *Tribune*. In 1877 Riis saw the suffering that went on in slums such as New York's Mulberry Street

Bend. He dedicated himself to writing stories about the terrible situations some immigrants endured. In this way, he fought what he called the battle with the slums (*Making* 20, 31, 76–78, 126–132).

People living in slums suffered from overcrowding. Riis wrote that he gave up trying to count the number of children living in one tenement building after he reached 128 in forty families. Noting that truant officers tried to identify these children, Riis added that the public schools could not admit them because of overcrowding. Without adult guidance or opportunities for advancement, these children grew up to be savages. Riis believed they could have succeeded as mechanics, but unions barred immigrants from the trades (*How* 135–138).

Riis believed the unhealthy environment in which these people lived caused the immigrants to act in ways that other people thought was less than human. Thus, even while portraying depraved actions, he always made clear that these people could learn to act better. For example, he explained how immigrant mothers often abandoned their children and how those children frequently died as a result. Riis did not believe the mothers acted carelessly; they wanted to help their children. Poor women came in rags to foundling homes carrying children wrapped in newspapers. Sometimes they left a message such as this: "Take care of Johnny, for God's sake. I cannot." In other cases, the mothers left children on the doorsteps of rich families. Unfortunately, most of the children left on doorsteps died of exposure. For those few children who lived, it fell to the city nurseries, the missions, and hospitals to save their lives. These children were not much more fortunate; many died in these institutions as well. Because these institutions were overwhelmed with large numbers of children, they often sent the older or the disobedient children into the streets. On their own, the children became what Riis called "Street Arabs" who roamed in gangs, slept outdoors, and stole (*How* 137–163).

For Riis, the saloon threatened poor people most of all, yet its allure was understandable. In a tenement neighborhood, wrote Riis, the saloon was the one bright and cheery place. There were no coffeehouses, reading rooms, or decent clubs. In the poorest ward in New York City in 1889, however, homeless people found enough money to support 485 saloons. Although the law prohibited children from drinking, Riis showed pictures of young boys carrying "growlers," large buckets used to carry cheap beer or rum. Once trapped by alcohol, these young men turned to crime (*How* 165–182).

Like other reformers of his day, Riis urged the improvement of housing for immigrants, complaining of problems such as the high incidence of disease and death caused by inadequate or broken toilets and baths, extreme overcrowding, and the absence of parks and playgrounds (Lubove 81–85). Similarly, he thought that architectural changes could help schools become more effective by introducing into the children's lives opportunities to play in sunlight surrounded by flowers. Riis praised the construction of the Letter H school, a design he attributed to C. B. J. Snyder. Copied after the Hotel de Cluny in Paris, these schools took up the middle of a block, extending from one street through to the other. The wings of the building formed a letter H and enclosed two open yards, giving students almost an acre of asphalt where they could play games or exercise. Riis wrote that under the red-tiled roof of the building were gymnasiums and bright, well-lighted classrooms. In other more crowded areas, such as Hester Street, fences were placed around the roof, creating a playground where two thousand children could dance to the music of a band. According to Riis, these school buildings offered a dramatic change from the tenements. He asserted that the buildings taught the children many moral lessons because they were places where children could be happy (*Battle* 348–363).

Riis encouraged his readers to support the New York City Board of Education that in 1898 had opened thirty-one playgrounds. This was part of what was called the play movement, begun in Boston by advocates such as Marie E. Zakrsewska. They placed piles of sand in the yards of chapels or nurseries and hired neighborhood women to supervise. As the idea spread to other cities, educators adopted it and the movement spread from the construction of parks to the building of playgrounds as part of schools (Liles 294–295).

Another popular movement Riis supported was the use of school buildings as social centers. This was part of the effort to reduce the temptation for both young and older immigrants to frequent saloons. He wanted schools to provide meeting places for youth clubs and adult social organizations. Riis wrote that teaching about democracy was only part of the job of education. Schools had to be places where people could be together. For that reason, Riis would compel all children to attend public schools and he would ask the schools to allow the children, their parents, and other members of the community to use the schools as well. He described his successful efforts to have administrators open classrooms at night for students to hold club meetings. Riis thought the schools should welcome the adults of the neighborhood to use assembly halls to hear lectures and music. The school should host meetings for political parties and trade unions. Neighborhood residents should attend dances in the schools, and mothers and fathers should meet in those buildings to trade gossip as they did on the rooftops and in the saloons (Riis, *Battle* 372, 405–407).

In the early twentieth century, school planners constructed buildings that would allow the community use the school. For example, in 1911 Fletcher Dresslar published a survey of U.S. schoolhouses. He advocated that every high school include an assembly room on the central axis of the first floor in a place easy to enter and leave. Although windows were necessary for light, they should be too high to be a distraction for audience members. He recommended that the room have a stage of ample proportions with dressing rooms on both sides. On the stage, diploma exercises, plays, lectures, and concerts could be held. Such assembly rooms would foster a deeper loyalty to the school and the academic ideals it represented than athletic events offered (Dresslar 34–38).

Most important, however, journalists such as Riis supported a change in the way people governed schools. Riis took pride in his contribution to the removal of the system of ward boards that had developed in New York City from the common school movement. Residents elected representatives to these local neighborhood boards, and these representatives decided where schools would be built and hired the teachers to staff them. Riis wanted a centralized system that allowed a citywide board to appoint experts to manage the schools. Such trained administrators would select the best teachers for the schools, he argued. The only opposition Riis noted to this reform came from Tammany Hall politicians. They complained that the central board members would bring in teachers from other states instead of hiring the daughters of the neighborhood residents as had the ward trustees. Riis argued that this practice hurt the schools because the best new teachers came from Massachusetts and had achieved national reputations for their work (*Battle* 347–348).

The second author-reformer, Joseph Mayer Rice, was trained as a physician but wrote several articles detailing the need for school reform. From January to June 1892, he observed more than twelve hundred classrooms in thirty-six cities across northeastern United States. In addition, he visited twenty institutions for training teachers. Rice complained that people often resigned the welfare of their children to ward politicians who placed the children in classrooms unfit for habitation. However, Rice noted that board members acted differently in different cities. In some cities, members tried to be objective and careful. In other cities, members were selfish and uncaring. Likewise, the superintendent, when well chosen, could be a strong force for good education (Rice 9–13).

On the other hand, Rice believed that the teachers constituted the greatest problem in education. Even the best-trained teacher in the United States was ill prepared compared to teachers in Germany. However, most of the teachers in the United States did not have any education beyond grammar school, wrote Rice, and they were hired because boards were free to hire whoever they pleased. As a result, board members hired teachers to please influential people, and once the board appointed the teachers, they would not fire them no matter how they performed (13–16).

Rice suggested three solutions: First, divorce the schools from politics. This meant that supervisors had to be free to act in ways that would serve the interests of the students. When board members imposed their wishes on who should be hired or fired, problems resulted. Second, supervisors had to improve the professional abilities of teachers by discussing educational methods and helping them apply those suggestions in practical situations. Finally, everyone needed to recognize how important it was for teachers to improve (Rice 16–19).

In describing what he found in the schools, Rice characterized the teaching methods in many schools as mechanical, and he felt this happened because teachers stayed too close to an academic curriculum. That is, the teachers drilled facts into students' minds and heard them recite lessons they had memorized. In general, he contended, teachers exhibited cold, unsympathetic attitudes toward the children. But Rice also noted that there were some schools operating on what he called a scientific or progressive model of instruction. In this manner of instruction, teachers sought to learn more about the psychological development of children. They did not mindlessly follow textbooks but tried to adapt instruction to the minds of the children. Instead of a cold environment, according to Rice, the progressive school was glowing with life and warmth, and the students happily pursued nature and artistic studies (19–24).

Rice believed that the more gentle and interesting method of teaching was more effective. In schools where the students worked at tasks that made sense to them, they learned to read, write, and do arithmetic better than those students who were subjected to continual drill and repetition. He feared that schools would persist in the old type of education because school officials were corrupt. Until those people were voted out of office, educational problems would remain (Rice 24–27).

The muckraking journalists opposed the traditional academic curriculum as Eliot and Harris had expressed it. Consequently, they thought their calls for change in school governance would bring about changes in curriculum. Their hope was that a new breed of administrator with a more enlightened business-minded board of education would diversify the curriculum rather than force all students to study the same materials.

Was School Governance Improved?

Riis's and Rice's articles gained widespread attention and focused concern on school governance. Reformers complained that when people had moved into cities, they brought with them the manner of school governance typical in rural areas. Although situations differed among specific cities, in general there was a system of subdistrict or ward boards filled with trustees or board members elected from the neighborhood. Until 1911 in Pittsburgh, for example, there were thirty-nine such boards and each was responsible for choosing teachers, raising funds, and building schools. Usually, representatives from such subdistrict boards sat on a central or districtwide board. Thus, not only was the system fragmented, but the body charged with overseeing the whole was also large and cumbersome. However, as a result of campaigns fueled by the stories of people such as Riis and Rice, the central school boards were reduced in size and took more control. In 1893, in the twenty-eight cities having populations of 100,000 or more, there was an average of 21.5 central board members per city. In 1913 the average dropped to 10.2 central board members per city (Tyack 88–89, 126–127).

Unfortunately, it is not clear whether placing the authority for school governance in a smaller, central board made up of people elected at large in the city was an improvement. It was a political battle. The people who supported the reforms to create what they called a nonpolitical school board were usually highly educated and members of elite families. The people who opposed the changes were politicians or teachers who viewed the reformers as snobbish intruders (Tyack 148). For example, in New York City in 1894, Nicholas Murray Butler, president of Teachers College at Columbia University, used the popularity of Riis's and Rice's articles to direct a reform bill through the state legislature that established a board of superintendents, increased the power of the central board, and drastically limited the authority of the ward board. The teachers unanimously opposed it. Butler argued that this resistance was the result of corruption from Tammany Hall. But the teachers were not trying to protect politicians; they worried about the ways in which reformers wanted to change their profession (Urban 27–29).

Before Butler's bill passed, teachers were promoted to different grade levels and to administration by seniority or years of experience. Thus, the person who knew the school the best became the administrator. This was a reward for the teacher's dedication and a guarantee of stability for the school. Reformers made clear that they wanted to do away with this system, calling it political and open to corruption. They preferred a system whereby administrators were selected by training and examination (Urban 32).

It is not clear, however, that the administrators chosen by training and examination were better than those who had worked in the system for years. In fact, the teachers often complained that the new administrators who had never taught in public schools lacked the intuition and practical insight that came from long and intimate association with classrooms. Nonetheless, school boards or superintendents chose administrators without consulting teachers. In 1894, when the superintendent of Cambridge, Massachusetts, suggested that teachers should elect representatives to councils that could evaluate prospective administrators and curriculum proposals, the school board ignored the request. When that superintendent left, the board increased the superintendent's authority instead of acting on the idea of councils (Urban 33–36).

Further, the teachers were probably not as bad as Rice suggested. For example, during the discussions about Butler's proposed changes in New York, a journalist new to the city wrote that she had expected to find the schools in the miserable condition Rice had described. Because the teachers did not rise in mass to protest these allegations, she assumed they were true. However, she visited a variety of schools and found intelligent, well-bred teachers working pleasantly with happy, well-trained students. Likewise, other supporters contended that the school trustees were not corrupt politicians, claiming instead that the trustees were more attentive to the needs of the school and the neighborhoods than distant central officials could be (Tyack 152–153).

Although Riis criticized the sensitivities immigrant voters showed in defending opportunities for their daughters to be teachers, it is not clear that out-of-state teachers were better than local teachers. That is, people raised in the area often knew the neighborhood and spoke the language of their students. Not only did they represent models of Americanization for the students, but also teaching jobs represented opportunities for immigrants to work their way out of slums.

It should be noted that Riis did not approve of people remaining in their ethnic groups. Even his ideas about a healthy childhood seemed to widen the distance between immigrant parents and their children. For example, although Riis praised the Jewish community for its industriousness and drive for knowledge, he contended that Jewish religious education was regressive. He hoped that the contrast between the attractive public schools and the dark, inhospitable Hebrew schools found in the tenements might encourage the children to leave their faith and embrace the ways of the United States (Fried 55–56).

Whether needed or not, the reforms gave control of the schools to new groups. The people elected to those positions tended to be prominent men of business who were well known throughout the city. Ethnic and minority groups who had dominated the ward boards were excluded. Thus, by 1927, when George Counts did a survey of the social composition of school board members, he found that the typical city board of education comprised six members. One member was usually a housewife, and the other five were often men who were bankers, lawyers, physicians, or business executives. Sometimes, one member was a salesman, clerk, or laborer. Counts worried that when the business elite controlled the schools, they would insist that the lessons reinforce the ideas of their social class. Students would not learn that there were alternative views, such as those of labor unions, he argued (Counts, *Social* 79, 92–95).

To some extent, Counts had cause to worry. As centralized reforms spread throughout the United States, elite reformers tried to prevent socialists and radical progressives from using school buildings for community meetings, claiming that such events would unnecessarily increase the cost of education. However, as more educators urged that schools become social centers, ethnic groups gained access to school buildings. Sometimes to the dismay of the board of education, they used their meetings to preserve their language and culture. As a result, while elite groups gained control in most cities, numerous voluntary organizations fought to make schools responsive to neighborhood concerns. Although events unfolded differently in various cities, these struggles kept school curriculums from serving exclusively any one group (Reese, *Power* 200–208, 250–251).

How Were Schools Changed to Meet the Needs of the Students?

In addition to changing the type of people who controlled the schools, the reforms often accelerated the tendency of schools to include industrial training. Journalists argued that new immigrants to the city needed industrial training to learn about their new homeland rather than the academic program recommended by Eliot and Harris. This became such a popular idea that in 1918 meeting the needs of the large numbers of pupils with varying capabilities was expressed as the second reason the Commission on the Reorganization of Secondary Education wanted to change the curriculum from the strictly academic one offered by the Committee of Ten and the Committee of Fifteen.

Journalists such as Riis attached considerable importance to industrial training. He praised especially the twenty-one industrial schools maintained by the Children's Aid Society, a private philanthropy. He believed these industrial schools transformed tough street urchins into respectable citizens and cost far less to run than prisons. Containing more than five thousand pupils, these schools enrolled children less than five years of age in kindergartens and offered other studies for children ranging from ages five to fourteen. More than 10 percent of the students could not speak English. In those industrial schools, students learned how to read, write, and do arithmetic. For the girls, the schools offered instruction in sewing, cooking, and dressmaking. The boys learned carpentry, wood carving, and printing (Riis, *Children* 197–208).

In fairness, neither Riis nor his associates created the idea of using industrial training to help deprived persons. Schools such as Oberlin and Mount Holyoke had long offered students chances to work on campus while studying. However, Hampton Normal and Agricultural Institute became a famous model when U.S. General Samuel Chapman Armstrong became the principal. Reminded of the manual labor school founded by his missionary parents on the island of Maui in Hawaii, Armstrong created a curriculum to train a cadre of African Americans who could go forth and teach in elementary schools (Gregg 4–5).

Supported by the Freedman's Bureau and several private philanthropists, Hampton opened in 1868 with two teachers and fifteen pupils. By 1921 the school had more than 2,300 students and more than 150 staff members. The students were over the age of sixteen. The primary aim of education at Hampton was character development through hand work. This ideal persisted. Even in 1917, long after the Emancipation Proclamation, professors at Hampton argued that because African Americans felt the influence of slavery that made work with the hands beneath the dignity of free human beings, all students had to work in shops, laundries, kitchens, offices, farms, and gardens where they learned that with labor came independence and self-reliance (Gregg 8–9).

In 1878 Hampton opened its doors to forty Native Americans, called ex-prisoners of war, belonging to the Kiowa, Comanche, and Sioux tribes. Representing the first attempt of the U.S. government to support education for Native Americans, the Hampton experiment led to the creation of what were called Indian Schools. At Hampton the enrollment of Native Americans reached its peak in 1887 with 160 students. As in the case of African American students, these Native American men and women were expected to return to their homes and demonstrate what they learned at Hampton. A few of the former Native American students worked outside reservations in occupations such as stenographers and railroad employees. In 1912 the government stopped its appropriations for such students, but several Native Americans continued to enroll and to graduate from the Institute (Andrus 89–93).

When Armstrong began Hampton Institute, he omitted Latin and Greek from the curriculum and adapted the courses to the life students would lead. The instruction included subjects such as correct use of English, mathematics, geography, and the principles of moral science and political economy. His successors continued the practical emphasis so that the study of mathematics was connected to the problems of the sawmill. An arithmetic room was fitted with counters for buying and selling so that all transactions of daily life could be enacted. Insurance policies, tax bills, and mortgages served as part of the arithmetic curriculum. However, some instructors complained that the curriculum was too narrow to broaden students' horizons. For example, continual practice in the application of arithmetic to the problems of daily living was insufficient to prepare a person to be a schoolteacher. Consequently, in 1913 the faculty added academic courses that would help develop intelligent citizens who could make intellectual and vocational contributions to the community (Doerman 30–32).

One of the most famous graduates of Hampton Institute was Booker T. Washington, who became an apostle of Armstrong, spreading the idea of industrial training. He wanted every African American to receive industrial training, and he discouraged African Americans with academic interests from pursuing those studies. Although Washington seemed to counsel African Americans to accept segregation, he implied that because trade training for Blacks would soften prejudice among Whites, it could lead to an integrated society.

How Did Booker T. Washington Use Industrial Education at Tuskegee Institute?

Booker Taliaferro Washington wrote that he was born a slave on a plantation in Franklin County, Virginia, in 1858 or 1859 and grew up without a birthday or a name beyond "Booker" until he attended his first school after his family moved to Kanawha County, West Virginia. In the fall of 1872, Washington walked five hundred miles to enroll in Hampton Institute. Finishing his studies in 1875, he credited the school and its founder, General Samuel Chapman Armstrong, with teaching him to love labor for its financial rewards and for the independence that comes from "the ability to do something the world wants done" (Washington 1, 34–35, 45–47, 73).

A forceful and convincing speaker, Washington earned national fame when he spoke to the Atlanta, Georgia, Cotton States and International Exposition in 1895. The purpose of the exposition was to demonstrate the industrial advancement enjoyed by the South since the Civil War. Washington had asked the directors to allow African Americans to erect a large attractive building on the grounds showing the progress of the freedman in hopes that such a demonstration would make it easier for the two races to be friends. In addition to granting his request, the directors asked Washington to make a short speech during the opening exercises. In the five minutes he took to make his address, Washington outlined how education could improve race relations (Washington 196–216).

Washington began his address by comparing the condition of African Americans to that of a crew of a ship lost at sea. Dying of thirst and spotting a friendly vessel, the sailors cried out for water. They heard the reply, "Cast down your bucket where you are." It happened that the distressed vessel was off the shore of the mouth of the Amazon River and surrounded by fresh water. Using this metaphor, Washington urged African Americans to recognize the possibilities inherent in cultivating friendly relations with their neighbors. Repeating the refrain "cast down your bucket," he recommended that African Americans develop capacities in agriculture, mechanics, and domestic service. To the White people who sought immigrant labor for factories, he recommended that they "cast down their buckets where they are" and look to the eight million Black people whose habits they knew and who had worked for them without strikes or labor wars. Although he called for integration in industrial areas, he did not recommend social integration. Instead, he claimed that in all things purely social, the two races could be as separate as the fingers, yet they must be one as the hand in all things essential to mutual progress. Pointing with pride at the building on the exposition grounds representing the progress of African Americans, Washington acknowledged the generosity of philanthropists from the North and the South who made such accomplishments possible. In conclusion, Washington repeated his promise not to force social integration. The opportunity to earn a dollar in a factory is more important, he claimed, than the opportunity to spend a dollar at an opera house (Washington 218–224).

Washington's address became known as the Atlanta Compromise because he promised that African Americans would end the demands for equality they had made since Reconstruction in exchange for opportunities to work in industrial, agricultural, and domestic settings. Most important for this discussion, however, the speech captured the promise that lay behind the education Washington received at Hampton Institute and the training he offered at Tuskegee.

About fourteen years before his speech in Atlanta, on July 4, 1881, Washington opened a school in Tuskegee, Alabama, in a dilapidated shanty near a decrepit African American Methodist church. A year earlier, the Alabama legislature had granted an annual appropriation of two thousand dollars for teacher salaries for what was to be a normal school. Unfortunately, they did not give any consideration to acquiring land, erecting buildings, or obtaining tools or books (Washington 106–117).

When he began his class in Tuskegee, Washington was dismayed to find that most of his African American students wanted to learn subjects that would take them out of the fields or the kitchens. They considered the most practical thing an education could do was to enable its possessor to take the job of teacher and earn more money. Washington complained that the bigger the book and the longer the title, the more students wanted to study it, even though they lived in filth and needed skills such as carpentry to construct sound homes. After three months in the shanty, Washington arranged a loan of $250 from the treasurer of Hampton Institute and with it bought a nearby abandoned plantation (119–132).

From the beginning, Washington planned to have students do the agricultural and domestic work at Tuskegee Institute and erect the buildings. While performing these services, they were taught the best methods of labor so that the school received the benefit of their labor and the students learned a trade. In twenty years, the students constructed forty buildings. Although they had several problems learning how to manufacture bricks, they succeeded so well that they began to sell bricks to the neighboring White people. They did the same with carts, buggies, and wagons (Washington 148–154).

Being able to trade with the White neighbors was important to Washington. He wrote that something in human nature made an individual appreciate deserving individuals no matter what color of skin those individuals had. He believed that the White farmers softened their prejudices because of the tangible interdependence created when his school sold them objects. Interestingly, several parents of his students did not share this faith in the skilled trades. Many parents wrote letters complaining about their children working instead of studying. Although Washington ignored specific complaints, he went to as many communities and public meetings as he could to explain his program. The result was that enrollments increased (148–157).

At every opportunity, Washington impressed on students that they had as much interest in Tuskegee Institute as did any trustee, director, or teacher. To facilitate contact with students, he made arrangements for them to write him if they had complaints and to meet with him in the institute's chapel to discuss problems. At the same time, he insisted on what he called the gospel of the toothbrush. Taken from General Armstrong at Hampton, this idea meant that cleanliness was paramount. Any student who refrained from maintaining a high level of personal hygiene was forced to leave the institute. Washington credited this policy with bringing a high degree of civilization to students (Washington 163–176).

How Successful Was Washington?

If measured by their popularity, Washington and his program were most successful. However, over the years Washington's program had failed to prepare students for the types of work they might encounter as adults. Worse, it may have ignored essential political concerns. Washington was an important figure in his day. On December 16, 1898, then U.S. President McKinley took the occasion of the Peace Jubilee celebrating the end of the Spanish-American War to visit Tuskegee Institute. In a warm speech, McKinley congratulated the people of the institute for the good work they did and called favorable attention to the genius and perseverance of Washington who made it possible. In 1899 Washington toured Europe, where he spoke with important personages, visited farms, and delivered speeches. Queen Victoria of England invited him and his wife to tea in Windsor Castle. On his return, President Charles Eliot of Harvard conferred on Washington an honorary degree, and the newspaper stories in Boston and New York praised Harvard for making an excellent choice (Washington 267–308).

Even William Torrey Harris, who had been an influential member of the Committee of Ten and the Committee of Fifteen, declared that Washington's solution to what he called the "Negro problem" should be applied to all downtrodden people no matter their race (Curti 309). Others sought to apply the Tuskegee idea to education in Africa. Thomas Jesse Jones, who taught at Hampton College, served as educational director for the Phelps-Stokes Fund. The reports that came out under his direction recommended that African teachers adopt practices Armstrong had initiated at Hampton and that Washington carried out at Tuskegee (Cremin, *American Education 1876–1980* 221–223).

Despite its benefits, Washington's program of industrial training may not have been appropriate for the rapidly changing United States. As Washington popularized his ideas of industrial training for the masses, manufacturers were adopting machine production to replace the skilled artisans that Tuskegee trained. Mechanized agriculture was pushing farmers off the land. Furthermore, changes in business practices increased the difficulties small businesspeople faced. With the growth of large corporations, the use of credit on a vast scale, and the rise of mail order businesses and chain stores, African Americans trained in schools such as Tuskegee could not easily open their own shops in small towns (Curti 307–308).

More important, Washington may have established a poor educational model. This was the basis of the criticism that William Edward Burghardt Du Bois made against the Tuskegee ideal. Writing in 1903, Du Bois claimed it was a mistake for Washington to depreciate institutions of higher learning and advocate common school and industrial training. For one thing, Washington's school depended on African Americans trained in Black colleges to be teachers if for no other reason than there were not enough willing White people to teach African Americans (Du Bois 88–89).

Du Bois noted that after 1895 supporters of industrial training argued that training for work should precede intellectual education. Du Bois disagreed. He argued that in the American colonies, Harvard University preceded lower schools because the higher had to come before the lower. That is, the colleges had to train the teachers of the lower schools. It was not enough, warned Du Bois, that teachers know the techniques of instruction. Teachers had to be "broad minded cultured men and women able to scatter civilization among a people whose ignorance was not simply of letters but of life" (125–129).

According to Du Bois, the mistake in Washington's model was that it required all African Americans to give up higher education. The result of this belief was that colleges established for African Americans such as Atlanta, Fisk, and Howard suffered steady declines in financial assistance. It is important to note that Du Bois did not want to deprive African Americans who could profit from industrial training of the opportunity to attend a trade school; the South needed intelligent and trained workers. At the same time, however, he wanted those African Americans who could profit from college to have the opportunity to attend an academic college program. This talented tenth of African American college graduates should serve as preachers to leaven the Black church, as physicians to guard against disease among African Americans, and as lawyers to protect the property of the toiling masses of Black people (Du Bois 87–88, 134–139).

Du Bois believed that education should train ability, which would in turn bring about the political and social advancement of African Americans. His views on integration were not as straightforward. When Washington advocated social segregation, Du Bois opposed it to some extent. For example, in 1921 he claimed that segregated schools meant that social segregation would continue through life. He also noted that social circumstances meant that sometimes people had to accept segregated schools. In 1934 Du Bois began an extended controversy with other leaders of the National Association of the Advancement of Colored People (NAACP) that led to his resignation as the editor of the journal *Crisis.* He disagreed with the NAACP policy of seeking integration at all costs. Instead, he urged African Americans to recognize that White Americans would not accept them and to organize their own economic and social power no matter how much segregation that implied. He added that when African Americans tried to remove all segregation, they denied the accomplishments of Negro churches, Negro newspapers, and Negro schools (H. Moon 128, 184–214).

Did Industrial Education Have to Separate Students?

Industrial education did not have to lead to segregation. A proponent of more integrated or democratic approaches to the problems of poverty was Jane Addams, a founder of the settlement house movement in the United States. Addams did not dislike industrial training, but she wanted to mix it with other approaches that opened the possibilities for all people to live together. As a result, like Riis, Addams credited such training in the public schools with teaching immigrant families to live in the United States. For example, Addams described an Italian girl who studied cooking at the public school. In their former village in Italy, the girl's mother had mixed the bread batter at home and taken it to a village oven where many women baked together. In the United States, the mother was on her own and unable to understand the more complicated American cooking stove. Fortunately, the girl had learned at school how to use the stove and could show her mother how to bake bread. According to Addams, through the daughter the school taught the mother, a former village dweller, about modern urban life and changed the habits of the entire family (182–183).

On September 18, 1889, Addams, Ellen Starr, and Mary Keyser moved into a dilapidated but solidly built mansion called Hull House near the junction of Blue Island Avenue and Halstead and Harrison Streets in Chicago, Illinois. For Addams the settlement house was an experimental effort to solve the social problems engendered by a large city. She and the other settlement house residents pledged to regard the entire life of their city as organic, to make every effort to unify it, and to protest the overdifferentiation of groups in the city. Early on the residents of Hull House took up many different activities. One of the residents set up a public kitchen to teach the women in neighboring immigrant families how to cook the inexpensive, nutritious food available in Chicago. This was important because the food that immigrants had prepared in their former countries was expensive or difficult to obtain in Chicago. Hull House provided a coffeehouse and a gymnasium where the neighborhood children and young adults could gather and play. Like Riis, Addams feared that without such places the young people would visit the local saloons. In their tenements, they did not have rooms to entertain guests. Further, Hull House set up a coal cooperative association to provide low-cost heating, and began the Jane Club to provide shelter to women on strike against factories (Addams 98–106).

Hull House members held classes to teach immigrants about the United States and organized musical bands, theater productions, an art museum, and craft clubs; however, the spirit of the educational endeavors may be best represented by the labor museum. This museum came about because Addams noticed that European immigrant women could not control their U.S.-born children. These children looked down on their parents who appeared lost in the new country. As Addams sought a way to help families bridge the European and American experiences, she saw an old Italian woman spinning yarn for a pair of stockings. Addams thought that young people who worked in textile factories should be interested in this older form of the industry. According to Addams, if young people saw that the machinery found in factories evolved from the simple tools their parents used at home, they might begin to revere their past, thereby laying the basis for sound progress. In the neighborhood, Addams found people spinning thread in different ways that were characteristic of different countries. She invited several women to come to Hull House and arranged them in a room so that the methods of spinning appeared sequentially. Her aim was to show that industry developed when workers in different countries exchanged ideas and techniques even though those workers spoke different languages or followed different religions. Later, Addams brought in lecturers on industrial history to explain these transitions and the painful social changes that followed technological innovation (Addams 172–174).

Addams considered the labor museum a success. She recalled one triumph that involved an Italian girl named Angelina who came to Hull House for cooking class every Saturday evening while her mother went to spin in the labor museum exhibit. Angelina always left her mother at the front door while she went around to the back door. Addams thought that Angelina did not want people to identify her with her mother because the older woman wore a kerchief over her head, boots, and a short petticoat. One evening Angelina saw her mother surrounded by a group of visitors from the University of Chicago's School of Education. They told her that her mother was the best stick-spindle spinner in the United States. When Angelina inquired about this, Addams told Angelina how her mother had grown up in a small, secluded village in Italy governed by narrow religious and social conventions, and had experienced an unsettling shock when she came to the United States. Angelina began to talk with her mother about life in an Italian village. After a short period, Angelina allowed her mother to bring a box of homespun garments to Hull House. The box contained clothes Angelina had regarded as uncouth and forbidden anyone to see. More important, Angelina walked into the labor museum beside her mother (Addams 176–177).

John Dewey became a friend of Jane Addams. When he accepted a professorship at the University of Chicago in 1894, Dewey regularly visited Hull House to observe, give lectures, and join the residents for dinner. In 1897 he served as a trustee for the settlement house. As a result of his association with Hull House and Jane Addams, Dewey became more fully aware of the miseries that exploited people suffered. He shared with Addams a desire to make democratic ideals function in industrial settings. According to his daughter, Jane, Dewey's experiences in Hull House gave a sharper and deeper meaning to his faith in democracy as a guiding force in education (Wirth 23–24).

From 1896 to 1904, Dewey ran his own laboratory school in which he took an experimental perspective similar to the one Addams had relied on in establishing Hull House. Dewey thought the laboratory school could be an opportunity to test his pedagogical theories and his ideas about philosophy and psychology. The school would show the truth of Dewey's views and give him the chance to modify them as needed. In 1916 he summarized the articles he wrote about his laboratory school in *Democracy and Education,* which he wrote as a textbook to guide teachers and administrators in public schools who wanted to make their classrooms more educative (Cremin, *American Education 1876–1980* 167–173).

Most important, Dewey's curriculum took the idea of the labor museum and expanded it. For Addams the labor museum was a way to help people appreciate the gifts each person could offer. In Dewey's school, students engaged in activities that helped them trace the evolution of academic subjects. As a result of such experiences, Dewey believed that students would understand the society in which they lived. Thus, Dewey took the hopes that Harris had expressed for the academic subjects and showed how industrial training, when conceived as an introduction to academics, could lead to what Harris had called self-determination. As discussed in Chapter four, this was the idea that a person achieved individuality by immersing himself or herself in the collectivity.

How Did Dewey Use the Ideal of Democracy to Construct a Curriculum?

Dewey called his lessons "active occupations." Dewey thought that most ideas could achieve a synthesis, so this term may have suggested a relation to industrial training. Or it may have expressed a relation to the labor museum. At any rate, the term implied that these were things to do rather than learn. Because the fundamental concerns of human beings have been about food, shelter, and clothing, Dewey thought these activities would tap everyone's instincts and reveal a great deal about social organizations. For example, Dewey thought that gardening could be taught as an avenue for knowledge about the place of agriculture in human history and lead to a study of botany. As students matured, their interest in gardening could prompt them to conduct scientific experiments in things such as seed germination. Because Dewey believed that the sciences grew out of these disciplines, it seemed reasonable for students to retrace these steps. Therefore, he defined education as the reconstruction of experience. In it students reconstructed the experience of the human race, but their aims grew out of their present activities in the home and neighborhood. As students participated in these activities, they took on new aims that led to other activities (*Democracy* 194–202).

Dewey believed this method could be applied to traditional school subjects. In learning geography, for example, students should gain the power to perceive spatial connections to ordinary acts. Learning history was to gain the power to recognize human connections among human activities. Dewey thought that teachers could allow the subject matters to penetrate into students' living experiences if teachers kept faith with the interdependence of human beings and nature. He urged teachers to include nature study with geography and to reveal how these influenced the development of differences in civilizations, thereby relating history to geography, and to begin historical studies with the current situation with all its problems. Ultimately, Dewey believed that industrial history gave the most insight into social affairs because it showed how human beings have extended dominion over the natural world (*Democracy* 207–218).

For Dewey, active occupations were superior to traditional school activities because they built on the students' interests. Traditional school activities might appear to foster interest, discipline, and intelligent thought because students worked on problems, answered questions, completed tasks, and overcame difficulties. But for the students, these classroom problems did not come from personal experience; they came from the textbook. Consequently, as far as students were concerned, the real problem was to earn a grade. Not surprisingly, they observed the teacher's behavior and modified their own actions to fit the teacher's requirements. Had they felt the problem was genuine, they would have directed their attention to the activity itself. Dewey believed that laboratories, shops, gardens, dramatizations, plays, and games offered opportunities for schools to reproduce situations found in life. They enabled students to apply ideas in ways that reflected genuine experiences. In order to foster thinking, Dewey argued, five conditions were needed:

1. The pupil had to be involved in an ongoing activity that was important to the student for its own sake.
2. A genuine problem had to develop in the experience.
3. The student had to have the information and make the observations needed to deal with the difficulty.
4. The student had to devise possible solutions.
5. The student must test the proposed solutions (*Democracy* 152–163).

Naturally, if students learned best when they had an active interest in the work, teachers would do better under similar conditions. But Dewey found that in schools administrators took their ideas of educational goals from what was current in the community and imposed those goals on teachers. In turn, the teachers imposed those aims on the students. This reduced the work of teachers and students to that of slaves. To counter such authoritarianism, Dewey recommended that teachers treat statements about educational aims, such as "Prepare a class to study medicine," as suggestions for observing or planning. Proper educational aims would be founded on the intrinsic activities and students' needs. The aims should cooperate with the students' activities. Finally, the aims must not be ultimate but must lead to other aims (*Democracy* 106–110).

Instead of taking aims from outside the classroom, Dewey believed the system of active occupations located the aims within activities. As a result, life in the classroom was much easier. Dewey argued that if teachers thought of aims as part of a process of activity and observation, they would not have to cajole or threaten students to keep order in the classroom. In other words, he believed that interest and discipline were aspects of an activity that had an aim. Any activity continuously develops; it has a beginning, a middle, and an end. For students to follow the activity as it unfolds, they must identify with the objects in the experience; this is what it means to have an interest. Similarly, students must attend to the ways those objects change; this is what it means to be disciplined. Therefore, Dewey thought that teachers should think of the students' capabilities as related to the subject matter because the activity, as it developed, held them together (*Democracy* 110, 123,137–138).

Dewey's idea of subject matter was related to his conception of aims. The things school taught were not found only in organized bodies of knowledge, although these compendiums of information were important. When Dewey described subject matter, he said that it consisted of the facts observed and the ideas suggested in the course of an activity having a purpose. As a result, the subject matter varied among people. From the point of view of the teacher, subject matter was the accumulation of the experiences of humankind that could be used to understand new experiences. In school, for example, teachers could use their knowledge of subject matter to think about the cruder activities of the students. A teacher who knows a great deal about music could perceive possibilities in the inchoate musical impulses of students. On the other hand, the pupils' understanding of subject matter followed three different stages: The first was some form of skill or content of ability. The second was communicated or social knowledge that comes from other people's experiences, and the third was a rationally organized body of material. Unfortunately, teachers thought about subject matter as an organized body of information, and they taught it that way. As a result, students failed to recognize the usefulness of the information (*Democracy* 180–193).

Perhaps Dewey's view of science best illustrates the distinctions among these conceptions of subject matters. He thought science was most important as a study because it had emancipated humankind from slavish devotion to custom. In fact, he hoped it could work similarly for students. This did not mean that students should learn scientific truths; such material is not science to the pupil. Instead, they should learn how science improves people's ability to do things. More important, Dewey argued, they must learn how science modifies and enlarges the desires people feel. As a result, science served in the curriculum as it had in society: It emancipated human beings from local or temporary incidents of experience and opened intellectual vistas (*Democracy* 219–230).

This process of liberation was what Dewey thought schools should do for everyone because he equated education with social life. That is, he contended that as people shared experiences, they improved the quality of their experiences. Although he believed that people learned from every social arrangement, he noted that complex modern societies set up institutions specifically designed to educate young people. These schools had three important functions: (1) to simplify the features of society the young should acquire, (2) to eliminate the unworthy features of the environment, and (3) to help the children escape the limitations of the social group into which they were born. A problem Dewey noted was that teachers tried to fulfill these functions by telling children what they should know. Although books, lectures, and written work transmitted a great deal of information, these methods did not help children develop attitudes such as a sense of cooperation. To develop cooperation, for example, children had to engage in shared activities such as games or projects in which individuals adjusted their behavior to fit with the actions of others (*Democracy* 9, 19–20).

Because Dewey believed that education took place in a social group, he had to specify which type of social order would promote the most growth for its members. He offered two standards by which to measure the value of any social life. The first was how numerous and varied were the interests the people shared. The second was how full and free was the interplay with other groups. Thus, although it might appear that a criminal could increase the ability to steal, a group of criminals shared limited interests and, because of their burglary, set themselves apart from everyone else. When Dewey applied his standards to measure the value of different political systems, he found that a democratic system was superior. In such a system, people could interact freely with each other, reconstruct their social habits, and hold a wide range of interests. This meant that in such a system the aim of education was more education (*Democracy* 81–85, 100).

Dewey used the ideal of democracy to construct a curriculum. Thinking that a democratic system that allowed free and full exchanges within and among groups provided the most opportunities for growth, he looked for an analogous method of teaching. He found it in his definition of education as a reconstruction of experience that added meaning to the experience and increased the person's ability to direct the course of subsequent experience (*Democracy* 54–61, 68).

The problem with Dewey's system was that teachers tended to prepare students for the future. They tried to teach students some skill or information that the students might need in later life. Unfortunately, when teachers told students what they needed to know, students learned to look to the future rather than take advantage of the opportunities in the present. To some extent, this was the problem with the industrial training movement. It tried to prepare students for the lives they were likely to lead. As a result, it separated vocational training from academic training on the grounds that academic training served no future activity. Dewey feared that the economically gifted students would pursue traditional cultured education while the masses would receive technical training. Thus, social divisions would increase, and the education of both groups of students would weaken. The students of the humanities would be unable to find cultural elements in useful activities, and the vocational students would never learn the higher meanings of their trades (*Democracy* 306–320).

Were Addams's and Dewey's Proposals Appropriate?

Addams and Dewey were enormously popular. Addams became a nationally recognized figure, and in 1931 she received the Nobel Peace Prize. Hull House grew far beyond its original mansion, occupying more than a city block. In 1961 the city of Chicago removed the buildings to make way for a campus of the University of Illinois, but the trustees took up other decentralized operations. The social settlement movement that began with Toynbee Hall and Hull House spread throughout the United States, Europe, Asia, and Japan. As a result, most nations established national organizations, and an international federation began in 1922.

In the 1970s, however, some historians complained that Addams did not truly serve the immigrants but instead tried to control them. Paul Violas argues that the organic community Addams tried to foster depended on elitism. The women of Hull House sought to direct the workers and the immigrants who came to their doors. In so doing, Violas claims, Addams sought to replace the traditional controls that had existed in the rural communities from which these people had come with advice from experts, which they would follow on their own ("Jane Addams" 81–83).

Like Addams, Dewey became enormously popular. His books were translated into dozens of languages and spread around the world, and he garnered the reputation of being one of the most important philosophers in the United States. Although Dewey's ideas formed the core of practices that later became known as progressive education, in the early 1950s as he neared the end of his life Dewey complained that many of the changes he had recommended were adopted in superficial ways. The schools remained authoritarian (Zilversmit 3, 167–168).

It is not easy to locate the problems. One possibility was that many commentators found it easy to caricature Dewey's pronouncements and to attack their own misrepresentations. Some of his supporters defended him in the same way. Dewey may have exacerbated these problems himself by, for example, writing in an awkward style. Perhaps more important, when his disciples distorted his ideas, Dewey did not clearly correct them (Cremin, *Transformation* 237–238).

Ironically, in a sense Dewey predicted that his ideas would fall from favor. In 1901 he wrote that educational reforms pass through stages in which they are praised widely, attempted for a short time, criticized as failures, and rescinded. He blamed these recurring cycles of reform and retrenchment on the lack of clear standards to evaluate schools, an over concern that students acquire technical proficiency in some skills and mastery of certain information, and the minimal role teachers played in creating the curriculum (Kliebard 74–75).

Some critics attributed the failure of Dewey's ideas to his being overly optimistic. He did not discuss power relationships in society, apparently operating on the belief that truth and its demonstration would triumph. From this perspective, Dewey appeared to be an individual who described how things in schools should be arranged but who neglected to offer a strategy for achieving that objective (Zilversmit 176–177).

Critics often attack Dewey for not serving more pluralistic goals. For example, during World War I he brought a graduate seminar to study Polish immigrants in Philadelphia. In the course of the research, he found that Polish immigrants wanted to retain their Polish identity. They held their Catholic religion tightly, wanted to serve in the Polish Army that was being formed in exile, and sought the restoration of the Polish monarchy. He believed their attitude reflected an unthinking allegiance to tradition. In his report, he contrasted them unfavorably to a small group of Polish Jews who were willing to join the U.S. Army and sought the establishment of a socialized democracy in Poland after the war (Karier 92–93).

According to Clarence J. Karier, this example illustrates how Dewey wanted to make the masses accept science and the scientific method as the keys to social improvement. Dewey and the liberals who followed him wanted schools to teach students to accept this new and different way of life (106–107). But the critics such as Violas and Karier who attacked Addams and Dewey overstated their case. Several historians accuse them of misrepresenting the characters they described (Ravitch, *Revisionists* 129–138).

Whereas Violas and Karier may have been overly critical of Dewey, other historians contend that Dewey wanted to preserve cultural differences (Ravitch, *Revisionists* 130). This statement is equally exaggerated. Dewey did not praise diversity for its own sake. For him, artificial or permanent divisions among people prevented growth. On the one hand, Dewey noted that older cultural ways could provide the basis for forming hypotheses to be tested in approaching a problem. After people evaluated the success of the proposals, they should adopt the best. However, if people held to a particular way because it was traditional, progress would not take place. Most important for Dewey, progress was not simply achieving the ends that people had always sought. Progress also meant that people should use their experiences to enrich previous purposes and to form new ones (Dewey, *Democracy* 225). For example, building a road makes traveling from one place to another easier and makes civilized human interaction possible. People's interests may turn from questions of survival to artistic efforts. If a calamity destroyed all roads, all sources of electric lighting, and all the furniture, people would regress to more primitive states and hold more basic desires. Therefore, Dewey would not want people to hold firmly to traditional values any more than he would want them to hold to traditional means of accomplishing something.

Did the Efforts to Enhance School Success Encourage Diversified Curricula?

It is probably the case that Dewey's educational ideas fell into disfavor for the same reasons that diminished the hopes of the Committee of Ten that all students would pursue an intelligently conceived program of liberal studies. One of these reasons was that many educators contended that children failed when schools offered similar programs to a wide range of children. As discussed earlier, this was the third reason the Commission on the Reorganization of Secondary Education called for a change in the curriculum. The report noted that many changes in educational theory took place between 1893 and 1918.

Educational researchers found many reasons to change the curriculum. For example, in 1909 Leonard Ayres published reports about the progress of students throughout grade levels in several large cities. In every school, he found some children who were older than they should be for the grade they attended. Although different cities held students behind at different rates, the averages were high. For example, in Medford, Massachusetts, 7 percent of the students had not advanced as they should, while in Memphis, Tennessee, 75 percent of the African American youth were overage for their classes. On average, 33 percent of the students in city schools were behind their appropriate grade level. According to Ayres, the problem of students repeating grades or leaving school was not new. It was not caused by increasing enrollments nor was it getting worse as schools enrolled new pupils (1–7).

Ayres noted that students who were overage for their grade rarely graduated. Generally, schools carried all children through the fifth grade, took one-half to the eighth grade, and passed one in ten through to high school. Unfortunately, these failures were not balanced by students making rapid progress. For every child who was ahead of his or her appropriate grade level, there were eight to ten who made slow progress. Ayres concluded that the courses of study found in most schools suited unusually bright children. Other students found the material too difficult to master (1–5).

To reduce school failure, Ayres made four general suggestions. First, he recommended changes in compulsory attendance laws. That is, better enforcement of compulsory attendance laws would ensure that students were present in school. This was necessary to reduce school failure. Further, laws should compel attendance long enough for students to finish high school. Most states required children to attend only until age fourteen, which encouraged leaving before graduation (Ayres 7).

Second, Ayres proposed some changes in the course of study so that more children might pass. One change called for flexible grading, which would allow students who failed a portion of the work to repeat only the part they failed. He approved of plans such as the Batavia system, in which students did group work part of the time and individual work part of the time. Under this system, teachers spent more time with students who needed extra help. Another plan from Cambridge, Massachusetts, divided grades 6 through 9 into four tracks. The students in the longest track took six years to complete the course. The students in the shortest took only four years. Options allowed students to change tracks if they found the work easy or difficult (Ayres 193–197).

Third, Ayres thought that cities should make some provision for children of immigrants. Immigrant children did not fail excessively in school. That is, the percentage of children of foreign-born parents in the schools did not influence rates of failure. Many cities with high rates of students whose parents were foreign-born had good rates of school promotion, while some cities with few immigrants had high rates of failure. In fact, he noted that a greater proportion of native White people were illiterate than were native White people whose parents were foreign-born. Furthermore, the children of immigrants had better rates of school attendance. However, the groups succeeded at different rates. Children from German families had the best records, followed by Americans, Russians, English, Irish, and Italians. Although Ayres found that students often overcame the handicap of not knowing English, he thought immigrant children should receive some sort of special instruction. School people in several cities placed a foreign-born child who did not speak English in one of the lower grades until the child picked up English. Finding this system unjust, Ayres recommended that cities imitate the New York and Cincinnati schools and establish separate classes for the students who did not speak English (5–7, 196–197).

Fourth, Ayres wanted schools to keep better records. He argued that if the aim of the common school was to furnish an elementary education to as many students as possible, educators had to find out why students failed. He recommended that each school maintain a general census and continuous record cards for each student. These cards were to contain information about the student's entrance, enrollment, attendance, and academic progress by school year. Such personal cards could make problems more visible and reduce one cause of grade repeating. Portable records might make it unnecessary for students to repeat work or grades when they transferred from one school to another (Ayres 199–215).

Ayres's arguments influenced his contemporaries to make schools more flexible in order to help students make the transition from elementary to high schools. For example, one of the advocates of the junior high school was the superintendent of Berkeley, California, schools, Frank Forest Bunker, who supported his views by quoting Ayres. In January 1910, Berkeley schools placed grades 7, 8, and 9 in separate buildings. Several administrative problems ensued. The buildings had not been constructed with this pattern in mind, so pupils had to travel to new locations. The teachers and principals did not receive the higher pay offered to teachers at senior levels although they had to be qualified for secondary work. However, students had an opportunity to ease into the more individualistic and scholarly nature of high school. At the same time, there were fewer discipline problems because the older students were separated from the younger. The schools offered more flexible promotion plans such as the Batavia system that Ayres had recommended. In addition, the students from small elementary schools could form new and wider peer groups before moving to the larger high schools. The plan worked. Although Bunker did not know how many students had left the district high school before he implemented the junior high, he noted that with the junior high, only about 16 percent of the class dropped out after the ninth grade. This was considerably less than the 60 percent rates of school leaving Ayres had found previously (Bunker 102–114).

Another advantage of the junior high was that it allowed students to explore vocational options more than had been possible in elementary schools. Bunker wanted the students to hear clerics talk about the ministry, businesswomen to explain the opportunities for women, educators to describe teaching as a profession, and plumbers to reveal the possibilities in their trade. At the same time, in the junior high students could receive more industrial training than they had in the elementary schools. Bunker noted that the principal of a junior high school in a neighborhood of families who earned their living through unskilled labor substituted practical courses for academic ones. Instead of English, his teachers offered a sort of business English course in which students learned to write letters and make applications. Instead of algebra, the students took business arithmetic, which included making budgets. They took measurement classes in which they used railroad timetables to calculate distances between cities. As a result of these course changes, the size of the ninth grade in that neighborhood grew rapidly (137–148).

In a short period, school districts changed the traditional arrangement of eight elementary grades and four secondary grades. A popular variation was to add a junior high school so that there would be six grades of elementary school, three grades of junior high, and three grades of high school. By 1920 there were 883 junior high schools nationwide (Krug, *Secondary School* 33–34).

Most important for this discussion, the calls for curriculum flexibility and increased attention to vocational courses offered a new and more humanitarian reason for educators to ignore the recommendations of the Committee of Ten. They thought that by changing the curriculum they could keep more students in school.

How Did Psychologists Encourage the Development of a Diversified Curriculum?

Another change in educational theory that took place between 1893 and 1918 was the shift in educational psychology from philosophic speculation to a more empirical basis. In large part, this came from what was called the child-study movement. Writing in 1911, G. Stanley Hall claimed that twenty-five years earlier education had been based on what he called "sonorous metaphysical platitudes" that mystified listeners. The foremost educator who used such psychologies was W. T. Harris, who acquired almost papal authority among educators. According to Hall, the view of psychology changed, and educational reforms began as a result of the child-study movement. From various studies of how children learned and grew, schools began to change to fit the child (G. Hall, *Educational Problems* iii–vii).

To some extent, Hall initiated the child-study movement. After studying with Harris, Hall went to Germany for postgraduate work where he gathered materials on pedagogy. In 1880 he began a series of lectures at Harvard on the history of philosophy and pedagogy. Many teachers from the Boston public schools attended his lectures because Hall made the authority of science reinforce the romantic ideas spread by Francis Parker, the superintendent of Quincy, Massachusetts, schools. Parker encouraged teachers to let children be themselves in order to ascend through natural stages to maturity. What Hall did was to extend Parker's idea of letting children develop naturally into a view that education should be based on a scientific study of child development. It was science, Hall claimed, that would show how children developed naturally (Ross 103–124).

Although Hall blended the romantic idea that nature would direct children's growth in the best way with calls for better scientific studies of children, the idea that science should play a role in education was not new. In the 1830s, for example, in Hanover, an English territory in Germany, Johann Friedrich Herbart advocated a science of teaching. However, his idea of being scientific was to be mathematical. That is, Herbart discarded the notion of faculty psychology and considered the mind to be formed by experiences. He believed that new sensations fit together with other previously acquired ones to form what he called an apperceptive mass. Thus, for Herbart,, the science of psychology was to present mathematical descriptions of the encounters among perceptions (Dunkel 51–54).

This conception of the mind led Herbart to formulate four steps of teaching. Although he used different terms at various times to describe these steps, he placed them in the same general order. In the first, often called "clarity," the student observed the qualities or characteristics of an object. In the second, often called "association," students linked the concept or object to other sensations acquired earlier. The third was "system," which was necessary for association to take place. Finally, the structure had to be constructed out of "principles," which was the last step (Dunkel 74–75).

In the last years of the nineteenth century, Herbart's ideas became popular in the United States. In 1895 a group of reformers founded the Herbart Society; its three most energetic supporters were Charles DeGarmo, Charles McMurry, and his brother Frank McMurry. Together, they introduced Herbart to teachers in the United States. For a time, Francis Parker and John Dewey joined in their efforts. But educators' formal attachment to Herbart soon declined. In 1902 the Herbart Society changed its name to the National Society for the Scientific Study of Education and officially removed its connection with Herbart (Dunkel 120–122).

Although Herbartianism faded quickly, prominent educators continued to publish adaptations of his ideas. For example, in 1903 Charles McMurry published *The Elements of General Method Based on the Principles of Herbart.* Following his mentor, McMurry defined the aim of education as moral excellence to which all activities and studies in the schools must contribute. He claimed that as a result of the introduction of studies such as history, drawing, manual training, and physical culture, the schools no longer had to depend on old traditions of instruction or on textbooks. However, the danger was that the curriculum would become a mass of unrelated lessons. Therefore, McMurry urged teachers to think of the relative value of the studies. Instead of placing the formal studies in the center of school life as Harris had done, McMurry urged that history and natural science become the center. Above all, he urged, educators should allow students to follow their inherited spontaneous energies to acquire the best available cultural materials (12–13, 82–83).

According to McMurry, the practical key to the problems of education was Herbart's concept of apperception, which implied nine important conclusions.

1. Knowledge must be used. Teachers should not drill students on information whose only use is in a test.
2. Newly acquired ideas are always related to formerly learned ones.
3. Students must understand new information to learn it.
4. New ideas must be related to the ideas learned earlier.
5. Teachers must know what students already know if they are to connect new lessons to that old information.
6. Students cannot learn skills without having mastered some concepts on which the new material depends. For example, they should be able to multiply before they tackle division.
7. Lessons should build on experiences students had at home and during their infancy. Thus, natural science would focus on materials found in the neighborhood.
8. Teacher and students must become aware of the power that comes from being able to use their knowledge.
9. Lessons must constantly work toward the building of general concepts (McMurry 280–292, 331).

As these nine conclusions indicate, McMurry disapproved of an exclusively literary education for all students. However, the main authority for his nine conclusions was their connection to Herbart's ideas. While he offered teachers suggestions of what to do with students besides read, the value of his ideas was their connection to the great teacher's philosophy. On the other hand, Hall claimed that teachers should base their ideas on studies of the children (Dunkel 123).

The central method Hall used to study children was questionnaires. For example, from 1894 to 1895, Hall and his students compiled fifteen questionnaires on particular topics such as children's fears and distributed them to more than eight hundred correspondents throughout the country. These included teachers in normal schools, superintendents, principals, and other teachers. The questionnaire listed possible fears, asked for information about the age at which they appeared, their intensity, manifestations, causes, and effects. Recipients of these questionnaires answered them and provided copies to students or coworkers to answer. Some went to classrooms to observe children before answering. As a result, in that one year Hall received more than twenty thousand responses (Ross 290–291).

Although the methods Hall used were impersonal and appeared objective, the questions were vague. As a result, much of his information was fragmentary and inconclusive. This did not stop Hall from drawing on it as he chose while supplementing his findings with personal reminiscences. Not surprisingly, few psychologists other than his students at Clark University where he was president imitated Hall's methods (Ross 290–292).

Despite the problems with his research, Hall was extremely popular as a public speaker, claiming that science would show the proper direction for teachers. For example, when Hall addressed the problems in kindergartens, he contended that Friedrich Froebel's book *Education of Man* was so badly organized that no one could understand it. He noted that the strength of the book was the way it asked women to be attentive to children. Despite these problems, the kindergarten movement in the United States had become a sect, Hall claimed, wherein women tried to implement exactly Froebel's suggestions. According to Hall, the result was that the work in the classroom was ill conceived. Teachers tried to help students acquire abilities they would attain naturally at a later date. He pointed out that Froebel's occupations overworked children, made them sit still when they would rather move, and required that they use fine or small muscles they had not yet developed. Therefore, he concluded, educational improvement would come when kindergarten teachers opened themselves to the scientific movement of the age (G. Hall, *Educational Problems* 2, 15, 18).

Although Hall began his educational work in 1880, he took several years to write his central book explaining his position. In 1904 Hall published *Adolescence: Its Psychology and Its Relations to Physiology, Anthropology, Sociology, Sex, Crime, Religion, and Education.* Acknowledging that he could not fully demonstrate his belief in a genetic psychology, Hall contended that children developed in a pattern that recapitulated the evolution of the human race. If teachers recognized the similarity in those stages of development, they would avoid many errors in the classroom. According to Hall, the ages from eight to twelve represent the stage during which the child begins to move outside the home circle. This stage reminded him of the stage in evolution when people in warm climates began to shift for themselves. Thus, children revel in hunting and fishing. Unfortunately, instead of letting youth play as they should, teachers make them sit and read (G. Hall, *Adolescence* Vol I, viii–xii).

The next stage was adolescence, which suggested a stage in human history when the developments of civilization appeared to be possible. Although this was a time of rapid growth, schools and churches failed to recognize the special needs and dangers confronting children. Hall claimed that one such need was to protect girls from overwork and thereby establish normal periodicity, the regular occurrence of menses (G. Hall, *Adolescence* Vol 1, xiii–xvii).

When he turned to the question of education, Hall complained about the influence colleges had on elementary and high schools. He pointed to the Committee of Ten and the Committee of Fifteen in this regard. One result was to standardize programs, giving certain lessons at set periods of time. However, the children at different stages of development attend to different things (*Adolescence* Vol 2, 508–509).

Hall complained that the three central ideas of the Committee of Ten were wrong. The first idea was that every subject should be taught the same way to every student no matter what vocation those students would follow. Hall thought this principle ignored differences in children's interests, abilities, and the use to which ideas would be applied. The second idea was that all subjects were of equal educational value if taught well. According to Hall, this notion overlooked how courses in science were more useful than lessons in Greek. The third idea was that a high school education that prepared students for college also prepared them for life. In Hall's estimation, such a consideration was true only if life was an endless series of examinations similar to those that students take in college courses. Instead of concentrating on literary studies, Hall urged high schools to adopt wider diversity in the curricula and offer more varied methods of instruction than using textbooks and giving examinations (G. Hall, *Adolescence* Vol 2, 510–526).

Did Studies of the Transfer of Training Weaken the Rationale for the Liberal Studies?

Another change in educational theory occurred when psychologists cast doubt on the psychological rationale for a unified program of liberal studies. This work came from scientists such as Edward Lee Thorndike, who built on Hall's general framework but used more sophisticated methods. As a result, Thorndike transformed the child-study movement into educational psychology (Ross 347–348).

The educational theory Thorndike criticized was called the transfer of training. The Committee of Ten's report argued that when the main recommended subjects were taught consecutively and thoroughly, they would all train the powers of observation, memory, expression, and reasoning. In making this assertion, the Committee of Ten fell back on the Yale Report of 1828. The theory was that a person could learn something—Latin, for example—that was unrelated to something else—accounting, for example—and the first study, Latin, would aid the later efforts, accounting, because the brain had become stronger or better in certain ways.

In 1901 Thorndike published a series of articles stating that improvement in one mental function did not influence the efficiency of other mental functions. Working with

R. S. Woodworth, Thorndike concluded that those entities once labeled faculties, such as sense discrimination, attention, memory, observation, or accuracy, did not exist. It was unreasonable to speak of narrow functions such as attention to words or accurate discrimination of lengths. Instead, he argued that the mind appeared to be a machine that reacted in particular ways to particular situations. Thus, what was called the faculty or function of attention was a collection of several abilities rather than a particular trait (Thorndike and Woodworth 249–250).

The experiments Thorndike and Woodworth conducted were constructed in the following manner: Subjects performed tasks until they developed a level of proficiency. At that point, they applied the skills those tasks required to other tasks. For example, subjects learned how to estimate the size of rectangles. When they achieved a degree of proficiency, they had to estimate the size of other shapes. However, the ability to estimate the size of the new shapes was different. That is, the more similar the new shape was to the original shape the more likely subjects were to estimate correctly. The more unlike the original shape, the less likely subjects were to estimate the size of the new shape (Thorndike and Woodworth 249–250).

According to some accounts, Thorndike's experiments destroyed the grounds on which claims for a unified curriculum could be built because they showed there was no direct transfer of abilities from one activity to another. It was not that simple, however. For one thing, Thorndike expressed his conclusions in scientifically cautious words. A more accurate illustration of the influence of the experiments and the reasons why fewer educators justified their courses on the grounds of mental discipline appeared in Thorndike's introduction to education published in 1912.

Written for students in colleges and normal schools preparing to be teachers, *Education: A First Book* offered an overview of the field. Thorndike defined mental discipline as an increase in the student's general powers to respond well in thought, action, and feeling. He acknowledged that this was a reasonable aim for all educators. The question was how to achieve such improvements in all capacities. After reprinting the description of his experiments as a chapter, Thorndike concluded that the disciplinary value of any training was a question of fact to be measured, not an article of faith to be believed. He called for more experiments of various methods of teaching and of different subjects. At the same time, Thorndike criticized the tendency to justify studies on the sole grounds that they would be useful to students in later life. Except in the case of skills such as reading and writing, these claims often turned out to be false. On the other hand, he added, the capacity of any study to improve students' abilities in other functions was not clear either. For example, geometry could not improve a student's reasoning powers if the student only memorized the information. As a result, unless someone could prove that courses such as geometry offered general improvements such as advancing students' abilities to reason from general principles, those courses should not be required of all students (Thorndike 1, 42–45, 112–122).

In the conclusion of his text, Thorndike noted that schools were offering more varied curricula than had been the case some years earlier. However, these changes were not complete enough to suit him. In the case of elementary schools, Thorndike contended that most offered what he called a traditional program of studies concentrating on reading, writing, and arithmetic. Thorndike predicted this uniformity would change, as it had in the high schools. He noted that in 1910 high schools required the same number of academic courses as they had in 1890, but the number of courses such as bookkeeping, stenography, manual training, mechanical drawing, and domestic science had increased dramatically. Thorndike offered two simple explanations for these changes. People did not believe that children should be taught the same things children were taught fifty years earlier. Most important, school size and student enrollment had increased. With larger facilities and more teachers, schools could offer more things to a greater variety of students (Thorndike 268–275). Therefore, Thorndike noted that his studies did not destroy the old curriculum. At best, they aided a process already under way.

At any rate, Thorndike accurately predicted the changes that occurred particularly among the high schools. Although the movement for vocational education began quickly, it soon overtook other educational reforms. In 1906 the Massachusetts Commission on Industrial Education called for more direct training in the high schools, and it recommended separate vocational schools. The NEA appointed a committee to consider the place of industry in public education. In 1910 this committee responded with similar recommendations. As a result of these recommendations, Massachusetts, New York, Connecticut, New Jersey, and Wisconsin established state systems of vocational education (Krug, *Secondary School* 370–372).

In compiling these reports, commission members disparaged the older form of manual training as too much a school subject and not sufficiently tied to a vocation. For example, in the 1906 report of the Massachusetts Commission on Industrial Education, the authors complained that manual training was taught as a cultural subject used to stimulate other intellectual efforts. As a result, they saw it as disconnected from the problems of having a job, as were the traditional subjects (Massachusetts Commission 72).

As advocates of vocational education began to look for federal support, they established in 1906 the National Society for the Promotion of Industrial Education. This group lobbied Congress for legislation aiding industrial training in high schools. Although the society's first efforts failed, Congress set up a commission to study the matter. In February 1917, Congress passed the Smith-Hughes Act, which established the Federal Board for Vocational Education and appropriated funds for teacher training and salaries in agriculture, trade and industrial training, and home economics (Krug, *Secondary Schools* 372–373).

Minnesota offered an indication of how rapidly vocational education spread. In 1915 school authorities complained that farms in these largely rural districts had changed. Therefore, the schools must change as well. In the days when farms produced most of their own clothes, food, and furniture, schools could offer cultural activities and children would develop manual skills at home. In the twentieth century, farmers bought those items in stores and children had less to do at home. Therefore, educators argued that children had to learn manual skills at school. With industrial training, the state superintendent of schools said, the child who left after high school would have the skills necessary to get a job. As a result of this attitude, the legislature passed laws and the schools adopted programs encouraging industrial training. In 1908 a total of 5,864 men and women in Minnesota high schools studied industrial subjects such as manual training, cooking, sewing, and agriculture. By 1913 the total had grown to 23,882. The greatest jumps in enrollment were in areas such as cooking, sewing, and agriculture—those more vocational in nature than typical of manual training (Foght 33).

Vocational education spread at the same time high school enrollments increased. In the 1889–90 school year, fewer than 300,000 students, or about one-half of one percent of the total population, attended high school. These numbers grew dramatically. By 1914–15, about 1,500,000 students—1.5 percent of the population—enrolled (Krug, *Secondary School* 31).

Industrial education grew because it was a popular addition for students who did not have an interest in academic subjects such as geography or history. Thorndike's psychological studies did not cause teachers to offer different courses for different students. But by weakening the ideas of formal discipline, they may have reduced the number of reasons why teachers should try to convince students they should learn things such as mathematics and foreign languages. Faced with unruly, unwilling, or dull students whom the newly enacted compulsory education laws prevented them from expelling, teachers and administrators had to offer those students something else to do.

Perhaps for a similar reason, educators adopted special classes that allowed students to stay in school but segregated them from the regular classes. At any rate, special classrooms appeared in schools immediately after compulsory attendance laws took effect. For example, in 1897 Pennsylvania adopted compulsory attendance legislation, and special schools appeared in Philadelphia in 1898. Likewise, in 1902 Maryland adopted compulsory school attendance laws. Shortly thereafter the superintendent of Baltimore's schools said that they would have to make some provision for boys who were unmanageable in the regular classroom. In 1903 Baltimore introduced some ungraded classes for those pupils who for a variety of reasons did not make normal progress (Tropea 29–30).

Did Diversified Curricula Reinforce Social Biases?

When educators adopted diversified curricula, critics complained that they destroyed the idea of schools as a ladder up which aspiring children could climb. They feared that the schools became a series of ladders that reached in a variety of directions, with some leading higher than others. For example, John Dewey predicted that vocational courses would be for the masses and the humanistic or cultural studies would be geared to the well-to-do elite. As early as 1876, William T. Harris, whose ideas dominated the reports of the Committee of Ten and the Committee of Fifteen, complained about the tendency to provide a semitechnical education to the children of common laborers and to offer the children of wealthy people studies in cultural subjects. Instead of supporting such differences, he urged colleges to require students to think and write clearly in English. This would improve the high schools, which would produce citizens who could build a better society. However, reformers did not worry about reinforcing social class distinctions. They promised that diverse programs allowed students to prepare for the futures they could reasonably expect.

Some observers argued that the diversified curriculum did not distort the ideal of the academic high school until much later. For example, David Angus and Jeffrey Mirel compiled patterns of courses that students took in U.S. high schools from 1890 to 1995. They found that from 1890 to 1920, vocational education made important changes in high school curricula. However, they also found that large numbers of the students who could stay in school did not take vocational courses. The overwhelming percentage of these students took traditional academic courses in English, mathematics, science, and social studies. The classes for which enrollments declined were in the foreign languages, and the fields of English and social studies absorbed most of the students who avoided foreign languages. Angus and Mirel argue that the idea of curriculum differentiation did not gain control, nor did students enrolled in courses other than academic ones, until the 1950s (53–54, 117–119).

Although most people thought of U.S. high schools as places where students learned the academic skills that helped them participate in a strong, democratic society, educators tried to weaken this ideal. Despite many educators efforts to diversify the curriculum, the high schools were so much a product of Harris's principles that, as late as 1948, Henry Pochmann contended that most people thought of them in ways that matched Harris's proposals (Pochmann 114). However, professional educators argued that Harris's five basic academic subjects did not serve students from a modern society. They complained that students disliked academic subjects and dropped out before graduation. As a result, high school educators added pressure to meet students' individual needs with a mixture of academic and vocational studies. This caused critics to complain that educators did not appreciate the value of intellectual activities. In reply, educators pointed out the problems of trying to bring together different types of people under uniform academic instruction. However, academic conservatives indicated that curriculum differentiation frustrated the democratic aims of the high school. This statement continued until the 1960s.

TIMELINE
1890–1915

1890 Harvard University President Charles W. Eliot objected to high school and college academic standards

1892 C. W. Eliot pushed the NEA to define distinctions between high school and college

1892 Joseph Mayer Rice wrote about corruption and weak teachers in U.S. school systems

1892 The NEA formed the Committee of Ten to write a report on high school expectations and college requirements

1894 Nicholas Murray Butler passed a bill through the New York legislature to reform school administration

1894 John Dewey accepted a professorship at the University of Chicago

1895 The NEA's Committee of Fifteen reviewed elementary school programs

1895 B. T. Washington addressed the Atlanta, Georgia, Cotton States and International Exposition

1895 The Herbart Society was founded

1897 Pennsylvania adopted a compulsory school attendance law

1897 John Dewey served as a trustee for Hull House

1898 President McKinley visited Tuskegee Institute

1899 B. T. Washington toured Europe, met Queen Victoria, and received an honorary degree from Harvard

1901 John Dewey observed that most educational reforms passed through popular and unpopular phases

(continued)

TIMELINE Continued

1901 Edward Lee Thorndike argued that improving one mental function does not help other mental functions

1902 Maryland adopted a compulsory school attendance law

1902 The Herbart Society was renamed the National Society for the Scientific Study of Education

1903 Charles McMurry published a book based on Herbart's principles

1903 W. E. B. Du Bois criticized Tuskegee for encouraging African Americans to give up higher education

1904 G. Stanley Hall published a book on adolescence

1906 The Massachusetts Commission on Industrial Education recommended separate vocational schools

1906 The National Society for the Promotion of Industrial Education was established

1909 Leonard Ayres published his survey of students' progress in schools

1910 Berkeley schools divided grades 7 through 9 by building

1910 The NEA recommended separate vocational schools

1911 Fletcher Dresslar surveyed U.S. school buildings

1911 G. Stanley Hall supported the child-study movement

1915 Minnesota schools adopted industrial training programs

1918 NEA sponsored the Commission on the Reorganization of Secondary Education

CHAPTER

6 Science, Sexism, and Theology: 1918–1930

A woman welds with a blowtorch.

OVERVIEW

In 1918 the National Education Association's Commission on the Reorganization of Secondary Education released what is often called the Cardinal Principles Report, which contradicted the views of the Committee of Ten. According to the commission, the cardinal principles came from an analysis of the activities people undertook in modern society. Other

Social Class Discrimination and Sexism

- Cardinal Principles–Activity Analysis
- Scientific Curriculum Making
- Home Economics
- Business Training
- Social Studies
- Project Method
- Catholic Schools

educators called this method scientific curriculum making, asserting that it provided an objective way to decide what students needed to learn to become contributing adults in society. Although such a view appeared to accommodate the diversity that existed in society, it led to proposals that justified segregation and maintained social inequities. This problem became clear in the education of women and the development of the social studies.

The home economics movement began as an effort to prepare women to assume civic leadership, but its direction changed after the Cardinal Principles Report and home economics reinforced gender inequalities. Furthermore, women took business training, which offered work outside the home. Unfortunately, after 1918 such work fell into sexually segregated domains, and business courses prepared women for those limited domains. In a similar way, the social studies were developed by a subcommittee of the NEA's Commission on the Reorganization of Secondary Education. The Committee on Social Studies changed the aim of courses such as history from teaching students to make judgments to enabling them to explore their society. However, the aim of citizenship served a popular aim of Americanization in which immigrants, African Americans, and Native Americans learned to adjust to the demands of mainstream society.

As the idea that schools should help students meet the needs they would have as adults became popular, some educators argued that schools should meet the needs children had as children. In 1919 a group of educators formed the Progressive Education Association, dedicating themselves to using science in ways that would enable each child to develop freely and fully. They claimed the laws of learning indicated that children had to be free to choose their own projects. The argument was that when schools met these childhood needs, children would grow into productive, democratic adults. Ironically, sexism reappeared in these projects.

Despite the possibility that science served a wide range of social aims, studies of course selection indicated that schools using scientific methods of constructing curricula reinforced class distinctions. That is, children from lower-class families studied vocational programs to prepare for low-income jobs, while children from wealthier families pursued courses that led to college. But the fact that curricula were built around science did not cause this discrimination. Catholic educators looked to more theological models of curriculum building, yet parochial schools experienced problems with sexism similar to those found in public schools.

Why Did Educators Seek to Reorganize Secondary Education?

In 1890 Charles W. Eliot called the attention of the National Education Association (NEA) to the problem of articulation between high schools and colleges. As a result of his appeal, the NEA's Committee of Ten met and decided in 1893 that all students should study the same courses whether or not they were planning to attend college. However, in 1918 the NEA sponsored another committee, the Commission on the Reorganization of Secondary Education, to reconsider the same problem. The Committee of Ten and the Commission on the Reorganization of Secondary Education were organized in a similar fashion. They were steering committees that coordinated the work of several subcommittees. In the case of the NEA's Commission on the Reorganization of Secondary Education, it directed the work of sixteen committees that evaluated several different subject areas. These included the Committee on Business Education and the Committee on Social Studies. The aim of each committee was to determine how well its assigned subject met the needs of the students in secondary schools and satisfied democratic ideals.

Most important, the Commission on the Reorganization of Secondary Education presented a report that reversed the conclusions of the Committee of Ten. Instead of calling for similar programs for all students whether or not they intended to attend college, this new report called for different courses for different students. Furthermore, instead of listing the courses that students should take, the new report described the objectives that all people needed to achieve to prepare them for life in a democratic society.

According to the commission, education in the United States had to be guided by the meaning of democracy. For members this meant that each member of society should have the opportunity to develop his or her personality through activities designed for the improvement of society as a whole. Consequently, people should learn the knowledge, develop the interests, and cultivate the habits that will earn them appropriate places in society and that will help them use those stations to improve society. Therefore, the commission concluded that educators could decide how to reform curricula by analyzing the activities of the individual (Commission on the Reorganization 9–10).

The commission decided that people belonged to families, vocational groups, and civic groups. They had a margin of time to spend in leisure. Most important, they needed good health to pursue all these activities. They also had to acquire certain tools such as reading, writing, and mathematical skills to participate in these groups. Finally, all people had to have an ethical character. In this fashion, the commission arrived at its seven cardinal principles for education: health, command of fundamental processes, worthy home membership, vocation, citizenship, worthy use of leisure, and ethical character. However, the report noted that schools could meet these principles with specific courses, such as a course on health, or they could integrate the objectives into other courses. For example, need for cooperation between home and community in safeguarding health could be a topic in a social science course (Commission on the Reorganization 9–11).

The commission added that education should be varied to meet the different aspects of the vocational, civic, and leisure lives of the different pupils. Therefore, they recommended that elementary education be devoted to the needs of pupils aged six to twelve years. Secondary education should be broken into junior and senior parts. In the junior high school, students should explore their attitudes and select their future type of work. In the senior high school, students should receive training in the fields they selected. This meant that the curriculum should provide the students opportunities to pursue vocational fields such as agriculture, business, and household arts, and it should provide the necessary experiences for those students with academic interests. Despite this variety, the commission thought that high schools could provide unity to society in three ways. First, the social studies would teach students about society while courses in English and literature would introduce them to culture. Second, students would mingle socially in the building as they pursued their different courses. Third, students would engage in common activities such as athletics, social events, and some aspects of school governance. Thus, the comprehensive high school that embraced all curricula in a unified organization should be the standard type of secondary school in the United States. They felt it was best suited to the needs of the democratic society (Commission on the Reorganization 17–24).

It is not clear how much influence the Commission on the Reorganization of Secondary Education had on education. According to some historians, its impact was insignificant. Henry Perkinson contends that the cardinal principles began the tradition of committees throwing vague, universally appealing slogans at educational problems. Educators used the cardinal principles to convince themselves that schools were giving each child an equal opportunity to advance when there was little evidence this was true. The report could not help because it avoided the important controversies, such as the question of whether academic preparation was more important than vocational training. Perkinson notes that the principle of vocation was buried in the middle of the list of objectives while academics was not listed and could only be assumed under the principle of fundamental processes (148–149).

However, other historians such as David Angus and Jeffrey Mirel argue that the commission's report marked a shift toward the dominance of educational professionals. According to their interpretation, the commission's report steered around the educational debates of the day, such as the place of vocational education, in ways that called for professional curriculum planning to be done by faculty in colleges of education and their allies in school administration. In that way, Angus and Mirel contend, the report tried to give educators the power that university academics and lay people held over the selection of studies (14–19).

Most important for this study, the commission's report seemed to exacerbate the social biases inherent in a differentiated curriculum. As noted in Chapter 5, John Dewey warned in 1916 that a differentiated curriculum would mean one course of study for wealthy people and another for the less fortunate. Unfortunately, the commission's report seemed to justify efforts to change the curriculum in ways that validated the prejudices people in the 1920s felt about the way to improve society and the appropriate place of immigrants, African Americans, and women. The commission's suggestions appeared to turn subjects or programs that had liberal intentions into ones that reinforced existing social arrangements.

Did Educators Create Improved Curricula by Analyzing the Activities of Individuals?

The NEA's Commission on the Reorganization of Secondary Education adopted scientific curriculum making as its model. Franklin Bobbitt advocated this approach of determining what to teach by analyzing the activities of the citizens. In 1918 Bobbitt noted that educators used what he called scientific methods to make budgets, measure the effectiveness of different procedures, and evaluate the progress of students. Bobbitt thought scientific thinking should also be applied to the curriculum. In such a process, Bobbitt wrote, the first task of curriculum makers was to discover the total range of habits, skills, abilities, forms of thought, valuations, and ambitions that students needed for their prospective vocational labors, civic duties, language requirements, religious obligations, and social activities. Although his list included all aspects of human life, Bobbitt cautioned teachers to concern themselves only with those competencies not learned in life. As an example, he offered W. W. Charters's work compiling a list of common grammatical errors from which he arranged courses of study in oral and written language. Bobbitt assured his readers that this model of scientific curriculum design suited all aspects of adult life. For example, investigators could determine the skills workers needed or the portions of mathematics and science workers used in their jobs. Although this method meant that educators were also social reformers, it did not mean that teachers had to reconstruct everything. For example, Bobbitt claimed, if farmers in the school district ignored progressive agricultural practices, teachers should impart the missing skills in an orderly way to the students. However, the list of skills a teacher would select should represent only a portion of those the students needed. The students could learn the rest by further study. Thus, a curriculum rested on an understanding of what ought to exist in civics, morals, vocation, sanitation, recreation, and family life. Teachers' lessons rectified people's shortcomings in each of these areas (Bobbitt, *Curriculum* 41–52).

In 1922 Bobbitt went to Los Angeles, California, with several of his graduate students to construct the curriculum for the city's secondary schools. First, he and his graduate students put together a list of several hundred abilities that students should attain as a result of their school work. Second, the twelve hundred high school teachers selected those items from Bobbitt's list that were appropriate to their circumstances. They could add any they felt were lacking. The result was a list that covered ten classes of everyday life including such things as social communication, development of personal powers, development of mental efficiency, and religious activities. The abilities ranged from the specific to the general. For example, under physical efficiency, one ability was soundness of physique. Another ability listed under the same classification was ability to employ setting-up exercises for corrective and emergency purposes when nothing else is available. From the larger list, each department in the high schools selected those that the teachers of their subjects could achieve. For example, teachers of literature selected objectives such as the ability to use reading as a means of observing people indirectly. From these objectives, the teachers drew up activities. In this case, the literature instructors wrote that the students would read literature that reveals life and institutions in different countries. Finally, teachers drew up a list of assumptions on which their objectives and activities rested. For example, neither knowledge nor skill in literary production is necessary for those who use literature (Bobbitt, *Curriculum-Making* 1–47).

Educational philosophers criticized Bobbitt's ideas. In 1927 Boyd Bode pointed out that Bobbitt's questionnaires did not reveal useful information. When Bobbitt tried to discover what skills the people in Los Angeles thought the students needed to learn, he found that people generally agreed on these skills. But Bode argued that this popular agreement was twofold and meaningless. The agreement was twofold because the people in Bobbitt's sample acknowledged either the need for students to learn specific mechanical skills such as renewing washers in faucets or they agreed to vague objectives such as students needing to protect themselves from social, economic, and political fallacies. Because such agreements could not provide direction for improvement, Bode concluded they were meaningless. Therefore, he claimed that Bobbitt chose his objectives haphazardly. Most important, Bode believed that because Bobbitt set adult activities as the final patterns for a child's growth, he disregarded the need for the progressive transformation of the pupils' experience in the direction of wider social insight (*Modern* 80–88).

Although experts such as Frederick W. Taylor believed that the efficiency movement would not force workers to work harder, the new efficiency-minded administrators thrust a wide range of new tasks on teachers. In addition to imparting academic skills, teachers acted as social workers watching students at school and visiting their homes to ensure that they cared for their health. In the newly created homerooms, teachers acted as advisors and completed clerical tasks such as maintaining attendance rolls. Teachers administered mental tests to determine what courses students might pursue. They administered achievement tests to show how much students learned and how well the teacher performed his or her tasks. Furthermore, teachers instilled feelings of patriotism in students. According to many teacher representatives, the tasks grew too rapidly and encompassed too many areas to be accomplished in a reasonable fashion (Rousmaniere 54–74).

Did Educators Offer Separate Studies for Women?

Following its principle of determining the aim of education by analyzing the activities of individuals, the NEA's Commission on the Reorganization of Secondary Education suggested that women should be trained for different duties than men. In its 1918 report, the commission asserted that its third cardinal principle, worthy home membership, required the school to develop in students those qualities that would make an individual a worthy family member. In a literature class, for example, the reading selections could idealize the human elements that make up a home. However, the report complained that girls were not receiving the preparation in homemaking skills they needed to be wives and homemakers. Even those women preparing to enter wage-earning occupations would need such training. The report noted that after a few years these female wage earners began the homemaking that was their lifelong occupation. Therefore, the report urged that schools consider the training of women to properly manage homes to be as important as any other goal. Male students should learn to appreciate the value of a well-appointed home and the skills required to maintain it. In this way, men would learn to cooperate effectively (7–8).

Despite these calls for a different education, more women attended and finished high schools than men. For example, in 1909 Ayres had found that in the high schools, 57 percent of the pupils were girls and 43 percent were boys. For every 100 girls who entered high school, there were 79 boys. Although dropout rates were high, 31 percent of the girls continued to the fourth year of high school, while only 25 percent of boys made it that far. Among elementary schools, Ayres found a similar bias. Boys were 13 percent more likely to repeat grades than girls, and 17 percent more girls continued to the final elementary school grade. Ayres concluded that schools were better fitted to the needs of girls than they were to the needs of boys (7, 157).

In making these observations, Ayres ignored many other reasons for the discrepancies in school success. For example, boys may have left school to go to work. This might have been particularly the case for African Americans, for whom the disparity in graduation rates between the sexes was greater. School graduation may not have helped Black men find employment, whereas it was necessary for Black women to become teachers (Tyack and Hansot 171–172).

Although women performed better than men in secondary schools, educators argued that women needed different courses in high schools for two reasons. First, women dropped out of high school because they found the courses uninteresting, irrelevant, or unsuited to their abilities. Second, homemaking courses afforded women the opportunity to prepare for what they would do in the future.

This emphasis on homemaking was not surprising. Since the Civil War, increasing numbers of women worked for wages. By 1920 roughly half the nation's female population age twenty and older had worked for a wage. Most of them worked between the ages of fifteen and twenty-five. The most appealing area of work was in business, where clerical opportunities opened up for women. In fact, these positions became identified as women's work, and more than 80 percent of such positions were filled by women. However, most women's working careers were short, and few women older than twenty-four held jobs. Consequently, as high school education became more popular, women dominated two fields of study: home economics, which was clearly labeled as a course for women, and business. Ironically, educators rarely openly stated that business courses were for women. Yet most of the students enrolled were female (Rury 93–96, 151).

Did the Home Economics Movement Reinforce Gender Inequalities?

The home economics movement took an important change of direction at about the time the Commission on the Reorganization of Secondary Education released its report. It began in the 1890s as a movement to train women for positions of institutional leadership. After 1911 the home economics movement emphasized preparing women for their lives as wives and mothers. In part, this change of focus took place because of changes in the leadership of the movement.

Ellen Richards was one of the founders of the home economics movement. Before her efforts, home economics instruction in schools was analogous to manual training for boys. It focused on teaching girls to cook and sew. Domestic science taught women how to become effective servants. However, Richards tried to turn home economics toward professional training by educating young women to be leaders in their homes and their communities.

A graduate of Vassar, Richards studied chemistry at the Massachusetts Institute of Technology and taught there until her death in 1911. In the 1890s, she became involved in the New England Kitchen, which served inexpensive nutritious meals to immigrants in Boston. Richards took the dishes from the kitchen to her chemistry lab to test their nutritive value. However, the Kitchen failed to change the eating habits of immigrants who saw in the Yankee food a veiled attempt to Americanize them. In 1897 Richards joined the Boston School of Housekeeping. Originally founded to teach immigrants to be effective domestic servants, the school failed to attract students because the women could obtain employment without training. Richards redesigned the curriculum to teach young women scientific theories they could use to manage institutions. In fact, one of Richards's students, Marion Talbot, left the School of Housekeeping to become the dean of women at the University of Chicago (Stage 20–25).

Richards succeeded in having Wellesley and Smith Colleges offer domestic science courses. In 1893, however, Bryn Mawr College rejected the proposal on the grounds that the subject lacked intellectual content. When other colleges rejected her proposals, Richards turned her attention elsewhere. From 1899 to 1907, Richards met with interested people in the summers at Lake Placid, New York, to define and advance home economics. Attendance at these conferences grew from eleven to seven hundred people. Although they had difficulty deciding what to call their field, Richards and the other conference members settled on the term "home economics" because it blended domestic science, economics, sociology, and what Richards called euthenics, or the science of controlling the environment (Stage 25–27).

In 1909 the Lake Placid conference became the American Home Economics Association (AHEA). In its constitution, the group declared as its aim the improvement of the conditions of living in the home, the institutional household, and the community. To achieve this broad aim, the association petitioned schools and colleges to recognize subjects related to the home in their curricula. The U.S. commissioner of education praised the AHEA for stimulating the development of practical courses in home economics. Columbia University opened a school of household arts, and the Santa Barbara, California, State Normal School opened a school in manual arts and home economics. The University of Wisconsin offered similar courses, as did Stout Institute in Menomonie, Wisconsin. These programs were established to train teachers to work in the public schools (U.S. Bureau of Education 11, 175–178).

After Richards's death in 1911, members of the AHEA disagreed about the proper direction of home economics. Because she defined the home as the entire community, Richards had asserted that home economics was a training ground for good citizenship. Therefore, she and her disciples had trained women to reform public facilities. But efficiency experts such as Catherine Frederick took a narrower view of the home and tried to turn the movement away from training career women. In returning to the simpler origins of the field, they sought to teach women how to decorate the house, plan balanced meals, and care for their own children instead of trying to improve the lives of immigrant children (Stage 29, 31).

Despite the change in direction, vestiges of the former, more exalted efforts remained. As a result, critics claimed that home economics suffered because its supporters disagreed about their aims. For example, in 1915 David Snedden, an advocate of vocational education, worried that courses such as cooking devoted too much attention to abstract principles of science at the expense of practical instruction. He complained that courses such as the physics of the household could not help anyone understand housework. Although acknowledging that teachers knew the aims of classes in which students learned and applied skills, he found that teachers could not explain why students should learn the skills they did. In part, the aims were confused, Snedden argued, because the home economics programs had been used to train professionals such as future teachers and to shape effective housewives. Unfortunately, he noted, these aims differed (263–289).

Despite the confusion in aims, the home economics programs spread. In 1917 Congress approved the Smith-Hughes Act that, besides providing federal funds to agricultural and industrial training, supported homemaking education and signaled acceptance of homemaking as a career. As a result, more schools offered these courses. By 1920 six thousand high schools included home economics in the curriculum, and land grant colleges in all but eight states offered home economics programs (McGrath and Johnson 12–13).

Even with federal and private support, home economics courses suffered from low student enrollments. In 1910 only 3.8 percent of the students in grades 9 through 12 took homemaking courses. This rose to 12.9 percent in 1915. Although the figures continued to increase, they did so slowly. By 1928 only 14.3 percent of the students took home economics. When George Counts surveyed the high school curriculum in 1923–24, he found that only 4.7 percent of the total recitation time was spent on home economics (Krug, *Secondary Schools* 477–478).

Some advocates of homemaking argued that immigrant families could profit most from this aspect of education. They believed that immigrant women did not realize the importance of good nutrition and cleanliness. According to these home economists, even destitute families could improve the health of their members by employing proper homemaking techniques. Despite these assertions, home economics courses were least popular in the Northeast where large immigrant populations lived. However, immigrant women may not have pursued home economic courses because they did not think of housekeeping as a profession for which one prepared; women were not paid to keep their homes (Rury 144–146).

The aim of training wives and mothers seemed to permanently mark the field as a study appropriate for women. Despite efforts to include men, the field remained female dominated. For example, in the 1930s, some textbooks in home economics contended that the material and the problem-solving skills were appropriate for both boys and girls. The authors wrote descriptions to include men and frequently used the masculine pronoun to refer to a student. Nonetheless, in the 1938–39 school year, less than one percent of the students enrolled in home economics courses were boys (Apple 92).

In time, home economists came to praise the confusion of aims that marked the field. In 1933 Lita Bane complained that home economists did not know if they were teaching a course that was part of general education to improve home and family living, or if they were training students to work in fields such as hospital dietetics or teaching. Bane urged home economists to concentrate on service to the family. But in a little more than ten years, Bane came to praise the situation she had criticized. In 1945 she wrote a school text with Mildred Chapin in which the authors noted that the study of home economics prepared people for a variety of tasks in addition to improving family life (Brown 430–431).

In short, home economics illustrated how the Commission on the Reorganization of Secondary Education validated the prejudices people felt about the role of women. In the 1890s, the home economics movement was an effort to enhance the prominence of women in society. After the 1918 report, home economics lost that direction.

Did Business Education Segregate Women?

In 1918 the Commission on the Reorganization of Secondary Education urged commercial educators to broaden their scope. Through its Committee on Business Education, it called for more general rather than specific preparation. In response, schools developed courses in business organization and store practice to train students in more professional aspects of commercial life. In addition, schools adopted other courses such as economics and commercial geography to explore broad social values common to all human activities (Haynes and Jackson 56–57; Krug, *Secondary School* 452–453). Although such business training would appear to be gender neutral, this was not the case. In the same way that home economics reinforced the separate nature of women's work, business education validated the separate domains that characterized most business enterprises.

Business education did not become a popular field in public schools until after World War I. Although the report of the Commission on the Reorganization of Secondary Education influenced the growth of this field, it was not a determining factor. Commercial training such as bookkeeping had long existed, but private business or commercial schools satisfied the demand. Tuition fees varied from $50 to $200 for a school year of about ten months. Students paid these high fees to earn comparatively low salaries, but the school excelled at teaching technical skills such as bookkeeping or, after 1872, stenography. By the end of the nineteenth century, such private business schools were popular. For example, in 1876 in New York City there were 137 private commercial schools. By 1886 the number grew to 239. During the same period, enrollments in those schools rose from 25,234 to 47,176. When parents objected to public school officials about the need to send their children to private schools for instruction, business education expanded into the public high schools. As the typewriter gained acceptance in businesses in the 1890s, courses in typing and related skills such as stenography appeared in public school curricula. However, typing and stenography courses were offered as additions to the more academic programs in public schools rather than as part of business programs. Many commercial courses were offered in shorter, two-year programs. By the 1920s, though, most schools expanded business courses to four years (James 3–48; Krug, *Secondary School* 444–446).

Business training in public schools grew at a rapid rate. In 1893 the number of students enrolled in public school business courses was 15,220. By 1915 that number increased to 208,605. This was an increase of 1,270.5 percent, much greater than the increase of students in high schools in general. In those same years, 1893 to 1915, enrollments in all public high schools grew from 254,023 to 1,328,984. This was an overall increase of 423.1 percent (Haynes and Jackson 51–52).

Although many students studied business, they selected from a narrow range of courses. In 1915 one-half of the students in Boston took commercial courses. In San Francisco and Philadelphia, one-third of the students were enrolled in business programs. New York, Cleveland, Boston, and San Francisco had their own public business high schools. By 1919 one-fourth of all students in secondary schools studied business. However, six courses or subjects took up 90 percent of the recitation time. These were bookkeeping, typing, stenography, commercial law, commercial arithmetic, and commercial geography. Other subjects—salesmanship, accounting, office practice, spelling, and penmanship—took up most of the remaining 10 percent (Krug, *Secondary School* 446–449).

Besides broadening the studies, commercial educators reformed instruction. For example, in 1913 Ellwood Cubberley claimed that the typical high school business program included American history, bookkeeping, typewriting, and stenography as well as commercial geography, penmanship, and commercial law. Everything was theory, Cubberley complained, or taught by drill and repetition so that students acquired narrow skills and memorized information but did not apply their lessons to business practices. As a result, the learning was ineffective. By 1926, however, Cubberley found improvements. In many high schools, the bookkeeping department managed the accounts for athletic teams, such social affairs as proms, and the cafeteria. In other schools, the commercial department monitored the required program in wood shop. In these cases, the wood shop instructor issued a payroll to each student. The commercial department maintained a bank in which the students deposited their earnings. In order to pass shop class, students had to accumulate a particular sum, perhaps fifty dollars, in their accounts ("Commercial Education" 7–8).

It is important to note that most businesses did not divide their tasks into men's and women's spheres until after World War I. Before 1890 clerical work was a way for men to enter companies and begin a career. As businesses grew and government regulation increased, companies found that they had to maintain regular correspondence and careful records. These jobs became routine and offered little chance for promotion. Eventually, employees became segregated to some extent; tasks such as typing fell to women whereas bookkeeping was reserved for men. At any rate, by 1920 clerical work was considered a feminine domain (Rury 95–96).

Despite this division of labor, the educational requirements of male and female students in business schools did not vary. In most high schools, boys and girls who enrolled in business courses followed the same requirements. Some cities such as Boston offered single-sex business high schools for girls that offered training for jobs such as telephone operator and salesperson. Detroit sought to establish different requirements in commercial courses for men and for women. However, even when the men and women students attended the same school building and followed the same general program, some classes enrolled mainly women. This separation reflected the practices found in businesses. For example, after 1910 stenography became an increasingly popular course, and by 1927 in this class 85 percent of the students were women (Rury 152–153).

Thus, the report of the Commission on the Reorganization of Secondary Education did not call for distinct training for women entering business. In fact, it contradicted the tendency to offer segregated training by requesting that vocational training be more general than specialized. However, the courses women took in public high schools reflected the biases that existed in the business enterprises where they would seek employment.

Did Educators Use Science to Reinforce Gender Distinctions?

Another way the Commission on the Reorganization of Secondary Education reinforced social biases was its advancement of scientific curriculum making. The problem was that this model of practical curriculum planning did not include any mechanism to test the assumption that women had a separate domain from men.

In 1921 W. W. Charters, a leader in scientific curriculum making, wrote about the reorganization of women's education. First, according to Charters, the administrators or the faculty of a women's college had to determine the ideals for which the school stood. Although such ideals were opinions rather than facts, Charters felt that any list was acceptable if it grew out of careful deliberation. Second, the college should list the activities that women undertook, and, third, the faculty should select those activities that were of primary importance. Fourth, the faculty had to determine how those activities could be best performed. For example, if writing letters neatly was important, the college could collect methods to write neatly. Finally, the faculty had to justify their selections (Charters, "Reorganization" 228–230).

In his article, Charters urged administrators in women's colleges to follow his steps of job analysis to develop the curriculum. In 1923 he described his efforts to construct the curriculum for a school for women, Stephens College in Columbia, Missouri. First, he identified the activities women undertook in their lives by soliciting from women the diaries they kept of a normal week, interviewing one hundred women, and analyzing the duties in vocations suitable for the college's graduates. He divided these activities into the categories of vocational, social, and personal. At the same time, he had faculty members determine among themselves what ideals should control the education. Later, a group of outstanding women and men in various fields evaluated their conclusions (*Curriculum Construction* 328–329).

The activities Charters found important for women focused on areas such as foods, clothing, physical hygiene, communication, reading, and participation in vocations. He broke these activities into parts. For example, within the category of foods he placed items such as the care of food, the disposal of waste, and the preparation of food. He made similar classifications for housewives and for professional women such as secretaries. The required subjects would encompass activities carried on by married and unmarried women, which included such things as clothing, care of health, mental hygiene, and English composition. Charters added a course on aesthetic activities such as music and theater and a course on personal finance or consumer training. Because Charters assumed all women did these things, he argued that they could be required subjects for women in vocational schools or in liberal arts colleges ("Review and Critique" 375–378).

Boyd Bode criticized Charters's ideas of job analysis in the same way he had challenged Bobbitt's. Bode found that the list of functions Charters drew up was reasonable for certain fixed jobs such as spelling or some secretarial tasks. Yet more complicated tasks involving judgment could not be easily taken apart. Second, although Charters could determine the tasks people performed in daily life, he could not show that they should perform these tasks or learn to do them better. This decision was more complicated, according to Bode. For example, Charters's method of job analysis could not tell people what they should do in the future. At best it prepared students for the functions adults performed when the curriculum was being developed. It could not predict what functions people would need twenty-five years later (Bode, *Modern Educational Theories* 95–118).

Applied to women's education, Bode's criticisms were particularly apt. Although Charters could design a curriculum to teach women to perform the tasks most women did, he could not determine whether they should be taught those skills. If women lived and worked in a status subservient to men, Charters's model prepared women to function well within that separate and inferior role. Charters's system contained no mechanism to indicate whether social change was warranted.

However, this did not mean that all scientific considerations of education were essentially sexist. Such investigations could lead to more liberating insights. For example, in 1923 Willystine Goodsell, a professor of education at Teachers College, complained that several scientists advocated distinct types of education for women on the basis of physiological and psychological differences. The most eloquent of these, she wrote, was G. Stanley Hall. According to Goodsell, Hall presented three explanations of the unique place of women. First, males were more likely to vary physically and psychologically and therefore could be agents of progress. Second, men thought differently than women. Third, intellectual pursuits hurt women during their menstrual periods. After describing Hall's views, Goodsell showed them to be unsupported by scientific evidence (*Education* 68–98).

Another method of justifying separate and distinct training for women was what Goodsell called a social view, which claimed that because women play an essential role radiating joy among family and friends, their education should equip them appropriately. This meant more domestic training. Goodsell pointed out that women were working outside the home in increasing numbers and needed vocational training in manufacturing, professional service, and clerical work to perform those functions. If this trend led to women turning their backs on housework and childrearing, Goodsell recommended that professional domestics and nurseries take on these tasks (*Education* 99–119).

Goodsell noted that critics of coeducation had warned that young women would injure their health if they participated in the same activities as men. She pointed out that no studies proved this to be a reasonable fear. In fact, she found more compelling evidence that young women developed strong, healthy bodies when they participated in organized and vigorous sports. She acknowledged that girls matured faster than boys, but she thought this caused them to be better students than the boys, not weaker. Some studies by Thorndike showed that women excelled in humanities and men in the sciences. Although Thorndike attributed this to physiology, Goodsell thought the differences were due to social circumstances (*Education* 121–129).

Although Goodsell criticized the prevailing views that called for distinct training for women, she was not pessimistic. She concluded her book by noting that women's traditional sphere would continue to break down. She also hoped that philosophic inquiries similar to hers would enable women to play larger and more useful roles in the twentieth century (*Education* 349–350).

Did the Social Studies Reinforce Social Prejudices?

Many commentators consider the report of the Committee on Social Studies, a subcommittee of the NEA's Commission on the Reorganization of Secondary Education, as the founding document of the field. In fact, it did not create the social studies. As a result of the report, however, many public schools adopted the model it recommended. According to the commission's report, social studies was a new field formed by joining together traditional subjects such as history, geography, economics, and sociology in ways that helped students meet the principle of citizenship. Although the social studies could have led toward the progressive transformation of the student's experience in the direction of wider social insight, more frequently it prepared students to accept society as it was presently constructed. Unfortunately, this caused social studies teachers to pass on social prejudices as if they were scientific truths.

The Committee on Social Studies was one of sixteen committees that functioned under the guidance of the NEA's Commission on the Reorganization of Secondary Education. Each committee sought to determine how well its assigned subject met the needs of the students and satisfied democractic ideals. The Committee on Social Studies, which met from 1913 to 1916, defined the social studies as those subjects whose content related to the organization and development of human society and to people as members of social groups. These subjects included geography, history, economics, political science, and sociology. The aim of the social studies was to cultivate good citizenship. Thus, from their social studies students would develop loyalties to their city, their state, and their nation that were tempered by a sense of membership in a world community. Graduates of programs developed by schools whose goal was social efficiency aimed at developing these attributes (Committee on Social Studies 17).

It is important to note that the Committee of Ten had, in its report of 1893, also considered the aim of studies such as history, civil government, and political economy. However, the Committee of Ten did not believe that these disciplines fostered loyalties within students as the new commission wanted. Instead, the aim of disciplines such as history and civil government was more cerebral, training students' judgment, preparing them for intellectual enjoyment, and helping them, when they were mature, to exercise a salutary influence on national affairs. In addition, the Committee of Ten thought that courses in history and civil government gave students opportunities to use their knowledge of ancient languages. However, this view contradicted the report of the Committee on Social Studies, which wanted teachers to tailor instruction to their local situation and to the interests of students. In the new social studies, even the study of history was more present-oriented than it had been for the Committee of Ten.

The report of the Committee on Social Studies did not list topics to be covered, nor did it give teachers a pattern from which to organize the subject matter. It suggested broad areas of study, described the principles that should govern instruction, and offered some examples. The report offered two cycles for secondary schools to follow. The junior cycle, intended for grades 7 through 9, included geography, European history, American history, and civics. The senior cycle was intended for grades 10 through 12, and included European history and American history. The senior cycle also offered a culminating experience called the problems of democracy. These were two complete and similar cycles because the junior high school was becoming popular, and students often left school after junior high or went on to vocational preparation. Nonetheless, the senior cycle was broader and more intensive (Committee on Social Studies 17–20).

To describe the first cycle, the report offered the course of study in the Indianapolis, Indiana, schools as a model. In that case, teachers included studies of history and civics with geography. Organized around social problems, seventh-grade geography urged students to determine how geography influenced human history. For example, when the students studied Argentina, they determined why the Argentine Republic had a better opportunity for future development than any other country in South America. Although seventh-grade history was a separate course, it was taught to show the ways in which present conditions had developed. For example, students learned that the U.S. government had its beginnings in Europe many years before the New World was discovered (Committee on Social Studies 25–28).

By the eighth grade, geography was no longer a separate subject but a significant aspect of history, and community civics became an important addition. Closely coordinated with history, community civics taught how a national community came into being. However, this class focused on such elements of welfare as health, protection of property, recreation, education, and transportation rather than on the machinery of government. Most important, in community civics classes the lessons related to the students' lives. The teacher might begin by showing how the selected element of social welfare was important to the students and to other people in the community. At this point, the class might visit a local agency to observe what took place, demonstrating to the students how they should act so that their welfare and that of the community could be enhanced. In the ninth grade, the discussions extended beyond local agencies to national and international relationships that showed how communities depended on each other (Committee on Social Studies 28–31).

The report of the Committee on Social Studies noted that the Indianapolis schools had adapted courses in arithmetic to teach civics. Although called community arithmetic, this was not a separate course. Instead, the title indicated that students solved arithmetic problems that reflected tasks they would do in their homes or neighborhoods. Some problems related to food, clothing, or domestic economy such as using market quotations to calculate the cost of a given meal. Other arithmetic problems concerned things relevant to the industries in the area. In this case, students determined the hourly wage of a worker when given the total salary (Dunn 23–26).

In ninth grade, civics instruction became vocational in order to help students choose their vocations and behave while working. Therefore, the course considered the social significance of work, the social value and interdependence of all work, and the social responsibilities of the worker. For example, the committee described the vocational enlightenment course in Middletown, Connecticut. Students first considered the characteristics of a good vocation, and then they examined eighty or ninety professions in some detail. Finally, they discussed how to choose a vocation, how to prepare for it, and how to carry it out (Committee on Social Studies 33–35).

The Committee on Social Studies hoped that the addition of civics courses to the seventh, eighth, and ninth grades would interest students and keep them in school. Because the sixth and eighth grades marked the end of particular educational segments, many students stopped attending school at these points. The committee hoped that students would find the courses in civics and the problems of democracy more attractive than traditional history courses, providing reasons for them to stay in school (Committee on Social Studies 21).

Although community civics was developed in urban settings, the course could be conducted in rural locales. For example, the report described how in Berea, Kentucky, the students learned about roads. They examined the ways roads were constructed and then practiced arithmetic by determining the cost of hauling produce to market and by comparing the benefits the road provided to the expense of maintaining the roads. The results of these computations indicated the value of the roads, and the students expanded their study of local roads to an analysis of roads in European countries. This led to a history of the development of roads. These activities culminated in a consideration of the way roads aided the development of human cooperation and community (Committee on Social Studies 36).

The committee recommended that as much as possible students should obtain the materials for study from local sources. In examining the protection of property in rural classes in Delaware, for example, the teachers asked the following types of questions: What insects, birds, and animals destroy property in your community? What plant and animal diseases prevail in your locality? Why should the federal government interest itself in these questions? The students were told to go to the state agricultural college to obtain appropriate bulletins and to ask their parents if they used these services (Committee on Social Studies 37).

Similarly, the committee concluded that the study of history should function in the present. The report described how a teacher approached young women in a high school of practical arts who came from working-class families and were uninterested in academics. The teacher began the history lesson on medieval craft guilds by asking the girls' parents to take their daughters to their workplaces during a holiday. She wanted the students to visit the parents' work even if their jobs were as mundane as carrying mortar for bricklayers. In school the students explored how their parents' crafts had changed. From two hundred girls, the teacher heard reports on seventy-five occupations and the ways they developed from the medieval craft guilds to the trade unions. The teacher considered the lesson a success because students were interested in learning and their parents enjoyed telling them about their jobs (Committee on Social Studies 52–53).

The report of the Committee on Social Studies recommended imitating Hampton College by having a culminating course called the Problems of Democracy that would focus the subject matters of history, sociology, economics, and political science on issues the students should understand. For example, in the area of the economic relations of immigration, the report suggested a study of the standards of living of immigrants and Native Americans. The commission gave as examples two social problems that students investigated in the Hampton College curriculum. The first was to compare the impulsive actions of crowds to the deliberative acts of individuals and to evaluate the results of each. The second was to evaluate the power and the effects of tradition (Committee on Social Studies 57–60).

What Was the Source of the Biases in the Social Studies?

When the Committee on Social Studies proposed that schools combine the traditional courses of geography, history, economics, political science, and sociology into the social studies in ways that would teach citizenship, it marked the beginning of social studies as a school subject. However, this was not a new idea. In 1865 the American Social Science Association formed to study and propose solutions to problems such as social injustice and poverty. The members wanted to use education to advance its ideas. In 1887 the U.S. commissioner of labor supported this effort, arguing that the study of social science could help form good citizenship (Saxe 3–4, 110).

Most important for this discussion, the recommended instruction in the social studies was similar to what some people thought should be given to immigrants in New York City and to African Americans and Native Americans at Hampton College. The chairperson of the NEA's Committee on Social Studies was Thomas Jesse Jones, who developed those ideas. In his correspondence, Jones claimed that he wrote the report. However, Arthur William Dunn, the committee's secretary who had worked with the Indianapolis schools, claimed he wrote it. At any rate, the committee's report emphasized Jones's idea that school subjects should teach students to understand the essentials of a good home, the duties and responsibilities of citizenship, the cost and meaning of education, the place of labor, and the importance of thrift. Jones developed these ideas in his own life, in his work with other immigrants, and in his teaching experiences at Hampton College. Although Jones thought that science proved the truth of his idea, they remained his personal biases, which he brought into the social studies (Nelson 85).

Born in 1873 in Wales, Jones immigrated with his family to the United States in 1884. Although he spoke only Welsh when he arrived in the United States, Jones entered Washington and Lee College in 1891. He received a doctoral degree in sociology in 1904 from Columbia University, where he also served as director of the University Settlement House for immigrants in the Lower East Side. In his dissertation, Jones made a detailed study of one urban block in New York City. He noted that teachers harmed the pupils by treating them as individuals. He believed that the schools should train all students to abandon their individual national characteristics and move to the higher, more developed Anglo-Saxon ideal (Correia 98–106).

On graduation Jones moved on to teach in Hampton Institute in Virginia, which offered a curriculum of industrial education. While at Hampton, Jones devised a curriculum in the social studies. The social studies did not teach industrial skills, which the Hampton curriculum emphasized, but Jones thought his approach to the sciences prepared African American and Native American students to function as proper citizens and to act in a socially responsible manner. For example, according to Jones, one of the most important truths revealed by these social studies was that races, like individuals, must grow from one stage to another. As a result of the social studies, Jones wanted African American students to regard the difficulties their race must pass through as the natural difficulties through which almost every race must pass. He wanted them to avoid thinking of these difficulties as the oppression of the weaker by the stronger (Jones, *Social Student* 5).

One lesson clearly demonstrated how Jones justified existing segregation. In a lesson designed to demonstrate to his African American and Native American students the importance of saving money, Jones began student discussions by considering the way these groups, though poor, squandered money when it was available to buy things to suit their tastes. Examples he gave were that African Americans bought useless ornaments instead of substantial garments they could wear for long periods, and Native Americans bought ponies for display instead of cattle to improve their farms. Following this discussion, Jones had students conduct a survey of saving institutions in which they compared the faulty practices of honest but ignorant Black bankers and insurance agents to the practices of the old-line White firms. In this way, according to Jones's curriculum statement, students came to understand the unwillingness of White companies to insure African Americans, and they saw the need for reforms of Black businesses (Jones, *Social Studies* 12–14).

Jones was particularly proud of the way he and his students used U.S. Census Bureau bulletins. Jones wrote lists of questions to guide students in using the reports. These questions asked students to describe the situations in which people lived and to compare the conditions of White and Black people. According to Jones, studying the actual social conditions as described in the census had four benefits:

1. It helped students develop an impersonal scientific attitude toward social problems.
2. It afforded the opportunity for careful reasoning.
3. It imparted knowledge of actual conditions.
4. It taught simple statistics and advanced literacy (Jones 18).

Jones left Hampton College in 1909 with the reputation of being among the leaders in minority education. After working with the U.S. Census Bureau and Howard University, Jones was appointed educational director of the Phelps-Stokes Fund, a private, New York-based philanthropy endowed by its namesake to construct model tenements for poor people and to advance the education of Native Americans and Black people in the United States and Africa. In this capacity, Jones conducted studies of the education in the United States and Africa (Correia 110). Most important for this discussion, he chaired the NEA's Committee on Social Studies to determine the role of the social studies; his bias in favor of preparing immigrants, African Americans, and Native Americans to adjust to the demands of society's existing conditions permeated the work. His ideas were popular because they fit into a model of Americanization that was widespread. However, by 1921 this model of helping immigrants disappeared because Congress passed legislation restriciting immigration. This policy of exclusion remained until 1965.

Did Educators Use Scientific Surveys to Justify Their Own Preconceptions?

Educators used science to reinforce their own perceptions of what would improve schools and society in what became known as the school study movement. In the first decade of the twentieth century, many aspects of social life such as municipal organizations, recreation, and housing were the subject of organized study. Educators seized on this popular idea and claimed that they could improve the schools if they subjected them to scientific study. Unfortunately, these studies were often not objective, nor were they completed carefully. Instead, they were opportunities for a small, interrelated group of people to advance their ideas of how schools should operate.

In 1907 Pittsburgh city schools adapted the land surveys made by civil engineers to make a study of their institutions. In 1910 the schools in Boise, Idaho, introduced an innovation by inviting the superintendent from Indianapolis schools to survey their schools. It soon became a trend to import experts from outside the schools to conduct surveys. For example, in 1911 three prominent educators, including the U.S. commissioner of education, surveyed the Baltimore schools. The resulting report was 102 pages and considered the system of supervision, the training of teachers, the elementary curriculum, and the physical condition of the schools. From 1911 to 1913, a university professor and eleven associates conducted a survey of the New York City schools. The report cost almost $100,000 and filled three volumes, yet it was so critical of the administrative system that the school committee did not accept nor publish part of the report. In 1915–16, Leonard Ayres conducted a survey of the schools in Cleveland, Ohio. His report advanced vocational education programs and tests of reading to measure the achievement of the pupils. After 1915 school districts began to call on the federal government to conduct surveys. The U.S. Department of Education began to do nationwide surveys. The first was a survey of what was called Negro education (Judd 10–11, 13–17).

The rationales for importing experts were that they would have adequate prestige to present a convincing set of recommendations and they would provide objective information. But the outcome of the surveys was predictable. They were generally conducted by a small group of university professors who had achieved fame in school administration. These individuals held generally the same ideas of what was needed to improve schools. For example, favoring a model used in business corporations they recommended changes such as having central administrators select textbooks and faculty. As a result, these school surveys were not accurate assessments of what each district needed. Instead, they were ways for the school reformers discussed in Chapter 5 to reduce the power of neighborhood or ward school trustees (Tyack 129–147).

An example of the political use of school surveys took place in New Mexico. The citizens of that state had been divided on the merits of using Spanish in the instruction of Spanish-speaking children. Some people thought children should learn Spanish in those rural areas where the language was common. Citizens in the more urban section felt that everyone should speak English. In 1915 the state legislature adopted an act that allowed school districts to teach Spanish at any grade level and that permitted the use of Spanish to explain any concept to a student. Another law called for the special training of fifty teachers to teach in the Spanish American communities. In 1917 the legislature required teachers to be able to teach reading in both Spanish and English. The legislature strengthened this law two years later by requiring teachers in rural areas inhabited by Spanish-speaking people to be proficient in reading, writing, and speaking Spanish. Although this represented a victory for the people who favored Spanish, the intention was not to teach Spanish but to help the students who did not already know English. To some extent, the New Mexico Department of Education tried to weaken the effects of the law by reminding teachers that instruction should be in English (Getz 30–36).

The department's view favoring English prevailed, in part at least, through the help of outside experts and a school survey. In 1920 the New Mexico Board of Education invited three experts, George Strayer, William Bagley, and Ellwood Cubberly, to survey the schools in the state. Of the three, only Bagley visited New Mexico, touring the state for eight days. In their final report, the experts disapproved of the policy of providing separate and special preparation for teachers destined to work in Spanish-speaking areas. Instead, they urged streamlining teacher training and saving money by having all teachers attend the same courses of preparation (Getz 37–38).

Was It Beneficial to Separate Children according to Ability Levels?

A more controversial aspect of the application of science to curricula was the tendency to use science to predict students' abilities. A few years before World War I, researchers created mental measurements to evaluate and improve instruction. After the war, these became increasingly popular aspects of school life. From 1910 to 1913, several researchers conducted studies comparing the relative merits of different methods of teaching reading. Subsequently, from 1914 to 1920, researchers developed standardized tests of reading ability so that teachers could assess the achievements of groups of students (Gray 101–102). In spelling, research focused on discovery of words written by adults, arranging them in appropriate sequence for different grades, determining effective ways of teaching, and measuring results (Horn 107). Before 1910 researchers began developing standardized tests in arithmetic that led to changes in the texts because test makers distributed sets of practice problems to teachers. By 1925 elementary school teachers bought millions of copies of these exercises each year (Buswell 125).

Perhaps the most important imposition of the mental measurement movement was through the development of tests of mental ability or intelligence. In 1905 Alfred Binet introduced his first scale of intelligence. Various researchers applied the idea of such testing in the United States, but it was not until World War I that the measures were used on large groups. The U.S. Army used these tests to classify individuals according to their abilities and to reject candidates unfit for service. Soon schools began using the tests as means to direct students into programs appropriate to their abilities and to place students of similar aptitudes together in the same classes to facilitate instruction. The tests were not supposed to be the sole measure, however. They were to be used in conjunction with other information such as school attainments, opinions of teachers, and indications of the student's interests (Colvin 26–27, 33, 44).

Many educators claimed that intelligence testing would improve instruction. Advocates argued that the tests reduced school failure by allowing counselors to place children in programs and in levels appropriate to their abilities. In 1915 one junior high school tried to sort the children according to their grades, measures on achievement, and intelligence tests. After two years, the educators called the experiment a success because most students appeared happy and successful and few left school early (Trabue 177–179). Advocates of such mental measurements argued that intelligence testing and homogeneous grouping enabled high school teachers to adapt instruction and choice of materials to the needs of the group. In such settings, competition was fair and all students had incentives to work hard. In mixed ability classrooms, these advocates noted, the slower students might give up because they could not equal the work of the brightest students (Miller 205–209).

Gender bias in the testing was not a big obstacle for such advocates. For example, although professors at Goucher College for Women acknowledged that most tests were designed for men and ill adapted for women, they used these mental tests to make judgments about applicants and about students in their programs. According to one professor, the tests enabled administrators to place students of similar abilities in the same sections of required courses. Further, the tests could aid in diagnosing academic difficulties by determining whether problems were the result of poor prior training or deficient abilities. In fact, professors at Goucher College tried to use the intelligence test scores of the women pupils to set the grades. Their hope was to arrive at grades that measured what the students had actually achieved rather than grades that reflected the students' innate abilities (Rogers 248–251).

However, many critics complained about the problems with mental testing. William Bagley complained that using the tests to classify children could lead educators to restrict students' opportunities to learn. He warned that the tests did not measure the students' ability as much as they measured the students' achievement. Similarly, Black scholars such as Horace Mann Bond responded to arguments linking intelligence to inheritance that made Blacks and immigrants appear genetically inferior. Bond pointed out that scores of many White Southerners were lower than those of many Black Northerners. To him, environment seemed to be the important variable (Urban and Wagoner 221).

Could Science Liberate Students?

Although scientific measures seemed to serve some groups more than others or to reinforce whatever inequalities already existed in society, a group of educators thought they could use science to free students from any external constraints and allow them to grow as much as possible. In 1919 this group of educators formed the Progressive Education Association (PEA) and selected as their honorary president Charles W. Eliot, former chairperson of the Committee of Ten. In its founding statement of principles, the PEA dedicated itself to helping the fullest and freest development of the individual based on the scientific study of his or her mental, physical, spiritual, and social characteristics. In general, members were associated with small private schools. However, they hoped to transform the entire U.S. school system. Although this aim sounded grandiose, they did actually move in this direction. In 1924 they began a journal, *Progressive Education.* In 1926 they employed a full-time professional director, and John Dewey agreed to become their honorary president. However, by 1930 leadership of the association shifted from the original founders to the professors at Teachers College at Columbia University, who took over control of the association; the organization then began to exercise extensive influence among public school people (Cremin, *Transformation* 240–250).

One reason why the professors at Teachers College took over the PEA was that the schools that were part of the organization followed a model called the project method that William Heard Kilpatrick, an important member of the faculty, had popularized. In 1918 Kilpatrick proclaimed there was a way to use what he called the laws of learning to help children grow naturally. He adapted the ideas of Edward Thorndike, a psychologist, to show that children learn when they pursued activities they enjoyed. According to Kilpatrick, learning was the creation of bonds in people's minds that joined a stimulus to a response. The child's desires provided the motive for reacting, made the inner resources available, and guided the actions toward a reasonable end. The satisfaction of those desires fixed those bonds so that the child developed habits or character. Thus, the project method was built around children's desires. To some extent, Kilpatrick borrowed the idea of the project method from vocational educators who had used similar terms. In Kilpatrick's hands, however, the project method did not prepare children for future activities; it enabled them to enjoy the work they were doing (*Project Method* 2–9).

Teachers had long used home projects to teach students some skills associated with a trade. For example, in farming communities the students who lived on farms recorded the cost of feeding a cow in a particular way, compared the cost with feeding another cow in a less expensive manner, and measured the milk production of both. In this way, students determined whether an expensive diet enabled the cow to produce more milk and thus was worthwhile. Through such a project, students learned arithmetic and agriculture.

Kilpatrick changed the meaning of the term "project method." For him the project method entailed a wholehearted, purposeful activity taking place in a social environment. He believed that when teachers allowed students to set their own purposes and work to a conclusion, students learned to solve problems, think independently, and become honest, cooperative citizens. Projects were bad, he contended, when the aim was to enable students to grasp the subject matter easily. According to Kilpatrick, there were four different types of projects. First, a producer's project required students to do something. Second, a consumer's project required a student to use and enjoy something. The third was a problem project, in which students solved an intellectual difficulty. Fourth, through a specific learning project the student's purpose was to acquire some degree of knowledge. In all projects, however, the students should initiate the process because when they accomplished their own purposes they learned more than they did under any form of coercion. However, Kilpatrick allowed that sometimes teachers had to direct students toward activities such as the specific learning project (*Foundations of Method* 344–367).

In a scientific way, Kilpatrick's students sought to prove the superiority of the project method. For example, from 1917 to 1921, Ellsworth Collings compared the progress of the students in three rural schools in McDonald County, Missouri. One school was the experimental school, which contained forty-one students. The other two schools served as controls. One had twenty-nine students and the other thirty. In most respects, the schools were identical. The students ranged from six to fifteen years of age; their abilities, school success, and attitudes toward school were the same, and they came from similar backgrounds (Collings 4–10).

The biggest difference between the control and the experimental schools was the curriculum. The control schools implemented the traditional subject curriculum, which was published in book form and consisted of 220 pages outlining the amount of work the teacher was to do each quarter of each term. The text contained lists of supplementary books and materials in agriculture, cooking, and manual training that teachers should use in conjunction with the subjects. In the experimental school, the curriculum was defined as the purposes of the boys and girls in conjunction with the cooperation of the supervisor and the teacher. These purposes became projects (Collings 13–14).

In all cases, the school day ran from nine o'clock in the morning until four o'clock in the afternoon. In the control schools, the curriculum moved along quickly with the students changing activities every ten to twenty minutes. Students took one hour for lunch and two ten-minute recess periods during the day. In the experimental school, there were four blocks of about an hour and a half, a thirty-minute lunch period, and a thirty-minute playtime after lunch. Story projects, in which students read aloud, sang, or listened to phonographs, came first in the day. Hand projects followed. In these, students made or did things such as construct rabbit traps or prepare cocoa for lunch. Excursion projects came last; these were opportunities for the students to learn more about the community in which they lived (Collings 25, 47–48).

In the control schools, the curriculum followed a traditional program. For example, in geography students considered why countries such as Greece depended on ocean trade. In history they read about the early problems and successes of the pioneers in Missouri. In nature study, they gathered flowers, learned their names, studied the parts of the flower, and played games to reinforce these lessons. In arithmetic students measured things in the room. They learned the number facts and counted money (Collings 25–43).

In the experimental school, on the other hand, the projects were generated by the students, and the teacher helped them pursue their ideas. For example, after a student asked why a local family experienced recurring cases of typhoid, the students decided to ask the family if they could visit. The family invited them to come, and the students began seeking information about the causes of typhoid. They made a list of things to check during their visit such as drinking water, waste disposal, and food sources. After careful consideration of what they discovered, the students decided that flies probably transmitted the disease among members of the household. The project led to concerns about exterminating these insects or keeping them away from the home. As a result, students visited other farmers to see how they controlled flies. They found various ways to dispose of animal manure and rubbish, and they made garbage pails and fly traps. They wrote an extensive report, which they delivered to the family that suffered from typhoid. The family accepted the report and carried out the recommendations. As a result, typhoid did not appear in that house during the next year. This project led the students to investigate other diseases in the community and to deliver a report to the townfolk during a community meeting (Collings 54–66).

Collings thought that several conditions and steps made the projects effective. Most important, the teacher had to allow the students freedom to select their own purposes in order to ensure that they wanted to do the work. Although the projects could be individual, they were often group activities. In either case, the teacher talked with the pupils to select the project and to decide how to carry it out. As the group talked about what they wanted to do, one student wrote the ideas on a board. The students and the teacher selected one of the ideas. This choice was placed on a project bulletin board along with the related ideas. In this way, students could see alternatives as they proceeded with the project. The first criterion for selecting a project was practicability, or whether the students were capable of planning, executing, and evaluating their project. The second criterion was that it led to other activities. These activities could be similar, as when a girl made an apron for her doll and then a cap, or the activities could branch into new areas, as when the girl made dishes and furniture for her doll. In the second case, the activities branched because the processes, sewing and pottery, differed. In all cases, the students had to carry out the projects. They conferred with the teacher, but the students planned how to accomplish their aims, and they had to execute the plan. Collings suggested that the teachers and students label the projects in order to organize the day. That is, each day the different groups did more than one project. However, Collings suggested that similar types of projects should take place at the same time. Those that were noisy should be done at one time and projects that were quiet could be done together. Finally, the students must decide how to evaluate the success of the project and carry out the evaluation themselves. In the case of the typhoid investigation, the family's freedom from sickness was a happy measure. Of course, each step, the results, and ideas for further action appeared on the project bulletin board and in the students' project folders (Collings 317–335).

When it came time to determine the effectiveness of the project method, Collings was gratified to find that the project method was successful. At the end of the four-year period, he administered to the students standardized tests in reading, handwriting, arithmetic, composition, spelling, American history, and geography. Although they took similar tests when the experiment began, the tests were not identical. Consequently, a simple measure of growth was not available. Nonetheless, on the available measures students in the experimental school out-performed the students in the control schools. At the same time, they exceeded national standards on the standardized tests. The students in the experimental school seemed to develop improved attitudes toward school. More students stayed in the experimental school than in the control schools. Daily attendance was higher, tardiness was lower, truancy decreased, and there was less corporal punishment in the experimental school than in the control schools. More students finished the eight-year course and more students went on to high school. The experimental school seemed more attractive to parents; more parents visited the experimental school, attended the annual meeting, and used the experimental school facilities than did control school parents. In public elections, more parents of experimental students voted for things such as school tax levies and starting a consolidated school than did parents of students in the control schools. Therefore, Collings concluded that his experiment demonstrated that the curriculum could be drawn entirely from the students' interests. When the school worked that way, student success increased. The students' attitudes improved and the parents felt closer connections to the school (Collings 225–269, 339–342).

Significantly, Collings's efforts to break the authoritarian model of education did not lead him to confront the notion of gender segregation. For example, in describing the way the projects linked and led to other activities, Collings compared the projects of a girl, Christine, and a boy, Jim. Christine proposes to sew a dress for her doll. Jim decides to build a table. In Collings's example, Christine chooses her project and thereby learns more. The teacher suggests to Jim that he undertake the table construction and he learns less. However, to the feminist reader, these examples and similar ones may suggest that within the project method gender biases could have been frequent.

Was the Project Method a Good Method of Instruction?

It is not clear whether the project method was a valuable contribution to curriculum making. Certainly, many people approved of the innovation, and it became a popular model. However, then contemporary philosophers of education complained that Kilpatrick's ideas offered little that was new. This was particularly unfortunate, they added, because the project method appeared to offer a democratic approach to education. If educators thought deeply about the meaning of democracy, they could offer suggestions that would be most helpful.

Despite the warnings of such philosophers, schools offered more combinations of scientific curriculum making and project methods. They diversified the curriculum in efforts to meet the students' needs. Unfortunately, the effect was to reinforce biases among the social classes.

After Kilpatrick advertised his project method, educators in various parts of the country imitated it. The schools Collings studied were located in rural McDonald County, Missouri. The parents had been born and raised in the communities. They were of English extraction and most of them owned farms of forty to eighty acres where they raised dairy cattle or small fruits, or engaged in general farming. The communities had almost no organized social life. Religious ceremonies were held irregularly, and there were no community meetings, fairs, or recreations beyond occasional parties at individual homes. The teachers averaged twenty-two years of age and about three years of teaching experience. They had high school diplomas and two years of teacher training (Collings 10–13).

Thus, Collings's experiment demonstrated that the project method could serve conservative, rural communities. He contended that it brought the members of a community together in democratic activities. However, through the Progressive Education Association, the plan became popular in public and private schools that served upper- and middle-class urban children. In general, these schools advertised a scientific yet liberating approach to learning. Disparaging traditional subject matter curricula, the teachers gave students opportunities to experiment, and they thought of their work as administrators and teachers as experiments. Whereas the purest applications of the project methods seemed to occur in private schools, public schools combined the project method with some version of scientific curriculum planning.

For example, in a private school, the City and Country Day School in New York City, Caroline Pratt taught in a way similar to the project method. One activity she encouraged with her eight-year-old students was to develop a school store that bought all the supplies for the school. In this activity, students would learn geography, history, arithmetic, and science. The students obtained a loan from the school to buy the supplies, set up books to keep track of paying it back, and set about finding out what supplies to buy and where to get them. In the process, they learned where the supplies originated. The teacher kept copious records to determine what the students had learned. Another teacher in the school organized a different set of activities. These were to investigate the lives of Native Americans and the White settlers. The students sought out information from a range of books and other resources and then created dramas, paintings, and stories to convey what they found. Pratt called her approach experimental although she acknowledged that it resembled Kilpatrick's project method. According to Pratt, the difference was that the project method was concerned with schoolwork. She wanted to make it possible for students to have integrated experiences and thereby live integrated lives (328–332).

In Denver, Colorado, Jesse Newlon instituted a program that combined the project method with scientific curriculum making. The key feature of Newlon's program was that teachers formed study committees that worked under the guidance of professors from nearby universities. Specialists on different subjects and a competent librarian helped them. Although the teachers had difficulty finding ways to fit all the material they felt was essential into projects, the cornerstone of the curriculum was purposeful activity. Thus, they tried to work out ways to show pupils that the material was useful. For example, in home economics the committee surveyed the activities girls participated in at home. Similar job analyses of commercial practices in Denver businesses determined the curriculum in business courses. These tasks became the curriculum as Charters had recommended. The Committee on Social Studies planned a three-year program that was divided into large units. These units were broken down into projects for the students (Newlon and Threkeld 229–238).

Despite the apparent popularity of the project method, philosophers found the concept inadequate. For example, when Boyd Bode criticized other exponents of a science of education, he was equally critical of Kilpatrick's project method. He noted that traditional teachers had used projects for many years and, for example, had students play store to learn arithmetic. However, the teachers knew that students could not learn the entire subject in this way. If they tried, the learning would be discontinuous, random, and too immediate. Bode acknowledged that Kilpatrick countered this problem by admitting there were essentials students had to learn whether they wanted to or not. However, Bode argued that this admission caused Kilpatrick even more problems. That is, the project method was supposed to be effective because the students showed interest in the activities. By saying that students had to learn some things they did not like, Kilpatrick reduced this motive for learning. In fact, Bode thought that Kilpatrick reinforced the unfortunate alternation between free play and the teacher-imposed work that was typical of most classrooms. Bode concluded that Kilpatrick weakened his own revolutionary goal of having schools change the pupils' scale of values and their outlook on life (*Modern Educational Theories* 141–165).

Bode did not disparage the efforts to reform education. In fact, he noted that the concern for educational change came from wider efforts of social change. However, he warned that questions of curriculum reform could not be answered until people knew what sort of culture they wanted. Usually, educators had simply tried to restyle old ideals. He argued that if democratic ideals were appropriate, these would be more complicated than simply spreading more education to more people or fitting them to social life. Bode lamented that educators tended not to engage in the complicated thought necessary in order to shape the educational objectives and teacher training to align with the meaning of democracy (*Modern Educational Theories* 329–348).

Despite Bode's criticisms, schools continued to blend the academic curriculum, the project method, and scientific curriculum making. Educators hoped that such combinations would enable schools to serve democracy. Such diversified curricula were supposed to provide all students with the opportunities to develop their talents and find appropriate places in society. Unfortunately, the comprehensive high schools and the junior high schools that resulted from this conception of education did not advance democracy as much as they seemed to sort the students according to gender and the social class from which they came.

In 1922 George Counts published *The Selective Character of American Secondary Education,* a study of the high school enrollment patterns for three years in Seattle, Washington; St. Louis, Missouri; Bridgeport, Connecticut; and Mt. Vernon, New York. The sample included 17,265 students. When Counts compared the students' parents' occupations to the number of males in each occupation, he found that the students from families in which the father or guardian was a manager, a professional, or a proprietor of a business had a better representation in proportion to their representation in the population than did students who came from families of miners, personal service workers, or laborers. Not surprisingly, when he sought the same information for students *not* in high school, Counts found the picture to be reversed. That is, in comparison to their representation in the general population, more children from families of laborers did not attend high school than children of proprietors, professionals, and managers. When Counts looked at the enrollments in courses, he found that those students from groups that were poorly represented in high schools tended to take practical or vocational courses instead of academic studies leading to higher education. This was even more true for girls than for boys. Therefore, he concluded that the high school was serving the occupational groups from the upper strata of society (5, 32–33, 48, 69–73, 87).

To show that the differences in enrollment patterns derived from social rather than personal factors, Counts looked at the intelligence test scores of the students in the different courses. He found surprising similarity in mental abilities among the students in different tracks. In other words, the median scores on intelligence tests of boys and girls in the college preparatory, scientific, teacher preparation, or commercial courses were not appreciably different (127–129).

Did Catholic Schools Avoid Sexism?

The problems of bias in schools about gender or social class did not come from the application of science, although such distinctions were helped by scientific curriculum making, the use of school surveys, and the introduction of scientific measures of students' abilities. The experiences among Catholic educators illustrates that science did not carry the bias. Although Catholic schools followed what might be called a theological model of curriculum, Catholic educators had difficulties similar to those of public school educators when they considered the education of women.

In 1900 there were about 3,800 parochial Catholic schools enrolling around 900,000 students. These were staffed almost exclusively by teaching sisters or nuns. Although the bishop or archbishop of the diocese or archdiocese was responsible for all the schools, parish priests controlled their parish schools because few dioceses had school boards or superintendents. In addition to diocesan efforts, religious communities invested in Catholic secondary education (Gleason 40–41).

Unlike public educators, Catholics created single-sex schools. At first the curriculum was different, but soon the schools offered girls the same curriculum that boys received. For example, of the more than about six hundred Catholic academies for girls, all were run by religious women and many of them began to metamorphose into colleges. One such religious community, the School Sisters of Notre Dame, founded an academy for girls in Baltimore in the 1860s. Within a decade, it offered collegiate courses, and in 1896 the state chartered it as the College of Notre Dame of Maryland. Six women graduated three years later (Gleason 89).

When Catholic women's academies began in the eighteenth century, the curriculum centered on what Catholics called the four R's: reading, writing, arithmetic, and religion. In addition, the students learned sewing and French. By the end of the nineteenth century, however, the traditional curriculum in a Catholic woman's academy began to parallel that found among the boys: English grammar, rhetoric, literature, logic, history, geography, astronomy, arithmetic, bookkeeping, several sciences, and penmanship. Latin appeared in the girl's schools by 1908. The curriculum shifted from training in what might be called the ornaments to education in the sciences and mathematics as the academies began to offer collegiate degrees. They made these changes because people criticized the women's schools for offering unsubstantial courses (Burns 242–243).

As in the case of public schools, in the nineteenth century there was no direct path from Catholic elementary school to Catholic college, yet many Catholic women pursued higher education. By 1870, 20 percent of the teachers in New York City were Irishwomen. Three decades later, the same was true of other cities with sizable Irish concentrations. Although some religious schools began to offer them higher education, by 1907 almost two thousand Catholic women attended non-Catholic normal schools or colleges. In addition, many women attended the Catholic Summer School. Similar to the Chautauqua movement, this summer school offered four- to six-week sessions combining intellectual and recreational opportunities in places such as Lake Champlain, Maryland, and Louisiana (Gleason 27–28).

In 1884 the Third Plenary Council urged Catholics in the United States to provide Catholic boys and girls with elementary schools, high schools, and colleges where they could learn while surrounded by an atmosphere of piety. Many parish priests tried to open high schools, but few succeeded because such schools drew pupils from only one small district. They were also small and poorly organized. In 1900 the archbishop of Philadelphia opened the first central high school for boys. Drawing students from the entire city, it was large enough to have classrooms, special rooms for manual arts and mechanical arts, laboratories, a chapel, eighteen lay faculty, and two priests who served as administrators. Four years later, the Catholic Educational Association (CEA) approved this model of a diocesan high school, and the idea spread. In 1912 a similar school for girls opened in Philadelphia. However, Catholics did not build junior high schools because the expense of the separate buildings was excessive (Burns, Kohlbrenner, and Peterson 247–249, 252).

In general, the curriculum in the central or diocesan Catholic high schools was the same as the curriculum in the public high schools except that religion played a prominent part. As the curriculum in the public high schools expanded to include more practical subjects, the diocesan Catholic high schools offered these newer practical courses as well. As a result, the spread of Catholic high schools paralleled the explosive growth of the public high schools. In 1900 there were about 50 Catholic high schools. This number grew in 1915 to about 1,300 with 74,600 students. By 1930 there were about 2,230 Catholic high schools and 242,000 students. It is important to note that Catholic high schools grew while the percentage of students attending private schools declined. In 1900 about 39 percent of all secondary pupils in the United States attended private high schools. However, this percentage dropped to less than 9 percent in 1924 (Burns, Kohlbrenner, and Peterson 253–255).

As the central high school movement spread among Catholics, controversies increased about the education desirable for women. In 1907 Thomas Edward Shields, a priest, used the device of a dialogue among seven fictitious characters to describe the controversies surrounding the Catholic education of women. In *The Education of Our Girls,* Shields showed the range of opinions found among Catholics, from conservatives who feared that higher education made women unfit for motherhood to liberals who thought women and men should attend the same schools and study the same intellectual materials. The conclusion to which Shields brought his characters was that women must be able to pursue higher education, but it should be in a segregated and religious setting. That is, the training had to be separate because the women had to learn things suited to their gender such as domestic science. These were supposed to enable them to serve as allies to men and to bring unique qualities to the family and the world even when they became professionals. Their education had to be religious because without this element they would not learn to be ethical.

Cardinal Gibbons, the archbishop of Baltimore and the nominal head of the Catholic Church in the United States, approved of Shields's book. However, Shields sparked controversy by urging Catholic teachers to adopt the progressive ideas of educators such as Kilpatrick. In 1902 Shields became a professor of psychology in the Catholic University of America. He had his own publishing company and produced in 1906, for the correspondence school he established, a text, *The Psychology of Education,* for Catholic school teachers. He published and distributed a journal, the *Catholic Educational Review,* to which he regularly contributed articles. In 1908 Shields delivered a speech to the Catholic Educational Association in which he advocated that religion teachers build on the students' experiences and lead them to understand the doctrines. Conservative critics complained that Shields's ideas of teaching distorted the philosophy of the church, and thereafter his influence in the CEA was limited. Nonetheless, Shields continued to publish textbooks that teachers used in Catholic schools. These were widely adopted, and his ideas spread until he suffered a heart attack in 1917 and his books fell into disuse (Walch 119–124).

Because Catholic educators organized their curriculum around a different set of principles, they faced considerable opposition, although in external appearance Catholic schools were roughly similar to public schools. For example, in 1922 the Masons and the Ku Klux Klan prevailed in Oregon to elect Walter Pierce as governor. Although 90 percent of the children in the state attended public schools, Pierce's supporters had made campaign speeches accusing private schools, especially Catholic ones, of corrupting the children. Shortly after taking office, the state legislature passed and Pierce approved mandatory attendance at public schools. Before this requirement took effect, opponents appealed to the U.S. District Court where, in 1924, they won. The state's attorneys appealed to the Supreme Court, arguing that public schools encouraged students' patriotism. On the other side, the private schools' lawyers contended that students should not be forced to believe any particular ideal. In 1925 the Supreme Court justices rendered their decision in *Pierce v. Society of Sisters.* Although they agreed that schools should encourage good citizenship, they did not think this requirement removed the right of parents to prepare their children for additional duties. Thus, the justices decided that Catholic children could not be forced to attend public schools if their parents wanted to send them to private schools (Walch 156–158).

To some extent, these controversies in the United States prompted Pope Pius XI to issue the lengthiest statement about education and the first papal encyclical to speak to the entire church about education. In 1930 he wrote *Christian Education of Youth.* In it he referred to the Oregon school case, discussed coeducation, and spoke about the proper methods of teaching. Written in response to many requests for a statement about sound principles of education, his letter synthesized all previous church pronouncements on education and became the reference point for any discussion of the position of the Catholic Church on education (Gabert 83). Most important for this discussion, although the encyclical placed theology at the center of Catholic education, it called for the separate education of women.

In his letter, Pius began by noting that education was the means by which human beings perfected themselves. As a result, it had to include Christian religion. He held that the family had the first right and obligation to educate children, but the civil society had preeminence over the family because its aim was the well-being of the community. The church was supreme in its domain, which is the eternal salvation of humankind. The Catholic Church undertook the obligation to teach every branch of learning, culture, and physical education because these helped in the development of religion and morality. It offered this education to the faithful and to those people and countries not yet Christian. This was not an effort to impose on people, the pope added, but an effort to have all levels work in harmony because the natural order should always be in harmony with the supernatural (Pius XI 3–11).

The pope noted that the family's inviolable right to educate the children derived from the fecundity communicated from God. It was expressed in canon law, which held that parents have an obligation and the right to educate their children as well as to feed, clothe, and house them. Because this education included religious training, parents had to keep their children out of schools filled with impiety. In this context, he praised the Supreme Court for its defense of parents' rights (Pius XI 14–15).

On the other hand, the pope noted that the state was obligated to protect and foster individuals and families. Therefore, the government must protect the rights of the children if the parents ignored them. This obligation meant that the state should create its own schools if no others existed, and it should set standards to ensure that all citizens possessed the physical, intellectual, and moral culture needed for the common good. In such supervision, however, the state had to avoid giving militaristic training or usurping religious duties. Whereas the duties of the state fall under civic education, the church is responsible for anything in human affairs that is sacred or refers to the saving of souls (Pius XI 16–20).

Although Catholic institutions admire and respect scientific research, the pope went on, several problems resulted from excessive faith in science. Calling these myths of naturalism, he decried the tendency not to discipline youth but to allow them freedom in developing. Sex education was foolhardy because it inspired the actions it was designed to prevent, and coeducation was harmful because it prevented men and women from developing different tendencies. The sexes were designed to complement each other in marriage, he wrote, and should be trained apart during adolescence. Pius XI asked Catholics to institute separate high schools for boys and girls unless Christian prudence forbade them. Further, he recommended attention to family education, which could take place in catechisms, schools, and churches. Calling schools complementary to the church and the family, he asked that Catholic schools be set up independently of secular ones and that the church supervise the selection of texts, hiring of teachers, and formation of the curriculum. In this way, everything in the children's education would be founded on religion (Pius XI 22–30).

The pope asked that all learning in Catholic schools reinforce religious instruction. He supported continued training in Latin, and asked pastors and religious organizations to encourage their members to become teachers. He praised associations that warned parents about objectionable materials in films, theaters, and books. All of these efforts, he concluded, would enable young men and women to coordinate the activities of their earthly life with the supernatural (Pius XI 32–37).

As the pope urged, Catholics in the United States tried to organize their schools following theological principles rather than scientific ones. To prepare women and men for marriage, they sought to separate the sexes with separate schools. When they could not afford to build separate high schools, coeducation resulted, as the encyclical indicated it might. As in the case of public schools, Catholic girls attended Catholic high schools more frequently than did Catholic boys. By 1936 there were 1,945 Catholic high schools in the United States, with 124,265 men and 160,471 women students (Buetow 226, 260–261).

In general, the curriculum in Catholic schools remained traditional. Although some Catholic schools embraced the diversification urged by the Commission on the Reorganization of Secondary Education in 1918, most schools retained a traditional curriculum. To justify the conservative approach, Catholic educators returned to the papal encyclical, which urged caution in abandoning the old and tested subjects. Nonetheless, Catholic schools usually removed Greek, reduced the emphasis on Latin, and added some business and a few vocational courses. However, they retained a curriculum steeped in classical humanism on the grounds that it enhanced the students' abilities to reason (Bryk, et al. 30–32).

Ultimately, sexism remained a problem in Catholic schools even though they were not organized around the principles of science that dominated public schools. Hence, it seemed that the problem derived from the culture the schools served more than from the processes educators used. Although Catholic schools tried to follow a theological rather than a scientific model, they exhibited biases similar to those found in the public high schools that adopted the recommendations of the cardinal principles report. The counter-example of the Catholic schools indicates that the biases common in the culture had more influence over school affairs than other organizing ideals.

Did Science Cause School Curricula to Become Biased?

As public school educators adopted the views of the NEA's Commission on the Reorganization of Secondary Education, the comprehensive high school became the U.S. model. In these schools, educators organized the curriculum using some form of what they called science. This included analyzing people's daily activities, conducting surveys, and following the students' patterns of development and interests. Although educators hoped that such schools would be more flexible and thereby allow all students to succeed, the flexibility seemed to reinforce cultural biases.

Ironically, Catholic educators struggled with the same problems even though they claimed to be less dependent on science and were less flexible in their curricula. Although Catholic educators often asserted that women should receive a distinct training that prepared them for marriage, the differences disappeared as women studied the same subjects as men. Pope Pius XI warned against coeducation, but he did not indicate what women should study beyond urging that their education should be permeated with religion as it was for men.

During the 1920s, problems of bias became severe. This was a period of intense nativism exacerbated by a countrywide drive against Bolshevism, often called the Red Scare. In 1921 Congress restricted immigration, and in 1924 President Coolidge signed the Johnson-Reed Act, which extended immigration restrictions to their furthest point yet. Calling that decade the Tribal Twenties, John Higham pointed out that longstanding nativisms continued prewar trends. The hatreds were directed against Catholics, Jews, and southeastern Europeans. As a result, the Ku Klux Klan, established in 1915, reached heights of popularity and spread through the midwestern states. However, Higham also noted that these intense feelings burned themselves out. By 1923 the public began to react against the domination of the Klan as the economic prosperity that developed after 1924 made xenophobia appear unnecessary and as traditional values began to restrain those biases (Higham 255, 265–266, 298, 324, 329).

Despite the decline of ethnic prejudices, public school and Catholic school educators succumbed to the prevailing biases in society. When educators tried to consider the differences in students' abilities and interests, they prepared people from different groups in ways that perpetuated social inequities. For example, in fitting women for the social life then available, Charters developed curricula that continued the separation of the genders. Catholic educators faced similar problems. Although philosophers such as Bode asked educators to think about the kind of culture they wanted, there was no simple way to solve the problem of gender bias in schools. Even when teachers used the project method to give students opportunities to choose classroom activities, social biases seemed to influence the students' choices. Educators tried to integrate groups and to advance democracy, but the curricula advanced some groups and held others back.

TIMELINE
1918–1930

1918 The NEA's CRSE released the Cardinal Principles Report

1918 Franklin Bobbitt applied the scientific method to determining school curriculum

1918 William Heard Kilpatrick developed the laws of learning and the project method

1919 The Progressive Education Association was established

1920 William Bagley surveyed New Mexico schools

1921 The United States began a forty-four year period of excluding immigrants from social improvements

1921 Congress restricted immigration

1922 F. Bobbitt and his students created the curriculum for Los Angeles' secondary schools

1922 George Counts published a study of high school enrollment patterns

1922 Oregon elected Walter Pierce governor

1923 W. W. Charters reviewed his curriculum for Stephens College for women

1923 Willystine Goodsell objected to G. Stanley Hall's view on women

1924 President Coolidge signed the Johnson-Reed Act

1924 The PEA began the journal *Progressive Education*

1924 The U.S. District Court did not allow the Oregon legislature to require attendance at public rather than private schools

1925 The Supreme Court declared that Catholic children could attend public schools

1926 John Dewey became the honorary president of the PEA

1930 Teachers College at Columbia University took control of the PEA

1930 Pope Pius XI wrote *Christian Education of Youth*

CHAPTER

7 The Great Depression, Critical Thinking, and Hispanic and Native Americans: 1930–1940

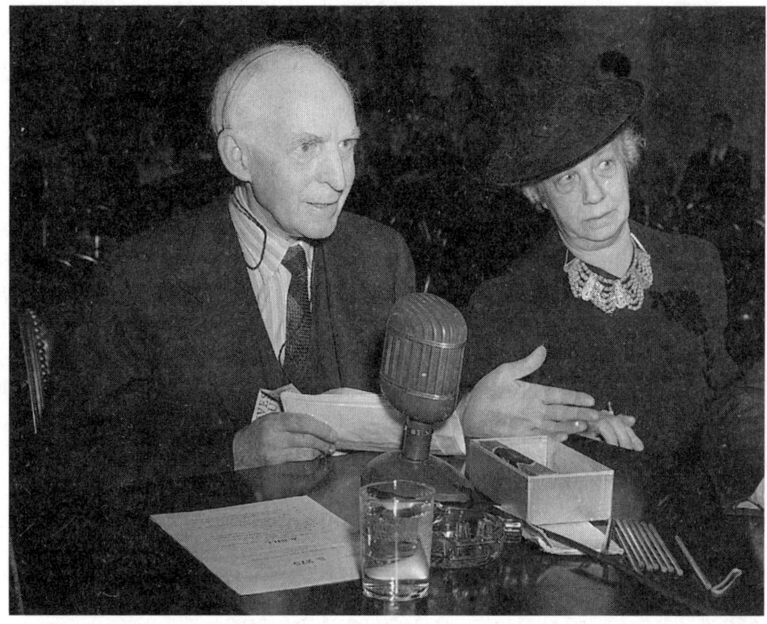

Charles and Mary Beard

OVERVIEW

As a result of the Great Depression, which began in 1929, educators became concerned about social problems. Although most teachers ignored invitations to join political organizations and lead social change, they took three different approaches to reform society. First, they tried to teach students to understand and solve social problems. This idea spread

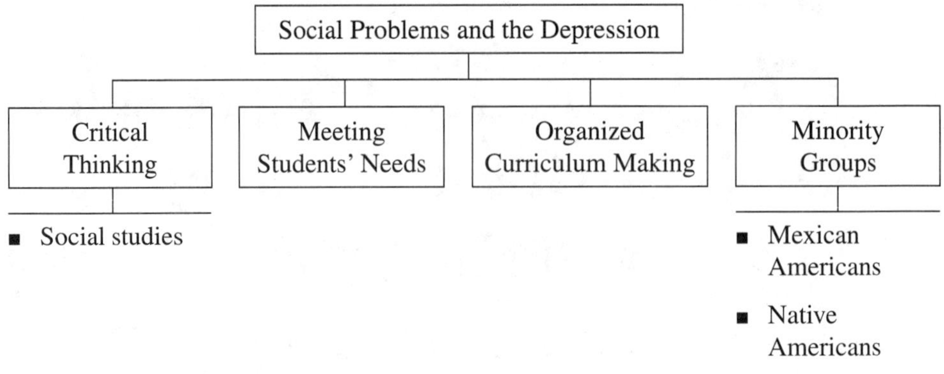

as historians agreed that the social studies could teach students to be active and critical citizens. Second, progressive educators argued that when high school students learned to pursue their own interests, they learned to participate actively and intelligently in social affairs. Thus, they contended, their aim of using science to encourage the fullest and freest development of the child served the reconstruction of society and educators tried to combine educational theories in order to enhance school people's abilities to serve the needs of students as they matured. The third approach was the most popular. Educators suggested that administrators should involve parents, teachers, and citizens in curriculum construction. Called organized curriculum making, such endeavors were supposed to prevent small, elite groups from determining the curriculum and allow all people to share in the material benefits that education represented. Unfortunately, each of the four approaches was flawed by an inadequate conception of democracy and social reform.

When the New Deal spread into areas that had been without economic assistance, federal welfare improved conditions for Hispanic Americans and Native Americans. The curriculum reforms imitated the movements that other schools had experienced earlier. Building on the idea that students should learn about their communities, teachers adapted the curriculum to the unique situations of these minority groups. Although such an approach appeared philanthropic, it threatened to isolate the groups more thoroughly or to lead the students to abandon traditional society completely.

How Did the Depression Affect Schools?

When the stock market crashed in October 1929, schools operated normally for some time. For example, in Waukegan, Illinois, near Chicago, the home of blue-collar workers and lower-level managers, several buildings sported new additions or were themselves nearly new in the fall of 1930. Unfortunately, by December 1931 the schools were in trouble, and by the next year the local newspaper called for cuts in education. First the board paid teachers in a mixture of cash and promissory notes. Then it cut the teachers' pay by 20 percent. Finally, it cut programs, courses, and supplies. Thus, by the 1935–36 school year, Waukegan spent about $55 per student, down from about $75 per student in 1920. The impact of these financial cuts was devastating. As the board dismissed special teachers, these reductions weakened or ended programs in instrumental music, penmanship, manual training, and domestic science. For four years, the board did not buy textbooks. As a result, one fifth-grade class had only one history textbook, from which the teacher read aloud to the students (Zilversmit 77–79).

Many other city school boards cut programs and released teachers during the depression. For example, in 1931 the Chicago school board claimed it could no longer pay the city's teachers. For the next two years, teachers were paid for only four of the nine months they worked, and they received their salaries in the form of warrants, which were redeemable for less than their face value. To some extent, the mayor helped the teachers by paying them for some of the work they did in 1931 and preventing authorities from arresting teachers who had not paid taxes on their vehicles. Nonetheless, in 1933 the school board closed all junior high schools and the city's junior college; reduced the number of kindergarten teachers, physical education teachers, and music teachers; and eliminated all coaching positions. In all, almost fifteen hundred teachers lost their jobs and the remaining teachers taught substantially larger classes (Urban and Wagoner 244–246).

On the other hand, some cities strove to maintain teachers and programs despite severe problems. For example, in Detroit nearly 28 percent of the jobs related to the automobile industry were eliminated within a year of the stock market crash. The assessed value of property dropped from $3 billion in 1930 to $1.7 billion seven years later. Further, almost 35 percent of the taxes for 1932–33 were not paid. This was a greater percentage than any other city in the United States. In the face of this financial disruption, a prominent banker persuaded the mayor of Detroit to appoint a citizen's committee to advise the administration about the crisis. In 1930–31, Detroit schools had a budget of about $18 million, the largest share of municipal spending. Not surprisingly, the citizen's committee demanded cuts in school spending. However, labor leaders wanted to maintain teachers and their salary levels. In a compromise, labor leaders recommended making sure that all teachers were U.S. citizens and Detroit residents. Further, they suggested removing married women from the faculties and reducing what they considered extraneous programs such as night schools, summer schools, manual arts, home economics, music, art, and physical education (Mirel 90–92).

Although Detroit's school board could not resist all efforts to reduce costs, members tried to avoid firing teachers or severely cutting their salaries. In July 1932, however, the Detroit school board agreed to reduce salaries at a rate suffered by other city employees. Further, the board preserved courses in art, home economics, and physical education by contending that their elimination would diminish the schools and ultimately cost the taxpayers more money. In part, the Detroit board of education resisted calls from business leaders to reduce the schools' budget because in the public's opinion business leaders had failed to preserve their own companies. Consequently, their advice was suspect. Further, Detroit's labor leaders decided not to press their opposition to extra programs. In all, a formidable array of interest groups in Detroit, ranging from the American Legion to the Socialist Party, protested cutting school programs (Mirel 93–109).

During the depression, wealthier school districts did not feel such pressures. For example, in Lake Forest, the home of Chicago's successful businesspeople, the schools engaged more teachers, added new buildings, and offered new courses during the depression even though the schools did not enroll more students (Zilversmit 70–71).

Despite the difficult times, high schools continued to grow across the nation. In 1929 about 4,400,000 students were enrolled in grades 9 through 12. By 1938 the number of students enrolled in high schools grew to about 6,700,000. To some extent, the depression forced students *into* high schools. From 1928 to 1930, before the depression, high school enrollments grew by a total of about 490,000. However, from 1930 to 1932, during the depression, those enrollments increased by a total of about 700,000 (Krug, *Shaping* 218).

In general, however, school districts across the country cut courses in home economics, foreign languages, physical education, and algebra. On the other hand, most school districts retained courses in manual training, agriculture, and bookkeeping. Although academic courses were often the least expensive to teach, school boards did not always save them. In fact, there was no clear pattern of favoring academics over practical courses. Budget cutters in most school districts sought to reduce teachers' salaries (Krug, *Shaping* 214–217).

In most cases, teachers tried to protect their jobs during the 1930s by joining unions. The two most popular organizations were the National Education Association (NEA) and the American Federation of Teachers (AFT). The NEA was founded in 1867 by school leaders and was devoted to improving educational administration. In 1909 Ella Flagg Young became the first female president and she turned the organization toward the concerns of teachers. However, in 1917 the NEA moved its headquarters to Washington, D.C., hired an executive secretary, and recruited leaders from the administrative ranks of state normal schools. As a result, the NEA became a powerful lobby for education. The organization grew during the anti-union era so that by 1920 it had 20,000 members, a number that grew to more than 200,000 in 1930. During the depression, the NEA unsuccessfully sought federal aid for education. It was more successful in requiring states to help finance education. Such state funding helped rural schools because farm failures diminished the local tax base (Urban and Wagoner 167, 212–213, 228–229, 252–253).

The AFT was formed in 1916 by a group of local teachers associations in Chicago. In a short period, the American Federation of Labor granted the AFT a charter, and other large city groups joined. By 1920 the AFT included about one hundred local units. At the same time, new leaders from New York who were steeped in socialism replaced the original founders, who had concerned themselves with protecting jobs and salaries. As a result, in the 1920s, when a fear of foreigners, communism, and unions spread across the nation, memberships in the AFT declined rapidly. The membership rolls recovered in the 1930s, though, as teachers faced economic hardships (Urban and Wagoner 227–228, 252).

Did Teachers Try to Reshape Society?

Hoping to direct society's widespread disillusionment with capitalism, several intellectuals urged teachers to engage in overt political action to reform society. For example, in February 1932 George Counts delivered a speech to the Progressive Education Association (PEA) in which he challenged the organization to indoctrinate students against the evils of capitalism. He wanted teachers to show students that the country required a socialized economy. Although association members were sympathetic, they were uncertain whether teachers should indoctrinate students. Nonetheless, the PEA set up a Committee on Social and Economic Problems with Counts as a member. In 1933 the committee presented its report, *A*

Call to Teachers of the Nation, to the delegates of the PEA. The report called for teachers to band together in a powerful organization militantly devoted to stripping the privileged caste and building a new social order. During the annual meeting, however, many members of the PEA complained that the report was overly socialistic and its acceptance by the organization would hurt those teachers and administrators who worked with conservative school boards. In a compromise, the PEA published the report but disavowed any connection with the findings (Bowers 18–19, 35–37, 41).

In other ways, radicals tried to direct teachers' unions to wider political aims. In New York and Philadelphia, teachers who were members of the American Communist Party took over or influenced unions. Ironically, this was further than George Counts wanted to go. Late in the decade, Counts ran for and won the presidency of the AFT on the basis of ridding the union of this alien ideology. Nonetheless, during the depression the AFT concentrated more on teachers' jobs and salary scales than on social reconstruction. As a result, its membership grew (Urban and Wagoner 251–252).

Instead of engaging in direct political action, many educators thought they could reshape society by helping students become critical thinkers through the social studies. Since 1916 many school districts had set up one cycle of three courses including a ninth-grade civics class for junior high school students and another for senior high students with a twelfth-grade course called Problems of Democracy. This pattern followed the recommendations of the NEA's Committee on Social Studies. However, the school districts did not follow the recommendations of the report and designed the courses in ways that had the students investigate local problems (Barr, Barth, and Shermis 26–27).

Before the depression, social studies educators complained about the superficial ways the school districts instituted social studies. In 1922 Harold Rugg presented the results of a survey of the content of courses in 1,180 schools. He found that the new names for social studies courses disguised traditional approaches to the subject matter. For example, in history classes the students learned countless facts about political and military developments in the United States and in ancient and medieval times. Rugg was pleased to find that most high schools offered a course in community civics in which they learned how cities were planned and communities developed, and that the texts for these courses discussed some social problems such as immigration and racial conflicts. However, he noted that civics was only a half-year elective course that few students could take, and in the texts the social problems were superficially treated. As a result, Rugg concluded that in most schools students read specific assignments and answered specific questions from the teachers. He added that they rarely learned how to organize and carry out investigations into local problems ("Do the Social Studies?" 1–24).

With these complaints in mind, Rugg worked with a research staff to write a series of textbooks illuminating social problems in the United States. First, the authors identified three hundred important problems on which they based the series. Second, the authors tested students in grades 3 through 12 to determine their ability to understand concepts in order to probe the issues. Third, the authors drew up a list of generalizations used by what Rugg called frontier thinkers in about sixty books. In 1926 Rugg signed a contract with Ginn and Company to produce the series, and the first volume was ready in 1929. By 1939 the publishers sold about 1,320,000 copies of the texts and nearly 2,700,000 workbooks (Kliebard 174–175).

Entitled *Man and His Changing Society,* Rugg's textbook series fit the altered interests of teachers during the depression. It asked students to think about the ways society should be reformed. By 1937 it consisted of eight volumes for the elementary schools and six volumes for the junior and senior high schools. At the elementary level, the texts portrayed the advance of civilization in ways that integrated descriptions of economics, political and social life, mechanical arts, and aesthetic arts. According to the texts' preface, the series introduced students to the conditions and problems they would confront as citizens of the world. The books claimed that when schools integrated subjects such as history, geography, and civics they helped the students use facts from a range of sources to understand modern life and how it came to be. Thus, texts presented history when it could help a student understand the present and introduced geography when spatial relations clarified contemporary problems. According to the preface, this did not reduce the amount of history or geography students learned, but instead increased it and made it relevant. The center of the series was a set of problem-solving activities in workbooks that encouraged the pupils to actively study the society around them. The hope was that they would learn to participate in U.S. society and develop an understanding of other civilizations that would lead to increased tolerance (Rugg, *Changing* v–ix).

Paradoxically, the strength of the textbook series turned out to be its weakness. Critics complained that Rugg's books had an anticapitalist theme. The most influential of these critics was Orlen K. Armstrong who argued that Rugg's series cast doubt on the motives of American heroes, criticized democracy to advance socialism, condemned the idea of private property in favor of collectivism, and portrayed religious faith as outmoded. Although Rugg and his supporters defended them, they did not revise them, and school districts stopped ordering them after 1940 (Kliebard 177–178).

Did Historians Accept the Integrated Social Studies as a Replacement for History?

The transition of history as a school subject to the social studies reflected the uneasy relationship that exists in the United States between intellectualism and practical affairs. Yet historians tend to overlook the complex arguments involved in this shift. Instead, they portray the change as the victory of certain educators over academicians. For example, in a chapter explaining the origins of what he called the shopping mall high school, David Cohen writes that by 1930 social studies replaced the traditional courses of history, complaining that one of the effects of this change was that it reduced the academic demands on students because the new courses were designed to permit all the students to pass (Powell, Farrar, and Cohen 251–252). In a similar manner, Herbert Kliebard describes the creation of the social studies in 1916 as the triumph of the social efficiency experts who wanted all school subjects to help people adapt to the social order. Kliebard describes Harold Rugg's effort to create a social studies text that would serve the social reconstructionists as they sought to teach students to become critical thinkers (125–128, 200–208).

But the story was more complicated. In 1892, when the NEA appointed the Committee of Ten to investigate the requirements for admission into college from high school, the committee formed ten smaller groups or conferences of experts (each of which had about ten members) assigned to examine specific subjects such as Latin, mathematics, and history. In its report, the Committee of Ten considered the aim of studies such as history, civil government, and political economy. These disciplines strived to train the students' judgment, to prepare them for intellectual enjoyment, and to teach them how to exercise a salutary influence on national affairs when they became adults. In addition, the Committee of Ten thought that courses in history and civil government provided the students opportunities to use their knowledge of ancient languages.

To describe the proper purpose and methods of teaching history, the American Historical Association (AHA) formed the Committee of Seven. In 1899 this committee had surveyed the practices of secondary schools in large cities and small towns. From the 250 replies the committee received, members found that schools taught the subject differently. The members were pleased to find that many teachers used materials besides textbooks, tried to arouse the students' interests, and sent students to libraries to do independent research. They attributed the use of these practices to the recommendations of the Committee of Ten in 1893. Nonetheless, after comparing the schools in the United States to those in Germany, France, and England, which some members visited, the committee called for more attention to history in secondary schools (Committee of Seven 429–436).

To describe the value of the study, the Committee of Seven pointed out several ways in which history helped students. For example, it could show students the steps human beings took to create civilization; it helped the pupils learn how to think about political and social problems that were similar to those they would confront as adults; it gave students a broader knowledge and elicited a more intelligent spirit that came from a familiarity with people from other times; and it cultivated judgment by seeking the causes for several effects. In this way, history developed the scientific way of thinking. Finally, according to the report, historical studies enabled students to acquire library skills (Committee of Seven 437–441).

As a result of the many benefits of the study of history, the Committee of Seven recommended that some form of history be studied each year from grades 7 to 12. After surveying the courses offered by many schools, the committee recommended that four blocks of history be studied sequentially. The first was ancient history, followed by medieval and modern European history. English history was third and U.S. history last. The committee recommended that teachers use textbooks because any other method would lead to confusion. Yet the report added that the classes might use more than one book so that students could compare accounts. The report also suggested that students use other materials to help them explore events more fully (Committee of Seven 446–447, 475–479).

In 1905 the AHA appointed the Committee of Eight to consider the problems of teaching history in elementary schools. To make its study, the committee sent questionnaires to 250 superintendents around the country and found that most elementary schools gave attention to the teaching of history. To explain the value of teaching history, the committee pointed to the report of the Committee of Seven. Following the conclusions of that earlier committee, the Committee of Eight recommended that history in elementary schools should cover all the events students could understand and that these should be drawn from political, social, industrial, educational, and religious activities (viii–x).

In the main, the Committee of Eight thought that history in the elementary school should concentrate on U.S. history with the aim of explaining the society in which students lived. This did not mean it had to be contemporary history, however. Writing before the adoption of the junior high schools, the committee recommended that sixth-grade students learn those features of ancient and medieval life that contributed to American civilization. Geography had to play a role in such explanations. In the seventh grade, the settlement of the colonies should be considered and, in the eighth, students would cover the political, industrial, and social growth of the new nation. To keep students' interest, the committee recommended that teachers endeavor to make the lessons fit together in stories that revealed new developments. To illustrate how this might be done, the committee presented outlines of topics covering those grade levels (Committee of Eight x–xvii).

According to one set of commentators, the Committees of Seven and Eight were dominated by historians. On the other hand, the NEA Committee on Social Studies in 1916 was dominated by educators. The point these commentators make is that academic scholars were more likely to favor a textbook orientation than were teachers who faced students daily (Barr, Barth, and Shermis 19–25). These commentators probably overstate the separation between academics and instructors. Although the AHA committees recommended what might be called a textbook approach, they did so because they feared that teachers with only modest training could not be trusted to create effective courses. Further, the AHA committees tried to find ways to make that approach interesting. Finally, the AHA's committee members were aware of the problems of teaching in public elementary and secondary schools. Although only one of the members of the Committee of Seven was a teacher, three others had been. On the Committee of Seven, three members were superintendents of schools and two taught in normal schools. Only two members were from colleges.

How Did the Depression Influence Historians?

The work of the AHA committees appeared to be inadequate. In 1923–24, the AHA commissioned a study of the teaching of the social sciences. This report described teachers and administrators faced with increasing numbers of students, confronted by changing social conditions, and confused by the conflicting recommendations of learned committees. As a result, in 1929 the AHA appointed the Commission on the Social Studies in the Schools. Including noted historians and prominent educators among its members, this committee reviewed textbooks, courses of study, and books about teaching and prepared a statement of objectives for the courses. In 1932 the AHA published its first report entitled *A Charter for the Social Sciences in the Schools.* Written by Charles Beard, a famous historian, in consultation with the other commission members, this report recommended that social studies integrate disciplines such as history, sociology, political science, and economics (v–xii).

Beard gave three reasons why there should be integrated courses rather than separate or fixed studies of the social sciences. These reasons can be seen as a combination of the earlier idea of exercising the students' minds and the later concern with teaching students to think critically. First, there was constant change in the intellectual disciplines and in society. Second, in an industrial society people should learn to think rather than to memorize facts and information. Third, in a democracy students had to learn to participate intelligently in politics (*Charter* 21–44).

Beard looked for a division of labor in improving social studies. On the one hand, historians and other scholars should devote more attention to the larger aims of their disciplines and the relations among those areas of study. On the other hand, Beard thought that the authors of manuals for schools could draw on such scholarly work to construct reasonable textbooks. However, Beard noted that a serious problem existed among the teachers. Secondary school educators did not engage in active scholarship. As a result, he complained, they were content to adopt the views of the community and distort the social studies (*Charter* 81–92).

For Beard and his commission, the fundamental purpose of the social studies was to help students develop rich, multifaceted personalities. The social studies should equip students with the practical knowledge and the ideals necessary to succeed in a changing world. This meant that students should be informed, aware that the environment as well as individuals can be changed, and imbued with the highest aspirations of humankind (*Charter* 96–97).

Although Beard wanted students to recognize the claims of different cultures, he did not advocate multicultural social studies. Beard wanted the students to learn to be imaginative and critical rather than tolerant because he thought these traits were the forces for social progress. When students left the schools, he wrote, they entered a pluralistic world of competing allegiances. The home, the gang, the industry, the business each had its own system of correct behavior. The child must learn about this pluralism and how to cope with it intelligently. Therefore he advocated that teachers discuss these loyalties with a high level of rationality (*Charter* 113–114).

In addition to the *Charter for the Social Sciences,* Beard wrote another book for the commission in 1934. Entitled *The Nature of the Social Studies in Relation to Objectives of Instruction,* it treated the problems of the social sciences as a whole and described the objectives teachers should aim for to make the content useful in guiding society. In this text, Beard articulated the thesis that marked his career in the AHA. This was the view that there can be no science of society because none of the social sciences could be as exact as the natural sciences. At best, Beard argued, social sciences could predict within broad limits what might happen under certain conditions. For example, economists might use historical data to predict what would happen to wages and prices if a country's currency remained inflated.

When Harry Elmer Barnes reviewed Beard's *Nature of the Social Studies,* he noted that the commission's series of books aroused controversy among historians. Although he considered them important contributions to efforts to reconstruct U.S. society in reasonable ways, he complained that the series did not acknowledge the work other educators and previous commissions had accomplished. Nonetheless, Barnes praised Beard for recognizing that the social sciences did not offer unlimited value to efforts for social reform because such efforts had to be guided by ethical considerations. According to Barnes, the irony Beard pointed out was that objectivity in the social sciences was diminished by the same degree to which ethics entered the study of society (97–98).

Most important to this discussion, Beard made the same point to the AHA when he became president. In January 1934, Beard delivered his presidential address, "Written History as an Act of Faith." Quoting Benedetto Croce, he defined history as contemporary thought about the past. This definition repudiated the doctrine held by historians during the end of the nineteenth and the beginning of the twentieth century who sought to describe the past as it had happened. According to Beard, conservative historians after the French Revolution sought this perspective because they wearied of history as propaganda. As historians recognized the obstacles to objectivity, they borrowed two formulas from natural science. The first was that every event had a cause and if historians could reveal these they would discover the laws of social change. For Beard, Karl Marx illustrated this model. The second was that historians borrowed the images of Darwin, describing successions of cultures as organisms that rose, grew, competed with other societies, and fell. Oswald Spengler represented this ideal. According to Beard, historians tired of these searches for objectivity and adopted a formula that made all events relative to time and circumstance. Calling this scheme historical relativity, Beard noted that history could not become absolute because such inquiries serve the ideas and interests of certain groups during particular times. To avoid the dangers of believing that history was a record of chaos or of treating it as either Marx or Spengler envisioned, Beard urged historians to use the scientific method, but at the same time to acknowledge the biases implicit in their selection of topics and their treatment of materials ("Written History" 219–229).

Beard's presidential address sparked controversy from members of the AHA who called the ideal of objectivity a noble dream that had led its believers to write sound and masterly books. Beard replied to these criticisms with a paper entitled "That Noble Dream." According to Beard, the idea that historians could divorce themselves from their predilections and record the truth contained several assumptions: (1) the historian could know this thing called history; (2) the historian could view the historical record objectively; and (3) the events of history had some organization that the historian could understand. Unfortunately, Beard added, these assumptions were impossible. For example, historians cannot see the past objectively but must rely on documents that cover only part of the events. Further, the documentation represents only part of the past. In addition, when historians recorded events, they used some ethical considerations and they brought with them the biases of their own times. Thus, Beard concluded, these limits destroyed the idea of history as objective. He called for more open meetings among historians at which subjects ranged beyond the political histories historians commonly wrote. He urged historians to reach into economic, racial, sexual, and cultural interests. At the same time, he recommended that historians describe the assumptions under which they worked ("Noble Dream" 74–87).

What Methods of Curriculum Planning Did Historians Recommend?

As the controversy among historians proceeded, various members of the AHA's Commission on the Social Studies in the Schools explored alternatives for teaching the social studies. One such idea was to begin the instruction of history with the present and move backward to the past. This was an effort to ensure an adequate discussion of contemporary issues. However, the ideal of an integrated approach to the study of society came from Leon Marshall, author of several history texts, and his daughter, Rachel Marshall Goetz (Barr, Barth, and Shermis 30).

Marshall and Goetz's text was similar to a text that social studies educator Harold Rugg wrote and published at about the same time. Both texts integrated the social science disciplines. However, Marshall and Goetz's approach was less likely to suffer criticism from the conservatives who attacked Rugg for being socialistic. Because Rugg structured his texts around issues or problems, critics could easily complain that he portrayed the United States in a poor light. Marshall and Goetz organized their approach around what they called the processes of living, allowing them to point out that their text exposed students to ways of living common to all societies. According to Marshall and Goetz, five groups of fundamental human activity made social life comprehensible. These activities included adjusting to the external world, continuing biologically, guiding human motivation, developing social organization, and directing cultural improvement. Their text explained each of these and compared the ways people in different societies undertook them (2–11).

By organizing the instruction around five processes of living, Marshall and Goetz believed teachers could build on the students' familiarity with each process. And because the processes were universal, the lessons offered an overview of data for social living at all times and in all places. Although Marshall and Goetz wanted students to realize that the physical environment influenced the society or culture that lives in it, they pointed out that change was not always progress. For example, cultural advances that brought material improvement also often led to war. Consequently, they hoped the social studies would teach students how to direct the culture toward increasingly better living (11–45).

To explain how such an organization might work, Marshall and Goetz presented explanations of each of the five processes. For example, in adjusting to the external world the students could learn about the increasing control people have exercised over the physical environment, including the ways people made light. Artificial illumination extended through the following points on a continuum: simple fires, lamps of fat, candles, and gas jets. Similar stories of fighting famine through food preservation might be explained. In all these cases, students made certain fundamental observations. One was that the ability to live well depended on changes in the environment. Another was that although such changes should have led to the creation of different types of human beings, they did not. A third observation was that as people found new ways to do things, their culture changed (Marshall and Goetz 49–53).

In keeping with their aim of teaching students to evaluate change, Marshall and Goetz urged teachers to present the advantages and disadvantages of the choices. Such investigations extended into controversial areas. For example, when they considered complicated matters such as the development of economic systems, Marshall and Goetz noted that the collective systems in practice in the Soviet Union improved life for many people but caused suffering for others. Capitalistic systems such as that found in the United States caused a disproportionate distribution of wealth and at times broke down. Yet they contended that it produced high living standards for many people. In another controversial example, under the theory of biological continuance Marshall and Goetz considered different forms of family life: monogamy, polygamy, and polyandry. But the authors did not argue that one view was best. Instead, they wanted students to learn that the mating arrangements were aspects of a culture, and if those aspects were to be planned, such planning would be complicated (70–71, 109–111).

How Did Other Historians React to the *Charter for the Social Sciences*?

Although Marshal and Goetz tried to avoid the problem of indoctrination that historians identified in the social studies, their efforts may not have been enough. In his book *That Noble Dream,* Peter Novick described the difficulties that historians faced trying to decide if they could be objective in their work. Novick claimed that the AHA never officially accepted or endorsed its commission's report. He contended that the problem stemmed from the fact that after World War I historians looked back on the participation of many of their colleagues in the war effort. They complained that during the war, history writing turned into propaganda to show the rightness of the struggle to subdue Germany. According to Novick, historians worried that within the social studies, they would have to serve as the propaganda department of the government. Not surprisingly, he added, they complained that the commission's report expressed an explicit frame of reference that historians would have to adopt (Novick 190–191).

Despite Novick's account of the controversies, the AHA continued its support of the social studies. In 1934 the AHA assumed responsibility for editing the magazine *The Social Studies* for teachers of history, social studies, and social sciences; this magazine eventually became the journal for the National Council for the Social Studies (NCSS). In 1937 the AHA and the NCSS established the journal *Social Education,* which was to appeal to junior high school and high school teachers. Unlike the *American Historical Review,* the official journal of the AHA, *Social Education* carried articles debating the nature of the social studies, evaluating its aims, and describing appropriate methods of instruction.

In its second issue, *Social Education* described the evolution of the social studies movement. According to the editors, the 1916 report of the Committee on Social Studies represented a rebellion of school people against the requirements imposed by the various committees of the AHA and enforced by the College Entrance Examination Board (CEEB). Although the 1916 report presented a practical program for junior and senior high schools, the conservative colleges and the CEEB did not recognize the new subjects in the social studies. As a result, in 1934 the CEEB established a Commission on History, which presented its report in 1937 (Editor 77–78). According to Novick, the CEEB commission paid little attention to the social studies and reinforced the teaching of history as a separate subject (191–192). However, Novick's interpretation of the CEEB report seems to be only partially true.

The CEEB commission began its investigation into the study of teaching history by surveying current practices. The commission sent questionnaires to 250 schools and 75 universities. They found increasing attention being paid to social studies among all schools, even private ones, although there was more resistance among prestigious preparatory schools. However, there was no agreement about what social studies should cover, and universities made no consistent requirements concerning what the students should study (CEEB 546–548).

In its definition of history, the CEEB commission made it possible for students to study history in a manner consistent with the social studies. The commission defined "history as the study of man in society from his dim beginnings to the present day" (548), adding that the study should be undertaken in as broad a manner as possible. Therefore, the members preferred courses in world civilization over any political, social, or cultural history. Most important, according to the report, such a study should enable students to understand the fundamental problems human beings faced in their social evolution.

In one sense, the commission did challenge the social studies movement. The report noted that high schools tended to emphasize history courses as a means to prepare students to become good citizens. As a result, although the commission's report agreed that a study in history could not be fully objective, members did caution against including only those aspects of history tied to contemporary concerns (CEEB 549).

However, they made two other recommendations that brought courses in history closer to the aim of the social studies. First, to limit the material that the CEEB examination would cover, the commission recommended that teachers concentrate on the history of Europe, Egypt, and the New World. At the same time, they urged that the study of ancient history, which concerned Greece and Rome, be reduced in favor of more contemporary studies. Second, when describing the methods of instruction, the report recommended that teachers present the units of civilization as evolving cultures. To describe the fundamental problems that history courses should discuss, the authors borrowed the framework of social process that Marshall and Goetz presented in their book, *Curriculum-Making in the Social Studies* (CEEB 550–556).

How Did Historians and Social Studies Teachers React to the CEEB Report?

One member of the CEEB commission, Tyler Kepner, refused to sign the report. In a minority opinion, he complained that the report turned the study of history into courses in sociology, and that the method the report recommended (the format suggested by Marshall and Goetz) had been considered without success for more than twenty years in limited circles (CEEB 565–566).

In a subsequent article, Kepner, director of the social studies for Brookline, Massachusetts, public schools, described five problems with the commission's report. First, he disliked the practice of commissions handing down blueprints to teachers. In this case, historians were trying to control the social studies curriculum and exclude the other disciplines that should be involved. Second, members of these commissions ignored the needs of the average pupil in the average classroom. Third, those plans overlooked the fact that many teachers were not trained to teach the curricula they defined. Fourth, the textbooks were not written to build on those plans. Finally, the commission drew up its plans without considering whether the citizens in the communities wanted such curricula (Kepner 81–87).

The teachers of history at Phillips Exeter Academy endorsed Kepner's objections, arguing that the effort to teach broad courses that confront fundamental problems would force teachers to skim the surface of many events. These teachers argued that such a social processes approach would leave students with a thin layer of unrelated facts (Teachers 258).

However, Alan Lake Chidsey, headmaster of the Pawling School, complimented the work of the CEEB commission in trying to provide some organization to a field in which different experts expected teachers to follow different directions. He contended that

Kepner's complaints were ill founded. For example, Chidsey asserted that there was no difficulty in studying social problems. Any historical study should be considered as a broad sociological investigation. Second, although Chidsey acknowledged that teachers might not be prepared to use the new system and it might ask a great deal of students, he did not think that justified remaining in a system that forced students to memorize dates, places, and events (Chidsey 256–257).

The editors of *The Social Studies* who printed the CEEB report chided the commission for ignoring the 1916 report on the social studies. They complained that the commission was premature in endorsing the social process approach of Marshall and Goetz because teachers were not trained to use it and texts built around it had been neither written nor printed. However, they contended that these problems could be resolved in time. In general, therefore, they favored the approach (CEEB 567).

In 1937 the CEEB published a report of another subcommittee for the Commission on History: the Subcommittee on the Other Social Studies. This report reinforced the recommendation that broad courses covering the development of civilization should be studied. The subcommittee added that the contribution from studies in economics, government, and sociology was to help students understand the problems of contemporary society such as those relating to standards of living and economic security (Subcommittee 262–263).

Scholars disagree about the result of these controversies. Novick contends that history did not disappear from high school curricula. He attributes the staying power of history as a school subject to three factors: (1) school people failed to form a coherent program of the social studies; (2) school boards distrusted the progressive ideals found in the social studies; and (3) the older ways of teaching were difficult to overcome (Novick 192). However, Kliebard points out that although many high schools retained courses that were named history, those classes were organized along the lines of the social studies (125).

Of these two interpretations, Kliebard's may be more accurate. However, it overlooks the ways in which historians changed their own profession and moved it in a direction closer to that found in the social studies. Although many historians refute Beard's call for wider, more open approaches to history, his appeals mirrored the general mind-set that Marshall and Goetz wanted students to acquire as they pursued the social studies. In that way, controversies over the social studies reflected questions about the nature of intellectual activities more than they represented struggles for the control of the curriculum.

Did Educators Think the Reorganization of Schools Would Lead to Social Reform?

In a manner similar to that of social scientists such as Beard, progressive educators began to claim that their ideal of allowing children the freedom to develop on their own also encouraged the children to become active and critical citizens. In April 1930, the members of the PEA met to discuss how the high schools could better develop the powers of young people and equip them to rebuild the national life that the depression had disturbed. Although they discussed many options, they found each revision would prevent many students from moving onto college. Consequently, the PEA established the Commission on the Relation of School and College to seek an agreement that would allow secondary schools the freedom to attempt fundamental reconstruction. The twenty-six members included teachers, principals, college deans, and evaluation specialists. Their efforts became known as the Eight-Year Study (Aikin 1–2).

The members of the PEA commission complained that the high school had grown too rapidly to develop a definite purpose. Originally a preparation for college, by the 1930s high schools offered diplomas that enhanced an individual's chances of economic success. As a result, enrollments grew from about one million students in 1900 to tens of millions in 1930. But high school did not help most students. The PEA members noted that about half of those who entered failed to graduate and only a third of the graduates went on to college. Further, high school courses did not give students an appreciation of the American heritage. They did not prepare students for the responsibilities of community life nor did they develop the students' creative energies (Aikin 3–6).

The Eight-Year Study should have offered the opportunity to test the effectiveness of a curriculum such as the project method, but it did not. By 1930 curriculum planners combined methods such as traditional academic programs, the project method, and scientific curriculum making to fit what they conceived to be the needs of the schools. Consequently, when the PEA enlisted thirty high schools to begin experimental programs of reconstruction and asked more than three hundred colleges and universities to enroll the graduates of those schools, they asked the high schools to share two principles of curriculum revision. The first was that students would work together at activities that satisfied their desires and solved problems they faced in everyday life. The second was that the schools would help students understand and appreciate the democratic way of life (Aikin 16–18).

The thirty schools included public and private institutions; some were large and others were small. Beginning in 1933, each of these experimental schools began to change their curricula, although the amount they changed varied. Those that retained the traditional subjects encouraged students to engage in independent longtime research into topics of their choice. Some schools tried to fuse subjects such as English and social studies. Other schools engaged in extended cultural studies in which the students tried to understand the daily life of people in countries such as Greece and China. A representative example was a school in Denver, Colorado. There, the teachers built a core curriculum around a study of problems that high school students confronted. As a result, each unit had a central idea to which the teacher related experiences for the students; under the category "personal living," students explored their vocational interests and aptitudes (Aikin 48–62).

In most of the thirty schools, students usually worked together in small groups, a method in keeping with the aim of encouraging an appreciation of democracy. Teachers helped students select project goals, plan activities, and execute them. In such classrooms, students used fewer textbooks. They searched through library resources, bulletins, and pamphlets, and movies and radio programs were important sources of information and ideas. Thus, instead of lessons to be learned, the schoolwork in the thirty schools focused on problems to be solved (Aikin 77–85).

Democracy extended to the organization of the thirty schools. Many schools set up policy councils during which teachers and administrators planned programs together. To ensure that every student had one person who knew him or her, a counselor worked with the same students throughout the four-year program and visited their homes if possible. Further, to facilitate communication between the school and the home, students received carefully written statements of their progress instead of a card with letter grades or numbers (Aikin 25–39).

The first experimental class graduated in 1936 and about two thousand of the graduates entered the colleges participating in the study. To determine the effect of the revised curricula, for the sake of comparison each student from one of the thirty schools was paired with a graduate of a traditional high school. Thus, although there was no specific control group, evaluators made comparisons within the same colleges of students of similar sex and age as well as similar scholastic aptitude scores, racial background, religious affiliation, size and type of secondary school, social class of family, and geographic location of home. In this way, researchers could learn if the students from the thirty experimental schools developed intellectual capacities, developed citizenship skills, attained personal vocational goals, showed a concern for the contemporary scene, and held positive attitudes toward their contemporaries (Chamberlin, et al. 1–9, 206).

The results were positive. The graduates of the thirty schools earned slightly higher grades than the comparable students. They received more academic honors and were judged to be more intellectually curious and able to think in more precise ways. Most important for the aims of encouraging social reform, the graduates of the thirty schools demonstrated more resourcefulness in new situations, participated in more service activities, and showed a more active interest in world affairs. Therefore, the evaluators concluded that the graduates of the thirty schools had greater success than the comparison graduates of traditional schools. Furthermore, the graduates of the more radical schools had more success than the graduates of the schools that used less experimentation, and these benefits were not dependent on the students' native abilities. Students with high and low intellectual abilities profited from the experimental instruction (Chamberlin, et al. 207).

Did the Interesting Lessons Lead to Social Reform?

As curriculum planners mixed ideas about curriculum making, they gave their combinations new names. For example, in the 1930s a new name to describe a curriculum approach appeared among educators: the activity movement. Before 1929 U.S. educational indexes did not include the topic "the activity movement." Yet by 1934, many schools sought to include the activity of the learner in the educative process. Similarly, educators in Mexico, France, and Germany worked to bring more activity into the schools (Mossman 1–3).

The term "activity method" meant many different things. Some educators defined it as letting students follow their own interests. Other educators applied it to any opportunity students had to learn by doing. In other cases, it meant training students through their senses or developing lessons in which the students cooperated. In general, the idea implied that the students had opportunities to teach themselves instead of waiting for someone to instruct them (Woody, "Historical Sketch" 32–34).

Several supporters claimed that the activity movement was based on the philosophy of John Dewey and the way he constructed his laboratory school curriculum. However, Dewey criticized overzealous applications of the idea. Although he acknowledged that allowing students to move around satisfied psychologists' findings that children depend on motor experiences to learn, Dewey warned that teachers did not solve educational problems by giving students the freedom to move around and do things. Activities could be rowdy, thoughtless, or mechanical. Consequently, the question remained of which direction the curriculum should take. Until teachers recognized that experiences were complex, fluid phenomena that stretched far into the future, Dewey concluded, activities in the classrooms would not be helpful ("Comment" 82–86).

William Heard Kilpatrick, who had popularized the project method, noted that the activity movement was confined to elementary schools. He thought it was an effort to correct the excessive dependence on textbook lessons. From fifteen books that represented the most authoritative statements, Kilpatrick isolated in the activity movement the elements of the curriculum, the methods of planning, the roles of the teacher and the students, and the evaluations. According to Kilpatrick, proponents of the activity movement shared the view that children should learn by engaging in activities that were part of their process of living. Although some authorities wanted teachers to plan these activities, the majority favored the view that teachers would guide the pupils as they selected activities from the experiences they developed. Kilpatrick also found that these authors felt that the activities in which students engaged were the educative processes separate from or independent of subject matter ("Definition" 45–46, 62–63).

In acknowledging the activity movement as a protest against intellectualism in schools, Kilpatrick approved of it. He saw this anti-intellectualism as a way to reform society, contending that the activity program seemed to be based on the view that individuals learn when situations make demands on them. He called this the best understanding of psychology. Because education was the cumulative result of these events, teachers using the activity method forgot education and focused on life. Such an orientation contrasted with traditional education, which, he argued, limited school study to subject matter imposed by teachers. In Kilpatrick's view, traditional teaching was a static, autocratic method that forced new generations to repeat the processes of previous ones. The activity model was thus the way of democracy and of a growing civilization directing itself to ever better things ("Statement" 200–202).

Not everyone supported the activity movement as enthusiastically as Kilpatrick. Boyd Bode complained that the activity movement included a disparate range of educational ideas and thought that supporters might improve their practices if they reconsidered Dewey's definition of education as the reconstruction of experience. For Bode, this phrase suggested how to direct the curriculum. He also warned teachers against treating each child as a detached unit. Lessons had to show students how they related to each other as members of a social organization ("Comment" 78–81).

Similarly, critic Ernest Horn found thirteen different definitions of the movement. However, he complained that these definitions restated old principles with which most educators would agree, including points such as recognizing that children's play is important and emphasizing thinking over memorizing. Horn warned teachers not to be misled by slogans, suggesting that they should think more deeply about what they attempted to teach and the effect the lessons would have on the students. The answers to such questions were not easily discovered, Horn noted ("Comment" 195–197).

Although commentators noted that the activity curriculum was confined to elementary schools, in 1935 the National Council of Teachers of English (NCTE) published a commission's report indicating how this model could be used to shape the curriculum in elementary, secondary, and college classrooms. In this plan, the entire curriculum of the school would be chosen to reflect the desirable experiences most people have or should have in life. Any experiences that students could not have directly would come vicariously through literature. The role of English as a subject matter in such a setting was to provide the communication necessary to conduct the social activities. In such a unified curriculum, all subjects were integrated with everyday life (Hatfield vi–5).

The NCTE commission divided the curriculum into experience strands, which were subdivided into units. Within each strand, the units would include several similar experiences organized to develop students' skills. For example, in oral communication the experience strands covered activities such as conversing, telephoning, and discussing and planning. The first unit in the strand, "Conversation," might include the social objective of talking with a small group about home experiences. The enabling objectives included waiting to speak until another speaker finished, speaking loudly, and speaking in complete sentences. These strands and units were not tightly organized into grade levels but arranged as steps in a reasonable progression adapted to the students' needs and capacities. Although the NCTE commission noted that teachers must evaluate the students, members could not give clear directions on how this might be done. They urged teachers to consider vague measures such as composition power, social spirit, and poise more than mechanical measures of composition or retention of facts about literature. The commission wanted the curriculum in schools at all the levels to parallel the present and future experiences of the students (Hatfield vi–vii, 6–9).

The members of the NCTE curriculum commission realized that a single curriculum would not be suitable for children in a wealthy suburb, a city tenement, or a farming community. Nor could it serve children in New Hampshire as well as Mexican American children in Texas. But the members thought such a school program would put an end to artificial divisions such as the separation of practical from theoretical knowledge and prevent the splitting up of intellectual life into fragments. Most important, it would provide students the chance to see life and to live it as a whole (Hatfield v, 14).

The activity movement expressed the hope that it was a revolutionary act to give students freedom to follow their interests and to engage in activities that resembled everyday life. Supporters believed they were following the philosophy of John Dewey and making the schools more democratic. Despite his warning that freedom would not teach children to reshape society, the teachers seemed to believe that such simple changes were enough to allow schools to produce intelligent, self-assured individuals who could confront the severe social problems of the depression. Such freedom seemed the way to accommodate the needs of diverse groups and improve society. Although the principle encouraged separating students according to their interests, the teachers hoped that different groups of students would come together to work on projects of mutual interest and social significance.

Did Educators Combine Opposing Theories of Students' Needs?

As the activity movement illustrated, many educators persisted in efforts to construct an appropriate curriculum by meeting students' needs. The idea received such prominence that in 1938, in *Progressive Education at the Crossroads,* Boyd Bode warned that the concept of needs could distract educators from thinking deeply about the complex and contradictory relationships that make up a democracy. That is, teachers could think they were being democratic when they catered to students' desires. Claiming that this approach resembled the superstitious reverence for childhood found in Rousseau, Bode contended that it led to anti-intellectualism in the classroom that was evident when teachers did not plan long-range classroom lessons in a coherent way (62–72).

Heeding Bode's warning about the need for coherent planning, educators thought this could be accomplished by uniting conflicting concepts of students' needs, which would lead to a democratic theory of education. Unfortunately, their efforts reinforced a shallow conception of democracy, which became clear in an extensive effort undertaken by the Progressive Education Society. Interestingly, Bode was a member of this team of authors, but he withdrew after one year.

In 1939 the PEA published the report of its Commission on the Secondary School Curriculum. Written by V. T. Thayer, Caroline Zachry, and Ruth Kotinsky, this report, entitled *Reorganizing Secondary Education,* argued that the schools could advance the ideals of democracy and improve society if they met the students' needs. According to Thayer, Zachry, and Kotinsky, it was not simple for schools to meet the needs of students as they matured because needs had been construed differently for children and for adolescents. In elementary schools, the teachers viewed the children's needs as desires or wishes that were intrinsic within the children. This was a perspective made popular by William Heard Kilpatrick who advocated the project method described in Chapter 6. On the other hand, in secondary schools teachers thought of adolescent needs as the social demands they would meet as adults. This was a view more in line with the ideas of Franklin Bobbitt described in Chapter 6 (Thayer, Zachry, and Kotinsky 20–25).

Other educators had made the same observations, and they tried to meld the ideas of Kilpatrick and of Bobbitt. However, the results were usually some form of uneasy compromise. For example, in Winnetka, Illinois, an elite suburb of Chicago, Carlton Washburne developed an approach that blended Kilpatrick's project method with Bobbit's scientific curriculum making in what he called an individual instruction technique. This consisted of setting up specific units of achievement, preparing diagnostic tests to cover these units, and designing self-instructive, self-corrective practice materials to teach the information. The process began when teachers decided on what Washburne called the common essentials: the ideas or pieces of information and knowledge that students needed to learn. The levels of achievement were identified from statistical records showing what a slow but normal and diligent child could accomplish in a year. Once the materials were drawn up, however, students could work as long as they wished to accomplish the tasks. Washburne found that children could work on these materials in the morning and achieve mastery. In the afternoon, they engaged in projects of a creative nature including dramatizations, preparing a school paper, giving concerts, and engaging in student government assemblies. The report card provided both a record of the student's progress through the individualized academic work and a section illustrating the student's development of the attitudes and habits essential for cooperative living (Washburne 220–225).

Thayer, Zachry, and Kotinsky yearned to make a more complete synthesis, so they merged Kilpatrick's and Bobbitt's views of needs by considering the concept of needs to be both personal and social. They believed this could be done if the needs referred to relationships.

Thayer, Zachry, and Kotinsky believed studies indicated that adolescents needed to learn about four types of relationships or areas: immediate social relationships, wider social relationships, economic relationships, and personal living. These relationships included things that were personal to each child yet extended into the society in which the children lived. Teaching about these relationships was the job of schools, they continued, because society had changed to the point at which traditional approaches no longer worked easily and no other agencies helped children understand these important aspects of life (30–50).

Although critics such as George Counts contended that Thayer, Zachry, and Kotinsky focused on helping individual students grow but ignored the need to restructure society, the authors themselves did not think this was the case. Thayer, Zachry, and Kotinsky appeared to believe that the best way to improve society was to help each person reform himself or herself. When schools facilitated personal growth, they fulfilled the democratic tradition.

For Thayer, Zachry, and Kotinsky, two essential elements in a school advanced democracy. First, everyone had to value diversity. In meeting students' needs in social relationships, for example, teachers should use the differences in students' backgrounds to develop an appreciation of the contributions made to American life by different national and racial groups. Teachers should at all times foster the students' sense of security in their origins and confidence in their uniqueness. The aim was to help students recognize that all people differed from each other and that they could contribute their differences to the wider social group. At the same time, students should not believe that social problems were due to the presence of minority groups (Thayer, Zachry, and Kotinsky 325–327).

Second, the schools had to be organized democratically. Thayer, Zachry, and Kotinsky urged educators to adopt democratic methods of administration and curriculum building, including regular meetings of student councils that took part in forming school policies. In addition, students should learn how schools failed as democratic institutions. For example, students should learn how the schools had designed courses in home economics and civics to Americanize the children of immigrants and separate them from their parents. Thayer, Zachry, and Kotinsky thought that if students knew about these denials of the ideal of democracy, they would try to correct similar failings in their own times. Studies in all the subject matters demonstrated that society profits when different cultural groups contribute to the common good (Thayer, Zachry, and Kotinsky 323–341).

Thayer, Zachry, and Kotinsky hoped the curriculum could be constructed in a similarly cooperative manner by having teachers, subject matter specialists, and child-development experts contribute insights from their different perspectives. Their idea differed from organized curriculum making in that they wanted to include only those people who had an expertise that illuminated an educational problem, rather than include representatives of all the groups in a community or a state. To illustrate the process, Thayer, Zachry, and Kotinsky held up the report of the Committee on the Function of the Social Studies in General Education as an example of democratic curriculum design that also promoted the development of democratic attitudes among students (Thayer, Zachry, and Kotinsky 414–417).

Composed of specialists in the social sciences, social studies teachers, and educational theorists, the Committee on the Function of the Social Studies defined the role of the social studies teacher as using the resources of the social studies to meet the needs of adolescents and to develop the characteristics of behavior essential to democracy. According to the committee, any form of curriculum organization could achieve this end. Consequently, they did not recommend a radical revision of the curriculum such as replacing the academic subjects with what was called the functional curriculum, in which lessons were organized around problems or needs common to youth (12–23).

The Committee on the Function of the Social Studies claimed that schools should meet the needs of adolescents by helping them understand the relationships within which they lived, because these interactions played a central role in the students' pattern of development. To aid in such instruction, the committee identified a useful division of relationships into immediate personal-social, social-civic, economic, and personal living, claiming that the social studies offered resources for the study of these areas. For example, books such as Booth Tarkington's *Seventeen* or Mark Twain's *Tom Sawyer* could stimulate discussions of behavior in personal-social associations at different stages of growth. Students might observe children in a nursery or elementary school to consider the problems of development. They could also visit city council meetings, interview political leaders, and review newspaper reports of local issues. For cumulative activities, the students could present roundtable discussions, write articles for a student newspaper, or make reports to the class (Committee on the Function 67–189).

Thus, the Committee on the Function of the Social Studies claimed that students would learn about democracy if teachers applied the subject matter from the social studies in ways that illuminated the types of relationships found in society. Unfortunately, the committee pursued a shallow idea of democracy. For example, although its report held that students should cherish the contributions made by different racial and national groups because these groups advanced society, the committee did not notice that if society is enriched by these contributions, everyone including the people in the different groups would be changed. Philosophers call this process a dialectic because each group advances but retains elements that position it in opposition to other groups. The committee's report did not contain anything as sophisticated as a dialectic. As a result, it implied that groups contributed to the progress of society yet remained the same.

Why Did Planners Want to Include Community Members in Curriculum Planning?

In 1922, when Franklin Bobbitt asked twelve hundred teachers to work together to design the curriculum of Los Angeles schools, he started a movement that spread to other cities. Soon the process grew to include teachers, administrators, and citizens in many walks of life. Called organized curriculum planning, this process helped schools integrate the ideas of the many different people who worked in them and those whom they served.

The advocates of organized curriculum making argued that their methods enabled U.S. schools to ensure that democracy prevailed in the United States. Writing in 1935, Hollis Caswell and Doak Campbell contended that U.S. schools should encourage the equitable distribution of the material wealth made possible by industrialism. This meant that education had to become social engineering. Unafraid of this radical suggestion, Caswell and Campbell stated that their process of organized curriculum making gave local citizens the opportunity to choose such a program (21–22).

According to Caswell and Campbell, four influences kept the schools from developing a curriculum that would meet the nation's social needs. First, most educators could only conceive of curricula as logically organized subject matters. They pointed out that by 1929 few schools blended courses in history and geography into the social studies or allowed students to explore their communities. Second, teachers slavishly followed textbooks. Third, small politically organized groups of citizens campaigned to make the curriculum suit their own interests. As a result of these citizen campaigns, by 1929 every state required its schools to teach about the evils of alcohol consumption and celebrate temperance day. Fourth, the achievement test movement and college admission standards forced schools to adopt instruction that enabled their students to do well by those measures (Caswell and Campbell 38–60).

The process of organized curriculum making was simple. In general, a consultant served as coordinator. This individual worked with a steering committee to solicit the involvement of large numbers of people from various parts of the community or the state, divide them into committees, and assign each group a particular task. For example, in 1929 the state superintendent of Florida chaired a steering committee of eighteen members to improve instruction in the schools. First the committee hired two consultants from George Peabody College. Caswell directed the formation of the elementary program, and Campbell conducted the discussions about the secondary curriculum. The steering committee set up several subcommittees to deal with the various subject matters such as language arts, mathematics, and social studies, and hired additional consultants from other colleges to lead these subcommittees. Taking a list of basic objectives devised for the state, these subcommittees formulated the objectives for the special fields and developed appropriate materials that included units of work, lists of reference books, teaching aids, and suggested procedures. The subcommittees passed on their reports to a general committee that prepared courses of study for publication. In 1933 Florida's department of education published the elementary course of study and courses of study for language arts, social studies, home economics, foreign languages, and commercial courses (Caswell, et al. 364–366).

The project in Florida had mixed results. According to Caswell, one advantage was that it made teachers aware of the value of formulating a basic philosophy with consistent objectives and procedures. However, the project designers took care not to impose strict lesson plans on the teachers; the curriculum materials were guides that teachers could adapt to their own situations. A second advantage was that the program developed leaders within the states who helped expand the projects between 1937 and 1949 when statewide curriculum building became popular. Caswell complained, however, that many Florida teachers ignored the materials developed during the project (Caswell, et al. 366–367).

Despite the limited success of organized curriculum making, the procedures spread rapidly. According to the curriculum laboratory at Teachers College, in 1937 seven-tenths of the cities with more than 25,000 residents had such curriculum development programs. Slightly less than half the cities with populations of 5,000 to 25,000 instituted such organized programs, and about a third of the cities with less than 5,000 inhabitants had similar curriculum improvement programs (Caswell, et al. 45).

Defining curriculum as all the experiences that children have under the teachers' guidance, Caswell and Campbell believed that curricula were best formed through the cooperative efforts of individuals such as administrators, teachers, subject matter specialists, psychologists, sociologists, and philosophers. The process began with a statement of guiding principles that were based on a coherent point of view. From this followed a statement of the aims of education. Because these were social demands, the aims would be aspects of the democratic ideal in the United States. Therefore, members of the community could help select them. The next problem was to define the scope of the curriculum so that each of the students' experiences led into the next. Caswell and Campbell thought that teachers should be able to organize the experiences around the purposeful activities or interests of the students and orient them toward life in society. Furthermore, there should be an identifiable core of things to learn to which the skills and information from different subjects contributed. Finally, the curriculum had to provide for continuous evaluation of the program and the students, and this evaluation should stimulate new learning activities (69, 80, 110, 124, 184–186, 373–375).

Caswell and Campbell employed several types of committees to draft such a curriculum including administrative, production, editing, and advisory committees. To encourage teachers to use the materials, they tried to involve every teacher in the city's schools and appointed them to various levels within the committees. For example, in 1932 the state of Virginia initiated study courses for all teachers and hired Caswell and Campbell as consultants. They prepared a small bulletin listing seven topics such as the definitions of curriculum, objectives, and subject matter. High school principals, exemplary teachers, and other consultants served as directors of the local groups. About 15,000 teachers participated in these study groups (Sidney Hall 340–341).

Organized curriculum making involved many individuals besides professional educators. Because the aims of education were social, Caswell and Campbell called on local citizens to explore their preferences. For example, during the Virginia program a committee of professional educators prepared a tentative statement of the aims of education, which they gave to one hundred representatives of civic groups. When the aims had been revised according to the suggestions of these groups, they were sent to fifteen hundred individuals. The committee on educational aims tabulated their replies and used them to produce a revised report. According to Caswell and Campbell, such participation reduced the ability of special interest groups to impose on the curriculum, and it made for closer connections between home and school (Caswell and Campbell 477–479).

Did Organized Curriculum Making Lead to Social Reform?

Caswell and Campbell thought that organized curriculum making would allow schools to shape a curriculum to fit the needs of their communities. By the 1940s, such organized curriculum making became statewide rather than citywide projects so that the curriculum served a region rather than a single community. Even so, it is not clear that organized curriculum making served the functions of encouraging individuals such as classroom teachers to invest in the programs, nor did these projects encourage experimentation in local classrooms to suit the particular needs of the students.

In 1930, for example, Guy Whipple noted that what usually happened during the subcommittee meetings was that teachers called in textbook agents, who outlined a program based on books the agent sold. These subcommittees then wrote their objectives directly from those textbooks. In another case, the board of education offered a course of study as an example that the teachers were to adapt to their particular situation. Unfortunately, the teachers feared they would lose their jobs if they changed the course of study and so followed it exactly as the board had designed it. Consequently, the teachers did not really contribute to the curriculum development in ways that made them appreciate the schools' objectives, and the board did not encourage the experimentation the committee members wanted (367–368).

On the other hand, some educators claimed that because the organized curriculum programs encouraged experimentation or differences in the curricula among local schools, they weakened democratic ideals. For example, William Bagley complained that it sounded democratic to have teachers make up lists of educational objectives they thought appropriate to the local schools, but this neglected two important needs: (1) the students did not develop the elements common to all good education, and (2) they did not learn what they needed in order to adapt to different communities. These were problems, he noted, because most of the students would move to other parts of the country when they became adults (Bagley, 145–146).

Bagley believed that schools enhanced democracy by offering as high a level of common culture as possible. This meant that many elements in the school programs had to be the same in different parts of the country. Although Bagley acknowledged that school curricula had to be revised to include new scientific findings and artistic advances, he thought that all curricula should offer students the most reliable skills and information produced in the past. In addition, he wanted students to acquire traits such as cooperation with other people, courage in the face of disappointment, and willingness to face facts. According to Bagley, these skills and traits formed the base of human progress. His fear was that curriculum development became a consensus-building exercise among different groups of people who emphasized what was popular at that moment, leaving out the development of skills students needed to live and work together (Bagley 139, 157, 210–211).

Despite these criticisms, organized curriculum making became firmly established in U.S. public schools. To some extent, this can be explained by acknowledging that advocates were correct in claiming that such a process encouraged everyone to invest in the curriculum. However, a considerable degree of the popularity of organized curriculum making was due to the development of the office of the superintendent of schools and the vulnerability under which these officials worked.

Developed late in the nineteenth century, the office of school superintendent grew in importance as city school boards reduced the role of trustees or ward boards. Following the model of a business corporation, board members delegated the authority for planning, hiring, and purchasing to this central executive. By the twentieth century, candidates aspiring to be superintendents attended universities where they received special training to carry out these increased functions (Urban and Wagoner 194–195).

At the same time, however, newspapers and magazines became more popular and increased the power of public opinion. As a result, the security of school superintendents declined even though these officials acquired increased power to change schools. As early as 1909, school superintendents complained at the ease with which relatively small pressure groups drove them from office. Seeking to protect themselves from public criticism, school administrators adopted policies that were widely praised in other parts of the country. For example, in 1911 Frederick Taylor became nationally famous for expressing the principles of efficiency that would improve factories and businesses. Almost immediately school administrators claimed they followed Taylor's plans, hoping that people would perceive this adoption of a popular idea as a strategy in the best interest of schools (Callahan 42, 52–54).

In a similar spirit, school superintendents gravitated toward organized curriculum making. Because this process involved the input of representatives of every possible opposition group, critics could not complain that the superintendent made a mistake in constructing the curriculum. Further, as with the efficiency movement, the superintendents learned about organized curriculum making at the universities where they trained for their jobs. That is, professors of education such as Caswell and Campbell taught their students the value of school surveys and organized curriculum making. In fact, these professors often had their graduate students who would soon become superintendents somewhere serve as assistants in a curriculum project. Therefore, the process probably became popular not because it combined the views of different groups in the community but because it insulated the curriculum from any criticism.

One effect of the organized curriculum movement was that it reinforced the drive to have students study what was important or relevant to them. Thus, secondary schools offered different programs for different students. Usually, the elementary schools concentrated on some sort of basic education, but this model differed for some minority groups. In these cases, although educators followed the same model of meeting students' needs, this principle led to separate schools that either threatened to isolate the groups more thoroughly or lead the students to abandon their traditional culture completely. Two examples illustrate these problems.

Did Hispanic Education Lead to Social Reform during the Depression?

During the depression, U.S. President Franklin Roosevelt's New Deal spread money to areas that had been deprived during the prosperous years of the 1920s. In New Mexico, the infusion of federal funds to a poor state boosted the economy. In schools these funds influenced programs such as vocational education and music and arts. Because many of these projects reinforced Hispanic culture, the federal aid to education from the New Deal enabled New Mexico schools to preserve cultural diversity (Getz 11).

Since the turn of the century, there had been considerable disagreement among the citizens of New Mexico on the merits of using Spanish in the instruction of Spanish-speaking children. These children were concentrated in rural, poverty-stricken villages. From 1918 to 1924, however, one county school superintendent in New Mexico, Nina Otero-Warren, tried to promote Hispanic culture through the schools. She collected Hispanic stories, plays, and songs, which she published in her book, *Old Spain in Our Southwest.* As superintendent she encouraged teachers to discover what games the students' parents played and to use them in physical education instead of mainstream American pastimes such as baseball. She suggested that in those communities where the adults practiced traditional weaving, tin work, or pottery, these crafts should be taught in the schools. She thought that teachers of Spanish-speaking children should speak Spanish, although she would not allow them to use the language during instruction. Otero-Warren reserved the use of Spanish for the playground or artistic activities (Getz 41–45).

However, Otero-Warren's ideas were not popular among New Mexico educators. In fact, when the depression began the New Mexico department of education recommended that all Spanish-speaking students receive only English instruction. As a result, the teachers suppressed all Spanish in school buildings, separating Spanish-speaking children and forcing them to take an intensive course in English that was conducted only in English, then returning them to the general classroom. Unfortunately, this direct method retarded the students' progress through the grades by at least one year and subjected them to humiliating experiences on the playground (Getz 38–39).

In 1933, as federal relief funds began to reach the state, Otero-Warren became state supervisor of education in the Education Division of the Works Projects Administration. Working in adult education, Otero-Warren obtained special permission to use bilingual instruction and materials that built on the experiences of adults. At the same time, schools spread throughout the state. Federal funds supported the construction of 257 new schools and the remodeling of 56 more. The funds also paid for the construction of twenty-three gymnasiums, six libraries, and nine auditoriums. These construction projects paid wages to local workers who in turn paid local taxes to operate the schools. Most important, the federal programs responded more to local needs than to the requirements of any central agency. As a result, educators were encouraged to adapt the programs to the unique situations their students faced (Getz 103–106).

Nearly everyone involved in the New Deal in New Mexico advocated using the federal funds to maintain the state's distinct character in a manner similar to that articulated by Otero-Warren. This meant looking for a way to preserve the village setting and promote traditional arts and crafts. To expand this thrust, the state department of education hired a sculptor, Brice H. Sewell, as supervisor of trade and industrial education. Before his state appointment, Sewell had taught in the San Jose Training School, where he was in charge of handicrafts. Following his interests, he promoted the development of village craft industries that utilized raw materials found in the rural villages in the Spanish-speaking sections of New Mexico (Getz 107–109).

In Chupadera, a small town without any agricultural or manufacturing resources, Sewell's administration opened one of the first vocational schools and craft workshops under the provisions of the Emergency Education Act. This school turned the community into a center for the production of handmade rawhide and wood furniture, activities by which most of the families sustained themselves. In Taos a similar school taught Spanish colonial ornamental ironwork. These ventures were so successful that by 1936 vocational schools teaching crafts spread throughout most of Hispanic New Mexico. Although Sewell expected these handicrafts to make the villagers financially independent, the crafts he introduced were different from those introduced in the mainstream communities in the eastern and western parts of the state. These more advantaged students learned subjects better designed to meet the needs of the industrialized community such as auto mechanics, welding, and commerce (Forrest 108–109).

Of course, the New Deal in New Mexico extended far beyond educational programs. It included projects to build roads, public buildings, and hospitals; to translate a wealth of Spanish documents; and to protect the soil. In 1940 the New Deal culminated with large, coordinated rehabilitation programs such as the Taos County Project, in which seventeen agencies joined to plan land use programs, libraries, roads, water facilities, and health care facilities. In outlying villages, the project built community centers for adult education classes and recreation. A county bookmobile extended library resources, and a health association brought medical care to thousands of people who had never had it. Unfortunately, the attack on Pearl Harbor and the entry of the United States into World War II took many of the people and much of the federal money away from these projects (Forrest 148–150).

Most reformers thought the war was a temporary delay in the rehabilitation of New Mexico's villages. Such was not the case. Although the villages survived, they did not become self-supporting. In 1986 the Hispanic counties of northern New Mexico remained one of the most resistant pockets of poverty in the United States. In a peculiar way, the New Deal's educational program contributed to this failure. On the one hand, the handicraft-training movement ended too quickly to provide the long-term benefits for which Sewell had hoped. For example, in 1941 there was virtually no trace of the San Jose Experimental School, although it had been enthusiastically supported only six years earlier. On the other hand, the effort gave importance to the Spanish language, the community culture, and the historic arts. Though the specific arts and crafts they encouraged did not help the residents become financially independent, the schools did teach students the benefits of education and introduced them to more affluent lifestyles than the subsistence level at which they lived. Thus, the movement designed to keep people in the villages gave many people an education that made village life appear unattractive. Not surprisingly, the young people left the villages, and from 1940 to 1960 the rural population of New Mexico declined by almost 30 percent (Forrest 129, 156, 175–179).

Did the Curriculum for Native Americans Improve during the Depression?

In the same way that the New Deal encouraged New Mexico teachers to use Spanish and to develop traditional arts and crafts, it encouraged teachers of Native Americans to tailor instruction to the students' particular needs. This was especially true among the Navajo.

In the 1930s, the Navajo people constituted the largest tribe of Native Americans in the United States, with a population of about 45,000. They lived on a reservation of almost 24,000 square miles in northeastern Arizona that extended over the borders of New Mexico and Utah. Although the tribe had grown, the members had not attended schools. In 1868, when the then-10,000 Navajo moved to that reservation, the U.S. government promised to provide a school and a teacher for every thirty children who attended. For their part, the Navajo promised to compel their children to attend. Unfortunately, neither side kept those promises. In the 1880s, the U.S. government began establishing and operating boarding schools in cities such as Grand Junction, Colorado, and Phoenix, Arizona. Some Navajo children attended these boarding schools. One school operated by the government opened on the Navajo reservation in the 1890s. More typically, the federal government contracted missionary societies to provide schools. This system ended in 1901 (Bailey and Bailey 168).

The number of Navajo attending schools increased as the number of schools increased. In 1890 there were 89 Navajo students out of a school population of about 6,000 children. Only about 2 percent of adult Navajo had any formal education at that time. In the first years of the twentieth century, the U.S. Commissioner of Indian Affairs began constructing boarding and day schools on the reservation. By 1908, 770 children attended school, and enrollments rose to almost 2,000 by 1932. By 1930 almost one-third of the Navajo had experienced some formal education (Bailey and Bailey 168–169).

These changes were not made easily. In 1920, after Congress learned the extent of illiteracy on reservations, it empowered the secretary of the interior to secure the enrollment of eligible Native American children in schools. At the same time, Congress warned that it would close any schools that were not filled to capacity. As a result, in 1922 local officials strived to place each Native American child in school every day. Although nationwide more Native American children entered schools, one-third of all eligible Native American children out of school were Navajo. One reason for their resistance was that Navajo parents needed the children at home to tend to sheep (L. Kelly 172–175).

In 1926 the U.S. Department of the Interior commissioned the Institute for Government Research, chaired by Robert S. Brookings, to undertake a report on conditions among Native Americans in general. This was the first major report on the status of these people. In 1928 the commission delivered its report, which concluded that an overwhelming majority of Native Americans were extremely poor and not adjusted to the economic and social system of the dominant White civilization. Their health was bad, and their living conditions encouraged the spread of disease. The commission contended that there were two main reasons for this extreme poverty: the land Native Americans farmed was poor, and their traditional social system did not serve them well in the new economic conditions. Although this conclusion suggested that the government should educate Native Americans to take care of themselves, the commission found that such education had failed because the U.S. Indian Service did not appropriate enough money to hire adequate personnel to teach the Native Americans to earn decent wages and to live at a level that promoted health and decency (Institute for Government Research 3–10).

In its 1928 report, the Institute for Government Research argued that the U.S. Indian Service's policy of sending Native American children to boarding schools was grossly inadequate. At these schools, students were fed at a cost of eleven cents a day. Although teachers tried to supplement the students' diet with food and dairy products produced by the school, they could not provide sufficient amounts nor enough variety for the children to maintain their health. Frequently, students contracted tuberculosis; the dormitories were overcrowded, and medical services were inadequate. In addition to these uncomfortable conditions, students above the fourth grade had to work on the school grounds performing dangerous tasks such as operating heavy equipment in the laundries that would be prohibited by child labor laws in many states (11–13).

The Institute for Government Research noted that these boarding schools employed a curriculum that had no relation to the needs of the students. The commission members found that teachers expected the same performance from students who encountered English for the first time as they did from those who spoke English at home. Worse yet, according to the report, discipline was restrictive instead of developmental. Misbehaving children were placed in limited quarters. Finally, the report noted that when students successfully completed their education, there was no effort to help them find appropriate work. In fact, the skills or trades they learned at the schools, such as harness making, were not the kind from which people earned a living (Institute for Government Research 13–14, 384).

In the 1920s, Native American schools did not follow the practices of curriculum formation popular among public schools. For example, at that time, as described in the section on organized curriculum making, public school boards often produced courses of study and encouraged teachers to adapt them to the needs of the students in the classrooms. The boards revised these courses of studies regularly to fit them to changing social conditions. But although the schools run by the Indian Service served many different tribes with different languages and customs, the service had produced a course of study in 1915 and expected every teacher in all the schools to follow it exactly. By 1927 they had not revised this course of study. The service expected teachers to concentrate on basic instruction in reading, writing, and arithmetic and to teach students through mechanical drill and repetition exercises. Although members of the commission of the Institute for Government Research thought students should learn community civics, they found no such course nor did they locate any teachers attempting to instruct Native American students in the history or traditions of Native Americans. Such instruction was essential, the Institute for Government Research contended, if students were to understand the place of their people in modern society. To revise the curriculum and provide reasonable instruction, however, the Indian Service needed more money. Conditions were so bad that all schools lacked libraries and most had only a few old textbooks (370–374).

The Institute for Government Research condemned the system of off-reservation boarding schools. At these schools, students worked half the day and studied the other half, and the tasks they performed were often dangerous and harmful to their health. Consequently, the report urged, all Native American children up to grade 6 should be sent to Native American day schools where they could pursue academic studies. However, the report urged that these studies avoid drill and repetition of spelling words and instead recommended new programs similar to those used in public schools with courses appropriate to the students' cultural backgrounds (375–376).

In response to this report, the Commissioner of Indian Affairs sought at least two important changes in education. First, the commission took the students from boarding schools and placed them in public schools or day schools on the reservation. This change in policy satisfied Native American groups such as the Navajo Tribal Council and the members of Congress. It did not influence school attendance because there were too few school buildings. To some extent, this changed during the depression. In 1935 funds from two federal programs initiated nationally to alleviate the problems of the depression—the Public Works Administration and the Works Progress Administration—went to the construction of forty-seven schools for Native Americans (L. Kelly 176–181).

Second, the commissioner dropped the uniform course of study that had been required in all Native American schools. Instead of imparting only academics, instruction focused on four topics: health, land and livestock conservation, civic participation, and manual skills. In these schools, the language of instruction was English. However, in some cases the students studied their own language and culture to better learn English and to enhance civic participation. For example, in some Navajo reservation schools, Navajo as a written language was introduced to facilitate English instruction (Jones, *Navajo* 53, 57; L. Kelly 181).

In 1939, under its then education director Thomas Jesse Jones, the Phelps-Stokes Fund published a report about the problems facing the Navajo people. The investigators found that the Navajo people held tenaciously to their language and their customs and resisted the Americanization undergone by millions of European immigrants. But the Navajo faced a crisis. The arid reservation land was threatened by erosion and overgrazing. Although the land could support about 550,000 sheep or goats, the Navajo had accumulated more than 1,250,000. Jones's report pointed out that in 1933 the U.S. Bureau of Indian Affairs began programs to reduce soil erosion. However, the conservation measures clashed with the customs of the Navajo who distrusted the White experts. Not surprising, as they had previously experienced European Americans as ruthless exploiters. As a result, the inquiry staff of the Phelps-Stokes Fund asserted that soil conservation, personal health, and family life for the Navajo depended on this tribe learning about modern civilization (Jones, *Navajo* vii, 2–3, 39).

The investigators for Phelps-Stokes found the administrators on the Navajo reservation better able to help the people than had been the case a decade earlier. More money had been spent on buildings. But although capable and attentive personnel directed educational programs, almost half the eligible children on the reservation did not attend school, and of those that did attend, almost half were in grade 1 or below. The investigators thought the primary reason for this lack of interest in education was that the Navajo were in the midst of a cultural shift. The old values had fallen and the new Western ideals had not yet taken firm hold. Investigators believed, however, that some educational changes had to be made to alleviate the problems of poverty and severe soil erosion on the reservation (Jones, *Navajo* 39–40).

In 1939 most Navajo students attended reservation day and boarding schools although some went to public schools, mission schools, and boarding schools off the reservation. These off-reservation options were considered unsatisfactory by the investigators for the Phelps-Stokes Fund because the children encountered prejudice and the distances they had to travel were great. To Jones and his staff, reservation day schools seemed to be the best option. There were also problems with the curricula of the Indian Service Schools. When the commissioner of Indian Affairs freed the teachers from the course of study that concentrated on basic academic skills, he left them without a curriculum guide. Worse, Jones found the teachers unable or unwilling to prepare reasonable guides for their students. As a result, the teachers were frequently bewildered about what to teach and when to teach it. Although these teachers had been trained in teachers' colleges, few could speak the Navajo language. However, Jones and his staff were impressed with facilities for adult education found in many of the day schools. They noted admirable areas for shop production, where residents made items such as baby cribs and chairs; for cooking, where the residents learned to perform functions such as baking bread and canning fruits; and for shop repair, where the residents sharpened tools and fixed automobiles (Jones, *Navajo* 41–43).

Most important, the Phelps-Stokes investigators were dismayed because the schools did not hire native Navajo to be teachers. Although the White women who taught in the reservation day schools were well trained, they could not easily communicate nor understand the problems in the Navajo hogans, or homes. Most of these teachers left their jobs after a short time. To improve the schools, Jones and the other investigators suggested that administrators hire teachers fitting three criteria: (1) the teachers should feel an affection for the Navajo; (2) they should have at least a working knowledge of the language; and (3) they must be able to endure the loneliness of reservation life (Jones, *Navajo* 45–46).

According to Jones, the reservation teachers employed a version of the project method that called for students to work on activities related to their interests and home life. Because most of the students would remain on the reservation, all the schools tried to provide knowledge to control the environment, establish health habits, and create attitudes favorable to the soil conservation policy. Unfortunately, teachers did not have adequate supervision or technical assistance to make these projects lead to academic instruction. That is, Jones and his investigators contended that when the teachers stopped using a uniform course of study and replaced it with a project method that had students investigate things around the reservation, they had such an aversion to making the students memorize skills associated with reading, writing, and arithmetic that they ignored these basic academic skills. As a result, very little instruction prepared students to enter the mainstream of American life. In part, Jones thought, the problem was that resources and personnel were spread too thin. In 1939 the Commissioner of Indian Affairs divided the Navajo reservation into ten school districts, nine of them centered on boarding schools. The principal of a boarding school also supervised three to six day schools for the younger pupils (Jones, *Navajo* 47–57).

Consequently, the investigators recommended that several small one-room schools be distributed throughout the area to replace the few large day schools. Traveling teachers would regularly visit these sites. The Phelps-Stokes commission found the day schools and the boarding schools too expensive and unrewarding. Although the schools provided a wide range of services to both children and adults, only about one-fourth of the population took advantage of them. The children were needed at home, and the families moved as many as four times a year, putting children out of reach of school buses. For the curriculum, the report suggested that the basic instruction emphasize reading, writing, and arithmetic. This did not mean a return to drill and memorization, according to Jones and the commission members, because these subjects could be taught in ways that imparted the social essentials. For example, arithmetic could be used to teach lessons in health, agriculture, or home life (Jones, *Navajo* 57–70).

How Did the Depression Influence Teachers and the Education of Minorities?

The depression encouraged teachers to think about their responsibilities as agents of social change. Although they joined unions, they would not use those associations to lead political movements. Those teachers more concerned with the intellectual disciplines such as history and sociology turned to the social studies to teach students to become aware of their society, critical of its many imperfections, and desirous of improving it. Educators shared the concerns felt by many academicians. At the same time, those teachers who might be called more child centered turned to projects that would regenerate the students' creative energies such as the Eight-Year Study and the activity movement. A third group of educators sought to involve many different types of people in curriculum building. Called organized curriculum building, this model wanted citizens, parents, teachers. administrators, and subject matter specialists to work together in enormous projects to define the goals and materials for an education appropriate for a specific city or state.

The thrust of these reforms was to adapt instruction to the specific needs of the students so as to improve the democratic society. Educators who wanted teachers to reconstruct society complained that the child-centered reformers ignored pressing social issues. However, the advocates of building curricula around the students' needs thought they were teaching children to act independently and think intelligently. They hoped such citizens would reform society. In a similar manner, the organized curriculum makers seemed to impose a course of study—determined by consensus—on everyone. However, they thought they were allowing the best ideas of all people to come together in a plan that would benefit everyone. Thus, although the instruction was aimed at individual children, it should improve a society all people shared.

The flaws in these approaches became most evident when the models were applied to minority groups such as Mexican Americans and Native Americans who received segregated educations. This was caused by differences in language or extraordinary distances between homes and schools. Although these groups suffered during prosperous times, federal funds to end the Great Depression brought the progressive ideas of curriculum reform such as the activity movement to their schools. In those segregated settings, the progressive models of meeting people's needs became opportunities to strengthen the traditional culture. To some extent, this was a benefit. Such education could reinforce the ties among members of the community and might reduce some problems that beset their particular area. In general, however, the schools worked against the communities they meant to strengthen. Sometimes students learned skills that did lead to opportunities to achieve more comfortable living conditions. At other times, students had enough exposure to the wealth available outside their communities that they chose to leave. Therefore, no curriculum option could help the people in these different communities retain their traditional ways of life and, at the same time, profit from the improved standards of living found in the wider society. These goals appeared to conflict with each other.

TIMELINE
1930–1940

1930 The PEA met to begin the eight-year study of high schools

1932 George Counts challenged the PEA to combat capitalism

1932 Detroit and Chicago schools cut teachers' salaries, programs, courses, and supplies due to the stock market crash

1932 Virginia offered to all teachers in the state study courses based on Hollis Caswell and Doak Campbell's methods

1932 The AHA published its first report, *A Charter for the Social Sciences*

1933 Nina Otero-Warren became New Mexico's supervisor of education and encouraged bilingual instruction

TIMELINE Continued

1933 Chicago closed all junior high schools

1933 The PEA's Committee on Social and Economic Problems presented its report, *A Call to Teachers of the Nation*

1934 Charles Beard delivered his AHA presidential address

1934 AHA began editing the magazine *The Social Studies*

1935 NCTE published a report supporting the activity curriculum

1937 AHA and NCSS established the journal *Social Education*

1937 CEEB published a report on history education

1939 PEA published the report *Reorganizing Secondary Education*

1939 Thomas Jesse Jones, heading the Phelps-Stokes Fund, published a report on the Navajo struggles

1939 The Navajo reservation was divided into ten school districts

CHAPTER

8 War, Democracy, and Isolation within Minority Groups: 1940–1954

New Crossett High School for Whites

OVERVIEW

Some historians argue that after World War II the federal government began to intrude into local school affairs. According to this interpretation of education history, government officials wanted to use elementary and secondary schools to meet national objectives in foreign policy and economic development. Although such an interpretation accounts for some of the evidence, it ignores the fears educators had of government intervention and the reasons they gave for enacting particular policies.

As the 1940s began, educators contended that schools could restore the economic prosperity lost during the depression if all people had the opportunity to receive an ap-

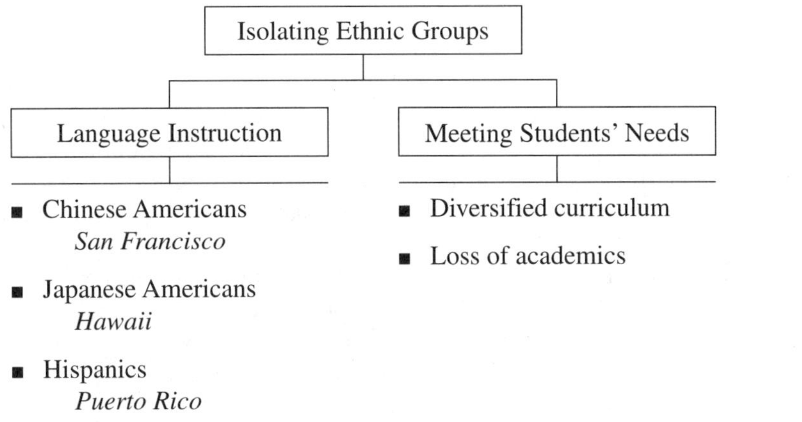

propriate education. Ironically, one aspect of this desire to improve everyone's status—the need for all people to communicate—isolated those minorities for whom English was not the native language. Three cases illustrate this tendency: the Chinese students in San Francisco, the Japanese children in Hawaii, and Spanish-speaking residents of Puerto Rico. In these cases, the view that all citizens in a democracy should share a common language resulted in different actions. However, in all of them, this democratic principle weakened the possibility of equal opportunity.

Nonetheless, educators argued that World War II made imperative three tendencies of reform already under way in U.S. elementary and secondary schools:

1. Courses became more practical.
2. The federal government increased financial support of local schools, and national associations tried to direct reforms in local school districts.
3. Educators emphasized the democratic traditions for which the nation fought.

After the war, educators continued to emphasize making the schools more democratic. They claimed that one way the country could demonstrate its appreciation of the sacrifices young people made to win the war was for schools to meet the students' needs. Thus, educators called for high schools to offer a range of courses that appealed to various types of students. These schools divided the students among several programs, and the divisions followed social class lines. Unfortunately, educators could not reduce the problems of segregation because their aim of meeting the needs of youth did not provide any reasonable direction but was instead vague and indeterminate.

How Did Educators Try to Rebuild Elementary and Secondary Schools after the Depression?

Some historians contend that since World War II U.S. schools have become an agency of the federal government and serve its purposes. For example, Joel Spring contends that since World War II federal involvement in education has reinforced one specific tradition in U.S.

education. During the nineteenth century, public schooling expanded in the United States for a variety of reasons such as maintaining communities, increasing morality, Americanizing immigrants, and preparing the population for industrialization. In the twentieth century, public education became a way to separate students according to abilities, to guide them into specific programs based on their abilities, and to prepare them for particular slots in the national labor force (Spring, *Sorting* 1–2).

Spring's perspective explains some of what happened in U.S. education, but it overlooks educators' fears of government intervention and the reasons they gave for enacting particular policies. It is possible that the increased federal involvement in schools that took place was an unintended consequence of educators' desire to help students adjust to the relationships they would develop. The diversified curriculum was intended to meet the different needs of various students. It is true, as Spring suggests, that educational commissions often claimed that schools enhanced society's wealth. However, their stated aim in making this observation clear was to advance the common good, not to provide a means of profit for powerful elites.

In 1940 the National Education Association (NEA) commissioned its Educational Policies Commission (EPC) to determine the relationship between education and the economic advancement of society. Entitled *Education and Economic Well-Being in American Democracy,* the EPC's report noted that at least two-thirds of high school age youth were enrolled in secondary schools, and a million youth attended colleges and universities in the hope that their education would provide them with increased wealth and social position. However, such opportunities were not extended to all young people on the basis of their ability to learn. Instead, the opportunities for education were reduced by factors such as belonging to a poor family, living in a region with insufficient wealth to afford public schools, being a member of a minority group such as African Americans, or living in a rural area. According to the EPC, these limitations hardened the divisions separating the social classes. Although there were complex reasons for these inequalities, the EPC asserted that the primary cause was financial (1–3).

According to the EPC, the Great Depression had aggravated educational inequities. From 1930 to 1936, the national income diminished by almost one-half; total expenditures by federal, state, and local agencies for public education diminished from $2,417,000,000 to $2,237,000,000. Although public spending during the same period had increased, public schools suffered because the federal government had been more successful in raising funds than had states or local districts. A large portion of the federal money went to establishing social security, relief, and military preparedness. However, the EPC warned that failing to provide equal educational facilities for everyone would suggest that society rejected the ideal of equality of opportunity (*Education and Economic* 3–5).

In surveying the factors that increased productivity in an economy, the EPC noted that an efficient system of education increased the value of the workers, a nation's primary wealth, in several ways:

- Education enhanced the workers' interest in self-improvement.
- When the workers had increased vocational intelligence, output per worker increased.

- Through education workers could transfer to fields in which their skills were needed.
- Health education improved productivity by letting people work for more years.
- Education increased people's willingness to conserve natural resources, which would extend productivity.
- Because children of different social classes worked together in the common schools, they learned to accept leadership from people who had risen to authority through intelligence and effort.

For all these reasons, the EPC declared that education improved the culture and its productivity (*Education and Economic* 7–32).

According to the EPC, traditional education could not ease the economic problems confronting the American people in what the EPC called the new corporate age. For example, because people worked for large industries, schools had to teach students about industrial relations and develop cooperative attitudes among workers, managers, and citizens. The EPC thought schools should enhance general mechanical and scientific competency. Although the EPC called on colleges and universities to help the public understand economic problems, the members thought that elementary schools could set the foundation of such understandings by teaching skills needed to read reports, record orders, and understand research findings. The EPC also called for more consumer education, especially in areas such as food consumption, clothing needs, shelter requirements, and health expenses. At the same time, the EPC called for consumer training to help students understand public expenditures, proper saving habits, and social responsibility (*Education and Economic* 33–74).

The EPC called for a vocational education that was aligned with the community's economic needs. However, they noted that this required extensive study because changes in industry rendered some specific training unimportant but made other sorts of skilled workers essential. Not only did vocational education have to take account of such trends, but the school also should guide youth in choosing careers based on their capacities, abilities, and the opportunities in the community. To the EPC, guidance services were most important because they enabled students to make wise decisions about their futures (*Education and Economic* 75–94).

According to the EPC, wise public policy should provide the amount of education that enabled people to earn the most income possible after paying for the cost of schooling. If schooling was to provide social mobility, it had to be free; otherwise, costs would exclude some people who needed it. But some children required more than free tuition. Without food, clothing, medical aid, and shelter, some children could not attend school. Because income was related to the level of education people attained, EPC members reasoned that children should be required to attend school for at least ten years. Although committee members wanted the average length of education to be fourteen years, they realized that several factors such as individual capacity influenced any person's ability to profit from schooling. Nonetheless, evidence available to the EPC showed that students who received aid to attend higher education often performed better than students whose families sent them. Finally, the report noted that many states maintained separate and inferior schools for African Americans. Although the EPC did not call for the racial integration of schools, the committee observed that uneducated Black people represented a burden, and therefore it called for equal expenditures for schools of all races (*Education and Economic* 103–152).

As the EPC report indicated, if the high schools were to contribute to the economic well-being of the country, they had to adopt an appropriate curriculum. However, at least one group argued that more vocational courses were not the answer. In 1940 the American Council of Education, an organization of colleges, universities, private secondary schools, state departments of education, and city school systems, established the American Youth Commission (AYC) to determine which courses students should take and how these classes should be organized. Entitled *What the High Schools Ought to Teach,* the AYC report listed three reasons why high schools should change their curricula. First, the number of students attending high schools had increased rapidly. In 1900 there were less than 700,000 students in all the high schools in the United States. By 1939, according to the report, there were more than 6,500,000. According to the report, this increase was caused in part by compulsory education laws inspired by desires to lengthen and improve the period of adolescent development and by efforts to keep children out of the labor force. Second, new courses grew out of increased contributions to knowledge and efforts to prepare youth for the problems of organized society. Third, the problem of youth unemployment forced high schools to find ways to build student morale and develop potential abilities. Although vocational education appeared to be a solution to these problems, the AYC found that vocational courses were often narrowly focused and did not prepare students for the work that was available (1–10).

The AYC listed four elements needed in a program of secondary instruction: (1) reading as a subject of instruction; (2) the ability to work steadily for eight hours; (3) social studies instruction that taught students how to act appropriately and understand the problems of community life; and (4) some instruction about personal problems such as maintaining physical and mental health (10–27).

In keeping with the view that schools should offer practical instruction, the AYC contended that in mathematics, instead of following complicated and abstract materials, the students should learn how an equation works, how a table of numbers can become a graph, and the basics of functional relations. Additionally, the benefit of studying a foreign language was that it helped students understand the structure of languages in general. This understanding could be obtained more easily, the report claimed, if students took a general course in language rather than tried to master any particular foreign tongue (27–29).

Although reports such as this may reinforce Spring's view that national organizations redirected elementary and secondary schools to serve national interests, the problems at issue are more complicated. The desire for a uniform national language has long been a part of what historians such as John Higham called the pattern of American nativism. In their eyes, the unwillingness of people in the United States to learn different languages was a character fault. However, educators decided that instruction in foreign languages was unnecessary in the United States. Instead, they held that all students should learn to speak correct English because the citizens in a democracy must communicate with each other. Unfortunately, they could not easily identify what level of mastery of English the students should attain. In some cases, educators' distaste for foreign languages went beyond trying to forge one country out of many peoples and became a tool to exclude non-English-speakers from participation in the school or the community. Two examples—the Chinese American students in San Francisco and the Hawaiian American and Japanese American students in Hawaii—illustrate this tendency.

How Did the Need for Correct English Affect Chinese Students?

According to Victor Low, San Francisco offers the clearest example of educators who pushed the need for understandable English speech to the point at which it became a tool for exclusion. Perhaps even more disappointing, the teachers who succeeded were probably members of a class that Peter Kwong calls the "Uptown Chinese." In 1987 Kwong assigned this name to the more than 30 percent of Chinese Americans who held professional jobs, graduated from universities, and earned incomes above the national average. At the same time, more than 30 percent of Chinese Americans held low-paying jobs as manual and service workers. Kwong calls this group the "Downtown Chinese." Kwong contends that the Uptown Chinese profited from holding the Downtown Chinese in place (4–7). Although this phenomenon also occurred in the case Low chronicled, he noted that school administrators used English fluency to maintain discrimination, and in their desire to excel, the Chinese American teachers in the system exacerbated the problem.

With the advent of World War II, Chinese Americans in San Francisco made strides in overcoming the segregation that had marked their earlier educational experiences. When Madame Chiang Kai-shek visited the United States in 1943, the media welcomed her and portrayed the Chinese people as natural allies of the United States, a relationship exemplified by their struggles against Japanese aggression. At her request, Congress repealed discriminatory immigration laws. Further pressure for change came from Chinese American men who had served in the U.S. Army. Many of these soldiers married in China because there were many more Chinese men than Chinese women in the United States. In 1946 Congress approved the War Brides Act, which allowed these men to bring their families home with them. Other changes followed. In 1947 California removed a state code prohibiting Chinese Americans from buying real estate, and many Chinese Americans bought homes outside Chinatown in San Francisco. In a more sweeping gesture, the California legislature and Governor Earl Warren repealed the section of the education code calling for racial segregation. In practice, these reforms caused few changes. In part, the practice of having neighborhood schools perpetuated segregated education. However, the superintendent of San Francisco schools removed the phrase "Oriental School" from the name of the Commodore Stockton School, which had been built in 1915 exclusively for Chinese American students who could not enter the other school buildings (Low 133–132, 142–143).

Despite the legal end of segregation, Chinese students who entered San Francisco attended the Chinatown schools. From 1948 until 1955, about 1,600 war brides and about 1,500 Chinese children settled in San Francisco. San Francisco schools offered some programs to help these people overcome their limited English-speaking ability, and one building in Chinatown, the Washington Irving School, held orientation classes for the war brides, guiding them through the city and helping them learn about their new homes. Galileo High School offered a year of basic instruction in reading, writing, and arithmetic before the new Chinese students enrolled in regular courses. In the elementary schools, special classes, called "Opportunity Classes," offered lessons in English to the younger children before they joined the regular classes. Americanization classes taught English, geography, and citizenship. However, the schools did not address many of the problems the newcomers brought to the Chinatown area. For example, many children worked long hours at dangerous jobs, and some of the older boys lived on the streets gathering food and clothing through petty crime. Instead, the San Francisco schools channeled its resources into other districts, in part because Chinese students often had records of high academic achievement and because Chinatown had a reputation of taking care of its own problems (Low 135–146).

The influx of Chinese immigrants spurred the San Francisco schools to hire Chinese American teachers. From 1926 until 1946, San Francisco schools hired about one Chinese American teacher a year. By 1951 four more teachers were added. The rate increased so that by 1959 a total of seventy-one Chinese American teachers had served in the district since 1926. Even this small number of appointments was closely controlled. From 1943 until 1959, for example, San Francisco schools hired a total of six female and fourteen male teachers to teach in secondary schools. Most of these were assigned to the junior high school level, and no Chinese American woman taught at the senior high level before 1959 (Low 146–154).

In general, administrators assigned Chinese American teachers to Chinese-speaking students. Consequently, as the Chinese American population spread northward and westward into the city, more schools became known as "Chinatown schools" and hired Chinese American teachers. Despite a large pool of candidates, however, from 1943 until 1954 San Francisco schools seemed to abide by an unspoken quota, employing only three Chinese American teachers in any one school. Even the elementary school that had enrolled only Chinese American students since its founding in 1915 employed only three Chinese American teachers out of a total faculty ranging from twenty-two to twenty-seven teachers. This practice of having only three Chinese American teachers together in one school caused the district to place newly hired Chinese American teachers in other sections of the city that were considered less desirable. Generally, those teachers tried to work themselves into the Chinatown schools (Low 154–158).

One reason there were few Chinese American teachers was that administrators and teacher educators held distorted views of language fluency. Although they could speak and understand English, Chinese Americans had difficulty passing the training programs to become teachers in San Francisco offered by the local colleges. The teacher educators and school officials decided that Chinese Americans who had an accent, such as dropping the final "l" in words or not correctly making a "th" sound, could not teach. As a result, Chinese Americans who wanted to become teachers took a speech test at the local state teachers college. Those who failed had to take compensatory classes until they passed (Low 169–179).

Not surprisingly, because Chinese American teachers learned and worked under severe restrictions, they reacted by instituting teaching methods that hurt the students. When Victor Low interviewed former Chinese American teachers in San Francisco, he found that these teachers had tried to gain approval from their superiors and advance to a more secure or better position by demanding of their students strict discipline, assigning a great deal of seat work, and emphasizing the quieter activities of reading and writing instead of speaking. According to Low, however, this worked against the students because, in San Francisco through the 1940s and 1950s, colleges used speech tests to approve teaching applicants, yet the teachers in the elementary schools emphasized written English instruction for Chinese American children rather than spoken language exercises (Low 169–179).

How Did Concerns about English Influence Schools in Hawaii?

Hawaii offers another example of the way in which language requirements worked to exclude a segment of the population. On the one hand, educators followed principles similar to those outlined in the AYC report *What the High Schools Ought to Teach.* Instead of valuing bilingual training, they emphasized opportunities for all people to learn English. In order to help their children advance socially and economically, non-native-English-speakers often tried to send their children to English-speaking schools. For those non-native-English-speakers who wanted to become teachers, educators made excessive demands and turned concern for proper English into a device to exclude applicants. However, by the 1960s and 1970s, concern for preserving the native Hawaiian language led educators to establishing public schools where the language was spoken.

For many years, commentators thought that the eight islands of Hawaii offered the opportunity to test solutions to problems affecting other parts of the United States. The land mass was about 6,400 square miles, and only the coastal fringe of each island allowed agricultural and industrial development. In this small area, a wide range of different peoples lived and worked together. Therefore, individuals or small groups of researchers could assess the results of experiments in universal education and race relations. For example, in the 1930s, one commentator wrote, children in schools spoke freely of their ancestry, proudly claiming race mixtures of Scotch, German, Hawaiian, and Chinese. There were no race lines drawn in the school system. Children of all races played, studied, and lived close together. Similarly, among the teaching staff people of different races worked side by side demonstrating interracial understanding and friendliness toward the students (D. Crawford i–iii, 195–196).

Despite this picture of racial harmony, World War II brought the end of two different educational endeavors that had developed as people sought to work out the ways in which groups who spoke different languages could live and work together. The first was the English Standard school system, which allowed middle-class White students to preserve their language, but reinforced the tendency of Japanese students to retain their native Hawaii Creole English and continue working in lower-status positions. The second effort was the Japanese Language schools.

The English Standard schools had roots in the origins of Hawaiian education. In 1820 the Prudential Committee of the American Board of Commissioners for Foreign Missions sent two Protestant ministers, a physician, a mechanic, a printer, and their wives and children to Hawaii. They were soon joined by other missionaries who knew the Hawaiian language and began committing the language to written form. By 1822 they had printed the first short text in Hawaiian and had set up schools for almost 300 adults. The idea of conveying messages with symbols fascinated the native Hawaiians. Taking instruction as a form of recreation, about 15,000 adult Hawaiians enrolled in various schools within a few months. At the same time, the missionaries printed more books. By 1825 they had 16,000 primers and 13,500 catechisms, and by 1830 they had more than twenty different books and had imported more materials. Furthermore, they established special schools. In 1836, for example, the missionaries opened a manual labor school for boys on Oahu, and two years later they started a similar school for girls on Hilo (Wist 16–30).

As students in the adult programs graduated, some of them became teachers and the educational aims shifted from adult training to child education. However, the missionaries began to relinquish control of the schools, turning over responsibility for education to the government. Although Hawaii was ruled by a king, school governance was democratic. The school laws of 1840 provided that each village would elect a school committee, which would act with the local missionary to select a teacher and set up taxes to support the school. This law was similar to that instituted in New England (Wist 23, 50–52).

Because the missionaries came to Hawaii with their families, they felt conflicting obligations. On the one hand, they wanted to continue their work on the islands. On the other hand, they wanted their children to have American educational advantages. As a result, in 1842, Daniel Dole, his wife, and Marcia Smith opened a separate school named Punahou for thirty-four students, fifteen of whom were boarders. The curriculum imitated the manual training found in two other boarding schools on the islands. Academic courses were elementary, with advanced work available from tutors. By 1854 the curriculum advanced to offer what was called a college program, but it never moved beyond being an elementary and secondary preparatory school. It was from this school that General Samuel C. Armstrong, the founder of Hampton Institute discussed in Chapter 5, graduated (Wist 104–106).

In 1848 the Reverend Richard Armstrong, General Armstrong's father, became the government superintendent of Hawaiian schools. He made two changes in the curriculum. First, he advanced vocational education by introducing agricultural education for boys and homemaking for girls. Second, he confronted the problem of language. By 1850 English was the language of commerce, and the monarchs spoke English as well as Hawaiian. Consequently, in 1854 the Hawaiian legislature authorized establishment of a few classes in English and a few English schools if the local board could collect $400, which the government would match. Because learning English was important for social advancement, these English schools became popular. By 1888 less than 16 percent of the pupils attended schools where the language of instruction was Hawaiian, although there was a fee attached to attendance at the English schools. The rate of change continued so that by 1894 only about 2 percent of the public schools in Hawaii carried out instruction in Hawaiian (Wist 54, 68–73).

Although the instruction in public schools was in English, White students attended private schools following the tradition established by the missionaries. However, in the 1920s the public schools began a system of territorywide English Standard schools. These were different in two ways from the select English schools of the 1850s: the students did not have to pay any tuition, and most of the students in these English Standard schools were White. This represented a dual system supported by the territorial department of public instruction, which was mandated to provide equal support to all public schools on the islands. However, these segregated schools brought middle-class White students to public schools for the first time in Hawaii (Stueber 27–28).

Critics called the English Standard schools discriminatory because the entrance requirements depended solely on the ability to speak and write English. There were no tests of other academic skills. Articles in Japanese newspapers in Hawaii complained that children whose first language was not English could not fairly compete with children for whom English was the first language. Nonetheless, the English Standard schools continued as elite institutions. In 1925 they enrolled 2 percent of the population of Hawaii public schools. Before they closed in 1947, they enrolled about 9 percent of the student population. By World War II, Caucasians constituted about half the students in the English Standard schools, whereas they represented no more than 2.5 percent of the students in the regular Hawaii public schools. Interestingly, other groups such as Hawaiians, Portuguese, and Chinese were represented in about the same proportions as in the other public schools. These ranged from 20 to 7 percent. However, the Japanese accounted for about 8 percent of the students in the English Standard schools, whereas they represented about 55 percent of the students in regular schools (Tamura 110–113).

Closed out of the English Standard schools, some Japanese students found private schools to be avenues for upward mobility in Hawaii. Between 1925 and 1947, about 40 percent of the White students in Hawaii attended private schools. Although Japanese students remained a minority in private school enrollments, their presence grew during that same time. In 1925 there were 561 Japanese students in private schools in Hawaii; by 1947 the number grew to 2,465. In 1925, however, this was only 2 percent of all Japanese students, and in 1947 the increase represented only 7 percent of all Japanese students. Thus, the overwhelming majority of Japanese students remained in public schools where they made up 47 percent of the student population in 1920. At that time, each one of the other ethnic groups such as Hawaiians, Part-Hawaiians, Portuguese, and Chinese contributed about 10 percent apiece to student enrollment. The Japanese students represented a majority in the public schools evenly distributed around the islands. From 1925 to 1947, of the Japanese in private schools, 30 to 50 percent attended Catholic schools. These Catholic schools offered religious training, but the graduates also learned to speak Standard English, whereas the students in the public schools retained their native Hawaii Creole English (Tamura 95, 107–119).

In the 1920s, Japanese students in Hawaii tried to become teachers. In response to mounting applications from candidates who appeared ill suited because of poor language skills, the Territorial Normal and Training School, which became part of the University of Hawaii in 1931, began administering oral language exams for entrance. Prospective students gave a five-minute speech to a seven-member board whose members eliminated applicants who appeared to have incorrigible speech habits. According to the president of the Normal School, of all groups the Japanese students had the most problem with English (Tamura 198–199).

Language differences led to many difficulties for the Japanese students. In 1934 the Japanese junior high students who had been born in Hawaii scored two years below national norms on verbal tests. However, they were two years above such norms on nonverbal tests. Housing segregation and the lack of opportunity to hear Standard English contributed to this discrepancy. In addition, many Japanese claimed that they chose to speak their Hawaii Creole English because it was the language of their families and represented a friendliness that, for them, Standard English lacked (Tamura 199–202).

World War II led to the racial integration and closing of the English Standard schools. Fearing a Japanese invasion following the attack on Pearl Harbor, more than 1,800 White students left the English Standard schools and moved to the mainland. As a result, in 1944 White children numbered only 21 percent of the total student body. Meanwhile, Asian students constituted 35 percent of the total in the English Standard schools. By 1946 the enrollment of White students in the English Standard schools fell to less than half the number in 1941. In 1948 the territorial legislature ended new enrollments in the English Standard schools. Because students already enrolled could continue, the last students graduated and the segregated programs ended in 1960, a year after Hawaii achieved statehood (Stueber 32–33).

English did not remain the language of instruction in all public schools in Hawaii. With the rise of concerns about bilingual education in the 1960s and 1970s, native Hawaiians complained that the school policy of integration and universal use of the English language in teaching threatened the continued existence of the Hawaiian language. As a result, the Hawaii Constitution of 1978 required that schools promote the study of Hawaiian culture, history, and language. In most schools, these programs introduced students to native Hawaiian culture through elder or native speakers or various activities recreating past traditions. In 1983 the Hawaii board of education approved the use of Hawaiian as the language of instruction in the school on Niihau, a small, privately owned island populated almost entirely by Hawaiians who retain their language and culture. Previously, students from Niihau traveled to the island of Kauai for public schooling (Kape'ahiokalani, Benham, and Heck 197–203).

Were Japanese Students Encouraged to Study Their Native Language?

The language question in Hawaii became more complicated as Japanese families set up Japanese language schools for their children in order to preserve their culture. In this case, educators' desire to advance the English-speaking abilities of their students worked against U.S. military and political interests.

In 1885 the U.S. government recruited laborers from Japan to work in Hawaii. Within seven years, these workers opened Japanese-language schools for their children. These schools did not replace the government-sponsored English schools. Instead, by 1920 about 98 percent of the more than 20,000 Japanese students who attended English schools also attended Japanese-language schools where they learned the language, religion, and the culture of their parents' home (Tamura 147).

In 1920 a federal survey commission reported that the Japanese-language schools represented a serious obstacle to the public schools of Hawaii. At that time, there were about 160 such schools with an enrollment of about 20,000. In addition, about 2,000 students attended twenty Chinese- and Korean-language schools. According to the survey, there were three reasons why these schools impeded efforts in the public schools. First, the curriculum materials about Japanese culture that were prepared in Japan appeared subversive to the aims of American education. Second, since the children sometimes attended Japanese-language school before and after public school, their instructional day was extremely long. Third, the schools were not supervised by the Hawaii Department of Instruction as were other private schools. Further, the teachers in the Japanese schools came directly from Japan and had no training in American education (Wist 170–171).

Although the federal commission recommended closing these schools, the Hawaii legislature enacted provisions that required the teachers to prove they knew American history and could read, write, and speak English. The Japanese teachers had to pledge to abide by the regulations of the Department of Public Instruction and to teach the students to become good U.S. citizens. However, the students could attend no more than one hour a day. Finally, the Department of Instruction required pupils to have finished the first two grades of American public school. The department reserved the authority to select courses and texts; it decided that those books had to assume the students' primary language was English (Wist 171–173).

Several of the foreign-language schools filed suit in the territorial courts and finally in the federal courts. In 1927 the U.S. Supreme Court declared unconstitutional the Hawaii laws restricting Japanese-language schools. Drawing on the *Pierce v. Society of Sisters* case discussed in Chapter 6, the Supreme Court justices concluded that because the students attended public schools, their parents could teach them additional lessons in whatever subjects they wished as long as those lessons did not disturb society or harm the children's morals (Tamura 148–149).

Following Japan's attack on Pearl Harbor in 1941, the military government closed all Japanese-language schools and confiscated their properties. Worse, of the Japanese Americans sent from Hawaii to mainland internment camps, the teachers and priests from these schools made up the greatest part (Stueber 32–33). In 1943 the territorial legislature prohibited students up to grade 5 from attending any foreign-language school. The Chinese challenged this law and won in 1947. As a result, some Japanese-language schools reopened on the islands (Tamura 160).

The controversy about Japanese-language schools was complex. It was not clear whether the schools encouraged Japanese nationalism. Some former students remembered singing the Japanese national anthem and bowing reverently before the picture of the Japanese emperor and empress. Others claimed they learned to cheer "banzai" on important occasions. However, some educators claimed that the lessons in moral education, called *shushin,* advanced acculturation to the United States. Although those values had Japanese origins, they were compatible with American values. According to Eileen Tamura, the revised textbooks in the Japanese-language schools taught the students to exemplify attributes such as duty, honesty, perseverance, industry, courtesy, cooperation, and courage. Tamura believes that the only virtue in conflict with traditional American values was filial piety because it subordinated individual initiative to family loyalty (Tamura 154–155).

Ironically, when the territorial legislature limited or destroyed the Japanese-language schools, it acted against the U.S. national and military interests that it sought to serve. During the war, some of the graduates of these Japanese-language schools served in U.S. military intelligence translating captured documents and interviewing prisoners. In these roles, they provided important information to the U.S. military. Most important, they learned those language skills in the Japanese-language schools (Tamura 160–161).

During World War II, military officials sent about 1,100 Japanese Americans to the mainland concentration camps. In addition, they held about 1,500 Japanese Americans in concentration camps in Hawaii. However, these were small percentages because Japanese Americans constituted more than one-third of the islands' labor force. Despite the discrimination and intolerance those camps represented and encouraged, Japanese Americans advanced economically and politically in Hawaii. By 1980 Japanese Americans represented about one-fourth of the state's population and about one-third of the labor force. Yet more than 60 percent of the state's dentists, more than 25 percent of the lawyers, and 20 percent of the architects were Japanese Americans. By 1985 more than 60 percent of Hawaii's state legislators were Japanese Americans (Weinberg 60–65).

As a result of World War II, educators moved more quickly toward the goal of integration. The war ended segregation in the English Standard schools, but when the Japanese sought to preserve their language and culture through special schools, the territorial government closed them. If the uniform instruction in English was supposed to serve national interests, it backfired with the closing of the Japanese-language schools because that foreign-language instruction had served the nation's interests during the war.

Did the Language Question Advance Democracy in Puerto Rico?

In Puerto Rico, questions about the language of instruction illustrated yet another set of problems associated with language training. In this case, the problems differed from those found in San Francisco or Hawaii. The language question for Puerto Rican school people was whether instruction should be carried out in English or Spanish or both. The important point is that Puerto Rican educators decided the question by applying the same principles found in the AYC report *What the High Schools Ought to Teach:* They did not value the ability to speak more than one language. These educators believed that language study should enable students to understand their community and communicate with people who lived around them. Unfortunately, the result of their educational strategy was that Puerto Ricans became even more separated from people on the mainland of the United States.

In 1898 the U.S. government seized from Spain what was then officially called Porto Rico. Almost immediately the U.S. military governor claimed that the island would soon be the gem of the Antilles. In keeping with this promise, the new government built roads, schools, and hospitals, and in 1932 the island's name was changed to Puerto Rico. U.S. industries paid premium prices for Puerto Rican sugar, and islanders did not have to pay federal taxes. Yet in 1936, after touring the island, U.S. Secretary of the Interior Harold Ickes declared the slums of San Juan to be the worst he had ever seen, and in 1942 a missionary from the city of Mayagüez on the island wrote Eleanor Roosevelt, the wife of the U.S. president, to tell her of the children starving in her school (C. Goodsell 3–7).

Part of the problem was population. In 1940 Puerto Rico, which is one hundred miles long and thirty-two miles wide, held 1,869,255 people. This gave it a population density of 546.1 per square mile. At that time, the population density of the continental United States was 50 per square mile. Even Haiti, the most densely populated republic in the Western Hemisphere, had a density of 327 per square mile. Another part of the problem was that the United States did not have an extended development policy for the island. Instead, the federal government offered temporary aid such as hurricane relief, or tied the island's development to other aims such as military defense (C. Goodsell 7–8).

In 1941 U.S. President Franklin Roosevelt appointed Rexford Guy Tugwell as the governor of Puerto Rico. Unlike the seventeen previous governors appointed by U.S. presidents, Tugwell had experience in the island and was committed to encouraging economic development. A former professor of economics at Columbia University, Tugwell had developed a strong friendship with Luis Munoz Marin, a leader of the Popular Democratic Party. In 1940 this party won a majority of seats in the Puerto Rican Senate, and Munoz became president of the Senate. Munoz Marin's party adopted the slogan "Bread, Land, and Liberty." The three parts of this campaign included redistribution of wealth through taxes and public assistance, enforcement of a then forty-year-old U.S. law limiting corporate ownership of land to five hundred acres, and development of the economy by protecting industries and increasing the availability of credit (C. Goodsell 12–13).

True to the campaign promises, in the spring of 1942 the Puerto Rican House and Senate approved and Tugwell signed a significant portion of the legislation. These policies had three major effects: They transformed the single-crop agricultural economy of the island into a diverse, industrial one, they advanced the standard of living to the highest level in Latin America, and they converted the island's colonial status into a more autonomous model. As a result, commentators called these policies an administrative revolution. These bills gave control of municipal water systems to a Water Resources Authority, created a governmental planning agency, established an administrative budget agency, authorized the establishment of two developmental agencies, and reorganized the University of Puerto Rico. The cooperation between Tugwell and Munoz Marin lasted until 1946, when Jesus T. Pinero, a citizen of Puerto Rico, became governor. After the U.S. Congress amended the Jones Act to change Puerto Rico's governorship from an appointive to an elected position, Munoz Marin was elected governor in 1948 and remained in office until 1965 (C. Goodsell 2, 22–23, 58–59, 203–204).

For a time, politicians such as Munoz Marin who preferred independence ignored questions about the desirability of the relations between the United States and Puerto Rico. They sought to raise the living standard, and in school affairs, they debated the issue of the language of instruction. Regarding the latter issue, educators did eventually ask whether Puerto Rico should ultimately separate or integrate with the United States. In 1898, when the United States invaded the island, schools began to teach in English and imported teachers from the mainland. Yet many Puerto Ricans wanted to be autonomous. The movement for autonomy had begun when the island was a Spanish colony, and it continued during U.S. control and achieved some victories in 1948, when the governor was elected by the people. The biggest break came in 1949. Spanish became the language of instruction in island schools. At best, schools offered English as a foreign language (Gutierrez 1).

In Puerto Rican schools, the language policy varied over the years. From 1898 until 1900, English was supposed to be the medium of instruction. However, from 1900 to 1903, Spanish was the medium of instruction in the elementary grades and English was a subject for special study. In high schools, this pattern was reversed. From 1903 until 1917, the policy reverted to English as the language of instruction and Spanish was taught as a subject. In 1917 the U.S. Congress granted citizenship to Puerto Ricans through the Jones Bill, which also separated the powers of government into administrative, judicial, and legislative branches, with a two-chamber house and senate. At the same time, schools adopted a bilingual language policy that provided for Spanish and English to alternate as subjects and as the languages of instruction. That is, in the first four grades, Spanish was the medium of instruction; grade 5 was transitional, with half the subjects taught in Spanish and half in English. In grades 6 through 12, English was the medium of instruction (Gutierrez 30, 72, 79).

The policy of bilingual education did not satisfy many politicians. Writing from 1915 until 1930 in the island press, Epifanio Fernandez-Vanga, a prominent academic, director of the San Juan school district, and member of the Popular Democratic Party, claimed that the instruction in schools did not help anyone become bilingual. He thought that it hindered students intellectually and spiritually. In fact, he feared that the U.S. government sought to increase its control of Puerto Rico by teaching in English. According to Fernandez-Vanga, Puerto Ricans had to speak and read the Spanish language to preserve their national identity. Ironically, Fernandez-Vanga turned the movement for autonomy on itself. Before 1898 the leaders of the movement for autonomy considered Spain the oppressor. Although Fernandez-Vanga was born in 1880, he ignored the oppressive role Spain had played in Puerto Rican history and called on Puerto Ricans to take pride in their Spanish heritage, urging Puerto Rican citizens to resist what he called the United States' illegal efforts to control the island (Gutierrez 79–87).

In 1929 Luis Munoz Marin made a similar argument. He published an article in the *American Mercury* in which he complained that bilingualism kept Puerto Ricans from holding a true identity. Claiming that the conditions under Spain had been good, he feared that the use of the English language would weaken the movement for Puerto Ricans to control their own affairs. By the 1940s, however, Munoz Marin moderated his separatist rhetoric and worked effectively with U.S. officials. In fact, he cooperated closely with U.S. governor Tugwell. However, Munoz Marin's Popular Democratic Party maintained the view that the true issue was the establishment of a Republic of Puerto Rico through the will of her people (Gutierrez 97–99, 112).

During the 1940s, the Puerto Rican Teachers Association (PRTA) advocated teaching English in the schools. Since its founding in 1911, the PRTA endorsed teaching in Spanish, but the organization did not achieve the status to exert influence until 1940. By that time, the PRTA divorced the political sphere from the educational sphere. That is, instead of emphasizing cultural goals, PRTA members argued that instruction should be in Spanish because it was pedagogically more effective. They noted that students could not learn to be bilingual because their environment was Spanish speaking (Gutierrez 108, 112–118).

In 1945 Pedro Cebollero conducted a study for the Puerto Rican Council for Higher Education to determine a school language policy. He noted that up to that time Spanish had been the language of instruction for only four years in the history of U.S. control of the island, whereas English had been the language of instruction for thirty years. He offered three pieces of evidence against continuing the English-language program. First, officials admitted the failure of the policy by instituting periods during which instruction was in Spanish. For example, teachers used Spanish in the lower grades, and they reserved English for the upper grades. Second, several studies in Puerto Rico demonstrated that elementary school students did not learn subjects such as mathematics, history, or science when English was the medium of instruction. Third, in other places such as French West Africa, Dutch East Indies, and Ceylon, the vernacular was the language of instruction in the elementary grades (Cebollero 169–171).

Further, Cebollero argued, studies of adults in Puerto Rico demonstrated that Spanish was sufficient to satisfy their needs. Had several different languages been spoken on the island, as was the case in the Philippines, or had the vernacular been inadequate to express many ideas, it would make sense to use English as the language of instruction. But Spanish was the common language of the island and in that language people could express their ideas (Cebollero 172–173).

According to Cebollero, teachers rejected the policy to teach in English because it made instruction more difficult. For example, when teaching mathematics they had to correct the English or reject the answer if it was incorrectly expressed. As a result, *all* classes became classes in English grammar and vocabulary, and instruction in the other subjects was slow. Worse, Cebollero argued, students could not come to grips with real situations that required thinking, planning, and action because the artificial language severed the connection between the school and the community (173–174).

However, Cebollero approved of using English as the medium of instruction in some subjects in high schools. This was reasonable because much of the material to be studied was written in English and the number of high school students was small. Because most of those students were preparing to attend universities in the United States, they needed the practice with the language (175–176).

Despite the findings of researchers such as Cebollero, educators may have recommended that instruction be conducted in Spanish so that schools would employ more Puerto Ricans as teachers. When the United States invaded Puerto Rico, about 15 percent of the population was literate and not more than 0.5 percent had attended school beyond the elementary grades. In an effort to increase education, the newly established Bureau of Education in the U.S. Department of the Interior built schools, printed texts, and imported teachers from the United States. By 1900, of the 322,000 children of school age, about 38,000 attended schools. Teachers came from the United States in increasing numbers that reached a peak in 1925 with 244. However, as bilingual education became an open question, the number of teachers imported from the United States dropped to 75 in 1934 (White 209–219).

Despite these complex motives, local support for Spanish as the language of instruction accelerated even while officials in Washington tried to retain bilingual education in Puerto Rican schools. In 1934 Jose Padin became Puerto Rico's commissioner of education and ended the practice of bilingual education in all grades. He reinstated the policy of using Spanish as the language of instruction in the elementary school and English in the high school. When the U.S. government opposed his policy, he resigned in 1936. His successor, Jose Gallardo, reinstated bilingual instruction. However, in 1942, Gallardo ordered elementary school teachers to use Spanish for instruction. The next year the U.S. Senate Committee on the Territories met in San Juan. As a result of their investigation, Gallardo returned the schools to a policy of bilingual education. In 1945 the island legislature approved a bill making all schools use Spanish as the language of instruction. The governor vetoed it. The legislature overruled his veto, but in 1946 U.S. President Truman vetoed the bill, complaining that although the plan might be pedagogically sound, it was politically sensitive because federal administrators were discussing the political status of Puerto Rico. He feared the bill might disturb those deliberations. In reply, the PRTA filed a suit, as did a Puerto Rican parent against the government. These two lawsuits were aimed at making Spanish the language of instruction. Before these suits could be decided, Luis Munoz Marin became governor; he appointed Mariano Villaronga as commissioner of education in 1949.

By administrative decision, Villaronga made Spanish the language of instruction in island schools. His decision stayed in force (Gutierrez 102–108, 122).

Thus, bilingual instruction ended in Puerto Rican schools for the same reasons that schools on the mainland exaggerated fluency in English. That is, educators thought the students should learn the language spoken by the members of their communities. Although such a policy was practical, it was also isolationist. In the case of Puerto Rican children, it meant they were more completely removed from life on the mainland.

How Did World War II Influence U.S. Elementary and Secondary Schools?

As the cases in San Francisco, Hawaii, and Puerto Rico illustrate, educational policies followed the same general principles set out in the AYC report *What the High Schools Ought to Teach.* These included making the courses more practical, emphasizing the problems of the community and the government, reducing the importance of studies such as foreign languages, and ensuring that students mastered the language of their community. However, the effects of those principles often varied. During and after World War II, educators applied these AYC principles even more widely.

In general, World War II had three effects on elementary and secondary schools:

1. The appeal of traditional courses declined even further, and the courses those schools offered became more practical.
2. Educators consciously tried to teach students the democratic traditions for which the country waged the war.
3. The federal government began to contribute more money to local schools for specific educational programs, and educators turned to national organizations to direct the reform of local school districts.

In December 1941, after the Japanese destroyed the U.S. Pacific fleet in Honolulu, the United States abruptly entered World War II. In a message delivered to teachers in 1942, President Franklin Roosevelt asked them to help the government mold men and women who could fight through to victory. He asked every schoolhouse to become a service center, and he hoped that in the schools all young people would learn the wisdom and patience needed by those who would bring a lasting peace (National Institute on Education and War iii).

In order to decide how schools should help the war effort, the U.S. Office of Education established a Wartime Commission immediately after the Japanese attacked Pearl Harbor. In August 1942, this commission called a nationwide meeting of more than seven hundred prominent educators that included university deans; city school superintendents; and representatives of teachers associations, parents associations, and the National Catholic Welfare Conference. In their final statement, the committee asserted the need for teachers to join other sectors of the country in the war effort. To commission members, this was an opportunity for teachers to take pride in their work, serve young people, and help the nation. They recommended that the curriculum be adapted immediately to prepare for the demands of the armed forces. This meant, for example, that courses in mathematics should use problems drawn from aviation, navigation, and industry. Industrial arts courses should teach skills related to war needs, and schools should offer a greater number of home economics courses that focused on home care of the sick and home management under war conditions. Social studies courses should cover the war aims. In addition, courses should be established to introduce students to the armed forces to lessen the time needed for induction (National Institute on Education and War xiii–xv).

Although educators agreed to join in an all-out effort to win the war, they were not sure what "all out" meant in schools. The Educational Policies Commission (EPC) of the National Education Association (NEA) approved an answer in December 1942. According to the EPC, the instructional problems differed between elementary and secondary schools. Because the younger students would probably not have to participate in the fighting, they should be prepared for citizenship in a peaceful and democratic world. Thus, they would learn the basic academic skills, the elements of good health, and the need for community service. The EPC cautioned teachers to limit discussions of the war and avoid efforts to make the students hate or fear the enemy. Instead, they recommended that teachers emphasize the ideals of freedom and equality. Music and art, for instance, could express the war aims. On the other hand, secondary students had to be taught the skills needed by the war industries and the fitness required by battle. This meant that every able-bodied boy had to receive preinduction training as prepared by the U.S. Army and the U.S. Office of Education. All students had to receive guidance to direct them toward needed occupations. In order to help with this task, the War Manpower Commission sought to compile statistics on the skills needed by various industries (EPC, *What the Schools* 1–11).

The EPC used the war as a reason to continue criticism of teaching academic subjects in secondary schools. For example, the EPC noted that there was no need for all students to take extended courses in mathematics. Instead, most students needed to know how to perform fundamental operations of arithmetic. Those students who could pursue more mathematics should receive instruction related to wartime uses, with problems drawn from aviation, navigation, and industrial management. In foreign languages, the EPC found no value in exposing many students to a year or two of French, Spanish, or German. Instead, a few students should study languages such as Russian, Chinese, Japanese, and Italian to the point at which they could speak and write fluently. According to the EPC report, study of the ancient languages of Greek and Latin should be severely limited because they had little practical application. Further, the EPC wanted students to study the requirements for maintaining good health, strong muscles, and good character. Although the EPC cautioned teachers against fostering a hatred of the enemy among students, the report did encourage teachers to emphasize that the United States must win the war, that people must preserve democracy, and that they must develop plans for international cooperation. Further, the EPC urged teachers to show that to make a lasting peace, national sovereignty had to be limited, and each country should adopt economic policies that more equitably divided wealth among its citizens (*What the Schools* 16–30).

In 1943 the NEA published the *Wartime Handbook for Education.* This manual incorporated many of the ideas found in the pamphlet produced by the EPC, although it omitted references to limiting national sovereignty, expanding international cooperation, and founding a just economic order after the war. Nonetheless, it followed the same practical orientation that governed the EPC. Instruction in elementary schools was to encourage obedience to expert authority and emphasize basic academic instruction. The NEA recommended that elementary students study more history in order to understand why wars begin and what effects they have.

Extracurricular activities such as paper drives and Junior Red Cross work were encouraged to help the war effort. In secondary schools, the NEA recommended changes such as increasing vocational programs, taking advantage of the government-sponsored program for planting victory gardens and producing vegetables for school lunches, and offering preflight training for future pilots. In citizenship, the NEA called for a study of the war and opportunities to understand and appreciate democracy. Further, the NEA urged that racial and national prejudices be reduced. For example, the NEA recommended that teachers expose the fallacies of the Nazi's beliefs about racial superiority. In English classes, students could contribute to patriotism by studying the meaning of democracy and by encouraging activities such as debating societies in order to understand the function of public opinion. In art and music classes, students contributed to the war effort by producing posters supporting the war effort and assembling bands to play for recruits leaving for training camps.

Other organizations made similar suggestions. In 1942 the *New York Times* conducted a survey among 7,000 students in thirty-six colleges that revealed even educated citizens knew little about the history of the United States. Although the U.S. Office of Education contended that thirty-eight states required secondary schools to teach a course in U.S. history and most other states did the same without the formal requirement, the American Historical Association, the Mississippi Historical Association, and the National Council for the Social Studies formed a committee to conduct a survey of teaching practices and of elementary and secondary school texts. This committee decided the problems lay in inadequate teacher preparation. The committee recommended that history be emphasized in all social studies courses at all levels, and that this study stress continuous awareness of the relations between the United States and other countries; it could not be isolationist. In a similar effort, the National Council for the Social Studies issued a statement entitled *The Social Studies Mobilize for Victory* that described programs secondary schools could adopt to advance war aims. This statement recommended social studies programs that were similar to the original three-year sequence discussed in Chapter 6. However, it added that teachers should give special attention to the economic, social, and political aspects of world relations in the study of U.S. history (Kandel 94–99).

Ultimately, educators made modest changes in the curriculum during the war. However, one subject expanded a great deal: physical education. This trend began when the physical exams required by the Selective Service Act of 1917 revealed that many young men were unfit for duty in the armed services because of maladies such as infected teeth, tuberculosis, venereal disease, eye defects, and heart lesions. After the war, physical educators claimed that they could prevent young men from being unable to serve their country. Some skeptical educators warned that these promises were empty because regular exercise could not alleviate defective vision. Nonetheless, many people embraced the idea of physical education in schools. By 1921 twenty-eight states had passed legislation about physical education. Most made it mandatory (Krug, *Secondary School* 389–390).

The growth of physical education was steady. From 1922 until 1928, the percentage of all students in grades 9 through 12 taking physical education courses increased from 5.7 percent to 15 percent. Although the percentages remained low, actual numbers grew rapidly. Enrollments nationwide in physical education increased from 123,568 in 1922 to 435,383 by 1928. This continued so that by 1934, 50.7 percent of the students in grades 9 through 12 enrolled in some form of physical education. As enrollments in physical education increased, the activities within the classes changed. Instead of formal gymnastics, more time was devoted to organized play, dancing, and swimming. However, most school districts had inadequate facilities for physical education and few had sufficient personnel for the programs (Krug, *Secondary School* 391–392).

Although military preparedness was one reason for the growth of physical education between the wars, it may not have been the most important reason. Physical education classes may have enjoyed increasing popularity in the period between the world wars because these courses fit the model of the comprehensive high school. Because these large schools had to serve different sorts of students, there had to be some classes that all students could take. Physical education classes and homeroom were two periods when all students could be together. Students did no homework for physical education so they were not separated by intellectual ability, and large groups of students could attend one class. Further, physical education classes were relevant because the students learned about their bodies. Most important, students enjoyed phys ed (Angus and Mirel 96).

In some locales, physical education classes represented opportunities for teachers to tie the instruction closer to the home lives of the students. For example, as discussed in Chapter 7, Nina Otero-Warren, an educational administrator in New Mexico, encouraged teachers to find out what games the students' parents had played in their villages. She recommended that they play those games instead of the more common baseball during the organized play in physical education. Through such activities, Otero-Warren reasoned, the children not only took exercise but learned about the culture of their parents.

Despite the increased enrollments in physical education before World War II, the percentage of men who failed the physical exam for induction into the armed services was the same as it had been during World War I. Nevertheless, shortly after the end of World War II nearly every state legislature increased the number of hours of physical education that students had to take and called for improvements in physical fitness and health programs. Enrollments in physical education increased. In the 1948–49 academic year, 91 percent of junior high school students and 69 percent of high school students took physical education. Thus, by the post–World War II years physical education had the largest registration of any subject, with the exception of English, in the overall secondary program (Krug, *Secondary School* 392–393).

Did the Federal Government Influence Education during World War II More Than It Had during World War I?

In 1917 the federal government encouraged educators to support the war, but those efforts were feeble in comparison with the efforts expended in 1942 and 1943. There were three reasons for this difference. First, the high schools were far less popular in 1917 than they were in 1942. Second, after the United States entered World War I, the fighting lasted another nineteen months and was contained in Europe; the United States entered World War II in 1941 and the war lasted until 1945. Third, in 1917 neither educators nor government officials could agree on the way the schools could help the war effort. Prominent educators lacked a strong central organization to plan activities, and different federal bureaus made separate demands on schoolteachers. The only coordinated effort encouraging teachers to support World War I was the publication of the semimonthly periodical *National School Service,* which published articles explaining the war effort. However, the journal did not begin until September 1919 and the war ended in about two and a half months. In 1942 the EPC and the Wartime Commission of the Office of Education provided a central focus for cooperative efforts between educators and government officials to coordinate reforms (Todd 223–225).

Despite the lack of coordination during World War I, teachers sought to help the war effort. In 1917 in schoolrooms, the study of current events brought the reality of the war closer to students. In sewing rooms and manual training shops, pupils made articles for the armed forces. Boys and girls worked in gardens or helped farmers to raise food for school kitchens. They sold thrift stamps and bonds to neighbors to finance the war effort. Physical and health education became important to prepare young people for the war effort. In short, in World War I as in World War II, schools emphasized practical courses. However, in 1917 teachers did not emphasize the democratic way of life to prepare students for the peace (Todd 232–233).

On the other hand, in 1942 the federal government turned immediately to schools as part of the nation's defense. For example, for the 1942–43 fiscal year the government appropriated $94 million for vocational training of students below college level that was designed to prepare workers for war plant production. Most important, in order to build a lasting peace the government encouraged educators to persist in their efforts to enhance democracy in the schools (NEA, *Wartime Handbook* 11, 18–19).

Despite increased federal contributions, high school enrollments fell for the first time in many years. In 1939–40, high school enrollments exceeded 7.1 million. However, in 1941 enrollments fell and continued to decline to more than 6 million in 1943. This decline was not caused by young people joining the military, nor did it come from a decrease in the high school–age population. Instead, students dropped out of high schools to take jobs (Angus and Mirel 80).

In 1943 several city school superintendents complained that the number of students applying for permanent work permits was twice what it had been when the war began. In response, the U.S. Office of Education, the U.S. Department of Labor, and the Children's Bureau issued a plea for students to go to school. This statement argued that the nation would survive the war and have an honorable future. However, the statement added, this requires that all students receive an education that will advance the democracy during the coming peace. Therefore, people must realize that educational programs had been determined after years of development; students had a right and an obligation to complete them without distractions (Kandel 86–87).

How Did Educators Want Schools to Serve Democracy after the War?

During World War II, many educators maintained the view that traditional subjects were useless for most students, but they had held this view before the war began. The war gave them opportunities to criticize academic subjects even more. After World War II, educators maintained their antipathy toward academic subjects, and they used national organizations to spread this view around the country. However, they expressed this idea not so that schools could better serve the nation, but because they feared that unless they did the national government would take control of the schools.

In 1944 the National Education Association published a report of its Educational Policies Commission (EPC) entitled *Education for All American Youth.* The report began with the warning that the federal government could create a national system of education that would replace the traditional system of local and state control of schools. According to the report, if the federal government took control of local schools, it would happen in part because the federal government had refused to provide adequate assistance to local and state school systems. Another reason the federal government might take over schools was that schools refused to teach any subjects except traditional academic subjects that were irrelevant to the students' lives. However, the report warned, everyone would suffer if the federal government took over schools because such a large system would be unable to respond to local conditions, and the uniform curricula that might result would favor certain groups or social classes of students (*Education for All* 1–10).

The report contended that all children differ in ability, occupational interests, access to educational facilities, type of community in which they live, family background, mental health, and physical well-being. However, all youth have several traits in common. They need to know how to fulfill their obligations as citizens, and they should understand their culture. Finally, they need to know how to maintain their physical health and to develop their capacities to think rationally (*Education for All* 11–17).

Later, in a summary of its EPC report, the NEA expanded the list to ten needs that all youth have in common despite their other differences: the need to develop salable skills; to maintain good health and fitness; to understand the rights and duties of citizens in a democracy; to recognize the significance of the family; to know how to purchase and use goods and services; to understand the influence of science on human life; to appreciate art, literature, music, and nature; to use leisure time wisely; to develop respect for persons; and to learn to think rationally (NEA, *Planning* 3–10).

To illustrate how teachers and boards of education might frame a curriculum, the EPC presented two fictitious examples of postwar school improvement. One was set in a rural area given the name "Farmville." Here the students went to a common secondary school for grades 7, 8, and 9. In this building, all the students studied the same curriculum designed to teach them to understand their world, think clearly, express themselves articulately, and master scientific and mathematical processes. For these students, guidance was offered by classroom teachers. In the consolidated high school that served the area, the students followed different courses in vocational preparation, intellectual development, and recreational pursuits. However, they remained together in courses that taught about citizenship, family living, health, and cultural heritage. For these students, guidance came in three ways, beginning with a course in which all students explored work available in the world. During this experience, students met with counselors to map out an educational plan that would meet their vocational interests. Finally, teachers and counselors exchanged information about the students. In this way, teachers could adapt instruction to the students' interests and abilities and the counselors could adjust their recommendations (EPC, *Education for All* 29–47).

The EPC's recommendation for urban areas was presented in a fictitious example named "American City." In this case, the schools offered a similar program that allowed students to work together to learn those things they needed in common and provided opportunities to pursue those studies tailored to their particular interests. However, because the school was in an urban setting, more students finished high school. They had a wider range of vocational programs, and work experience directly related to their vocational training could be chosen. Similarly, guidance was an important component even for those students who had left full-time school (EPC, *Education for All* 171–196).

The point is that EPC members offered a compromise in which students could pursue their individual interests some of the time and work together during other parts of the school day. In their example of the city school's curriculum, health and physical fitness concluded the day and brought students together from all walks of life. In the area of social living, teachers worked in what the report called unified courses in common learnings. These took up three periods in grades 7 through 10 and one period in grades 11 and 12. The board of education offered a two-year program after the twelfth grade called the community institute, which consisted of liberal arts training or specific vocational training, and in these two years common learnings took up one period a day. In the tenth grade, for example, in social living the students studied the American city at work, which led to other topics such as family life, labor unions, community health, and personal problems. In grade 11, students learned how to participate intelligently in civic affairs and began to seek the connection between problems in the city and the nation. In grade 12, the curriculum returned to personal problems. Within these common learnings courses, teachers served as counselors to the students. Because the teachers observed the students in a variety of situations, they could help them select their courses of study and plan for their future. However, the vocational training programs divided the students into different fields such as business education, retail and wholesale selling, and homemaking. Other schools added things such as agriculture, airplane mechanics, and machine trades. Finally, the college preparatory programs offered another set of tracks that divided the students for part of the day (NEA, *Planning* 44–47).

According to one historian, the report *Education for All American Youth* was a major work that was considered to express the widely shared beliefs of educators of that time (Hampel 35–37). However, in meeting the students' needs, educators did not think of themselves as serving the interests of the national labor force. They thought they were helping all students lead full and rewarding lives.

In the 1950s, Did Educators Think It Was Important to Meet the Students' Needs?

Following the spirit of the EPC, many educators believed that everyone would benefit if teachers strived to meet the needs of youth. During the 1950s, educators proclaimed that when schools met the students' needs, the education of students with disabilities would improve, the schools could protect the national security of the United States, and social ills such as juvenile delinquency would end.

As the decade began, educators' belief in the importance of meeting students' needs was so strong that they thought such an approach would solve the problems facing children they called exceptional. In 1950 the subject of the forty-ninth yearbook of the National Society for the Study of Education (NSSE) was the education of exceptional children, defined as those who deviate from the average in physical, mental, emotional, or social characteristics to the extent that they require educational services to develop to their maximum capacity. The committee added that the education of exceptional children was required of any democracy in which all people were considered equal. The committee divided the objectives of such education into four groups: self-realization, human relationships, economic efficiency, and civic responsibility. These were identical to the objectives that the Educational Policies Commission had selected for all children, demonstrating educators' belief in the equality of education for all children (Kirk, et al. 3–4).

According to the NSSE yearbook committee, exceptional children needed special education services because they could not develop within regular group classes, which were too large and were run by teachers who were not qualified to help these children. However, the committee was not willing to suggest that exceptional children should be segregated. Committee members acknowledged that there was a great deal of controversy about whether placements in special classes were beneficial. They decided the modern conception was that special education classes were similar to hospital visits: They provided the special services these students needed for a time but not permanently. Indeed, the committee added, such special education could be administered for part of the day while the students spent the rest of the day with a regular class. The committee did acknowledge that some children might have to stay in a special residential school (Kirk, et al. 4–11).

No census of exceptional children had ever been taken. In 1930 a White House Conference on Child Health and Protection identified 3,000,000 children in elementary schools who required special treatment. In the 1947–48 academic year, approximately 365,000 exceptional children were enrolled in special schools or classes. Although this was an increase from 1940 when there were 313,722, the committee said that the number should have been closer to 400,000 (Kirk, et al. 6, 12).

According to the yearbook, the growth in special education had come about by some states enacting legislation requiring statewide programs. By 1949 forty-one states had laws authorizing or requiring special education services. Thirty-four of those states made financial appropriations to help districts meet the cost of such services. Some states offered special appropriations to selected teacher education programs to prepare people to work with exceptional children (Kirk, et al. 13–14).

Among the committee's recommendations were the call for a wide range of services for students with all types of disabilities and the extension of these services to rural and urban settings. Early identification of disabilities would help, the committee added, and the programs had to extend from elementary through secondary schools. However, they wanted all levels of government to be involved to coordinate the delivery of services to these children (Kirk, et al. 14–16).

In the 1950 NSSE yearbook, various authors wrote about the specific kinds of exceptional children who required special treatment including students with visual, acoustic, and orthopedic disabilities. In addition, an article authored by Merle Sumtion, Dorothy Norris, and Lewis Terman described the education of gifted children, complaining that people often thought of democracy as meaning identical opportunity for all people. However, the authors claimed, this hurt gifted children and robbed society of the benefits such children could offer as adults. Therefore, they suggested that people follow John Dewey's definition of a democracy as a place where society demanded some return from people and offered each person the chance to develop his or her unique talents (260–261).

In their article, Sumtion, Norris, and Terman described the Stanford study of gifted children that Terman had begun in 1921. The study selected about 1,500 children whose intelligence quotient on the Stanford-Binet scale ranged between 135 and 200, and followed them through their education and into their careers to identify the traits that were typical of gifted children and the factors that influenced their development. By 1945 the men were employed as professionals or in higher business occupations at a rate seven or eight times greater than students from a random group. The number of college teachers, lawyers, and physicians was twenty or thirty times the norm for a random group. Although the members of the gifted group did about eight times better in school than a normal group, they should have done even better. One problem was the result of ineffective counseling in high school and college. Another difficulty was that gifted students were subjected to curricula far too easy for them during the elementary and high school years. Furthermore, in college professors often restrained these students' creative abilities. The authors concluded that schools should identify the gifted students, offer them enriched programs, and provide for moderate acceleration of all their programs. In these ways, the schools would meet the needs of these children and enhance society's general welfare because gifted children could contribute to society (Sumtion, Norris, and Terman 271–279).

Second, educators claimed that when schools met the students' needs, they would enhance military preparedness. Beginning in 1947, the United States was locked in a cold war with its former ally in World War II, the Soviet Union. Education was an important weapon in this struggle. For example, in 1951 the governor of Illinois and the state superintendent of public instruction called a meeting in Chicago of nationally known experts in the military, industry, agriculture, medicine, and social welfare to discuss how the schools could enhance national security. Noting that newspapers told of the bitter war in Korea and acrimonious debates in the United Nations, these experts decided that the nation faced two challenges. First, the United States had to present the ideals it represented in ways other nations could accept. Second, the United States had to maintain adequate military might to prevent surprise attacks. Most important, the members agreed, the schools could protect the nation from communist aggression. Warning against teachers indoctrinating the students, the committee members listed several ways the schools could preserve the nation included ensuring that all people were literate, preparing people to accept personal sacrifice, and helping them believe in a national ideal. Education would contribute to national security by better identifying the individual needs of the students and offering training that was geared to their needs, interests, and abilities (Sanford, Hand, and Spalding 1–7, 32–40).

In general, the committee in Chicago suggested that elementary schoolteachers continue to help students learn to function in groups of peers by having them plan objectives and undertake activities with other students. They wanted students to learn to think critically and evaluate their own work. At the same time, the committee recommended avoiding traditional academic practices such as separating children from their age mates when the children failed to meet what they called arbitrary standards. Instead, they called for curricula that encouraged students to actively participate in learning and for lessons that aided in the understanding of community life such as exploring the stress that national defense caused families (Sanford, Hand, and Spalding 102–116).

Regarding the secondary school curriculum, the Chicago committee published reports explaining how specific subject areas might function. For example, the writers warned against eliminating agricultural education during a national emergency as happened in World Wars I and II. They called for the continuation of flexible programs allowing students to work on farms and attend schools. They also recommended having students in art classes make posters or illustrations promoting other patriotic drives such as urging people to buy savings bonds. Foreign-language instruction could produce some people who could act in military intelligence or diplomatic services, but for most students foreign-language instruction led to an increased understanding of their own language and culture rather than to fluency. In mathematics, the students could learn to apply the facts and concepts to daily life. In science, students should confront problem solving, the importance of the conservation of natural resources, the biological basis of human relations, the difficulties facing consumers, and ways to survive during an emergency (Sanford, Hand, and Spalding 122–138, 139–143, 162, 184–193, 206–220).

The third tendency was the faith expressed by many educators that when schools met the students' needs many social problems would disappear. For example, in 1953 the National Society for the Study of Education issued a yearbook entitled *Adapting the Secondary-School Program to the Needs of Youth.* The chairperson of the yearbook committee, William G. Brink, asserted that educators had always organized their programs to meet the students' needs. However, from time to time they changed their ideas about what those needs were. An early emphasis was on intellectual attainment; other conceptions included the behaviors associated with responsible citizenship and job preparation. When many youth failed to pass Selective Service exams, health needs became popular educational concerns. However, educators experienced several conflicts, such as whether to stress the immediate needs of youth or their future needs, whether individual or social needs should take priority, and whether needs should be specific or general. Brink noted that most organizations published general lists and emphasized good citizenship, health, and wise use of leisure. The concern for students' needs came from the peristent fact that although secondary schools had grown, almost half the students left before graduation, and more boys than girls dropped out early. He attributed this failure to impediments in reading skills that prevented academic success and to inadequate guidance programs that failed to provide students with realistic goals based on an understanding of their capacities (2–8).

Brink claimed that if schools paid more attention to the needs of youth, there would be less juvenile delinquency. Schools should attend to the problems students face in their peer groups because the anxieties they face as a result of social stratification could impede learning. Further, as the size of families dropped but more mothers worked outside the home, schools had to help students learn more about home and family living. Finally, because technology had caused many changes, students needed guidance to select reasonable jobs. Workers had to receive repeated job training to adapt to technological changes, and people needed to learn how to profit from increased leisure time (Brink 8–17).

Did Educators Criticize the Ideal of Meeting the Needs of Youth?

Despite the optimism some educators displayed about meeting the needs of youth, academic critics complained about what they saw as the mindless devotion to students' needs. The criticism became so severe that the organization most closely associated with this ideal, the Progressive Education Association, disbanded. One of the more intelligent critics of progressive education was Arthur Bestor. In 1952 Bestor criticized the EPC's list of the ten common needs of youth. As described earlier in this chapter, this list included items such as developing salable skills, understanding the significance of the family, and knowing how to purchase goods intelligently. According to Bestor, by 1952 this list of needs represented the philosophy of most U.S. public schools; that is, school people contended that they tried to meet these needs. However, Bestor found the items on the list to be vague, and he was dismayed to note that the list did not mention the role of subject matters such as history or mathematics. Furthermore, Bestor warned, when educators ventured into areas such as personal living in which they had no special competence, they were violating the students' privacy. More important, in making such intrusions educators ignored their fundamental duty to enhance students' intellectual abilities (414–419).

In the same spirit, Bestor criticized a movement called life adjustment education, which had originated at the same time that the EPC published its list of the common needs of youth. Proposed in 1945 by Dr. Charles Prosser, life adjustment education was based on the view that academic programs in high schools served only about 20 percent of the students who were preparing for college. Vocational programs served only about 20 percent of those expecting to work immediately after high school. As a result, nearly 60 percent of the students did not receive an appropriate education. In 1946 the U.S. Office of Education held regional conferences to determine how high schools could help these students for whom neither academics nor vocational training was adequate. In 1947 the Office of Education held a national conference and published the results in a bulletin that recommended offering these students functional experiences in practical arts, home and family life, health and physical fitness, and civic competence. Also, in the area of self-realization and use of leisure, members suggested ideas offered by the EPC such as that students needed to learn adult diversions such as wood carving or chess (Division of Secondary Education 15–17, 63–65, 74–75).

According to Bestor, the main problem with life adjustment education was that advocates did not believe that traditional intellectual disciplines could satisfy the needs of students. It appeared that members of the conference valued academic subjects only as preparation for college. As a result, when the members considered how schools could advance self-realization and use of leisure, they ignored traditional subjects as a means to enrich people's lives. Further, committee members considered the mass of students as lacking the intelligence to use leisure wisely when traditionally people developed this ability without special training (Bestor 427).

Although the Progressive Education Association disbanded in 1955, critics continued to attack the ironies inherent in the idea of meeting students' needs. For example, in 1961 in "Need and the Needs-Curriculum," B. Paul Komisar criticized the idea that educators could build a curriculum based on students' needs. He noted that the term "need" had several interpretations. It could refer to a social or institutional prescription such as learning to follow rules, or it could refer to students' desires such as the need for recognition, affection, or achievement. Thus, Komisar decided, almost any curriculum could be said to meet the students' basic needs, and as a result of this ambiguity the general proposal for schools to meet the students' needs was trivial, vague, or indeterminate. Interestingly, Komisar suggested that the slogan was popular precisely because it lacked clear meaning. Administrators could defend their actions against an antagonistic audience by claiming that their school met the students' needs (37–41).

An article written by an educator who wanted to devise programs to meet the students' needs illustrates Komisar's complaint. In the NSSE yearbook quoted earlier, Harold Alberty listed six types of secondary school programs that he claimed met the needs of youth. Alberty organized these models on a continuum extending from a traditional model of separate subjects that were taught rigorously to programs in which teachers and students made up the lessons spontaneously (118–139). Inadvertently, perhaps, Alberty showed with his continuum that any conceivable program could be considered as meeting the needs of youth. That is, the most authoritarian, teacher-directed curriculum and the most open, student-led classroom could meet the students' needs.

It should not be surprising that by the mid-1950s the popular press was ridiculing such progressive notions as learning to function in groups and not requiring students to master predetermined information, strategies that the Chicago group supported. There are at least six reasons why the progressive education movement fell into public disfavor. First, although most progressive educators thought schools should meet the students' needs, educators could not agree about what this meant nor how to do it. They formed factions that fought each other instead of cooperating to advance their common interests. Second, progressives seemed to be more adept at criticizing traditional classroom practices than at offering positive alternatives. Third, these progressive educators expected teachers to know a great deal and to work extremely hard. Their expectations were excessive, and few teachers tried to follow the progressive prescriptions. Fourth, after most schools adopted elements of the progressive movement, progressive educators continued to argue for the goals they had already won. For example, some educators could not stop complaining that when desks and chairs were bolted to the floor, students could not work together. They continued making these criticisms even after most schools installed movable furniture. Fifth, at the end of World War II most people held conservative political ideas and as result disliked anything that sounded radical, especially in education. Sixth, as progressive educators came to dominate colleges of education and their own professional associations, they neglected the coalitions of businesspeople, union leaders, farmers, and parents who had supported them earlier. As a result, they lost the public support they had once garnered through such innovations as organized curriculum making. Finally, in the 1950s popular writers such as David Riesman and William H. Whyte Jr. ridiculed the notion of students learning to function in groups as an effort to create conformity (Cremin, *Transformations* 347–351).

Did Educators Try to Serve the Students' Needs or the National Labor Force?

The beginning of this chapter quoted Joel Spring, who complains that educators tried to design a system of schools through ability groupings, guidance counselors, and vocational training to strengthen the nation's labor force. However, Robert Hampel contends that educators in the 1940s and 1950s made the choices they did because they did not carefully think out the compromises they were working out. Following this line of reasoning, one might argue that educators made the choices they thought would advance democracy but that those compromises undermined this goal.

For example, despite the criticisms of people such as Arthur Bestor, the EPC's list of the ten common needs of youth and life adjustment education represented efforts to cater to the diversity found within the schools that educators wanted to create. That is, many members of the life adjustment movement proposed that small school districts join with other districts, thereby forming larger schools. These life adjustment educators believed that small schools were understaffed, underfinanced, and unable to provide different opportunities to the various types of students who would attend these larger, consolidated buildings. Therefore, conference members noted that schools had to offer adequate guidance facilities to direct individual students to the best methods of satisfying their interests. Likewise, conference members valued opportunities for common learning in order to teach students to work together. Consequently, the life adjustment movement attempted to provide for individual differences within an integrated social setting (Division of Secondary Education 17).

Furthermore, educators tried to make the school attractive to all students. As a result, occasionally intellectual instruction, which was the primary job of the school, was pushed to one side as other, competing needs took precedence. In other words, when school people sought to serve the students' personal and social needs, they believed they were helping each child to develop his or her talents and that they were teaching students to appreciate the differences among cultural groups. In pursuing these goals, they hoped to improve society.

In this way, the diversified high schools symbolized the educational aims educators held after World War II. Within those large buildings, many different groups of students were supposed to come together and select their studies from different programs such as vocational, academic, and general studies. The teacher and later the guidance counselor was supposed to help students make intelligent choices among these options. Although educators thought of this as improving democracy, they disregarded the importance of academic subjects.

According to Robert Hampel, the educators' decision to offer academic studies in high schools for only a few students was one of the compromises they made to maintain the growing institution. He contends that the public distrusted people who understood abstract ideas. Generally, people valued practical knowledge and pleasant personalities more than intellectual achievements. Further, in the 1940s people associated academic study with the severity of the former generation. They wanted to make school fun and rewarding. Thus, open discussions, relevant topics, extracurricular events, and a choice of programs seemed to mark educational progress (12–17).

Hampel's conception seems accurate in the case of educators adopting the AYC's unwillingness to value fluency in foreign languages. Thus, as the experiences in San Francisco, Hawaii, and Puerto Rico illustrated, the progress toward physical integration did not match the changes in educational theory. Children of different groups attended separate buildings, and language differences exacerbated the segregation. In San Francisco and Hawaii, Asian people suffered because boards of education would not hire teachers who spoke nonstandard English. In other cases, such as in Puerto Rico during the periods when English was the language of instruction, teachers complained that the students did not learn about their Spanish-speaking communities. Yet when they did study in Spanish, Puerto Rican society moved further from the U.S. mainstream culture.

Although educators thought the best way to produce a good curriculum was to design it in ways that met the needs of the students, this model did not give direction to curriculum planners. Philosophers contended that the idea of meeting the needs of the students could justify any program those planners wished to create. Thus, a program that encouraged assimilation, such as the use of English as the language of instruction in Hawaii, could be said to meet the students' needs. However, a program that reinforced segregation could be considered to meet the students' needs, as in the case of Puerto Rico, where educators adopted Spanish as the language of instruction. The concept of meeting the child's needs was so vague that people could argue that teachers met the needs of students with large comprehensive high schools that offered vocational programs, liberal arts courses, and opportunities for students to learn to adjust to life in society. Other people could argue equally well that small private schools with academic programs met their students' needs. The ideal did not provide a means for choosing among these claims, thereby reducing the danger inherent in pursuing any goal too strongly. As a result, claiming that they wanted to serve the needs of the students, educators urged the closing of Japanese-language schools in Hawaii even though these schools served the diplomatic and military interests of the country.

TIMELINE
1940–1954

1940 The EPC presented its report, *Education and Economic Well-Being in American Democracy*

1940 The American Council of Education established the AYC

1940 Luis Munoz Marin became president of the Senate in Puerto Rico

1941 The United States entered WWII after the Japanese destroyed the American Pacific fleet in Honolulu

1941 Franklin D. Roosevelt appointed Rexford Guy Tugwell as Puerto Rico's governor

1942 A missionary teacher in Mayagüez, Puerto Rico, wrote Eleanor Roosevelt about her starving students

1942 Jose Gallardo, Puerto Rico's commissioner of education, established Spanish-language instruction in elementary schools

1942 The Puerto Rican House and Senate signed legislation that changed Puerto Rico's colonial status into a more independent relationship

(continued)

TIMELINE Continued

1942 The *New York Times* surveyed college students about U.S. history knowledge, with disappointing results

1942 F. D. Roosevelt addressed U.S. teachers to motivate them to mold patriotic, strong students during wartime

1942 The U.S. Office of Education's Wartime Commission decided to include aspects of the country's war involvement in school curriculum

1942 The EPC and the NEA agreed to gear classrooms toward U.S. enthusiasms and wartime needs during the war

1943 The NEA published the *Wartime Handbook for Education*

1943 The U.S. Senate Committee on the Territories met in San Juan and changed the education policy back to bilingualism

1943 Madame Chiang Kai-Shek visited the United States, persuading the United States to repeal discriminatory immigration laws

1943 The Hawaii territorial legislature prohibited students up to grade 5 from attending any foreign-language school

1944 The NEA published the EPC report encouraging physical fitness for youth

1945 World War II ended

1945 Dr. Charles Prosser proposed life adjustment education for high schools

1945 Pedro Cebollero studied the school language policy in Puerto Rico

1946 Congress approved the War Brides Act

1946 The U.S. Office of Education met to discuss high school students' options other than vocational training or academic studies

1946 Jesus T. Pinero became governor of Puerto Rico

1947 The United States and the Soviet Union entered the cold war

1947 California allowed Chinese Americans to buy real estate

1947 Chinese Americans successfully contested the law preventing children from attending foreign-language schools

1947 The English Standard schools in Hawaii closed

1948 Munoz Marin assumed his position as Puerto Rico's governor

1949 Munoz Marin appointed Mariano Villaronga Puerto Rico's commissioner of education

1949 Spanish replaced English as the language of instruction in Puerto Rican schools

1950 The NSSE published a study on exceptional children and the most beneficial education suited to their needs

1951 The governor of Illinois and the state superintendent of public education met with other important figures in Chicago to make schools more beneficial to national security

1953 The National Society for the Study of Education issued a yearbook, *Adapting the Secondary School Program to the Needs of Youth*

CHAPTER

9 Desegregation, Academics, and the Comprehensive High School: 1954–1964

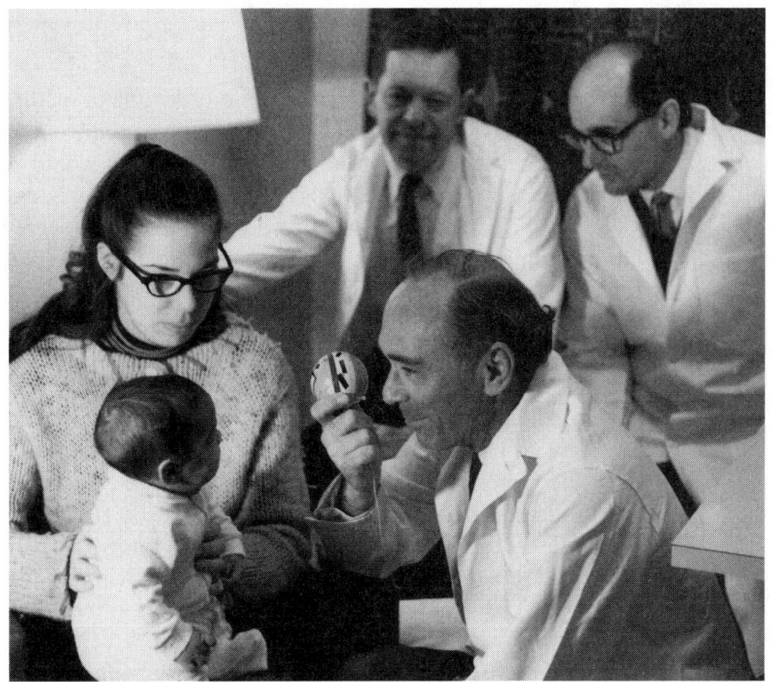

Jerome Bruner

OVERVIEW

From 1954 to 1964, the federal government increased its intervention into local school affairs. The federal programs came from two distinct sources: the federal courts, which in 1954 outlawed the racial segregation of schools, and the administrative branch and Congress, which in 1958, fearing the technological advances of the Soviet Union, authorized

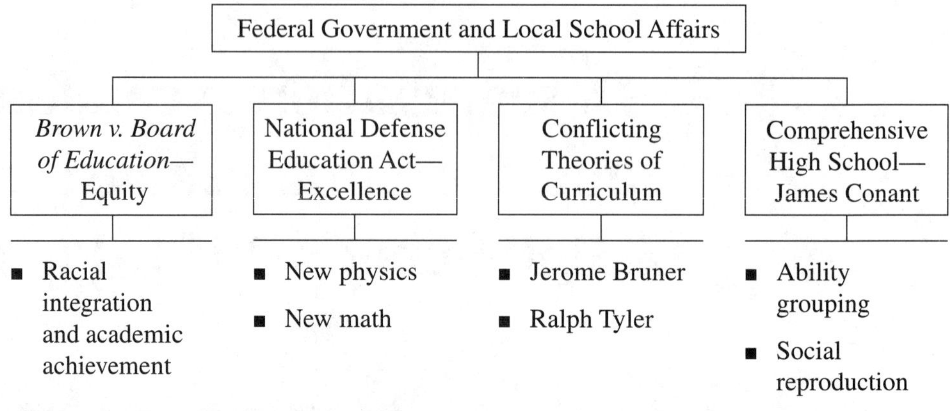

funds for the improvement of academic programs in mathematics and science to produce scientists whose inventions would protect the nation from foreign invasion. Although both actions were extensions of the view that education would advance democracy throughout the nation, they required schools to protect democracy in contradictory ways.

On the one hand, the Court's decision to outlaw segregation was an effort to provide equity throughout the schools. It also constituted a curriculum proposal; the justices hoped that racial integration would help African American students perform better in schools because all children would learn that no race was inherently superior. On the other hand, the efforts to improve instruction in science and technology sought to enhance the opportunities for some students to excel academically. This inevitably encouraged some sort of elitism.

Although both tendencies could negate each other, educators thought that the comprehensive high school would solve the problem. These large schools offered gifted children the opportunity to pursue advanced academic studies, and other students could enroll in courses teaching them to adjust to social life. Unfortunately, ability grouping turned into a form of racial or ethnic segregation within schools because members of certain racial groups and social classes enrolled in distinct programs. At the same time, many courses lacked an academic focus so that not all gifted children received the stimulus they needed.

Administrators and teachers favored the comprehensive high school because it allowed them to retain a larger number of different students. However, educational researchers claimed that the comprehensive high school demonstrated the ways in which schools reproduced existing social inequities.

What Caused School People to Racially Integrate the Schools?

Before 1950 few local districts had racially integrated schools. In some districts such as Dayton, Ohio, administrators boasted of a tradition of racially integrated schools. However, they enacted policies that segregated the students. In 1954, with the culmination of a well-crafted legal campaign that took many years, the U.S. Supreme Court decision in the *Brown* case changed many people's ideas.

In 1896 the Supreme Court had ruled in *Plessy v. Ferguson* that a state did not have to require racial integration. If the voters in a state approved, the only thing a state had to provide was equal facilities in separate areas for African Americans. In 1954 the justices did not reverse the conclusion of *Plessy v. Ferguson* with their *Brown* decision. Instead, they quoted a judge in the lower courts who had decided that African American students segregated in separate public schools developed feelings of inferiority that retarded their academic progress. In addition, the justices quoted modern psychological authority that supported this finding. As a result, the justices concluded that separate education was unequal education (Clark 158–159).

By linking the academic progress of African American children to the racial integration of schools, the Supreme Court justices implied that the desegregation of schools was a curriculum matter. That is, patterns of pupil attendance influenced what students learned and how they performed. To justify their contention, the justices cited a study by Kenneth Clark. In this study, Clark and his wife demonstrated that three-year-old children recognized racial differences. The researchers asked children to distinguish between a brown doll and a white doll that were dressed alike. When asked to hand over the Negro doll or the White doll, they did so 75 percent of the time. Researchers asked the children which doll they liked best, which doll was bad, or which doll had a nice color. The majority of the African American children favored the white doll and rejected the brown doll (Clark 18–23).

To Clark and to the Supreme Court justices, these responses demonstrated the evil effects of segregated schools. The justices ordered racial mixing to reverse the damage in the hope that integration would illustrate to the students that no racial group was inherently superior to any other. In a short period of time, the Supreme Court made several other decisions to end the segregation of parks, golf courses, airports, and bus terminals. In these later cases, however, the justices did not mention the psychological effects of segregation (Salomone 43).

Because desegregation was a legal issue, it was an inevitable but unfortunate development that the controversy over racial integration devolved into a dispute over who had authority to decide local school affairs instead of a question about the best way to make one nation out of many peoples. Lawyers for the NAACP filed subsequent suits challenging federal officials to uphold the decision and seeking to expand the definition of racial integration. On the other side, conservatives in southern states began to form what they called massive resistance to uphold what they saw as their legal rights.

After making its decision, the Supreme Court asked officials in various southern states to join conferences to investigate the effects of the *Brown* decision. No official responded. Instead, in states such as Mississippi, legislatures approved constitutional amendments permitting state funds to support tuition in private schools and passed laws forbidding White students to attend integrated elementary or secondary schools (Bartley 67–81).

Other southern politicians went even further. In 1956 101 members of U.S. Congress from the states of the former Confederacy signed South Carolina's Strom Thurmond's Declaration of Constitutional Principles. Commonly known as the Manifesto, this document argued that state governments could join in massive resistance to the federal government. The rationale was that state governments could interpose their authority between the citizens and an agency of the federal government such as the courts (Bartley 108–149).

Ironically, the first test of the theory of interposition came in Little Rock, Arkansas—ironic because unlike South Carolina, for example, Arkansas had a tradition of moderation in racial matters. In fact, the governor, Orval Faubus, who took a public stand against the integration of Central High School, had previously tried to remain neutral in race matters. In 1954 the school board instructed the superintendent of Little Rock schools to construct a plan to comply with the federal court order. However, on September 2, 1957, Governor Faubus ordered troops from the Arkansas National Guard to send away any Black students who wanted to enter the previously all-White Central High School. U.S. President Dwight D. Eisenhower ignored the theory of interposition and ordered troops from the 101st Infantry from Fort Campbell, Kentucky, to escort nine Black students into the building. On September 24, 1957, pictures in national newspapers showed troops pushing White students toward the school with bayonets pointed inches from their backs (Blossom 73–127).

As the NAACP lawyers filed more suits, other cities in the South instituted more successful programs of racial integration, but, as in Little Rock, these plans depended on Black children wanting to enroll in previously all-White schools. Consequently, a few Black children would transfer from all-Black schools and attend schools that had been designated as all White. For example, in Greensboro, North Carolina, the transition to integrated schools in 1957 was peaceful as six African American students applied to transfer to previously all-White schools. Although most cities desegregated the schools peacefully, the cities where people resisted loudly and violently dominated the newspapers.

In 1958 the NAACP awarded the Springarn Medal for contributions to racial advancement to the nine African American students who integrated Central High School in Little Rock and to Daisy Bates, president of the Arkansas NAACP. Although this symbolized the importance the organization placed on school integration, it overlooked the problems such a strategy placed on Black teachers who worked in the all-Black schools. If their school districts resisted integration, they had to remain silent or lose their jobs (Lomax 124–125).

In several southern states, legislatures abolished teacher tenure and passed laws prohibiting teachers from joining the NAACP. In some southern districts, boards of education racially integrated school faculties by removing Black principals, replacing them with White counterparts, and demoting Black teachers. In 1965 Florida replaced more teachers than any other state because it used the National Teacher Examination to determine promotion or tenure (Commission on Professional Rights 7).

The use of the National Teachers Exam as a tool of segregation extended back to 1940. At that time, the NAACP won a verdict from the U.S. Court of Appeals prohibiting Virginia schools from paying Black teachers less than equally qualified White teachers. As a result, Florida and South Carolina turned to the National Teachers Exam to justify racially separate salary schedules. Because the scores of White teachers usually exceeded those of Black teachers, school districts such as the Palm Beach County schools in Florida could divide teachers into salary groups based on test results. In that city, there were four salary levels. No African Americans were in the highest group, and 60 percent of the Black teachers were in the lowest. Despite the fact that the National Teachers Exam segregated teachers, federal courts permitted the practice because the tests were graded by machines that could not deduce the race of any exam taker (S. Baker 60–62).

In 1965 U.S. President Lyndon Johnson ordered the U.S. Department of Health, Education, and Welfare (HEW) to prohibit any displacement of teachers based on race. Unfortunately, East Texas, where Johnson had lived, had an exceptionally high number of teacher displacements. In this section of Texas, when a school district desegregated, White teachers moved to formerly African American schools but Black teachers never went to White schools. In one district, the superintendent released all Black principals, Black teachers, Black bus drivers, and Black cafeteria workers. These practices were possible because East Texas schools did not offer teachers tenure. There was no provision for rehiring teachers no matter how well they performed their work, and school districts could disregard formal qualifications for teaching. Thus, one district decided that teachers did not need a college degree to hold a job (Commission on Professional Rights 13–28).

Surprisingly, the displaced African American teachers and principals in East Texas did not organize into an occupational caucus to protect their rights, nor did they appeal to local professional associations. The local teachers' organizations were dominated by White teachers who were not sympathetic to the African Americans' problems. When the Black teachers and principals complained to the HEW office, they found no relief. The HEW staff totaled six officials to service complaints from Arkansas, Texas, Louisiana, and Oklahoma. They were so overloaded that they had difficulty even acknowledging receipt of letters (Commission on Professional Rights 52, 24–28).

What Caused People to Improve the Instruction of Academics?

During World War II, Americans saw how technological advances such as the atomic bomb diminished the value of previous measures of power such as superior numbers of soldiers. Before the war ended, U.S. President Franklin Roosevelt wrote Dr. Vannevar Bush, then director of the Office of Scientific Research and Development, asking him to prepare a study of postwar science. Entitling his report "Science, the Endless Frontier," Bush recommended that a new agency be created to advance American science. However, Congress did not act on Bush's proposal until 1950, when it created the National Science Foundation (NSF) as an independent agency of the executive office of the presidency to develop a national policy for the promotion of basic research and education in science (Science Policy Research Division 1–3).

In 1952 Congress voted the NSF a budget of \$3.5 million to disburse grants for research. The program was popular among members of Congress, who voted in 1953 to increase the budget to \$4.75 million. About \$1.7 million supported doctoral research programs. However, the NSF began to support science education in the form of summer institutes for science teachers from small colleges. In 1955 Congress increased the NSF budget to \$12 million and its grants to \$10 million (Marsh and Gortner 15–17).

Although people accepted giving federal money to scientists who promised to improve national defense, they disputed the reasonableness of extending federal aid to education because they feared federal control. Even those educators who acknowledged the need for some federal assistance sought to limit it in order to preserve local control. For example, in 1956 the Committee for the White House Conference on Education reinforced the view that the federal government should have a minimal role in education. Although this committee called for people to emphasize the importance of education and to double the amount of money spent on schools, the members were careful to urge that the bulk of the money come from local and state governments. They thought federal funds should be for school buildings and allocated on an emergency basis (4–6).

At the same time, in Congress there were three obstacles to extending federal aid to public schools. First, several politicians felt that the people in each community should control the local schools through a locally elected or appointed board of education. To these people, local and state support was adequate; federal aid would only bring federal control. Second, because the federal government could not support organized religion, some politicians did not want any federal money to go to private schools. These politicians faced an equally strong group who believed that federal money must be extended to private or church schools if federal monies were going to public schools. Third, southern legislators who opposed the *Brown* decision feared that federal aid would become another weapon to bring about the racial integration of schools (Clowse 41–43).

On October 4, 1957, an event of worldwide interest changed the picture of federal aid to education: The Soviet Union launched the first Earth-orbiting satellite. Called Sputnik, this satellite was carried into space by a three-stage rocket twenty times more powerful than the one the United States planned to launch later in the year. For weeks before this event, President Eisenhower was busy with the racial problems in Little Rock, Arkansas. In his first public responses to Sputnik, he denied that the Soviet Union had any superiority over the United States. At the same time, however, he conferred with eminent scientists on the Science Advisory Committee of the Office of Defense Mobilization who suggested that he appoint a scientific advisor to the White House and that he consider ways to avert a shortage of scientific personnel that would allow the Soviet Union to surpass U.S. technology. Educators took advantage of the crisis to seek financial aid to schools (Clowse 5–12).

Newspapers claimed that the Soviets had beaten the Americans into space because U.S. schools lacked intellectual standards. They argued that Soviet scientists were better trained than Americans. However, because the space programs in the Soviet Union and the United States were directed by former German rocket scientists, at least one critic complained that the problem was not educational; the Soviet Union's German scientists were better than the United States' German scientists. Despite these controversies, on October 20, 1957, Eisenhower announced that he wanted the federal government to strengthen math and science training (Clowse 13–14).

In reaction to the Soviet success with Sputnik, the congressional Committee for Labor and Public Welfare held hearings from January to March 1958 to determine what action the federal government should take to strengthen education. According to some commentators, one of the most impressive witnesses to appear before the committee was Dr. Wernher von Braun, director of the U.S. Army Ballistic Missile Agency (Clowse 84).

Born in Germany, von Braun received a doctorate in physics from the University of Berlin and headed the missile program in Peenemünde, Germany, during World War II. He came to the United States in 1945 and joined the U.S. missile program. In his testimony, von Braun drew on his experiences in Europe and the United States to contrast the education in U.S. high schools to that found in European schools. First, in the United States teachers tried to help all students graduate, whereas European schools ruthlessly selected and trained the best students, who had to pass stringent examinations to move up the grades. Second, in the United States von Braun found high schools spending time on family life or human relations, which did not happen in German schools. European schools did not try to make learning fun or relevant for the students. They administered required courses and ignored social adjustment. Third, in teacher training European universities did not consider methods of teaching important. Instead of teaching people how to teach, von Braun added, European universities asked if a person knew the subject and was inspired to communicate that subject to the students (63–67).

In his conclusions, von Braun drew three recommendations from his comparison. First, he endorsed the suggestion that the federal government should set up some sort of an inspection agency to establish national standards for requirements for graduates of high schools, colleges, and universities. Second, he recommended that the schools offer increased opportunities for gifted students. Von Braun believed that teachers hurt their students by pacing instruction to the slowest child; young students accepted inspiration and rose to challenges. Therefore, the United States should imitate the Soviet Union in encouraging young children to excel, in sifting them constantly, and in giving the best opportunities to the top performers. Third, von Braun asked all Americans to eschew anti-intellectualism. He reminded the congressional committee that single-minded people such as Thomas Edison contributed a great deal to society. Although these people were not always well adjusted, he added, they worked well and lived in a world of their own. Such geniuses have to be accepted for what they can do (67–69).

After hearing from several witnesses and conferring among themselves, members of Congress drafted and adopted the National Defense Education Act (NDEA). This legislation was written to avoid the three obstacles traditionally blocking federal support of schools. First, although critics contended that if progressive educational practices ended, state and local tax support of local schools would be adequate, supporters of the NDEA countered that the bill corrected weaknesses in the schools that the current crisis revealed. Second, to break the deadlock about aid to religious schools, the NDEA authorized assistance to parochial schools provided the funds went only for testing and upgrading science, math, and foreign-language instruction. This appeased politicians who wanted to maintain a separation of church and state while also appeasing Catholic educators who would have blocked federal aid to schools if it excluded parochial institutions. Finally, to win the support of southern politicians, HEW officials promised that the department would not withhold funds from states in which schools were racially segregated unless Congress empowered the department to do so (Clowse 128–135).

In August 1958, with Eisenhower's support, the House and Senate approved the NDEA. Up to the end, the most outspoken critic of the NDEA was Strom Thurmond, senator from South Carolina, who was convinced that HEW officials were lying and would withhold federal money from segregated schools. Thurmond claimed that taxes from southern voters would support schools in other parts of the country. However, many members of Congress from the southern and border states where segregation was the issue ignored Thurmond's complaints. They either chose not to vote on the bill or supported it (Clowse 136–138).

Congress divided the NDEA into several sections and made distinct annual appropriations for each. For example, in fiscal year 1961, Title II allocated about $83 million for loans to help students attend colleges or universities. Title III offered around $70 million in financial assistance to strengthen science, mathematics, and foreign-language instruction. To identify and encourage able students, Title V offered about $15 million for guidance, counseling, and testing. In the area of language study, Title VI offered about $8 million to help increase the scope and quality of foreign-language instruction. Title VII used about $5 million to enhance the utilization of media such as television, radio, and motion pictures. Vocational education was supported by Title VIII. Finally, Title X disbursed almost $3 million to improve the statistical services of state education agencies and to survey the effects of federal programs on higher education. The U.S. Office of Education directed all of these services. However, Title IX established a special service in the National Science Foundation (U.S. Department of Health, Education, and Welfare 1, 6–55).

In 1963 the U.S. Office of Education declared that the NDEA had improved education in all levels from elementary schools to graduate programs. According to an HEW report, NDEA funds strengthened the teaching of science, mathematics, foreign languages, and vocational education. The report claimed that schools enjoyed improved counseling and testing services and that worthy students found it easier to attend college. The Office of Education measured success by counting the amount of funds distributed and the number of projects supported. For example, from 1959 to 1962, Title III projects involved a total of $323.6 million for the improvement of science, mathematics, and foreign-language instruction. As a result of those funds, 11,121 classrooms or laboratories were remodeled to improve science instruction (U.S. Department of Health, Education, and Welfare 1, 12–13).

Although the Office of Education claimed that the NDEA was a success, the effects of NDEA activities were not clear. Little effort was made to prove that the money was spent effectively. For example, the Office of Education did not define what constituted a science project. As a result, state departments of education used the money to encourage reforms they thought were important. New York offered the funds to school districts that already exceeded state guidelines. Mississippi directed the funds to districts that fell below minimum standards. Maine favored consolidated districts in its disbursements. Because the deadlines for applications came quickly, administrators in many school districts and states tried to spend all they could receive. Consequently, many school districts spent the money on large buildings such as planetariums that provided diversions for the students as well as on teaching aids. Sometimes these buildings did not fit into well-thought-out instructional plans, but they consumed large amounts of money and impressed parents and community leaders. Not surprisingly, in 1959, of the $23 million disbursed among 8,947 Title III projects, more than 8,000 projects accounted for less than half the funds. The remaining 940 projects received the greatest part. In 1960, under Title III 47,976 projects absorbed $46.3 million, yet 10 percent of these projects cost more than $20 million (Marsh and Gortner 52–56).

These tendencies raised the question of whether the spending brought improvement in science learning. Of course, the money advanced schools in other ways as well. For example, state departments of education in the Northwest tended to send the funds to large urban school districts. In the past, those big cities had not received a reasonable portion of regular state aid. Title III of the NDEA gave state officials a chance to redress these inequities (Marsh and Gortner 92).

State departments of education could spend the federal money as they saw reasonable and appropriate because Congress did not put stipulations on the NDEA. In fact, seeking to avoid excessive federal control, the provisions of the act forbade the Office of Education from controlling the disbursement of the funds and prohibited state legislatures from placing prerequisites on the money (Marsh and Gortner 76–77).

However, as described in Chapter 11, by 1965, when Congress passed the Elementary and Secondary Education Act, attitudes changed. The size of the grants grew enormously. At the same time, television news programs showed mayors and the local police in southern cities brutally mistreating civil rights demonstrators. Consequently, people came to fear misconduct by local officials more than they dreaded the federal controls over local school districts. Therefore, Congress required the agencies that received federal aid from grants such as the Elementary and Secondary Education Act to prove they spent the money appropriately and effectively. In the 1970s, President Richard Nixon tried to reduce federal government oversight by providing all federal funds in the form of block grants, which state education agencies could spend as they wished. However, neither Nixon nor his successor, Ronald Reagan, succeeded in combining federal funds into block grants.

How Did Prominent Scientists Try to Change the Teaching of Science in Elementary and Secondary Schools?

Before the NDEA passed, Congress sent funds to the National Science Foundation to support scientists as they tried to change the teaching of science. From 1952 to 1955, NSF budgets grew steadily. Much of this money supported doctoral-level research in universities. However, a portion supported the development of college-level courses for high school science teachers in schools and colleges. In 1956 NSF's annual report urged the development of high-quality science education in elementary and secondary schools to prevent a shortage of scientists during the coming decade. One effort to improve the instruction of young people came from Professor Jerrold R. Zacharias of the Massachusetts Institute of Technology (MIT) who proposed that a high school physics course be built around ninety films, each about twenty minutes long. Each film would be complete in itself, have a teacher's guide, and offer questions for discussion and research. Most important, the content would introduce students to physics as done in the present day with a study of particles, followed by a consideration of the laws of force and motion, and leading to the mathematics needed to compare theory and experiments. In 1956 Professor Zacharias convened a group of eminent scientists, who called themselves the Physical Science Study Committee (PSSC), to expand the project (Marsh and Gortner 16–21).

The PSSC began evaluating existing physic textbooks. The results were depressing. Often the books covered too much material, devoted little space to physics, and paid excessive attention to practical applications. Worse, sometimes the texts misrepresented the concepts they *did* present. Hoping to correct the situation, the NSF awarded the PSSC $300,000 to study the feasibility of creating teaching materials for a new high school course in physical science (Marsh and Gortner 18–23).

In December 1956, forty-eight physicists and educators from Cornell University, Bell Laboratories, the University of Illinois, and the California Institute of Technology gathered at MIT to debate the framework of such a course. They decided to create a one-year course that would demonstrate the unity and regularity of the physical world. The format would trace the way scientists had created the picture of science that extended from the atom to the universe. The text would show how scientists tried to discover the laws of physical science by observing physical phenomena. Approving the results of the conference, the NEA granted PSSC almost $300,000 more for the coming year (Marsh and Gortner 30–35).

Zacharias enlisted more scientists, consultants, photographers, artists, engineers, and technicians to help in the work. By the summer of 1958, the group had created a text and illustrated it with experiments that called for easily available materials such as bricks and soda straws. They tested these materials in more than twenty high schools and then revised them. Another group wrote an accompanying laboratory manual. In addition, the Educational Testing Service, which constructed the College Entrance Examinations, devised, revised, and distributed a series of classroom tests and a new College Entrance Examination for the PSSC (Marsh and Gortner 18–38).

In the summer of 1958, the PSSC offered five summer institutes spread throughout the country. A total of 326 teachers attended these programs to learn how to teach the new course. In the fall of 1958, about 250 schools had classrooms that offered the PSSC material. The numbers grew rapidly. In 1959 more than 625 schools offered the course, and by 1961 more than 75,000 students enrolled in it (Marsh and Gortner 47–50).

In 1964, looking back over his accomplishments, Zacharias considered the fall of 1960 to be the date when the course revision ceased being an experiment and became an established course. Thus, he noted, the preparation took about four years, involved about eight hundred schools, and included about one thousand teachers. This constituted about 8 percent of the secondary high school physics teachers at that time (Zacharias and White 79).

How Did Specialists Change Subject Matters Such as Mathematics?

The PSSC inspired mathematicians to produce an innovation called "new math." As in the case of the PSSC, the distinguishing feature of the groups who produced the new math was that they were composed of academic specialists rather than educators. As a result, these new curriculum projects tried to draw the students' attention to the discipline of mathematics rather than to the applicability of mathematics or its relevance to their lives outside school.

In 1951 a committee of professors at the University of Illinois began a model of new math by publishing a list of mathematical competencies that high school students would need before entering the college of engineering. The success of this endeavor led the university to create the University of Illinois Committee on School Mathematics (UICSM), which was charged with creating a curriculum that would help high school students acquire the competencies the earlier committee had listed. The first effort was tried in the university's laboratory school and in two Illinois public schools the next year. Based on what was called "guided discovery," UICSM directed the students to understand concepts such as number, variable, function, equation, and geometry. Although discovery methods of teaching were common, the coordinator of the UICSM project believed that when students attempted to verbalize their discoveries, they actually impeded their ability to assimilate them. Consequently, the UICSM materials suggested that students not explain their discoveries nor read descriptions of what they were supposed to have found. Instead, teachers were supposed to test the students' understanding by having them apply their discoveries to new situations. This system demanded considerable preparation by teachers. As a result, by September 1957 the UICSM program had spread to only twelve schools (Hayden 100–107).

In February 1958, a more influential effort to create new math began when a group of research mathematicians including the presidents of the American Mathematical Society (AMS) and the Mathematical Association of America (MAA) convened in the Mathematics Meeting of the National Science Foundation at MIT. The AMS was an association of theorists and the MAA served college teachers. Hence, the mathematicians who attended this conference had held themselves aloof from matters of elementary and secondary curricula. Nonetheless, the participants at this Cambridge Conference, as it was called, decided to hold a writing seminar for five weeks in the summer to prepare a model secondary mathematics curriculum and to arrange publication of monographs on mathematics that would interest secondary students. In order to retain their isolation, in April 1958 the AMS appointed eight individuals without direct connection to the association to carry out the resolutions of the conference. Calling themselves the School Mathematics Study Group (SMSG), this committee applied to and received from the NSF $100,000 to devise a practical program to improve instruction in mathematics in elementary and secondary schools (Wooten 10–14).

The SMSG appointed a twenty-six-member advisory committee that included a wide cross section of the nation's mathematicians. The advisory committee and the director of the SMSG, Professor Edward G. Begle of Yale University, employed forty-five people to work in the writing group that summer. Twenty-one were college teachers of mathematics, twenty-one were high school teachers, and the remaining participants came from the Rand Corporation, Bell Telephone Laboratories, and the American Association for the Advancement of Science (Wooten 13–16).

This first writing session began on June 23, 1958. The participants divided themselves into subgroups. One subgroup began outlining a curriculum for grades 7 and 8, and the other four subgroups took on the tasks for grades 9, 10, 11, and 12, respectively. These curricula were to be suitable for college-capable students, and they were to contain the best and most appropriate mathematics possible. On July 19, the summer seminar ended, but, work on the project continued. In September the NSF extended an additional $1,200,000 to the SMSG. With this funding, the director moved into four large rooms at Yale University to coordinate preparation of materials, training of teachers to use the materials, and trials in secondary schools (Wooten 17–45).

During the year, participants divided themselves into four panels. The first panel devoted itself to editing and testing the materials produced during the summer for use in the seventh and eighth grades. The second panel began writing sample textbooks for grades 9 through 12. A third panel began producing monographs on different subjects in mathematics that would serve as supplements for gifted students. Finally, the fourth panel turned to the work of preparing teachers to use the materials correctly. This was a concern because many of high school mathematics teachers were poorly prepared. For example, some experts estimated that more than 25 percent of the mathematics teachers in the United States had not studied calculus. Thus, the SMSG panel on teacher training began producing teacher study guides in set theory, geometry, and algebra (Wooten 48–53).

The materials constructed for the seventh and eighth grades provide an idea of the curriculum reforms the group had in mind. First, they decided not to present separate courses in algebra or geometry. Although these would appear in the later grades, in junior high the emphasis was on mathematical structure so examples were drawn from arithmetic, geometry, and algebra. The panel members found that contemporary texts offered a considerable amount of what they called social mathematics. This was material applied directly to life situations. However, the panel decided to use social math only to illustrate mathematical ideas rather than to show the practicality of mathematics. Thus, although practical applications appeared in the texts, these applications were secondary to the exposition of mathematical concepts. Further, panel members decided to omit drill and review. Instead, they chose to provide for skill maintenance in new settings. The most important aims were to appreciate abstract concepts, develop a precise vocabulary, and learn experimentation and proof (Mayor 1–3).

To test the materials for the seventh and eighth grades, the SMSG set up experimental centers in different cities around the United States. In these centers, a director recruited suitable teachers and selected classes to try out the materials. The director of each center distributed the materials to the teachers, and after the teachers tried a unit the director administered an evaluation questionnaire and relayed their responses to the SMSG. Because the centers were near universities, mathematics professors could act as consultants to teachers (Wooten 46–47).

Hoping to test the new textbooks in 1959–60 the academic year, SMSG had to write the six secondary texts and teacher's manuals within six weeks. To accomplish this monumental feat, Begle retained the services of more than one hundred writers, including the participants of the original summer seminar. Using the sample texts and teachers' responses as points of departure, one group met in Ann Arbor, Michigan, in June 1959 to write seventh- and eighth-grade texts. In general, they divided the work among teams of two or three people while a coordinating committee went over everything to ensure that the style and presentation throughout was consistent. At the same time, another group met in Boulder, Colorado, to write texts for grades 9 through 12. This group was divided into subgroups that were assigned different grade levels. Although each group delegated work somewhat differently, in general teams of two to six people would write first drafts of chapters, which other teams would then revise. Thus, writing, rewriting, discussing, and criticizing continued throughout the process. Despite the haste and resulting confusion, by the fall of 1959 six textbooks and several individual units were ready for testing in forty-nine centers with a total of 26,000 students (Wooten 61–82).

For the seventh- and eighth-grade levels, the texts departed from the traditional review of mathematics and drill that had dominated the field. Instead, these new texts made computation only one aspect of the subject and concentrated on reasoning. They traced the historical development of mathematics, explaining different numeration systems. Most important, these new texts did not offer practical applications as previous books had. Instead, the authors concentrated the students' attention on mathematics itself. In a similar fashion, the ninth-grade algebra text contained the same content found in traditional texts. However, the authors presented a picture of the structure of algebra through Socratic questioning that led students to discover the basic properties (Wooten 83–85).

In January 1960, the NSF added $1,700,000 to the SMSG. With these new funds, SMSG held another writing session with eighty-seven participants in June 1960 at Stanford University. Faced with a huge amount of information from test results and teacher questionnaires, the writers divided themselves into smaller teams to tackle revisions. At same time, a new group of writers began to work on texts for elementary schools. These authors faced two unique problems. First, elementary school teachers were ill prepared to teach mathematics; twenty-nine states required no mathematics training for elementary school teachers. Second, most people thought of mathematics teaching as having the students memorize algorithms. Therefore, few people knew how to teach mathematics to young children (Wooten 97–99).

In August 1960, the SMSG completed the textbooks for college-bound secondary youth, and Yale University Press took over the publication and distribution of the texts. In September the SMSG received a further grant of $1,184,200 from the NSF. One year later, in the fall of 1961, SMSG moved from Yale to Sanford University (Wooten 105–109).

It is important to note that the SMSG did not devote itself to the development of materials for a narrow band of students. Three efforts illustrate this commitment to a more general teaching of mathematics. First, in 1960 a panel of writers considered developing materials for non-college-bound students. Some pilot studies indicated that these students could learn the same material as other, faster students if it was presented slowly. Consequently, this panel worked from the same general outlines used by the other SMSG writing groups (Wooten 101).

Second, a center for SMSG opened in Puerto Rico. This center worked closely with the center at Stanford to translate the SMSG materials into Spanish. The texts were available in September 1962 and aimed at improving the mathematics education of Spanish-speaking citizens of the United States (Wooten 130–131).

Third, in 1966 the SMSG began a special curriculum project to determine how to teach mathematics to what were called culturally disadvantaged primary school children. In 1964 the SMSG set up experimental schools in Boston, Chicago, Miami, Detroit, Oakland, California, and Washington, D.C. Local school officials chose participants by selecting children whose families earned less than $2,000 to $4,000 per year and whose homes lacked books, examples of parental reading, or stimulation to succeed. The students who made up the comparison groups lived in middle-class neighborhoods of the metropolitan area. All students used the same SMSG materials. The initial pilot study found that the students labeled disadvantaged did not respond in uniform ways to the materials. Some did well while others did not. This led researchers to wonder whether these children shared intellectual tendencies (Leiderman, Chinn, and Dunkley 1–3, 89).

How Successful Were the Efforts to Revise the Subject Matters?

The efforts to make the subject matters correspond to the structure of academic disciplines enjoyed an initial success. However, by the end of the 1960s, as more criticisms of the revisions appeared, their popularity faded. Early empirical studies showed that the revisions were worthwhile. For example, in November 1961 the SMSG reported the results of a study to determine the short-term effects of using their mathematics texts. In comparing the progress of students using SMSG texts with those using traditional texts, this evaluation showed that the SMSG students had about the same mathematical skills as students using traditional texts. However, the SMSG students had significantly greater understanding of the subject matter of mathematics. This was an important finding because the authors feared that students would not develop the ability to add and subtract as they worked through the discovery exercises in the texts (Wooten 105–109). Not surprisingly, participants in the efforts thought they succeeded to revise the subject matters. For example, in 1966 Stephen White, a journalist who worked with Zacharias in the PSSC, claimed their films and writings revolutionized the teaching of physics and became the vanguard of a radical reform movement in all education (7).

Given the reformers' enthusiasm, their ideas spread. By 1966, in the United States seven different groups produced courses labeled as new mathematics. These included the University of Illinois Committee on School Mathematics, the University of Maryland Mathematics Project, the SMSG, the Greater Cleveland Mathematics Program, the Committee on the Undergraduate Program in Mathematics, the Committee on Mathematics for the Non-College Bound, and the Minnesota School Mathematics Center. Of these groups advancing new math, the SMSG had the greatest influence in secondary education. In the mid-1960s, commentators estimated that more than 10 percent of the students in secondary schools in the United States used SMSG textbooks. Nonetheless, these groups were similar in that they sought to present mathematics as a many-sided but unified discipline. They wanted to give students a sound understanding of basic principles, and they introduced mathematical ideas to the students earlier than traditional programs. Often, these programs introduced concepts to young children, such as the idea of sets in order to give meaning to number, that were new and startling to parents unfamiliar with mathematics (Johnson and Rahtz 6–11,19–23).

Furthermore, this type of curriculum revision spread to Europe. In 1958 the Organization for European Economic Cooperation asked the MAA to make a survey of mathematics instruction in its member nations, an effort to be supported by a grant from the U.S. National Science Foundation. The first such effort took place in November 1959 when educators and mathematicians from Europe and the United States met at the Cercle Culturel de Royaumont in Asnières-sur-Oise, France. After hearing comments from members of the SMSG in the United States, members of this conference decided there should be changes in mathematics curricula in European schools. Reforms would seek to better prepare students for university study and give all students a tool for use in daily life (B. Moon 43–48).

The participants at the Royaumont conference created an executive committee similar to the SMSG to produce outlines or synopses from which teams of mathematicians in various countries could produce their own texts. The following year many of the participants from Royaumont met and announced that a team of master mathematicians had met and formulated a unified approach to the entire curriculum for secondary school students. In 1963, during a second conference held in Athens, Greece, participants reported that a great deal of significant study, writing of new textbooks for secondary schools, and reeducation of teachers had taken place in various countries. Furthermore, as in the United States, mathematicians in several European countries began to develop materials for elementary school children (B. Moon 50–56).

Despite these signs of success, the curriculum revision movement encountered difficulties. Because the texts could startle people unfamiliar with mathematics, problems arose. Four complaints were widely heard: (1) the SMSG model ignored applications of mathematics; (2) the texts were too rigorous and symbolic for most students; (3) the content for each grade level was too great to be covered in an academic year; and (4) the time devoted to practice of computational skills was inadequate (Johnson and Rahtz 17–20).

As complaints mounted, educators acknowledged the success of the reforms but admitted shortcomings as well. For example, writing in 1966, John Goodlad contended that the reforms started by the PSSC and the SMSG were more widespread than previous curriculum reform movements had been. As a result, students were studying material that differed from that offered ten years earlier. Unlike earlier reforms, which originated from some understanding of the characteristics of youth and society, the PSSC and SMSG model derived from the academic disciplines. To demonstrate his point, Goodlad listed five characteristics of the PSSC and SMSG approach to curriculum:

- The disciplines were separated rather than fused around some integrating issue.
- The movement tried to organize the curricula around the primary structural elements in each field.
- Instead of organizing the courses around social applications, the courses were organized to present the discipline in orderly ways.
- The students used inductive methods of learning.
- The materials came in packages that contained complete units.

Goodlad noted that the texts often failed to present the essential concepts of a discipline, substituting generalizations that came from those concepts. Further, packaged curricula prevented teachers from building on students' interests. In this regard, Goodlad told a story of a teacher who asked students to stop looking at a turtle a boy brought to class and turn to the crabs that were the subject of the day's lesson ("Where Precollege" 1–11).

Perhaps as a result of these complaints, some elementary and secondary schools adopted the innovations too slowly to satisfy the innovators. For example, in 1967 Robert Davis, former member of the SMSG and director of a project for producing supplementary materials for elementary students at Syracuse University, complained that as far as he could see the mathematics revolution had not taken place. He noted that schools had long resisted innovation. Although Davis complimented the work of the PSSC and the SMSG, he thought their efforts were inadequate unless educators in elementary and secondary schools and in teacher training institutions realized the important need to modify curricula to help meet what he called the emerging crises in technology (1–19).

Popular songs and comedians ridiculed the new math. More important, in 1973 Morris Kline published *Why Johnny Can't Add: The Failure of New Math.* According to Kline, the new math was misleading or incorrect. For example, a fundamental premise of new math was that students would not have to rely on rote learning if the subject were taught logically in ways that revealed the underlying reasoning. However, Kline believed this was a half truth. Positive and negative numbers and fractions might be introduced in a logical fashion to a child, but irrational numbers such as the square root of two could not be explained and therefore had to be postulated. Further, when texts in new mathematics depended on deduction they misrepresented the ways in which mathematicians worked. There was much more intuition and messy thinking in real mathematics, Kline argued, than the texts implied (24–31, 48–49).

In some texts, Kline found only the illusion of rigor. The authors took simple topics and cloaked them in what he called "prissy pedantry" to give them the impression of deep mathematical insight. Kline thought the problem was that the textbook authors had an inordinate concern for precision in language. As a result, their statements were correct but unclear. This was particularly obvious when the texts explained operations by referring to sets of numbers instead of the numbers themselves. The problem became even worse when the texts used symbols instead of words to explain ideas. Kline observed that sometimes texts in elementary mathematics used more elaborate notations than those that appeared in writings of theoretical physics, engineering, or computer science (59, 72–73).

Most important, Kline asserted, the general thrust of new math was misdirected. That is, the new math texts tried to teach what the authors called the structure of mathematics. Consequently, teachers had to interest young children by showing the order that permeated every branch of mathematics. Unfortunately, Kline thought, the subject presented in this way held no significance to either young children or adolescents. Students had to see mathematics work in real situations in order to appreciate its power (82–83).

In all, new math did not survive the 1960s. However, it did not completely fade away. Through the 1990s, new math remained a part of most elementary and secondary textbooks although it appeared in more compromised forms. These compromises were necessary because the movement to make it modern faded as groups such as the SMSG that sponsored it disbanded. Ironically, as Sputnik brought home the threat of war and encouraged the effort to upgrade science and mathematics curricula, the military may have sped the decline of new math. During the Vietnam War, in the 1970s, students rebelled against technology and related subjects as part of their disaffection from the war (B. Moon 240–244).

Could the Structure of a Discipline Capture the Students' Interest?

Although the new curricula faded, they illustrated an important national disagreement about how courses should be organized. One group thought that students could find a subject interesting on its own terms, whereas another group thought that students become interested in a subject when they recognize its relevance to their lives.

When Kline argued that children appreciate the value of a subject by recognizing its practicality, he struck at the heart of the effort to reassert the dominance of academic subjects. The central concept of the new physics and the new math was that students could learn to think as subject matter specialists did. To some extent, this sounded like John Dewey's aim in using occupations as lessons that led students to an understanding of subject matter. As pointed out in Chapter 5, Dewey had children plant gardens in order to become familiar with biology, meteorology, and history. However, in 1960 Jerome Bruner claimed that it was unnecessary for children to begin their lessons with a practical activity. He believed that if the subject matter was well taught, it would be exciting.

In 1959 Bruner was chairperson of a conference of thirty-five scientists, scholars, and educators at Woods Hole on Cape Cod sponsored by the National Academy of Sciences.

The aim of the conference was to examine the process involved in imparting to young students a sense of the substance and method of science. Conference members divided into five work groups. Each group prepared a separate report about the subject its members considered. As chairperson, Bruner wrote a document reflecting the general themes of the conference. This appeared as *The Process of Education* in 1960 (Bruner vii).

Bruner noted that an individual's interests came from internal satisfactions and external rewards. Both of these attractions could be called into action if teachers enabled students to grasp what he called the structure of a discipline. First, the excitement of discovering how ideas related to each other in a subject would be appealing. This relationship of ideas or concepts in mathematics or physics or history was the structure of the discipline and represented the way of thinking characteristic of scholars who were expert in the area. Second, by learning through discovery students would develop the attitudes and values of intellectuals, for whom rewards abounded in the wider society. For example, although Bruner acknowledged that people had often thought of education as a means to a better job, he asserted that the Sputnik crisis had made Americans aware of the need to place academics on a level equal with athletics and social adjustment (Bruner 72–75).

For Bruner, however, the primary reason for focusing instruction on the fundamentals of a subject was that such fundamental ideas could be applied to other problems in school and in life. Learning served the future in two ways: a person learned something in one setting and applied the skill in another, and an individual transferred principles and attitudes to a new activity. This second type of transfer of training was the most important. Texts written by the PSSC and SMSG sought to encourage such transfer by making central the pervading and powerful ideas and attitudes relating to physical science and mathematics. Further, as both these examples illustrated, the most able scholars in the fields had to decide what constituted the fundamental ideas of a subject. These were the people who should write the textbooks (Bruner 17–19).

Drawing on the conclusions of Jean Piaget, Bruner acknowledged that children learn differently than adults and that they learn differently at different stages of their development. Children about five years old were in what he called the preoperational stage and tended to think about relationships between experience and action. Although these children could manipulate the things in the world around them, they lacked the idea of reversibility. That is, they did not realize that objects can be changed and returned to their former state. Consequently, they could not grasp mathematical concepts that depended on the conservation of quantity. These children would not realize that a set of objects divided into subgroups remained the same total number of objects. When the children reached about six to ten years of age, according to Bruner, they entered the concrete operational stage of development in which they began to accumulate information about the world and to use their new understandings to solve simple problems. At the age of ten to fourteen, children began to use formal operations, constructing hypothetical propositions, imagining possible variables, and recognizing some relationships that could be tested (Bruner 31–39).

Despite these differences, even young children could learn the fundamentals of the subjects provided that teachers presented the basic concepts in ways that helped the children pass progressively from concrete thinking to more formal operations. This should not be done in a particular or mechanical sequence. For example, Bruner recommended that children learn to face problems that challenged them and thereby forge ahead in their development (39–40).

Consequently, for Bruner the curriculum in all the grades focused on the fundamentals of a subject. Calling this the spiral curriculum, Bruner argued that the material taught at any grade level should be something that, when fully developed, was worthy of an adult knowing it. In literature, for example, the curriculum could be built around an awareness of tragedy. This could begin for young children with a retelling of great myths or use of children's classics. In later grades, teachers could build on students' earlier reactions to create more explicit understandings of tragedy with themes such as loyalty or identity (52–53).

In taking the position that the fundamentals of the subject matter were most important, Bruner took issue with the central idea of the progressive movement, which had been that the subject matter had to be made relevant to the lives of students. This notion had become an important idea in curriculum construction and evaluation throughout the United States. For example, Ralph Tyler was a well-known advocate of including students' needs in the curriculum. He was the former director of evaluation for the Eight-Year Study conducted by the Progressive Education Association, and in 1949 he wrote what may be the most widely read book in curriculum study, *Basic Principles of Curriculum and Instruction.* Tyler listed four questions that he thought any person developing a curriculum had to answer:

1. What educational purposes should the school seek to attain?
2. What experiences can the school provide to attain those purposes?
3. How can the school organize the experiences?
4. How can anyone determine if the purposes have been attained?

Tyler did not answer the questions; he suggested methods for studying them (*Basic Principles* 1–2).

The question of goals was most important to Tyler. Unlike Bruner, however, he did not think about whether the material to be learned was similar to what a scholar understood. Instead, Tyler meant that the materials students use, the activities they engage in, and the tests they take should be defined by the objectives. The information to determine what the objectives should be came from several sources. First, the learners themselves provided information. Because education was a process to change students' behaviors, educators should identify the necessary changes in the behavior patterns that the school should produce. This model of need represented a gap between what the child was and what he or she was to become. Therefore, Tyler recommended that teachers construct conceptions of acceptable norms the students should acquire. Second, children have certain psychological needs, such as a need for affection or status. The school could provide the information or skills to help children satisfy these basic needs as well as initiate activities that enable them to meet some of these needs. This model portrayed needs as tensions within students that had to be resolved before the students could reach equilibrium (*Basic Principles* 3–8).

In addition to looking at the learners themselves, Tyler suggested that information to select educational objectives should come from studies of contemporary life outside school, suggestions from subject specialists, ideas from philosophy, and findings of psychologists. Thus, Tyler did not overlook the concern for subject matter, but he limited it. He complained that teachers frequently chose the subject matter on the basis of what a person needs to be a scholar in that field. Instead, teachers should select subject matter according to the ways it can contribute to daily life for most people. Therefore, instead of creating mathematics courses as training for mathematicians, Tyler wanted a method of instruction that applied arithmetic to contemporary problems (*Basic Principles* 16–27).

In 1977 Tyler reconsidered what he had written and compared those ideas to the curriculum revisions of the PSSC and SMSG. He remained convinced that he had been right and contended that the curriculum reformers such as Bruner overlooked two factors: the learner's active role and what he called the influence of the nonschool environment ("Tyler Rationale" 395).

Complaining that these materials were often constructed by subject matter specialists with little or no consideration of the needs or interests of the students, Tyler wrote that these materials were designed for teachers to deliver to the students. This implied, he argued, that teachers need not construct lessons and that learning should be a passive activity. This could not work, Tyler asserted, because learners must see the ways they can use what they learn. They will not carry on the behavior unless they can succeed in it and see that it will be valuable in various situations they encounter. Therefore, Tyler approved of teachers devising lessons that encouraged students to use outside the school the materials they learned in class. These might include having arithmetic problems for which the students select the lowest price for foods ("Tyler Rationale" 396–397).

Regarding the nonschool environment, Tyler suggested that teachers form community councils to assess educational needs and identify resources. At the same time, teachers might teach students how to take advantage of contemporary society such as ways to find beneficial programs on television ("Tyler Rationale" 399–400).

At first glance, Tyler's accusation that the SMSG or Bruner wanted students to be passive is ridiculous. An essential aspect of all the new math programs was that students discover ways in which the concepts related to each other. Discovery learning was not a passive activity. The misunderstandings arose from conflicting notions of the role of the subject matter, the doctrine of interest, and the role of the teacher.

First, the PSSC, SMSG, and Bruner wanted schools to prepare students for academic study in college. As a result, the primary aspect of elementary and secondary schools was to prepare students to think in the same patterns that scholars used. However, Tyler saw subject matter as something that helped students understand themselves and their society. For him, academics were tools for better living. Second, the PSSC, SMSG, and Bruner believed the subject matter to be fascinating in its own right. However, Tyler thought this attitude was an old-fashioned view inherited from the Committee of Ten, arguing that children wanted to learn things that were practical and at which they could succeed. Finally, the PSSC, SMSG, and Bruner were concerned that teachers could not determine what was fundamental about a subject area. Teachers were often inadequately trained or lacked the interest to pursue the subject matter itself. Consequently, they needed the assistance provided by textbook series, films, seminars, and teaching manuals in order to enable the students to relate the concepts in important and exciting ways. However, for Tyler these texts and guides restricted teachers' abilities to involve the community in curriculum planning. Unless there was a widespread effort to include the members of the community, psychologists, and subject matter specialists, the curriculum would be artificial and removed from the students' interests.

It is important to note that both educational views could serve the ideas of integration. That is, as noted previously, academic specialists such as the SMSG tried to find ways to use the new curricula with different sorts of people in the hope that everyone would appreciate the structures of the disciplines. Further, Tyler, continuing his work with the Eight-Year Study, sought ways for students to pursue their own interests in ways that served the common good.

Why Did Educators Turn to James Conant to Resolve Contradictions among Different Educational Aims?

For most educators, the comprehensive high school offered a means of bridging the apparent contradiction between educational aims that concentrated on acquisition of subject matter and aims that sought to meet the students' needs. In this effort, they were aided by James Conant, whose ideas became prominent for four reasons. First, federal officials trusted his judgment. For example, on November 7, 1957, when Eisenhower stated that he wanted programs to improve the instruction of math and science, he incorporated in that speech several parts of a lengthy telegram Conant had sent him. In this speech, Eisenhower claimed that high schools were generally good; however, foreign-language instruction was weak. Many able students were interested in science and mathematics, but these students had to be selected by nationwide testing programs and encouraged to pursue scientific studies. To achieve these ends, schools needed better laboratory facilities and more qualified teachers, Eisenhower concluded. These were ideas that Conant had championed long and hard (Clowse 54–57).

Second, Conant was prominent and popular among educators. Trained as a chemist, Conant became president of Harvard University and helped organize scientific programs such as the research that led to the atomic bomb. He was an advisor to the National Science Foundation and the Atomic Energy Commission. After the war, he served as high commissioner and ambassador for West Germany. Furthermore, he was involved in elementary and secondary school reform. In 1944 he had been a member of the EPC when it made its report advocating that schools meet the common needs of youth. In 1951 he became the commission's chairperson when it made its revised report. In 1956 he contacted the president of the Carnegie Corporation of New York. With the corporation's sponsorship, Conant and a staff of educators began a study of high schools in the United States. The investigators visited 103 schools in twenty-six states. Conant claimed to have visited at least fifty-five of the schools in order to compensate for his lack of direct experience in high school activities (Passow 1–13).

The third reason Conant could influence school people was that he was ready to take advantage of the opportunity. The Sputnik crisis caused school board members to ask how they should organize their schools and what subjects they should offer. For Conant, the timing was perfect. He had finished his study titled *The American High School Today* in 1956 and was ready to give them the answers (Passow 13).

Finally, as noted earlier, the NDEA offered federal funds for counseling, guidance, testing, foreign-language study, and vocational education. Therefore, school districts had a financial incentive to adopt Conant's views.

Many of Conant's suggestions were identical to or extensions of the recommendations found on the reports of the EPC in 1944 and 1952. For example, he believed that the number of high schools had to be reduced. Instead of many small schools, educators needed to create larger comprehensive high schools with diversified curricula for different students. In addition, he noted that in all the schools he visited, the academic students were not sufficiently challenged. Able boys avoided foreign languages and specialized in math and science. On the other hand, able girls avoided math, science, and foreign languages. Therefore, he advocated what came to be known as ability grouping (Conant, *American* 40).

The body of Conant's report consisted of twenty-one recommendations. For example, he urged that elementary and secondary schools employ one full-time counselor for every three hundred students. These people should have had experiences in teaching. However, unlike the EPC, Conant thought teachers could not act as counselors. Instead, these counselors were to use aptitude and achievement tests to direct students, especially bright ones, into an appropriate track of elective courses (*American* 44–45).

Likewise, Conant recommended the formation of individualized programs but without designations such as college preparatory, vocational, or commercial. The general education programs Conant wanted all students to take included four years of English courses, two years of history including U.S. history, a year of mathematics, and a year of science. In all courses, including the subjects required of all students, the schools should group the students by at least three different levels of ability. This would mean that the most able, the average, and slow students would be segregated from each other. In such a system, Conant thought, the bright and the slow students could receive instruction suited to their capabilities (*American* 45–49).

To enhance the education of the academically talented students, Conant urged a program of four years of mathematics, a foreign language, and English, with three years of science and social studies. Such a program should require fifteen hours of homework each week. Highly gifted pupils should be identified and allowed to take advanced courses that would prepare them for achievement tests. With suitable scores, the students could receive college credit for those courses. In addition to this academic preparation, high schools should offer diversified programs to develop marketable skills such as typing, home economics, retail trade, vocational agriculture, or industrial trades (*American* 51–63).

Thus, Conant preserved the notion of the high school as an institution that brought all people together while at the same time allowing each student to pursue specific courses tailored to his or her abilities and appropriate to society's needs. This would not be an institution that forced bright students to waste time, nor would the courses be so advanced that most students failed them. To bring these different students together, Conant suggested two activities. First, homerooms would hold a cross section of students of high, moderate, and low ability. The homerooms would elect representatives to student councils, and the homeroom periods would be a time for students to discuss issues of school policy and governance. Second, the twelfth-grade social studies courses would include a cross section of students in which students would discuss problems of democracy in the United States. As a result, students would develop an understanding of the free society and foster mutual respect among different types of people (*American* 74–76).

Conant's first report was an instant success. For several weeks, it was high on the best-seller list. Professional organizations of educators endorsed the report, and Conant traveled widely explaining to school and parent groups how to organize schools. He was featured in a film that portrayed a school in Oakland, California, and another in Labette County, Kansas, to demonstrate how his recommendations could be applied in different settings (Passow 21–24).

Conant may not have caused a change as much as he heralded something that was already happening. At any rate, the consolidation of small school districts took place rapidly. At the end of World War II, in 1945, there were about 100,000 school districts in the United States. In 1980 there were only about 16,000. Yet, over the same period, the total enrollment in elementary and secondary schools grew from 23 million to about 40 million. More and more students went to larger schools (Ravitch, *Troubled Crusades* 327).

Did the High Schools Offer Equal Opportunity?

The basis of Conant's proposal was that children of ability would be able to move ahead in academics while other children could move into the areas that suited them. This represented a major change in high schools. For many years, critics complained that the high school served a few students and ignored the rest. Years later Conant found that students did not have equal opportunities. Therefore, he worried that students could not advance according to their abilities.

In 1967 Conant issued his second report, entitled *The Comprehensive High School.* He wrote that the high school was called comprehensive because the entire secondary program for a town or neighborhood could be offered under one roof. One school might contain a girl who would marry at eighteen, a boy who was destined to become an atomic scientist, and the future captain of industry. It was distinctly American, Conant added, because Americans chose to adopt an elective system of education. In place of elite institutions for academically successful students, towns created one institution to provide a general education for all future citizens, excellent instruction in academic fields for some students, and first-class vocational training for other students. Of course, there were exceptions. Some urban districts had separate vocational institutions; few cities had separate academic high schools (*Comprehensive* 3–4).

To gather information for this second report, Conant's team sent questionnaires to 18,500 schools across the United States. They received replies from more than 15,000 of them. Within this sample, Conant found that the percentage of graduates who continued full-time education fell into what might be called a normal distribution. That is, a few schools had almost no students going on and a few schools had nearly all their graduates continuing their education. About three-quarters of the schools had somewhere between one-fourth and three-fourths of the students continuing. The size of the schools varied. In some states, as many as 80 percent of the schools held less than 500 students. In another state, only 5 percent of the schools enrolled less than 500 students. Only about 6 percent of the schools had a student body that exceeded 2,000 students. Conant devoted his attention to medium-sized high schools, which had student bodies of about 800 to 2,000 and offered comprehensive programs. Using this range, Conant avoided what he called the extremes of large urban schools or small rural ones, which had their own special problems. Nonetheless, even in this sample of middle-range schools he found a surprising inequality of opportunity (*Comprehensive* 1–12).

To Conant's surprise, the size of the school seemed to influence only two things. Larger schools were more likely to have wide programs in foreign languages and opportunities for advanced placement. The most crucial variable was the size of the faculty. Teacher salaries constituted about 80 percent of the annual school budget, Conant estimated. Therefore, a school's greatest expense was a large faculty. As a result, some schools had enough teachers for a student-teacher ratio of about 11 students to one teacher, whereas other schools had a ratio of about 38 to one. However, when a school had less than 17.4 to one, it was likely to offer instruction in calculus; provide four years of instruction in foreign languages; allow students to study English, math, science, a foreign language, social studies, physical education, art or music in the same year; provide advanced placement courses; and keep the average pupil load for teachers below 120. Schools with a student-teacher ratio of 26.5 to one were unlikely to offer these things (*Comprehensive* 13–19).

The schools failed to realize several goals Conant had recommended in his first study. First, in 1959 Conant had thought there should be one full-time guidance counselor for every 250 to 300 students. In 1967 he found that only about 14 percent of the schools had a counselor for 300 students or less. Second, in 1959 he had recommended that the schools use ability grouping. In 1967 he found that almost 97 percent of the schools surveyed separated the students by aptitude. However, whereas Conant wanted ability grouping to be implemented subject by subject so a student might take an advanced English class and a lower-level mathematics course, many schools divided students by tracks so that they studied all subjects in the same type of classes. Most schools followed his earlier recommendations about requiring three or four years of social studies and a course in the problems of democracy for seniors. They adopted his idea of elective programs for the highly gifted, and about 40 percent of the high schools offered these students the opportunity to earn advanced placement credit from a college for courses in history, mathematics, or English. However, the idea of a student studying a foreign language in order to be competent in it seemed extreme to most educators. In almost all schools, students could not take four years of one foreign language; schools usually offered two years of Latin and two years of French or Spanish (Conant, *Comprehensive* 23–51).

Thus, although Conant criticized the fact that students in some schools had more opportunities than students in other schools, he did not attribute the differences among the schools to things such as social class or race. For example, Conant tried to determine if there was a relationship between the number of students planning to attend college and the type of program the school offered. There was not. Schools that did not send many students to college had adequate foreign-language and mathematics programs in the same proportion as schools that sent most of the students to college. Therefore, Conant attributed the problems to the unwillingness of some elected officials to spend the money to hire enough teachers, or to complicated patterns of school finance that sent more money to some districts than to others. These were things that concerned citizens could change (*Comprehensive* 19–22, 70, 80).

Consequently, Conant retained his optimism. In his second report, he criticized educators for failing to realize the ideal of the comprehensive schools. Between these two reports, Conant wrote *Slums and Suburbs,* described in Chapter 11. As a result, he was aware of racial segregation and the inequities that affected many schools. He was convinced that had the ideal of the comprehensive high school dominated education one hundred years earlier, there would be no segregated schools (*Slums* 7–8).

Did the Differentiated Curriculum Increase Opportunities for Different Students?

Conant took the idea of a comprehensive high school that offered different courses for the different types of students from his work with the EPC in 1944 and 1951. Although this report represented the views of many educators in elementary and high schools, intellectuals criticized the idea as undemocratic. For example, in 1958 John Latimer, a dean at George Washington University, argued that high school students were not prepared for training to become scientists or engineers. Looking at surveys collected by the U.S. Bureau of Education, he found that from 1890 to 1910 most high school students enrolled in what he called cumulative subjects. These were courses such as foreign languages, mathematics, and science whose advanced levels built on earlier instruction. By 1949 the number of subjects increased dramatically. More important to Latimer, half of the students took courses such as business, home economics, physical education, or art that cultivated a skill or provided an opportunity for self-discovery. Because these classes were not as difficult as the cumulative subjects, they may have saved many students from failing high school. However, Latimer feared they may have prevented many other students from trying to succeed (59–77).

Latimer's solution was for high schools to teach mathematics, science, foreign languages, history, and English to every student. He thought it was a disservice to offer non-academic, practical, or vocational courses to students with lower than average learning abilities. When differences had to be accommodated, the instruction among ability groups should differ in quantity not in kind. Thus, students would learn at their own paces and within their own abilities those subjects that Latimer thought made life in the modern world possible (134–135).

In a similar vein, in 1964 three philosophers of education, Harry S. Broudy, B. Othanel Smith, and Joe Burnett, complained that the idea of having different courses open to different students fragmented the curriculum and weakened the ideal of an education for democracy. The problem was that vocational courses were often offered to children from low-income families in cities, while suburban schools offered children from more prosperous families college preparatory courses. These inequities were perpetuated by educators who thought that vocational courses prevented students from dropping out of school by promising a job on graduation. Broudy, Smith, and Burnett did not believe such courses prevented social problems. They argued that those graduates would not have the knowledge and skills for job mobility and would become unemployed as the economy changed (10–16).

According to Broudy, Smith, and Burnett, all students should learn material helpful in dealing with life. This common curriculum would cover five general areas: (1) the symbolics of information, which included English, foreign language, and mathematics; (2) the basic sciences including general science, biology, physics, and chemistry; (3) developmental studies, covering the evolution of the cosmos, social institutions, and culture; (4) exemplars, which included art, music, drama, and literature; and (5) molar problems, covering the typical social problems of the day (246–247).

Acknowledging that not all students learned equally well, Broudy, Smith, and Burnett, thought the subjects could be differentiated by levels. Therefore, they called for an ungraded secondary school in which students would proceed at their own pace. Within that structure, the content would be offered in different levels of instruction. In each level, students learned the concepts and any logical operations essential to the subject. However, in the higher levels of instruction students approached the complexity and sophistication that experts used. The lower levels would use simpler language and offer less complex information. Most important, students proceeded individually and mixed levels among the subjects, going faster in some and slower in others (Broudy, Smith, and Burnett 252–258).

Despite the arguments of Latimer or of Broudy, Smith, and Burnett, most high schools continued the tradition of offering different course materials for different students. The curriculum reforms that followed the NDEA changed courses for the top students. In 1949 only 18 schools in six states offered courses in advanced chemistry and physics. By 1961 that number grew to 937 schools in forty-nine states. This rate of change was greater than the increase in enrollment. Between the same years, enrollments grew by about 50 percent while the increase of advanced science courses was nearly 2000 percent. Although new courses were added for the brightest students, the lower-level students continued to receive practical courses such as mathematics for modern living (Powell, Farrar, and Cohen 286–287).

In fact, despite the emphasis popular critics placed on mathematics and science, only a few students took these courses. In 1948 about 55 percent of the students in grades 9 to 12 studied some mathematics. By 1963 this percentage rose to about two-thirds of the students. However, enrollments in other courses such as health and physical education increased from about 69 percent in 1948 to more than 102 percent. More revealing, the courses in mathematics that most students took were practical or general mathematics courses, not the academic college preparatory courses. Instead, students enrolled in household biology, science for modern living, or everyday physics (Angus and Mirel 116–119).

Unfortunately, the comprehensive high school with tracking appeared to sort the students by social class or ethnic background. At the least, non-White students seemed to fall more commonly into lower-ability group classes and into low-status vocational programs. Important evidence in this regard was accumulated by John Goodlad, then dean of the Graduate School of Education at the University of California at Los Angeles. In the 1970s, he began collecting detailed information about thirty-eight schools, which included elementary and secondary schools in thirteen different communities. Jeannie Oakes, one of his research assistants, undertook an extensive study of the practice of grouping students according to their abilities and its effects in twenty-five of these schools.

Entitling her book *Keeping Track: How Schools Structure Inequality,* Oakes found that students from minority groups or low-income families appeared in disproportionately large percentages in the bottom-ability groups. Specifically, she noted that among the twenty-five schools she studied, White students enrolled in the higher-track English and math courses in percentages that greatly exceeded their proportion in the schools. In a corresponding manner, smaller percentages of White students were enrolled in the lower-track courses than appeared in the student bodies as a whole (65–67).

Among vocational courses, the relationship between ethnicity and tracking was more complex. The enrollment of White and non-White students in all vocational courses seemed to indicate that these groups were fairly represented in each school. Looking more closely, however, Oakes found that non-White students were more likely to receive specific training for low-level occupations, whereas higher-status vocational training was more likely to be offered to White students. Furthermore, non-White students more often took courses held off the school grounds and thus were more likely to be separated from the other students. Worse, students began these courses when they were as young as twelve years old (Oakes 157–167).

Oakes argued that these biases appeared because almost all schools used three criteria to decide how to sort students into ability groups: scores on standardized tests, teacher and counselor recommendations, and students' and parents' choices. Each of these worked against poor and minority students. First, these students consistently scored lower on standardized tests than White students. Second, teachers and counselors often made assessments of students on the basis of language, behavior, and dress. Finally, test scores and counselor recommendations together influenced students and parents in making their own decisions. Thus, two subjective opinions forced a third (Oakes 5–14).

Tracking might appear to be reasonable if it were a way for overworked educators to provide the best education possible to the students who would most profit from it. But this did not happen. The students who went on to colleges and universities in the 1970s were less academically prepared than those who went on in the 1930s. For example, in the 1930s the students who went on to college had taken four years of science and four years of mathematics, but only about 12 percent of the students who made it to fifth grade entered college. By contrast, in the 1970s about 75 percent of the students who made it to fifth grade graduated from high school and half of those went on to college. However, these students needed only one science course beyond general science, and only a fraction had taken a course beyond first-year algebra. Thus, the rigor of academic preparation diminished in order to allow more people to enter college (Powell, Farrar, and Cohen 289–291).

Why Did High Schools Sort Students into Ability Groups?

There are two explanations why ability groups became popular. The first was expressed by Oakes, who feared there was something wrong with capitalism that caused schools to track students and discriminate against minorities. Although she could not make a direct connection between the social system and school practices, the evidence she found did reinforce the accusations radical critics made of schools. For example, when Oakes looked at the classroom climates, she found that teachers of higher-track students felt that students wanted to learn, whereas teachers of the lower-track students believed they had to control the students at all times. Not surprisingly, the students in the high-track classes saw the teachers as more concerned about them than did the students in the lower tracks. High-track students were more likely to go on trips, write reports, and do research or other activities designed to involve them in learning than were lower-track students. Low-track students were more likely to feel excluded from classroom activities. As a result, Oakes concluded, the students least likely to do well went to the lowest tracks, where they endured negative relationships and had less chance to become involved in their own learning. In these ways, she argued, schools prepared these students to stay at the bottom of institutions and society (Oakes 113–135).

Oakes asserted that her findings confirmed the correspondence hypothesis of Samuel Bowles and Herbert Gintis. These theorists argued that the social relationships in schools produce a class of students who will become workers and other classes who will become managers. The lower groups learn to obey external authority and conform to the needs of the workplace while the higher groups learn to internalize rules and work cooperatively with other people. Oakes added that other theorists such as Paul Willis had shown that working-class children often rebel against schools and reject any school learning. The result is that their rebellion places them in lower tracks and in factory jobs as adults. Acknowledging that the differences between the views of Bowles and Gintis and those of Willis demonstrate the schools' roles in the reproduction of social inequalities to be complicated, Oakes concluded that research seemed to confirm that schools had such an effect (118–122).

Oakes was so convinced that her research showed the dangerous effects of tracking that she predicted there would be several legal suits claiming that ability grouping was racially discriminatory. To some extent, Oakes was correct as alternatives to tracking appeared through reforms such as inclusion of children with learning disabilities and cooperative learning (Weaver 366–367).

However, there was a second explanation for the popularity of the comprehensive high school with ability grouping or tracking. Instead of contending that high schools served a totalitarian and powerful elite, this explanation held that comprehensive high schools were popular because they offered things students wanted. They offered college preparation to those who could profit from it and life adjustment training to those who needed it.

In 1985 Arthur G. Powell, Eleanor Farrar, and David K. Cohen contended that the nature of high schools was determined by the aim to offer something to all students. People in the United States expected the entire adolescent population to attend and to graduate from high schools. Educators tried to accomplish this task by making numerous accommodations so that everyone was satisfied. As a result, the high school became similar to a shopping mall where everybody could find something, but there was no one thing everyone had to have. Consequently, the variety of curricula exceeded the variety demanded by the range of differences among students. Not only did schools offer different courses, but teachers also offered differences within subjects. For example, to meet graduation requirements in English, a school could offer courses such as applied communication, junior English, and advanced junior English, each covering different material and making different demands on the students. Schools also provided an extra curriculum of sports and other nonacademic activities. Finally, a services curriculum addressing social or emotional problems such as a divorce resource group or an adolescent parenting program often carried academic credit (Powell, Farrar, and Cohen 1–2, 21–34).

Other historians agree with Powell, Farrar, and Cohen. In 1999 David L. Angus and Jeffrey E. Mirel argued that beginning in the early twentieth century, high schools in the United States took on a custodial mission. From 1964 to 1975, educators tried to respond to protests from women and minorities about unfair treatment, offering different courses designed to appeal to the distinct groups. With curricular differentiation, educators could satisfy those complaints, open buildings and classrooms to new groups, yet retain the essential nature of the institution. Angus and Mirel claim that schools remained stable because educators retained the view that they must meet the needs of youth. During the 1960s and 1970s, high schools around the country offered many new courses that promised to help students develop their personalities for the well-being of society. Unfortunately, the diversified curriculum segregated students by ethnic group and social class (Angus and Mirel 122–161).

TIMELINE

1954–1964

1954 In the *Brown* case federal courts outlawed racial segregation of schools

1955 The National Science Foundation budget increased to $12 million

1956 One hundred one members of U.S. Congress from former Confederacy sign a Manifesto to resist racial integration

1956 The Committee for the White House Conference on Education declared that the government should involve itself only minimally in education

1956 James Conant began his study of high schools, explained in his book, *The American High School Today*

1956 The NSF promoted change in elementary and secondary science courses

1956 Professor Jerrold R. Zacharias established the PSSC to improve physics courses

1956 Forty-eight physicists and educators debated the structure of a new physics course designed by the PSSC

1957 Nine African American students enter previously all-White Central High School in Little Rock, Arkansas

1957 Eisenhower emphasized that science and math courses needed to improve

1957 The Soviet Union launched the satellite Sputnik

1957 Eisenhower announced that the U.S. education system needed improvement

1958 Several southern states abolish teacher tenure, prohibit teachers from joining NAACP, replace Black principals with White counterparts, and demote Black teachers

1958 Research mathematicians participated in the Cambridge Conference

1958 The SMSG carried out the plans of the Cambridge Conference

1958 The SMSG held its first writing session to devise a curriculum for teaching math in grades 7 through 12

TIMELINE Continued

1958	The PSSC offered five summer seminars using its new textbook
1958	The U.S. Congress approved the NDEA
1958	The congressional Committee for Labor and Public Welfare held many hearings on education improvement
1958	The Organization for European Economic Cooperation asked the MAA to survey methods of math instruction in various countries
1959	The MAA held a conference in Asnières-sur-Oise, France
1959	The SMSG published textbooks
1960	As chairperson of a conference, Jerome Bruner published *The Process of Education*
1961	Various divisions of the NDEA allocated money for educational purposes
1962	The SMSG made its texts available to Spanish-speaking Americans
1963	The U.S. Office of Education commended the NDEA's work on schools
1963	The MAA held a conference in Athens, Greece

CHAPTER

10 The Civil Rights Movement, Christian Day Schools, and Multiculturalism: 1964–1980

A lone police officer faces a crowd of civil rights protestors.

OVERVIEW

As described in Chapter 9, the U.S. Supreme Court made the racial desegregation of schools a curriculum issue by suggesting that such practices would improve the academic progress of African American students. However, from 1954 until 1964, few schools desegregated. This changed during the civil rights movement. From 1964 to

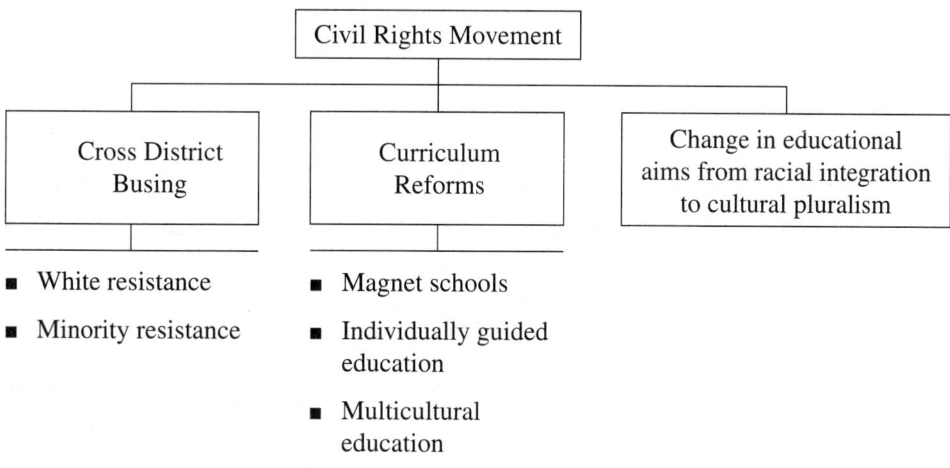

1969, the U.S. Department of Health, Education, and Welfare (HEW) required many local school districts to racially integrate in order to be eligible for federal funds. With the election of President Richard Nixon, this pressure weakened. Interestingly, although the U.S. Civil Rights Act allocated resources to support curriculum improvements, HEW officials did not spend this money to develop courses that would reinforce the goals of racial integration. As the drive for racial integration increased, many groups resisted mechanisms such as busing to bring different students together. In part, these problems derived from a conflict of worthy aims that lay behind the 1963 March on Washington. These aims were the pursuit of racial integration and personal rights. For example, while civil rights advocates claimed that African American children had a right to attend integrated schools, conservative political leaders argued that people had the right to attend neighborhood schools. Other African American groups joined the conservatives, contending that segregated schools supported by Black parents improved the education of Black children. Similar conflicts appeared among religious groups.

Although curriculum planners did not take advantage of the resources available through the Civil Rights Act, they did try to implement some curriculum changes to enhance racial desegregation. For example, school boards offered special programs such as individually guided education and magnet schools to advance racial desegregation. But while these programs could support racial integration, they could contradict that aim as well.

Many educators suggested that ethnic studies or what became known as multiculturalism was a necessary first step for racial harmony. However, in 1974 conservative parents in Kanawha County, West Virginia, argued that ethnic studies encouraged a type of moral relativism that destroyed the basis of human community. Educators did not seek to resolve these controversies. Instead, they sought procedures that would allow everyone to retain his or her views and still attend the same building. Thus, educators abandoned the progressivist ideal of creating a democratic society and instead embraced a model of pluralism that allowed each group to maintain its values.

How Did the Pursuit of Civil Rights Change in the 1960s?

With the Montgomery, Alabama, bus strike, the pursuit of racial equality changed in three important ways: (1) public demonstrations became an important part of the continued legal campaign for equal rights; (2) for a while the focus moved away from the racial integration of schools; and (3) several organizations began to compete with the NAACP, seeking to remove barriers preventing African Americans from using public facilities such as city buses, airports, and voting places.

On December 5, 1955, after turning down an offer to assume the presidency of the city of Montgomery, Alabama's, chapter of the NAACP, Martin Luther King, Jr. accepted his election as president of the newly organized Montgomery Improvement Association. From this event, a national hero emerged. After successfully desegregating the city buses, King was elected president of the newly formed Southern Christian Leadership Conference (SCLC). The SCLC sought to spread their activities over the South (King, *Stride* 42, 154).

The SCLC represented an alternative to the domination of the NAACP because the SCLC was a loose federation of affiliate organizations whose local leaders engaged in local protests about particular incidents. Although the NAACP usually offered legal and financial support to such demonstrators, its leaders preferred to follow well-coordinated, long-range programs planned by experts. Furthermore, the formation of the SCLC encouraged the growth of a wide variety of groups, some of which did not seek racial integration. For example, many African Americans joined Elijah Muhammad and the nation of Islam, called the Black Muslims, when the popular press criticized their desire to separate completely from White America. This negative publicity attracted people who liked such a program (Lomax 104–106, 178–192).

African Americans turned to organizations such as the SCLC because the pace of racial integration was slow. Although the Supreme Court had called for desegregation in 1954, only 9 percent of the Black students in the South attended racially integrated schools by 1963, and most of these schools had only token integration. To speed up the process, the SCLC chose to demonstrate in Birmingham, Alabama, during April 1963 because the city was the symbol of racial intolerance. The Easter weekend included an important shopping day. Further, a new city administration had taken office, so a demonstration could set the stage for negotiations to desegregate lunch counters, fitting rooms, and drinking fountains; to place African Americans in important positions in business and industrial concerns; and to establish a biracial committee to develop a timetable for desegregation in the city (King, *Why Can't* 18, 54).

At the height of the protest, on May 2, 1963, wave upon wave of demonstrators marched on Birmingham's Sixteenth Street Baptist Church. By this time, more than 2,500 people had gone to jail. Frustrated, the police dropped the posture of nonviolence they had taken until then. On May 4, 1963, newspapers carried pictures and stories of Birmingham police officers clubbing prostrate women, of police dogs attacking young children, and of pressure fire hoses sweeping people down streets. These events and their publicity strengthened protestors' resolve, weakened the confidence of the White business leaders, and caused buyers to avoid stores where trouble took place. On Friday, May 10, 1963, U.S.

President John F. Kennedy devoted the opening minutes of his press conference to a discussion of the Birmingham demonstration. Later that day, the city's business leaders signed an accord agreeing to the demonstrators' demands. On the crest of this victory, demonstrations began in other cities such as Savannah, Atlanta, and Nashville. Because there was no executive committee or master plan to guide the movement, A. Philip Randolph proposed a March on Washington to unite protestors (King, *Why Can't* 99, 109, 122).

On August 28, 1963, nearly 250,000 people journeyed in every conceivable form of transportation to hear Martin Luther King, Jr. tell of his dream. In his momentous speech, King offered his hope as a refrain:

> When we let freedom ring,...we will be able to speed up the day when all God's children, Black men and White men, Jews and Gentiles, Protestants and Catholics, will be able to join hands and sing the words of that old Negro spiritual, "Free at last! Free at last! Thank God almighty, we are free at last!"

This speech expressed the aspirations of the civil rights movement as it called on all citizens to engage in social action to ensure that all people enjoyed the same human rights (Bellah 213, 249).

With the March on Washington, the means by which schools were integrated changed. Before 1963 the pace of racial desegregation in the South was slow because for each school district there had to be a federal or state trial, and the judge had to order the district to desegregate. But the pictures of peaceful marchers threatened by dogs in Birmingham, Alabama, turned public sentiment against segregation. Consequently, Congress passed and, on July 2, 1964, President Lyndon Johnson signed the U.S. Civil Rights Act giving federal bureaucrats the power to alter entire school districts without court trials. Title VI of the Civil Rights Act said that no person could suffer discrimination in any program funded by the federal government. Thus, the Office of Education within the HEW could make the decision to suspend federal funding by itself (Orfield, *Reconstruction* 13).

This change was important. From 1954 to 1964, the pace of desegregation was slow because the NAACP or some other advocacy group had to bring each individual school district to trial, which took time and money. Appeals dragged the process out even further. However, when HEW obtained the power to impose financial sanctions on segregated districts, things moved more quickly. From 1964 until 1969, HEW staff caused six hundred administrative proceedings against segregated school districts. The effect was startling. In 1964 only 2.3 percent of southern African Americans attended desegregated schools. In 1965 that number grew to 7.5 percent, and in 1966 it became 12.5 percent (Salomone 58, 64–65).

What Curricular Changes Enhanced Racial Integration?

When Congress approved the 1964 Civil Rights Act, legislators included Title IV to offer technical and financial assistance to school districts undergoing racial desegregation. Unfortunately, in 1973 the U.S. Commission on Civil Rights found that "with few exceptions, funds expended under this title have been wasted, their objectives blurred, and their purposes thwarted" (*Title IV* 1–6, 41). The commission found three reasons for this failure: First, Congress allocated relatively little money for these purposes. Second, the programs had a low priority with federal officials, in part because they disagreed how they should be spent. Some officials felt that Title IV programs should concentrate on problems of school desegregation such as improving human relations among the pupils and the staff, whereas other officials wanted to spend the money strengthening academic programs. Further, the commission found that state and local educational officials ignored the Title IV offices in their areas.

With the March on Washington and the resulting legislation, federal officials had the opportunity to direct a social transformation. However, those officials were not convinced that curriculum change was an important part of that evolution, although they had the means at their disposal to encourage extensive curriculum revisions. As a result, the racial desegregation of schools represents a missed opportunity because there was a model of how to construct such a curriculum that would help students understand a social change that was currently in progress.

The model appears in Dewey's 1900 essay "School and Social Progress." Dewey argued that the innovations of his laboratory school were part of the larger social evolution then taking place. In a short period, Dewey had seen the frontier close, factories expand, and cities grow. The social repercussions were enormous. Families broke up as people moved from farms to make new lives in the cities. People needed new skills and habits to live and work, yet many people could depend only on their own resources to survive in these new conditions. As discussed in Chapter 5, Dewey's curriculum focused on what he called occupations that re-created for the child the opportunities for cooperative activity once common in rural communities. Most important, through those occupations children learned how the industrial revolution had transformed society. Thus, through building houses or planting gardens students came to learn about geography and biology but also about history.

The point is that HEW officials could have encouraged educators to plan curricula in the spirit of Dewey that would have shown students the benefits of racially and ethnically integrated societies. They did not. The problem was not that federal officials ignored curriculum, but that during the 1960s, the priority in curriculum development was designing programs to compensate for the deficits minority children suffered. Thus, curricular theorists sought ways to help minority children increase their academic skills and become the equals of other children. They did not think about social transformation as a whole.

Ironically, as will be discussed more fully in Chapter 11, the programs of compensatory education could increase segregation. The federal involvement became dramatic in 1964 when Congress opened the War on Poverty and, in 1965 with the Elementary and Secondary Education Act, Public Law 89–10, allocated almost $2.5 billion to schools, much of which went to children suffering from poverty. Further, in 1977 in *Milliken v. Bradley II,* the Supreme Court ordered the state of Michigan to pay for the harm caused by segregation in Detroit. This case followed *Milliken v. Bradley I,* which is discussed later in this chapter. In the first case, the Court decided not to require the integration of urban and suburban schools. However, in the second decision, the Court decided that state governments should pay cities to develop programs of remedial education for those urban schools whose students remained overwhelmingly minority and lacked reasonable levels of academic skills.

Consequently, the remedial or compensatory education for minority children in Detroit was a substitute for the meaningful racial integration that the court denied.

Was the Effort to Racially Desegregate Schools Successful?

Court-ordered desegregation did not permanently change the patterns of student attendance. By 1991 the extent of racial segregation in public elementary and secondary schools was the same as it had been before 1971 when the Supreme Court approved transporting children away from neighborhood schools to different school buildings in order to bring about racial integration (Orfield and Eaton 54–55). Three things happened to blunt the drive for desegregation.

First, HEW's ability to racially desegregate schools lasted only a short time because HEW officials encountered political problems as they sought to enforce their guidelines. In 1965 the U.S. House Education and Labor Committee heard testimony that the Chicago, Illinois, school board had drawn attendance boundaries in ways that maintained racial segregation. In September 1965, HEW sent a team to investigate racial segregation in Chicago. Before the study was completed, HEW officials notified the Illinois state superintendent to defer further grants to Chicago. A public controversy exploded, and political leaders such as Chicago's Mayor Richard Daley complained to President Lyndon B. Johnson, who requested an immediate settlement. Unfortunately, because they acted before receiving a report, HEW officials lacked the information they needed to justify their actions. Interpreting Johnson's message as a directive, HEW officials released federal funds. The problems did not end in Chicago but extended throughout the department, marking the end of HEW's control over racial desegregation. When Richard Nixon took office as president in 1969, federal officials announced that they would rely on litigation rather than withholding funds. As a result, the next five years showed a decline in the number of reviews being held until 1974, when no school district was reviewed (Salomone 64–69).

While HEW officials faced difficulties, lawyers for the NAACP's Legal Defense and Educational Fund enjoyed success in forcing racial integration. They were able to make sure that schools used effective means to desegregate, and they pushed racial integration into the North.

Throughout the South, school districts offered African American children the opportunity to attend White schools. Although these freedom of choice plans existed on paper, school districts often prevented Black children from leaving Black schools. As a result, in *Green v. County School Board of New Kent County,* which the Supreme Court decided in 1968, the justices affirmed that whatever plan the district used, it had to make a difference in the enrollment patterns. In 1971, while deciding the appropriate means to racially desegregate schools in the consolidated school districts of Charlotte and Mecklenberg in North Carolina, the Supreme Court approved transporting students away from neighborhood schools (*Swann v. Charlotte*).

In addition to verifying that school districts desegregated, NAACP lawyers pushed racial equality into the North. This was difficult because lawyers had to prove that public officials had denied Black children the right to attend certain schools. Because the constitutions of many southern states required separate schools for Black and White pupils, lawyers could show that school boards prevented Black children from entering some schools. However, many northern states forbade such segregation, and school officials in those states argued that the people segregated themselves by choosing to live in certain neighborhoods. Nonetheless, in 1972, in a case called *Keyes v. School District No. 1, Denver, Colorado,* NAACP lawyers proved that officials manipulated attendance zones, assigned teachers, and selected school building sites in ways that created the racial segregation of schools. As a result, the Denver schools had to desegregate (Salomone 49–50).

As the NAACP enjoyed success, however, public resentment increased, generating the second obstacle to the drive for desegregation. In 1971, when the justices approved busing for racial balance, they had cautioned against subjecting children to hardships such as long bus rides. Nonetheless, a public protest developed against busing. In Congress legislators attempted to draft legislation prohibiting the use of federal funds for busing. Even President Nixon profited from and contributed to the unpopularity of school desegregation. In February and March 1972, Nixon asked the courts to call a moratorium on efforts to achieve racial balance. In exchange, he offered $2.5 billion to aid disadvantaged children within urban schools. During his second presidential campaign, the Republican party called for a constitutional amendment to end school busing for racial balance. When Nixon's opponent, George McGovern, said that citizens must pay for a century of segregation with school desegregation, Nixon won by a landslide (Metcalf 144–145, 428).

The third thing to blunt the drive for desegregation was that NAACP lawyers suffered such a major defeat in 1974 that it dissipated the public pressure to draft a constitutional decision against busing for racial balance. In the case of *Milliken v. Bradley,* the NAACP wanted the Supreme Court to force fifty-two suburban school districts to integrate with the city schools of Detroit in a large metropolitan plan. The lower courts had agreed with the NAACP lawyers because, by 1973, the student bodies of the city schools were 70 percent Black, whereas in the metropolitan area the schools were only 19 percent Black. Thus, the lower courts agreed that if desegregation were limited to the city, many schools would retain nearly all-Black student populations. However, the Supreme Court justices decided that the NAACP lawyers had not shown that public officials caused the segregation; therefore, there was no legal requirement to correct it (U.S. Commission, *Statement* 84–88).

Despite this setback, racial integration continued in several cities and people came to accept the policy. For example, Boston, Massachusetts, schools implemented a desegregation plan in September 1974 that required busing of 17,000 of the 80,000 students in the system. A controversial aspect of the plan was the attempt to exchange students between Roxbury High School, in the heart of a Black area, and South Boston High School, the pride of a White Irish enclave. When the Black children arrived from Roxbury, mobs in South Boston threw stones at the buses. However, by 1976 people in Boston surrendered to the inevitability of school busing, and the following year school busing lost its influence in city elections (Formisano 66–75).

Social scientists disagreed about whether busing caused White or middle-class people to leave cities and move to suburban areas. In 1975 James S. Coleman and his colleagues released information showing that when a city desegregated its schools, such White migration lasted for only one year. However, if the proportion of Black students rose too quickly, other White families left, and the population of the city became increasingly Black and the population of the suburbs became White. Although they thought that these effects differed in different cities, they found the trends to be consistent.

Other social scientists disagreed with Coleman. In February 1976, Thomas F. Pettigrew and Robert L. Green argued that Coleman's conclusions were true only about the trends from 1968 to 1969. They contended that research conducted later showed that cities for which the desegregation plans were more than five years old or which included the city and its surrounding suburbs, such White flight did not take place (Pettigrew and Green 1–53). But in May 1976, Coleman contended that the situation was worse than he had supposed. According to his studies, White people continued to leave the cities to avoid desegregation plans even after the plans had been in place for five years (Coleman 217–224).

In August 1976, the U.S. Commission on Civil Rights accepted Pettigrew and Greens's version of events. The commission reported that White people had been leaving the cities for the suburbs since the 1950s. They attributed this migration to four factors: relocation of employment, desire for more living space, higher incomes, and fear that property values declined as minorities moved into a neighborhood. Interestingly, when the same commission looked at the experiences in cities such as Boston in 1976, the members concluded that desegregation works. Their report claimed that school officials and local leaders could engineer a peaceful transition to school desegregation. However, they warned that a peaceful opening day was only the beginning of a successful process. A second generation of problems arose that could jeopardize the goal, including classroom segregation, inequitable disciplinary procedures, low minority participation in extracurricular activities, and absence of multicultural, bilingual education (U.S. Commission, *Fulfilling* 152–163). As if to show the wisdom of the commission's report, that same year several cities such as Dallas, Texas; Dayton, Ohio; and Flint, Michigan, implemented cross-district busing plans without civil disturbances.

Despite the promise that desegregation could work, the U.S. district courts decided in 1986 in *Riddick v. School Board* that school districts could dismantle their desegregation plans once they were declared unitary. The Supreme Court confirmed such a ruling in 1991 in *Board of Education of Oklahoma v. Dowell.* One year later, in *Freeman v. Pitts,* the Court decided that desegregation plans could be disbanded even if they had been only partially successful.

Why Was Cross-District Busing for Racial Desegregation of Schools Controversial?

Racism was one reason why people opposed busing for racial balance. However, opinion surveys found that gradually people lost much of the racial prejudice that caused the initial protests. In 1959, 72 percent of the Whites surveyed in the South expressed an objection to sending their children to school with African American children, whereas only 7 percent of the White population in nonsouthern states objected to racial integration. By 1980, only 5 percent of Whites in the South and in the North objected to racial integration for their children. However, 77 percent of the White population opposed school busing (Rossell 10–16). Thus, White people came to accept the idea of sending their children to school with members of other racial groups, but they opposed the mechanism that made it possible.

A second reason why people opposed cross-district busing may be that events during the summer of 1963 changed people's ideals. In the first half of the twentieth century, the progressive ideal of democracy encouraged the drive for racial integration. Such hopes continued after 1963, but the words of freedom and human rights became expressions of more desirable ideals. That is, when the civil rights movement showed that African Americans, linguistic minorities, and women held a second-class status, these groups sought independence for themselves. The search for group identity became important. One of the ironies of this change was that some groups segregated themselves in order to cement their identities.

In his campaigns, Martin Luther King, Jr. built coalitions among divergent groups. Ironically, however, he offered a metaphor that illustrated the shift from a democratic to a pluralistic image of society. In his "I Have a Dream" speech in Washington, King used gospel hymns to evoke the image of different people joining hands while singing about the value of freedom. This was a vivid picture, but a contradictory one. The people are singing about a value that could pull them apart rather than about an emotion such as love that could unite them.

No matter what King's metaphor meant, when he praised the right of people to be individuals his affirmation released such a range of responses that all groups used the words of freedom to support their own visions. For example, people who protested the racial integration of schools justified their resistance on the grounds of freedom and individual rights; they contended that parents had the right to send their children to neighborhood schools.

In general, the arguments about school desegregation were contests of human rights. For example, in 1971 the school board of Dayton, Ohio, followed the suggestion of the Ohio department of education and set up an advisory committee that would hold open meetings to receive suggestions about ways to reduce the racial segregation in schools. In their report, the advisory board to the Dayton board of education recommended that the city schools join with the suburban schools to provide a quality, racially integrated education for all children. It asserted that Black children had the right to attend racially integrated schools. When this report reached the board, newly elected conservative members rejected the recommendation on the grounds that people had the right to send their children to a neighborhood school. In neighborhood schools, teachers knew the families and the parents participated in school activities. The conservatives believed that such a sound education would produce adults able to live in an integrated society (Board of Education, *Minutes* 15–26).

Each of these conflicting rights had some basis in decisions of the Supreme Court. For example, the view that Black children had the right to attend racially integrated schools came from a misreading of the *Brown* decision. In making its decision in 1954, the Court relied on social science evidence showing that segregation caused Black children to suffer diminished self-concepts. Further, in 1968 in *Green v. County School Board of New Kent County*, the Court said that during desegregation reasonable numbers of Black children had to enter previously White schools. From this, people assumed that Black children had a right to attend an integrated school.

But the Court had not clearly stated this right. In *Keyes v. School District No. 1, Denver, Colorado,* most of the justices agreed that the school board could not use the excuse that it preserved neighborhood schools in order to defend actions that racially segregated children. However, in his dissent from this decision, Justice Lewis Franklin Powell, Jr. cautioned against cross-district busing because he thought the neighborhood school reflected a desire of citizens for a sense of community in their schools. Finally, in 1974 in *Milliken v. Bradley I,* the court resisted the NAACP's plea to integrate Detroit schools with surrounding suburban school districts, but the justices accepted the NAACP's request that pupils in the Detroit schools desegregate. Thus, the justices decided that segregation could be acceptable if it was the inadvertent result of people choosing to live in different suburban school districts rather than urban ones. The justices ordered the city schools in Detroit to desegregate because the city school board officials had caused segregation in trying to preserve neighborhood schools. Because there was no such evidence about suburban school officials, their students did not have to participate.

Did Minority Groups Resist the Racial Integration of Schools?

Some Black activists felt that the drive for racial integration diminished the chances of minority groups developing political influence. In 1967 Stokely Carmichael and Charles Hamilton called for Black power, asserting that, in order to be successful, African Americans had to control their own organizations. In their book, Carmichael and Hamilton disavowed the civil rights movement, nonviolence, and integration. Recalling their experiences with the Student Nonviolent Coordinating Committee (SNCC), they stated, that White, middle-class people who wanted to participate in Black community groups could play supportive roles (83).

In 1960 African American students from universities such as the Agricultural and Technical College at Greensboro, Tennessee's Agricultural and Industrial University, and Fisk University sat at lunch counters where they were refused service. On being arrested, these students received financial aid and guidance from the NAACP and the Congress of Racial Equality (CORE), but the students decided they should start their own organization to encourage students on all college campuses to set up their own nonviolent protests. The organization became racially integrated and engaged in voter registration drives, freedom rides, and sit-ins (Lomax 139–141). However, Carmichael and Hamilton, argued that in 1966 the White people working in SNCC understood that it should become an African American organization; therefore, those White workers accepted their removal from SNCC.

Likewise, Carmichael and Hamilton urged Black parents to take control of aspects of the public schools in their communities such as hiring and firing of teachers, selection of teaching materials, and determination of standards; they argued that professional educators demonstrated an insensitivity to the needs and problems of the Black child. Carmichael and Hamilton acknowledged that Black parents in the Ocean Hill-Brownsville section of New York City had tried to control their own schools but claimed that those parents failed because they did not have their own permanent and powerful organizations (166–167).

Not surprisingly, Martin Luther King, Jr. disagreed that Black organizations lost their power when they fused with White groups; he dismissed as myths Carmichael and Hamilton's suggestions that the Irish, the Italians, and the Jews rose to power through separatism.

Instead, he said that the only way minority groups could improve their status was by joining into coalitions with White people. King warned that 10 percent of the population by itself cannot induce the other 90 percent to change a way of life (*Where Do We Go* 58–59).

Unfortunately for King, when riots broke out in major cities such as Detroit, political extremists on both sides of the color line attracted larger, more receptive audiences. In July 1967, forty-three people died and more than $125 million worth of property was destroyed in Detroit during six days of violence and destruction. One month later, regular columns appeared in Detroit newspapers urging African Americans to control their own schools. In answer to this pressure for community control, in 1970 the state legislature passed and the governor signed a bill that nullified a desegregation plan and instead divided Detroit city schools into eight regions giving Blacks political control of four of those regions. It was at this point that the NAACP turned to the federal courts with the case *Milliken v. Bradley* and demanded the racial integration of the city and the suburbs (Mirel 311–343).

Ironically, some departments of the federal government encouraged Black separatism even while the HEW required school districts to racially desegregate. In November 1966, Congress approved the Demonstration Cities and Metropolitan Development Act, also known as Model Cities. This bill required citizens in individual cities to develop a comprehensive and coordinated plan that focused a variety of resources on the problem of poverty. In making its approval, Congress dropped a requirement for racially integrated housing and prohibited using school busing as a precondition for assistance (Sundquist, *Making Federalism* 79–82).

Not surprisingly, Model Cities programs encouraged segregation. In May 1967, the U.S. Department of Housing and Urban Development (HUD) approved seventy-five applications for planning grants. The program in Dayton, Ohio, differed from most other Model Cities programs. Community residents in an almost exclusively African American part of Dayton known as the Inner West devised and administered the Model Cities Demonstration Project. This came about because young, militant Black separatists challenged city administrators and demanded community control. When the planning council tried to gain control over the area's schools, the school board resisted. Nonetheless, from 1967 until 1975, when Congress ended allocations to these projects, the members of the planning council of Dayton's Model Cities Demonstration Project argued that the racial desegregation of schools would weaken the council's educational programs. Ironically, during that same period the Dayton public schools received pressure from HEW and the federal courts to desegregate all the schools (Watras 113–128).

Because the Model Cities program was established to encourage urban renewal, the biggest share of the several million dollars that went to Dayton's Model Cities Demonstration Project paid for educational innovations. A community schools program kept school buildings open from seven in the morning until ten at night. In those buildings, people found adult education classes, recreational activities, and personal services. The planning council recruited African Americans to become administrative interns who earned credits toward certificates of school supervision while learning to become change agents in the schools. Finally, teachers learned to work in teams and to advance courses in Black awareness. Several programs were tied to enhancing Black children's self-concept. Guidance and counseling programs worked to prevent children from developing bad attitudes. The planning council invited prominent African Americans to give inspirational talks to the children. At the same time, Head Start enrolled preschool children in the program's target area (Watras 113–128).

In other cities, other minority groups sought to preserve neighborhood schools to protect their children. The most successful were the Chinese families in San Francisco who raised the issue of bilingual education discussed more fully in Chapter 12. In March 1970, the Chinatown office of San Francisco legal services filed the case *Lau v. Nichols,* contending that the English-only instruction their children receive in public schools was inadequate. A short time later, in May 1971, a group of Chinese leaders asked the school board not to include Chinese immigrants in the Chinatown section as part of the court-ordered racial desegregation plan. They feared that sending Chinese children outside of the neighborhood schools would be a hardship. When the desegregation plan went into effect, one thousand Chinese American students enrolled in private, so-called "freedom schools." To attract the students back to public schools, the district exempted them from the desegregation plan. Finally, in 1974 the justices of the Supreme Court decided that the equality of education required by the 1964 Civil Rights Act compelled the San Francisco schools to offer more bilingual education. The San Francisco school district sought to meet this commitment by exempting bilingual teachers from layoffs and expanding resources available to them even though the district endured declining budgets (Kirp 103–104, 108, 114–115).

How Did Christian Day Schools Respond to the Civil Rights Movement?

In the 1960s, Christian day schools grew at an amazing rate, and this growth can be attributed in various ways to the racial integration of schools. By one estimate, beginning in the 1960s two new such schools started every day so that by 1984 there were from 9,000 to 11,000 Christian schools with a total enrollment of nearly one million students. Many of these schools took over private segregationist academies that formed in resistance to the racial integration of schools. However, it is not fair to say that the Christian day schools offered an alternative to racial integration. By the 1980s, most Christian schools professed nondiscrimination. Although the representation of Black students was small, many Christian schools enrolled some Black students (Carper 110–129).

In general, the connection between racial integration and Christian schools was indirect. These schools flourished because evangelical Christians gave up supporting public schools, complaining that teachers and texts weakened respect for authority and loosened standards. At the same time, some educational researchers found that as the public schools underwent racial desegregation, administrators stopped enforcing behavior rules and allowed students and teachers to decide how to run affairs (Grant 45–49). Consequently, insofar as the public school people overemphasized tolerance, these evangelical Christians' concerns were a reaction to the civil rights movement.

For example, in 1970 a U.S. district court judge ordered the schools in Nashville, Tennessee, to desegregate faculties and students. To avoid this requirement, many students enrolled in private schools. In 1969 only 9 percent of the county's first graders attended private schools; by 1978 this portion grew to 20 percent. However, these schools did not entirely exclude African American children, and the student body in one Christian school was entirely Black. When asked why they chose these schools, parents reported that they feared the values that would appear in the racially integrated schools and wanted their children to be taught self-discipline, diligence, and etiquette (Pride and Woodward 126–162).

In other cases, the founders of private segregationist academies and Christian schools said they came forward to meet a community need caused by racial desegregation. An example of such an irony took place in 1973 when the U.S. district court ordered the schools in Memphis, Tennessee, to racially desegregate the students. In reaction, a group of community members calling themselves Citizens Against Busing (CAB) opened twenty-six schools enrolling more than five thousand students. CAB members claimed they did this to offer people an alternative and thereby prevent the violence that took place in other cities. Shortly, several church people founded Christian schools in Memphis. They felt that instruction in the CAB schools was poor, and they wanted to give students a better education (Nevins and Bills 26–34).

From 1973 to 1975, two researchers visited eleven then newly developed private schools in South Carolina, Georgia, Alabama, and Tennessee. These schools were not tied to any denomination that had a tradition of parochial education. Only two of the schools had the word "Christian" in their names, yet the curriculum was a blend of religion and patriotism. Teachers called themselves "born again" Christians and they taught that evolutionary theory contradicted the truth of the Bible. When the researchers examined the students, they found them to have high ideals and to express a morality that sought moral absolutes. Therefore, the researchers concluded that although the public schools were far better equipped and the public school teachers far better trained, public school students would learn that morality depends on situations and thus they would be less happy than the students in the private schools (Nevins and Bills 113–114).

How Did Catholic Schools Respond to the Civil Rights Movement?

Whenever public schools in a large city had to racially desegregate, the Catholic schools usually refused to accept new transfer students in an effort to avoid encouraging White flight. The effectiveness of such a directive could vary; Catholic schools usually did not have a strong central organization and individual principals or parish priests could ignore such a request. Thus, Cardinal Medieros's request that Boston Catholic schools not accept transfer students fleeing desegregation was ineffective. More than two thousand pupils transferred into the Catholic schools when the Boston public schools desegregated (Formisano 196–214). On the other hand, in some cities such as Dayton, Catholic school enrollments did not increase when the city's public schools initiated cross-district busing.

More important, Catholic schools faced problems similar to those faced by public schools because many were organized by parishes that followed geographic boundaries. For example, in 1968 a group of influential liberal Catholics in Dayton drafted a proposal to racially integrate the Catholic elementary schools, contending that Black children had the right to an integrated education. When the Cincinnati archdiocesan school board commissioned hearings about the proposal for Dayton, several conservative Catholics argued that busing children away from their parish schools to other Catholic schools attended by minority children would violate the rights of the parents who contributed to the construction of their school. These conservatives also complained that sending the child away from the parish school would weaken the relationship the family should form with their priest, who controlled the education in the school and the activities in the church. To support their positions, they quoted many church documents that spoke of the need for a strong parish community to advance the faith (Watras 207–231).

Although the Cincinnati archdiocesan school board did not adopt the conservative position, the Dayton-area Catholic elementary schools never desegregated. However, from 1968 until 1970, about forty White suburban Catholic children attended St. James, an urban African American Catholic school in Dayton, and celebrated Mass at that parish. About the same number of Black children from St. James traveled to a suburban Catholic school.

Like other religious groups, Catholics hoped that everyone would recognize the love God has for all people and stop prejudging other groups. At times, this faith in religion seemed to excuse Catholics from pursuing more positive acts to cause racial integration. At other times, circumstances seemed to prevent the best-willed people from desegregating the schools. Two examples illustrate these difficulties.

In 1955 New Orleans, Louisiana, Archbishop Joseph Rummel appointed a committee to study racial segregation in the archdiocesan schools. The committee recommended a grade-by-grade process of integration. When Rummel agreed to begin this process, segregationists burned a cross near his home, picketed a local seminary, and turned in empty church collection envelopes at Sunday Mass. They vowed to withhold contributions until assured there would be no school integration. Rummel gave in and turned his attention to the national level, helping to write the 1958 U.S. Catholic bishops' statement "Discrimination and the Christian Conscience," which called racism an affront to God. However, this statement also warned people to be prudent in changing society. Following this caution, Rummel waited until 1960 when the New Orleans public schools desegregated. In 1962, after public unrest subsided and there was no threat that the state legislature would withdraw finances from integrated schools, the New Orleans Catholic schools adopted an open enrollment policy that allowed Black Catholic children to apply to enter any Catholic school. The schools desegregated peacefully as 150 Black children attended thirty formerly all-White schools (Watras 62–63).

In 1967 the Chicago archdiocesan school board adopted an open enrollment policy, which seemed to cause some schools to move from desegregation to resegregation. For example, in 1968–69 the Academy of Our Lady on Chicago's southwest side had an enrollment of eighteen hundred young women and was located in a neighborhood that had a population about 13 percent non-White. By 1972–73, the neighborhood was almost completely Black. During those five school years, White student enrollment declined by 963 students and minority enrollment in the school increased to just under half the total enrollment. Worse, the school changed from having a budget surplus to showing a deficit of $100,000. Fearing such rapid racial tipping would turn the school into an entirely African American institution, the principal and the school's alumnae board tried to impose quotas on African American admissions in an attempt to retain a racially integrated institution. The Chicago archdiocesan school board rejected their plan, and the local Catholic newspaper criticized their scheme for being racist. As a result, the school's survival became questionable (Moses, 99–106, 169–176, 244–245).

What Curriculum Models Were Popular in Public and Catholic Schools during Desegregation?

When the federal government supported strengthening the curricular offerings in schools in areas undergoing racial transformation, experts often introduced individually guided education (IGE). For example, from February 1968 until February 1971, the U.S. Department of Education funded a Multiple Motivation Program in Dayton, Ohio, under Projects to Advance Creativity in Education. The aim was to improve educational services in neighborhoods undergoing population change in the hope this would give White middle-class people a reason to remain in those changing neighborhoods. The Multiple Motivation Program served an area of Dayton where newly arrived, lower-class African Americans were replacing White middle-class residents. Seven schools, including a Jewish academy and a Catholic elementary school, received monies to form school community committees and improve activities to end White flight (Watras 131–140). Although Multiple Motivation sought to improve schools in a racially integrated neighborhood, it used the same IGE model found in the Model Cities Demonstration Project that served a nearly all-Black neighborhood on the other side of Dayton.

IGE owed some of its popularity to the ideals of the civil rights movement although it was not specifically part of the effort to racially desegregate schools. The federal government and private philanthropies supported this idea. For example, between 1965 and 1968, Herbert Klausmier at the Wisconsin Center for Individualized Schooling created a plan for school improvement. In 1971 the U.S. Office of Education funded his efforts to set up individualized education programs around the country (Fleury 216–222).

Another model of individually guided education came from the Institute for the Development of Educational Activities (/I/D/E/A/), then an affiliate of the Charles F. Kettering Foundation, which helped John Goodlad in California form the League of Cooperating Schools. The Kettering Foundation took the ideas Goodlad tried in the League of Cooperating Schools, formed them into the Change Program for Individually Guided Education, and offered the program to schools without charge (Fleury 15–16).

The key idea of the IGE program was that the particular school building was the important element of change. That is, the teachers and the principal in the building had to determine what the change would be and how it would happen. The Kettering Foundation offered consultants to help building personnel engage in the process. As in the League of Cooperating Schools, however, these consultants brought suggestions from their experiences in other buildings; they did not impose a general model of proper education (Goodlad, *Dynamics* 96).

IGE's aim was to encourage children of all ages and all types to be successful. Thus, although the words *diversity* and *tolerance* did not appear in the literature, these ideas were not far from the program's aims. The /I/D/E/A/ staff drew up a list of thirty-five outcomes to describe the conditions that should prevail in a school that encouraged the continuous growth of students, administrators, faculty, and staff. These included dividing the building into learning communities, giving each learning community a cross section of teachers and aides to work with at least two age groups of students. Further, each student had an advisor to help him or her plan an individual learning program (Paden 23–26).

As part of the IGE process, the learning community members met regularly to select broad goals. From these wider aims, individual students selected some goals and turned them into personal objectives with activities to achieve them. The teachers monitored and gathered information about each student's progress, and the teachers set goals for their own development and helped evaluate each other's progress.

Although it was initially popular, IGE faded after 1975 for three reasons. First, private philanthropies and state agencies stopped supporting it. Second, the advocates of IGE rarely sought objective measures of academic learning such as standardized test scores; they evaluated the success of the model by improvements in the students' desire to learn (Fleury 222). Third, IGE lost popularity because of bureaucratic tendencies. That is, when a school district hired a new superintendent, that person wanted to be identified with innovation. As a result, new superintendents may have chosen to discontinue programs begun by their predecessors.

Individually guided education was consonant with the civil rights movement; students enjoyed some freedoms, they had responsibilities, and they cooperated. Although the name implied that students worked alone, this was only supposed to happen occasionally. Instead, the program focused on small groups. In clusters of three to thirteen, the students could brainstorm, accomplish specific tasks, or evaluate their own efforts. However, IGE did not imply any form of social order, because it was a model of school planning. Thus, it could function in a racially segregated community as it did in Dayton's Model Cities Demonstration Project. On the other hand, it could serve the aims of racial integration as it did in the case of the Multiple Motivation Project.

Did Magnet Schools Encourage Racial Integration?

A popular model of advancing racial integration was the magnet school. The idea behind magnet schools was to offer an attractive program in a geographic area populated by lower-class minority students. Because it was the quality of the school that attracted middle-class or White students, desegregation took place by means of personal choice. Many people suggested the idea of magnet schools to address different problems. In 1963 several civil rights groups asked the Los Angeles school board to begin a program of racial desegregation that included magnet schools. In 1969 Catholic educators in Dayton recommended such an idea as a compromise proposal among several ideas to desegregate Catholic elementary schools. Not surprisingly, politicians found the idea attractive in the face of public resistance to busing. Thus, in 1976, after McGovern's disastrous loss, the Democratic party's platform called for a variety of mechanisms incorporating individual choice, such as magnet schools, to bring about racial desegregation (Orfield, *Must We Bus* 157, 276, 432).

Surprisingly, magnet schools did not become widespread. In 1983 only about 4 percent of the nation's high schools, including magnet schools, offered specialized curricula. Nonetheless, the Carnegie Foundation for the Advancement of Teaching urged that all large urban areas develop magnet schools for gifted and talented students (Boyer 20, 239).

The idea of magnet schools retained popularity among conservative politicians who otherwise decried racial desegregation. For example, in 1981 the Reagan administration won congressional action to rescind the Emergency School Act of 1972, cutting off the one remaining significant source of funds for programs of racial integration. Only the magnet school portion of these funds was restored (Orfield and Eaton 16).

Despite the fact that most people could accept magnet schools as a means of racial integration, they were not clearly effective in this effort. First, magnet schools did not involve many children. In some cities, as few as 2 percent of the children took part in magnet schools. Second, magnet schools did not racially balance themselves. In 1977, for example, in a sample of 216 magnet schools, seventeen had less than 20 percent minority students and seventy-four had from 60 to 100 percent minorities. Third, magnet schools appeared to be expensive. Specialized equipment, small classes, innovative administrators, and excellent teachers required money. However, exact costs were difficult to determine and may have dropped over time. Some districts called some buildings magnet schools but did not invest adequately in the programs to justify the name. Fourth, case studies of some magnets indicated that they drained morale and commitment from teachers and administrators not included in the schools. Fifth, because these magnet schools appeared to be most available to middle-class students, they may have prevented those children from mixing with peers from lower social classes. As a result of these problems, most commentators agreed that magnets could reduce racial segregation only if they were part of a larger mandatory plan (Hochschild 70–78).

One researcher disagreed. In 1990 Christine Rossell compared the desegregation effectiveness of mandatory magnet plans with voluntary ones. For Rossell, a voluntary plan was one in which the parents had the most freedom in selecting the school for their children because neither school officials nor court officers forced assignments. Although she had difficulty placing the twenty school districts she studied in the proper categories, two examples stood out. Cincinnati, Ohio, represented one of the most voluntary models; the district lacked any numerical goals. On the other hand, Dayton, Ohio, forty-five miles to the north, represented a mandatory model; the U.S. District Court judge had ordered the Dayton city schools' board of education to mix pupils in all schools to a ratio of White and minority students equivalent to the district's ratio as a whole, plus or minus 15 percent. Obtaining her data from the U.S. Office of Civil Rights, Rossell determined that mandatory plans caused the most White flight and had the least racial desegregation (183–216).

However, another researcher, Brian Fife, studied the same twenty school districts that Rossell used and came to the opposite conclusion. He found that the most coercive models were the most effective. Fife noted that to some extent the different conclusions reflected different statistical measures of racial desegregation. However, when Fife used Rossell's operational definitions, he still found the mandatory plans more effective.

Whether or not they worked, magnet schools functioned in the same way individual education did. Rather than speaking directly to the ideals supporting racial integration, the magnet schools tried to bring about racial integration by offering what people saw as quality education. The hope was that the problems of diversity would take care of themselves in these good schools.

Did Multicultural Studies Enhance Racial Integration?

One curriculum model that confronted the problems of diversity and racial integration was ethnic or multicultural studies. However, this was by no means a uniform approach. Such instruction seemed to follow a progression. An early effort in this regard was changing the textbooks. In the early 1960s, the NAACP and the National Urban League called on educators to use textbooks that portrayed the contributions and experiences of African Americans. Publishers worked to produce books to meet this criterion. Similarly, other minorities such as Mexican Americans, Native Americans, Asian Americans, and Puerto Rican Americans asked for more reasonable treatment of their groups in textbooks. However, several state departments of education recognized that schools lacked texts with relevant materials about minority groups woven into the fabric of the book. As a result, they offered guides to resources for teachers to use as administrators bought new books. For example, in 1974 the Ohio department of education offered the guide *Providing K–12 Multi-Cultural Curricular Experiences* as a resource to teachers to use between the time old texts were phased out and new books purchased. The guide presented facts about events and famous members of four minority groups listed in chronological order.

In general, when school districts implemented an ethnic studies program, the teachers aimed it to the type of minorities in the school district. School districts responded most frequently to the demands for Black studies programs. As a result, publishers created materials to explore the problems and the contributions of African Americans. Teachers taught the courses to Black students (Banks 16–17).

Unfortunately, a Black studies program could turn into an anti-White episode. For example, in 1968, three years after the Sausalito, California, board of education voluntarily desegregated the schools, the district hired a Black power advocate, James Toliver, as a teacher. At Toliver's recommendation, the district began a Black studies program, hired some members of the Black Panthers' Party from nearby Oakland as consultants, and named another Black power advocate, Sidney Walton, as principal of the school. Walton was the author of *The Black Curriculum* in which he argued that the Black community members, Black faculty members, and Black students had to show White people that they would die to achieve their aims. Some parents complained to the school board about violence and militancy, but other parents said that the district was trying to reach Black children in an innovative manner. In February 1970, the education committee of the Marin County grand jury responded to White parents' complaints of reverse racism. In the controversies that followed, Black students boycotted a school and Black Panther members tried to intimidate the school board by bringing guard dogs and steel staves to meetings. Subsequently, the superintendent resigned, two board members who supported the Black separatist administrators lost a recall election, and new board members who supported racially integrated education took their places (Kirp 204–210).

One problem with multicultural education was the tendency to focus on African Americans as if there were only two cultural groups, Blacks and Whites. Thus, in 1975 James Banks offered teaching strategies for what he called ethnic studies. Holding up the idea of the melting pot as an unrealized myth, Banks asserted that ethnic groups were intensifying efforts to glorify their pasts and develop pride among their members. Banks called on teachers to help students learn how to understand how the many different groups in U.S. society interacted in order to teach the students to be tolerant. Such lessons, he argued, would benefit all children whether or not they belonged to a minority group (5–9).

According to Banks, the criterion for selecting the content of an ethnic studies course was whether the material would enable students to develop valid generalizations about their social world and to acquire the skills to influence public policy. During the study of minority cultures, students could learn that human beings have the same basic needs but that people in different groups learn to satisfy them in different ways. Banks thought such lessons in what he called cultural literacy were important for White children because White ethnic groups tend to think their culture is superior to all others. He hoped that when White students understood ethnic minorities, they would appreciate the humanity of minority group members (19–21).

Banks wanted ethnic studies to have an interdisciplinary perspective. That is, he believed students should consider ethnic problems from disciplines such as anthropology, political science, and geography. When Banks selected the important concepts that anthropology could lend to ethnic studies, he listed ideas such as cultural diversity. For example, he wrote that many African Americans spoke Standard English on the job and used Black English at home or with friends (53–55).

When Banks discussed the role that the discipline of history might play in ethnic studies, he cautioned teachers to help students uncover the biases of historians. He complained that "throughout history, history has been written by the victors and not by the vanquished" (75). As a result, students read histories of Native Americans written by White historians who had little empathy for the culture. To correct this flaw, he urged that history be taught through the eyes of the minority.

Banks asserted that many ethnic problems within U.S. society were conflicts of values. However, he urged teachers not to force children to accept any one set of values but to develop a system of clarifying their own. Typical values such as respect for authority and honesty might not help minority children. For example, Puerto Rican American children might not respect police officers when they know these officials may kill their friends and neighbors during a protest against U.S. injustice. Or African American slaves may have had to lie and steal in order to gather enough food to avoid starvation. Therefore, teachers should instruct that "no values are functional for all times, settings, and cultures." Instead, students should learn the processes they could use to obtain values. Banks offered a method of value clarification that included defining value problems, describing value-relevant behavior, naming values exemplified by the behavior, determining conflicting values, hypothesizing about the source of the values, naming alternative values, hypothesizing about the consequences of the values, and stating reasons for the value choices (108).

Beyond this discussion of values, Banks did not treat questions of religion or spirituality. Theology was not one of the disciplines he thought should contribute to ethnic studies. At best, religion appeared in stories about the rise of Native American prophets who in the eighteenth century urged their tribes to resist White settlers, and in descriptions of religious dissenters such as the Puritans who, Banks claimed, did not tolerate dissent among their own members.

Thus, for educators such as Banks, multicultural education enhanced integration because it helped all students learn to be more tolerant. Unfortunately, the basis for that tolerance was a type of relativism in which traditional values were as acceptable as any other form of values. In a short time, conservatives complained that multicultural education led to a form of assimilation rather than integration because their form of valuing was omitted.

Did Any Groups Disagree with the Aims or the Methods of Multicultural Education?

As values clarification and multicultural texts became popular, conservative groups protested against them. In September 1974, school board member Alice Moore and several conservative parents complained that English language arts textbooks purchased by the Kanawha County, West Virginia, school board made slang appear as acceptable as Standard English, portrayed respect for authority as foolish, and claimed ethical norms were dependent on the situation. They claimed these books threatened the children's belief in God. The resulting strikes by parents and sympathetic coal miners made national news. Disturbances continued until the school board removed some of the most offensive titles and agreed to allow children whose parents objected to the books to read something else (Cowan 19–21).

The textbooks were published by reputable firms such as D. C. Heath, Scott-Foresman, and Silver Burdett Company and were selected from a recommended list distributed by the West Virginia state board of education. In choosing these books, the local selection committee followed the suggestions that the state superintendent of schools had made to all school districts: language arts textbooks should indicate that the United States is a multiethnic nation, show a variety of viewpoints, illustrate the contributions of minority groups, and assist the students in examining their own self-image.

The books contained stories and essays by noted authors such as Langston Hughes, Norman Mailer, James Baldwin, and George Orwell. Some stories spoke of college radicals and resistance to the draft during the Vietnamese crisis, whereas others mentioned consensual unions between men and women. Some books described the problems minority groups faced. Although these stories made it appear that Black people stole, used drugs, and were angrier than Whites, the parents did not focus on this element of the texts. They took the view that the books were part of a national conspiracy to weaken traditional religion. As a result, two parents filed the case of *Williams v. Kanawha County School Board* in U.S. District Court claiming that the texts imposed a religion of secular humanism. Judge K. K. Hall dismissed the suit, saying that he could find no effort to establish religion in the books. If the parents were unhappy with the schools, they should express their displeasure at the voting booths, not in the courtroom.

Although Judge Hall did not find any attempt to establish religion in the books, the exercises did trivialize religion. For example, in one text the students read creation stories including parts of Genesis from the Bible. A reading comprehension exercise invited the students to invent their own gods and write their own creation stories. The parents complained that this implied God is a myth created by humans.

According to Alice Moore, the protesting school board member, this relativistic approach was at the heart of the controversy. Later, Moore wrote that there were two ways to teach morality in schools. One approach was absolutist; it recognized moral law as immutable and absolute, determined by God. The other approach was relativistic, recognizing no authority outside human beings to determine right from wrong. When public schools approached such moral questions as stealing, the teachers had to choose one approach or the other. Whichever view prevailed, it injured parents who believed otherwise. Thus, Moore concluded, the only solution was to strip the schools of all moral instruction ("Moral Education" 225–226).

To some extent, the Kanawha County school board adopted Moore's approach. The members decided that if a parent objected to his or her child reading any book, the child could be excused from the assignment. The books remained in the classrooms, but the supplementary texts that caused the biggest problems stood unused. This approach did not satisfy the textbook supporters. Reverend James Lewis, an Episcopal minister who approved of the books, complained this was a nonsolution showing that "the liberal community is morally bankrupt, no longer having ideals that it's willing to fight and die for" (Candor 188).

How Did Educators React to the Complaint That Multicultural Texts Undermined Traditional Values?

In general, educators refused to try to bring together the two value orientations to which Alice Moore referred, the absolutist and the relativistic. Instead, they reacted to the Kanawha County textbook controversy by looking for ways such disputes could be avoided so that everyone could study together in relative peace. This approach began in October 1974 when the Teacher Rights Division of the National Education Association (NEA) agreed to inquire into the controversy in Kanawha County. The NEA panel did not try to evaluate the texts or the supplementary materials, and they acknowledged the sincere and urgent concerns the parents expressed. The problem, the panel concluded, came from a clash between rural and urban groups in the county.

School districts in West Virginia comprise entire counties, which can include many different types of communities. In the 1970s, Kanawha County was the most important industrial area in the state with chemical plants, printing firms, and glass manufacturers. It contained the capital of the state, Charleston, with a population of around 70,000. Outside the city were small country towns, general stores, and subsistence farms that could be reached only by way of winding, bumpy roads that ran among the hills and hollows. To the members of the NEA panel, Kanawha County was made up of two culturally polarized communities that lived miles apart but held values separated by light years (Teacher Rights 8–9).

According to the NEA panel, fundamentalist religious beliefs were an expression of the culture of Appalachia, and these lay behind the textbook controversy. In former times, such religious faith enabled people to withstand the hardships of mountain living. Although these hardships had lightened, the panel believed this religion served as a bulwark against the psychological and social stress of integration into the wider society (Teacher Rights 13–15).

The NEA panel feared that the protest left teachers frustrated and afraid, had driven out a superintendent, and gave students a lesson in demagoguery. Unable to unite the clashing cultural orientations, panel members looked for ways to protect the schools from excessive public reaction. They concluded that the administrators had failed to plan effectively. Therefore, they urged school administrators to anticipate any adverse public reaction to language arts textbooks and create a system for handling complaints that distinguished between legitimate concerns and irrational objections. Finally, the panel wrote, school administrators had to respond promptly to the first complaints. With these recommendations, the NEA panel hoped to help everyone. NEA panel members wanted teachers to have the academic freedom to select appropriate materials as well as protect the rights of the parents to inquire about their children's educational reading materials (Teacher Rights 55–63).

Although subsequent textbook protests took place, they lacked the extensive media coverage the Kanawha County dispute suffered, partly because parents followed manuals showing how to complain effectively. In 1979 Connought Coyne Marshner wrote *Blackboard Tyranny* as a road map for parents seeking to become politically active in behalf of their rights (322). In her book, Marshner advises parents about the way to begin a complaint by visiting the teacher, then the principal, and finally complaining to the local board members. She suggests that people remain calm and rational and construct permanent political organizations to petition legislatures about grievances. Marshner saw her book as an alternative for parents who wanted their children to receive intensive basic skills instruction, yet did not want to move to home schools or private academies.

Another reason why subsequent textbook protests drew less publicity is that school district administrators instituted the policies recommended by the NEA panel. In 1986 Edward Jenkinson published a handbook that warned school people about what he called the school protest movement, calling Marshner one of its spokespersons. Noting that the courts are unreliable protectors of academic freedom, Jenkinson urged school districts to adopt policies stating that the responsibility for the selection of instructional materials is delegated to the professionally trained and certificated staff. In those policies, administrators should outline the composition of textbook selection committees, the procedures for complaints, and the dissemination of information to parents. In these ways, wrote Jenkinson, the administrators could prevent division in the community and protect the teachers' right to teach and the students' right to learn (Jenkinson 23).

Was the Kanawha County Dispute a Clash of Cultures?

Interestingly, if educators saw the Kanawha County dispute as a reaction against a common approach to advance racial or social integration, they refused to think the materials were at fault. Thus, in 1977 the Association for Supervision and Curriculum Development (ASCD) called multicultural education a tool to eliminate discrimination with regard to race, sex, class, and disabilities. The ASCD committed itself to the process of ensuring that all curriculum materials offered a realistic treatment of cultural pluralism (C. Grant 1).

Most educators acted much as the NEA panel had. Instead of thinking there was a difficulty in the overly relativistic approach of the materials, educators saw the protest as signaling the need for more and better multicultural efforts. For example, one of the authors of a textbook series involved in the controversy in West Virginia agreed with the NEA panel that the problem was a clash of cultures. James Moffett had developed for Houghton Mifflin a textbook series entitled *Interaction.* This series of books, readings, films, activity cards, and tapes offered what he called "thoroughgoing individualization." When the protestors focused on his series along with others, the company salespeople stopped pushing his books, sales declined, and the publisher dropped the series. Looking back on the incident, Moffett criticizes the publishers for being overly sensitive and profit conscious. The textbook protestors gave into a will to ignorance that Moffett calls agnosis, which he claims derives from a human need to conform to the ideas of a particular group rather than seek the wider claims of humankind (236).

Moffett agrees with the NEA panel that there was a culture of Appalachia and that the textbook protestors held to this cultural orientation. However, there are two problems with the view that the textbook conflict was a clash of cultures. First, it was hard to prove that the protestors in Kanawha County were fundamentalist mountaineers. Evidence that there was a clash of cultures came from surveys conducted by reporters for the *Charleston Gazette.* When the reporters asked 386 voters at the September polls if they favored or disapproved of the books, they found that 41.2 percent opposed the books, 27.2 favored them, and 31.6 percent were undecided. These answers differed by locality; those who favored the books tended to be from the city of Charleston and those who opposed tended to be from rural areas such as Alum Creek (Moffett 35). However, when Alice Moore, the school board member, who started the controversy, ran for reelection in 1976, she won by the largest vote ever cast for a school board member, carrying every voting district in the county including those in both rural and urban areas (Moore, Letter). These election results suggest that, even if Kanawha County was a multicultural community, something about her complaints made sense to everyone.

The second problem with the theory that the textbook controversy was a clash of cultures is that other conservative authors who did not share the Appalachian heritage complained that public school textbooks ignored religion, traditional family values, and conservative political and economic positions. For example, in 1987 Paul C. Vitz examined sixty representative social studies texts from reputable firms such as McGraw-Hill, Macmillan, and Allyn and Bacon for students in grades 1 through 4. He looked at another twenty textbooks for grades 5 and 6. Vitz found glaring omissions. One text edited a story by Nobel laureate Isaac Bashevis Singer and removed references to religion. Thus, in the original story the main character "prayed to God" and later remarked "Thank God." In the textbook, however, the words "to God" were omitted and the expression "Thank God" became "Thank goodness" (Vitz 1–4).

As complaints about secular humanism gathered momentum among conservatives, groups of parents filed suits to modify texts. They were momentarily successful. In March 1987, U.S. District Judge Brevard Hand, in *Smith v. Board of School Commissioners of Mobile County, Alabama,* found that forty-four textbooks purchased by the Alabama public schools promoted a religion that he called secular humanism. Although secular humanism was at best a form of atheism, Hand thought it was a religion because it denied all religions. This view did not stand for long. In August 1987, the U.S. Court of Appeals for the Sixth Circuit voted unanimously to reject Hand's decision. Chief Judge Pierce Lively wrote that the plaintiffs did not produce any proof that students had to affirm their belief in any practice mentioned in the stories. Thus, the appellate judges agreed with a decision one month earlier by the Supreme Court that reversed a Louisiana law requiring the balanced treatment of creation science and evolutionary science. The justices labeled it a poorly disguised way to bring religion into the school.

In the midst of this legal conflict, educators sought to evaluate the problems. In August 1987, the ASCD held a panel to comment on religion in the curriculum. The panel noted that in response to conflicting pressures some textbook publishers removed or understated the role of religion in founding and developing the country. This overreaction, panel members added, extended into classrooms where teachers mistakenly thought the Supreme Court had ruled against any mention of religious faith. The solution they recommended was simple. Teachers, textbooks, and instructional materials should provide adequate treatment of diverse religions and their roles in U.S. and world culture. Although people should be sensitive to other people's beliefs, everyone should realize that teaching about religion is acceptable under the U.S. Constitution (ASCD 36).

Did Educators Abandon Integration?

In the ASCD statement of 1987, the panel members did not define what they meant by religion. Consequently, they seemed to be saying that educators could not trespass on any belief that appeared spiritual. Similarly, Alice Moore, the protesting school board member from Kanawha County, contended that there was no way to accommodate both educators who favored multicultural texts and fundamentalist parents. According to Moore, the texts represented a relativistic model and the parents wanted a more absolute approach to thinking about values—there was no way to bring them together. Although the ASCD urged teachers not to interfere with any person's beliefs, Moore behaved as though people holding either perspective about morality should alter their perspective. Consequently, instead of asking each group to recognize problems with their own views, everyone sought textbook-adoption procedures that could bring peace, give each group the things it wanted, and allow schools to operate.

The danger of such compromises was that people used the idea of respect for other groups' values to avoid exploring existing problems. In the case of the Kanawha County textbook dispute, when parents objected to equating religion and myth, educators and textbook protestors could have considered more deeply what a myth is. This would have led them to a rich bibliography of works by theologians and anthropologists. By not doing so, educators seemed to abandon the faith in evolution, change, and progress exemplified by progressives such as John Dewey.

Furthermore, multicultural educators used the words *democracy* and *pluralism* as if they were the same. However, these terms are not synonymous. In as much as pluralism means that different groups live and work apart, it contradicts the spirit of democracy that Jane Addams created in Hull House. Although Addams encouraged immigrant groups to read poetry and show art from their native lands, she did not help immigrant groups retain their cultural identities. She saw herself building bridges among the groups, so she set up kitchens to change people's traditional eating habits and introduced former rural dwellers to the mysteries of urban sanitation.

Multiculturalists might have seen Addams as destroying cultural identities by advancing a melting pot theory. However, multiculturalism did not solve the problems of diversity as much as it changed them. For example, in 1998 Jane Ayers Chiong complained about school requirements that forced students to identify themselves as one race even if each of their parents belonged to separate racial groups. She surveyed school forms and federal documents found in an urban school district and in a suburban district, and in March 1992, she interviewed thirty public school teachers from those schools. She found that federal forms and standardized tests wanted students identified as belonging to a racial category. When the students had difficulty categorizing themselves, the school personnel did it for them. Although the teachers Chiong interviewed believed in multiculturalism, they used materials or discussed issues in ways that implied all people belonged to one of many different traditions. Shortly after Chiong's research, the U.S. Office of Management and Budget recommended abolishing the policy of assigning people to only one racial category. However, Chiong fears that schools might not change enough to help multiracial children form cohesive yet multiple identities (1–15, 69–102, 111–112).

In an integrated society, the category "multiracial children" may not exist. If the different groups contribute to the formation of a larger whole, multiracial children would be evidence of its success. However, as an advocate of multiracial children, Chiong takes a multicultural perspective. She believes the children should be treated as a unique group or, more correctly, an infinite number of special groups. Thus, separation, integration, or assimilation are not so much choices among methods as they are choices about the types of problems people want to confront.

How Did the Civil Rights Movement Change Educational Aims?

The changes caused by the racial integration of schools were extensive. The civil rights movement began as an effort to speed up the slow pace of racial integration. Racial desegregation of schools can be considered a curriculum change because it was supposed to increase the academic performance of African Americans. Unfortunately, there were no curricular changes to help children understand the nature and the direction of the transformation then under way. Instead, curricular reforms were aimed at improving the effectiveness of schools undergoing racial integration. These included the IGE model, magnet schools, and multiethnic or multicultural education. Although there were several types of multicultural education, the type that became most well known sought to teach the students that each group had its own sense of values and that these were not superior to those of any other group. However, conservative educators argued that such relativism undercut traditional values. Textbook protestors in West Virginia complained that multicultural texts cheapened the values they wanted their children to learn. Multicultural educators did not think about the conflict between absolute and relativistic value orientations but viewed the problem as a clash of cultures that could be solved by increased efforts in multicultural education. According to the protestors, this represented the very sort of assimilation that multicultural education disparaged. It implied that everyone had to adopt the view that values depend on the group rather than some absolute sense of truth. Thus, the racial integration of schools turned from an effort to mix Black students and White students in the same classrooms into a question of which value orientations advance a sense of community.

Educators tended to see the problems as deriving from people's limited appreciation of differences. Perhaps they did. But the unwillingness of educators to question the basis of multicultural texts was another form of cultural blindness.

Nonetheless, as the drive for racial integration diminished, educators focused on the conception of individual rights. Although the concept of personal freedom was popular, it led to a conception of the world as a place where individuals should lead separate lives and pursue particular goals. Such a view overlooked the idea that personal freedoms flourish in the midst of social obligations and benefits. Curricula could have been formed that demonstrated the ways in which societies were changed and developed through exchanges. However, the view that people should not judge different cultural standards suited a society in which highways encouraged people to move out of cities to settle in suburbs that some sociologists called lifestyle enclaves. Unlike the ethnically diverse neighborhoods found in many nineteenth-century cities, these were communities where people who shared the same interests and occupations lived together. In so doing, they affirmed each others' patterns of dress, recreation, and taste (Bellah, et al. 71–75).

However, schools and neighborhoods did not have to be segregated. Many options such as metropolitan reorganization, educational parks, or dispersal of low-income housing succeeded in many cities. Unfortunately, people lacked a reason to try them. To some extent, civil rights advocates contributed to this problem. As they concerned themselves with legal requirements, pedagogical preferences, and the need to fight racism, the calls for racial integration often sounded like pleas for people to sacrifice individual opportunities and extend aid to underprivileged people.

It is not surprising that after a short period, schools became racially segregated again. The percent of Black students in intensely segregated schools had declined during the 1980s. However, from 1986 until 1991, racial segregation rose to the level that had existed before the U.S. Supreme Court's first busing decision in 1971. Further, because few efforts had been expended to integrate Latino students, they had always been more likely than African Americans to attend segregated schools. More important, the academic achievement of students in these segregated schools was low (Orfield and Eaton 54–55, 65–67).

TIMELINE
1964–1980

1964 Congress opened the War on Poverty and Lyndon Johnson signed the Civil Rights Act

1965 The U.S. House Education and Labor Committee heard testimony that the Chicago school board used attendance boundaries to maintain segregation

1965 HEW investigated Chicago's attendance policies, but federal officials would not financially punish the school system

1966 Congress approved the Demonstration Cities and Metropolitan Development Act, which focused on poverty

1967 Stokely Carmichael and Charles Hamilton promoted black organizations

(continued)

TIMELINE Continued

1967	The Chicago archdiocesan school board adopted an open enrollment policy, resulting in majority White schools turning majority Black
1967	Racial riots in Detroit killed 43 people
1968	*Green v. County School Board of New Kent County* determined that schools had to change their enrollment patterns
1968	The Cincinnati archdiocesan school board objected to Dayton-area Catholic elementary schools planning to desegregate
1968	James Toliver began Black power programs in the Sausalito, California, schools
1969	Richard Nixon became the U.S. president
1970	Chinese Americans protested English-only instruction in San Francisco schools during *Lau v. Nichols*
1970	The Michigan state legislature gave Blacks in Detroit control over four city school regions
1970	The U.S. district court ordered Nashville schools to desegregate but lost students to the private schools
1971	Chinese immigrants asked the San Francisco school board to let their children attend their neighborhood schools
1971	The U.S. Office of Education funded Herbert Klausmier's IGE programs
1971	Schools in Dayton, Ohio, established an advisory committee that held open meetings to discuss methods of desegregation
1971	The Supreme Court approved busing children to schools
1972	Denver, Colorado, schools were compelled to desegregate after the *Keyes v. School District No.1* case
1972	Richard Nixon had the courts call a moratorium on racial integration issues
1973	The U.S. Commission on Civil Rights stated that Title IV of the Civil Rights Act, concerning racial desegregation in schools, had failed
1973	The U.S. district court ordered Memphis schools to desegregate, but citizens formed CAB and established new schools
1974	West Virginian parents argued against ethnic studies and multicultural tests
1974	NAACP suffers major defeat in *Milliken v. Bradley* and failed to integrate Detroit's suburban and urban schools
1974	The Ohio department of education offered *Providing K–12 Multi-Cultural Experiences* to teachers
1974	Boston implemented a desegregation plan for the schools
1974	The NEA attempted to effect a compromise between protesters and the school board in Kanawha, West Virginia
1975	James S. Coleman published evidence of White migration to the suburbs
1975	James Banks introduced teaching strategies called ethnic studies

CHAPTER

11 The Culture of Poverty, Compensatory Curricula, and Federal Funding: 1964–1998

Young children play during a Head Start program.

Culture of Poverty

- James Conant
- Michael Harrington
- Oscar Lewis
- Frank Riessman
- War on Poverty
- ESEA 1965
- Project Head Start
- Cultural Deprivation
  Racial segregation
- Failures of Compensatory Education

OVERVIEW

Throughout the 1950s, many African Americans moved from rural sections of southern states to northern cities. Several authors argue that these new immigrants and other people who remained poor suffered from a culture of poverty that prevented them from taking advantage of the general social progress. In his 1964 State of the Union Address, President Lyndon Johnson declared war on poverty in the United States. As part of the largest federal allocation to public schools up to that time, Johnson's administration disbursed almost $1 billion in the 1965–66 fiscal year to develop innovative educational programs for children who lived in poverty. Most of these programs were designed to compensate for cultural characteristics all these children were supposed to share. Unfortunately, studies failed to show that programs such as Head Start helped the children succeed in schools. As a result of the controversies about the effectiveness of poverty programs, President Richard Nixon announced the formation of the National Institute of Education to gather information about educational interventions. Critics argued that the ideas of cultural uniqueness and the need for special programs to help disadvantaged children justified segregated educational programs. However, in administering special aid federal officials designed programs that encouraged racial integration. Thus, through several plans, courts linked racial desegregation and compensatory education. In other cases, however, compensatory education programs separated the lower-class children from their affluent peers.

Sociologists developed the idea that poor people shared a distinct culture of poverty in order to facilitate the development of educational programs. The hope was that schools would initiate new curricula to compensate for the cultural disadvantages under which these children suffered. Although sociologists soon discounted the idea, educational theorists preserved variations of the model under terms such as cultural resistance theory. These efforts to help students by studying the nature of the learners and their families shared a conservative theme. That is, the aim was to find ways by which low-income students could master the same material as other children. Consequently, unlike efforts to fashion an activity curriculum in the 1930s, compensatory education in the 1960s, 1970s, and 1980s reinforced traditional notions of subject matter, thereby intertwining models of segregation and assimilation.

Did Urban Schools Face Unique Problems in the 1960s?

During the 1950s, approximately a quarter of a million African Americans moved each year from rural southern farms to northern and western industrial cities. Although they pursued better lives, many of these people settled in unattractive neighborhoods. Because they had poor educations, they often had to accept low-paying jobs or welfare. More important, their children could not break out of these conditions. African American children constituted the largest percentage of students leaving schools before graduation because traditional educational programs seemed unable to help them (Bailey and Mosher 8).

As the public became aware of the problems in the cities, several authors argued that urban schools should offer different programs designed to reduce the problems of poverty although the National Defense Education Act encouraged many schools to strengthen their academic programs. For example, in 1961 James Conant, former president of Harvard University, contrasted what he called the city slums and the wealthy suburbs of the ten largest cities: New York, Chicago, Los Angeles, Philadelphia, Detroit, Baltimore, Houston, Cleveland, Washington D.C., and St. Louis. In the suburbs, Conant found attractive homes and spacious school buildings that differed from the crowded tenements and dilapidated school buildings he found in the slums. Part of the problem was financial. Suburban districts spent almost twice as much per student per year than city schools. Another part of the problem was social discrimination that prevented African Americans from earning enough money to afford decent housing. Furthermore, Conant warned, the large numbers of African American children who dropped out of school without any prospect of employment represented social dynamite (*Slums* 1–3).

Conant believed that urban schools needed different programs than suburban ones. He argued that "what a school should do and can do is determined by the status and the ambitions of the families being served" (1). In one slum area, only 10 percent of the parents had graduated from high school and one-third had completed elementary school. Therefore, in urban schools Conant found teachers setting up classes to help the mothers of schoolchildren learn to read, thereby changing the family attitude toward academics. More organized approaches utilized remedial reading clinics, nongraded programs for overage pupils, and special school and community teams to integrate the efforts of students, teachers, parents, and employers. Conant found an example of these efforts in the Great Cities Program for School Improvement formed by superintendents of the country's largest city schools. At the other end of the spectrum, suburban parents tended to be college graduates who expected their children to go to college. Consequently, in the suburban schools he found rigorous academic programs to prepare students for college (*Slums* 25, 60–61, 80–91).

Conant did not believe that racial integration of schools would solve the problems of poverty. Such a view implied that all-Black schools were inherently inferior. In fact, he recommended that urban students be grouped by abilities even if this resulted in racially segregated classes. Guidance counselors could disguise these tracking procedures by individualizing students' programs without putting them in tracks labeled "college preparatory," "vocational," or "commercial," thus increasing remedial work, effective guidance, and appropriate vocational training in urban schools (*Slums* 29–31, 63–66, 146–147).

Conant expressed the popular view that urban schools should differ from suburban schools because the teachers had to cope with different conditions. Yet it is important to note that by concentrating on family differences, Conant rejected the implication that inherited or genetic differences caused African American youth to fail in schools (*Slums* 17).

Was There a Slum Culture?

In 1962 Frank Riessman extended Conant's concern about family patterns. Riessman argued that teachers had not understood that poor people had a culture different from that of affluent people. Therefore, the teachers had not been able to help the students whom he called culturally deprived. Although Riessman used the term "culturally deprived" because it was popular, he disliked the term because he thought the poor possessed a culture of their own developed from coping with a difficult environment. For him, culturally deprived children came from cultural and racial minorities who shared what he called slum life with hardened criminals, prostitutes, and winos. However, they disliked this criminal element and kept apart from it. Riessman estimated that the culturally deprived constituted a large group: In many cities, one of three children was culturally deprived (1–4).

In listing the characteristics of the culturally deprived, Riessman wrote that they felt alienated from the wider society and expressed their frustration by believing political leaders were corrupt. Although culturally deprived people wanted a better standard of living, they disliked the middle-class values of prestige and individual status, preferring security and grouped membership. Furthermore, culturally deprived people were anti-intellectual, preferring to learn in physical ways by manipulating objects or seeing pictures. This tendency expressed itself in an affection for sports and heroes who doggedly overcome difficult situations (25–30).

Although Riessman noted that culturally deprived children failed in school, he thought this happened because they held unique ideas of what constituted a valuable education. That is, whereas the more affluent groups favored academic training, the lower social classes valued vocational and practical education. This meant that teachers who tended to value learning for its own sake worked with students who did not take the same view. When the students failed, Riessman argued, they developed negative attitudes toward schoolwork (11–15).

Rather than challenge racial segregation, Riessman offered several suggestions for teachers to improve the education of culturally deprived children:

1. Teachers should select reading materials that recognize the differences between middle-class and lower-class life and display the positive aspects of life in slums by portraying culturally deprived individuals in favorable ways.

2. Teachers should teach culturally deprived students the skills that middle-class children learn at home such as how to ask and to answer questions, how to study, how to relate to adults such as the teacher, and how to take tests.
3. Teachers should capitalize on the child's culture. For example, the students may tend to be inflexible and traditional. But this permits teachers to have students memorize and repeatedly practice such basic skills as number facts.
4. Spirituals, jazz, and blues might lead the culturally deprived children to art and music just as Black history might lead African Americans to history or social studies.
5. Teachers should build on the affection of culturally deprived children for action and manipulation of objects by offering them opportunities to role-play historical situations and create fictitious stores and banks to learn arithmetic and economics.
6. Urban schools should hire more male teachers because the more masculine, sports-minded culturally deprived children disliked a school that had a feminine atmosphere (19–37).

In evaluating models of school improvement, Riessman considered Higher Horizons, a project begun in 1956 in a junior high school in New York City. The Great Cities Program for School Improvement created several similar efforts in thirteen other cities seeking to encourage children from low socioeconomic homes to prepare for and attend college. Higher Horizons improved the children's reading ability, increased their intelligence test scores, and reduced discipline problems and absenteeism. In this program, counselors used several measures besides written intelligence tests to place children in classes. They offered extensive information about colleges and careers, and teachers used texts that portrayed minority men and women in professional capacities such as doctors and lawyers. Administrators organized special remedial reading programs, planned field trips to art museums and concerts, and kept the school buildings open at night so that parents and children could find quiet places away from noisy home situations to read and study (Riessman 98–102).

Despite Higher Horizons' apparent success, Riessman remained skeptical. Although the program considered the conditions in which deprived children lived, it ignored their culture. For example, teachers appeared not to realize that deprived children had trouble with tests because they did not know how to take such tests, had little motivation to take them, and distrusted the examiners. Further, the program did not try to consider the frustration that deprived people feel (109–111).

Was the Culture of Poverty a New Phenomenon?

Like Riessman, Michael Harrington contended that poor people had their own culture. In 1962, Harrington argued that the nature of poverty had changed because the conditions made people different. The problems stemmed from the irony that while people in the United States celebrated the then highest standard of living in the history of the world, nearly 50,000,000 citizens were poor. This other America, as he called it, consisted of unskilled workers, migrant farmworkers, the aged, and the minorities who did not share in the general progress because their entire environment, their lives, and their values prevented them from taking advantage of opportunities. Harrington acknowledged that during the depression many people were poor. Because they were many, however, they could find labor leaders and politicians to help them. In the 1960s, there were fewer poor people and they lacked representatives. Worse, when they did receive help, such as when a school opened in a poor neighborhood, the poor remained deprived. Parents wanted the children to go to work to earn money, and the students felt pent up in the building, dropped out as soon as the law allowed, and, lacking adequate education, never found decent employment (Harrington 1–11).

According to Harrington, the poor were invisible. People who lived in poverty stayed off the beaten track. Their homes were in the country away from highways or set in parts of cities where middle-class people rarely ventured. Whereas affluent children attended suburban schools, poor children stayed in city schools. Urban renewal projects isolated poor people even more. When these projects removed decrepit houses in order to replace them with new, expensive apartment houses, the poor moved into already crowded older slums. Furthermore, when people who lacked proper nourishment and medical care left their neighborhoods, they dressed like more affluent people; mass production had made clothes readily available (2–5).

The problem was that the poor shared a culture of poverty, a cycle that people could not escape and a force that twisted their spirits. For example, poor people were sick more often and for longer periods than middle-class people because they lived in unhygienic conditions, had poor diets, and could not obtain adequate medical care. Thus, they lost wages and could not afford better housing, food, or medical care. Suffering more daily stress, they had more psychiatric problems than did affluent people. Not surprisingly, those lower-class people who avoided serious psychological problems became rigid, suspicious, and fatalistic because everything seemed to turn against them (Harrington 16,129–146).

Although Harrington advocated increased social security, expanded minimum wage protection, and guaranteed comprehensive medical care for everyone, he asserted that there was no simple solution to poverty. Instead, he called on all Americans to engage in a crusade to change the entire environment of the poor. This was essential, he thought, because poverty stemmed from an interdependent system or culture. Harrington asked the federal government to direct this fight; it had the necessary funds, and by nature of its central authority it could coordinate programs of housing, welfare, and urban improvement. Unfortunately, because poverty was invisible, he feared that few people would realize the crusade was necessary (176–184).

How Did the Federal Government Begin the War against Poverty?

But Harrington's call for a moral crusade fell on receptive ears. One story is that as John Kennedy sought a way to distinguish his presidency, he read Harrington's *Other America* and ordered copies for his staff. Alternatively, Kennedy may not have read the book but known of Harrington's argument (M. Katz, *Undeserving* 82). Either way, by the spring of 1963 Kennedy was convinced that a broad war on poverty could unify a host of social programs and rally the nation to a generous cause (Sundquist 7).

Kennedy wanted to tie together four types of reform. The first was an effort to change the slum communities by offering vocational preparation, career counseling, and jobs. The second was a rejection of urban renewal projects that cleared away old buildings and the development of comprehensive efforts to solve the social problems of slums. The third was an attempt to include work training programs with the public financial assistance already given to the poor. And the final type of reform was to include literacy training along with vocational training for adults in order to help the chronically unemployed find work (Sundquist 9–18).

In addition to these social improvements, Kennedy tried to increase school funding. From 1961 until 1963, Kennedy asked Congress to support building construction and teacher salaries for public education. These requests aroused an array of powerful opponents. Organizations such as the U.S. Chamber of Commerce, the National Association of Manufacturers, and the American Farm Bureau opposed federal spending for any welfare purpose. The National Catholic Education Association challenged federal aid unless it went to Catholic schools as well as public schools. Furthermore, many members of Congress feared that if they approved money for teacher salaries, lobbyists from groups such as teachers unions would continually pressure them for increases. In the face of this opposition, Kennedy found two types of public school improvement that legislators could approve: teacher training and experimental instructional projects. The discovery of these acceptable channels of federal aid, combined with the growing public awareness of the problems of poverty, set the direction for efforts to federally fund local schools after Kennedy's assassination on November 22, 1963 (Bailey and Mosher 16–24).

On January 8, 1964, during his first State of the Union Address, President Lyndon B. Johnson called for heroic measures to abolish poverty in the United States. Following the recommendation of the President's Task Force on the War against Poverty, Congress passed and Johnson signed the Economic Opportunity Act of 1964 (EOA). This law created programs such as the Jobs Corps, the Neighborhood Youth Corps, and Adult Basic Education. But, most important, it created the Office of Economic Opportunity (OEO), gave the office independent status, and placed it in the office of the president with a mandate to implement a series of programs dealing with education, vocational training, health, welfare, social security, housing, urban renewal, migrants, and economic development (Bailey and Mosher 31–33).

When the Democrats won a landslide victory in the November 1964 elections, Johnson had reason to believe that the public accepted his call to build a Great Society. In keeping with Kennedy's tendency to rely on task forces, Johnson assembled fourteen working groups made up of experts to generate various parts of a program. The thirteen members on the task force on education selected proposals that centered on the improvement and equalization of educational opportunity. In a very few months, the task force recommendations were crafted into a legislative proposal, approved by Congress, and funded at close to the levels the administration wanted. This was public Law 89–10, the Elementary and Secondary Education Act of 1965 (Bailey and Mosher 37–40).

It is not clear whether the civil rights movement influenced the war on poverty. On the one hand, some presidential advisors contended that Kennedy had a loyal following among African American voters; therefore, he did not envision establishing a poverty program in order to hold their allegiance. Further, Johnson's aides argued that when they approached members of Congress about poverty legislation, they explained that this legislation was not designed to help Black people. At least one aide repeated, "Most poor people are not Black, most Black people are not poor." On the other hand, some presidential advisors contended that the speeches of Martin Luther King, Jr. provided justification for the planning and acceptance of the poverty programs (M. Katz, *Undeserving* 84–85).

On April 11, 1965, President Johnson signed the Elementary and Secondary Education Act (ESEA) in the one-room schoolhouse he had once attended. ESEA had been designed to overcome the traditional sources of resistance to federal funding for public schools. First, the money was for program development, not for buildings or salaries. Second, it fit the apparent consensus between school administrators and members of Congress that the federal government should support help for educationally disadvantaged children. Third, ESEA allowed public schools to make arrangements with private schools to provide services for needy children, thereby ensuring the support of Catholic educators (Bailey and Mosher 31–57, 64–68).

Most of the money approved for ESEA went to Title I, entitled "Better Schooling for Educationally Deprived Children." Unlike other programs in the war on poverty, the United States Office of Education (USOE) administered the ESEA rather than the newly created Office of Economic Opportunity. The job was enormous. For a period of fifteen months, nearly 25,000 school districts in fifty-four states and territories applied for more than $1 billion. All of the money had to help the educationally disadvantaged. However, few school districts had programs that fit the description, and fewer still had any personnel with experience in securing federal aid of any kind. Finally, ESEA demanded more accountability by requiring more exact measures of program evaluation than other social legislation had required in the past (Bailey and Mosher 100–101, 162–163).

Most important, the USOE took the assignment at a difficult time. First, in 1965 the USOE and its parent organization, the U.S. Department of Health, Education, and Welfare (HEW), changed several important departmental procedures and personnel. This caused internal chaos. Second, besides administering the ESEA, the USOE had to oversee the racial desegregation of public schools as required by Title IV of the Civil Rights Act of 1964. This meant that nearly 5,000 school districts submitted materials to the USOE to prove that they did not racially segregate students or faculty and therefore could receive federal aid. The USOE was swamped with work (Bailey and Mosher 78–90, 148).

Despite these difficulties, the work got done. USOE officials consulted with many state officials to construct reasonable procedures for Title I of ESEA. Although they allowed state officials some authority in determining which schools should receive the aid, USOE administrators believed that the money was properly disbursed. Originally, the administration estimated that 5.4 million children would receive services costing about $200 per child. It turned out that in the first fiscal year, 8.3 million children received services costing about $120 per child (Bailey and Mosher 114–119).

What Types of Curriculum Innovations Did the ESEA Sponsor?

During the 1965–66 school year and the summer of 1966, school districts around the country started about 22,000 Title I projects to help children who lived in poverty. For example, the school district in Buckhannon, West Virginia, spent Title I funds on extra teachers to reduce class size, a meal program, vision tests, and correcting glasses. The Grants Pass Oregon school district used the project money to hire teachers and aides who would work in pairs with ten children. The Wilburton, Oklahoma, school district hired a remedial reading teacher, a grade counselor, a speech counselor, and other specialized instructors to work with the children. Teachers in the Pennsury school district in Fallsington, Pennsylvania, found that field trips expanded the children's background and made it easier for them to learn to read (Subcommittee on Education 259–261).

The major focus of the first year of ESEA Title I funds was to provide educationally deprived children with more individual attention. At least 45 percent of the state boards of education emphasized the importance of innovations such as smaller classes, teacher aides, and teams of specialists who focused on the specific needs of each student. Most programs were concerned with developing reading and language skills. Another popular innovation was to offer cultural enrichment experiences to children, many of whom had never left the confines of urban ghettos. These included trips to zoos, visits to planetariums, and tours of museums. School districts serving Mexican Americans, Native Americans, and Puerto Rican children offered programs of teaching English as a foreign language. Many state boards claimed that to make these programs work they had to hire more able and sympathetic teachers (Subcommittee on Education 917–920).

In their reports to the USOE, program administrators claimed that the innovations made dramatic improvements. Unfortunately, more objective measures showed less promise. For example, in 1966 the National Advisory Council on the Education of Disadvantaged Children employed twenty-seven consultants to visit a sample of eighty-six school districts to evaluate the summer programs. Instead of strategically planned, comprehensive programs, the evaluators found that for the most part the projects were fragmented efforts at remediation or vaguely directed enrichment. As a result, the council could not find any widely accepted way of creating effective education for disadvantaged children, although the members believed an acceptable model was available. This model included four main ideas: (1) children should receive individualized instruction; (2) they should discover information or ideas instead of receiving them in lectures; (3) teachers should plan concrete experiences for the children and recognize that disadvantaged children are physical learners; and (4) parents had to be involved in school affairs, the children had to be well fed, and the schoolwork had to correspond to work in the community (National Advisory Council 3–9).

What Was an Example of a Curriculum That Followed an Acceptable Model?

In 1966 Hilda Taba and Deborah Elkins published an example of a curriculum for children of poverty that fit the requirements of the National Advisory Council on the Education of Disadvantaged Children. In *Teaching Strategies for the Culturally Disadvantaged,* Taba and Elkins described sequences of a curriculum originally developed in the 1940s for the children of European immigrants. Taba and Elkins used it in the 1960s with African American sixth and seventh graders in what they called a slum in a northern city. The authors found the curriculum to be appropriate for the two different groups because they shared problems of low self-confidence, poor academic skills, and unclear ambitions (v–vii).

As an example of a well-planned unit, Taba and Elkins described "The Family of Man." This unit consisted of small sequences related to each other. For example, one sequence was Human Hands. The teacher had the students trace their own hands on a piece of drawing paper and list the important things their hands did. Then the teacher placed the headings "work" and "play" on the board in the front of the classroom, asking the students to categorize the things their hands did under the appropriate heading. The next day the teacher read a story to the children and then asked them to itemize the things the people in the story did with their hands. This led to conversations about the relative importance of these activities (88–91).

The lessons moved from school to home because in the evenings the children recorded what they saw adults do with their hands. Each student wrote a paragraph summarizing his or her observations, and the teacher duplicated these and placed them in pamphlets for the students. The children assembled lists of occupations clipped from newspaper ads and made collages from pictures cut from magazines. They categorized or ranked these pictures according to value and the list of things that people did. Later, the students researched historical accounts to see what people in the past had done with their hands and how that work influenced the contemporary world (91–95).

Taba and Elkins urged teachers to tie the sequences together in ways suited to the characteristics of culturally deprived students. In this case, the first topic was concrete and the students' assignment was short. Subsequent lessons involved discussions that took more time and became increasingly abstract. Thus, according to Taba and Elkins, there were six advantages to their model:

1. Students had the chance to increase their attention spans.
2. Students developed verbal facility.
3. Students learned to think abstractly.
4. The lessons made connections between home and school.
5. The progression of activities encouraged students to explore the outside world.
6. The lessons moved into more traditional subject areas (88–95).

Taba and Elkins warned teachers that planning such sequences took time because they had to be organized around children's experiences. Furthermore, teachers had to be careful in determining children's prior experiences. For example, in trying to explain the need for government, one teacher had begun by asking the students if they belonged to any clubs. When the students said they did, she asked them to list the clubs to which they belonged. Unfortunately, these culturally deprived children had not actually joined social organizations, and the lesson fell apart. Like other culturally deprived children, when asked something by a teacher, the students had offered the answer they thought the teacher wanted (273–275).

Therefore, Taba and Elkins recommended that teachers diversify the approach to learning. With culturally deprived children, drawing hands, making booklets, and pasting advertisements are not useless play. These activities hold attention, provide appropriate starting points, and create a sense of accomplishment. Tape recorders can help students who have difficulty reading. These same recorders can play music that has a calming effect while the students cut and paste. Above all, urged Taba and Elkins, the teacher needs to take an interest in the students in order to find ways to help them feel good about themselves.

Describing this attitude as one of caring, they wrote about a teacher who helped a child through a citywide test. He came to her classroom during a free period and they read the questions together. According to Taba and Elkins, such generosity built trust that led to school success (264–281).

Did Classroom Materials Reinforce a Coherent Approach to Compensatory Education?

By the time Taba and Elkins offered their plan, corporations and entrepreneurs had produced a wide range of materials to help disadvantaged children. Attracted by the funds from ESEA, these businesses offered a wide range of materials and approaches to appeal to teachers in different parts of the country. Generally, these materials assumed that the deficits in the children's background caused school failure. However, they did not represent a coherent approach such as the one illustrated by Taba and Elkins.

Curriculum specialists prepared materials to expose children to sights, objects, and sounds not found in low-income urban neighborhoods. Books and lessons contained material about minorities and urban life. These texts emphasized the relevance of school for urban children. With programmed learning machines, children learned individually and avoided the shame of public failure (Rees 100–107).

The materials to prepare teachers to work in the inner city offered a range of activities to help prospective teachers manage the assumed problems and misbehavior of disadvantaged children. However, these kits ignored innovative academic curricula. For example, in 1969 Science Research Associates, a subsidiary of IBM, produced the *Inner City Simulation Laboratory* created by Donald Cruickshank. This kit offered a databook containing accounts of a school and the students in a classroom, replicas of the students' permanent records, and movies and pictures of the students. The records described the students as members of low-income minority families, many of whom received public assistance. Instructions enclosed in the kit asked prospective teachers to do several things: construct sociograms of the interactions in the classroom, describe alternatives for helping students with language problems, identify the students' apparent self-image, and predict the students' expectations of school. Kit materials described incidents with the students that revealed problems with aggressiveness, inability to defer gratification, and concrete rather than abstract orientation, and suggested that parents exacerbated the problems because they resorted to violence in disciplining the children, showed no interest in school, or lived away from the children. According to these materials, these conditions made teaching in the inner city school different than teaching in an affluent suburb.

Did Project Head Start Offer a Reasonable Curriculum?

As with many organizations that originated in Johnson's war on poverty, Project Head Start began with such speed that the planning committee could offer only a vague description of an appropriate curriculum. Head Start was not part of ESEA but grew out of an apparent failure of the Economic Opportunity Act of 1964. The EOA funded community action programs (CAPs) that sought to organize and employ adults living in poverty. This idea seemed to fit Harrington's idea of enlisting the poor people to fight poverty, and it had been tried in cities such as Oakland, California. However, because CAPs were separate from most state agencies, they earned a reputation for undermining the authority of local governments and misusing funds. As a result, many cities would not apply for CAP money. Faced with the possibility that there would be a surplus of more than $150 million in the first year's budget, Sargent Shriver, director of the Office of the Economic Opportunity (OEO), wanted to spend the money on preschool education. As the husband of John F. Kennedy's sister, Shriver shared the family's concern for the education of children with mental retardation. One of Kennedy's siblings was disabled, and his parents had founded the Joseph P. Kennedy, Jr. Foundation to work on the problems related to mental retardation. More important, Shriver believed that programs for young children would not arouse the public opposition caused by the CAP initiatives for adults. He was impressed by some research studies done with Black children at risk for educational failure. After a period of intense stimulation and efforts to change children's attitude toward school, researchers had found that the children's IQ scores increased (Zigler and Muenchow 2–14).

Despite Shriver's initial ideas, Project Head Start did not strive to improve the intelligence of children. Instead, three ideas served as its foundation. The first was to include family members. This strategy came about because a member of the planning committee, Urie Bronfenbrenner, took what he called an ecological view of child development. That is, all programs for children should involve the whole family in order to have lasting impact. Interestingly, different groups interpreted this proposal differently. For the planning committee, maximum feasible parent participation was the best way parents could learn about child development because they participated with the children in the daily activities of the program. Bronfenbrenner believed that this ecological approach served all families in all social classes because it improved family members' relationships. However, CAP leaders in different states interpreted this requirement as calling for parents to run the Head Start centers. CAPs had sought to enable economically deprived adults to develop alternative power structures in order to challenge any institution that threatened to reduce their ability to control their lives (Zigler and Muenchow 15–19, 101–103).

A second emphasis in Head Start was that the projects should not focus on only one aspect of the child such as academic abilities. Instead, the projects should improve several areas. Thus, children were to receive pediatric and neurological examinations; an assessment of nutrition, vision, hearing, and speech; as well as selected tests for problems such as tuberculosis, anemia, and kidney disease (Zigler and Muenchow 18–19).

A third point basic to Head Start was that the children required experiences of success in order to supplant the patterns of failure and frustration common to life in poverty. Consequently, the programs had to maximize opportunities for children to succeed at what they did (Zigler and Muenchow 18–19).

In the summer of 1965, Head Start began trials around the nation, enrolling about 500,000 children in hastily constructed programs. Most centers depended on volunteers, but two hundred colleges and universities offered six-day workshops to prepare more than 44,000 teachers. The Head Start planning committee did not specify an appropriate curriculum but asked all programs to meet the following four objectives: offer flexible schedules, encourage exploration and manipulation of the environment, develop imagination through activities such as puppetry, and provide opportunities to strengthen verbal skills. As a result, the various centers conducted their affairs in relative freedom with poorly trained personnel. Despite these problems, President Johnson announced in August that the summer trials had been successful and would become year-round programs (Zigler and Muenchow 36–55).

Did the Compensatory Education Programs Succeed?

In general, evaluations of compensatory programs to help children from low-income families were disappointing. In 1967 the U.S. Commission on Civil Rights compared the performance of four programs offered in schools with mostly Black students to the academic progress of Black students in mostly White schools in the same school systems. The results were uniformly in favor of racial integration. First, in Syracuse, New York, teachers imitated the Higher Horizons program, providing cultural enrichment and special classroom groupings, with remedial reading and arithmetic exercises. However, the Black students who were transported to White schools improved their academic performance almost twice as much as the students in the special project (*Racial Isolation* 128–130).

Second, when the Commission on Civil Rights looked at a Berkeley, California, program, members found that the teachers reduced class size, employed special staff, improved teaching materials, and involved community members. However, Black children who rode buses to attend formerly White schools learned faster than the African American children in this program (*Racial Isolation* 130–131).

Third, in Seattle, Washington, the school district transferred 242 children from two majority Black elementary schools to formerly all-White elementary schools. The remaining students in the two Black schools received intensive compensatory education and reduced class sizes. The African American students in the White schools did not have special programs and attended large classes. However, comparisons of their scores on reading tests administered at the beginning and end of the year showed that the transferred students learned more than those who stayed and had compensatory instruction (*Racial Isolation* 131–132).

Finally, the Commission on Civil Rights reviewed evaluations of the Philadelphia Education Improvement Program (EIP) that had been introduced in 1963. By 1965 this program included 33,000 children. Because the EIP sought to improve the quality of teaching, the teachers in EIP schools were younger on average than teachers in the district, more responsive to the students, and better able to handle complex subject matter. Almost all the students in these schools were African American. Over a two-year period, the school district traced reading achievement test scores of African American students in EIP schools, of African American students in segregated schools that were not part of the EIP, and of African American students who were transported to White schools. Unfortunately, there was no evidence that the EIP helped students. Although the test scores of EIP students started behind the other groups, the gap remained constant throughout the two years (*Racial Isolation* 132–137).

Despite these findings, the Commission on Civil Rights encouraged school districts to fund programs that included cultural enrichment, better teaching, and other educational services for children who lived in poverty. However, the members concluded that compensatory programs were not likely to succeed in racially and socially isolated school environments. Their report noted that many of these programs sought to improve the children's self-esteem. Unfortunately, the commission members heard testimony that the segregated school buildings where compensatory education took place implied an inferiority that contradicted these efforts (*Racial Isolation* 128–140).

At the same time, Head Start officials began to find disappointing results in preliminary studies of children who participated in the 1965 summer programs. Although the children from the summer programs had scored higher on tests measuring readiness to enter schools than their age-mates who had not been in Head Start, after a few months the two groups of children performed similarly. Several supporters of Head Start contended that the program had been too short. Consequently, the Johnson administration devised Project Follow Through to preserve the Head Start gains through the early years of elementary school (Zigler and Muenchow 56–57).

Despite efforts to improve Head Start, studies continued to show that the project failed. In 1968 the Office of Economic Opportunity commissioned Ohio University and Westinghouse Learning Corporation to make a nationwide study of Head Start programs. Researchers had the difficult task of setting up a method to determine if the 12,927 summer and full-year centers scattered over the continental United States had succeeded. They randomly selected 104 centers, from them chose a total sample of 3,968 children, and divided these children into two groups. In one group, they placed children who had attended Head Start programs in various parts of the United States. In the other group, they placed children who were eligible to attend Head Start programs but had not. All of the children were in the first, second, or third grade, and the two groups roughly matched the children according to sex, race, age, grade level, and attendance in the same school district. Researchers compared the children's cognitive abilities on well-known standardized tests such as the Stanford Achievement Test and the Illinois Test of Psycholinguistic Abilities. In addition, the research staff developed measures of affective development. The results were grim. Children who attended the summer Head Start did not score better than the other children on the tests of cognitive ability. Children who attended the full-year program scored higher in the first grade, but did not score better on measures of cognitive ability at grades 2 or 3. Finally, there was no improvement of affective development in areas such as self-concept or classroom behavior (Cicirelli 235–243).

Of course, some compensatory education programs enjoyed positive evaluations. For example, studies of the effectiveness of the television show *Sesame Street* indicated that children who watched learned basic skills such as counting, identifying the names of letters and numbers, and sorting objects. They also had improved attitudes toward children of different races. Primarily intended for disadvantaged children at home without Head Start, *Sesame Street* began in 1968 with curricular aims far more limited than those of a classroom. After its initial success, however, two problems appeared. First, the show expanded its goals in the second year. At first the show taught children to classify objects on the basis of a single criterion. In the second year, they moved to classifying objects on the basis of two criteria. Researchers found that children did not learn the more complicated material as thoroughly as they had learned the simpler. Second, the children most in need were least likely to watch. Although the program quickly acquired a large audience, middle-class children watched more frequently than children from lower-class families. Worse, the most disadvantaged children watched the least (Ball and Bogatz 11–24).

Why Did the Programs Fail?

There is no clear reason why compensatory programs failed. Possible explanations fall into six main categories: (1) the evaluations were inaccurate; (2) the war on poverty should have focused on something other than education; (3) the curriculum was of less importance than the peer group; (4) the disadvantaged students were genetically unable to take advantage of the special training; (5) the programs tried to change something that was not a problem; and (6) the programs themselves caused the failure.

An example from the first category appeared in 1970 when two statisticians argued that the Westinghouse and Ohio University evaluation of Head Start was incorrect. They claimed that the ways researchers chose the groups of children caused inaccurate results. When Head Start began, the teachers recruited the most needy children. Three years later, program evaluators sought untreated children in the same community to serve as the control group to compare to those children Head Start had already enrolled. The statisticians argued that the untreated children could have been more able at the outset than the group the teachers initially brought into Head Start. Thus, although the researchers found the Head Start children performing similarly to other children, it was possible that those Head Start children would have performed worse without the program. The statisticians concluded that this bias was a problem in evaluating any compensatory education program because the programs recruited the most needy children. In a true experiment, the participants in the control and the experimental groups had to be chosen at random (Campbell and Erlebacher 185–210).

An example from the second category of explanations came from Daniel P. Moynihan. Although Moynihan did not criticize compensatory education, he argued that educational changes alone could not succeed in improving the lives of underprivileged children. In March 1965, he advised President Johnson that the war on poverty should focus on strengthening the family structure of African Americans. Quoting sociologists such as E. Franklin Frazier, Moynihan argued that three centuries of injustice had distorted the lives of African Americans resulting in what he called a tangle of pathologies. As an example of this tangle, he demonstrated that from 1948 to 1962 the number of Aid to Dependent Children cases rose and fell with the rate of unemployment among African American males. Moynihan concluded that family instability reduced educational achievement (Rainwater and Yancey 93).

At first, Moynihan appeared to influence public policy. In June 1965, President Johnson gave a speech at Howard University that Richard Gordon and Moynihan had written claiming that the federal government had to create conditions enabling low-income families to stay together. Without strong families, the aid to schools and other forms of public assistance would not break the circle of poverty. After this speech, critics began to attack the ideas. Many civil rights leaders contended that Moynihan's report made the behavior of low-income people appear to be the reason for their poverty. Several scholars contended that the African American family was not disintegrating and the rise of female headed families was not as great as Moynihan implied. As a result of the controversy, his report diminished in importance (Rainwater and Yancey 125–130, 246–270).

The third category of explanations for the failure of compensatory programs was that curriculum did not influence children's academic achievement as much as peer group associations. An example of this possibility came from the largest survey of schools taken up to that time. In 1966 the U.S. Department of Health, Education, and Welfare released a survey concerning the availability of educational opportunities in the United States. Congress mandated this survey when it approved the Civil Rights Act of 1964. Directed by James Coleman, the survey revealed that most children attended segregated schools and that African American students had less access to physics, chemistry, and language laboratories. The minority pupils had fewer books in their libraries and insufficient textbooks. Yet these minority pupils needed good school facilities, curriculum, and teachers in order to succeed academically even more than did majority pupils (Coleman, et al. *Equality* 3–22).

Despite these differences in materials, Coleman noted that the schools were remarkably similar in the way they related to the achievement of their pupils when their socioeconomic backgrounds were taken into account. That is, the teachers' ability, the availability of books, or the condition of the school did not seem to influence a pupil's achievement as much as the educational backgrounds and aspirations of the other students in the school. Coleman claimed that this effect influenced White students less than it affected Black students. Consequently, if White pupils from homes supportive of education entered a school where most of the pupils did not come from such homes, their achievements might not differ from what they would have been in a school composed of students like themselves. However, if educationally weak minority pupils were placed with schoolmates with strong educational backgrounds, their achievement would improve (Coleman, et al. *Equality* 21–22).

Although Coleman's findings were a strong argument for racial integration, many educators expressed surprise at the possibility that schools did not influence achievement. Some educators argued that if spending money to train teachers, buy books, and equip learning laboratories could not improve the abilities of disadvantaged children, the underpinnings of compensatory educational programs were misplaced (Mosteller and Moynihan 28–30).

The fourth type of argument was that disadvantaged children were genetically unable to profit from special training. In 1969 Arthur Jensen claimed that standardized tests focused on a specific form of intelligence, and programs such as Head Start as well as schools sought to improve this type of intelligence. However, the children had to have the necessary neural structures to profit from these educational experiences. Unfortunately, these neural structures were inherited from the parents, and lower-class people appeared to have a different genetic makeup than middle-class people. Consequently, Jensen believed, genetics doomed compensatory education. Instead of trying to help poor children learn academics, schools should offer ways for the children to utilize the strengths they had. Thus, Jensen concluded, in order to realize the ideal of universal education, schools should provide a range of educational methods and goals to accommodate the diversity of mental abilities found among children (3, 111–117).

The fifth category of explanations for the failure of compensatory education was that the curriculum materials were built on unproven or false assumptions. For example, Irwin Katz contended that the materials for inner-city schools were based on four widely accepted notions of school failure. One explanation was that the authoritarianism of the parents and the parents' early withdrawal from supervising caused children to reject all adult authority. Another explanation was that the early experiences of African American children caused them to distrust all people and they carried this distrust to school. Another view was that during slavery African Americans developed patterns of childrearing that discouraged personal achievement, and they carried these practices to the present. A fourth view was that because most African American families were matriarchal, the children lacked father figures. As a result, the male children became impulsive and dependent. The point Katz made was that there was little evidence to answer important questions about these four different assumptions. For example, it was not clear that the personalities of poor children were specifically different from those of affluent children or that those differences led to school failure. Furthermore, there was little research showing that any unique personality traits among low-income children derived from their family life or if the traits could be modified in schools (13–27).

Another criticism of the assumptions underlying compensatory education came in 1970 from Joan Baratz and Stephen Baratz, who argued that programs such as Head Start failed because they were based on racist views such as that African Americans used limited and poorly structured speech. Accepting this assertion as true, Head Start programs sought to remedy this deficient language in order to help the children learn to think more complexly and thereby increase their success in school. Furthermore, evidence to the contrary did not weaken teachers' beliefs. When studies showed that Head Start did not increase the children's cognitive abilities, officials sought to increase the length of the programs. Although the Baratzes acknowledged that African American language was a hindrance in mainstream society, they denied that it hindered the development of abstract thinking. They claimed that African Americans used a structured language system. Therefore, Head Start programs should abandon a deficit model of poor children's language and accept the children's culture as valid. The Baratzes contended that teachers could use what they called the Negro dialect to teach children to succeed in school. In this way, the children would learn about the mainstream and at the same time maintain their cultural heritage.

The sixth category of explanation for the failure of compensatory education was that the programs themselves caused the failure. For example, in the 1980s Henry Levin noticed that disadvantaged students fell further behind other students each year they were in school. The teachers were not at fault because they retained hope and interest in the students. According to Levin, the problem was that compensatory programs slowed down instruction on the assumption that disadvantaged students needed extra time to learn. This caused both teachers and students to reduce their expectations and students to feel stigmatized; the rate of learning to decrease while mainstream students moved through more materials at increasingly faster rates; the repetition of low-level exercises to dull interest and prevent learning processes such as problem solving; and remedial programs to shut out the community of the home members from school activities (H. Levin 31–32).

Did the Failure of Compensatory Education Influence National Politics?

The controversy over the value of compensatory education offered President Richard Nixon a way to solve his own political problems. During 1969 Nixon had vetoed several bills calling for increased educational appropriations. National education groups resisted these vetoes and used them to criticize the administration. To relieve this ill will and create a distinctive educational policy, Nixon chose to emphasize research. On March 3, 1970, he proposed the creation of the National Institute of Education (NIE). Claiming that the federal government should not simply spend money on education, he asserted that the job of the institute would be to discover which programs offered the most return for the investment (Sproul, Weiner, and Wolf 33–34).

In June 1972, Congress passed and Nixon signed the NIE legislation. However, by then the NIE had few supporters. The leading advocate, Daniel P. Moynihan, had resigned his position as presidential advisor and returned to Harvard University, leaving the White House without anyone to advance the plan. Newspaper commentators described the formation of the NIE as Nixon's way of criticizing federal efforts to help schools. Educators feared that the institute was a way to fight the problems of schools with words rather than deeds. Although the American Educational Research Association (AERA) should have championed such an institution, the executive officer for the AERA gave only his personal views during congressional hearings about creating the NIE; the association had no provision for making public statements. Finally, most Congress members did not support the idea of educational research; they did not think it was something voters appreciated or considered useful. Despite these disadvantages, the NIE began with a budget of $110 million (Sproul, Weiner, and Wolf 66–77, 94).

Unfortunately, when Congress reconsidered the NIE budget, it reduced those appropriations. In 1974, for example, the Senate subcommittee on appropriations recommended that the agency receive no federal money. At best, the NIE received modest support from educational groups to restore its funds. National teacher organizations saw little to gain from the NIE and focused their lobbying on the multibillion-dollar budget of the educational division of the HEW. The president of the AERA submitted a statement on behalf of the institute but did not appear during congressional hearings. Local educators complained that NIE activities did not help elementary or secondary education. One state superintendent stated that the NIE repeatedly studied the same topics and never advanced (Sproul, Weiner, and Wolf 72–99).

Although critics feared that Nixon would use the NIE to cut educational budgets, the principle of federal aid to low-income students was entrenched. As a result, Nixon made little effort to cut ongoing ESEA projects, and educational aid to states and districts increased during his presidency. Further, the NIE persisted and came to support many important and successful projects (Cusick 137–141).

The failure of compensatory programs brought about three changes in those programs. First, educators disregarded the concept of cultural deprivation, arguing that the children from disadvantaged circumstances shared only the condition of being at risk for failure. Second, although evaluations of compensatory programs continued to reveal their failure, these studies often expressed the problems as indications of the need for increased efforts. Third, educators looked for procedures to improve entire schools or districts rather than looking for an effective curriculum. Each of these changes deserves further investigation.

Did New Measures or a Different Label Change the Curriculum?

The measures and the label changed as the failure of compensatory education became evident. By 1973 the National Advisory Council on the Education of Disadvantaged Children acknowledged that compensatory education did not improve children's academic achievement. However, they claimed that researchers should have considered other goals such as changes in affective behavior before judging the programs to be failures. Therefore, the council report recommended that programs be evaluated on the basis of the five following factors: attendance of students, number of discipline problems, math achievement, reading achievement, and parent attendance at meetings. Furthermore, although the council accepted the term "educationally deprived children," the report noted that these children came from varied backgrounds and suffered a range of disabilities that kept them from achieving at grade level. Because the children's needs differed, innovations might succeed in one school district and fail in another (National Advisory Council 7–20).

In view of this complicated situation, the council report recommended that school districts tailor their approaches in ways consistent with the needs of their communities. In 1973 the bulk of Title I ESEA funds supported basic skills instruction in reading and math. Because the legislation did not make this a restriction, however, some cities took different approaches. Educators in Rochester, New York, had used Title I ESEA funds to teach English as a second language. In 1971 in Riverside, California, educators used such funds to reduce dropouts caused by drug abuse, whereas school officials in Detroit had spent the monies on continuing education for pregnant adolescent women (National Advisory Council 20).

To spur innovation, the council report described 216 successful projects in different states. In general, however, among these reports there were repeated efforts to provide children with immediate gratification, individualized instruction, and specially designed reading materials. In Salt Lake City, Utah, for example, students practiced their reading and math skills by working at small assignments that were evaluated immediately. The students kept track of their progress using a flowchart and received rewards called "skins" that they could convert into cash (58). In Cleveland, Ohio, a clinician, a psychologist, a nurse, and a speech and hearing specialist examined the students. On the basis of the diagnosis, a remediation team wrote an instructional plan and a reading specialist carried out the remediation for one hour a day, five days a week (61). Finally, in Denison, Texas, students who needed special assistance in reading development went to a laboratory where teachers used high-interest materials with small groups of students to improve their basic reading skills (National Advisory Council 77).

ESEA Title I funds provided support for schools that enrolled a high percentage of students from low-income families. In 1981 Congress approved and President Ronald Reagan signed the Education and Consolidation Act. The programs for deprived children provided by ESEA Title I were transferred to Chapter I of this new legislation. The goal of Chapter I funds remained to provide support for districts heavily populated with low-income, low-achieving students. As was the case with Title I, the funds flowed to those students who needed special services. As a result, the children receiving the aid did not have to be poor. In fact, by 1976–77, only 42 percent of the students receiving Title I funds came from low-income families. Typically, however, Black and Hispanic students received the aid. Further, the amounts of money continued to increase. By 1988 Chapter I was budgeted at $4.3 billion. Most of this money went to increase reading and mathematics achievement of low-achieving students (Slavin 3–11).

Under Chapter I, as with Title I, the help was to be supplemental to regular class instruction. As a result, the predominant method of delivering remedial instruction to low-achieving students was in what were called "pull-out rooms." That is, during the school day students would leave their regular classrooms at predetermined times to visit a special teacher. This resulted in several problems. The remedial material was often not coordinated with the regular classroom instruction, so regular instruction was fragmentary. Students interrupted classroom lessons by leaving or entering at odd times, and they lost time traveling between classrooms. In addition, several studies indicated that instruction in these pull-out rooms was low-level training on processes such as perception and motor skills. It was often not academically based (Stein, Leinhart, and Bickel 145–159).

Because Chapter I served a wide range of students suffering from a range of disabilities, educators referred to the children as being at risk for failure. This term "at risk" became a nonspecific label for low-achieving youngsters who could profit from any one of a number of educational programs. For example, in a handbook written for teachers in 1993, Richard Sagor defined at-risk students as those unlikely to graduate on time with skills necessary for participation in work, cultural events, or civic affairs. He applied the label to children who suffered from some sort of physical handicap, developmental disability, or the unwillingness of the institution to help them. The suggestions he offered for teachers and administrators were as varied as implementing a multicultural curriculum and employing mastery learning (33–78).

In general, the changes in the methods of evaluating compensatory education made it more difficult for anyone to determine that the programs failed. At the same time, the definition of children who could profit from instruction supported by federal aid expanded, and more types of instruction were considered to be useful.

How Did Failure Indicate the Need for Extended Efforts?

Although research studies continued to show the weaknesses of programs such as Head Start, researchers expressed those failures as a need for increased efforts. For example, in 1985 evaluators released a synthesis of more than 210 evaluations of Head Start. Unfortunately, all the studies showed that Head Start programs did not provide lasting cognitive benefits. One year after enrollment in a Head Start program, Head Start children scored higher on tests of cognitive ability, social behavior, achievement motivation, and self-esteem than children in comparison groups. By the end of the second school year, however, there were no meaningful differences on any of these measures. This failure was true no matter how the studies were designed or what measures the researchers used (McKey, et al. 7–14).

While synthesizing the research, the authors found some positive results. For example, a few studies showed that Head Start children were less likely to fail a grade in school or to be assigned to special education classes. But the clearest successes were in the children's health. By providing medical and dental examinations, Head Start had reduced children's health problems, and the programs had also improved the children's motor development. Also on the positive side, the parents of the children praised Head Start programs, sizable numbers of them participated in the programs, and the children whose parents participated a great deal performed better on cognitive tests. Unfortunately, Head Start did not seem to have a long-term effect on the parents' childrearing practices, attitude toward education, or behavior toward health (McKey, et al. 14–21).

A comparison of the influence of the type of program was disappointing. That is, children in highly structured academic curricula showed more cognitive gains than children in traditional or Montessori curricula, but these gains faded over time. Interestingly, those programs that followed some theory of child development such as a Piagetian model seemed to make more immediate difference than programs that did not follow any similar theory (McKey, et al. 14–21).

Wanting to show Head Start in the best light, advocates found two ways that the analysis of studies suggested a need for increased efforts. First, they decided that early studies might have caused the disappointing results. After 1970 Head Start programs became better organized and the teachers were better trained. Thus, advocates argued more research was needed to see if these changes had beneficial effects. Second, advocates blamed elementary schools for not stimulating or supporting the children as effectively as the Head Start programs. In order for children to retain cognitive gains, Head Start programs and schools should use similar and developmentally appropriate methods. Therefore, advocates called for closer partnerships between Head Start programs and elementary schools (McKey, et al. i, 22–23).

How Did Reformers Try to Redesign Schools or Districts?

In the 1980s, Henry Levin found that students in compensatory education fell behind mainstream students because of the slow pace of remedial instruction. His answer was to accelerate the learning of these students so that they would catch up with the others. In other words, schools should abandon the idea of separate gifted programs and offer the same enriched education to all students. However, Levin did not offer a curriculum that would do this. Instead, he suggested that each school follow a process of reform wherein administrators and faculty members created a shared idea of academic excellence and a plan to achieve it (32–36).

In 1986 Levin established the Accelerated Schools Project at Stanford University to spread his message. By 1992 he claimed to have enabled more than fifty schools in California, Missouri, Illinois, and Texas to follow his plan. The schools followed three principles. First, the faculty and administrators worked together to draft a vision statement that became the measure for all subsequent actions. Second, the schools used the strengths of their students, such as the ability to work manually or a natural curiosity about life, to form appropriate instructional methods. They enlisted parents and community leaders to help. Third, all decision making was collaborative. This meant that administrators, teachers, parents, and students worked in task forces to decide the school's curriculum, instructional strategies, and governance. According to participants, this model of school reform was successful (McCarthy and Levin 250–263).

Private philanthropies encouraged even more wide-scale reform efforts. For example, in 1987 The Anne Casey Foundation in Greenwich, Connecticut, offered the City of Dayton, Ohio, and nine other cities $20,000 each to develop proposals targeting the needs of at-risk youth. The Casey Foundation named these programs New Futures to indicate that cities would enlist local leaders to create environments that encouraged children to succeed. The Casey Foundation took the view that the adolescents were at risk for academic failure, leaving school, and becoming pregnant because community institutions failed to equip them with the expectations, opportunities, and supports necessary to become responsible adults (Watras 306–307).

In 1988 the Casey Foundation awarded Dayton $10 million to fund its proposal. Four other cities, Lawrence, Massachusetts; Little Rock, Arkansas; Pittsburgh, Pennsylvania; and Savannah, Georgia, received similar awards. From local sources, Dayton added $10 million to fund the five-year undertaking (Watras 307).

Unlike the other cities, Dayton's plan concentrated on the schools. The program centered on two pilot middle schools where the teachers had joined together in clusters, each working with about 150 students. The New Futures program selected four objectives: to reduce school leaving, improve academic performance, enhance youth employment, and prevent teenage pregnancies. The key to the program was the use of twenty-five community associates hired to serve as case managers. Each associate would serve as an advocate for fifty students and introduce them to appropriate human service personnel who could enhance natural support systems such as family, friends, and church. These community associates were to become catalysts for changing the ways youth services and schools operated (Watras 307–309).

Unfortunately, after five years and $20 million, the New Futures project in Dayton could not show that it had increased graduation rates, improved employment opportunities or college admissions, or reduced teenage pregnancies. Although New Futures associates had not helped their students, they had collected extensive, accurate statistics showing that in Dayton too many children lived in poverty, too many teenage children had babies, and only 31 percent of the students in the Dayton city schools graduated on time. In 1994 the agency published a plea for citizens and governmental agencies to work harder to reduce these problems, released its employees, and closed its doors (Watras 316–318).

Did Anthropologists Think That Poor People Formed Unique Cultures?

The rationale for many innovations to help the poor was that low-income people had their own culture. Although in 1961 Frank Riessman used the term "culturally deprived" to describe the children who lived in poverty, he believed that these children and their families possessed a culture of their own developed from coping with a difficult environment (1–3). In keeping with the then popular concerns of educators, Riessman identified this culture among African Americans in urban centers, but he included other groups as well. When Michael Harrington adopted the term "culture of poverty," he applied it to a wide range of groups. For Harrington, the term expressed the idea that because of their material conditions poor people held a set of attitudes and values that hindered their ability to succeed. Although Harrington did not give anyone credit for this phrase, he borrowed it from anthropologist Oscar Lewis. Later, Lewis wrote that Harrington misunderstood the term's meaning (Rigdon 170, 244).

However, Lewis may have used the notion of a culture of poverty as superficially as Harrington. Lewis had studied with prominent anthropologists such as Ruth Benedict and Ralph Linton who trained him to keep his personal and political views separate from his work. His wife, Ruth Maslow, was the sister of the psychologist, Abraham Maslow. As he matured, Lewis thought of himself as going beyond his teachers and combining anthropology, psychology, art, and political persuasion. He and his many assistants wanted to retain their scientific orientation, but they concentrated on writing reports that avoided scientific jargon and precise methods of presentation. They wrote in ways accessible to any moderately literate person. Most important, he dedicated his life to showing the ways in which capitalism harmed lower-class people, and this crusade affected his conclusions (Rigdon 11–20, 135–149).

In 1959 Lewis used the phrase "culture of poverty" in his study *Five Families: Mexican Case Studies in the Culture of Poverty.* Trying to expand his concept, Lewis followed up his studies of the five families with intensive studies of two of the families in the *Children of Sanchez* and *Pedro Martinez.* In 1968 Lewis published a more complete explanation of his thesis in *A Study of Slum Culture.* Acknowledging that it might be more correctly called a subculture of poverty, he preferred the shorter form. This culture of poverty was the people's reaction to their marginal position in a class-stratified, capitalistic society and their way of coping with the realization that they would never attain the goals held by people in other social classes. Lewis thought this culture perpetuated itself from generation to generation so that by the time children were six years old, they could not take advantage of opportunities to improve (1–7).

Lewis argued that people in the culture of poverty did not participate in the dominant society. They were not members of political parties; rarely used museums, banks, or art galleries; and though they held middle-class values, they did not follow them. For example, women said they believed in marriage, but they did not legally marry. Instead, they lived with men. From these free unions, they had children and what appeared to be a marriage. However, if the men became unreliable or dominating, the women could easily leave them (7–8).

Among the families of people in poverty, Lewis noted several identifying traits. The protected stage of childhood common to the middle classes did not exist among the families in this culture. Children were initiated into sex early. Frequently, fathers abandoned wives and children. There was a tendency toward mother-centered families, a disposition toward authoritarianism, a lack of privacy, and a verbal emphasis on family solidarity that was rarely achieved because siblings competed strenuously for limited goods and maternal affection (10).

On the individual level, Lewis asserted, there were strong feelings of helplessness and inferiority. Other personality traits included weak ego structure, lack of impulse control, an inability to defer gratification, and strong present-time orientation. At the same time, there was a sense of resignation and fatalism and a widespread belief in male superiority. Although people were sensitive to status distinctions, they had no sense of class consciousness. They could not see connections between their own troubles and problems elsewhere in the world (10–11).

Although Lewis believed that the material conditions of poverty produced this culture, he believed that people could be desperately poor and not share it. This was because the core of this culture was destroyed by any movement that organized and gave people hope. For example, the civil rights movement accomplished more by improving the self-image of African Americans than by anything else. Further, the Castro revolution in Cuba had given impoverished Cubans a sense of power and importance that eliminated juvenile delinquency and attendant problems of poverty even though material conditions remained unchanged (Lewis 12–14). To prove this idea, the last project Lewis undertook before he died in 1970 was an effort to study the effects on poor people of socialism in Cuba (Gans, *War* 25, 157).

In the same way that mass movements could destroy the culture of poverty, traditional cultures could have little material wealth yet the people would feel integrated in society and not share the culture of poverty. Further, the culture of poverty differed in accord with national identity. That is, he argued, slum dwellers in Mexico had some closer identifications with the history and traditions of their country than did the low-income people in Puerto Rico. Thus, the Mexicans moved further away from the core characteristics of the culture of poverty (Lewis 16–17).

Lewis acknowledged that there were strengths to the culture of poverty. For example, living in the present enhanced people's capacity for spontaneity and their enjoyment of the sensual. However, Lewis refused to idealize the poor. In order for the victims of the culture of poverty to join the middle class, he claimed, they needed psychiatric treatment. Because masses of people could not receive such care, revolutionaries might seek to organize the poor and thereby give them a sense of belonging, power, and leadership. Consequently, although Lewis believed that poor people should have more economic opportunities, he thought that it was easier to eliminate poverty than reduce the influence of the culture of poverty (19–21).

Other anthropologists made similar arguments about various groups. For example, from October 1957 until May 1958, Herbert Gans lived in the West End of Boston, Massachusetts, among native-born Americans of Italian parentage. Gans was a sociologist and an urban planner. Because many critics complained that professionals use middle-class values to direct urban renewal projects, Gans wanted to find out what a slum was like. In

1961 he published the results of his participant observation research in *The Urban Villagers,* in which he claimed that West-Enders were not frustrated in their pursuit of middle-class values. Their way of life constituted a distinct working-class subculture that bore little resemblance to middle-class life (*Urban* xiii–xiv).

Gans noted that the culture was a satisfactory way of adapting to the opportunities society made available, though he doubted that it was as beneficial for people as the professional upper-middle-class subculture. As an urban planner, Gans noted that the values of this subculture prevented the people from participating in formal organizations. They allowed political machines and labor unions to defend their interests. When these failed, they turned to authoritarianism and violent protest to express their views. Gans found that West-Enders could not understand the need for bureaucracies to set objectives and make plans. Instead, the people in the working-class culture depended on family and friends for help. Although this insulated them from the wider society, they rejected professional caretakers such as medical specialists and psychotherapists even when there was no cost. At the same time, their dependence on their own group, the low value they assigned to privacy, and the general conservatism of working-class people penalized any who deviated from this mind-set. However, Gans distinguished this culture from the culture of lower-class people; he thought that the female-based lower-class family bred pathologies among men such as unwillingness to develop skills to hold jobs, doubts about self-worth, and personal instability that led to alcoholism, drug addiction, and mental illness (*Urban* 295–305).

In 1965 Jack Weller made similar observations about life in contemporary Appalachia. Weller was a Presbyterian minister in Whitesville, West Virginia. A native of New York, Weller found that the usual ways of working with people and with committees failed in West Virginia. On reading *Urban Villagers* by Gans, Weller came to the conclusion that the people of southern Appalachia were similar to Boston's West-Enders. Although Weller thought that most people living in Appalachia belonged to this folk culture, not all people bore its stamp. When Weller listed the values of this group, he included many that Lewis had chronicled: fatalism, present orientation, and a belief that only friends and family will help in times of need. Like Gans, Weller noted that the lower-class elements of this culture were pathological. He could see no advantages to the way the people in his area lived. They resisted new ideas, had overly permissive childrearing practices that led to lives based on personal feelings, and lacked long-term goals. To show the limits this culture placed on people, Weller recalled talking to a mother whose son had become interested in rock formations and started collecting rocks. "I finally shamed him out of it," she proudly announced (3–8, 150–160).

Whereas Weller's interest in the ways of Appalachians was ministerial, lawyers used the concept of a culture of Appalachia to win court cases. Kai Erickson was drawn to Buffalo Creek, West Virginia, as a consultant in a suit against the Pittston Company. One of that company's subsidiaries, Buffalo Mining Company, owned a dam made of a massive pile of coal waste. In February 1972, the dam collapsed, sending a thirty-foot wave down the valley that killed 125 people and destroyed more than one thousand homes. The survivors banded together, selected a leader, and employed the firm of Arnold and Porter to represent them in court. They won $13.5 million (Stern ix–10, 299).

An important part of the case was Erikson's testimony that the disaster disrupted the sense of community that was more important to these people than it might have been to others. Erikson characterized the culture of Appalachia as a tangle of contradictory tendencies. First, the mountaineer loved tradition but respected personal liberty. Second, the culture was characterized by a contrast between self-assertion and resignation. Third, the people were group-centered and self-centered at the same time. Fourth, they took pride in the ability to survive hardship but feared illness to the point of hypochondria. Fifth, they strove for independence yet possessed a need for dependence. In fact, to Erikson, it appeared that mountaineers became independent because the group expected it of them. According to Erikson, these people suffered more severe emotional disorders as a result of the flood than mainstream people had suffered in similar disasters. A collective trauma quickly followed the individual shocks people felt and persisted long after the community was destroyed (84–93).

Were the Anthropologists Wrong?

To some extent, the failure of compensatory education disproved the theory of a culture of poverty although the concept might have collapsed on its own. That is, Lewis's concept of a culture of poverty did not arise from his case studies. Although his subjects were members of a broad lower-income group, they differed so much that they did not clearly represent a cultural orientation. For example, in *Five Families* Lewis chose people who had varied lifestyles and different incomes; one was relatively wealthy. This differentiation occurred because Lewis made the culture's criteria fluid. However, it weakened his thesis; he could not show what these people shared (Rigdon 52–55).

When the war on poverty began in the 1960s, Lewis found himself attacked by critics on both sides. On the one hand, he seemed to be arguing that capitalism caused the problems of poverty. Consequently, conservatives argued he was mistaken. On the other hand, he appeared to argue that poor people had certain characteristics that had to change. Thus, left-wing writers argued that Lewis thought poor people made their own troubles. Sometimes Lewis defended his notion of the culture of poverty by calling it an idea to be tested. At other times, facing left-leaning critics, he called the culture an adaptation that enhanced the people's chances of survival. Finally, in 1968 he backed away from the thesis and claimed that he had never intended the concept to be a summary of his case studies (Rigdon 87–99).

In 1968 Charles Valentine published *Culture and Poverty* to criticize the then popular conceptions of poverty. He claimed that scholars such as E. Franklin Frazier, Nathan Glazier, and Daniel P. Moynihan repeated the theme of the disorganization of life of low-income urban African Americans. Calling these studies exaggerated, he noted that they presented the poor as lacking any culture. On the other hand, Valentine noted, Lewis presented a theory of an international culture of poverty, but the behaviors he listed were not patterns as much as random acts. Although Valentine found the work of Herbert Gans methodologically superior to that of the other scholars, he criticized Gans for writing that lower-class people manifested pathological behaviors. Gans had based this observation on other people's reports. Therefore, Valentine concluded, the problem with all the assessments of the culture of the poor was that researchers failed to offer sufficient documentation to prove their assertions. Not one of them demonstrated that the people they described actually held the values or engaged in the behaviors that the researcher reported (20–21, 70–76, 112, 127).

In 1982, writing an expanded edition of *Urban Villagers,* Herbert Gans retracted the description of the lower class as pathological. Despite the fact that rates of mental illness are higher among the lower class than the working class, he acknowledged that most people in any group were not pathological. He added that his comment had turned a shortcoming of the U.S. economy into a medical problem, thereby diverting attention from the necessary policies designed to reduce the economic and political inequalities that cause the pathologies. Gans also withdrew his statements about the pathological nature of the matriarchal African American family. Even though female-headed families increased more rapidly among Blacks, they had become increasingly numerous among White families since World War II. Single-parent families appeared pathological because there were higher delinquency rates among boys from single-parent families. However, Gans conceded that this difference may have resulted from judges sentencing such boys to correctional institutions because they believed a mother alone could not control them (*Urban* 287–294).

In his revision of *Urban Villagers,* Gans maintained his view that there was a working-class subculture. However, he saw this culture as situational rather than a condition passed from parents to children. That is, whereas Lewis saw the culture of poverty as permanent, Gans saw the culture as changeable. According to Gans, parents developed an orientation because of the constraints with which they coped, but they did not pass this view on to their children. As a result, Gans decided that poor people and working-class people could accept opportunities for economic advancement as well as people in any other class. Their culture did not condemn them to poverty as Harrington had asserted (279–284).

Although sociologists backed away from the idea of a culture of poverty, a version of the notion continued among educational researchers. In 1977 Paul Willis published a study of twelve working-class nonacademic lads from a small English city he called Hammertown. Entitling his book *Learning to Labor,* Willis sought to show how working-class kids obtain working-class jobs. In his study, Willis showed that the lads reproduced themselves as working-class adults similar to their parents. That is, by resisting the schools' authority, disrupting classes, being truant, and refusing to acquire credentials, the lads disqualified themselves from the opportunity to enter middle-class jobs. Their single choice was unskilled manual labor (Aronowitz ix–xiii).

Other studies followed building on the idea that lower-class children failed because they resisted the schools' dominance. For example, in a study of Jamaican teenage boys in Toronto, Canada, Patrick Solomon decided that the children formed their own culture in order to resist the school. These students in a lower-track vocational high school called themselves the "Jocks." They exaggerated their language, a patois from the West Indies, in order to increase the distance between themselves and other students and teachers. They wore special clothes such as army digs and sported a Rasta look with long unkempt or braided hair. They disregarded school rules and treated other students with contempt. Solomon called this behavior resistance, and he believed it was rooted in the social status of the Jamaican people in Canada. However, he thought the structure of the school exacerbated the difficulties. For example, by not knowing the Jamaican culture, the teachers were vulnerable to the Jocks' complaints that a particular rule violated their heritage. Further, by encouraging the Jocks' interest in athletics, the school increased their academic failures.

Did Compensatory Education Increase Racial or Social Segregation?

The critic William Ryan argued that the folklore surrounding the ideas of cultural deprivation and the culture of poverty forestalled questions about larger social changes. Calling it "blaming the victim," Ryan contended that these approaches sought to change the child and ignored suggestions to change the system such as bringing about racial desegregation or opening school governance to community residents (33–35).

To some extent, Ryan was correct. For example, the *Inner City Simulation Laboratory* described earlier reinforced the idea that, because most schools had distinct groups of children, segregation was reasonable. At the same time, however, the *Inner City Simulation Laboratory* taught prospective teachers that children from low-income homes thought differently than children from advantaged homes. The hope behind such an effort was that prospective teachers would become more tolerant and better able to offer constructive lesson plans. This was the aim of many ethnic sensitivity courses that boards of education offered practicing teachers and administrators when desegregation took place.

Furthermore, the term "cultural deprivation" did not have to imply racial segregation. Martin Duetsch, a professor of early childhood education, thought that low-income children learned differently than affluent children. However, he believed that racially mixed schools were essential to the creation of democratic social order. In his perspective, the concept of cultural deprivation could help teachers work with diverse, heterogeneous classes. He warned teachers against grouping students by abilities because this would segregate the classrooms (281–294).

Although Ryan charged that school boards and administrators used the concept of cultural deprivation to reinforce their own authority, this was not always the case. For example, in Dayton, Ohio, arguments of cultural deprivation justified a procedure to allow neighborhood residents to control the schools. This happened in 1969 when a group of residents from an inner-city neighborhood wrote the 1969 application to HUD for the Model Cities Demonstration Project. HUD granted more than three million dollars for the comprehensive plan. However, the residents did not take control of the schools (Watras 298–299).

On a policy level, the federal funds that were designated to improve schooling for educationally deprived children did not have to increase segregation. In fact, when the USOE began to administer the ESEA in 1966, officials tried to ensure that Title I money would not contradict desegregation efforts. To prevent local school administrators from justifying the segregation of African American children by saying that the children could be best served when they were in separate projects designed to compensate for their shared disadvantages, USOE officials allowed the money to follow the children if they had to be transported away from one school to another building for remedial work (Bailey and Mosher 149–150).

Although Ryan saw compensatory educational programs as substitutes for desegregation, the courts did not view it that way. In 1977, in the case about the racial desegregation of Detroit and its suburbs, the Supreme Court ordered the school district to implement compensatory programs along with the racial desegregation of some of the buildings. The aim was to eradicate the harmful effects of districtwide segregation and prevent them from recurring (Orfield, et al., *Dismantling* 147–148).

To some extent, Ryan was correct. Compensatory education did not complement court-ordered desegregation in Detroit, Michigan; Little Rock, Arkansas; Austin, Texas; or Prince George's County, Maryland. In these cases, policymakers had not examined the needs of the pupils in order to select appropriate compensatory programs. They chose programs that were popular and fit the limits of the budget. At the same time, the courts did not require the school districts to show how the students would benefit from compensatory programs such as reduced class size or remedial reading. Nor did the courts require the school districts to demonstrate that the programs worked. As a result, in these cities the compensatory programs became temporary benefits rather than permanent repairs of segregation (Orfield, et al., *Dismantling* 148–174).

Although it is not clear whether compensatory education reinforced segregation, it did replace other, more innovative ideas about the curriculum. Compensatory education programs became popular about the same time as the revisions of the teaching of mathematics, social science, and physics brought about by the Defense Act of 1958. However, the ESEA and the Defense Act had opposing effects on schools. On the one hand, to improve national defense scholars conceived of the subject matter in imaginative ways. On the other hand, in compensatory education educators did not change the conception of the subject matter; they tried to present it in ways the students could grasp. Despite its failure, the orientation of compensatory education dominated the curriculum innovations if for no other reason than ESEA offered considerably more money to local schools than the Defense Act. In this way, educators missed the opportunity to fully use federal monies to revitalize thinking about subject matters.

Most important for this discussion, the extensive funding made available through the ESEA for compensatory education overshadowed the federal money available through Title IV of the Civil Rights Act of 1964. Title IV money should have been used to develop curricula that would have advanced the racial integration of schools. Curriculum theorists did not apply to use this money to develop courses of study that would teach students why racial and social integration was important. Instead, they applied for funding to develop courses to help children from low-income families master school subjects. Consequently, the curriculum developed during the civil rights movement did not point to the major social transformation favoring racial integration that was taking place at the time. In some ways, curricula worked against the change while claiming to support it.

TIMELINE
1964–1998

1964 Lyndon Johnson declared war on poverty in his State of the Union Address

1965 Daniel P. Moyhihan suggested that President Johnson focus his war on poverty on strengthening the African American family structure

1965 President Johnson signed the Elementary and Secondary Act of 1965

1965 Head Start enrolled financially disadvantaged children

(continued)

TIMELINE Continued

1966 Hilda Taba and Deborah Elkins published *Teaching Strategies for the Culturally Disadvantaged*

1966 About 22,000 Title I ESEA projects began nationwide

1967 Studies by the U.S. Commission on Civil Rights showed good educational results from racial integration

1968 The Office of Economic Opportunity commissioned a nationwide study of Head Start programs

1969 Science Research Associates of IBM produced *Inner City Simulation Laboratory,* a study of low-income minority students

1969 Nixon vetoed several bills providing for more education funding

1970 President Nixon proposed the establishment of the National Institute of Education

1972 Congress passed the NIE legislation

1973 The National Advisory Council on the Education of Disadvantaged Children acknowledged that compensatory education would not improve the children's academic achievement

1974 The U.S. Senate decided that the NIE should receive no federal money

1986 Henry Levin established the Accelerated Schools Project at Stanford University

1987 The Anne Casey Foundation offered ten cities money to aid at-risk youth with specific programs

CHAPTER

12 The Advocates—Feminism and Special Needs: 1964–1998

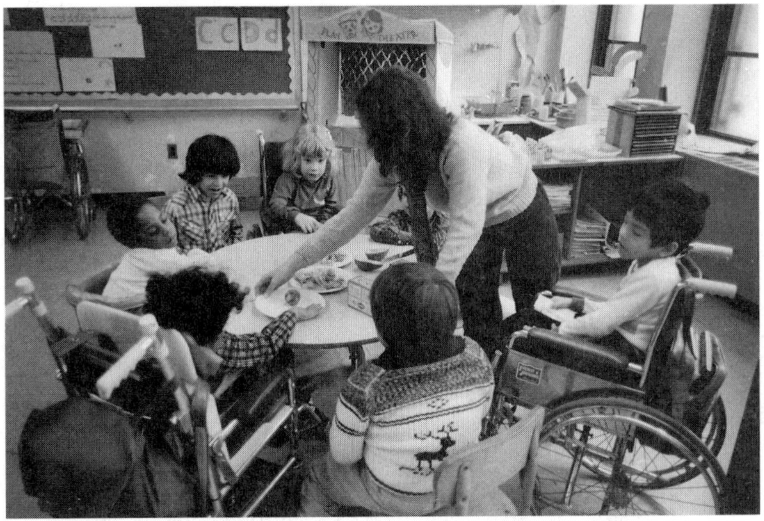

A teacher passes out food to children with special needs.

OVERVIEW

Some policy analysts argue that the result of increased federal assistance to local schools was the development of educational programs serving national interests. Although partly true, such a view overlooks the ways in which advocates of special interest groups campaigned for control. In the late 1960s, advocates of linguistic minorities, children who were disabled, and women tried to persuade the federal government to adopt legislation that would force educators to follow particular models of curriculum planning. These advocates claimed that educators had denied the rights of their constituents. Using this argument, they recruited parents and special teachers to join their organizations, hired lawyers who had worked for the NAACP, filed litigation in federal courts, and used the resulting legal

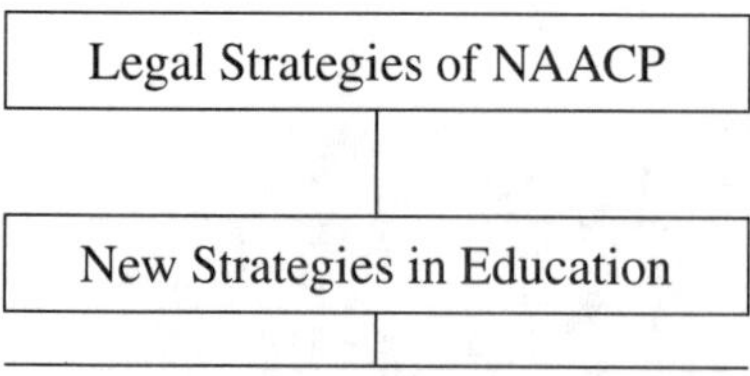

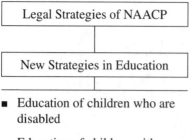

- Education of children who are disabled
- Education of children with limited English proficiency
- Education of women

victories to shape federal legislation. Advocacy groups that supported the education of disabled children were the most successful. As a result of the efforts of lobbyists for organizations such as the Council for Exceptional Children (CEC), Congress demanded that all local districts follow a particular process of curriculum planning. This represented an extensive intrusion of the federal government into local school affairs. Surprisingly, the advocacy groups for special education encountered such little resistance that they called their efforts a quiet revolution. Advocates for linguistic minorities and women were not as successful.

The curriculum proposals for children with disabilities were simplistic. Although they called for as little segregation as possible, the process of determining the lessons was legalistic. As a result, it tended to devolve into a mechanical notion of rehabilitation. In the case of linguistic minorities, questions arose about the role of public schools in preserving the family heritage. For example, should bilingual education programs teach Hispanic children Spanish if they spoke only English? The least successful of the groups were women. In part, the failure of women's advocates resulted from their constituents turning from political efforts to a desire to transform society by integrating family, love, and work. Although the rationales for these reforms implied segregation of the different groups, the advocates moved toward what they called inclusion.

How Did Advocacy Groups for Children with Disabilities Originate?

According to Joel Spring, since World War II federal involvement in education has turned public schools into tools to separate students according to abilities, guide them into specific programs based on their abilities, and prepare them for particular slots in the national labor force. Most important, Spring adds, when the federal government took part in the racial desegregation of schools, this action set the precedent for the national regulation of education (*Sorting* 1–2).

While the federal government's intervention in the racial desegregation of schools set the pattern for future educational reforms, it did so because advocacy groups for linguistic minorities, children who were disabled, and women thought they could follow the pattern set by the NAACP. According to Rosemary Salomone in her book *Equal Education under the Law,* advocates for these groups claimed that school officials had violated the children's rights and sought federal intervention on their behalf.

Although the most successful were advocates for special education, the officials who participated in the effort did not credit their success to their imitation of the NAACP. For example, writing in 1976, director of governmental relations for the Council for Exceptional Children (CEC) Frederick J. Weintraub credited the advance of special education to "hundreds of thousands of individuals who devoted their energies over the years to improving public policies for exceptional children" (Weintraub and Abeson 2). To show what a complicated process this was, he noted that "there are over 16,000 school districts, 50 state governments, one federal government, numerous other governing authorities and subunits all creating policies" (1).

Despite the distracting details, the advance of special education followed an augmenting pattern. Beginning in the 1960s, national advocacy groups recruited parents to form local organizations and state coalitions. These groups pressured school districts to change. Claiming that local officials violated the rights of the disabled, coalitions of advocates for special education asked the federal government to make changes in local or state affairs. While the national organizations lobbied the Congress, local advocacy groups sued in federal courts. Their lawyers had often worked on behalf of the racial desegregation of schools, and they used the same arguments for children with disabilities. That is, the lawyers contended that children with disabilities lacked the opportunity to adapt successfully to society when schools excluded them. Finally, advocates used the legal victories to encourage legislators to sponsor legislation requiring specific procedures of curriculum planning.

Although the successful campaign for federal assistance began in the 1960s, advocacy groups for special education began in the nineteenth century. In general, these organizations were professional associations. For example, the American Association of Instructors of the Blind (AAIB) began in 1853 and formally organized in 1871. Because members were superintendents of residential schools for people who were blind, members of various legislatures called on this association when faced with decisions about blindness. Further, these professionals sought to dominate other associations of persons with vision impairment. For example, in 1895 people who were blind formed the American Blind People's Higher Education and General Improvement Association. However, in 1905 this organization opened its membership to anyone interested in people with vision loss and changed its name to the American Association of Workers for the Blind (AAWB). Members of the more professional AAIB joined the AAWB and tried to move its policies in line with those of the other organization (Ferguson).

Other organizations grew in similar ways. In 1876 a group of superintendents formed the American Association of Superintendents of State Schools for the Feebleminded. This association grew into the American Association on Mental Deficiency, and many of its members attended meetings of the National Conference of Charities and Corrections, where they found a wider forum. By 1949 these members of professional associations to help people with mental retardation actively joined with parents in local school districts. The next year, in 1950, forty-four delegates from twenty-three organizations in thirteen states formed the National Association of Parents and Friends of Mentally Retarded Children (President's Panel, *MR* 37–39). In 1952 this organization became the National

Association for Retarded Children and in 1980 changed its name to the Association for Retarded Citizens (ARC). In 1991 the organization became The Arc, removing any stigma associated with the word *retarded* (The Arc 2–4).

The Council of Exceptional Children was founded at Teachers College of Columbia University in 1922 by twelve professionals concerned with children who had special needs. This meant that CEC members attended to the education of gifted and talented children and of children with disabilities. At the same time, the CEC enrolled professionals as members and became an international organization (Colachio 50–51; Levine and Wexler 15–16).

In addition to these professional associations, a few parents of children with disabilities formed local and temporary advocacy groups during the first half of the twentieth century. For example, according to the President's Panel, in Cuyahoga County, Ohio, five mothers protested because public school officials refused to admit their children in 1933. School administrators responded by opening a special class for their children (*MR* 37–39). However, it is not clear what the parents gained in this action. Special classes for children who were called backward or mentally defective appeared in several city schools throughout the first thirty years of the twentieth century. Because many different types of children with disabilities were grouped in the same classroom, these special classes may have separated children with all sorts of difficulties and eased teaching in the regular classes more than they met the needs of the children with special needs or the concerns of their parents (Barry Franklin 46–47).

As early as 1958, the CEC and the National Association of Retarded Children had joined to support enactment of Public Law 85–926, Expansion of Teaching in the Education of the Mentally Retarded. In general, the organizations to advance the education of persons with disabilities sought to cooperate with school and public administrators. For example, in 1962 the President's Panel on Mental Retardation called attention to the needs of children with physical disabilities. However, in its message the President's Panel cautioned against using legal means to force a community to provide adequate care for persons with mental retardation. The report added that advocates should not use legal means such as the courts and the legislature except as a last resort. The President's Panel called for federal agencies such as the Department of Health, Education, and Welfare (HEW) to exercise national leadership in developing educational services for children with mental retardation. These agencies of the federal government could act in partnership with state agencies, local governments, and voluntary organizations (President's Panel 149, 178–180).

The CEC cooperated with the National Education Association to promote passage of the Elementary and Secondary Education Act of 1965 (ESEA), Public Law 89–10 (Colachio 51–52). However, special educators did not benefit as they might have. Although Title I of ESEA could have directed money to children with disabilities, the staff in the U.S. Office of Education decided to use it only for low-income children (Salomone 143–144).

In 1966, during the debates about the renewal of ESEA, the CEC lobbied people such as Wayne Morse, chair of the Senate Committee on Labor and Welfare. Within a short period, an extensive array of interest groups such as the American Psychological Association, the National Association of Mental Health, and the Association for Children with Learning Disabilities joined to ask for three things. First, they called for federal funds for states to educate children with disabilites. Second, they wanted an specific bureau within the Office of Education to administer programs for the children with physical disabilites.

Third, they claimed that each child should have a free, appropriate public education (Levine and Wexler 20–28).

With surprisingly little debate about the special education sections, Congress approved and President Johnson signed in 1966 a bill that became Public Law 89–750. This bill renewed ESEA, and it contained a new Title VI authorizing $50 billion for 1967 and $150 million for 1968 to help in the education of people with disabilities. Most important, Title VI created the Bureau of Education for the Handicapped (BEH) in the Office of Education. It also mandated formation of the National Advisory Committee to act as a consultative body to the BEH and to Congress. As a result, advocates for the many different types of people with disabilities had a single position within the federal government from which to exert combined influence (Levine and Wexler 29–33).

In order to advance the process of lobbying, advocates for people with disabilities linked their campaigns with the then popular drive for civil rights. For example, in 1968 the International League of Societies for the Mentally Handicapped adopted a Declaration of General and Specific Rights of the Mentally Retarded, asserting that people with mental retardation have the rights accorded to more fortunate people. According to this declaration, each child with mental retardation had a right to proper medical care and "to such education as will enable him to develop his ability and potential to the fullest possible extent" (Lippman and Goldberg 7).

Using their increased presence in the U.S. Office of Education, advocacy groups for special education lobbied Congress. In 1970 Congress responded by replacing Title VI with the Education of the Handicapped Act, added the category of special or learning disabled to the list of physical disabilities, and authorized $630 million to be spent for the education of people with physical disabilities (Levine and Wexler 34–37). Congress also added to ESEA the opportunity to provide services to gifted and talented children (La Vor, 101).

How Did Local Advocacy Groups Advance Special Education?

In order to take advantage of their surprising legislative successes, special educators depended on citizen efforts. However, these so-called grassroots movements were not spontaneous uprisings of disaffected parents and citizens. Frequently, professional members of the advocacy groups organized the citizens' actions. Once national advocacy groups recruited some teachers and parents to form local organizations and state coalitions, these groups pressured school districts to change. Claiming that local officials violated the rights of people with disabilities, coalitions of advocates for special education recruited more parents and teachers and made changes in local or state affairs. Vermont offers an example of such state-level pressure from special educators.

In 1969 Vermont State Representative John Alden submitted a bill modeled on an Illinois Education for the Handicapped law that was reputed to be the best in the nation. Jean Garvin, state director of special education and pupil personnel services; Sister Janice Ryan, from Trinity College; and Hugh McKenzie, head of special education at the University of Vermont, began raising support for the bill from members of interest groups such as the Vermont chapter of the Association of Retarded Children and the Vermont Association for

Children with Learning Disabilities. When Alden's bill died in committee, Garvin, Ryan, and McKenzie began drafting a replacement. In 1970 Alden became a state senator, and he introduced the new bill as S.98 (Riley 312–313).

Garvin, Ryan, and McKenzie began to raise support for S.98. Trinity College sponsored a Political Action Day in September 1971 with representatives from national organizations such as the Council of Exceptional Children. Participants at this meeting formed the Vermont Committee for the Handicapped (VCH). Special education faculty at the University of Vermont began developing county organizations, asking everyone to contact members of the education and the appropriations committees in the state legislature. On November 4, 1971, the VCH organized a demonstration of more than 250 people at a meeting of the state Senate Education Committee. At Garvin's urging, the state board of education voted during November 1971 to lend its support to S.98. And in January 1972, county groups of parents and special educators who had formed to pass Alden's bill began publishing a newsletter to circulate among themselves (Riley 315–317).

The strongest opposition came from the governor of Vermont, Deane Davis, who on January 5, 1972, complained that the special education legislation would be too expensive and incite unnecessary litigation. When Vermont's Senate Education Committee reviewed an amended version of Alden's S.98 in January 1972, Garvin, Ryan, and McKenzie testified that the governor's objections were unfounded. Although VCH members asked the senate not to compromise, the committee approved a mild version of S.98 (Riley 317).

Fortunately for special education advocates, in 1973 the Vermont Appropriations Committee discovered more than $400,000 the governor had placed in an unused budget account. With the public aware of the existence of this money, the legislature could use it to fund the special education bill (Riley 320).

Other interest groups began to support the special education legislation including the American Civil Liberties Union, the Vermont Diocesan Council, the Vermont Superintendent's Association, and the National Association of Social Workers. When committee deliberations threatened to kill the bill, a newspaper reporter wrote an article accusing the governor of holding S.98 ransom to obtain approval for legislation concerning campaign expenses. Suffering public criticism, the committees released the bill, and it came to the house for a vote just before the Easter holidays. In one morning, Vermont's house and senate approved the legislation (Riley 318–322).

How Did Advocacy Groups Establish Children's Right to an Appropriate Education?

To make effective appeals to Congress, the advocates for special education tried to establish a right to education for children with disabilities in federal courts. Some legal cases were extensions of racial desegregation suits. For example, some school districts used tracking systems to reintroduce racial segregation. The first case demanding access to public schools for children with mental retardation began on January 7, 1971, when the Pennsylvania Association for Retarded Citizens (PARC), a state affiliate of the ARC, filed a case in U.S. district court against a list of defendants beginning with the commonwealth of Pennsylvania. Other advocacy groups, such as the American Association of Mental Deficiency, the CEC, and the ARC, joined as friends of the court.

PARC v. Commonwealth began in 1969 when members of PARC complained during an annual meeting about conditions at the Pennhurst State School and Hospital which was one of the nine residence facilities for people with mental retardation under the supervision of the Pennsylvania Department of Public Welfare. At that time, the facility had 3,013 residents and a bed capacity of 2,126. Although newspapers had published reports of overcrowding and inhumane treatment, the state legislature had not acted. Parents and members of PARC called on the organization to stimulate reform. As a result, PARC resolved to retain counsel and file any necessary legal action against the Department of Public Welfare to close or improve Pennhurst. At the same convention, PARC members adopted A Bill of Rights for Pennsylvania's Retarded Citizens, which was similar to the one adopted a year earlier by the International League of Societies for the Mentally Handicapped (Lippman and Goldberg 16–22).

PARC's bill of rights had no legal bearing on the case. Instead, imitating *Brown v. Board of Education,* the PARC case rested on the claim that Pennsylvania statutes violated the Fourteenth Amendment of the U.S. Constitution. Represented by Thomas K. Gilhool, an attorney who had previously worked in civil rights cases, PARC contended that children with mental retardation did not have equal access to an education. Official exclusions, postponements, waiting lists, and excusals kept these children out of public schools (Lippman and Goldberg 22–24).

There was no contest. After testimony by four witnesses for the plaintiffs, the officials of the commonwealth of Pennsylvania consented to enroll children with mental retardation in publicly supported educational programs. These were to be as similar as possible to the education available in most public schools and supervised by state department of education personnel (Lippman and Goldberg 31–32).

In the consent agreement, the state of Pennsylvania agreed to search out and find all children requiring special education. As part of this effort, agencies such as county mental health offices notified parents through public news releases, messages to professional groups, and civic and neighborhood organizations of the services available to these children. Radio and television spot announcements broadcast these messages through the state. State senators and representatives included notices in their letters to constituents. The Liquor Control Board enclosed announcements in consumer packages of the search for children with mental retardation. At the same time, the Pennsylvania department of education began to plan ways to educate the expected increase of 53,000 children with disabilities. In these actions, the state Department of Education worked under the supervision of a court master in the same way that school districts did when ordered to racially desegregate pupils and faculty (Lippman and Goldberg 37–44).

In 1972 advocates of special education won a second major victory in *Mills v. Board of Education of the District of Columbia.* A year earlier the board of education of the District of Columbia public schools admitted that it had an affirmative duty to provide an appropriate education to several children who suffered from behavioral problems, hyperactivity, emotional disturbances, or mental retardation. By January the board had failed to comply, so the plaintiffs filed again. In his decision, U.S. District Court Justice Joseph

Waddy quoted several cases concerning racial segregation, arguing that they demonstrated that these children have a right to an education on equal terms with the education a state provides to other children. Waddy forbade the public schools of Washington, D.C. to exclude a child unless the board of education provided adequate alternative education, a prior hearing, and a periodic review of the child's progress.

Although this litigation followed patterns established in racial segregation cases, there was an important difference between suits for special education and suits for racial integration of schools. Lawyers supporting children with disabilites did not have to work through lengthy appeals that reached the Supreme Court as did lawyers for the NAACP. By 1994 the Supreme Court heard at least seven cases involving special education (Thomas and Russo 50). However, between 1954 and 1994, the Supreme Court rendered decisions in more than three dozen cases involving racial desegregation of public schools (Russo 297–309).

How Did Federal Litigation Determine the Process of Planning a Child's Curriculum?

In 1972 Paul R. Dimond was a lawyer for the plaintiffs in the *Mills* case. He also worked with Nathaniel Jones and the NAACP Legal Defense Fund to racially desegregate schools and public housing in Dayton and Columbus, Ohio; Detroit, Michigan; and Wilmington, Delaware. In 1973 he outlined the ways that decisions in civil rights law could be applied to the education of people with disabilities.

In his article in the *Hastings Law Journal,* Dimond noted that a body of litigation contested the incorrect assignment of minority children to classes for children with educable mental retardation. Dimond disagreed with educators who believed that these cases pointed out the problems minority children have taking the verbal portion of the IQ test. He felt the cases called for a complete reform of placement procedures. That is, these cases demonstrated how school authorities excluded these children from public education by arbitrary and capricious processes (1091–1108).

In posing the question of whether a state can deny a child access to a public education, Dimond acknowledged that the U.S. Supreme Court held in *San Antonio Independent School District v. Rodriguez* that education is not a constitutionally guaranteed right. However, a body of lower court decisions continued to uphold the obligation of school authorities to justify any act that prevents a child from receiving an education. Thus, Dimond argued, because the state has an interest in educating its citizens, its officials cannot exclude some groups (1091–1108).

Dimond contended that school officials created the problems. Teachers, administrators, school boards, even parents and students wanted the children in any particular classroom to be the same in age, intelligence, ability, character, and culture. As a result, Dimond believed, the solution should be a fair procedure for assigning children to various educational programs. If court cases sought these procedures, justices would not have to make educational decisions; they would only have to list the procedures that school officials must follow in making them (1108–1110).

In other cases in which decisions could impose a burden on the person, such as dismissal from employment or the *PARC* and the *Mills* cases, Dimond found that the following steps protected everyone: The child must have an opportunity for a hearing. There must be a public notification of the opportunity for special education, a full expert evaluation of the child's needs, and the development of a specific educational plan. Finally, officials had to give the plan to the family, notifying them of their right to appeal to a hearing officer. If requested, school officials had to call the meeting promptly and prove the appropriateness of the proposed placement. The hearing officer had to be independent of the school and all records made available to the parents (1111–1118).

Dimond argued that the right to a hearing was reasonable and important. It was a reasonable request because it did not ask justices to involve themselves in school administration; they could restrict themselves to determining whether the school's procedures preserved the child's right to due process. It was important because the hearings protected the best interests of the child. For example, if school officials chose not to serve those interests, parents would learn the proper avenues of appeal. In this way, Dimond concluded, when legal suits were limited to questions about proper procedures, they resulted in decisions that provided the best possible education (1124–1127).

Using Dimond's rationale, ARC and CEC lobbyists sought to convince members of Congress that suitable statutes could remedy the problems that the federal courts had already acknowledged faced children with disabilities. Officials from NARC contacted parents who could testify before Congress about the children's needs. The CEC contacted special education professionals willing to inform Congress about the conditions within schools. The members of ARC and CEC testified at national hearings, advised congressional staff about the appropriate structure of the bill, and wrote letters outlining their concerns. As a result of the combined actions of these organizations, the definition of an appropriate education as found in the legal cases appeared in the Education for All Handicapped Children Act, Public Law 94-142 of 1975 (Colachio 132–135).

What Was the Model of Curriculum Mandated by PL 94-142?

On November 29, 1975, President Gerald Ford signed Public Law 94-142, the Education for All Handicapped Children Act. Charged with administering the law, the U.S. Bureau of Education for the Handicapped opened the process to public deliberation. More than 2,200 people participated in sessions in which the rules were discussed. After publishing the proposed rules in March 1977, the BEH received more than 16,000 written comments. On August 32, 1977, the U.S. Department of Health, Education, and Welfare implemented the law (Levine and Wexler 113–116).

Because the advocates for special education used legal cases to shape the legislation, the law mandated an adversarial process of curriculum planning. For example, in the regulations, the BEH made clear that every school district had to follow the process outlined in the law or suffer the withdrawal of federal funds for children with disabilities. These rules required school districts to alert parents to the services available for these children. They had to establish nondiscriminatory testing, such as tests that assess specific areas of educational need in addition to any test of general intelligence. At the same time, parents had to be able to obtain an independent evaluation from a qualified examiner not affiliated with the school district. From these evaluations, parents, teachers, any special teachers, and consultants would draw up an individual educational plan (IEP) that stated the child's present level of educational performance, the annual goals and short-term instructional objectives to reach them, a statement of the specific educational services the child would receive and the extent to which the child could attend regular classes, and a schedule for review that would be conducted at least annually. If the parent or school officials disagreed with the decision, the school district had to provide a qualified impartial hearing officer to rule on the matter. Above all, the parents and the public had to have access to all the information on which the decisions were based. Furthermore, everything had to be done in a language the parents could understand. Thus, the specific activities for each child would differ depending on his or her disability. However, the process was the same for all children who were identified as disabled.

Critics complained about three things: The requirements would be expensive, parents and schoolchildren would seek special education placements too frequently, and too many uninformed parents would complain about what they believed to be improper treatment. To determine if these were reasonable criticisms, the Council of the Great City Schools (CGCS) sponsored a descriptive study of thirty-three school districts, including the largest school districts in the United States, over a three-year period ending in 1988. The study refuted many of these speculations. First, the CGCS study found that the school districts made substantial progress in reducing the number of inappropriate referrals for expensive testing by instituting alternatives to address the children's needs before considering special education services. Second, the study found that the enrollment of special education students constituted about 10.5 percent of the total enrollment, which was a little lower than the national average. Furthermore, over half of the districts reported fewer than five complaints by parents each year. Although five large cities reported significant numbers of complaints, most of them were settled prior to formal hearings. When the hearings did occur, the school districts prevailed (Research for Better Schools v–vii).

How Successful Were the Advocacy Groups for Special Education?

Three measures might indicate the extent of the success of the advocates for special education. First, advocacy groups for special education grew in a short period of time. ARC comprised 23 member organizations in 1950; by 1960 ARC had 681 state and local chapters and 62,000 members. In 1975 ARC grew to 1,700 state and local chapters and 218,000 members. Likewise, CEC grew from 5,000 members in 1950 to 70,000 by 1980 (Levine and Wexler 15–16).

Second, as a result of the increased federal funds and requirements, local school districts established more special education facilities. In 1965 there were 5 to 7 million children needing special education services, but only 25 percent of them attended appropriate private or public school programs, which were staffed by a total of about 71,000 teachers (U.S. Senate Subcommittee on Health 13–45). In 1977 the number of public school students classified as disabled increased to 3.7 million, and by 1990 that number rose to 4.6 million. This increase was even larger than it seems. From 1977 to 1990, public school enrollments declined by 3 million students. Consequently, the percentage of all public school students classified as disabled grew from 8.5 percent in 1977 to 11.4 percent in 1990. The number of special education teachers grew even faster, rising by more than 50 percent between 1978 and 1990 (Hanushek, et al. 35).

However, researchers disagree whether this increase in special education services diverted money from other types of education. For example, one group of researchers asserts that special education was roughly twice as expensive as the education of mainstream children. From this estimate, they conclude that the increase of special education students and teachers from 1980 to 1988 must have cost $3 billion out of a national aggregate of $54 billion for all school expenditures (Hanushek, et al. 36). On the other hand, researchers from the Economic Policy Institute estimate the cost to be much higher. In a detailed study of nine typical U.S. school districts, they collected data on total spending for special education and calculated its share of the total spending for K–12 programs. From this analysis, they conclude that the biggest share of new funds coming into school budgets went to special education: "Special education growth consumed 38 percent of net new funds in 1991" (Rothstein and Miles 49).

Third, advocacy groups for special education used their extensive public support to protect the legislation. For example, in 1983 Terrel Bell, secretary of education at the time, announced his intention to narrow the restrictive regulations that the U.S. Rehabilitation Act of 1973 and PL 94-142 placed on local schools. This was in keeping with the Reagan ideal of allowing school districts local autonomy. However, Bell dropped this proposal and retained the restrictions when he received more than 23,000 letters of protest (Salomone 164–165).

How Did Advocacy Groups Encourage the Adoption of Bilingual Education?

The advocacy groups for linguistic minorities differed from those that served children with disabilities. The difference was that some groups supporting linguistic minorities began as political associations whose aim was to advance the social and economic integration of immigrants into U.S. society. For example, from 1920 to 1929 more than 500,000 people emigrated from Mexico to the United States. These people joined together to help each other. In 1918 a fraternal society in southern Texas, the Order of Sons of America (OSA), superceded the former mutual aid society, Liga Mexicanista de Beneficencia y Proteccion, and expanded its concerns to voter registration, citizenship applications, and representation in jury selection. In order to coordinate the activities of groups such as OSA, several prominent Mexicans met in 1929 in Corpus Christi, Texas, to form LULAC, the League of United Latin American Citizens (Marquez 15–17).

In general, LULAC sought equal education and ethnic integration. However, LULAC members generated controversy by taking the position that although the Mexican heritage was equal to any in the world, it was part of Mexican Americans' past. In the 1930s, LULAC urged Mexican Americans to learn English and to speak it in their homes. Some LULAC members argued that Mexican Americans who lived in the United States should abandon any desire of returning to Mexico, give up ethnic enclaves, and absorb the customs of the dominant culture (Marquez 19–25).

Because education was an important concern to LULAC, the organization began the Little School of 400 in 1956. On completing a study of school failure among Mexican Americans, the president of LULAC sought the cooperation of the Texas Teachers Association. A teacher in Baytown, Texas, drafted a list of four hundred essential English words for Mexican American children to learn before they entered first grade. During the summer, two schools began the program with a total of sixty students. Of these, only one student failed and had to repeat the first grade. The next summer, the program spread and LULAC volunteers ran programs in six schools in southern Texas. The Texas legislature adopted this model, and from 1960 to 1964 more than 92,000 Mexican American children attended similar preschools for non-English-speaking children (Marquez 51–52).

At the same time, professional educators organized efforts to help linguistic minorities. In 1965 the National Education Association (NEA) surveyed the Mexican American children in the southwestern region of the United States. In their report *The Invisible Minority,* the NEA committee noted that there were 1.75 million Mexican American children in Arizona, California, Colorado, New Mexico, and Texas. The region once belonged to Mexico, and these people spoke a language and held a culture different from most of the population. The NEA committee asserted that these Mexican Americans did not try to assimilate nor did they strive to succeed as did the English-speaking Americans. Consequently, poverty was prevalent among Mexican Americans in this region (Committee on Education and Labor 169–177).

The NEA was most concerned that the Mexican American children failed academically. In California in 1960, for example, more than half of the males and nearly half of the females more than fourteen years old with Spanish surnames had not gone on to school beyond the eighth grade. In the general population, however, less than 30 percent of the males and 25 percent of the females had not gone beyond the eighth grade. According to the report, Mexican American children left school at a high rate because they started school with a language disability, and each year their academic performance fell behind that of their English-speaking peers (Committee on Education and Labor 177–179).

The NEA committee traced the language problem to the children's homes. For example, in 1965 a study of six hundred Mexican American adults in San Antonio, Texas, found that 71 percent of the parents spoke only Spanish to each other. Thus, although the children knew some English, the language of their home and childhood was Spanish. In schools they had to use a language foreign to them, and frequently the parents could not help. Although some schools reduced the content of most subjects to give the children time to learn English, this caused them to fall behind even more. The NEA report noted that some schools forbade the children from speaking any Spanish and punished them for lapsing into it on the playgrounds. One member of the committee reported that teachers in one school admonished the children, "If you want to be American, speak American." However, the NEA report concluded that such compulsion caused the children to withdraw, to feel inadequate, and to fail (Committee on Education and Labor 179–186).

The NEA survey did discover several encouraging programs. In Laredo, Texas, English-speaking and Spanish-speaking students were encouraged to speak, read, and write in both Spanish and English. In Albuquerque, New Mexico, some Hispanic parents realized their children spoke a flawed Spanish, and they wanted the schools to enhance the children's skills in Spanish and foster pride in their culture. As a result, Albuquerque schools offered language placement exams to provide native Spanish-speaking children with appropriate Spanish instruction. In Pecos, New Mexico, the NEA team found a teacher who was born in Chile conducting Spanish classes for Spanish speakers. The board of education in Merced, California, used money offered by the state for compensatory education to provide Spanish courses for Spanish speakers. In Pueblo, Colorado, a native Spanish speaker taught Spanish to all fifth- and sixth-grade Mexican American children, although the teacher was untrained in language instruction. Schools in Tucson, Arizona, initiated a pilot project in Spanish literature for native Spanish-speaking high school students. In El Paso, Texas, the majority of teachers were native Spanish speakers, and they offered courses in English and Spanish. The schools in Phoenix, Arizona, had classes in basic skills such as reading and writing in Spanish for the Spanish speaking. These classes covered cultural topics to foster pride in their heritage among the students (Committee on Education and Labor 184–196).

NEA members were careful not to recommend that all schools pursue the same goal. They did suggest that for all native speakers of Spanish schools should offer instruction in the early grades in both languages, that English be taught as a second language, and that correct Spanish be taught to Mexican American children. The report explained that native Spanish-speaking children needed advanced Spanish literature courses. However, the NEA committee called for more trained bilingual teachers who could speak, write, and read Spanish and English with cultured correctness. This meant that universities had to train teachers who spoke Spanish and that schools had to recruit them (Committee on Education and Labor 197–205).

Professional organizations formed to reduce similar difficulties. In March 1966 in New York City, personnel from the U.S. Bureau of Indian Affairs and members of the Modern Language Association, the Center for Applied Linguistics, the National Association for Foreign Student Affairs, the National Council of Teachers of English, and the Speech Association of America officially formed TESOL, Teachers of English to Speakers of Other Languages (Committee on Education and Labor 330). Because members faced a wide range of problems, the papers at the 1966 conference described several programs. Three papers from that conference illustrate the range of topics.

In the first paper, Paul W. Bell described two projects the Miami, Florida, public schools instituted to help children who had fled from Cuba with their families. One of the programs set up a series of steps to enable the children who did not speak English to master the language as quickly as possible. This meant the children had to be classified in one of three levels according to their abilities to speak and understand English. The amount and type of instruction the children received depended on their assigned level. Some studied English as a second language for three hours a day, spending the rest of the time on subjects such as art, music, and physical education that depended less on language. Other students spent less time on English and the rest of the time on subjects such as mathematics, art, and music at a level appropriate to their grade in school. In this case, teachers formed teams of three. Usually, a certified teacher worked with two Spanish-speaking aides recruited from Cuban refugee teachers who helped in the instruction. The other program was a bilingual elementary school founded in 1963. In grades 1 to 5, the children spent half of the day studying in Spanish and the other half studying the same material in English (Committee on Education and Labor 470–475).

In the second paper, Leo H. Salisbury described the problems facing native Alaskans, noting that these groups were not deliberately segregated on tribal reservations.

They lived in small, isolated villages ranging in size from fifty to fifteen hundred persons. Different groups of native Alaskans spoke different dialects or languages. Although compulsory education laws required the families to live close to schools, they migrated to traditional hunting or fishing spots during the summer months. Worse, in schools the children learned a language and skills unrelated to their family life. As a result, 60 percent did not reach the eighth grade, and the native Alaskans who persisted until high school left their homes to attend boarding schools. On graduation, the students had difficulty returning to their villages, yet they could not succeed in contemporary Alaskan cities without further education. Consequently, the U.S. Bureau of Indian Affairs offered scholarship money for native Alaskans to enter the University of Alaska. In the 1960s, about one-eighth of the entering first-year classes was native Alaskan. Unfortunately, half of these students withdrew in the first year and less than 2 percent graduated after four years. Salisbury described how the university offered special courses in anthropology, English, and communication in which native Alaskan students discussed cross-cultural problems. He found the most important experience to be an opportunity for the students to live for six weeks with a Western family. In this way, he wrote, they learned about the home life that awaited them should they leave their native communities (Committee on Education and Labor 476–484).

In the third paper, John B. King argued that the children who migrated from the rural South to live in low-income areas of northern cities faced problems similar to children born in Puerto Rico. According to King, teaching English as a second language would be a powerful weapon in the war on poverty. The curriculum could include instruction in the history and culture of these children's ethnic background as well as sequential lessons in listening, speaking, and thinking in Standard English (Committee on Education and Labor 485–491).

During the process to renew ESEA in 1967, the U.S. House of Representatives Committee on Education and Labor held hearings during which witnesses testified that the problems of linguistic minorities were pressing and existed in all parts of the United States. For example, in Hoboken, New Jersey, the population of Puerto Ricans rose from 3 percent in 1953 to 34 percent in 1967. At the same time, the population of foreign-born students was 9.4 percent, and this gave the Hoboken schools a student population with 43 percent linguistic minorities (Committee on Education and Labor 521).

Despite the agreement that something should be done to help linguistic minorities, witnesses did not agree on what should be done. When several people reasserted the NEA recommendations of teaching children their native language as well as English, other groups disagreed. For example, the American Spanish Committee submitted a statement that its members did not approve of teaching the Spanish language to children until high school. These Spanish-speaking parents wanted their children to learn English before they improved their Spanish (Committee on Education and Labor 517–520).

With little controversy, Congress approved and President Lyndon B. Johnson signed Title VII of ESEA, also called the Bilingual Education Act, in 1968. This authorized the use of federal funds to carry out imaginative elementary and secondary programs to meet the educational needs of children who came from an environment in which the dominant language was other than English and who attended schools with a concentration of low-income families. As a result, from 1969 to 1973, $117.9 million of federal support went to bilingual programs, most of which were in elementary schools (U.S. Commission, *A Better Chance* 171–172, 180–181).

The law did not specify whether the children would learn English or learn it in addition to their own language. However, in 1971, when HEW released its instructions for applying for the federal funds, it noted that the goal of bilingual education was to produce students who functioned well in two languages on any occasion. To some people, this implied that schools would teach children their native language as well as English. This was important because some educators believed that it was insufficient to teach English as a second language (ESL). ESL was a method of instruction developed in the 1930s for university students and foreign diplomats. In the 1950s, many elementary schools offered this instruction to non-English-speaking students in special classes away from their regular work. However, because ESL ignored the children's unique language and heritage, some educators feared that the children would come to dislike their culture (Crawford, *Bilingual Education* 27–28, 38).

How Did Advocacy Groups Use the Federal Courts to Support Bilingual Education?

In 1969 a member of the newly formed militant Mexican American Youth Organization, Jose Angel Gutierrez, returned to Crystal City, Texas, seeking an issue on which he could organize a movement to begin a third political party. Gutierrez had graduated from the Crystal City high school in 1962, and he asked the school board to sanction a homecoming celebration for former students. When the board refused, Gutierrez organized a boycott by Mexican Americans. At first, he persuaded 416 of the school's 673 students to stay home. As the strike wore on, the number fell to about 65 percent of the students. Parents and students joined to form Cuidadanos Unidos, and a group called Texans for the Educational Advancement of Mexican Americans offered to send teachers to help the children while they stayed out of school. National news media covered the events and federal mediators tried to ameliorate the situation. On January 6, 1970, the board agreed to the students demands. The members of Cuidadanos Unidos formed a political party and on January 23, 1970, filed applications to challenge the members of the school board in the coming election. Three candidates from Cuidadanos Unidos won seats on the Crystal City board of education. The party soon changed its name to La Raza Unida and for a short time competed with the two main political parties, Republicans and Democrats, in Texas state politics (Garcia 37–61).

Gutierrez's work in Crystal City is often cited as a model for Hispanic activists (Hammerback, Jensen, and Gutierrez 81). However, one of the most wide-reaching effects was the demand the students of Crystal City High School made for bilingual and bicultural education. In reaction to controversies similar to Crystal City's, director of the U.S. Office of Civil Rights, J. Stanley Pottinger, issued a memo on May 25, 1970, warning that all school districts with more than 5 percent national-origin-minority children must take affirmative steps to rectify any language deficiencies that would exclude them from effective participation in educational programs. Although Pottinger's memo did not indicate what the school districts had to offer, it warned against depending on English-language skills alone in assigning children to classes, cautioned against the use of tracking as a means to permanently separate children, and required contacting parents in a language they understood. Pottinger pointed out that school districts had to comply with these orders or they would be in violation of Title VI of the Civil Rights Act of 1964 forbidding discrimination on the basis of race, color, or national origin (U.S. Commission, *Excluded* 204–205). This was a serious threat because once a school district was found to be noncompliant, the federal government could deny it federal funds.

The biggest legal victory for bilingual education came in January 1974 with the Supreme Court decision in the case of *Lau v. Nichols*. In this case, the Human Rights Commission showed that in 1971 there were 3,457 Chinese students enrolled in the San Francisco school system who spoke little or no English. The plaintiffs who brought this suit did not urge any particular remedy. They agreed that teaching English as a second language would be acceptable, as would teaching the children in Chinese. Although the parents lost in the U.S. district court, they won in the U.S. appeals court and in the Supreme Court.

In writing the opinion, Justice William O. Douglas noted that although English was to be the basic language of instruction, the California Education Code allowed bilingual education. The justices based their judgement on the Civil Rights Act of 1964, which banned discrimination on the basis of race, color, or national origin in any program receiving federal financial assistance. It was obvious to the justices that the Chinese-speaking children received few benefits from the schools. Consequently, they ordered the district to take affirmative steps to rectify the language deficiencies. For example, any tracking system had to be designed to meet the language needs of the students.

In February 1974, the U.S. Department of Health Education responded to the Supreme Court's decision by issuing a memorandum clarifying federal regulations. The department reminded schools of the need to provide services for children of limited-English-speaking ability. However, the memo stated that the department had never indicated what form these services should take. For example, it had never adopted a position on whether schools should help the children maintain their original culture (Schneider 106).

In 1974 Congress had to reauthorize the Bilingual Education Act of 1968. U.S. Senators Edward Kennedy and Alan Cranston introduced the bills to expand bilingual and bicultural education. In part, the Senate was receptive to expanding the legislation because of the active involvement of ethnically based organizations. The most active was the Raza Association of Spanish Surnamed Americans (RASSA), which later changed its name to the National Congress of Hispanic Citizens. RASSA produced supportive materials, argued and lobbied during conferences, and was able to influence senators representing states with Hispanic voters. Such groups as the Puerto Rican Forum and, the Puerto Rican Association for National Affairs (PANA) argued for Puerto Ricans. Representatives from various Native American tribes and associations testified at hearings, and the U.S. Bureau of Indian Affairs urged the expansion of the legislation (Schneider 41, 63–65).

The series of reports of the U.S. Commission on Civil Rights on the education of Mexican Americans influenced the senators to act as well. In 1972 the commission released the third report in that series. Entitled *The Excluded Student,* this report focused on the linguistic and cultural problems Mexican American children experienced in schools and considered programs to alleviate those difficulties. The members found that schools excluded the Spanish language, the Mexican heritage, and the Mexican American community from participation in school affairs (11–12).

The U.S. Commission on Civil Rights found ten school districts in Texas that forbade students to speak Spanish on school grounds. Yet most of these districts had enrollments that were more than 50 percent Mexican American. If the students ignored the rule, they received detentions, suspensions, and sometimes physical punishments. Furthermore, in the Southwest only 4.3 percent of the elementary schools and 7.3 percent of the secondary schools included some form of Mexican American history in the curriculum. This was a problem because, according to several witnesses, the school texts supported the notion that the early settlers who came from Mexico wandered in confusion until the Anglo-Saxons came over the Rocky Mountains and brought order out of chaos (*Excluded* 13–20, 30–36).

Finally, according to the U.S. Commission on Civil Rights, the public schools did not invite Spanish-speaking parents to participate in school affairs. Few school districts employed community relations specialists. As a result, the most common communications between parents and school officials were written notices sent home with the children. In schools with more than 75 percent Mexican Americans, such notices were often in Spanish. However, in more integrated schools the notices were written in English. Parent–teacher meetings were also inaccessible because only about 2 percent of the secondary schools the commission surveyed conducted those meetings in Spanish. However, HEW had ruled against such practices because they denied equal access for Spanish-speaking people (*Excluded* 37–40).

In listing possible reforms, the U.S. Commission on Civil Rights approved of bilingual education because it permitted all children to become bilingual and bicultural. That is, children who spoke English could learn Spanish, just as those who spoke Spanish could learn English. Commission members were less inclined toward English as a second language (ESL) instruction. Noting that about 5.5 percent of the Mexican American students in the Southwest received some type of ESL instruction, the report noted that this instruction did not take advantage of the rich Mexican American heritage (*Excluded* 21–26).

As the U.S. Senate drew up legislation for bilingual education, the staff of the U.S. Commission on Civil Rights interacted with Mexican American lobbies and education groups. These three forces often participated in planning sessions, with Senate staff charged with drafting the legislation for bilingual education (Schneider 65).

During the congressional hearings and conferences, two issues arose repeatedly. One was whether bilingual education was supposed to establish a bilingual society. The second was whether bilingual education should include instruction in the children's cultural heritage. In line with Civil Rights Commission reports, the advocacy groups lobbied for instruction in the proper use of the native language as well as in English. They wanted to include lessons about the cultural traditions so that the children who were not proficient in English would not feel inferior to their peers. The final bill did not include these requirements, yet the lobbyists from the bilingual advocacy groups accepted the legislation. The law required that federally funded programs include native-language instruction and cultural enrichment, and it did not forbid such programs from persisting into the secondary schools, where students could acquire a sophisticated understanding of their own language. Although such dual instruction was necessary only as long as it took the students who were not proficient in English to learn as effectively as their peers, programs using only an ESL approach would not be acceptable, because ESL provided instruction in English without reference to the students cultural heritage (Schneider 128, 146–147).

That same year, 1974, Congress passed Title II of the Equal Opportunities Act. This bill was designed to prohibit the transportation of elementary or secondary school students to enhance racial desegregation. However, one paragraph of the law read as follows: "No State shall deny equal opportunity to an individual on account of his or her race, color, sex, or national origin by the failure by an educational agency to take appropriate action to overcome language barriers that impede equal participation by its students in its instructional programs" (U.S. Commission on Civil Rights, *Better Chance* 197). Although Congress did not define what appropriate action meant, the law allowed people to sue in federal court for redress. As discussed in a later section, African Americans used this law to force the Ann Arbor, Michigan, schools to include Black English in the curriculum.

Was Bilingual Education Effective?

In 1975 the U.S. Commission on Civil Rights visited several sites to examine bilingual bicultural education. The members liked what they saw. However, they complained that there were no systematic efforts to evaluate the results of these programs (*Better* 103–105). In 1978 such a survey was published. It was extensive, thorough, and disappointing to the advocates of bilingual education.

The U.S. Office of Education contracted with the American Institutes for Research (AIR) to produce the nationwide study of the impact of ESEA Title VII. During the 1975–76 academic year, AIR researchers gathered evidence from all Title VII Spanish–English bilingual education projects that had received funding for four or five years. The general design was to compare the performance of the students enrolled in the projects with similar students who did not participate. Initially, the researchers chose 11,500 students in 384 classrooms in thirty-eight sites across the United States, from which they sampled smaller groups at random for specific examinations (Danoff 10–12).

The results showed that the bilingual programs did not seem to help the children master academic subjects. That is, for second- to sixth-grade students, the achievement gains in English, reading, and mathematics were the same as they would have been without participation in the bilingual project (Danoff 22–23). In addition, the study indicated that bilingual programs did not serve the legislative goals. Less than a third of the students attended bilingual education classes to learn English. About 75 percent of the children in bilingual education programs either spoke only English or spoke English better than they spoke Spanish. When AIR researchers asked about the goals, they found that most project directors wanted the children to be fluent in both Spanish and English, and the teachers engaged in activities consistent with this aim. Further, when AIR researchers tested the children's ability to read Spanish, there was an increase in this ability among the students in the Title VII classes (Danoff 18–20). Although a major claim about the need for bilingual education was that it would increase children's affection for school, AIR researchers did not find this happening. In both groups, those in bilingual education and those not, the children held neutral feelings about their schools (Danoff 23).

Bilingual advocates complained that the AIR study was unfair because it collected a patchwork of classes labeled bilingual and compared the students in them to the students in regular classes. This treatment, advocates argued, did not allow investigators to focus on well-designed classes and examine their success (Crawford, *Bilingual Education* 87–89). Other researchers claimed that the AIR study was inaccurate. For example, K. N. Nickel noted that the two groups of students the AIR study compared were not similar. The students attending the non-Title VII classes had a better command of English than the students who attended bilingual Title VII classes. Further, because most of the teachers in the Title VII classes were not bilingual themselves, Nickel contended, the Title VII classes could not represent bilingual education (260–261). The lead researchers for the AIR study responded to Nickel's criticisms by claiming that they had used statistical controls to avoid these biases (Danoff and Coles 261–262).

Researchers went back and forth about the effectiveness of bilingual education. For example, in 1981 Keith A. Baker and Adriana A. de Kanter reviewed twenty-eight studies of bilingual education. They found that some programs helped some children. Nonetheless, they did not find enough evidence to justify the federal government relying on this method, and they believed that other models such as immersion in English might be more valuable. On the other hand, in 1985 Ann Willig conducted a meta-analysis of twenty-three of the same twenty-eight evaluations used by Baker and de Kanter. Employing different statistical procedures, Willig found the bilingual programs to be beneficial.

Did Bilingual Education Spread?

As researchers debated the effectiveness of bilingual education, advocacy groups continued to use the federal courts to advance their cause. Although *Lau v. Nichols* was the only case about bilingual education that the U.S. Supreme Court decided, federal district courts considered these issues and expanded the requirements for bilingual education to include African Americans. In July 1977, lawyers filed suit in federal district court on behalf of fifteen Black elementary school-age children who resided in a housing project. They claimed that the Ann Arbor, Michigan, school district failed to establish a program enabling the children to overcome the cultural, social, and economic deprivations that prevented them from making normal progress in schools. The court dismissed all of these allegations except the question of whether the children suffered from a language barrier that impeded their participation in school. During the trial, several experts testified about Black English contending that Black English differs from Standard English, that it underwent a long historical development, and that it flourishes in areas where there is a concentration of African Americans. The experts added that Black children who succeed in schools have to become bilingual (*Martin Luther King, Jr. Elementary School Children v. Ann Arbor School District Board,* 473F 3–9).

In its decision, the court directed the school board to submit a plan defining the steps it would take to identify the children who spoke Black English and describing the ways in which teachers would use that knowledge to help those students learn to read Standard English. In August 1979, the school board submitted a plan that called for training professional staff in identifying Black English, providing assistance to teachers in planning lessons and offering instruction that used Black English to learn Standard English, maintaining a link with the most current professional information on the educational effects of Black English, and establishing improved communications with the parents for suggestions and support. The lawyers for the children asked for several changes such as including a parents' representative on the teachers' supervision team. Although the court found these requests reasonable, they did not impose them on the school board. The court asked for more complete evaluation of the effectiveness of the students' instruction and declared that the plan complied with the Equal Opportunities Act of 1974 that required schools to take appropriate action to overcome language barriers (*Martin Luther King, Jr. Elementary School Children v. Ann Arbor School District Board* 24 Aug. 1979).

Why Did Some People Disagree with the Aims of Bilingual Education?

In 1977 Noel Epstein published *Language, Ethnicity, and the Schools,* criticizing the federal government for requiring local school districts to implement bilingual education even though evaluations of bilingual education were not positive and the direction such programs should take was unclear. Bilingual education advocates wanted the federal government to finance and promote pupil attachment to their ethnic language and history because advocates wanted to provide bilingual instruction to students who were already proficient in English. Further, Epstein complained, the U.S. Office of Civil Rights allowed some school districts such as San Francisco to segregate students and teachers in such bilingual programs in order to maintain the students' culture. According to Epstein, if such programs succeed in teaching children their native languages as well as English, the students will find English more useful and thus the native language will fade (1–4).

Epstein claimed he did not oppose parents seeking to maintain ethnicity among their children. For him, the central question was whether the federal government should take a role in encouraging students to feel an attachment to their ethnic languages and cultures. This might not promote better relations among groups, and within ethnic groups some people supported teaching the native language and others disagreed. Although bilingual educators claimed that such instruction led to school success, Epstein pointed out that research studies did not demonstrate these claims to be true (6–8).

Despite these criticisms, in August 1980 U.S. President Jimmy Carter sought to extend the federal regulations making bilingual education essential in schools where more than 25 percent of the students belonged to the same minority group. Public reaction was immediate, overwhelming, and negative. Congress voted to block Carter's changes, and in 1981 federal officials loosened the regulations to allow Fairfax County, Virginia, to conduct intensive ESL programs instead of bilingual education with cultural components because Fairfax schools enrolled students representing more than fifty languages (Crawford, *Bilingual Education* 42).

In April 1981, Senator S. I. Hayakawa of California proposed an amendment to the U.S. Constitution that would make English the official language of the United States. Although his proposal languished in a congressional committee, Hayakawa claimed that his amendment was necessary to counteract the ethnic chauvinism of Hispanic leaders who wanted to use public schools to advance their language and culture. He did not oppose people learning foreign languages; his son and daughter learned to speak and read Spanish fluently. However, Hayakawa wanted to prevent the United States from being torn apart by linguistic differences as were Canada, Belgium, and Sri Lanka (98–99).

An organization Hayakawa founded, U.S. English, supported efforts in forty states from 1986 to 1988 to make English the official language. Ten states passed such resolutions, among them states with high concentrations of foreign-language-speaking immigrants (Casanova and Arias 12). Although U.S. English, sometimes called "English Only," spent more than $18 million in these campaigns, the group's influence weakened in 1987. Several administrators and a prominent spokesperson, television personality Walter Cronkite, severed ties with the group when the chairperson wrote anti-Hispanic comments in a memorandum (J. Crawford, "What's Behind" 171–172).

In 1985, U.S. Secretary of Education William J. Bennett called bilingual education a failed effort and made clear his intention to allow funds from the Bilingual Education Act to finance methods of teaching children who were not proficient in English without using their native language. He claimed that since 1975 the U.S. Department of Education had required educational programs to be conducted in large part in the students' native language. Bennett argued that this reflected an arrogance on the part of Washington officials who believed that local school authorities could not be trusted to devise the best means to teach the students in their districts. Yet, he contended, after intensive federal support of more than $1.7 billion, there was no evidence that bilingual education helped the students. Consequently, he asked Congress to give local school districts the flexibility to find their own best ways of dealing with the problems (Bennett 359–362).

Congress did what Bennett wanted them to do. In 1984, when Congress reauthorized Title VII, it changed the law to allocate about 4 percent of the appropriations—up to $140 million—for special alternative programs that would not use the students' native language. When Title VII came up again for consideration in 1988, Congress increased the percentage of appropriations available for English-only instruction to 25 percent and stipulated that, in general, three years of bilingual education was adequate for a child. Although individual evaluations could lead to exceptions, programs would not maintain a longer transition to English instruction (J. Crawford, *Bilingual* 44, 83–84).

Why Were Special Education Advocates More Successful Than Bilingual Education Advocates?

There is no simple answer why one group of advocates succeeded more easily than another. Certainly, educators of people with disabilities did not have to fight against prejudice as much as did advocates of bilingual education; anyone's child could be born disabled. Another possibility is that teachers could not or would not make the commitment to learn another language. In California in 1985–86, only 25 percent of the elementary school-age children with limited English proficiency were taught by teachers fluent in their language. One district bilingual coordinator noted that the schools did not expect teachers to be fluent. Instead, they wanted teachers to have some acquaintance with the language, to know some phrases, and to be able to put the children at ease (J. Crawford, *Bilingual* 157). A third explanation is that special educators may have been able to capitalize on a widespread faith that research would find a way to overcome disabilities. Advocates for special education did not press for any particular curriculum idea; they asked for a process that elicited the best ideas and the financial support to make progress possible. On the other hand, bilingual educators wanted to advance the training in native languages and cultural traditions. Once empirical studies called this process into question, advocates could not easily deny requests for flexibility in choosing curricula.

Bilingual education may also have lost some support among Latino leaders. In a series of interviews of 241 Latino politicians and organizational leaders from 1978 to 1980, Rodolfo O. de la Garza found that 97 percent of the leaders supported bilingual education in principle and 67 percent strongly supported bilingual education that stretched from kindergarten through twelfth grade. Despite this apparent consensus, Garza noted several important distinctions. For example, some leaders were upset that bilingual education was implemented with teachers who were not fluent in Spanish. Other leaders felt that Mexican American students should not be segregated from other students from elementary school through high school. Some leaders thought that bilingual educators were promoting themselves, not the children (12–14).

How Did Advocates for Women Advance Their Cause?

Sophisticated arguments for what might be called women's liberation had been popular for many years. In 1949 Simone de Beauvoir argued in her book *The Second Sex* that women occupied a secondary position in the world similar to that filled by racial minorities. Following the philosophy of existentialism, she contended that there was nothing inherent in women's nature that justified this secondary status. Instead, it resulted from environmental forces such as education and tradition, which men controlled. Believing there was no reason for women to occupy inferior social positions and that the only bases for ideal human relations were independence and equality, de Beauvoir advocated things such as the expansion of colleges for women to enable women to learn the things that men learned (vi–viii).

Later, in 1963 Betty Friedan made a similar argument, warning against what she called a feminine mystique. Friedan contended that newspapers, teachers, and parents taught young women to seek fulfillment as wives and mothers; girls learned to view women who sought to be poets, physicists, or presidents as pitiful, neurotic, and unhappy. As a result, Friedan believed that women did not apply themselves to their studies in schools or colleges. They chose instead to marry and to help their husbands succeed. To weaken this mystique, Friedan urged women to learn to compete with men, to succeed in schools and colleges, and to fight for considerations such as maternity leaves and professionally run child care (11–12, 361–362).

Inspired by the success of the civil rights movement, the National Organization for Women (NOW) organized in 1966, and in 1968 the Women's Equity Action League formed. These groups imitated the strategies of the NAACP and, in the 1970s, made sex bias a national policy issue. Basing their arguments on the equal protection doctrine found in the Fourteenth Amendment of the U.S. Constitution, women's advocates turned to the federal courts to obtain equal access to jobs, schools, and athletic programs. Armed with some courtroom successes, they petitioned Congress to adopt the Equal Rights Amendment (ERA) to the Constitution. The ERA failed in 1982, however, and the Supreme Court refused to apply the same scrutiny to women's complaints that it did to those of race. Nonetheless, women's groups won battles over various amendments of the Civil Rights Act. For example, Title IX forced federal administrators to require universities to offer athletic scholarships to women (Salomone 112–136).

Part of the failure of the Equal Rights Amendment may be due to a change in what came to be known as the women's movement. In 1981 Betty Friedan claimed that the women's movement had reached a second stage. During the first stage, she wrote, women sought full participation in political and professional activities. During the second stage, women sought to transform society by integrating family, love, and work (26–28).

Women's advocates did not all take one direction and then shift toward another. However, the change Friedan described matched the general mood of the 1980s. For example, popular works of social criticism such as *The Culture of Narcissism* by Christopher Lasch, published in 1979, and *Habits of the Heart* by Robert Bellah and several coauthors, published in 1985, expressed reactions against the individualism and rationalism derived from the civil rights movement. These books explored more communitarian values. In line with this new emphasis, psychologists argued that women valued human relationships more than men did.

In 1982 psychologist Carol Gilligan published *In a Different Voice,* explaining how she heard women express a way of thinking about morality that was different from the way men disscused this topic. Working with Lawrence Kohlberg, Gilligan interviewed an eleven-year-old boy and an eleven-year-old girl as they thought through a situation called Heinz's dilemma. In this case, the children had to decide what the husband of a sick woman should do when a druggist charges more for a drug to cure her than the couple can pay. Asserting that human life is more valuable than property rights, the boy recommended theft, thinking the courts would excuse it. But the girl worried that the police might arrest the husband and this would drive the wife to despair. Since the girl told the interviewer that stealing is not right, her responses ranked a full stage lower on Kohlberg's progression of moral development than did the boy's because she seemed to be following a simple rule rather than evaluating a situation. However, the girl also said that if everyone discussed the problem, they would find another way. Therefore, Gilligan contended that the girl's responses displayed a deep-seated concern for the relationships among the married couple, the druggist, and the police that were different from the boy's views. This different perception justified her belief that these parties would ultimately cooperate (27–32).

Although Gilligan associated these different modes of thought with men or women, she noted that this association was not absolute. Referring to the work of other psychologists such as Nancy Chodorow, who claimed that mother–child relations form different orientations for males than for females, Gilligan believed the differences arose in a social context that often shaped distinct experiences for men and for women (1–2). Thus, for Gilligan men who were raised in ways similar to women could learn to think in the ways that women tended to think.

What Kind of Curriculum Offered a Feminine Approach to Morals?

In 1984 Nel Noddings published *Caring: A Feminine Approach to Ethics and Moral Education,* arguing that traditional philosophers studied ethics as principles that led to fairness. Calling this the voice of the father, she wrote that the voice of the mother had been silent. However, an important basis of ethical action was to be found in the feminine approach. That is, for Noddings ethical caring arose out of natural caring. Thus, people's desire to be good comes from the wish to remain in a caring relationship. When other people receive and respond to caring, they nourish this resolve. Thus, according to Noddings, teachers could build on these pleasant memories and add good associations to enhance moral education. As a result, Noddings believed, the primary aim of all education could be the nurturance of the ethical ideal (1–6).

To decide when an action is moral, Noddings followed a pattern similar to that expressed by John Dewey in *Democracy and Education,* who used two criteria to evaluate the worth of a social arrangement: Do the people consciously share many and varied interests? Do they enjoy full and free interplay with other forms of association? (Dewey 83). Following Dewey's pragmatic model, Noddings defined two criteria to establish the obligation to care: the existence of or potential for present relation, and the dynamic potential for growth in relation, including the potential for increased reciprocity (86).

Like Dewey's criteria, Noddings's standards were relativistic while providing direction. For example, in considering abortion, she argued, a mother could decide to maintain the fetus; this child was the product of love between her and a man for whom she cared. However, when the child grew up and became pregnant by a man who abandoned her, the mother could ethically help her own child, who was now a young woman, obtain an abortion. For Noddings, an absolute verdict about abortion was unimportant. The concern was whether particular actions enhanced the relationships among the people involved (86–89).

In her book *Caring,* Noddings did not recommend teaching this type of reasoning to children, although one could assume they would learn it. She explained that teachers must act as what she calls the "one-caring." Such a teacher should see the students as more important than the subject. Thus, although a caring teacher and a student would struggle together with mathematics, such a teacher would not show caring by doing everything possible to help the child learn; this would imply that the subject matter or the teacher's professional role was more important than the child as a human being (20).

For Noddings, some rules of teaching and forms of school organization enhanced caring. Teachers should allow students to learn all they wish about controversial subjects such as religion without being forced to accept a position. Students should engage in service activities to develop competence in caring. Subject matters should follow the range of human existence so that students could engage them in attitudes of aesthetical caring. This meant that students had to learn the history and applications of a subject matter, its potential for personal and recreational use, its epistemological problems, and the way those problems are resolved. This might call for increased emphasis on biographies that show how the subject influenced people's lives. Finally, students and teachers should work together for three or more years, work through a sort of contract system, and depend on external standardized achievement tests to provide grades (Noddings 182–187, 191–192, 195–199).

What Criticisms Did the Curriculum for Caring Suffer?

There were two important aspects of Noddings's aim to nurture the ethical ideal. The first was her assertion that ethical caring stemmed from natural caring and that this could be taught. The second was that her ambiguous attitude toward religion may have caused her to reject an important means of maintaining moral commitments.

In the first case, Noddings argued that since it was pleasurable to care and be cared for, people would want to continue those states. This desire would be the motivation to learn how to do good. Once inspired, students and teachers could work toward progressively more difficult types of caring. For example, she said, people could learn to share, or they could practice traits such as responsibility by taking care of pets. In these ways, students and teachers could become competent in caring (122–123).

However, some important educators were less convinced that students could learn to care. For example, in *Education at the Crossroads,* Jacques Maritain, a Catholic theologian, argued that educators labored under the misconception that everything can be taught. He contended that there could be courses in philosophy but not in wisdom. Most important, neither intuition nor love was a matter of training and learning; he held them to be matters of gift and freedom. However, Maritain did believe that natural sentiment was similar to caring. Thus, he urged teachers to foster what he called the fundamental dispositions of the true human person. These included a sense of cooperation with other people that he found to be as natural as the tendency to social and political life (22–23, 38).

In the second case, Noddings argued that personal relationships provided the basis for moral understandings that differed from the rules and principles often associated with religion (97). Further, she quoted stories such as the biblical tale of Abraham offering to sacrifice his son, Isaac, to show how religion could contradict an ethics based on caring (43–44). Noddings left open the possibility that religion could be a positive force, however, because she wanted children to be allowed to pursue religious faith if they chose.

There was some evidence that religion enabled people to be of service to others and to lead moral lives. In their 1992 book entitled *Some Do Care,* Ann Colby and William Damon published the results of extensive, semistructured interviews with twenty-three individuals who led intensely moral lives. They sought to locate the developmental principles that helped people form commitments. Although these individuals followed different occupations and fulfilled different roles, they all lived integrated lives and directed their personal goals toward moral commitments. To maintain this integration, they drew on a religious faith. Even those who did not hold to any formal religion believed in a transcendent ideal. Thus, Colby and Damon found that all twenty-three exemplars had a faith in something above and beyond the self that unified them and enabled them to fulfill their commitments (310–311).

Was There an Appropriate Method to Teach Women?

Shortly after Gilligan wrote that women reasoned differently than men, other psychologists contended that women learned differently. For example, in 1986 Mary Belenky and several coauthors interviewed 135 women asking them about their previous self-concepts and their personal relationships. Entitling the results of their research *Women's Ways of Knowing,* the authors contended that women followed a pattern of intellectual development that was distinct from that of men. Although Belenky and her coauthors did not interview men, they compared the results of their interviews with those of William Perry, who in 1970 had described how undergraduates at Harvard University changed their ways of knowing over time. Most of his subjects were men (Belenky, et al. 1–20).

According to Belenky and her coauthors, the simplest stage was for women to remain silent, seeking direction from some external authority. Although Belenky and her colleagues thought few women lived in silence, they believed this stage offered an anchoring point for their epistemology. The researchers found that sometimes women shifted to a contradictory view of truth as personal, internal, and subjective. Because the stage of silence represented an extreme denial of self, the women who made this change saw the movement as a liberating step toward autonomy and independent judgment. Furthermore, the researchers found that as women matured they blended the previous orientations and moved toward procedural knowledge or reason. Belenky and her coauthors identified two types of procedural knowers. Among the graduates of traditional liberal arts colleges, they found what they called "separate knowing." Women with this orientation espoused a morality based on impersonal procedures for establishing truth. Because such reasoning blended intuition and objectivity, the researchers found that it appeared to constrain some women. Other women jumped outside the traditional systems of reasoning and created their own frame. Calling this stage "connected knowing," the researchers found that these women perceived that all truth was a matter of context and that theories were models for approximating experience; in this highest stage of knowing, women sought to understand other people's knowledge and thinking.

In addition to deciding that women passed through various states of knowing, Mary Belenky and her coauthors outlined the way of teaching they thought would help women move through those stages. The traditional authoritarian model of education could not help, they claimed. Therefore, they borrowed the ideas of Paulo Freire to call for what they called "connected teaching," arguing that most schools used a form of banking education that implied teachers had the right answers and students had to find those answers. As an option, Belenky and her colleagues recommended that teachers think through problems with students and show the students the tentativeness of theories. This would help women recognize the relationships between people and ideas, thereby following women's natural pattern of growth. They identified this method of instruction as Freire's model of problem-posing education (190–229).

Did Freire Present an Appropriate Model for Women's Education?

The connected teaching that Belenky and her coauthors recommended was more therapeutic than Freire's problem-posing education. In *Pedagogy of the Oppressed,* Freire argued that the inescapable concern in today's world is the inability of people to become fully human. This appeared in the struggles for the affirmation of men and women as persons, the attempts to emancipate labor, and the will to overcome alienation. However, he added, this liberation was not something that anyone could give anyone else. According to Freire, people who were oppressed had to free themselves. If they accomplished this, new ways of thinking would free everyone. Unfortunately, oppressed people feared freedom and, when they sought reform, tried to become oppressors themselves. As a result, there had to be a way to enable oppressed peoples, even with their limited ways of thinking, to direct their own pedagogy (25–30).

Freire's answer was simple. The revolutionary educator had to engage in critical thinking with the students. This process would free them both. Freire called his method problem-posing education. Through it, the teacher and the student would see the world as something that was changing, and they would think about themselves and their world through a process of dialogue. However, Freire did not consider dialogue to be a technique that anyone could apply if properly trained. Dialogue could not exist without a profound love for the world and people. It required humility on the part of the teacher, and it demanded an intense faith in the ability of people to make and remake the world (56–71).

Thus, although Freire did not use the word, he saw caring as a necessary condition for revolutionary education. Such an attitude was not sufficient to provide problem-posing education. Good intentions could easily lead to cultural invasions, Freire argued. A kindly educator might approach laborers to offer them the knowledge the educator had put together. Though well organized, this plan implied that the workers were the objects of the actions, and it omitted their personal views of reality (74–76).

For Freire, the starting point of any liberating education was the concrete situation of the people and an awareness of their aspirations. Freire's curriculum was a process in which the teacher would present the situation and the people's feelings about the situation to the people as a problem. This was done in the form of some object or representation such as a picture that Freire called "codes." An effective code had the following characteristics: It was familiar to the people, it was neither overly explicit nor too enigmatic, and it was connected to historic or long-standing themes found in the people's situation (76).

Freire illustrated this procedure of a teacher using a code to listen to and challenge the students. A teacher in Santiago showed a picture of a drunken man on a busy city street to a group of tenement residents. They remarked that the drunk man was the only honest person in the picture. Like them, he worked hard for low wages, worried about his family, and drank to forget his problems. The residents connected the low wages they received with their alcoholism. This prepared them, Freire noted, to understand the ways they were exploited and to fight against them (99–100).

The process of developing this curriculum was complicated. To explain it, Freire offered an example of how an interdisciplinary literacy team might carry out a plan for adult education in a peasant area with a high percentage of illiteracy. The process involved five stages. First, the team went to the village, asked the villagers to join them, and with their help tried to record the daily life. Second, the members of the team, which now included some villagers, placed the contradictions of the situation into codes. They made some sort of representation, such as the picture of the drunk man on the city street. Third, they asked the villagers to describe what they saw in those codes. Fourth, they tried to determine systematically what they had actually found. They tried to make sure the codes were representative, effective, and led to increased liberation. Finally, they chose the best channel of communication for each theme. At each stage, team members sought the permission of and actively involved the people who were to learn from the materials. Most important, the investigators avoided any attempt to make the peasants accept the values of the team members. Freire cautioned that the only value the people should share with the team members was the importance of approaching reality and attempting to unveil it (91–102).

Interestingly, Freire influenced education in the United States in apparently contradictory ways. On the one hand, Belenky and her coauthors removed Freire's emphasis on social transformation and changed his method into a pattern of interaction between teachers and students marked by discussions that were cooperative and supportive rather than competitive and penetrating. The connected teacher, Belenky wrote, presented herself as a person and presented the objectivity of the subject matter as a personal issue (227). On the other hand, Peter McLaren acknowledged Freire as one of the important theorists who contributed to critical pedagogy. This was not a homogeneous set of ideas, McLaren cautioned. It was a body of work by different theorists who sought to empower the powerless and transform existing social inequalities and injustices (160, 194).

More in line with McLaren than with Belenky, Elsa Roberts Auerbach and Nina Wallerstein published a text describing how to use problem posing in adult classes for English as a second language. The key to this model was drafting the dialogues that language teachers had always used into codes that were the basis for reflection and action leading to social change. For example, one dialogue had ten short sentences made up of about six simple English words. The dialogue took the form of a series of questions and answers between a worker and his supervisor. The worker wanted safety gloves because he was handling dangerous materials. The supervisor said that he would get them later. The worker went to his factory committeeman to begin the process of filing a grievance. In the discussion that followed, the students talked about the National Labor Relations Act, the rights workers had under it, and the process of appeal should the employer try to punish workers who complain (Auerbach and Wallerstein 78–79). Thus, the dialogue and the activities inspired conversations about people's roles in reform while they taught the basic vocabulary and mechanics of English.

Do Women Think Differently Than Men?

After Gilligan's work became popular, psychologists debated whether there were different ways of thinking between the genders. In 1984 Lawrence Walker published a review of all the studies then available that used Kohlberg's measures and examined sex differences in the development of moral reasoning. These totaled thirty-one studies with 2,879 subjects who ranged in age from five to seventeen. Besides developing the survey, Walker used meta-analytic procedures to statistically combine the results of the more objective studies, reducing the impact of less carefully constructed studies. Although he found that a minority of studies revealed small sex differences in moral reasoning, he confidently concluded that the moral reasoning of men and women was remarkably similar (Walker 677–691).

In 1989 Martha Mednick, then a psychologist at Howard University, complained that theories of women's special nature appealed to political hopes rather than scientific truth. Mednick argued that an overwhelming body of evidence showed that men and women reasoned in similar ways. She added that feminist psychologists ignored this evidence, although it was readily available, and continued to assert that women thought differently than men. Mednick concluded that the assertions of psychologists such as Gilligan and Belenky persisted because they appealed to a cultural belief system. More important, when scholars focused on the differences between men and women, they ignored the need for structural social change. Consequently, an unfortunate outcome of the analysis of women was the growth of a mental health movement that supplanted a social change movement. To reinforce this allegation, Mednick quoted a then recent conversation with Simone de Beauvoir in which Beauvoir said that the new psychology was again defining women as the second sex (Mednick, "On the Politics" 1118–1123).

Even philosophers sympathetic to feminism warned against making too much of the differences between the genders. For example, Maxine Greene complained that those philosophers who searched for distinctive feminine ways of knowing or valuing omitted concern for human freedom. These philosophers were correct to make identity and relationships politically relevant. However, because they did not pay careful attention to the problem of freedom in community, they failed to help diverse human beings articulate multiple perspectives in multiple idioms in ways that they could form into something they had in common (85–86).

Did Advocates for Women Seek Separate Schools?

In general, women's advocates did not ask for separate educational experiences. They wanted the woman's perspective to be recognized as an important contribution. For example, although Carol Gilligan associated different modes of moral reasoning with men and with women, she noted that this association was not absolute, because it arose from social conditions. Thus, a boy could be raised to think more as women do. However, she protested the unfair nature of scales of moral reasoning that discounted reasoning built on a consideration of relationships. Similarly, Nel Noddings contended that philosophy suffered when ethical reasoning excluded what she called women's ways of thinking. Jane Roland Martin made a similar point about schools in her book entitled *The Schoolhome.* She wanted schools to take on the virtues of homes, as in Montessori's Casi dei Bambini, where caring attitudes encouraged students to learn academic material. Martin believed that schoolhomes would exalt domesticity and cure the separation of work and home in U.S. society. In them, boys would learn to replace violence with courage, and girls would learn to speak for themselves.

Nonetheless, during the 1980s and 1990s many people argued that single-sex schools would be especially helpful to women. Although there were some public and private schools and academies that accepted only women, American Catholics made a tradition out of building single-sex elementary and secondary schools. The encyclical letter of 1929 by Puis XI, *Divini Illius Magistri,* encouraged this separation. In that letter, the pope called on the faithful to realize that sex education and coeducation caused problems among children. However, in 1966 the Second Vatican Council published a document on education that appeared to reverse that position. It did not comment specifically on coeducation, but it did note that every person is entitled to a prudent sex education. As Catholic schools faced declining enrollments in the 1960s and 1970s, many single-sex schools combined to become coeducational.

In 1993 Anthony Bryk, Valerie Lee, and Peter Holland published the results of an extensive study of Catholic schools. Using complex statistical analyses, the authors compared the effects of single-sex schools for girls with the effects of coeducational schools. They obtained data on Catholic schools from the study High School and Beyond, initiated in 1980 by the National Center for Education Statistics. The authors concluded that in the separate institutions the girls developed more positive academic interests and behaviors, spent more time on homework, and experienced increased academic success, especially in science and reading. Although mathematics achievement did not increase, the female students had higher educational aspirations and became more concerned for sex role equity as a result of single-sex schools. Consequently, the authors argued, something positive was happening in single-sex schools even though Catholic educators viewed those segregated institutions as anachronisms (Bryk, Lee, and Holland 228–240).

Bryk, Lee, and Holland's research became part of a controversy over the value of single-sex schools. In 1998 the American Association of University Women published a report, *Separated by Sex: A Critical Look at Single Sex Education for Girls,* which was the product of a conference of sixteen scholars including Valerie Lee. Contrary to what Lee had argued, the committee agreed that there is no evidence that single-sex education is better for girls than coeducation. They concluded that no matter the educational setting, policymakers must identify the components of a good education. Nonetheless, conference members agreed that for some students single-sex programs produced positive results, although the long-term effects of such segregated education on boys and girls were unknown. Part of the problem, according to the researchers, was that single-sex schools could harbor sexism in the same ways that coeducational programs could. Another problem was that the programs among the single-sex schools varied so much that the schools had little in common except that the students were of one sex (1–3).

What Was the Effect of Advocates' Efforts to Legislate the Curriculum?

Advocates for special education, linguistic minorities, and women enjoyed different levels of success in legislating the curriculum. To succeed in courts and legislatures, advocates had to appeal using simple or narrow objectives. For example, part of the success of the NAACP was that it had asked that children be admitted into schools without regard to race. The narrowness of that plea gave it force. In this way, special educators had an advantage because they could claim that education should be something parents, specialists, and teachers agreed the child needed in order to overcome his or her deficiency. The process they demanded was one that called all these parties together to negotiate a curriculum for each child. It was a model that lawyers, judges, and congresspeople understood.

On the other hand, linguistic minorities could not make as direct an appeal because their aims were more splintered. Some advocates sought to teach the language and culture of the ethnic group more than they wanted to help the children learn English. Experts debated whether the children of immigrants needed special instruction in their native language to learn English. Further, teachers resisted the idea of learning new languages in order to teach the students.

Advocates for women won when they appealed for limited ends such as equal treatment in school athletics. On the other hand, when they contended that women learned things differently than men, they could not require school people to adopt their models. The best they could do was propose and explain. However, even this was helpful because it encouraged educators to think more deeply about the aims of education.

Women's advocates contended that women thought more about relationships than did men and that this perspective should be added to the schools. Such pleas for integration enhanced the ways people thought about the aims of education. By encouraging people to consider personal relationships as well as subject matter achievement, they asked that moral development take an important place in educational aims. These were not new ideas. In the project method and the activity movement of the 1930s, teachers considered the relationships among the students and their affinity for the subject matter as most important. Their aim was to have the ideas of democracy permeate the schools. However, these were not pleas for a dramatic style of integration that would remake education. For example, in concentrating on the relationships in the classroom, the teachers thought less about the need for wider social reform. At best, the hope was that when students learned to care for one other, they would transform society when they became adults. This was similar to what the progressive schools of the 1930s had tried to accomplish. Unfortunately, those earlier schools did not have wider social influences. Consequently, there was no reason to believe that the caring in the schoolhomes of the 1990s would reach beyond itself.

The point is that educators who sought to tailor education to children's disabilities, linguistic differences, or gender selected variations of the three alternatives that faced all minorities. At times they chose to separate; at others they chose to assimilate. In most cases, however, they adopted a model built on some form of integration.

TIMELINE
1964–1998

1965 The NEA surveyed Mexican American children and published the report *The Invisible Minority*

1965 The CEC and the NEA promoted the passage of the ESEA of 1965

1966 Various organizations gathered in New York to organize TESOL

(continued)

TIMELINE Continued

1966	NOW was organized
1968	The International League of Societies for the Mentally Handicapped adopted the Declaration of General and Specific Rights of the Mentally Retarded
1968	The Women's Equity Action League formed
1969	*PARC v. Commonwealth* started
1969	Jose Angel Gutierrez organized Mexican Americans into the group Cuidadanos Unidos in Crystal City, Texas, to boycott schools
1970	Crystal City agreed to the demands of Cuidadanos Unidos, which formed a political party and filed applications to run for election to the school board
1970	U.S. Office of Civil Rights Director J. Stanley Pottinger issued a memo to Crystal City schools warning them to follow the exact rules of affirmative action
1970	Congress replaced Title VI with the Education of the Handicapped Act
1971	PARC filed the first case demanding access to public schools for children with mental retardation
1972	*Mills v. Board of Education of the District of Columbia* forbade Washington public schools from excluding children with physical disabilities
1972	The U.S. Commission on Civil Rights published *The Excluded Student* as the third part of its series on Mexican American education
1974	Congress passed Title II of the Equal Opportunities Act
1974	Congress reauthorized and expanded the Bilingual Education Act of 1968
1975	AIR began researching Spanish–English bilingual education projects
1975	President Gerald Ford signed the Education for All Handicapped Children Act
1977	Lawyers filed a suit in federal district court arguing that schools did not accommodate Black English–speaking elementary students
1980	President Jimmy Carter extended the federal regulations on bilingual education
1980	The National Association for Retarded Children was renamed the Association for Retarded Citizens (ARC)
1981	California Senator S. I. Hayakawa proposed an amendment to the U.S. Constitution that would make English the official language of the United States
1982	The Equal Rights Amendment failed
1982	Carol Gilligan published *In a Different Voice*
1984	Nel Noddings published *Caring: A Feminine Approach to Ethics and Moral Education*

CHAPTER

13 Technology, Diversity, and Iconoclasm: 1980–2000

Boston teens on a youth pride march.

OVERVIEW

Social critics argued that as the twentieth century progressed people sought efficiency and harmony rather than new understandings of traditional values. Educational reform in the late twentieth century followed a similar pattern. Reformers in the excellence movement sought to make education more effective by subjecting students to identical measurements. At the same time, these reformers urged teachers or parents to choose their own curricula and to form their own schools. A different set of reformers, many of whom disliked the excellence movement, worked to make the schools safe places where administrators, teachers, and students accorded respect and dignity to gay, lesbian, and bisexual youth. Although these two sets of reforms seemed different, they could function together to make schools more efficient and harmonious. The problem was that advocates did not pursue deeper meanings in the contributions of previous educators. As a result, their reforms were superficial.

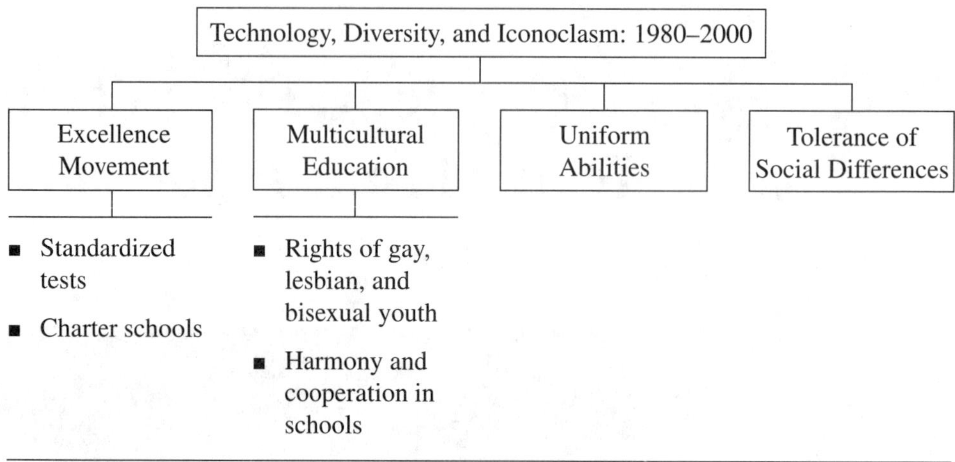

What Pattern of Changes Did Social Critics Find in the Wider Society?

Although the twentieth century brought increased affluence to most people in the United States, several critics complained that people paid for their comforts by giving up their traditional freedoms. In the 1950s, social critics such as William H. Whyte Jr. and C. Wright Mills complained that as more and more people worked for large corporations, these organizations posed new threats to traditional conceptions of personal freedom. For example, it became increasingly difficult for people to own their own businesses or control their own work. Although many people tried to start their own businesses, most people found it better to work for a large company and to move into a suburban community. As a result, U.S. society saw the rise of a white-collar class whose members developed an organization mentality that helped them work in teams with other similarly trained people. The problem, according to these critics, was that the large organizations, which included universities, discouraged people from pursuing traditional conceptions of intelligent thought and denigrated the value of personal genius.

In the 1970s, critics expanded these complaints, noting that the problem had spread around the world. For example, Jacques Ellul noted that by the twentieth century most traditional cultures gave way to technological societies, and teachers sought to integrate students into the wider social order. This meant that students learned to seek the same goals as other people in society. Ellul found that in a technological society education was the task of experts who used systems implemented by the state, imposed them on every person, and aimed them at social adjustment. Consequently, teachers measured the development of students by their adaptation to the people around them, and they trained students to be competent at various types of tasks. What the technological society lacked, Ellul noted, was the traditional idea that schools should produce a group called an intelligentsia that could provide moral understandings to direct and limit the technological efforts. As a result, in the technological society there was no way to restrain the development of techniques. Instead, people relied on technology to solve all problems to such an extent that society took on a different quality from the civilizations that had preceded it. More important, Ellul contended, the technological society spread around the world because traditional forms of social organization proved incompatible with the development of techniques. This occurred despite the best intentions of members of the more technologically advanced cultures (Ellul 124–125, 344–347).

By the 1980s, in the face of large corporations and technological imperatives, critics noted an ironical twist whereby people's desire for freedom and individual growth caused them to break down the mechanisms through which they traditionally resisted tendencies toward conformity. In 1985 Robert N. Bellah and his coauthors found that the American emphasis on individualism destroyed the traditional ties that existed among people. This was dangerous, they added, because those historical relationships created forces that limited the possibility of the majority of society exercising a tyrannical hold over everyone. In contemporary United States, the pattern worked in the following way. First, middle-class Americans rejected old-style social and political connections because they believed these relationships repressed their search for personal meaning. Second, society became more integrated economically, technically, and functionally, which required people to conform to the demands of larger institutions. Third, Bellah and his coauthor discovered that what they called the dominant culture of the manager and the therapist recognized the conflict between social and economic demands and personal desires. These managers urged people to make their particular segments of life into worlds of their own. However, when people took this advice they could no longer relate to their larger cultural setting and were powerless to recognize the source of their problems (Bellah, et al. vii, 50).

Educational reform in the late twentieth century followed a pattern similar to the model social critics found in the wider society. On the one hand, some reformers sought to make education more effective by subjecting students to identical measurements. For example, many states demanded that the students pass competency or proficiency tests before graduating from high school. Advocates claimed that these evaluative techniques would force teachers and schools to improve instruction. On the other hand, advocates for gay, lesbian, and bisexual youth worked to make the schools safe places where administrators, teachers, and students behaved toward one another with respect and dignity. Despite their differences, these two kinds of reformers could work together to improve school efficiency and culture. Unfortunately, advocates on both sides tended to ignore the lessons of the past and the contributions of previous educators.

How Did the Federal Government Try to Reform Education in the 1980s?

The educational reforms of the 1980s known as the excellence movement grew out of a shift in the federal government's involvement in education. In the late 1960s and the 1970s, the federal government aimed at providing educational equity for groups such as African Americans and children with disabilities. Although these efforts continued in the 1980s, the federal government returned to urging improved academic performance. Officials in the federal government blamed then current economic difficulties on schools, which, they said, failed to train competent workers. Several federal officials contended that these problems would disappear if state governments required high school students to take harder academic courses, spend more time in class, and pass standardized tests in order to graduate.

In the 1970s and early 1980s, the United States suffered difficult economic problems. Many cities in the midwestern states such as Flint, Michigan, and Dayton, Ohio, underwent severe recessions as industrial firms moved their plants. In 1977, U.S. President Jimmy Carter, a Democrat, asserted that the United States faced an energy crisis because Americans consumed too much foreign oil. This crisis caused national unemployment to grow to 7.5 percent and made inflation rise from 6 percent in 1976 to more than 12 percent. Interest rates soared to a high of 20 percent. When Carter claimed that Americans aggravated their own problems by wanting too much, business leaders claimed that he lacked a coherent strategy to tame inflation. Carter's Republican challenger, Ronald Reagan, used this criticism in the 1980 presidential campaign. Although Reagan promised to solve the economic problems, he could not. In 1982 unemployment rose to 11 percent. Bankruptcies and farm foreclosures reached record levels. The country's trade deficit increased from $25 billion in 1980 to $111 billion in 1984, and the national budget deficit grew to become the largest in the nation's history ("Reagan, Ronald W.").

As economic difficulties grew, President Reagan and Secretary of Education Terrell Bell appointed the National Commission on Excellence in Education (NCEE), which blamed public schools for the problems. Headed by David Gardner, former president of the University of Utah, NCEE included eighteen members from corporations, colleges, schools, and state governments. In 1983, after eighteen months of study, NCEE released its report *A Nation at Risk.* The committee claimed that a rising tide of mediocrity in U.S. schools threatened the former superiority of the United States in commerce, industry, and technological innovation. The report claimed that other nations surpassed U.S. educational attainments because U.S. schools had lost sight of the purpose of schooling (NCEE 5–6).

When NCEE members presented evidence showing that public schools failed, controversy centered around three points. First, NCEE complained that U.S. students performed badly on measures of academic achievement when compared to similar students in other industrialized countries. Second, they pointed out that the average achievement, as measured by standardized achievement tests, of high school students had dropped below the level attained by students in 1957. Finally, those standardized test scores, such as the College Board's Scholastic Aptitude Test (SAT) scores and the College Board Achievement Test scores, declined consistently from 1963 to 1980. The report claimed that average verbal scores declined fifty points and average mathematics scores dropped nearly forty points (NCEE 8–9).

NCEE members argued that students performed poorly on academic measures because schools diluted their academic programs. For example, the NCEE report noted that 42 percent of students enrolled in general track courses instead of more demanding college preparatory courses. In most schools, students chose electives such as physical or health education, work experience outside school, or personal development courses such as training for marriage and avoided difficult academic programs. Thus, although most schools offered intermediate algebra, only 31 percent of the students took it. Calculus was available in 60 percent of the schools, but only 6 percent of the students enrolled. Even the most science-oriented students in the United States spent about a third of the time that students in other countries devoted to classes such as mathematics, biology, chemistry, and physics. Further, the NCEE found that two-thirds of high school seniors did less than one hour of homework a night. Finally, the NCEE found that the cycle reinforced itself. As student reading levels dropped, textbook publishers lowered the reading levels and the difficulty of the material to meet market demands (NCEE 18–21).

To remedy the problems in high schools, NCEE members made recommendations.

1. The committee proposed what NCEE members called five new basic subjects of instruction. In order to graduate, students would take four years of English courses to help them read and write effectively. Students would also take three years of mathematics and science that were as demanding for the students who did not plan to continue their education as it was for the college-bound students. High school students would enroll in three years of social studies that would teach them things such as the fundamentals of the U.S. economic and political systems and the difference between free and repressive societies. The committee also added a new basic subject, computer science, which students would study for half a year in order to learn how to use a computer in their other courses. Concerning elementary and junior high school instruction, the report urged teachers to prepare the younger students for these academic experiences in the high schools (NCEE 24–27).

2. *A Nation at Risk* called for standardized tests of achievement at major transition points such as between high school and college. These tests would certify student accomplishment, identify students needing remedial work, and indicate what accelerated work could be implemented. Although NCEE members discouraged the federal government from administering such tests, they envisioned a time when all states would administer them (NCEE 28).

3. Schools should increase the time students spent on academic affairs. The NCEE report suggested that teachers assign more homework, that the school day be increased to seven hours, and that the annual calendar expand to include 220 days of classes.

4. Prospective teachers must show an aptitude for teaching, competence in an academic discipline, and high academic achievement.

5. Schools should implement mechanisms such as eleven-month contracts, merit systems of pay raises, and career ladders to encourage teachers to work harder at mastering their craft and their disciplines (NCEE 29–31).

Although these recommendations would increase the cost of running a school, NCEE offered no increased federal support. The report noted that the primary responsibility for funding these reforms should fall on state and local governments. The federal government should continue to supply aid to gifted students, socioeconomically disadvantaged students, minority and language-minority children, and students with disabilities. At the same time, the federal government would continue to protect students' and teachers' civil rights, support educational research, and provide student financial assistance in higher education (NCEE 32–33).

In general, NCEE members took the position that all students could learn if they had the time they needed to master it. Consequently, all students in all tracks or levels should learn the same material, but they should study the subject matter for different amounts of time. Taking their ideas from the arguments about mastery learning, NCEE members decided it might be reasonable for some students to finish school in eleven years and others in thirteen years (Tomlinson 18).

The ideas spread quickly. Within ten months, the U.S. Government Printing Office distributed more than 150,000 copies of *A Nation at Risk.* Several daily newspapers printed the complete report so that about four million citizens read it. Most important, state governments began to implement the suggestions. In 1983, the Education Commission of the States reported that every one of the fifty states appointed one or more commissions to survey the problems in education. At that time, there were 184 such commissions at work on such questions (Tomlinson 3–4; Peterson 3).

By 1984 the U.S. Department of Education claimed that the report *A Nation at Risk* brought education to the forefront of a political debate not matched since the Sputnik crisis in 1957. When department officials surveyed the actions in various states, they found that forty-eight of the states had commissions deliberating on high school requirements. Twenty-one states sought to improve textbooks. Eight states approved lengthening the school day, and eighteen adopted mandates lengthening the time of instruction (U.S. Department of Education, *The Nation* 11, 18).

Although Terrell Bell resigned from the position of secretary of education after less than four years, his successor, William J. Bennett, sought to advance the reforms initiated by *A Nation at Risk.* In 1986 Bennett produced the document *What Works: Research about Teaching and Learning.* It was similar to the NCEE report *A Nation at Risk* in two ways. First, it was short and clearly written. Second, in the same way that NCEE labeled its report an open letter to the American people, Bennett directed his report to parents who wanted to assist in the education of their children. Thus, both reports implied that school officials would not make the necessary changes on their own. In a foreword, President Reagan wrote that he concurred with his secretary that, armed with such information, the American people could fix their own schools. Department of Education Assistant Secretary Chester Finn, who supervised the compilation of the volume, explained why these politicians believed educators would not reform schools: Educators held to conventional wisdom about their profession so strongly that they overlooked obvious truths. For example, it noted that some research about the teaching of reading indicated that the phonics method gave students a better start when learning to read than what the document called the "look-say" approach. *What Works* contended that until the 1940s phonics instruction was used in most schools. Since then teachers had tried to teach students to identify a word at a glance rather than to sound out each letter. Although the report did not call the teacher's use of a look-say approach wrong, it claimed that, when applied judiciously, phonics instruction could help students identify words and sound out new ones (U.S. Department of Education, *What Works* v, 21).

What Works recommended what it called effective schools research, a set of findings comparing schools deemed successful with similar institutions that were not. According to the report, effective schools used strong instructional leadership, a schoolwide emphasis on basic skills, and high teacher expectations. As a result, the report suggested schools should focus on academic programs, establish fair and consistent discipline policies, and provide frequent opportunities for supervisors to observe teachers in action. In the classroom, teachers should plan instruction so that they used the time efficiently. They should explain exactly what students should learn, and they should demonstrate the steps to accomplish the task. Students should learn these carefully structured lessons by heart, and teachers should monitor their progress carefully, providing reinforcement for correct answers. In addition, teachers should require significant levels of homework (U.S. Department of Education, *What Works* 34–36, 41, 45–52).

What Works concluded with the observation that business leaders considered job applicants' basic academic skills more important than specific vocational training. Business leaders wanted schools to stress literacy, mathematics, and problem-solving skills. Whether or not Bennett and Finn accurately characterized the ideas of business leaders, business people did become involved in school affairs as a result of the publication of *A Nation at Risk.* In 1993 an organization of business people, the Conference Board, surveyed its members' efforts to improve schools over the previous ten years since the NCEE report appeared. Led by guidelines from the Committee for Economic Development, the National Alliance for Business, and the Business Roundtable, various corporations took part in a variety of ways. For example, Southern California Gas Company trained parents to become leaders in school communities, and the U.S. West Foundation provided a hotline and parent education network to help educators determine parents' needs. Businesses such as NEC Corporation and Apple Computer took part in mathematics and science programs such as the Models for Integration: Science and Technology (MIST) program in North Carolina. To prevent dropouts, the Coca-Cola Foundation instituted a Valued Youth Program that paid children labeled "at-risk" to tutor younger students. Whereas these first efforts attempted to provide general assistance to schools, a second wave of reform sought collaborations or partnering wherein businesses interceded to advise ailing school districts. For example, the Buenger Commission in Cincinnati lent executives to the public schools to help with school management and finance. In the third wave, businesses sought to bring about public policy initiatives. In Wisconsin, for example, businesses mobilized public opinion to support legislative changes leading to the state's school choice program. By the late 1980s, businesses took part in a fourth wave of reform that sought systemic changes. For example, business corporations helped states such as New Jersey to change the process of licensing teachers. They wanted to allow liberal arts graduates and adults experienced in other lines of work to become teachers without going through an extensive teacher training program (Conference Board 7–8, 16–20).

Despite this list of activities and accomplishments, the Conference Board found that its efforts did not improve school achievement. For example, Jerry Hume, chairperson of the board at Basic American, Inc., complained that the one-half of the applicants seeking work at his corporation could not pass a test of basic skills set at the eighth-grade level. Another business leader, Jerry Bowsher, argued that the problem required a total restructuring of the educational system. Among the problems he noted was that the leadership changed too quickly. He pointed out that from 1983 to 1993 there were five secretaries of education. When leaders changed so quickly they could not direct the fifty chief state school officers and more than 15,000 district superintendents to make substantial reforms (Conference Board 24–27).

Was NCEE Correct in Assuming That Public Schools Failed?

The report *A Nation at Risk* used three controversial sources of evidence to show what the authors called the failure of public high schools in the United States: They cited statistical comparisons of students in different countries on several special tests; they pointed out the average achievement of high school students; and they noted that the scores of SAT tests had declined consistently. These arguments convinced reformers. On the other hand, critics argued that the evidence was not as clear as the reformers made it appear.

In the first case, the NCEE report highlighted comparisons that the International Association for the Evaluation of Educational Achievement and the Educational Testing Service had conducted since the 1960s. For example, in the First International Mathematics Study, in a test given to seniors taking a math course, U.S. students ranked last behind eleven other nations. In the First International Science Study a few years later, U.S. students performed just as badly. These trends continued through the International Assessment of Educational Progress in Mathematics and Science and the Second International Assessment of Educational Progress administered in 1990–91. However, in 1991, on a test of reading abilities, America's nine- and thirteen-year-old children performed well (Ravitch, *National Standards* 84–86).

Critics refused to take these scores at face value, complaining that the researchers used invalid comparisons. That is, the researchers tested students in top-level schools in countries such as West Germany, the Netherlands, and Sweden. However, less than 20 percent of the student population in these countries attended these elite institutions. Researchers gave the same tests to students in U.S. high schools that were open to all students. As a result, the researchers compared the average achievements of the best students from several countries to the average of all the students in the United States. In such an unfair comparison, U.S. students had to perform poorly (Rotberg 296–297).

The researchers who conducted the tests acknowledged this problem. Several noted that it was pointless to compare average scores of students taking similar mathematics programs at similar levels in the different countries. Instead, they felt that a better question to ask was if the elite students in different countries perform similarly. Thus, for one test they compared the average scores of the top 5 percent of students in a specific age group in different countries (Bradburn, et al. 775).

Despite the statistical problems, researchers contended that some findings appeared clear. First, the best students in the United States scored lower on the international surveys than the best students from other countries. Second, when teachers presented more content to students, the students learned more and performed better on tests. Third, when a country offered a differentiated curriculum and tracked young students by their abilities, the performance of students on achievement tests was poor (Ravitch, *National Standards* 87–88).

The arguments in *A Nation at Risk* did not depend only on international comparisons. NCEE noted declines in achievement test scores in the United States. In the late 1970s, the authors of six major reviews of test-score trends argued that reading performance increased steadily until the mid-1960s. According to those reviewers, scores fell for the next ten or so years. Similar findings came from the National Assessment of Educational Progress (NAEP) when it began to create a national report card of educational achievement in 1969–70. Under supervision from the National Center for Education Statistics, NAEP administered tests in science, writing, and citizenship. In later years, it added tests in the other subjects such as art, mathematics, and social studies. The tests in science indicated a decline during the 1970s. The same thing happened when NAEP began assessing students' mathematics abilities in 1973. The next mathematics assessment in 1978 showed a decline (Stedman and Kaestle, "Literacy" 89, 91; Ravitch, *National Standards* 70–78).

In addition, NCEE pointed to declines in Scholastic Aptitude Test (SAT) scores to show the failure of public schools. The SAT provided more information than the NAEP because students had taken this multiple-choice test with verbal and mathematical sections during the 1960s. The high point occurred in 1963 when students taking the SAT had an average score of 478. By the late 1970s, however, the average score dropped to a low of about 420. Further, the number and percent of students taking the tests who scored above 600 declined. In 1972 about 116,590 students, or 11.4 percent of the total taking the test, scored 600 or above. In 1983 the number dropped to 66,292 students, or 6.9 percent of the total (Ravitch, *National Standards* 64).

Although NCEE claimed these achievement test scores indicated that the public schools failed, these scores stopped declining by the late 1970s and rose again after 1984. Several supporters of the excellence movement claimed this improvement was the result of the state-level reforms inspired by *A Nation at Risk.* However, critics thought that more complicated factors caused these shifts. For example, there may not have been a steady rise in SAT or achievement test scores until the 1960s. The studies that showed this increase were of such poor quality that they could not be trusted (Stedman and Kaestle, "Literacy" 89–90).

Although critics accepted the decline of test scores in the 1970s, they disputed the NCEE's explanation. According to NCEE, the SAT scores had declined because, during the permissive era of the 1960s, educators had lost their sense of purpose. Critics pointed out that this observation overlooked the changes in the number and type of students who took the tests. For example, in the 1970s more students from lower-scoring groups, such as minority groups and students not interested in academic programs, took the SAT. In addition, students took the test at a younger age because they had entered school earlier or been promoted automatically. According to the critics, the NCEE failed to take these changes into account (Stedman and Kaestle, "Great Test-Score" 132–133).

In 1989, John Jacob Cannell found that from 1974 to 1989 students' test scores on achievement tests such as the California Achievement Test and the Stanford Achievement Test rose steadily in all states. In fact, the rise was so steady that by 1988 all fifty states claimed that their average students' scores exceeded the national average. Cannell dubbed this impossible result "the Lake Wobegon effect," adopting the name from a radio show about a mythical town where all children were "above average." During the subsequent year, Cannell found that forty-eight of the fifty states reported scores above the national norm, and 90 percent of the elementary schools and 80 percent of the high schools exceeded the national norm.

Test makers and state officials accused Cannell of misusing statistics. Although researchers confirmed Cannell's basic conclusion that all states reported results exceeding the national average, they offered several possible explanations. For example, in 1989, after conducting a survey of forty-six state testing directors, Lorrie Shepard found the problem was that as the tests became more important, companies offered materials designed to help the students succeed on the tests. Some districts developed their own practice tests that imitated the actual test and provided instructional suggestions for teaching each objective. Because these materials had not been available earlier, the students performed better than the students with whom they were matched to determine placement against a national average. Unfortunately, Shepard noted, the increased scores did not mean the students learned more; they may have learned how to take the test, but they might be unable to apply the skills to other activities or incapable of performing better on other types of tests ("Inflated").

Did the Excellence Movement Achieve Its Objectives?

The excellence movement brought about a flurry of changes in schools and in the curricula they offered. However, most of these changes were superficial. To some extent, they prevented the major improvements that many reformers sought.

In response to *A Nation at Risk,* almost every state raised graduation requirements, created honors diplomas, and increased the number of academic courses needed to enter public universities. Although some states limited extracurricular activities and lengthened the school day, most states required students to pass standardized tests before graduating from high school or moving from one grade to another. The excellence movement was a regulatory movement for three important reasons. First, reformers consisted of people outside of education such as politicians, business leaders, and parents. In that way, it differed from the academic proposals of the 1950s and 1960s such as new math and new physics that had come from university professors. Second, during the 1980s politicians claimed to be concerned about education and needed some way to show their constituents they meant what they said. Because voters could easily understand these regulations, they became popular symbols. Most important, the reformers distrusted educators and wanted to pressure the teachers to change (Toch 38–39).

In some ways, the regulations succeeded. For example, enrollment in academic subjects increased. A study by the U.S. Department of Education compared the transcripts of 15,000 students who graduated in 1982 to the transcripts of students who graduated in 1987. Twelve percent of the students who graduated in 1987 fulfilled the requirements of NCEE. In 1982 only 2 percent had fulfilled those requirements. The percentages increased if researchers ignored the computer science and foreign-language requirements. In that case, more than 28 percent of the 1987 graduates met the requirements and 12 percent of the 1982 graduates did the same. These figures continued to advance so that by 1992, omitting computer science and foreign-language recommendations, 46.8 percent of the students met NCEE requirements (Toch 101–102; Ravitch, *National Standards* 95).

Despite this apparent success, most students did not receive the rigorous academic instruction that NCEE wanted. This happened for three reasons. First, schools offered several courses that administrators could count as academic when reporting to state administrators but that in fact were not. These courses carried names such as "science by investigation," "community science," or "fundamentals of general science." Second, teachers who knew little about academic subjects moved into those classrooms when enrollment in areas such as physical education declined. Older teachers who taught the nonacademic subjects but held more seniority replaced the younger but more academically trained teachers. Third, teachers did not explore new ways to teach academic subjects to students who possessed less ability. For example, instead of linking instruction to students' experiences, teachers depended on lectures and textbooks to convey the material (Toch 102–116).

Facing these apparent failures, reformers turned to standardized testing to encourage school reform. According to Chester Finn, Bennett's assistant secretary of education, the cycle worked in the following way. At first educational reformers thought students would learn more if school resources changed. Therefore, in the early 1980s they tried to extend the school day, require more academic courses, and reduce class size. However, Finn noted, these reforms did not seem to improve schools, so reformers decided to let school people use whatever means they chose to educate the students. Instead of mandating certain resources or means, reformers tried to hold teachers accountable through the testing program. Finn wrote that the first clear expression of this attitude came in 1986 from the National Governors Association when Tennessee Governor Lamar Alexander claimed that state leaders would regulate less if schools would produce more (Finn 124–125).

Finn acknowledged that this proposal depended on two conditions: The schools had to have clear goals and they had to use reliable tests to measure the students' achievements. An opportunity to set such goals and measures arose in 1990 when President George Bush and the state governors agreed to six national goals for schools. The third goal stated that by the year 2000, U.S. students would leave grades 4, 8, and 12 having demonstrated competency in subjects such as English, mathematics, science, history, and geography. Finn blamed the problems in working toward these goals on extensive resistance from groups of civil rights organizations, political conservatives protecting private schools, and companies producing their own tests. The controversies prevented President Bush from including such national standards and national testing in his America 2000 legislation proposals. Although President William Clinton supported such standards and tests, he also did not include them in his educational proposal called Goals 2000 (Finn 125–138).

Whereas Finn contended that political controversies in Congress prevented experts from developing national tests, Lorrie Shepard claimed that the proposal failed because it was poorly conceived. In 1991 the resource group for the National Education Goals Panel proposed a model for the national tests. They were to be tests based on world-class standards that would prevent students from learning by rote to answer low-level questions. The panel added that teachers would be free to use whatever means they wanted to teach the test material. However, when Shepard reviewed the panel's proposal, she found that five curricular and technical problems stood in the way. First, while the panel proposed that authorities from the fifty states and textbook companies should agree on the content of the new tests, this large number of people would not agree to include anything considered to be world class. The standards would be minimal so everyone could achieve them. Second, although the panel wanted the test to measure thinking ability, this would not happen. Once people became familiar with the content of the tests, they would help students memorize procedures or steps to obtain the answers. Third, teachers lacked the training to offer world-class material to students. Consequently, they would transform the performance assessments into steps that they could teach through drill and repetition. Fourth, these tests would encourage schools to track students so that only an elite corps would take the tests. Shepard noted that schools did this with advanced placement courses; administrators allowed few students to take advanced placement tests and receive the special credit. Fifth, offering these additional individual tests in several subjects would cost an inordinate amount of money unless they became traditional multiple-choice tests or teachers graded them. According to Shepard, neither option could work. The traditional tests invited memorization, and no one could expect teachers to grade the tests without extra pay (Shepard, "Will National Tests" 7–14).

Instead of the goals and testing that the National Education Goals Panel sought, most states adopted a form of minimum competency tests. Ironically, NCEE had warned against minimum competency tests, fearing that they fell short of what was needed. According to the report, the minimum would become the maximum (NCEE 20). Nevertheless, in 1985 fifteen states required students to pass a standardized test before graduating from high school. By 1987 the number of states imposing such tests on their students grew to twenty-four (Medina and Neill 6).

When politicians required students to pass competency tests to graduate from high school, they caused teachers and administrators to change their practices and the curriculum. Unfortunately, these changes did not meet the goals of the excellence movement nor did they improve the education of most students. In the 1986–87 school year, researchers from Research for Better Schools, Inc. conducted a survey of 277 school districts in Pennsylvania and 23 school districts in Maryland to determine how high-stakes testing affected the schools. In Maryland the high stakes were that students had to pass all four state competency tests to graduate. In Pennsylvania the stakes were lower because the state released average students' scores on achievement tests so that citizens could compare the performance of the different school districts. Not surprisingly, researchers found that in Maryland, where the stakes for the testing were higher, educators changed more to improve student scores. In Pennsylvania administrators sent lists of objectives to the teachers and asked them to be sure they covered such content in their classes. On the other hand, in Maryland, under administrative supervision, teachers redefined course objectives and changed course content so that students learned material covered on the tests. Further, Maryland school administrators supplied materials to help the students learn material specifically for the tests such as how to answer particular types of questions (Corbett and Wilson 3–5, 15–17).

As the use of standardized tests spread and their importance increased, teachers began to suggest that the standardized tests transformed the minimum level of learning into the maximum goal of instruction. In 1991 two researchers funded by the Spencer Foundation interviewed 360 elementary school teachers in 100 schools in two districts. Three-quarters of the teachers gave more emphasis to basic skills instruction and paid less attention to higher-level thinking or to extended projects as a result of the tests. More important, most teachers confessed that they taught to the test throughout the year. They did not confine such preparation to a few weeks before the test (Shepard and Dougherty 14–15).

In 1999 the International Reading Association issued a statement opposing high-stakes testing, which they defined as any test that administrators used to make important decisions about students, about the rating of different school districts, or about the determination of teachers' salaries. The IRA reported as its major concern the fear that testing became a way of controlling instruction. It was no longer a tool to gather information and to help improve students' reading abilities (International Reading Association 1).

Did Competency Tests Improve the Education of Minority Groups?

Advocates of standardized competency tests argued that such tests pointed out deficiencies in students' training and offered the opportunity for remedial attention. This argument influenced a decision about the legality of such tests when a civil rights organization, the Mexican American Legal Defense Education Fund (MALDEF), complained that White people used standardized tests to exclude minorities from schools and jobs. The federal court judge found that such tests could be part of plans to reform education.

In a case decided in January 2000, MALDEF lawyers argued that the state board of education unfairly discriminated against minorities or violated their right to due process when it required all students to pass the Texas Assessment of Academic Skills (TAAS) to graduate. The evidence seemed clear. In 1984 the Texas legislature began requiring students to pass a competency test to graduate. However, in 1990 the Texas state board of education replaced the former test with TAAS, which was designed to measure higher-order thinking and higher-problem-solving skills that the earlier test ignored. At the same time, the board set the cutoff scores at a 70 percent level. During the first administration of the TAAS in October 1991, minorities failed at extraordinary rates. Sixty-seven percent of the African American students failed and 59 percent of the Hispanic students failed. Among White students, the failure rate was 31 percent. Most interesting, the failures among minorities cut across lines of social class and economic status (*GI Forum* 5–6, 11).

The lawyers for MALDEF claimed that minorities in Texas did not receive an education equal to that of White students. They were underrepresented in advanced placement courses and in gifted and talented courses, and uncertified teachers taught a disproportionate number of minority students. Further, students with passing grades in classes such as English could fail that portion of the test. From this evidence, they concluded that school officials discriminated against minority students (*GI Forum* 7, 12).

In response, lawyers for the Texas Board of Education claimed that students who failed had seven additional opportunities to retake the exam and pass. Although the state board did not mandate remedial programs and those efforts varied from district to district, the lawyers pointed out that these oftentimes succeeded. Further, the board chose a passing level of 70 percent because this was the same percentage grade required to pass courses in Texas high schools. The lawyers for the state explained that the problem of students passing a course but failing the TAAS arose due to differences in measurement. Course grades included such things as effort and improvement, they argued, whereas the TAAS measured only mastery of subject matter (*GI Forum* 6, 7, 12).

When U.S. District Court Judge Edward C. Prado rendered his opinion, he noted that the MALDEF lawyers demonstrated the adverse impact of the TAAS on minorities. However, he countered the tests measured skills and knowledge that the state legislature and the board had decided were important for all students. Further, state officials possessed the authority to set the passing levels where they believed they should be. The only question the court could decide was whether such material and passing scores were fair. In this regard, the judge decided that the opportunities for remedial course work and for retaking the test reduced the problems of any inadequate education the minority students might have received (*GI Forum* 7, 12–13).

In his decision, Judge Prado acknowledged the problems in reforming schools by mandating tests. He observed that for a multitude of reasons minorities did not catch up to or keep up with majority students. Prado realized that state officials claimed the tests provided a means to help the minority students learn more, and that advocates for the minority students complained that the extensive opportunities for remedial assistance did not give the minority students an education but only helped them pass a test. However, Prado claimed, courts and judges could not answer the larger questions of what a student should learn or whether there should be special arrangements for minority students. At best, voters could address this question because elections could change the decisions of the legislators and the members of the board of education (*GI Forum* 15).

Although Judge Prado found that educators could use standardized tests to reform education, researchers argued that tests such as TAAS prevented schools from adapting their curricula in ways that would best serve their unique communities. In 1998 Anna Pedroza reported the results of her study of a small rural school district on the border of Texas and Mexico that she identified as Buena Vista Independent School District (BVISD). In a period of nine weeks, Pedroza interviewed sixty-five people including parents, teachers, counselors, administrators, and school board members about the ways that TAAS influenced instruction in their schools. In addition, she surveyed the district's educational reports, data reported in its public information system, and materials in area archives. The district enrolled about six thousand students, almost all of whom were Hispanic, qualified for free lunch, and had limited abilities in English. Interestingly, state officials recognized the BVISD elementary school as an exemplary institution, but identified the BVISD high school as a low-performing campus. This was because the state offered a Spanish version of the TAAS for elementary students and counted the results of only 40 percent of the students who had sufficient English-speaking skills. However, high school students lacked exemptions for language problems and had to take the English version. Pedroza found that the TAAS ignored the complex language experiences of these students. For example, school was the only place the students spoke English; the entire community with its close ties to Mexico spoke Spanish. More important, as the students moved into high school, the curriculum changed from bilingual instruction in the elementary schools to a model using English as a second language for the high school students. Because the students had to take the TAAS in English, the instruction reflected this goal.

Although critics complained that evaluation techniques such as competency tests limited the curriculum especially for minority students, advocates of the excellence movement continued to urge officials to implement more tests. In April 1998, the Center for Educational Reform, the Heritage Foundation, Empower America, and the Thomas B. Fordham Foundation sponsored a meeting for educational reformers, business leaders, and policymakers to discuss the state of education in the United States. Their report, *A Nation Still at Risk,* noted that poor instruction and inadequate preparation continued. However, the distance widened between good schools, where well-to-do children attend, and poor schools attended by economically deprived students. According to *A Nation Still at Risk,* the problem was that people with power in the schools did not want to change. As a result, they gave children of parents with adequate social class an excellent education and denied opportunities to the children of those who lacked money. The report offered two simple solutions. First, every school and student should meet demanding national standards measured by national assessment tests. Second, parents should have more opportunities to send their children to any school they chose such as different public schools, private schools, or parochial schools (*A Nation Still* 1–5).

Could Choice Improve Schools?

Conservative politicians had long argued that parents should be able to choose where to send their children to school. In 1981 Ronald Reagan suggested that parents receive tuition tax credits allowing them to deduct the cost of sending their children to private schools. Other politicians called for vouchers that would allow a parent to take the amount of tax money used to educate a child away from a public school and give it to the private school in which the child enrolled. According to the advocates of vouchers, they would function in ways similar to the way the GI Bill after World War II sent federal funds to any college or university that a former soldier attended. Although teachers' unions and associations of school administrators opposed these plans, two political scientists popularized the idea that parent choice would improve failing schools.

In 1990 John E. Chubb and Terry M. Moe argued that when parents and students could act as consumers and choose which schools to attend, this condition made schools more effective. Comparing public schools and private schools, they found that private schools produced more academic achievement because they functioned autonomously. In those settings, schools had clear goals, conducted ambitious academic programs, retained strong leadership, and expected high levels of teacher professionalism. They did this to attract and hold students. On the other hand, in public schools the bureaucracy stifled effective school organization and prohibited student achievement. Yet democracy required school bureaucracies. Voters elected board members who usually appointed superintendents who in turn hired other district officials who carried out the policies of the board and the superintendent. State governments granted these districts the authority to run the schools to which parents had to send their children. Consequently, although public school officials responded to elections, the democratically organized schools forced individuals and families to follow the policies created by the representatives of the majority of the voters (Chubb and Moe 5, 23).

To some extent, Chubb and Moe denied that they wanted a system of vouchers. However, they called for some mechanism that gave parents and students the ability to patronize any school they wished. Claiming that choice was a panacea, Chubb and Moe argued that market forces would improve schools. Therefore, they recommended that the public authority create a system in which public money flowed to schools. This strategy appeared similar to vouchers; however, under their plan, no school could charge more than the specified tuition so that rich families could not use local or state money to attend elite schools unavailable to families with lower incomes. To prevent complete equalization, Chubb and Moe suggested that some districts be allowed to contribute more than other districts. Thus, a family could choose a neighborhood that offered opportunities to attend better schools. Most important, schools should be free to define their missions and to reject any pupils who did not fit their requirements. However, they could not create racially segregated institutions. Schools had to have the freedom to define their missions, Chubb and Moe argued, because it provided real choices for consumers. Otherwise, the system returned to the uniformity found among public schools (Chubb and Moe 215–221).

Although Chubb and Moe thought that what they called market forces would create diversity among schools, experiences among Catholic schools illustrated that trying to use market techniques to support private institutions turned them into schools similar to their public counterparts. This happened to Catholic schools in low-income urban neighborhoods that changed their system of financing and reached out to families they did not traditionally serve. The result was that, contrary to the assertions of Chubb and Moe, consumer choice did not enhance educational diversity; it reinforced uniformity.

The changes took place in two ways. First, the Catholic schools sought competent financial assistance when the costs of education rose. In 1980 the average parish elementary school operated with a budget of $184,372. In 1993 the average cost rose to $547,838. Two-thirds of the increase came from expenses such as teacher salaries. Unfortunately, the average cost of Catholic schools in 1993 exceeded the total average parish revenue. Consequently, in 1990 the U.S. Catholic bishops called for the establishment of development efforts on behalf of schools in every diocese. In response, dioceses employed supervisors of development and Catholic high schools hired development directors who utilized professional marketing approaches to ensure successful fund drives and capital campaigns. Second, some Catholic schools changed the traditional pattern of funding. Under the former pattern, if a school was sponsored by a parish, the parishioners raised the money to build the school and contributed money from the parish funds to maintain it. As a result, families who belonged to the parish had priority for enrollment and their children paid a lower rate of tuition than children whose parents were not part of the parish. The new pattern, called cost-based, need-based tuition, originated in the archdiocese of Baltimore. In 1989 Archbishop William Borders asked schools to charge full tuition and change the parish subsidy into tuition assistance available to families who demonstrated financial need on a disclosure form administered by the archdiocese (Watras and St. John 402–403).

According to its supporters, cost-based tuition had two benefits. It allowed the newly created development directors to ask donors to fund attractive, long-range activities. People preferred to support such additions to a school rather than to subsidize tuition. At the same time, cost-based tuition removed difficulties that Catholic schools had in taking advantage of state support. For example, according to a report from Ohio's Buckeye Institute, in 1996 the state of Ohio offered vouchers for low-income children in the city of Cleveland that covered 90 percent of the tuition. However, the eight Catholic schools that accepted such students had set their tuition about $600 lower than the cost of educating them. The parish and the diocese made up the difference. However, when the schools accepted students with vouchers, they lost about $600 on each student in addition to the 10 percent of the tuition that the state would not cover (Watras and St. John 404–406).

Parish schools in low-income urban areas adopted the changes in Catholic school financing more often than schools in affluent suburbs. At least, this was the case in Cincinnati and Dayton, Ohio, where urban Catholic schools used cost-based, need-based tuition to attract minority students from the surrounding neighborhoods. Because most of these students were not Catholic, the schools did not try to form them in their faith. Instead, these urban schools in Cincinnati and Dayton pursued an aim called evangelization. In 1975, Pope Paul VI defined evangelization as bringing the good news of the Gospels into all strata of society. In evangelization, teachers tried to shape students' values to ideals consonant with those in the Bible. For example, a Franciscan Sister who served as the principal in a Catholic school in Cincinnati defined as evangelization her efforts to teach children to find alternative ways to deal with bad situations and to avoid drugs and violence (Watras and St. John 409).

How Did States Allow for Choice in Education?

Teachers' unions and school officials resisted plans that allowed parents considerable choice in public schooling such as vouchers or tuition tax credits. Consequently, despite the conservative political pressure to enact such policies, few states did. Some states began voucher programs, but they had legal problems because the money often went to religious schools, a practice that courts found unacceptable. However, a substitute proposal called charter schools began in Minnesota. This legislation grew out of Minnesota Governor Rudy Perpich's efforts to expand school choice. In 1985, Perpich, a Democrat, found support from a coalition that included the Minnesota PTA, agencies from the war on poverty, and the Minnesota Business Partnership. On the other hand, opposition came from teachers' unions such as the Minnesota Education Association and school administrators' organizations. Nonetheless, by 1988 the Minnesota legislature adopted Perpich's proposals that allowed high school students to enroll in some classes in nearby universities and to attend public schools in other districts or nonsectarian private schools (Nathan 58–59).

Support for the charter school concept came from Albert Shanker, president of the American Federation of Teachers (AFT). Disapproving of vouchers that opened schools to parental choice, Shanker wanted policies that would provide teachers with opportunities to create innovative new programs. He found the idea in a book by Ray Budde that compared teachers in experimental schools to explorers in the sixteenth century; they formed agreements with their school boards in the same way that explorers formed charters with their monarchs to set out on adventures and report their findings. As a result of Shanker's urging, the AFT endorsed the charter school idea at its annual convention in 1988. In Minnesota members of the Minnesota Federation of Teachers (MFT), a state branch of the AFT, joined with members of Minnesota's Citizen League and the CEO of a Minnesota computer business, Cray Research, to make suggestions for charter school legislation. However, the Minnesota Education Association (MEA), a rival union of the MFT, opposed the concept. After a series of compromises, the Minnesota legislature approved the proposal in 1991 that created the first charter schools (Nathan 61–69).

In 1992 California adopted a similar law, which allowed citizens to start new public schools or convert existing ones that were free from many restrictive state and district requirements but that were held accountable for some results and were subject to customer satisfaction. The idea spread quickly. By 1998 thirty-four states and the District of Columbia passed charter school legislation. These laws permitted 1,100 charter schools to open and enroll more than 250,000 students. In part, the money to support these schools came from state or district funds that paid for the education of each child. Thus, the charter schools competed directly with the public schools. Proponents claimed that such competition would encourage public schools to be more flexible and to meet the needs of the students and desires of the parents (Hassel 1, 8).

Another reason charter schools spread was that the federal government supported their growth. From 1994 to 2000, the federal government invested almost $400 million in public charter schools. U.S. President Clinton expressed pride in this endeavor, claiming that charter schools encouraged change by enhancing parent participation and promoting longer school years, higher academic standards, and improved character education. Consequently, in his budget message for fiscal year 2001, he requested $175 million to help cover the costs of opening new charter schools, hiring well-trained teachers, and acquiring more computers. To raise people's awareness of the contributions of charter schools, Clinton proclaimed May 1, 2000, through May 5, 2000, to be National Charter Schools Week (Clinton 2).

As part of the federal government's effort to support charter schools, Congress commissioned the National Study of Charter Schools. In its fourth report, published in 2000, researchers found a total of 1,605 charter schools in thirty-one states and the District of Columbia. These schools enrolled about 250,000 students, or 0.8 percent of the total number of students in the states where they operated. Since their origins in 1992, only 4 percent of the schools had closed. However, the charter schools tended to be small; the median enrollment was 132 students. Many of the charter schools had atypical configurations. They included all grades from kindergarten to twelfth, from kindergarten to eighth, or remained ungraded. About 70 percent of the charter schools in the 1998–99 school year were newly created rather than converted public schools. The charter schools did not disproportionately serve White or wealthy students, and in some states they served higher percentages of students of color than did public schools. However, they served somewhat smaller proportions of children with disabilities and children with limited English proficiency. Although many charter schools reported that they had primary control over critical areas of operations, most schools acknowledged that states monitored their financial records and reports of student attendance and student achievement (U.S. Department of Education, *The State* 1–3).

Did the Charter Schools Use Educational Innovations?

Despite the claims that charter schools would encourage experimentation, they did not seem to live up to that promise. For example, in 1994 Arizona passed legislation that freed charter schools from most regulations guiding public schools. Not surprisingly, charter schools spread rapidly in the state. By 1999 there were 351 charter school campuses serving about 40,000 students, which constituted about 5 percent of Arizona's public school enrollment. The most common type of charter school served elementary school-age children because owners could operate these schools easily. The median enrollment for charter schools was 110 students. Although advocates of charter schools claimed that these new schools would compete with public schools and cause them to improve, this was not true in Arizona.

In most districts, the public schools did not change. Those districts facing stiff competition from charter schools initiated customer service training for the staff and faculty. Thus, teachers learned how to welcome parents. At the same time, school district offices advertised the services available in public schools and compared standardized test scores with other districts. Some public schools offered more emphasis in phonics (Hess and Maranto 10, 12, 15).

In Arizona, charter school operators could determine their own curricula. However, they tended to use conservative approaches to the content. About 47 percent of the students studied in schools that advertised some sort of basic instruction of content. Schools implementing Montessori-type child-centered instruction enrolled about 35 percent of the students, and the remaining 18 percent attended arts-based, bilingual, or Waldorf programs. To some extent, religion crept into the curriculum of charter schools. One school taught creationism and another hung religious pictures on office walls. Most important, the gains in student scores on standardized tests matched the scores achieved by the same types of students in public schools. The charter schools produced a gain in math comparable to most public schools in reading and math. This was far below the gains predicted by advocates of charter schools (Hess and Maranto 15, 24, 26, 27).

Charter school advocates claim that their schools have not existed long enough nor reported test scores consistently enough for researchers to draw firm conclusions about the success that students experience in these schools. However, to meet critics' objections they cite several cases in which student test scores increased in charter schools over those of students in public schools. For more certain proof of the success of charter schools, advocates claim these schools involve parents more completely and cost less to operate than public schools (Finn, Manno, and Vanourek 74–96).

Some advocates complain that the charter schools have little freedom to experiment because the students have to meet state standards on things such as achievement tests. However, when the Edna McConnell Clark Foundation commissioned a study of charter schools in Texas, Massachusetts, California, and Louisiana, researchers found that charter school administrators and teachers believe their states' standards about assessment and curriculum frameworks provide direction for their programs. Because many of these educators come from public schools, they do not think of the standards as intruding on their work. However, the researchers noted that teachers' perceptions about standards differ depending on which social class the schools serve. Teachers in schools serving middle-class students think their students will perform well on standardized tests and they believe their curriculum matches the test questions. Teachers working with children labeled at-risk believe the standardized tests complicate their efforts to serve a diverse and needy student body. They plan few lessons to help them score highly. Thus, researchers have concluded that the mandated standards do not encourage educational improvement or the reduction of educational inequity in the charter schools. Interestingly, the researchers found parents unconcerned about the charter schools' compliance with state standards. Many parents thought the charter schools tested less than public schools, and they believed this showed the charter schools to be better for the children (Ascher, et al. 24–30).

Advocates claim that because charter schools lack the bureaucratic restraints found in public schools, they can experiment more freely and offer a better education than public schools. However, there are two problems with this view. First, in some cases large-scale private companies control charter schools. Second, school district bureaucracy can encourage innovation and experimentation.

The first problem is the intrusion of management companies that started schools to make a profit such as National Heritage Academies, the Leona group, Edison Schools, Inc., Mosaica, and Beacon Management. When these schools were established, some of the firms offered to provide only the services charter school operators needed such as attending to bookkeeping responsibilities. Other firms maintained total control over the schools. Sometimes these firms entered an area, convinced community leaders to allow them to start a school, constructed the facility, hired the teachers, selected the curriculum, and ran it. This raised questions about the possibility of charter schools encouraging truly local control. When a national, for-profit charter school corporation with sites in many states made the decisions about curriculum, teacher selection, and building management, parents and teachers could not do much more than accept those decisions or leave the school (Miron 5–7).

The second problem with the desire to enhance innovation by reducing restraints is that school district bureaucracy can encourage innovation. An example with magnet schools illustrates this possibility. In 1989 Dayton, Ohio, public schools applied to the U.S. Office of Education for a $4 million grant to establish twenty-five magnet schools in the city. Each of these schools emphasized a different academic area such as art, music, or foreign languages. They hoped their specialization would attract students of different ethnic and economic backgrounds. In 1992 the Dayton schools hired a team of consultants from Washington, D.C., to evaluate the magnet schools. The consultants found that parents and students approved of the magnet schools, that most of the students chose the schools for the particular focus, and that the students in the magnets performed better on basic skill tests than did students in conventional schools. However, the consultants also noted that the magnet themes were not well developed. Unfortunately, rather than find ways to strengthen the magnets, the Dayton school board adopted a proposal from a management study of the schools that recommended giving teachers in individual school buildings more control over their own operations, resources, and programs. The superintendent moved central office curriculum supervisors into an advisory capacity, reduced their number, and increased their range of operations. Although these supervisors were experts in particular fields such as art, music, or foreign-language instruction, the superintendent's view was that building principals could take charge of curriculum development. This failed to strengthen magnet themes because principals did not have the training to know what could be done, nor did they have the time to pursue such training. Instead, principals turned to teachers who volunteered for committees to make curricular suggestions. However, those teachers often lacked training or interest in the magnet areas. On the other hand, the subject area supervisors who occupied bureaucratic positions overseeing public schools could have enhanced educational experimentation. Before the superintendent reduced their numbers, these central office administrators brought together the teachers who worked in particular subject areas such as the arts or foreign languages. They held workshops to explore best practices in the field. Occasionally they arranged for the teachers to enroll together in university courses that demonstrated different instructional approaches. Once the superintendent reduced the number or influence of these supervisors, there was no mechanism by which to bring teachers who taught similar subjects together and to help them experiment. As site-based management spread in Dayton, many of the magnet schools drifted further away from their themes and returned to a traditional curriculum (Watras 273–277).

Did Schools Encourage Freedom and Tolerance?

Although the excellence movement encouraged uniformity in schools with techniques such as standardized testing, the advocates for various groups recommended that students and teachers show more tolerance for the differences in people's lifestyles. For example, in 1979 Joseph A. DeVito presented a paper to the Speech Communication Association in which he urged administrators and teachers to accord equal rights to gay and lesbian students. He suggested that administrators should hire gay and lesbian teachers to serve as role models, and that school policies should prohibit abusive language or criticism of the gay and lesbian cause.

DeVito's view persisted as a popular orientation. For example, in 1998 Richard A. Friend claimed that teachers and curriculum makers ignored the experiences of lesbian, gay, and transgendered people. As a result, members of these groups became invisible to majority youth, and heterosexual people thought of themselves as normal and morally correct. Friend called this condition heterosexism and asserted that these feelings of superiority justified harassment. He suggested that schools engage in what he called inclusive education to free the schools of hostility and make them safe for all students. It also included accepting views on homosexuality that differed from the views in the community. He called for the curriculum to consider lesbian and gay issues, and for teachers and texts to use gender-neutral language when talking about partner choice or families. He approved of gay–straight alliances that enabled people to understand homophobia, and he believed schools should hire counselors trained in helping people overcome homophobia.

Friend's recommendations for an education that enhances people's acceptance of homosexuality shares many points with ideas about sexual harassment. For example, a group of educators define sexual harassment as the abuse of power and authority that reinforces distinct standards for men and for women. According to their view, sexual harassment derives from the cultural belief that men are decisive and forceful while women are passive. Although state and federal laws prohibit sexual harassment, these educators complain that sexual harassment prevails in most schools, that women suffer from it more than men, and the most common form in secondary schools occurs among students. They recommend three strategies for schools. First, people should talk about it. Administrators can help by setting up school policies and complaint systems. Second, schools should infuse the curriculum with references to sexual harassment. They recommend that social studies teachers discuss the historical and cultural roots of sexual harassment. Finally, they recommend that school officials appoint a group of individuals to monitor the school's response to sexual harassment (Linn, et al. 106–120).

Educational organizations sought to advance the rights of gay and lesbian youth. For example, in 1987 Alex Molnar edited *Social Issues and Education: Challenge and Responsibility.* Within that volume, an essay by James Sears argued that educators had a social responsibility to promote human dignity and further social justice for gays and lesbians. The president of the Association for Supervision and Curriculum Development agreed with this position. Sears noted that the prejudice against homosexuality had religious roots that spread into concerns for social morality. Sears contended that educators had an obligation to resist these prejudicial attitudes, and he offered six steps they could take. First, teachers should examine their own feelings about sexuality and allow students to do the same. Second, they should replace myths with accurate information. Third, teachers should be responsive to the needs of gay and lesbian youth. Fourth, educators had to be vigilant in promoting the civil rights of all students. Fifth, administrators should hire gay and lesbian teachers. Finally, educators should speak out in the community in favor of gay rights legislation (Sears 89–95).

Many gay activists thought schools had to go beyond teaching tolerance and acceptance of gay and lesbians. In 1989 Eric Rofes published an article in the *Harvard Educational Review* urging people to open the classroom closet. He noted that in the 1980s, several gay and lesbian students forced schools to attend to their needs. For example, a male student threatened legal action if administrators prevented him from bringing a male date to the prom, and other students asked for information to prevent AIDS. However, Rofes thought that programs in Los Angeles and New York City offered important advances (Rofes, "Opening" 444–447).

According to Rofes, the Los Angeles Unified School District initiated Project 10 in 1985. Coordinated by a high school teacher, Project 10 offered a speakers bureau in order to bring gay and lesbian adults into the school, consciousness raising for school staff, and expansion of school libraries to include positive materials about homosexuality. In addition, the project offered counseling directly aimed at issues of sexual identity. In 1984 the project served about three hundred students (Rofes, "Opening" 447–448).

The second program Rofes complimented was the Harvey Milk School, named after the assassinated, openly gay San Francisco supervisor. Opened in 1985 by the New York City schools as an alternative school for students between the ages of fifteen and seventeen who could not continue in traditional high schools, the Harvey Milk School operated as a transitional school, teaching the students coping skills and methods of dealing with homophobia while focusing on acquiring an education (Rofes, "Opening" 448–450).

In 1997 Rofes complained that his article had made little difference although it appeared in academic readers in sociology, education, and psychology. Jesse Jackson included gays and lesbians in his rainbow coalition, and his rival in the U.S. presidential campaign, William J. Clinton, made gays in the military an important topic. However, Rofes found that no cities had opened schools or projects similar to the ones he had described in his paper. Worse, he believed that gay organizers ignored reforms such as charter schools that allowed advocates to create niche schools for particular populations. The most common change he found was the creation of gay–straight alliances in high schools. He yearned for schools appropriate for what he called "queer youth" (Rofes, "Schools" xii–xiv).

Although gay activists did not seek to start charter schools, several organizations tried to follow Rofes's suggestions. For example, in 1991 the Massachusetts Commission on Gay and Lesbian Youth urged educators to make schools safe for gay and lesbian students. The commission recommended training teachers to intervene in crises and to provide support groups that included gay and straight students. Further, the commission suggested that libraries include books favorable to gays and lesbians and that the curriculum include gay and lesbian issues. Another example was the Minnesota department of education, which issued a bulletin entitled "Alone No More: Developing School Support Systems for Gay, Lesbian, and Bisexual Youth." This bulletin noted that gay, lesbian, and bisexual students suffer from higher levels of suicide, drug abuse, and school absenteeism than other students. To counter these problems, the bulletin called for teachers to help students develop positive self-esteem by examining themselves on the issues and creating an inclusive classroom that was safe and respectful. Similarly, the bulletin called for administrators and staff to increase their awareness and concern for these issues.

Furthermore, in 1996 the National Association for Multicultural Education (NAME) labeled the following as social deficiencies: xenophobia, discrimination, ethnocentrism, racism, classism, sexism, and homophobia. In this way, the association added its name to the list of associations addressing the needs of gay and lesbian youth. Noting that many educators could not explain why it was necessary to fight homophobia, Cathy A. Pohan and Norma J. Bailey noted that gay and lesbian youth often attempted suicide, developed negative self-images, and engaged in risky sexual activities. Gay and lesbian youth often suffered violence and insults because their choices violated the moral or religious values of their friends and families. The authors rejected arguments that homosexuality was too controversial for the classroom, and proclaimed that all multicultural educators had an obligation to confront prejudice and commit themselves to fight for the dignity and rights of men and women who were gay.

Although other professional organizations used less excited rhetoric, they agreed with the need to help gay and lesbian students. In 1999 the National Association of School Psychologists adopted a position statement recognizing gay, lesbian, and bisexual youth as at risk for harassment, discrimination, and low self-esteem. Consequently, the association urged schools to adopt programs to meet the needs of these youth such as schoolwide inservice training, intervention with individual students, and the modeling of attitudes by school psychologists. The association's statement added that such programs had to include parents and other organizations committed to equal opportunity for education and mental health services for all children.

Was the Pursuit of Competence and Freedom Related to the Problems of a Technological Society?

Ironically, the recent educational reforms shared a similar problem related to the growth of the technological society. Advocates ignored the traditional role of schools in cultivating an intelligentsia that could offer moral direction. Instead, they looked for ways to make things work better or more harmoniously. This was at least partially true of the effort to improve schools by requiring more basic instruction and by using standardized tests to ensure that students learned the material. It was also a tendency in the efforts to improve the education of gay and lesbian youth. In fact, these two reforms could function together in the same school. Following the initiatives of the excellence movement, students would be held responsible for learning basic information. Employing multicultural educators and school psychologists, people in these efficient schools would respect the rights of each person to perform as well as he or she could.

Care is needed here. Students should learn to read and write and to do arithmetic, and multicultural educators and school psychologists should help students overcome their prejudices against their comrades. The problem with the recent reforms was that those changes did not build on the tradition or history of intellectual life. They were methods to make life in a modern industrial society more efficient and productive. Advocates on one side sought to enhance the ability of U.S students to compete in an international market. Advocates on the other chose to emphasize the benefits of mutual respect among peoples. Advocates on both sides looked for techniques or strategies to accomplish these ends and tended not to consider other, more profound values or moral judgments. To maintain their focus, advocates of each of these reforms repudiated the past rather than using the traditions of teaching to find ideas for the present. For example, many advocates of the excellence movement found the history of teaching to be a record of mistakes current practitioners should avoid. Consequently, they tended to distrust schools and teacher training institutions. On the other side, some multicultural educators contended that traditional views justified prejudices, and they looked to history for a record of conspiracies and deceptions by powerful people against minorities.

When reformers rejected history as a source of wisdom, they may have made intelligent reform more difficult to achieve. For example, if they had not repudiated the choices that progressive educators had made in their attempts to make schools more relevant and interesting, the members of the excellence movement could have sought the reasons that justified those choices and avoided the anti-intellectualism that corrupted them. Instead, by rejecting progressive attempts to make academic study more interesting, these conservatives turned to tests to improve teaching. However, the teaching that resulted concentrated on basic skills and information. It was academic instruction at its worst.

Likewise, those multicultural educators who wanted to reduce the prejudice that gay, lesbian, and bisexual youth suffered may have increased the problems of bigotry by condemning historical traditions. For example, in *Classical Educational Ideas,* Bernard Mehl claimed that the existence of racism and bigotry indicated the tragedy of modern technological society. Mehl noted that to solve these difficulties people turned to therapeutic techniques that might create feelings of community, or they invented romantic myths around which they could rally. Mehl contended that neither approach could succeed. As a result, he advised that instead of viewing bigotry as a problem to be solved, teachers should think of conditions such as homophobia as painful cries of humans caught in a society that demeaned the traditional ways people found meaning in the world. Thus, he argued, people should not repudiate history as a record of mistakes. They should look to history to find ways to promote full, human possibility within the present. Anything else, he believed, led to madness (205–213).

TIMELINE
1980–2000

1983 NCEE released its report *A Nation at Risk*

1985 Fifteen states required students to pass a standardized test before graduating from high school

TIMELINE Continued

1985 The Los Angeles Unified School District initiated Project 10, which made various efforts to promote openness toward gays in schools

1985 The Harvey Milk School opened in New York City as an alternative school for students who could not cope with surrounding homophobia

1986 U.S. Secretary of Education William J. Bennett presented his report, *What Works: Research about Teaching and Learning,* targeted toward parents

1987 Twenty-four states required students to pass a standardized test before graduating from high school

1988 Minnesota adopted Governor Rudy Perpich's proposal allowing high school students to enroll in some university classes and to attend schools in other districts

1990 President George Bush and state governors agreed to six national goals for schools

1990 The Texas state board of education raised the standardized testing requirements with the TAAS

1991 The Massachusetts Commission on Gay and Lesbian Youth encouraged educators to support their gay and lesbian students

1991 The National Education Goals Panel resource group proposed a national test model, which would expect world-class standards of the students

1991 The Minnesota legislature approved a proposal to form charter schools

1992 California allowed citizens to open new public schools or to convert certain existing ones into charter schools

1994 Arizona legislation exempted charter schools from most public school regulations

1996 The National Association for Multicultural Education addressed homophobia as one of its concerns

1998 The Center for Education Reform and other organizations sponsored a meeting concerning U.S. education that led to the report *A Nation Still at Risk*

1999 The International Reading Association issued a statement opposing high-stakes testing

1999 The National Association of School Psychologists urged schools to form programs to help gays and lesbians who suffered from social criticism and pressures

2000 MALDEF lawyers presented their case that the state board of education discriminated against minorities by requiring all students to pass the TAAS to graduate

CONCLUSION: WHAT SHOULD SCHOOL PEOPLE DO?

The thirteen chapters of this book describe several ways that educators from the colonial period to the last years of the twentieth century sought to solve the problems presented by the conflict between the desire for social unity and the need to respect differences among people. These chapters demonstrate that there was no solution to this problem. Instead, three alternatives continually reappeared. However, they did not reappear in exactly the same form. They were shaped by the concerns that dominated people's thinking during each particular period.

If the three alternatives fell on a continuum, assimilation would appear on one end and separation at the other end, with integration in the middle. If the continuum represented reality, it would have a large middle range and small sections at the end because few societies can coexist without changing each other. As novelists such as George Orwell have pointed out, slaves change their owners and servants direct the lives of their masters: None of the examples in the previous chapters represented pure separation or assimilation although most of them tended in one direction or the other.

The first chapter compares the differences among the Spanish, French, Dutch, and English colonies. The Spanish and the French missionaries tried to adapt the Christian faith to the Native American culture. Although the Dutch and the English tried to transplant a model of education from Europe, they could not retain it in any pure form. It changed so much that some historians argue that the colonial schools had different qualities than schools in the early republic. Therefore, these examples illustrate different types of integration.

The second chapter describes the efforts of early patriots who held different notions about how to make a strong republic. Some educators wanted to teach the different peoples in the land to hold the virtues they thought necessary to preserve the republic. Other patriots wanted to select the best potential leaders from each group and train them to serve the national government. In each case, these educators tried to find ways to teach children to be moral, able, and competent adults. As a result, they represent a form of integration at work.

Chapter 3 covers the common school movement. Although reformers such as Mann and Stowe wanted to impose the Protestant Bible on everyone, they thought this was a neutral model of education. And although frontier dwellers and Catholics considered the common school advocates to be narrow minded, reformers tried to blend the best views of all groups into an educational plan that would teach children to hold to the republican virtues of the early patriots. According to Mann, the common school referred to the hope that within its walls the children from all social classes and groups pursued the academic subjects emphasizing their common humanity. This was a strong statement in favor of social integration.

The fourth chapter describes many examples of educators trying to heal the wounds caused by the Civil War. Their efforts led to conflicting policies. Although segregation of racial and religious minorities grew, educators tried to bring people together. Thus, educators advanced the model of integration through textbooks and instructional methods such as manual training and the kindergarten. These innovations expressed the spiritual nature that educators believed all people shared.

The fifth chapter describes the ways in which educators adapted William Torrey Harris's interpretation of disciplining the mind to reinforce the importance of liberal arts training for all students. They argued that one course of study could train all students' human capacities no matter what their background or what they wanted to pursue in life. However, educators surrendered this notion for three important reasons including changes in society, changes in the school population, and changes in educational theory. As a result, schools offered industrial training and vocational education to help students follow different paths. At the same time, however, progressives such as Jane Addams and John Dewey sought ways for these new forces to bridge the distances between groups of people and generations.

Chapter 6 explains how educators adopted curricular differentiation or what educators today call tracking. Under this model, different students attended the same school. However, they studied different subjects depending on their abilities and their vocational interests. Critics complained that this led to segregation by social class and ethnic group. However, advocates called for new subjects such as the social studies and home economics to teach minorities and women how to succeed in the modern industrial society. Critics complained that even in the hands of the more socialistic progressives, the social studies, home economics, and the activity curricula segregated students in ways that appeared to reinforce social biases.

Chapter 7 describes an important shift in the social studies. Facing the dislocations caused by the depression, teachers no longer tried to help students adapt to the new order. Instead, they sought to help children think critically and solve the problems facing society. As World War II approached, educators turned to the social studies to teach children the value of democracy and the importance of diversity among peoples. Using methods of organized curriculum making, educators tried to form a consensus among teachers, parents, citizens, and experts about what children should learn. Critics complained that this model caused lower-class students to pursue vocational studies and upper-class children to pursue academics. They did not learn those things that people in a democratic society should share.

The eighth chapter observes the way progressive educators tried to build the curriculum on the students' home experiences. Although progressive educators believed this strategy captured students' interests, the lessons tended to avoid academics. The dangers of this approach became clearest in the educators' attitude toward language study. Because few students desired to speak a foreign language and everyone in a democracy should share a common tongue, progressive educators urged schools to stop teaching foreign languages. The emphasis on correct English hurt the efforts of Chinese people becoming teachers in San Francisco, and it delayed the assimilation of Japanese Americans in Hawaii. Ironically, in Puerto Rico the process worked in reverse. Puerto Rican teachers refused to teach English and maintained Spanish. In this way, they built school lessons around the children's home lives. However, by learning only Spanish, Puerto Ricans had difficulty availing themselves of the wealth and comforts that integration with the mainland would bring.

The ninth chapter describes how the federal government intervened in local school affairs. Federal officials started with two contradictory efforts. First, they tried to end the racial segregation of schools and thereby increase educational equity. Second, they attempted to improve the academic studies of mathematics and science, which moved toward educational elitism. Educators chose the comprehensive high school as a solution. Although such large buildings brought people together physically, they also separated them into different programs.

Chapter 10 explains how the civil rights movement changed local schools. Although federal officials forced schools to integrate their student bodies, curricular theorists did not try to find any curriculum model to demonstrate to students the importance of racial integration. In fact, the popular curriculum patterns such as individually guided education, magnet schools, and multicultural education separated the students more than they described why people of different races and ethnic groups should work and live together.

The eleventh chapter follows the development of the idea of a culture of poverty. This concept provided the rationale for most curriculum innovations of the 1960s and 1970s. In an effort to improve the academic performance of children from low-income families, curriculum makers borrowed ideas from anthropologists about the children's social backgrounds. Although large sums of money went into these attempts, they failed to improve the academic performance of children from low-income families. To some extent, the concept of a culture of poverty justified the segregation of low-income children. However, educators hoped this segregation would lead to integration later.

The twelfth chapter explains how advocates for three different groups—linguistic minorities, children who are disabled, and women—borrowed the strategies of the NAACP to advance their causes. In each case, advocates turned to the federal courts arguing that local school officials discriminated against their constituents. Of the three groups, the advocates for special education succeeded the most. Nonetheless, the three groups of advocates pursued some sort of separate training, which they thought would lead to integration and social progress.

The last chapter considers two recent trends: the excellence movement, with its demands for increased competency testing, and the effort to accord gay, lesbian, and bisexual youth the respect and dignity due to all people. Although these trends went in different directions, they had similar effects. That is, the advocates for each movement concentrated on techniques to make schools more effective or more harmonious. The result was that people ignored a search for values to bring people together and implied that fulfillment of personal desires brought social progress.

Although the educators described in each chapter worked on different problems in different ways, they tried to make one nation out of many groups of people. Because they succeeded in some ways and failed in other ways, their efforts illuminate three conclusions. First, no specific technique solves the problems of diversity. There are several reasons for this. The composition of the groups and their relative positions change as time passes. The conditions within which people apply the technique change, as do the aims people seek. Second, the best approach is to follow an idea to the point at which it breaks down. Trouble sets in when educators push beyond that point, as became clear in events such as the effort to use the Bible to bring people together during the common school movement, the desire to use the language of the community after World War II, and the attempts to apply the concept of a culture of poverty in classrooms. Finally, the fact that no techniques will solve the problems of diversity should encourage students to take new and deeper interest in understanding the efforts other people have made. If any particular model worked, teachers would have to learn only the method that would succeed. Because no one technique works, prospective teachers have to learn about all the possible variations that will limit the application of any plan. Teachers cannot be technicians. They have to be intellectuals.

APPENDIX

Acronyms

AAIB American Association of Instructors of the Blind

AAWB American Association of Workers for the Blind

AERA American Educational Research Association

AFT American Federation of Teachers

AFUC American Freedmen's Union Commission

AHA American Historical Association

AHEA American Home Economics Association

AIR American Institutes for Research

AMS American Mathematical Society

ARC Association for Retarded Citizens

ASCD Association for Supervision and Curriculum Development

ATS American Tract Society

AYC American Youth Commission

BEH Bureau of Education for the Handicapped

BVISD Buena Vista Independent School District

CAB Citizens Against Busing

CAP Community Action Programs

CEA Catholic Educational Association

CEC Council for Exceptional Children

CEEB College Entrance Examination Board

CGCS Council of the Great City Schools

CLSE Council of Learned Societies

CORE Congress of Racial Equality

CRSE Commission on the Reorganization of Secondary Education

EIP Education Improvement Program (Philadelphia, PA)

EOA Economic Opportunity Act

EPC Educational Planning Commission

EPC Educational Policies Commission

ERA Equal Rights Amendment

ESEA Elementary and Secondary Education Act

ESL English as a second language

HEW U.S. Department of Health, Education, and Welfare

HUD U.S. Department of Housing and Urban Development

I/D/E/A Institute for the Development of Educational Activities

IEP Individual Education Plan

IGE Individually Guided Education

LULAC League of United Latin American Citizens

MAA Mathematical Association of America

MALDEF Mexican American Legal Defense Education Fund

MEA Minnesota Education Association

MFT Minnesota Federation of Teachers

MIST Models for Integration: Science and Technology

MIT Massachusetts Institute of Technology

NAACP National Association for the Advancement of Colored People

NAEP National Assessment of Educational Progress

NAME National Association for Multicultural Education

NCATE National Council for Accreditation of Teacher Education

NCEE National Commission on Excellence in Education

NCSS National Council for the Social Studies

NCTE National Council of Teachers of English

NDEA National Defense Education Act

NEA National Education Association

NIE National Institute of Education

NOW National Organization for Women

NSF National Science Foundation

NSSE National Society for the Study of Education—formerly National Society for the Scientific Study of Education and the Herbart Society

OEO Office of Economic Opportunity

OSA Order of Sons of America

PANA Puerto Rican Association for National Affairs

PARC Pennsylvania Association for Retarded Citizens

PEA Progressive Education Association

PRTA Puerto Rican Teachers Association

PSSC Physical Science Study Committee

RASSA Raza Association of Spanish Surnamed Americans

SAT Scholastic Aptitude Test

SCLC Southern Christian Leadership Conference

SMSG School Mathematics Study Group

SNCC Student Nonviolent Coordinating Committee

TAAS Texas Assessment of Academic Skills

TESOL Teachers of English to Speakers of Other Languages

UICSM University of Illinois Committee on School Mathematics

USOE United States Office of Education

VCH Vermont Committee for the Handicapped

WORKS CITED

Addams, Jane. *Twenty Years at Hull-House.* 1910. New York: Signet, 1981.

Advisory Board to Dayton Board of Education. *Report of the Committee of 75.* Dayton, OH: Dayton Board of Education, 1971.

Aikin, Wilford M. *The Story of the Eight-Year Study.* New York: Harper and Brothers, 1942.

Alberty, Harold. "Designing Programs to Meet the Common Needs of Youth." *Adapting the Secondary Program to the Needs of Youth: Fifty-Second Yearbook of the National Society for the Study of Education.* Ed. William G. Brink, et al. Chicago: U of Chicago P, 1953. 118–140.

American Association of University Women. *Separated by Sex: A Critical Look at Single-Sex Education for Girls.* Washington, D.C.: American Association of University Women, 1998.

American Youth Commission. *What the High Schools Ought to Teach.* Washington, D.C.: American Council on Education, 1940.

Andrus, Caroline W. "Education of Indians." *Hampton Normal and Agricultural Institute: Its Evolution and Contribution to Education as a Land-Grant College.* Ed. Walton C. John. Washington, D.C.: GPO, 1923. 89–93.

Angus, David L., and Jeffrey E. Mirel. *The Failed Promise of the American High School, 1890–1995.* New York: Teachers College Press, 1999.

Apple, Rima D. "Liberal Arts or Vocational Training?" *Rethinking Home Economics: Women and the History of a Profession.* Eds. Sarah Stage and Virginia B. Vincenti. Ithaca: Cornell UP, 1997. 79–95.

The Arc. *Milestones.* Arlington, TX: The Arc National Headquarters, 1994.

Aronowitz, Stanley. Preface. *Learning to Labor.* Paul Willis. New York: Columbia UP, 1981.

ASCD Panel on Religion in the Curriculum. *Religion in the Curriculum.* Alexandria, VA: Association of Supervision and Curriculum Development, 1987.

Ascher, Carol et al. "Standards-Based Reform and the Charter School Movement in 1998–1999: An Analysis of Four States." Paper presented to the American Educational Research Association. New Orleans, LA. 24–28 April 2000.

Auerbach, Elsa Roberts, and Nina Wallerstein. *ESL for Action: Problem Posing at Work.* Reading, MA: Addison-Wesley, 1987.

Ayres, Leonard P. *Laggards in Our Schools: A Study of Retardation and Elimination in City School Systems.* New York: Charities Publication Committee, 1909.

Bagley, William C. *Education and Emergent Man.* New York: Thomas Nelson and Sons, 1934.

Bailey, Garrick, and Roberta Glenn Bailey. *A History of the Navajos: The Reservation Years.* Santa Fe, NM: School of American Research Press, 1986.

Bailey, Stephen K., and Edith K. Mosher. *E. S. E. A. the Office of Education Administers a Law.* Syracuse, NY: Syracuse UP, 1968.

Bailyn, Bernard. *Education in the Forming of American Society.* New York: Vintage Books, 1960.

Baker, Keith A., and Adriana A. de Kanter. *Effectiveness of Bilingual Education: A Review of the Literature,* 1981. ERIC Doc., fiche, ED215010.

Baker, Scott. "Testing Equality." *History of Education Quarterly* 1 (1995): 49–64.

Ball, Samuel, and Gerry Ann Bogatz. "Research on *Sesame Street.*" *Compensatory Education for Children, Ages 2 to 8.* Ed. Julian Stanley. Baltimore: Johns Hopkins UP, 1973.

Banks, James. *Teaching Strategies for Ethnic Studies.* Boston: Allyn & Bacon, 1975.

Baratz, Stephen S., and Joan C. Baratz. "Early Childhood Intervention: The Social Science Base of Institutional Racism." *Harvard Educational Review* 40.1 (1970): 29–50.

Barnes, Henry Elmer. "Review of *The Nature of the Social Studies.*" *American Historical Review* 40 (1934) 1: 97–101.

Barr, Robert D., James Barth, and S. Samuel Shermis. *Defining the Social Studies.* Arlington, VA: National Council for the Social Studies, 1977.

Bartley, Numan. *The Rise of Massive Resistance.* Baton Rouge: Louisiana State UP, 1969.

Beadie, Nancy. "Emma Willard's Idea Put to the Test: The Consequences of State Support of Female Education in New York, 1819–1867." *Educational Equity.* Ed. Karen J. Maschke. New York: Garland Publishing, 1997. 185–204.

Beard, Charles A. *A Charter for the Social Sciences in the Schools.* New York: Charles Scribners, 1932.

———. "That Noble Dream." *American Historical Review* 41 (1935) 1: 74–87.

———. "Written History as an Act of Faith." *American Historical Review* 39 (1934) 2: 219–231.

Beard, Charles, and Mary Beard. *The Rise of American Civilization.* New York: Macmillan, 1942.

Beatty, Barbara. *Preschool Education in America: The Culture of Young Children from the Colonial Era to the Present.* New Haven, CT: Yale UP, 1995.

Beauvoir, Simone de. *The Second Sex.* Trans. & ed. H. M. Parshley. New York: Alfred A. Knopf, 1983.

Belenky, Mary F., et al. *Women's Ways of Knowing.* New York: Basic, 1986.

Bellah, Robert et al. *Habits of the Heart: Individualism and Commitment in American Life.* New York: Perennial Library, 1986.

Bennett, William J. "The Bilingual Education Act: A Failed Path." *Language Loyalties: A Source Book on the Official English Controversy.* Ed. James Crawford. Chicago: U of Chicago P, 1992. 358–363.

Bentley, George R. *A History of the Freedmen's Bureau.* Philadelphia: U of Pennsylvania, 1955.

Bestor, Arthur E. Jr. "'Life-Adjustment' Education: A Critique." *Bulletin of the American Association of University Professors* 38 (1952): 413–441.

Blossom, Virgil T. *It Happened Here.* New York: Harper and Brothers, 1959.

Blow, Susan E. *Kindergarten Education.* Washington, D.C.: Department of Education, 1900.

Board of Education of the City School District of Dayton, OH. *Minutes.* 3 January 1972.

Board of Education of Oklahoma v. Dowell. 498 U.S. 237, 1991.

Bobbitt, Franklin. *The Curriculum.* Boston: Houghton Mifflin, 1918.

———. *Curriculum-Making in Los Angeles.* Chicago: University of Chicago, 1922.

Bode, Boyd. "Comment." *The Thirty-Third Yearbook of the National Society for the Study of Education: The Activity Movement.* Ed. Guy Montrose Whipple. Bloomington, IL: Public School Publishing, 1934. 78–81.

———. *Modern Educational Theories.* New York: Random House, 1927.

———. *Progressive Education at the Crossroads.* New York: Newson, 1938.

Bolton, Herbert E. "The Mission as a Frontier Institution in the Spanish American Colonies." *American Historical Review* 23.1 (1917): 42–61.

Bowers, C. A. *The Progressive Educator and the Depression.* New York: Random House, 1969.

Bowles, Samuel, and Herbert Gintis. *Schooling in Capitalist America: Educational Reform and the Contradictions of Economic Life.* New York: Basic Books, 1976.

Boyer, Ernest L. *High School: A Report on Secondary Education in America.* New York: Harper & Row, 1983.

Bracey, Gerald W. *Put to the Test: An Educator's and Consumer's Guide to Standardized Testing.* Bloomington, IN: Phi Delta Kappa, 1998.

Bradburn, Norman, et al. "A Rejoinder to 'I Never Promised You First Place.'" *Phi Delta Kappan* 72 (June 1991): 774–777.

Breitwieser, Mitchell Robert. *Cotton Mather and Benjamin Franklin: The Price of Representative Personality.* New York: Cambridge UP, 1984.

Brink, William G. "Introduction: The Youth-Needs Motive in Secondary Education." *Adapting the Secondary-School Program to the Needs of Youth: Fifty-Second Yearbook of the National Society for the Study of Education.* Ed. William G. Brink, et al. Chicago: U of Chicago P, 1953. 1–21.

Broudy, Harry S., B. Othanel Smith, and Joe R. Burnett. *Democracy and Excellence in American Secondary Education.* Chicago: Rand McNally, 1964.

Brown, Marjorie M. *Philosophic Studies of Home Economics in the United States.* East Lansing: Michigan State U, 1985.

Brown v. Board of Education, 347 U.S. 483, 1954.

Brumbaugh, Martin.G. "The Life of Christopher Dock." 1907. Trans. Martin G. Brumbaugh. *Life and Works of Christopher Dock.* New York: Arno Press, 1969. 11–23.

Bruner, Jerome S. *The Process of Education.* Cambridge, MA: Harvard UP, 1975.

Bryk, Anthony, Valerie Lee, and Peter Holland. *Catholic Schools and the Common Good.* Cambridge, MA: Harvard UP, 1993.

Buetow, Harold A. *Of Singular Benefit: The Story of Catholic Education in the United States.* New York: Macmillan, 1970.

Bunker, Frank Forest. *Reorganization of the Public School System.* U.S. Bureau of Education Bulletin No. 8. Washington, D.C.: GPO, 1916.

Burgess, Charles, and Merle E. Borrowman. *What Doctrines to Embrace: Studies in the History of Education.* Glenview, IL: Scott, Foresman, 1969.

Burns, Rev. J. A. *The Principles, Origin, and Establishment of the Catholic School System in the United States.* New York: Benziger Brothers, 1912.

Burns, J. A., Bernard J. Kohlbrenner, and John B. Peterson. *A History of Catholic Education in the United States.* New York: Benziger Brothers, 1937.

Buswell, G. T. "Contributions to Elementary-School Mathematics." *The Thirty-Seventh Yearbook of the National Society for the Study of Education: The Scientific Movement in Education.* Ed. Guy Montrose Whipple. Bloomington, IL: Public School Publishing Company, 1938. 123–128.

Butchart, Ronald E. *Northern Schools, Southern Blacks, Reconstruction: Freedmen's Education, 1862–1875.* Westport, CT: Greenwood Press, 1980.

Button, Henry Warren. "Committee of Fifteen." *History of Education Quarterly* 5.4 (1965): 253–263.

Butts, R. Freeman. *The College Charts Its Course: Historical Conceptions and Current Proposals.* New York: McGraw-Hill, 1939.

Calkins, N. A. *Primary Object Lessons for Training the Senses and Developing the Faculties of Children.* New York: Harper & Brothers, 1875.

Callahan, Raymond E. *Education and the Cult of Efficiency.* Chicago: U of Chicago P, 1962.

Campbell, Donald T., and Albert Erlebacher. "How Regression Artifacts in Quasi-Experimental Evaluations Can Mistakenly Make Compensatory Education Look Harmful." *Disadvantaged Child.* Vol. 3. Ed. Jerome Hellmuth. New York: Brunner/Mazel, 1970. 185–210.

Camus, Albert. *The Rebel: An Essay on Man in Revolt.* Trans. Anthony Bower. New York: Vintage Books, 1956.

Candor, Catherine. *A History of the Kanawha County Textbook Controversy.* Ann Arbor, MI: University Microfilms, 1976.

Cannell, John Jacob. "How Public Educators Cheat on Standardized Achievement Tests: The Lake Wobegon Report." ERIC Microfiche ED314454, 1989.

Carmichael, Stokely, and Charles Hamilton. *Black Power: The Politics of Liberation in America.* New York: Random House, 1967.

Carper, James. "The Christian Day School." *Religious Schooling in America.* Ed. James Carper and Thomas Hunt. Birmingham, AL: Religious Education Press, 1984.

Carr, Arthur Taylor. "Samuel Lewis: Educational and Social Reformer, 1799–1854." Diss. Western Reserve U, 1938.

Casanova, Ursula, and M. Beatriz Arias. "Contextualizing Bilingual Education." *Bilingual Education: Politics and Practice.* Ed. Ursala Casanova and M. Beatriz Arias. Chicago: U of Chicago P, 1993.

Caswell, Hollis L., & Campbell, Doak S. *Curriculum Development.* New York: American Book Company, 1935.

Caswell, Hollis L., et al. *Curriculum Improvement in Public School Systems.* New York: Teachers College Press, 1950.

Cebollero, Pedro. "A School Language Policy for Puerto Rico." *Politics and Education in Puerto Rico: A Documentary Survey of the Language Issue.* Ed. Erwin Epstein. Metuchen, NJ: Scarecrow Press, 1970. 169–176.

CEEB. "Report of the Commission on History." *The Social Studies* 27.8 (1936): 546–567.

Chamberlin, Dean, et al. *Did They Succeed in College?* New York: Harper and Brothers, 1942.

Charters, W. W. *Curriculum Construction.* 1923. New York: Arno Press, 1971.

———. "The Reorganization of Women's Education." *Educational Review* 62 (1921): 224–231.

———. "Review and Critique of Curriculum Making for the Vocations." *The Twenty-Sixth Yearbook of the National Society for the Study of Education: Foundations and Technique of Curriculum Construction Part I.* Ed. Guy Montrose Whipple. Bloomington, IL: Public School Publishing, 1926, 365–379.

Chidsey, Alan Lake. "Poor Old History." *Social Education* 1.4 (1937): 255–258.

Chiong, Jane Ayers. *Racial Categorization of Multiracial Children in Schools.* Westport, CT: Bergin & Garvey, 1998.

Chubb, John E., and Terry M. Moe. *Politics, Markets, and Schools.* Washington, D.C.: Brookings Institution, 1990.

Church, Robert L., and Michael W. Sedlak. *Education in the United States: An Interpretive History.* New York: Free Press, 1976.

Cicirelli, Victor G. "Head Start: Brief of the Study." *Britannica Review of American Education.* Vol. I. Ed. David G. Hays. Chicago: Encyclopedia Britannica, 1969. 233–243.

Clark, Kenneth B. *Prejudice and Your Child.* 2nd ed. Boston: Beacon Press, 1963.

Clifton, John L. *Ten Famous Educators.* Columbus, OH: R. G. Adams, 1933.

Clinton, William J. "Proclamation 7297 of 28 April 2000." *Federal Register* 65.86 (2000) 3 pp. Online. *LEXIS-NEXIS,* 3 May 2000.

Clowse, Barbara Barksdale. *Brainpower for the Cold War: The Sputnik Crisis and National Defense Education Act of 1958.* Westport, CT: Greenwood Press, 1981.

CLSE (Council of Learned Societies in Education). *Standards for Academic and Professional Preparation in Foundations of Education, Educational Studies, and Educational Policy Studies.* 2nd ed. Ann Arbor, MI: Caddo Gap Press, 1996.

Colachio, David P. *The Education for All Handicapped Children Act: A Historical Study of Public Law 94-142.* Diss. Texas A&M U, 1985. Ann Arbor: UMI 1985. 8605241.

Colby, Ann, and William Damon. *Some Do Care.* New York: Macmillan, 1992.

Coleman, James S. "Correspondence: Response to Pettigrew and Green." *Harvard Educational Review* 2 (1976).

Coleman, James, et al. *Equality of Educational Opportunity.* Washington, D.C.: GPO, 1966.

———. *Trends in School Desegregation 1968–1973.* Washington, D.C.: Urban Institute, 1975.

Collings, Ellsworth. *An Experiment with a Project Curriculum.* New York: Macmillan, 1925.

Colvin, Stephen S. "Principles Underlying the Construction and Use of Intelligence Tests." *The Twenty-First*

Yearbook of the National Society for the Study of Education: Intelligence Tests and Their Uses. Ed. Guy Montrose Whipple. Bloomington, IL, 1923. 11–44.

Commager, Henry Steele. "Schoolmaster to America." *American Spelling Book.* By Noah Webster. 1831. New York: Teachers College Press, 1962. 1–12.

Commission on Professional Rights. *Beyond Segregation: The Problem of Power.* Washington, D.C.: National Education Association, 1970.

Commission on the Reorganization of Secondary Education. *Cardinal Principles of Secondary Education: A Report of the Commission on the Reorganization of Secondary Education Appointed by the National Education Association.* Washington, D.C.: GPO, 1918.

Committee for the White House Conference on Education. *A Report to the President.* Washington, D.C.: GPO, April 1956.

Committee of Eight. *The Study of History in the Elementary Schools.* New York: Charles Scribner's Sons, 1912.

Committee of Seven. *The Study of History in Schools.* Washington, D.C.: GPO, 1899.

Committee on Education and Labor. *Hearings: Bilingual Education Programs.* New York: Arno Press, 1978.

Committee on Social Studies. *The Social Studies in Secondary Education: A Reprint of the Seminal 1916 Report.* ERIC Clearinghouse for Social Studies, 1994. ED374072.

Committee on the Function of the Social Studies. *The Social Studies in General Education.* New York: D. Appleton-Century, 1940.

Conant, James Bryant. *The American High School Today: A First Report to Interested Citizens.* New York: McGraw Hill, 1959.

———. *The Comprehensive High School: A Second Report to Interested Citizens.* New York: McGraw Hill, 1967.

———. *Slums and Suburbs.* New York: McGraw Hill, 1961.

Corbett, H. Dickson, and Bruce Wilson. "Raising the Stakes in Statewide Mandatory Minimum Competency Testing." ERIC Microfiche ED338641, 1989.

Correia, Stephen T. "Thomas Jesse Jones: Doing God's Work and the 1916 Report." Commentary to *The Social Studies in Secondary Education: A Reprint of the Seminal 1916 Report.* ERIC Clearinghouse for Social Studies, 1994. ED374072.

Counts, George S. *The Selective Character of American Secondary Education.* Chicago: U of Chicago P, 1922.

———. *The Social Composition of Boards of Education.* 1927. New York: Arno Press, 1969.

Cowan, Paul. "Holy War in West Virginia: A Fight over America's Future." *Village Voice* 9 (Dec. 1979). 19–21.

Crane, Verner W. *Benjamin Franklin and a Rising People.* Boston: Little, Brown, 1954.

Crawford, David Livingston. *Paradox in Hawaii.* Boston: Stratford, 1933.

Crawford, James. *Bilingual Education: History, Politics, Theory, and Practice.* Trenton, NJ: Crane, 1989.

———. "What's Behind Official English?" *Language Loyalties: A Source Book on the Official English Controversy.* Ed. James Crawford. Chicago: U of Chicago P, 1992. 171–177.

Cremin, Lawrence A. *American Education: The Colonial Experience, 1607–1783.* New York: Harper & Row, 1970.

———. *American Education: The Metropolitan Experience, 1876–1980.* New York: Harper & Row, 1988.

———. *American Education: The National Experience, 1783–1876.* New York: Harper & Row, 1980.

———. Preface. *Noah Webster's American Spelling Book.* 1831. New York: Teachers College Press, 1962. np.

———. "Horace Mann's Legacy." *The Republic and the School: Horace Mann on the Education of Free Men.* Ed. Lawrence A. Cremin. New York: Teachers College Press, 1957. 3–28.

———. *Traditions of American Education.* New York: Basic Books, 1977.

———. *The Transformation of the School: Progressivism in American Education, 1876–1957.* New York: Alfred A. Knopf, 1964.

Cuban, Larry. "Why Some Reforms Last." *American Journal of Education* 100.2 (1992). 166–194.

Cubberley, Ellwood P. "Commercial Education—Its History, Present Status, and Prospects for Future Development." *Business Education—A Retrospection.* Ed. Bernard A. Shilt. Chicago: South-Western Publishing, 1978. 6–9.

———. *Public Education in the United States: A Study and Interpretation of American Educational History.* New York: Houghton Mifflin, 1919.

Curry, J. L. M. *Address Delivered in Response to an Invitation of the General Assembly of Georgia.* Atlanta, GA: State Printer, 1889.

Curti, Merle. *The Social Ideas of American Educators.* 1935. New Jersey: Littlefield, Adams, 1978.

Cusick, Philip A. *The Educational System: Its Nature and Logic.* New York: McGraw Hill, 1992.

Danoff, Michael N. *Evaluation of the Impact of ESEA Title VII,* 1978. ERIC Doc., fiche, ED154634.

Danoff, M. N., and G. J. Coles. "AIR Researchers Respond to Nickel's Criticism." *Phi Delta Kappan* 61 (1979): 261–262.

Davies, John D. *Phrenology Fad and Science: A Nineteenth-Century Crusade.* 1955. Hamden, CT: Archon Books, 1971.

Davis, Robert. *The Changing Curriculum: Mathematics.* Washington, D.C.: Association for Curriculum Development, 1967.

Deutsch, Martin. "Dimensions of the School's Role in the Problems of Integration." *Disadvantaged Child.* Ed. Martin Deutsch. New York: Basic, 1967. 281–294.

DeVito, Joseph A. "Educational Responsibilities to the Gay and Lesbian Student." ERIC Microfiche ED184167, 1979.

Dewey, John. "Comment." *The Thirty-Third Yearbook of the National Society for the Study of Education: The Activity Movement.* Ed. Guy Montrose Whipple. Bloomington, IL: Public School Publishing, 1934. 81–86.

———. *Democracy and Education.* 1916. New York: Macmillan, 1966.

———. *The School and Society the Child and the Curriculum.* Chicago: U of Chicago P, 1990.

Diefenthaler, Jon. "Lutheran Schools in America." *Religious Schooling in America.* Ed. James C. Carper and Thomas C. Hunt. Birmingham, AL: Religious Education Press, 1984. 35–57.

Dimond, Paul R. "The Constitutional Right to an Education." *Hastings Law Journal* 24 (1973): 1087–1127.

Division of Secondary Education. *Life Adjustment Education for Every Youth.* Washington, D.C.: U.S. Office of Education, 1947.

Dock, Christopher. "Schul-ordnung." Trans. Martin G. Brumbaugh. *Life and Works of Christopher Dock.* New York: Arno Press, 1969. 99–149.

Doerman, Henry J. "The Academy and the Normal School." *Hampton Normal and Agricultural Institute: Its Evolution and Contribution to Education as a Land Grant College.* Ed. Walton C. John. Washington, D.C.: GPO, 1923. 24–35.

Dresslar, Fletcher R. *American Schoolhouses.* Washington, D.C.: GPO, 1911.

Du Bois, W. E. B. *The Souls of Black Folks.* 1903. New York: New American Library, 1969.

Dunkel, Harold B. *Herbart and Education.* New York: Random House, 1969.

Dunn, Arthur W. *Civic Education in Elementary Schools as Illustrated in Indianapolis.* U.S. Bureau of Education Bulletin No. 17. Washington, D.C.: GPO, 1915.

Editor. "Social Studies: Preparation for College or Life." *Social Education* 1 (1937) 2: 77–80.

Educational Policies Commission. *Education for All American Youth.* Washington, D.C.: National Education Association, 1944.

———. *Education for All American Youth: A Further Look.* Washington, D.C.: National Education Association, 1952.

———. *Education and Economic Well-Being in American Democracy.* Washington, D.C.: National Education Association, 1940.

———. *What the Schools Should Teach in Wartime.* Washington, D.C.: National Education Association, 1943.

Eliot, Charles William. "The Gap between Common Schools and Colleges." *Educational Reform: Essays and Addresses.* 1898. New York: Arno Press, 1969. 197–219.

———. "Undesirable and Desirable Uniformity in Schools." *Educational Reform: Essays and Addresses.* 1898. New York: Arno Press, 1969. 273–300.

Ellis, John Tracey. *Catholics in Colonial America.* St. Paul: North Central Publishing, 1965.

Ellul, Jacques. *The Technological Society.* Trans. John Wilkinson. New York: Vintage, 1970.

Ensign, Forest Chester. *Compulsory School Attendance and Child Labor.* 1921. New York: Arno Press, 1969.

Epstein, Noel. *Language, Ethnicity, and the Schools: Policy Alternatives for Bilingual-Bicultural Education.* Washington D.C.: Institute for Educational Leadership, 1977.

Erikson, Kai T. *Everything in Its Path.* New York: Touchstone, 1976.

Faculty of Yale College. "Original Papers in Relation to a Course of Liberal Education." *American Journal of Science and Arts* 15 (1829): 297–351.

Feinstein, Karen Wolk. "Kindergartens, Feminism, and the Professionalization of Motherhood." *International Journal of Women's Studies* 3.1 (1980): 28–38.

Ferguson, Ronald. *A History of the Efforts of the Organized Blind in Challenging Educational and Socially Constructed Policies (1940–1995).* Diss. Ohio State U, 1995. Ann Arbor: UMI, 1995.

Fife, Brian. *Desegregation in American Schools.* New York: Praeger, 1992.

Finkelstein, Barbara. *Governing the Young: Teacher Behavior in Popular Primary Schools in Nineteenth-Century United States.* New York: Falmer Press, 1989.

Finn, Chester E. Jr. "Who's Afraid of the Big Bad Test?" *Debating the Future of American Education: Do We Need National Standards and Assessments.* Ed. Diane Ravitch. Washington, D.C.: The Brookings Institution, 1995.

Finn, Chester E., Bruno V. Manno, and Gregg Vanourek. *Charter Schools in Action.* Princeton, NJ: Princeton UP, 2000.

Fleury, Bernard. *Whatever Happened to IGE?* Lanham, MD: UP of America, 1993.

Foght, H. W. *The Rural School System of Minnesota: A Study in School Efficiency.* Washington, D.C.: GPO, 1915.

Foner, Eric. *Reconstruction: American's Unfinished Revolution, 1863–1877.* New York: Harper & Row, 1988.

Formisano, Ronald. *Boston against Busing.* Chapel Hill: U of North Carolina P, 1991.

Forrest, Suzanne. *The Preservation of the Village: New Mexico's Hispanics and the New Deal.* Albuquerque: U of New Mexico P, 1989.

Franklin, Barry. *From Backwardness to At-Risk.* New York: SUNY, 1994.

Franklin, Benjamin. *The Autobiography of Benjamin Franklin.* 1771. New York: Airmont Books, 1965.

———. "The Idea of the English School." *Benjamin Franklin on Education.* Ed. John Hardin Best. New York: Teachers College Press, 1962. 152–171.

———. "Observations Relative to the Intentions of the Original Founders of the Academy in Philadelphia, June 1789." Ed. John Bigelow. *The Works of Benjamin Franklin.* Vol. XII. New York: G. P. Putnam's Sons, 1904. 74–104.

———. "Proposals Relating to the Education of Youth in Pennsylvania." Ed. George Willis et al. *The American Curriculum: A Documentary History.* Westport, CT: Praeger, 1994. 17–23.

Franklin, John Hope. "Jim Crow Goes to School: The Genesis of Legal Segregation in Southern Schools." *African Americans and the Emergence of Segregation, 1865–1900.* Ed. Donald G. Nieman. New York: Garland Publishing, 1994. 115–126.

Fraser, James W. *Between Church and State: Religion and Public Education in a Multicultural America.* New York: St. Martin's Press, 1999.

Freeman v. Pitts. 503 US 467, 1992.

Freire, Paulo. *Pedagogy of the Oppressed.* Trans. Myra Bergman Ramos. Rev. ed. New York: Continuum, 1997.

Fried, Lewis F. *Makers of the City.* Amherst: U of Massachusetts P, 1990.

Friedan, Betty. *The Feminine Mystique.* New York: Dell, 1963.

———. *The Second Stage.* New York: Summit Books, 1981.

Friend, Richard A. "Heterosexism, Homophobia, and the Culture of Schooling." *Invisible Children in the Society and Its Schools.* Ed. Sue Books. Mahwah, NJ: Lawrence Erlbaum, 1998.

GI Forum et al. v. Texas Board of Education et al. 87 F. Supp. 2d 667; 2000 U.S. Dist. *LEXIS* 153, 7 Jan. 2000.

Gabert, Glen. *In Hoc Signo? A Brief History of Catholic Parochial Education in America.* Port Washington, NY: Kennikat Press, 1973.

Gans, Herbert. *The War against the Poor: The Underclass and Antipoverty Policy.* New York: Basic, 1995.

———. *The Urban Villagers: Group and Class in the Life of Italian-Americans.* 1961. New York: Free, 1968.

Garcia, Ignacio. *United We Win.* Tucson: U of Arizona: MASRC, 1989.

Garza, Rodolfo O. de la. *Public Policy Priorities of Chicano Political Elites.* Washington, D.C.: Overseas Development Council, 1982.

Getz, Lynne Marie. *Schools of Their Own: Education of Hispanics in New Mexico, 1850–1940.* Albuquerque: U of New Mexico P, 1997.

Gilligan, Carol. *In a Different Voice.* Cambridge, MA: Harvard UP, 1982.

Gleason, Philip. *Contending with Modernity: Catholic Higher Education in the Twentieth Century.* New York: Oxford UP, 1995.

Goodlad, John I. "Where Precollege Reform Stands Today." *The Challenge of Curricular Change.* Colloquium on the Challenge of Curricular Change. New York: College Entrance Examination Board, 1966. 1–11.

———. *The Dynamics of Educational Change.* New York: McGraw-Hill, 1975.

Goodsell, Charles T. *Administration of a Revolution: Executive Reform in Puerto Rico under Governor Tugwell, 1941–1946.* Cambridge, MA: Harvard UP, 1965.

Goodsell, Willystine. *The Education of Women: Its Social Background and Its Problems.* New York: Macmillan, 1923.

———. *Pioneers of Women's Education in the United States.* New York: McGraw-Hill, 1931.

Gordon, Edward E., with Elaine H. Gordon. *Centuries of Tutoring: A History of Alternative Education in America and Western Europe.* New York: UP of America, 1990.

Grant, Carl A., ed. *Multicultural Education: Commitments, Issues, and Applications.* Washington, D.C.: Association for Curriculum and Development, 1977.

Grant, Gerald. *The World We Created at Hamilton High.* Cambridge, MA: Harvard UP, 1988.

Gray, William S. "Contributions of Research to Special Methods: Reading." *The Thirty-Seventh Yearbook of the National Society for the Study of Education: The Scientific Movement in Education.* Ed. Guy Montrose Whipple. Bloomington, IL: Public School Publishing Company, 1938. 99–106.

Green v. County School Board of New Kent County. 391 US 218, 1968.

Green, Elizabeth Alden. *Mary Lyon and Mount Holyoke: Opening the Gates.* Hanover, NH: UP of New England, 1979.

Green v. County School Board of New Kent County. 391 U.S. 430, 1968.

Greene, Maxine. *Dialectic of Freedom.* New York: Teachers College Press, 1988.

Gregg, James E. "History and Educational Philosophy." *Hampton Normal and Agricultural Institute: Its Evolution and Contribution to Education as a Land-Grant College.* Ed. Walton C. John. Washington, D.C.: GPO, 1923. 4–11.

Gutierrez, Edith Algren de. *The Movement against Teaching English in Schools of Puerto Rico.* New York: UP of America, 1987.

Hall, G. Stanley. *Adolescence: Its Psychology and Its Relations to Physiology, Anthropology, Sociology, Sex, Crime, Religion, and Education.* 2 vols. New York: Appleton, 1904.

———. *Educational Problems.* New York: D. Appleton, 1911.

Hall, Sidney B. "Cooperation in Virginia." *Educational Record* 14 (1933): 338–345.

Ham, Charles H. *Mind and Hand: Manual Training the Chief Factor in Education.* 3rd ed. New York: American Book, 1900.

Hammerback, John C., Richard J. Jensen, and Jose Angel Gutierrez. *A War of Words.* Westport, CT: Greenwood Press, 1985.

Hampel, Robert L. *The Last Little Citadel: American High Schools since 1940.* Boston: Houghton Mifflin, 1986.

Handlin, Oscar. *The Uprooted: The Epic Story of the Great Migrations That Made the American People.* Boston: Little, Brown, 1952.

Hanushek, Eric, et al. *Making Schools Work.* Washington, D.C.: Brookings Institution, 1994.

Harrington, Michael. *The Other America.* New York: Macmillan, 1962.

Harris, William T. *Psychologic Foundations of Education: An Attempt to Show the Genesis of the Higher Faculties of the Mind.* New York: D. Appleton, 1899.

———. "The Kindergarten Methods Contrasted with the Methods of the American Primary School." Kindergarten Department of the National Education Association. Nashville, TN. 17 July 1889.

Harris, W. T., and Duane Doty. *Statement of the Theory of Education in the United States.* 1875. Ann Arbor, MI: Xerox University Microfilms (American Culture Series, reel 620.7), 1974.

Harris, W. T., Wm F. Phelps, and Eli T. Tappan. "Report of a Committee on a Course of Study from Primary School to University, 1876." in Willis, George et al. Eds. *The American Curriculum: A Documentary History.* Westport, CT: Praeger, 1994. 73–83.

Hartz, Louis. *The Liberal Tradition in America: An Interpretation of American Political Thought since the Revolution.* New York: Harcourt, Brace & World, 1955.

Harveson, Mae Elizabeth. *Catharine Esther Beecher: Pioneer Teacher.* Lancaster, PA: Science Printing, 1932.

Hassel, Bryan C. *The Charter School Challenge: Avoiding the Pitfalls, Fulfilling the Promise.* Washington, D.C.: Brookings Institution, 1999.

Hatfield, W. Wilbur. *An Experience Curriculum in English.* New York: Appleton Century Crofts, 1935.

Hawke, David Freeman. *Benjamin Rush: Revolutionary Gadfly.* New York: Bobbs-Merrill, 1971.

Hayakawa, S. I. "The Case for Official English." *Language Loyalties: A Source Book on the Official English Controversy.* Ed. James Crawford. Chicago: U of Chicago P, 1992. 94–100.

Hayden, Robert W. *A History of the New Math Movement in the United States.* Diss. Iowa State U, 1981. Ann Arbor: UMI, 1981. 8209127.

Haynes, Benjamin R., and Harry P. Jackson. *A History of Business Education in the United States.* Cincinnati: South Western Publishing, 1935.

Hess, Frederick, and Robert Maranto. "Letting the Flowers and Weeds Bloom: The Charter Story in Arizona." Paper presented to American Educational Research Association. New Orleans, LA. 24–28 April 2000.

Higham, John. *Strangers in the Land: Patterns of American Nativism, 1860–1925.* New Brunswick, NJ: Rutgers UP, 1955.

Hinsdale, B. A. *Horace Mann and the Common School Revival in the United States.* New York: Charles Scribner's Sons, 1911.

Hochschild, Jennifer L. *The New American Dilemma.* New Haven, CT: Yale UP, 1984.

Hofstadter, Richard. *Social Darwinism in American Thought.* Rev. ed. New York: George Braziller, 1955.

Hofstadter, Richard, William Miller, and Daniel Aaron. *The United States: The History of a Republic.* 2nd ed. Englewood Cliffs, NJ: Prentice-Hall, 1967.

Honeywell, Roy J. *Educational Work of Thomas Jefferson.* New York: Russell, 1964.

Horn, Ernest. "Comment." *Thirty-Third Yearbook of the National Society for the Study of Education: The Activity Movement.* Ed. Guy Montrose Whipple. Bloomington, IL: Public School Publishing, 1934. 195–197.

———. "Contributions of Research to Special Methods: Spelling." *The Thirty-Seventh Yearbook of the National Society for the Study of Education: The Scientific Movement in Education.* Ed. Guy Montrose Whipple. Bloomington, IL: Public School Publishing, 1938. 107–121.

Howe, John. "Republicanism." *Thomas Jefferson: A Reference Biography.* Ed. Merrill Peterson. New York: Charles Scribner's Sons, 1986. 59–80.

Institute for Government Research. *The Problem of Indian Administration.* Baltimore: Johns Hopkins, 1928.

International Reading Association. "High Stakes Assessments in Reading: A Position Statement of the International Reading Association." ERIC Microfiche ED435084, 1999.

Jackson, Sidney L. *America's Struggle for Free Schools: Social Tension and Education in New England and New York, 1827–1842.* Washington, D.C.: American Council on Public Affairs, 1941.

James, Edmund J. *Commercial Education.* New York: J. B. Lyon, 1899.

Jefferson, Thomas. "Letter to Governor Wilson C. Nicholas." *Educational Work of Thomas Jefferson.* Ed. Roy J. Honeywell. New York: Russell, 1964. 230–232.

———. "Letter to Peter Carr." *Educational Work of Thomas Jefferson.* Ed. Roy J. Honeywell. New York: Russell, 1964. 222–227.

———. *Notes on the State of Virginia.* Ed. William Peden. Chapel Hill: U of North Carolina P, 1955.

———. "Plan for the Establishment of Ward Schools." *Educational Work of Thomas Jefferson.* Ed. Roy J. Honeywell. New York: Russell, 1964. 228–229.

———. "Report of the Commissioners Appointed to Fix the Site of the University of Virginia." *Educational Work of Thomas Jefferson.* Ed. Roy J. Honeywell. New York: Russell, 1964. 248–260.

Jenkinson, Edward B. *The School Protest Movement.* Bloomington, IN: Phi Delta Kappa Educational Foundation, 1986.

Jensen, Arthur R. "How Much Can We Boost IQ and Scholastic Achievement." *Harvard Educational Review* 39.1 (1969): 1–123.

Johnson, Donovan A., and Robert Rahtz. *The New Mathematics in Our Schools.* New York: Macmillan, 1966.

Johnson, Thomas. *The Oxford Companion to American History.* New York: Oxford, 1966.

Jones, Thomas Jesse. *Social Studies in the Hampton Curriculum.* Hampton, VA: Hampton Institute Press, 1906.

———, et al. *The Navajo Indian Problem.* New York: Phelps-Stokes Fund, 1939.

Judd, Charles H. "Contributions of School Surveys." *The Thirty-Seventh Yearbook of the National Society for the Study of Education: The Scientific Movement in Education.* Ed. Guy Montrose Whipple. Bloomington, IL: Public School Publishing Company, 1938, 9–20.

Kaestle, Carl. Introduction. *Joseph Lancaster and the Monitorial School Movement: A Documentary History.* Ed. Carl Kaestle. New York: Teachers College Press, 1973. 1–53.

———. *Pillars of the Republic: Common Schools and American Society, 1780–1860.* New York: Hill and Wang, 1983.

Kandel, I. L. *The Impact of the War upon American Education.* 1949. Westport, CT: Greenwood Press, 1974.

Kape'ahiokalani, Maenette, Padeken Ah Nee Benham, and Ronald H. Heck. *Culture and Educational Policy in Hawai'i: The Silencing of Native Voices.* Mahwah, NJ: Lawrence Erlbaum, 1998.

Karier, Clarence J. "Liberal Ideology and the Quest for Orderly Change." *Roots of Crisis: American Education in the Twentieth Century.* Ed. Clarence J. Karier et al. Chicago: Rand McNally, 1973. 84–107.

Katz, Irwin. "A Critique of Personality Approaches to Negro Performance." *Journal of Social Issues* 25.3 (1969): 13–27.

Katz, Michael B. *The Irony of Early School Reform: Educational Innovation in Mid-nineteenth Century Massachusetts.* Cambridge, MA: Harvard UP, 1968.

———. *The Undeserving Poor: From the War on Poverty to the War on Welfare.* New York: Pantheon, 1989.

Kaufman, Polly Welts. *Women Teachers on the Frontier.* New Haven, CT: Yale UP, 1984.

Kelley, Brooks Mather. *Yale: A History.* New Haven: Yale UP, 1974.

Kelly, Alfred H. "The Congressional Controversy over School Segregation, 1867–1875." *African Americans and the Emergence of Segregation, 1865–1900.* Ed. Donald G. Nieman. New York: Garland Publishing, 1994. 169–196.

Kelly, Lawrence C. *The Navajo Indians and Federal Policy, 1900–1935.* Tucson: U of Arizona P, 1968.

Kepner, Tyler. "The Dilemma of the Social-Studies Teacher." *Social Education* 1.2 (1937): 81–87.

Kett, Joseph F. "Education." *Thomas Jefferson: A Reference Biography.* Ed. Merrill Peterson. New York: Charles Scribner's Sons, 1986. 233–251.

Keyes v. School District No. 1, Denver, Colorado, 413 U.S. 189, 1972.

Kilpatrick, William H. "Definition of the Activity Movement To-Day." *The Thirty-Third Yearbook of the National Society for the Study of Education: The Activity Movement.* Ed. Guy Montrose Whipple. Bloomington, IL: Public School Publishing, 1934. 45–64.

———. *The Dutch Schools of New Netherland and Colonial New York.* 1912. New York: Arno Press, 1989.

———. *Foundations of Method.* New York: Macmillan, 1926.

———. *The Project Method: The Use of the Purposeful Act in the Educative Process.* 1918. New York: Teachers College Press, 1922.

———. "Statement." *The Thirty-Third Yearbook of the National Society for the Study of Education: The*

Activity Movement. Ed. Guy Montrose Whipple. Bloomington, IL: Public School Publishing, 1934. 200–202.

King, Martin Luther, Jr. *Stride toward Freedom.* New York: Perennial Library, 1958.

———. *Where Do We Go from Here: Chaos or Community?* New York: Bantam Books, 1967.

———. *Why Can't We Wait.* New York: Signet Books, 1964.

Kirk, Samuel, et al. "Basic Facts and Principles Underlying Special Education." *The Education of Exceptional Children: Forty-Ninth Yearbook of the National Society for the Study of Education.* Ed. Samuel Kirk, et al. Chicago: U of Chicago P, 1950. 3–17.

Kirp, David. *Just Schools.* Berkeley: U of California P, 1982.

Kliebard, Herbert. *The Struggle for the American Curriculum, 1893–1958.* 2nd ed. New York: Routledge, 1995.

Kline, Morris. *Why Johnny Can't Add: The Failure of New Math.* New York: St. Martin's Press, 1973.

Knight, Edgar J. "Calvin Stowe." *Reports of European Education.* Ed. Edgar J. Knight. New York: McGraw-Hill, 1930. 243–247.

Komisar, B. Paul. "Needs and the Needs-Curriculum." *Language and Concepts in Education.* Ed. B. Othanel Smith and Robert H. Ennis. Chicago: Rand McNally, 1961.

Korty, Margaret Barton. *Benjamin Franklin and Eighteenth Century American Libraries.* Philadelphia: American Philosophical Society, 1965.

Krug, Edward A. *The Secondary School Curriculum.* New York: Harper & Brothers, 1960.

———. *The Shaping of the American High School, Volume 2, 1920–1941.* Madison: U of Wisconsin P, 1972.

Kwong, Peter. *The New Chinatown.* New York: Noonday Press, 1987.

La Vor, Martin. "Federal Legislation for Exceptional Persons." *Public Policy and the Education of Exceptional Children.* Ed. Frederick Weintraub, et al. Reston, VA: Council for Exceptional Children, 1976. 96–113.

Lancaster, Joseph. "Improvements in Education as It Respects the Industrious Classes of the Community." *Joseph Lancaster and the Monitorial School Movement: A Documentary History.* Ed. Carl Kaestle. New York: Teachers College Press, 1973. 62–87.

———. "The Lancasterian System." *Joseph Lancaster and the Monitorial School Movement: A Documentary History.* Ed. Carl Kaestle. New York: Teachers College Press, 1973. 88–99.

Latimer, John Francis. *What's Happened to Our High Schools?* Washington, D.C.: Public Affairs Press, 1958.

Lau et al. v. Nichols et al. 414 US 563, 1974.

Leavitt, Robert Keith. *Noah's Ark: New England Yankees and the Endless Quest.* Springfield, MA: Merriam, 1947.

Leidecker, Kurt F. *Yankee Teacher: The Life of William Torrey Harris.* New York: Philosophic Library, 1946.

Leiderman, Gloria F., William G. Chinn, and Mervyn E. Dunkley. *The Special Curriculum Project: Pilot Program on Mathematics Learning of Culturally Disadvantaged Primary School Children, No. 2.* Stanford, CA: Leland Stanford Junior U, 1966.

Leloudis, James. *Schooling in the New South: Pedagogy, Self, and Society in North Carolina, 1880–1920.* Chapel Hill: U of North Carolina P, 1996.

Levin, Henry. "Beyond Remediation: Toward Acceleration for All Schools." *Making Schools Work.* Ed. Cheryl L. Fagnano and Katherine Nouri Hughes. San Francisco: Westview, 1993.

Levine, Erwin L., and Elizabeth M. Wexler. *PL 94-142: An Act of Congress.* New York: Macmillan, 1981.

Levy, Babette M. *Cotton Mather.* Boston: Twayne Publishers, 1979.

Lewis, Oscar. *A Study of Slum Culture: Backgrounds for La Vida.* New York: Random, 1968.

Liles, Jeffrey A. "Play Movement." *Historical Dictionary of American Education.* Ed. Richard J. Altenbaugh. Westport, CT: Greenwood Press, 1999. 294–295.

Linn, Eleanor, et al. "Bitter Lessons for All: Sexual Harassment in Schools." *Sexuality and the Curriculum: The Politics and Practices of Sexuality Education.* Ed. James T. Sears. New York: Teachers College Press, 1992.

Lippman, Leopold, and I. Ignancy Goldberg. *Right to Education.* New York: Teachers College Press, 1973.

Lomax, Louis. *The Negro Revolt.* New York: Signet Books, 1963.

Lord, John. *The Life of Emma Willard.* New York: D. Appleton, 1873.

Low, Victor. *The Unimpressible Race: A Century of Educational Struggle by the Chinese in San Francisco.* San Francisco: East/West Publishing, 1982.

Lubove, Roy. *The Progressives and the Slums: Tenement House Reform in New York City.* Pittsburgh: U of Pittsburgh P, 1962.

Lund, Leonard, and Cathleen Wild. *Ten Years after a Nation at Risk.* New York: Conference Board, 1993.

Lutz, Alma. *Emma Willard: Pioneer Educator of American Women.* Westport, CT: Greenwood Press, 1964.

MacMullen, Edith Nye. *In the Cause of True Education: Henry Barnard and Nineteenth Century School Reform.* New Haven, CT: Yale UP, 1991.

Mann, Horace. "Lecture VII." *Lectures on Education.* New York: Arno Press, 1969.

———. "Second Annual Report." *The Republic and the School: Horace Mann on the Education of Free Men.* Ed. Lawrence A. Cremin. New York: Teachers College Press, 1957. 34–43.

———. "Selection among Studies." *The American Curriculum: A Documentary History.* Ed. George Willis et al. Westport, CT: Praeger, 1994. 41–52.

———. "Twelfth Annual Report." *The Republic and the School: Horace Mann on the Education of Free Men.* Ed. Lawrence A. Cremin. New York: Teachers College Press, 1957. 79–112.

Maritain, Jacques. *Education at the Crossroads.* 1943. New Haven, CT: Yale UP, 1971.

Marquez, Benjamin. *LULAC: The Evolution of a Mexican American Organization.* Austin: U of Texas Press, 1989.

Marsh, Paul E., and Ross A. Gortner. *Federal Aid to Science Education: Two Programs.* Syracuse, NY: Syracuse UP, 1963.

Marshall, Leon C., and Rachel Marshall Goetz. *Curriculum-Making in the Social Studies: A Social Process Approach.* New York: Charles Scribners, 1936.

Marshner, Connought Coyne. *Blackboard Tyranny.* New York: Arlington House, 1979.

Martin Luther King, Jr. Elementary School Children v. Ann Arbor School District Board. 473 F. Supp. 1371, 1979.

Martin Luther King, Jr. Elementary School Children v. Ann Arbor School District Board. U.S. Dist. LEXIS 10198, 24 Aug. 1979.

Martin, Jane Roland. *The Schoolhome.* Cambridge, MA: Harvard UP, 1992.

Massachusetts Commission on Industrial Education. "Report." *American Education and Vocationalism: A Documentary History, 1870–1970.* Ed. Marvin Lazerson and W. Norton Grubb. New York: Teachers College Press, 1974. 69–76.

Massachusetts Governors Commission on Gay and Lesbian Youth. "Making Schools Safe for Gay and Lesbian Youth: Breaking the Silence in Schools and Families." ERIC Microfiche, ED367923, 1993.

Mayor, John. "The Junior High School Mathematics Work of the School Mathematics Study Group." *Philosophies and Procedures of the SMSG Writing Teams.* School Mathematics Study Group. Stanford, CA: Leland Stanford Junior U, 1965. 1–9.

McCarthy, Jane, and Henry M. Levin. "Accelerated Schools for Students in At-Risk Situations." *Students in At-Risk Schools.* Ed. Hersholt C. Waxman, et al. Newbury Park, CA: Corwin, 1992.

McClellan, B. Edward. *Moral Education in America: Schools and the Shaping of Character from Colonial Times to the Present.* New York: Teachers College Press, 1999.

McCluskey, Neil Gerard, ed. *Catholic Education in America: A Documentary History.* New York: Teachers College Press, 1964.

———. *Public Schools and Moral Education: The Influence of Horace Mann, William Torrey Harris, and John Dewey.* New York: Columbia UP, 1958.

McDonald, Forrest. *Novus Ordo Seclorum: The Intellectual Origins of the Constitution.* Lawrence: U of Kansas P, 1985.

McGrath, Earl J., and Jack T. Johnson. *The Changing Mission of Home Economics.* New York: Teachers College Press, 1968.

McKey, Ruth Hubbell, et al. *The Impact of Head Start on Children, Families, and Communities.* Washington, D.C.: GPO, 1985.

McKnight, Douglas. "Morality and the Public Schools: The Specter of William Torrey Harris." *Educational Foundations* 13 (1999) 4: 29–46.

McLaren, Peter. *Life in Schools: An Introduction to Critical Pedagogy in the Foundations of Education.* New York: Longman, 1989.

McMurry, Charles A. *The Elements of General Method Based on the Principles of Herbart.* 1903. London: Macmillan, 1910.

Medina, Noe, and D. Monty Neill. *Fallout from the Testing Explosion: How 100 Million Standardized Exams Undermine Equity and Excellence in America's Public Schools.* Cambridge, MA: National Center for Fair and Open Testing, 1990.

Mednick, Martha T. "On the Politics of Psychological Constructs." *American Psychologist* 44.8 (1989): 1118–1123.

———. "Education in American History." *Foundations of Education.* Ed. George F. Kneller. New York: John Wiley, 1963. 1–42.

Mehl, Bernard. *Classical Educational Ideas from Sumeria to America.* Columbus, OH: Charles Merrill Publishing, 1972.

———. "Education in American History." *Foundations of Education.* Ed. George Kneller. New York: John Wiley, 1963. 1–42.

Messerli, Jonathan. *Horace Mann: A Biography.* New York: Alfred A. Knopf, 1972.

Metcalf, George R. *From Little Rock to Boston.* Westport, CT: Greenwood Press, 1983.

Miller, W. S. "The Administrative Use of Intelligence Tests in the High School." *The Twenty-First Yearbook of the National Society for the Study of Education: Intelligence Tests and Their Uses.* Ed. Guy Montrose Whipple. Bloomington, IL, 1923. 189–222.

Milliken v. Bradley. 411 US 717, 1974.

Milliken v. Bradley. 433 U.S. 267, 1977.

Mills v. Board of Education of the District of Columbia. 348 F. Supp. 866, 1972.

Mills, C. Wright. *White Collar: The American Middle Class.* New York: Oxford UP, 1951.

Minnesota State Department of Education. "Alone No More: Developing a School Support System for Gay, Lesbian, and Bisexual Youth." ERIC Microfiche, 1994.

Minnich, Harvey C. *William Holmes McGuffey and His Readers.* New York: American Book, 1936.

Mirel, Jeffrey. *The Rise and Fall of an Urban School System, 1907–1981.* Ann Arbor: U of Michigan P, 1993.

Miron, Gary. "What's Public about Michigan's Charter Schools: Lessons in School Reform from Statewide Evaluations of Charter Schools." Paper presented to the American Educational Association. New Orleans, LA. 24–28 April 2000.

Moffett, James. *Storm in the Mountains.* Carbondale: Southern Illinois UP, 1988.

Moon, Bob. *The "New Maths" Curriculum Controversy: An International Story.* New York: Falmer Press, 1986.

Moon, Henry Lee, ed. *The Emerging Thought of W. E. B. Du Bois: Essays and Editorials from The Crisis.* New York: Simon & Schuster, 1972.

Moore, Alice. "Moral Education in the Schools: A Board Member's Perspective." *The School Law Newsletter* 6, 1976.

———. Letter to the author. 19 Dec. 1976.

Morgan, Edmund S. *The Puritan Dilemma: Story of John Winthrop.* Boston: Little, Brown, 1958.

Morris, Robert C. *Reading, 'Riting, and Reconstruction: The Education of Freedmen in the South, 1861–1870.* Chicago: U of Chicago P, 1976.

Moses, James. *Desegregation in Catholic Schools.* Ann Arbor, MI: University Microfilms International, 1978.

Mosier, Richard David. *Making the American Mind: The Social and Moral Idea in the McGuffey Readers.* New York: King's Crown Press, 1947.

Moss, Richard. *Noah Webster.* Boston: Twayne, 1984.

Mossman, Lois Coffey. "Statement of the Problem." *The Thirty-Third Yearbook of the National Society for the Study of Education: The Activity Movement.* Ed. Guy Montrose Whipple. Bloomington, IL: Public School Publishing, 1934. 1–8.

Mosteller, Frederick, and Daniel P. Moynihan. "A Path-breaking Report." *On Equality of Educational Opportunity.* Ed. Frederick Mosteller and Daniel P. Moynihan. New York: Random, 1972.

Murphy, Marjorie. *Blackboard Unions: The AFT and the NEA, 1900–1980.* Ithaca, NY: Cornell UP, 1990.

Murray, Rebecca. *History of the Public School Kindergarten in North Carolina.* New York: MSS Information Corp., 1974.

Nathan, Joe. *Charter Schools: Creating Hope and Opportunity for American Education.* San Francisco: Jossey-Bass, 1996.

Nation Still at Risk: An Educational Manifesto, A. np: Center for Educational Reform, 1998.

National Advisory Council on Education of Disadvantaged Children. *America's Educationally Neglected: A Progress Report on Compensatory Education, Annual Report to the President and the Congress.* Washington, D.C.: GPO, 1973.

———. *Summer Education for Children of Poverty.* Washington, D.C.: GPO, 1966.

National Association of School Psychologists. "Position Statement: Gay, Lesbian, and Bisexual Youth." ERIC Microfiche ED431983, 1999.

National Commission on Excellence in Education (NCEE). *A Nation at Risk: The Imperative for Educational Reform.* Washington, D.C.: GPO, 1983.

National Education Association (NEA). *Planning for American Youth: A Summary of Education for All American Youth.* Washington, D.C.: National Association of Secondary School Principles, 1944.

———. *Report of the Committee of Ten.* New York: American Book Company, 1894.

———. *Wartime Handbook for Education.* Washington, D.C.: National Education Association, 1943.

National Institute on Education and War. *Handbook on Education and the War.* Washington, D.C.: GPO, 1943.

NCATE. Proposed NCATE 2000 Unit Standards. 4 April 2000. Online. Available http://www.ncate.org/standard/m_stds.htm.

Nelson, Murry R. "Social Contexts of the Committee on Social Studies Report." Ed. Murry R. Nelson. *The Social Studies in Education.* ERIC Fiche ED 374072, 1994. 71–93.

Nevins, David, and Robert Bills. *The Schools That Fear Built.* Washington, D.C.: Acropolis, 1976.

Newlon, Jesse H., and A. L. Threkeld. "The Denver Curriculum-Revision Program." *Twenty-Sixth Yearbook of the National Society for the Study of Education: The Foundations and Technique of Curriculum Construction.* Bloomington, IL: Public School Publishing, 1926. 229–240

Nickel, K. N. "Experimentation, Extrapolation, Exaggeration: Thy Name Is Research." *Phi Delta Kappan* 61 (1979): 260–261.

Noddings, Nel. *Caring: A Feminine Approach to Ethics and Moral Education.* Berkeley: U of California P, 1984.

Nolan, Hugh J. *Pastoral Letters of the United States Catholic Bishops.* Vol. I. Washington, D.C.: U.S. Catholic Conference, 1983.

North, Douglas C. *The Economic Growth of the United States, 1790–1860.* Englewood Cliffs, NJ, 1961.

Novick, Peter. *That Noble Dream.* New York: Cambridge UP, 1988.

Oakes, Jeannie. *Keeping Track: How Schools Structure Inequality.* New Haven, CT: Yale UP, 1985.

Ohio Education Association. *A History of Education in the State of Ohio: A Centennial Volume.* Columbus: General Assembly, 1876.

Orfield, Gary. *Must We Bus?* Washington, D.C.: Brookings Institute, 1978.

———. *The Reconstruction of Southern Education.* New York: John Wiley & Sons, 1969.

Orfield, Gary, and Susan Eaton, et al. *Dismantling Desegregation.* New York: New Press, 1996.

Paden, Jon S. *Reflections for the Future.* Dayton, OH: Charles F. Kettering Foundation, 1978.

Panzer, Joseph J. *Educational Traditions of the Society of Mary.* Dayton, OH: U of Dayton P, 1965.

Passow, A. Harry. *American Secondary Education: The Conant Influence.* Reston, VA: National Association of Secondary School Principals, 1977.

Pedroza, Anna. A. "Bordering on Success: Mexican American Students and High Stakes Testing." ERIC Microfiche ED420713, 1998.

Perkinson, Henry. *The Imperfect Panacea: American Faith in Education 1865–1990.* 3rd ed. New York: McGraw Hill, 1991.

Perko, F. Michael, S. J. "By the Bowels of God's Mercy: Protestant and Catholic Responses to Educational Development in Cincinnati, 1830–1855." *Journal of Midwest History of Education* 11 (1983): 15–32.

———. *Time to Favor Zion: The Ecology of Religion and School Development on the Urban Frontier, Cincinnati, 1830–1870.* Chicago: Educational Studies Press, 1988.

Peterson, Paul E. "Did the Education Commissions Say Anything?" *Brookings Review* 2 (1983) 2: 3–11.

Petit, Sr. Mary Loretta, O. P. "Samuel Lewis: Educational Reformer Turned Abolitionist." Diss. Western Reserve U, 1966.

Pettigrew, Thomas, and Robert Green. "School Desegregation in Large Cities." *Harvard Educational Review* 1 (1976) 1–53.

Pierce v. Society of Sisters. 268 U.S. 510, 1925.

Pipes, Richard. *Russia under the Old Regime.* New York: Scribner, 1974.

Pius XI. *Christian Education of Youth.* Washington, D.C.: National Catholic Welfare Office, 1930.

Pochmann, Henry A. *New England Transcendentalism and St. Louis Hegelianism.* Philadelphia: Carl Schurz Memorial Foundation, 1948.

Pohan, Cathy A., and Norma J. Bailey. "Including Gays in Multiculturalism." *MultiCultural Education* 5 (Fall 1997): 12–15.

Powell, Arthur G., Eleanor Farrar, and David K. Cohen. *The Shopping Mall High School: Winners and Losers in the Educational Marketplace.* Boston: Houghton Mifflin, 1985.

Pratt, Caroline. "Curriculum-Making in the City and Country School." *Twenty-Sixth Yearbook of the National Society for the Study of Education: The Foundations and Technique of Curriculum Construction.* Bloomington, IL: Public School Publishing, 1926. 327–332.

President's Panel on Mental Retardation. *A Proposed Program for National Action to Combat Mental Retardation.* Washington, D.C.: GPO, 1962.

———. *MR 76 Mental Retardation: Past and Present.* Washington, D.C.: GPO, 1977.

Pride, Richard, and J. David Woodward. *The Burden of Busing.* Knoxville: U of Tennessee P, 1985.

Rabinowitz, Howard N. "From Exclusion to Segregation: Southern Race Relations, 1865–1890." *African Americans and the Emergence of Segregation, 1865–1900.* Ed. Donald G. Nieman. New York: Garland, 1994. 368–382.

Rainwater, Lee, and William L. Yancey. *The Moynihan Report and the Politics of Controversy.* Cambridge, MA: MIT Press, 1967.

Randall, Samuel S. *History of the Common School System of the State of New York from its Origin in 1795 to the Present Time.* New York: Ivison, Blakeman, Taylor, 1871.

Rauch, Eduardo. "The Jewish Day School in America." *Religious Schooling in America.* Ed. James C. Carper and Thomas C. Hunt. Birmingham, AL: Religious Education Press, 1984. 130–168.

Ravitch, Diane. *National Standards in American Education: A Citizen's Guide.* Washington, D.C.: Brookings Institution, 1995.

———. *The Revisionists Revised: A Critique of the Radical Attack on the Schools.* New York: Basic Books, 1978.

———. *The Troubled Crusade: American Education, 1945–1980.* New York: Basic Books, 1983.

"Reagan, Ronald W." *Encyclopedia Britannica.* Online. Britannica.com, 2000.

Rees, Helen. *Deprivation and Compensatory Education.* New York: Houghton Mifflin, 1968.

Reese, William J. *Power and the Promise of School Reform.* Boston: Routledge and Kegan Paul, 1986.

———. *The Origins of the American High School.* New Haven, CT: Yale UP, 1995.

"Report of the Committee of Fifteen." *The American Curriculum: A Documentary History.* Ed. George Willis et al. Westport, CT: Praeger, 1994. 95–108.

Research for Better Schools. *Special Education in America's Cities.* Washington, D.C.: Council of the Great City Schools, 1988.

Rice, J. M. *The Public-School System of the United States.* 1893. New York: Arno Press, 1969.

Rich, Thomas R. "The Western Literary Institute and College of Professional Teachers and the Common School Movement in the West, 1830–1840." Diss. Northern Illinois U, 1973.

Richard, Carl J. *The Founders and the Classics: Greece, Rome, and the Enlightenment.* Cambridge, MA: Harvard University Press, 1994.

Riddick v. School Board of City of Norfolk, Virginia. 784 F 2d 521. 4th circle, 1986.

Riessman, Frank. *The Culturally Deprived Child.* New York: Harper, 1962.

Rigdon, Susan M. *The Culture Facade: Art, Science, and Politics in the Work of Oscar Lewis.* Urbana: U of Illinois P, 1988.

Riis, Jacob A. *The Battle with the Slum.* New York: Macmillan, 1902.

———. *The Children of the Poor.* 1892. New York: Arno Press, 1971.

———. *How the Other Half Lives: Studies among the Tenements of New York.* 1901. New York: Dover, 1971.

———. *The Making of an American.* New York: Macmillan, 1923.

Riley, David P. "The Ins and Outs of Legislative Reform." *Public Policy and the Education of Exceptional Children.* Ed. Frederick Weintraub, et al. Reston, VA: Council for Exceptional Children, 1976. 312–323.

Rofes, Eric. "Opening Up the Classroom Closet: Responding to the Needs of Gay and Lesbian Youth." *Harvard Educational Review* 59.4 (1989): 444–453.

———. "Schools: Neglected Site of Queer Activities." *School Experiences of Gay and Lesbian Youth: The Invisible Minority.* Ed. Mary B. Harris. New York: Harrington Park, 1997. xiii–xix.

Rogers, Agnes L. "The Use of Psychological Tests in the Administration of Colleges for Women." *The Twenty-First Yearbook of the National Society for the Study of Education: Intelligence Tests and Their Uses.* Ed. Guy Montrose Whipple. Bloomington, IL, 1923. 245–252.

Rose, Willie Lee. *Rehearsal for Reconstruction: The Port Royal Experiment.* New York: Oxford UP, 1964.

Ross, Elizabeth Dale. *The Kindergarten Crusade: The Establishment of Preschool Education in the United States.* Athens: Ohio UP, 1976.

Rossell, Christine H. *The Carrot or the Stick for School Desegregation Policy.* Philadelphia: Temple UP, 1990.

Rotberg, Iris C. "I Never Promised You First Place." *Phi Delta Kappan* 71 (December 1990): 296–303.

Rothstein, Richard, and Karen Hawley Miles, *Where's the Money Gone?* Washington, D.C.: Economic Policy Institute,1995.

Rousmaniere, Kate. *City Teachers: Teaching and School Reform in Historical Perspective.* New York: Teachers College Press, 1997.

Rudolph, Frederick. *The American College and University: A History.* 1962. Athens: U of Georgia P, 1990.

Rugg, Harold. *Changing Governments and Changing Cultures: The World's March Toward Democracy.* New York: Ginn, 1932.

———. "Do the Social Studies Prepare Pupils Adequately for Life Activities?" *The Social Studies in the Elementary Schools* Ed. Guy Montrose Whipple. Bloomington, IL: Public School Publishing, 1923. 1–27.

Rury, John L. *Education and Women's Work: Female Schooling and Division of Labor in Urban America.* Albany: State U of New York P, 1991.

Rush, Benjamin. "A Plan for the Establishment of Public Schools to Which Are Added Thoughts upon the Mode of Education Proper in a Republic." 1786. *Essays on Education in the Early Republic.* Ed. Frederick Rudolph. Cambridge, MA: Harvard UP, 1965. 1–23.

———. "Thoughts on Female Education." *Essays on Education in the Early Republic.* Ed. Frederick Rudolph. Cambridge, MA: Harvard UP, 1965. 25–40.

Russo, Charles. "*Brown v. Board of Education* at 40: A Legal History for Equal Educational Opportunities in American Public Education." *Journal of Negro Education* 63.3 (1994): 297–309.

Ryan, James Edwin. *The History of the Manual Training Movement in the California Normal Schools.* Diss. U of California, Los Angeles, 1964. Ann Arbor: UMI, 1964. 64-9636.

Ryan, William. *Blaming the Victim.* New York: Pantheon, 1971.

Sagor, Richard. *At-Risk Students: Reaching and Teaching Them.* Swampscott, MA: Watersun, 1993.

Salomone, Rosemary C. *Equal Education under the Law: Legal Rights and Federal Policy.* New York: St. Martins Press, 1986.

Sanford, Charles W., Harold C. Hand, and Willard B. Spalding, eds. *The Schools and National Security: Recommendations for Elementary and Secondary Schools.* New York: McGraw Hill, 1951.

Saxe, David Warren. *Social Studies in Schools: A History of Early Years.* New York: SUNY Press, 1991.

Schmidt, George P. "Intellectual Crosscurrents in American Colleges, 1825–1855." *American Historical Review* 42 (1936): 46–67.

Schneider, Susan Gilbert. *Revolution, Reaction or Reform: The 1974 Bilingual Education Act.* New York: LA Publishing, 1976.

Schweninger, Lee. *John Winthrop.* Boston: Twayne Publishers, 1990.

Science Policy Research Division of the Library of Congress. *The National Science Foundation: A General Review of Its First Fifteen Years.* U.S. House of Representatives. Committee on Science and Astronautics. 89th Cong. 1st. Sess. Washington, D.C.: GPO, 1965.

Sears, James. "Well of Loneliness: Gay and Lesbian Youth." *Social Issues and Education: Challenge and Responsibility.* Ed. Alex Molnar. Alexandria, VA: ASCD, 1987. 79–100.

Selden, Frank Henry. *Manual Training.* Milwaukee, WI: American School Board, 1909.

Shea, John Gilmary. *Catholic Missions among the Indian Tribes of the United States, 1529–1854.* 1855. New York: Arno Press, 1969.

Shepard, Lorrie A., "Inflated Test Score Gains: Is It Old Norms or Teaching to the Test?" ERIC Microfiche ED334204, 1989.

———. "Will National Tests Improve Student Learning?" ERIC Microfiche ED348382, 1992.

Shepard, Lorrie A., and Katherine Cutts Dougherty. "Effects of High Stakes Testing on Instruction." ERIC Microfiche ED337468, 1991.

Shields, Thomas Edward. *The Education of Our Girls.* New York: Benziger Brothers, 1907.

Slavin, Robert. "Students at Risk." *Effective Programs for Students at Risk.* Ed. Robert E. Slavin, Nancy L. Karweit, and Nancy A. Madden. Boston: Allyn & Bacon, 1989.

Sluys, A. *Manual Training in Elementary Schools for Boys.* New York: Industrial Education Association, 1989.

Snedden, David. *Problems in Secondary Education.* New York: Houghton Mifflin, 1917.

Solomon, R. Patrick. *Black Resistance in High School.* Albany, NY: SUNY P, 1992.

Spencer, Herbert. "What Knowledge Is of Most Worth?" *Herbert Spencer on Education.* Ed. Andreas M. Kazamias. New York: Teachers College Press, 1966. 121–159.

Spring, Joel. *The American School, 1642–1990.* 2nd ed. New York: Longman, 1990.

———. *The Sorting Machine Revisited: National Educational Policy since 1945.* Updt. ed. New York: Longman, 1989.

Sproul, Lee, Stephen Weiner, and David Wolf. *Organizing an Anarchy.* Chicago: U of Chicago P, 1978.

Stage, Sarah. "Ellen Richards and the Social Significance of the Home Economics Movement." *Rethinking Home Economics: Women and the History of a Profession.* Ed. Sarah Stage and Virginia B. Vincenti. Ithaca: Cornell UP, 1997. 17–33.

Stedman, Lawrence C., and Carl F. Kaestle. "The Great Test-Score Decline: A Closer Look." *Literacy in the United States.* Ed. Carl F. Kaestle, et al. New Haven, CT: Yale UP, 1991. 129–148.

———. "Literacy and Reading Performance in the United States from 1880 to the Present." *Literacy in the United States.* Ed. Carl F. Kaestle, et al. New Haven, CT: Yale UP, 1991. 75–128.

Stein, Mary Kay, Gaea Leinhart, and William Bickel. "Instructional Issues for Teaching Students at Risk." *Effective Programs for Students at Risk.* Ed. Robert E. Slavin, Nancy L. Karweit, and Nancy A. Madden. Boston: Allyn & Bacon, 1989.

Stern, Gerald. *The Buffalo Creek Disaster.* New York: Vintage, 1976.

Stowe, Calvin. "The Bible as a Means of Moral and Intellectual Improvement." *Transactions of the Eighth Annual Meeting of the Western Literary Institute and College of Professional Teachers.* Cincinnati: James R. Allbach, 1839. 43–59.

———. "Education of Immigrants." *Transactions of the Fifth Annual Meeting of the Western Literary Institute and College of Professional Teachers.* Cincinnati: Executive Committee, 1836. 1–15.

———. "Report on Elementary Public Instruction." 1838. *Reports of European Education.* Ed. Edgar J. Knight. New York: McGraw-Hill, 1930. 248–316.

Stueber, Ralph K. "An Informal History of Schooling in Hawaii." *To Teach the Children: Historical Aspects of Education in Hawaii.* Ed. Alexander L. Pickens and David Kemble. Honolulu, HI: Bernice Pauahi Bishop Museum, 1982. 16–37.

Subcommittee on Education. *Notes and Working Papers Concerning the Administration of Programs: Title I of Public Law 89-10.* Washington, D.C.: GPO, 1967.

Subcommittee on the Other Social Studies. "Social Sciences in the High School." *Social Education* 1.4 (1937): 259–265.

Sumtion, Merle, Dorothy Norris, and Lewis Terman. "Special Education for the Gifted Child." *The Education of Exceptional Children: Forty-Ninth Yearbook of the National Society for the Study of Education.* Ed. Samuel Kirk et al. Chicago: U of Chicago P, 1950.

Sundquist, James L. "Origins of the War on Poverty." *On Fighting Poverty.* Ed. James L. Sundquist. New York: Basic, 1969. 6–33.

———. *Making Federalism Work.* Washington, D.C.: Brookings Institute, 1969.

Swann v. Charlotte Mecklenburg Board of Education. 402 U.S. 1, 1971.

Swint, Henry Lee. *The Northern Teacher in the South, 1862–1870.* 1941. New York: Octagon Books, 1967.

Taba, Hilda, and Deborah Elkins. *Teaching Strategies for the Culturally Disadvantaged.* Chicago: Rand McNally, 1966.

Tamura, Eileen. *Americanization, Acculturation, and Ethnic Identity: The Nisei Generation in Hawaii.* Urbana: U of Illinois P, 1994.

Taylor, Howard Cromwell. *The Educational Significance of the Early Federal Land Ordinances.* 1922. New York: Arno Press, 1969.

Teacher Rights Division. *A Textbook Study in Cultural Conflict.* Washington, D.C.: National Education Association, 1975.

Teachers of Phillips Exeter Academy. "Further Dissent." *Social Education* 1.4 (1937): 258.

Thayer, V. T., Caroline B. Zachry, and Ruth Kotinsky. *Reorganizing Secondary Education.* New York: D. Appleton-Century, 1939.

Thomas, Steven B., and Charles J. Russo. *Special Education Law: Issues and Implications for the 90s.* Topeka, KS: National Organization on Legal Problems of Education, 1995.

Thompson, Eleanor Wolf. *Education for Ladies, 1830–1860: Ideas on Education in Magazines for Women.* New York: King's Crown Press, 1947.

Thorndike, Edward L. *Education: A First Book.* New York: Macmillan, 1923.

Thorndike, E. L., and R. S. Woodworth. "The Influence of Improvement in One Mental Function upon the Efficiency of Other Functions." *Psychological Review* III (1901): 247–261.

Tinker, George. *Missionary Conquest: The Gospel and Native American Cultural Genocide.* Minneapolis: Fortress Press, 1993.

Toch, Thomas. *In the Name of Excellence: The Struggle to Reform the Nation's Schools, Why It's Failing, and What Should Be Done.* New York: Oxford UP, 1991.

Tocqueville, Alexis de. *Democracy in America.* Ed. Richard Heffner. New York: New American Library, 1956.

Todd, Lewis Paul. *Wartime Relations of the Federal Government and the Public Schools 1917–1918.* 1945. New York: Arno Press, 1971.

Tomlinson, Tommy M. "*A Nation at Risk:* Background for a Working Paper." *Academic Work and Educational Excellence: Raising Student Productivity.* Ed. Tommy M. Tomlinson and Herbert J. Walberg. Berkeley, CA: McCutchan, 1986. 3–28.

Trabue, M. R. "The Use of Intelligence Tests in Junior High Schools." *The Twenty-First Yearbook of the National Society for the Study of Education: Intelligence Tests and Their Uses.* Ed. Guy Montrose Whipple. Bloomington, IL, 1923. 169–188.

Trimmer, Sarah. "A Comparative View of the New Plan of Education Promulgated by Mr. Joseph Lancaster." *Joseph Lancaster and the Monitorial School Movement: A Documentary History.* Ed. Carl Kaestle. New York: Teachers College Press, 1973. 100–108.

Troen, Selwyn K. "Operation HeadStart: The Beginnings of the Public School Kindergarten Movement." *Missouri Historical Review* 66.2 (1972): 211–229.

Tropea, Joseph L. "Bureaucratic Order and Special Children, 1890s–1940s." *History of Education Quarterly* 27 (1987): 29–53.

Tryom, J. H., Ellen F. O'Connor, and Abbie Wilson. *Manual Training Cardboard Construction.* Springfield, MA: Milton Bradley, 1913.

Turner, Frederick Jackson. *The Frontier in American History.* 1920. New York: Holt, Rinehart, & Winston, 1967.

Tyack, David. *The One Best System: A History of American Urban Education.* Cambridge, MA: Harvard UP, 1974.

Tyack, David, and Elisabeth Hansot. *Learning Together: A History of Coeducation in American Public Schools.* New York: Russell Sage Foundation, 1990.

Tyler, Ralph. *Basic Principles of Curriculum and Instruction.* 1949. U of Chicago P, 1975.

———. "The Tyler Rationale Reconsidered." *The American Curriculum.* Ed. George Willis et al. Westport, CT: Praeger, 1994.

Unger, Harlow Giles. *Noah Webster: The Life and Times of an American Patriot.* New York: John Wiley and Sons, 1998.

Urban, Wayne. *Why Teachers Organized.* Detroit: Wayne State UP, 1982.

Urban, Wayne, and Jennings Wagoner, Jr. *American Education: A History.* New York: McGraw Hill, 1996.

———. *American Education: A History.* 2nd ed. Boston: McGraw-Hill, 2000.

Urofsky, Melvin I. "Reforms and Response: The Yale Report of 1828." *History of Education Quarterly* 1 (1965): 53–67.

U.S. Bureau of the Census. *Historical Statistics of the United States: Colonial Times to 1970.* White Plains, NY: Kraus International Publications, 1989.

U.S. Bureau of Education. *Report of the Commissioner of Education.* Vol. 1. Washington, D.C.: GPO, 1909.

U.S. Commission on Civil Rights. *A Better Chance to Learn: Bilingual Bicultural Education.* Washington, D.C.: U.S. Commission on Civil Rights Clearinghouse, May 1975.

———. *The Excluded Student: Educational Practices Affecting Mexican Americans in the South West.* Washington, D.C.: GPO, May 1972.

———. *Fulfilling the Letter and the Spirit of the Law.* Washington, D.C.: GPO, 1976.

———. *Racial Isolation in the Public Schools.* Vol. I. Washington, D.C.: GPO, 1967.

———. *Statement on Metropolitan School Desegregation.* Washington, D.C.: GPO, 1977.

———. *Title IV and School Desegregation.* Washington, D.C.: GPO, 1973.

U.S. Department of Education. *The Nation Responds: Recent Efforts to Improve Education.* Washington, D.C.: GPO, 1984.

———. *The State of Charter Schools: Fourth Year Report.* Washington, D.C.: GPO, 2000.

———. *What Works: Research about Teaching and Learning.* Washington, D.C.: U.S. Department of Education, 1986.

U.S. Department of Health, Education, and Welfare. *Report on the National Defense Education Act: Fiscal Years 1961 and 1962.* Washington, D.C.: GPO, 1963.

U.S. Senate Subcommittee on Health. *Hearings on the Education of Handicapped Children.* 89th Cong. 1st sess., Washington, D.C.: GPO, 1965.

Valentine, Charles A. *Culture and Poverty.* Chicago: U of Chicago P, 1968.

Van Doren, Carl. *Benjamin Franklin.* New York: Viking Press, 1938.

Vaughn, William Preston. *Schools for All: The Blacks and Public Education in the South.* Lexington: UP of Kentucky, 1974.

Vinovskis, Maris A. *The Origins of Public High Schools: A Reexamination of the Beverly High School Controversy.* Madison: U of Wisconsin P, 1985.

Vinovskis, Maris A., David L. Angus, and Jeffrey E. Mirel. "Historical Development of Age Stratification in Schooling." *Education, Society, and Economic Opportunity.* Ed. Maris A. Vinovskis. New Haven, CT: Yale UP, 1995.

Violas, Paul C. "Jane Addams and the New Liberalism." *Roots of Crisis: American Education in the Twentieth Century.* Ed. Clarence J. Karier et al. Chicago: Rand McNally, 1973. 66–83.

———. "Progressive Social Philosophy: Charles Horton Cooley and Edward Alsworth Ross." *Roots of Crisis.* Ed. Clarence J. Karier, et al. Chicago: Rand McNally, 1973. 40–65.

Vitz, Paul C. *Censorship: Evidence of Bias in Our Children's Textbooks.* Ann Arbor: Servant Books, 1986.

von Braun, Wernher. "Statement." *Science and Education for National Defense Hearings before the Committee on Labor and Public Welfare of the U.S. Senate.* 85th Cong. 2nd sess. Washington, D.C.: GPO, January–March 1958. 64–84.

Wagoner, Jennings L. Jr. *Thomas Jefferson and the Education of a New Nation.* Bloomington, IN: Phi Delta Kappa, 1976.

———. "That Knowledge Most Useful to Us." *Thomas Jefferson and the Education of a Citizen.* Ed. James Gilreath. Washington, D.C.: Library of Congress, 1999. 115–133.

Walch, Timothy. *Parish School: American Catholic Education for Colonial Times to the Present.* New York: Crossroad Publishing, 1996.

Walker, Lawrence J. "Sex Differences in the Development of Moral Reasoning." *Child Development* 55 (1984): 677–691.

Warren, Donald R. *To Enforce Education: A History of the Founding Years of the United States Office of Education.* Detroit: Wayne State UP, 1974.

Washburne, Carleton. "The Philosophy of the Winnetka Curriculum." *Twenty-Sixth Yearbook of the National Society for the Study of Education: The Foundations and Technique of Curriculum Construction.* Bloomington, IL: Public School Publishing, 1926. 219–228.

Washington, Booker T. *Up from Slavery.* 1901. New York: Penguin, 1987.

Watras, Joseph. *Politics, Race, and Schools: Racial Integration, 1954–1994.* New York: Garland, 1997.

Watras, Joseph, and Edward St. John. "Choice and Schools: An Analysis of Free Market Financing and Educational Values." *Catholic Education: A Journal of Inquiry and Practice* 1.4 (1998): 400–413.

Weaver, John. "Tracking." *Historical Dictionary of American Education.* Ed. Richard J. Altenbaugh. Westport, CT: Greenwood Press, 1999.

Weber, Max. *The Protestant Ethic and the Spirit of Capitalism.* Trans. Talcott Parsons. New York: Scribner's Sons, 1958.

Webster, Noah. "American Glory Begins to Dawn." *On Being American: Selected Writings, 1783–1828.* Ed. Homer D. Babbidge, Jr. New York: Praeger, 1967. 17–26.

———. "A Dissertation Concerning the Influence of Language on Opinions, and of Opinions on Language." *A Collection of Essays and Fugitive Writings.* Delmar, NY: Scholars' Facsimiles & Reprints, 1977. 222–228.

———. *Dissertations on the English Language.* 1789. Menston, England: Scholar Press, 1967.

———. "On the Education of Youth in America." 1790. Ed. Frederick Rudolph. *Essays on Education in the Early Republic.* Cambridge, MA: Harvard UP, 1965. 41–77.

———. *A Grammatical Institute of the English Language.* Part II. 1784. Menston, England: Scholar Press, 1968.

Weinberg, Meyer. *Asian-American Education: Historical Background and Current Realities.* Mahwah, NJ: Lawrence Erlbaum, 1997.

Weintraub, Frederick J., and Alan Abeson. "New Education Policies for the Handicapped." *Public Policy and the Education of Exceptional Children.* Ed. Frederick. J. Weintraub et al. Reston, VA: Council for Exceptional Children, 1976. 7–13.

Weller, Jack E. *Yesterday's People.* Lexington, KY: U of Kentucky P, 1966.

Wells, Guy Fred. *Parish Education in Colonial Virginia.* New York: Teachers College Press, 1923.

Welter, Rush. *Popular Education and Democratic Thought in America.* New York: Columbia UP, 1962.

Wertenbaker, Thomas Jefferson. *The Puritan Oligarchy: The Founding of American Civilization.* New York: Charles Scribner's Sons, 1947.

Westerhoff, John H. III. *McGuffey and His Readers.* Nashville, TN: Parthenon Press, 1978.

Whipple, Guy M. "What Price Curriculum Making?" *School and Society* 31 (1930): 367–368.

White, Stephen. *Students, Scholars, and Parents: An Exploration of the Ideas behind the New Math and Other Curriculum Reform.* New York: Doubleday, 1966.

White, Trumbull. *Puerto Rico and Its People.* New York: Grosset & Dunlap, 1938.

Whyte, William H. Jr. *The Organization Man.* New York: Simon & Schuster, 1956.

Willard, Emma. "Geography for Beginners." *Pioneers of Women's Education in the United States.* Ed. Willystine Goodsell. New York: McGraw-Hill, 1931. 91–96.

———. "Plan for Improving Female Education." Ed. Willystine Goodsell. *Pioneers of Women's Education in the United States.* New York: McGraw-Hill, 1931. 45–81.

Williams v. Board of Education of the County of Kanawha, 388 F. Supp. 93, 1975.

Willig, Ann C. "A Meta Analysis of Selected Studies on the Effectiveness of Bilingual Education." *Review of Educational Research* 55.3 (1985): 269–318.

Willis, George, et al. *The American Curriculum: A Documentary History.* Westport, CT: Praeger, 1994.

Wirth, Arthur G. *John Dewey as Educator (1894–1904).* New York: Wiley, 1966.

Wist, Benjamin O. *A Century of Public Education in Hawaii.* Honolulu: Hawaii Educational Review, 1940.

Woodward, C. Vann. *The Strange Career of Jim Crow.* 2nd ed. New York: Oxford UP, 1966.

Woodward, Calvin M. *The Manual Training School.* 1887. New York: Arno Press, 1969.

Woody, Thomas. "Historical Sketch of Activism." *The Thirty-Third Yearbook of the National Society for the Study of Education: The Activity Movement.* Ed. Guy Montrose Whipple. Bloomington, IL: Public School Publishing, 1934. 9–44.

———. *A History of Women's Education in the United States.* Vol. I. New York: Science Press, 1929.

Wooten, William. *SMSG: The Making of a Curriculum.* New Haven, CT: Yale UP, 1965.

Yezierska, Anzia. "Children of Loneliness." *The Work of Teachers in America.* Ed. Rosetta Marantz Cohen and Samuel Scheer. Mahwah: Lawrence Erlbaum, 1997. 223–235.

Zacharias, Jerrold R., and Stephen White. "The Requirements for Major Curriculum Revision." *New Curricula.* Ed. Robert W. Heath. New York: Harper & Row, 1964. 68–81.

Zigler, Edward, and Susan Muenchow. *Head Start.* New York: Basic, 1992.

Zilversmit, Arthur. *Changing Schools: Progressive Education Theory and Practice, 1930–1960.* Chicago: U of Chicago P, 1993.

INDEX

Ability grouping, 164–165, 261, 262–268, 299–300
Accelerated Schools Project, 318
Achievement tests, 362–373
Activity movement, 129–133, 192–194, 274, 299
Adams, John, 42
Adams, John Quincy, 56
Addams, Jane, 127–128, 132, 133, 293–294
Advocacy groups
  for bilingual education, 337–348
  for children with disabilities, 328–337, 347–348
  effectiveness of, 347–348, 356–357
  for women, 348–356
African Americans. *See* Blacks
Alford, John W., 83
Allen, Charles H., 99
American Civil Liberties Union (ACLU), 332
American Council of Education, 214
American Educational Research Association (AERA), 314
American Federation of Teachers (AFT), 180, 375
American Freedmen's Union Commission (AFUC), 83
American Historical Association (AHA), 183–190
American Home Economics Association (AHEA), 152
American Institute for Research (AIR), 344–345
American Mathematical Society (AMS), 251
American Social Science Association, 161
American Tract Society (ATS), 83
American Youth Commission (AYC), 214, 222, 226, 238–239
Angus, David L., 142–143, 148, 268
Apperception, 137
Armstrong, Orlen K., 182
Armstrong, Richard, 218
Armstrong, Samuel Chapman, 111, 122–123, 125, 218
Association for Retarded Citizens (ARC), 329–330, 332–335, 336
Association for Supervision and Curriculum Development (ASCD), 291, 293
Atlanta Compromise, 123–124
Auerbach, Elsa Roberts, 354
Aydelott, Benjamin P., 70
Ayres, Leonard, 134–135, 151, 163

Bagley, William, 163–164, 165, 200
Bailyn, Bernard, 17–18
Bane, Lita, 153–154
Banks, James, 287–289
Baratz, Joan, 313
Baratz, Stephen, 313
Barnard, Henry, 88
Barnes, Harry Elmer, 185
Batavia system, 134, 135
Beard, Charles, 55–56, 184–186, 190
Beatty, Barbara, 95–98
Beauregard, P. G. T., 85
Beecher, Catharine, 58–59, 61–62, 66, 67
Beecher, Lyman, 68
Belenky, Mary, 352, 354, 355
Bell, Andrew, 36
Bell, Paul W., 339
Bell, Terrell, 362, 364
Bellah, Robert N., 361
Bennett, William J., 347, 364, 365, 369
Bestor, Arthur, 236, 238
Bible education, 64–65, 69–72, 77, 103
Bilingual education, 163–164, 225–226, 281, 337–348
Binet, Alfred, 164
Blacks. *See also* Civil rights movement; Integration; Segregation
  Black English and, 288, 345–346
  cultural perspective of, 41
  industrial training and, 122–123, 124–127
  in Reconstruction period, 80–87
  social studies education and, 161–162
  War on Poverty and, 299–300, 303–304
Blow, Susan, 95–96, 97
Bobbitt, Franklin, 149–150, 156, 195, 197
Bode, Boyd, 150, 156–157, 170, 176, 193, 194–195

Bond, Horace Mann, 165
Borders, William, 374
Bowles, Samuel, 267
Brink, William G., 235
Brookings, Robert S., 204
Brosnahan, Timothy, 105–106
Broudy, Harry S., 264–265
Brown v. Board of Education, 242–243, 246, 278, 333
Bruner, Jerome, 256–258, 259
Bryk, Anthony, 356
Bullard, Charles, 68
Bunker, Frank Forest, 135
Bureau of Education for the Handicapped (BEH), 331, 335
Burnett, Joe, 264–265
Bush, George, 369
Bush, Vannevar, 245
Business education, 147, 154–155
Busing, 275–279
Butchart, Ronald, 83
Butler, Nicholas Murray, 101, 120, 121

Calkins, N. A., 91
Calvinism, 64, 68
Cambridge Conference, 251
Campbell, Doak, 197–199, 201
Camus, Albert, xiii
Cannell, John Jacob, 367–368
Cardinal Principles Report, *See* National Education Association, Commission on the Reorganization of Secondary Education
Carmichael, Stokely, 279–280
Carter, Jimmy, 346, 362
Caswell, Hollis, 197–199, 201
Catholic education
  civil rights movement and, 282–283
  compulsory attendance laws and, 116
  diversity and, 374–375
  Elementary and Secondary Education Act and, 303
  formation of Catholic schools, 102–106
  funding of, 70–72
  gender and, 146–147, 171–175, 356
  by missionaries, 2–8, 18
  monitorial method in, 36–37
  National Defense Education Act (NDEA) and, 247
Catholic Educational Association (CEA), 172, 173
Cebollero, Pedro, 224–225
Chapin, Mildred, 153–154
Charter for the Social Sciences, A (Beard), 184–185, 188
Charters, W. W., 149, 156–157, 170, 176
Charter schools, 375–379
Chase, Salmon P., 80–81
Chidsey, Alan Lake, 189–190
Child, Lydia Maria, 83
Children with disabilities, 233, 327–337, 347–348
Child-study movement, 136, 139
Chinese Americans
  bilingual education and, 281, 342, 345
  English instruction and, 215–217
Chiong, Jane Ayers, 294
Christianity. *See also* Catholic education
  Christian day schools, 106–107, 281–282
  Church of England and, 9, 10, 14–15
  colonial missionaries and, 2, 3–8, 18
  common schools and, 52, 64, 68–70
  Dutch Reform Church and, 8–10, 18
  Puritans and, 10–12, 16, 18
  religious tolerance and, 12–14
Chubb, John E., 373–374
Civil Rights Act of 1875, 86
Civil Rights Act of 1964, 271, 273, 281, 312, 325, 342
Civil rights movement, 249, 270–285, 320
  bilingual education and, 342–344
  busing and, 275–279
  Catholic schools and, 282–283
  changes in 1960s, 272–283
  Christian day schools and, 281–282
  individually guided education (IGE) and, 271, 284–285
  magnet schools and, 271, 285–286, 294
  minority resistance to, 279–281
  multicultural studies and, 271, 287–294
  War on Poverty and, 303–304
  women's rights and, 348–349
Clark, Kenneth, 243
Classroom materials. *See also* Textbooks
  in compensatory education, 307, 313
Clinton, William J., 369, 376, 380
Coeducation, 90, 175, 356
Cohen, David K., 182, 267–268
Colby, Ann, 351–352
Coleman, James S., 276–277, 312
College of William and Mary, 38, 41

Colleges
  articulation between high school and, 145–162
  gap between elementary schools and, 112, 172
  Latin and Greek instruction and, 41–45
  preparation for, 112, 113, 266
Collings, Ellsworth, 166–168, 169
Colonial education, 1–20
  of Christian missionaries, 2, 3–8, 18
  of Dutch colonists, 8–10, 19
  influence on twentieth-century education, 16–18
  of Puritans, 10–12, 16, 18
  religious tolerance and, 12–14
  resistance to, 14–16
Columbus, Christopher, 2, 4
Combe, George, 64
Comenius, John Amos, 91
Common schools, 51–78, 112, 135
  curriculum changes and, 63–67
  ideology and, 67–70
  loss of momentum, 75–77
  opposition to, 72–75
  popular press and, 57–58, 59, 61, 66, 67
  religious groups and, 70–72
  social changes and, 52–58, 77
  teacher training and, 58–63
  women and, 58–63, 66–70
Community action programs (CAPs), 307–308
Compensatory education, 274–275, 298, 302–315, 317–318, 324–325
Compulsory school attendance laws, 115–116, 134–135, 142
Conant, James, 260–264, 299–300
Congress of Racial Equality (CORE), 279
Coolidge, Calvin, 175
Corporal punishment, 61
Council for Exceptional Children (CEC), 328, 329, 330–331, 332, 335, 336
Council of Learned Societies in Education (CLSE), xi–xii
Council of the Great City Schools (CGCS), 336
Counts, George, 121, 153, 170–171, 180–181, 196
Cranston, Alan, 342
Crockett, Davy, 56
Cubberly, Elwood P., 16, 155, 163–164
Cultural deprivation, 324
Cultural perspective, 39–41
Culture of poverty, 297–326
  compensatory education and, 274–275, 298, 302–315, 317–318, 324–325
  nature of, 298, 301–302, 319–323
  Project Head Start and, 298, 307–311, 313, 316–317
  urban schools and, 299–301
  War on Poverty and, 274, 298, 302–309, 311, 315–316, 324–325
Curriculum. *See also* Advocacy groups; Textbooks
  common school, 63–67
  consolidation of, 112–114
  democracy in construction of, 129–133, 191–194
  diversified, 133–149
  Elementary and Secondary Education Act and, 304–309
  Great Depression and, 186–187, 197–201
  history, 186–187
  including community members in planning of, 197–199
  individually guided education (IGE) and, 271, 284–285, 294
  industrial training and, 122–129, 132, 141–143
  integration of schools and, 284–285
  magnet schools and, 271, 285–286, 294, 378–379
  mathematics, 250–253, 265–266
  meanings of, xi
  needs of students and, 119, 122–123, 146, 149–150, 194–197, 232–239
  organized curriculum building, 190–191, 199–201, 207–208
  post-World War II improvements in, 245–262
  racial integration and, 271, 273–277
  science and psychology in, 93–95
  War on Poverty and, 304–309
  for women's education, 350–354
Curry, Jabez L. M., 86–88

Daley, Richard, 275
Damon, William, 351–352
Darling, Noyes, 42
De Beauvoir, Simone, 348, 355
DeGarmo, Charles, 137
Della-Vos, M. Victor, 99

Democracy
curriculum and, 129–133, 191–194
pluralism versus, 271, 293
in Puerto Rico, 222–226
after World War II, 230–232
Desegregation of schools. *See* Integration
DeVito, Joseph A., 379
Dewey, John, 128–133, 137, 142, 148, 165, 192–193, 194, 234, 256, 274, 293, 350
Dimond, Paul R., 334–335
Diversity
Catholic education and, 374–375
common schools and, 77
of curriculum, 133–149
John Dewey and, 133
meanings of, xi
and multicultural studies, 271, 287–294, 379–381
Dock, Christopher, 13–14, 19
Dole, Daniel, 218
Doty, Duane, 90
Dresslar, Fletcher, 118
Du Bois, W. E. B., 82, 126–127
Dunn, Arthur William, 161

Eaton, John, 88
Economic Opportunity Act of 1964, 307–308
Educational psychology, 138–142
Education for All American Youth, 231–232
Education for All Handicapped Children Act (1975; PL 94-142), 335–337
Education for the Handicapped Act (1970), 331
Education Improvement Program (EIP), 309
Eight-Year Study, 190–191, 207–208, 258–260
Eisenhower, Dwight D., 244, 246, 260
Elementary and Secondary Education Act of 1965 (ESEA), 249, 274, 303, 304–309, 314, 315–316, 324–325, 330–331, 340–341, 344
Elementary school
consolidation of curriculum, 112–114
science instruction in, 249–250
World War II impact on, 226–232
Eliot, Charles W., 112, 116, 119, 122, 125, 147, 165
Elkins, Deborah, 305–307
Ellul, Jacques, 360–361
English as a second language (ESL), 341, 343
English instruction, 214–226. *See also* Bilingual education
Black English and, 288, 345–346
Chinese Americans and, 215–217
English Standard school system, 217–220, 222
Japanese students in Hawaii and, 219–222
in Puerto Rico, 223–226
Epstein, Noel, 346
Equal opportunity
bilingual education and, 344–345
in high school education, 262–264
Equal Rights Amendment (ERA), 349
Erickson, Kai, 321–322
Ethnicity/race. *See also* Immigration; Integration; Multicultural studies; Segregation; *specific ethnic groups*
bilingual education and, 163–164, 225–226, 281, 337–348
controversy regarding multiracial children, 294
Excellence movement, 361–379, 382
Exceptional students, 233–234, 261, 265, 285–286, 328–337

Farrar, Eleanor, 267–268
Fernandez-Vanga, Epifanio, 224
Fife, Brian, 286
Finn, Chester, 364, 365, 369
Ford, Gerald, 335
Franciscans, 4–5
Franklin, Benjamin, 22, 23, 24–29, 31, 32, 42, 45
Frederick, Catherine, 152
Freedmen's Aid Society, 81, 84
Freedmen's Bureau, 81–82, 83–84, 85, 87, 122
Free School Society, 34–35
Freire, Paulo, 352–354
Friedan, Betty, 348, 349
Friend, Richard A., 379
Froebel, Friedrich, 95, 96, 97–98, 138

Gans, Herbert, 320–321, 322–323
Garvin, Jean, 331–332
Gay and lesbian students, 379–381
Gender. *See also* Women
and Catholic education, 146–147, 171–175, 356
women's education advocates and, 348–356

Gender bias, 150–157
business education and, 154–155
gender segregation and, 150–157
home economics movement and, 151–154
intelligence testing and, 164–165
science education and, 156–157
social studies and, 158–162
Gibbons, Cardinal, 105, 173
Gifted students, 233–234, 261, 265, 285–286
Gilligan, Carol, 349, 352, 354–355
Gintis, Herbert, 267
Goetz, Rachel Marshall, 186–187, 189, 190
Goodlad, John, 255, 265, 284–285
Goodsell, Willystine, 157
Graded schools, 65–66, 86–87
Grant, Ulysses S., 86
Great Cities Program for School Improvement, 299, 301
Great Depression, 177–209
curriculum planning and, 186–187, 197–201
impact on schools, 178–180
rebuilding schools after, 211–215
social reform and, 190–194, 201–208
social studies and, 182–190
students' needs and, 194–197
teachers and, 179–182, 207–208
Greek instruction, 27–28, 31, 41–45, 74, 89, 92–93, 95, 100, 123, 227
Greeley, Horace, 73
Green, Robert L., 277
Greene, Maxine, 355
Green v. County School Board of New Kent County, 275, 278
Gutierrez, Jose Angel, 341–342

Hall, G. Stanley, 98, 136, 138–139, 157
Hamilton, Charles, 279–280
Hampel, Robert, 238–239
Hampton Normal and Agricultural Institute, 122–123, 125, 160, 161, 162, 218
Handlin, Oscar, 53–54
Harrington, Michael, 301–302, 319
Harris, William Torrey, 76, 80, 88–99, 101, 102, 103, 105, 107–108, 112, 113, 116, 119, 122, 125, 128–129, 136, 142–143
Hayakawa, S. I., 346–347
Hayes, Rutherford B., 84
Head Start, 298, 307–311, 313, 316–317
Hegel, Georg Wilhelm Friedrich, 89
Herbart, Johann Friedrich, 136–137
Higham, John, 175–176, 214
Higher Horizons (New York), 301, 309
High school, 65, 73–74, 75–76, 90
articulation between college and, 145–162
business education in, 155
Catholic, 146–147, 171–175
college preparation and, 112, 113, 266
Eight-Year Study of, 190–191, 207–208, 258–260
equal opportunity and, 262–264
growth of, 180, 191
home economics and, 153
rise of comprehensive, 148, 261–264
science instruction in, 249–250
World War II impact on, 226–232
Hispanic Americans
bilingual education and, 337–348
bilingual teachers and, 163–164
democracy in Puerto Rico, 222–226
New Deal and, 178, 201–203
standardized testing and, 371–373
History education, 182–190
Holland, Peter, 356
Home economics movement, 146, 151–154, 157
Horace Mann School (Boston), 100–101
Horn, Ernest, 193
Howard, Oliver Otis, 82
Hughes, John, 71
Hull House, 127–128, 132, 293–294

Immigration, 53–54, 106–107, 115–118
Chinese, 216, 281
compulsory school attendance and, 134–135
settlement house movement and, 127–128, 132
Individual educational plan (IEP), 336
Individualized instruction, 261
Individually guided education (IGE), 271, 284–285, 294
Industrialism, 54–55, 114–116
Industrial training, 122–129, 132, 141–143. *See also* Vocational education
Institute for Government Research, 204–205
Institute for the Development of Educational Activities (/I/D/E/A/), 284–285
Integration, 242–245, 270–282
busing and, 275–279, 295
concept of, xiii
curriculum and, 284–285

Integration *(continued)*
multicultural studies and, 287–294
poverty and, 299–300
Intelligence testing, 164–165, 234, 312
International Reading Association (IRA), 370–371
Ireland, John, 104–105

Jackson, Andrew, xiii, 34, 56
Jefferson, Thomas, xiii, 8, 22, 23, 37–41, 44, 45, 46, 49, 55
Jenkinson, Edward, 291
Jensen, Arthur, 312
Jesuits, 5, 7, 105–106
Jewish education, 107, 321
Johnson, Andrew, 87, 88
Johnson, Lyndon B., 245, 273, 275, 298, 303–304, 309, 310, 311–312, 331, 340
Jones, George, 68
Jones, Thomas Jesse, xiv, 125, 161–162, 205–207
Junior high school, 135–136, 148

Kanawha County, West Virginia textbook controversy, 271, 281–293
Karier, Clarence J., 133
Katz, Irwin, 313
Katz, Michael B., 73–75
Kennedy, Edward, 342
Kennedy, John F., 272–273, 302–303, 308
Kepner, Tyler, 189
Keyes v. School District No. 1, Denver, Colorado, 276, 278–279
Keyser, Mary, 127
Kilpatrick, William Heard, 165–166, 168–169, 170, 193, 195
Kindergarten movement, 80, 92, 95–98, 138
King, John B., 340
King, Martin Luther, Jr., 272–273, 278, 279–280, 303–304
Kliebard, Herbert, 44–45, 181–182, 190
Kline, Morris, 255–256
Kohlberg, Lawrence, 349, 354–355
Kotinsky, Ruth, 195–196
Ku Klux Klan, 173, 175–176

Ladies Society for the Promotion of Education in the West, 62
Lancaster, Joseph, 8, 14, 22, 34–37
Latimer, John, 264
Latin instruction, 27–28, 31, 41–45, 74, 89, 92–93, 95, 100, 123, 139, 171, 227
Lau v. Nichols, 342, 345
Leadership training, 37–39
Lee, Valerie, 356
Leloudis, James, 87
Levin, Harry, 313, 317–318
Lewis, James, 290
Lewis, Oscar, 319, 322
Lewis, Samuel, 58, 76, 77
Liberal education, diversified curriculum and, 133–149
Lincoln, Abraham, 82
Low, Victor, 215–217
Lutheran schools, 106–107
Lyon, Mary, 59, 66–67

Madison, James, 38
Magnet schools, 271, 285–286, 294, 378–379
Mann, Horace, 56–57, 61, 63–64, 71–72, 73, 75, 76
Manual training method, 98–102, 218
Maritain, Jacques, 351
Marshall, Leon, 186–187, 189, 190
Marshner, Connought Coyne, 291
Martin, Jane Roland, 355
Mathematics, post-World War II changes in, 250–253, 265–266
Mathematics Association of America (MAA), 251, 254
Mather, Cotton, 11–12
McDonald, Forrest, 23–24
McGovern, George, 276
McGuffey, William Holmes, 68–69
McKenzie, Hugh, 331–332
McKinley, William, 125
McLaren, Peter, 354
McMaster, James A., 103
McMurry, Charles, 137–138
McMurry, Frank, 137
Media. *See* Popular press
Mednick, Martha, 355
Mehl, Bernard, 12, 382
Military preparedness, 234
Milliken v. Bradley I, 274, 276, 279, 280
Milliken v. Bradley II, 274
Mills v. Board of Education of the District of Columbia, 333–334
Mirel, Jeffrey E., 142–143, 148, 268

Missionary teachers
in colonial period, 2–8, 18
in Reconstruction, 81, 83
Model Cities Demonstration Project, 280–281, 284, 285, 324
Moe, Terry M., 373–374
Moffett, James, 292
Moore, Alice, 289–290, 292, 293
Moral education, 24–37
Bible and, 64–65, 69–72, 77, 103
Benjamin Franklin and, 22, 23, 24–29
gender and, 349–352
Thomas Jefferson and, 22, 37–41
and Kanawha County, West Virginia textbook controversy, 271, 281–293
Joseph Lancaster and, 22, 34–37
Benjamin Rush and, 22, 29–30
Noah Webster and, 22, 30–34
Mosier, Richard, 68–69
Moynihan, Daniel P., 311–312, 314
Muckrakers, 116–119
Multicultural studies, 271, 287–294, 379–381
Munoz Marin, Luis, 223, 224, 225–226

National Assessment of Educational Progress (NAEP), 366–367
National Association for Multicultural Education (NAME), 381
National Association for the Advancement of Colored People (NAACP), 126, 243–244, 272, 273, 275–276, 279–280, 287, 327–329, 334, 348–349, 356–357
National Commission on Excellence in Education (NCEE), 362–371
National Council for the Accreditation of Teacher Education (NCATE), xii
National Council for the Social Studies (NCSS), 188
National Council of Teachers of English (NCTE), 193–194
National Defense Education Act (NDEA), 247–249, 261, 265, 299
National Education Association (NEA), 88, 91–93, 104–105, 141, 180
bilingual education and, 338–339
Commission on the Reorganization of Secondary Education (CRSE), 110, 114, 122, 134, 145–162, 175
Committee of Fifteen, 113–114, 122, 125, 139, 142
Committee of Ten, 110, 112–113, 114, 122, 125, 133–134, 136, 139, 142, 145–146, 147, 158, 182–183, 259
Educational Policies Commission (EPC), 212–214, 227–228, 230–233, 233, 236, 238
Teacher Rights Division, 290–291
National Education Goals Panel, 369–370
National Institute of Education (NIE), 298, 314
National Science Foundation (NSF), 245, 248, 249, 251, 253
National Society for the Promotion of Vocational Education, 141
National Society for the Study of Education (NSSE), 233–234, 235, 237
National Teachers Exam, 244–245
National Urban League, 287
Nation at Risk, A, 362–364, 366, 367, 368
Nation Still at Risk, A, 372–373
Native Americans
bilingual education and, 339, 340, 342
cultural perspective of, 41
industrial training and, 122–123
missionaries and, 2–8
New Deal and, 178, 203–207
Puritans and, 10
social studies education and, 161–162
New Deal, 178, 201–207
New Futures, 318
Newlon, Jesse, 169–170
New math, 250–253, 265–266
Nixon, Richard M., 249, 271, 275, 276, 298, 314
Noddings, Nel, 351–352, 355
Normal schools, 52, 57–63, 64–65, 69, 70, 76–77, 99, 219
Novick, Peter, 188, 190

Oakes, Jeannie, 265–267
Office of Economic Opportunity (OEO), 303, 304, 308, 310
Open enrollment policy, 283
Organized curriculum making, 197–199, 201
Otero-Warren, Nina, 201–202, 229

PARC v. Commonwealth, 333, 334–335
Parker, Francis, 136, 137
Peabody, Elizabeth, 96–97
Peabody Fund, 84–87
Pedroza, Anna, 372

Penn, William, 12–13
Perkinson, Henry, 148
Perpich, Rudy, 375
Pestalozzi, Johann Heinrich, 91
Pettigrew, Thomas F., 277
Philbrick, John D., 65
Phrenology, 64
Physical education, 228–229, 232
Physical Science Study Committee (PSSC), 249–250, 254, 255, 257, 259
Piaget, Jean, 257
Picket, Albert, 58, 65, 76–77
Pierce, Edward L., 81
Pierce, Walter, 173
Pierce v. Society of Sisters, 173, 221
Pius XI, Pope, 173–175
Plato, 10
Playgrounds, 118
Plessy v. Ferguson, 243
Pochmann, Henry, 143
Popular press
  common schools and, 57–58, 59, 61, 66, 67
  muckraker journalism and, 116–119
  progressive education and, 237
  public opinion and, 200–201
  science education and, 246
Pottinger, J. Stanley, 341–342
Poverty. *See* War on Poverty
Powell, Arthur G., 267–268
Prado, Edward C., 371–372
Pratt, Caroline, 169
Progressive education, 132–133, 237
Progressive Education Association (PEA), 146, 165–166, 169, 180–181, 190–191, 195, 236–237, 258
Progressive Era, 116–119
Project Head Start, 298, 307–311, 313, 316–317
Project method, 166–171, 193, 195
Prosser, Charles, 236
Psychology, education and, 94–95, 101, 138–142
Puerto Rico, 222–226
Purcell, John Baptist, 70, 72
Puritans, 10–12, 16, 18

Quakers, 12–14, 36

Rabinowitz, Howard, 85
Race. *See* Ethnicity/race
Raymond, William G., 99
Reagan, Ronald, 249, 286, 316, 362, 364, 373
Reconstruction, 79–88
Reissman, Frank, 300–301
Religious schools, 102–107. *See also* Catholic education
  Christian day schools, 281–282
  Jewish education, 107, 321
Rice, Joseph Mayer, 116, 119, 120, 121
Richards, Ellen, 151–152
Riessman, Frank, 319
Riis, Jacob, 116–118, 120, 121, 122
Rofes, Eric, 380
Rommel, Joseph, 283
Roosevelt, Franklin D., 201, 222–223, 226, 245
Roosevelt, Theodore, 116
Rossell, Christine, 286
Royaumont conference (1958), 254
Rugg, Harold, 181–182, 187
Rush, Benjamin, 22, 23, 29–30, 31, 39, 45, 49–50
Ryan, Janice, 331–332
Ryan, William, 324–325

Salisbury, Leo H., 339–340
San Antonio Independent School District v. Rodriguez, 334
Satolli, Francesco, 105
School choice, 373–379
School governance, 118, 120–121, 200–201
School Mathematics Study Group (SMSG), 251–254, 255, 257, 259–260
Science
  in curriculum, 93–95, 156–157, 165–168, 175–176
  John Dewey and, 131
  gender bias in, 156–157
  mental measurement movement, 164–165
  post-World War II changes in instruction, 245–247, 249–250, 265–266
  role in curriculum development, 93–95, 146–147
  scientific surveys and, 162–164
Sears, Barnas, 85–86
Sears, James, 379–380
Second Vatican Council, 356
Secular humanism, 289, 292–293
Segregation
  and ability grouping, 265–266
  in bilingual programs, 346

in Black education, 213–214, 244–245, 272–283
in Chinese American education, 215–217
compensatory education and, 324–325
concept of, xiii
gender, 151–157
of industrial training, 124–128
in Reconstruction era, 85
Selden, Frank Henry, 101–102
Sesame Street, 310–311
Settlement house movement, 127–128, 132
Seward, William, 70–71
Sewell, Brice H., 202, 203
Shanker, Albert, 375
Shepard, Lorrie, 367–368, 369–370
Shields, Thomas Edward, 172–173
Slade, William, 62
Sluys, A., 101
Smith, B. Othanel, 264–265
Snedden, David, 153
Snyder, C. B. J., 117
Social bias. *See also* Gender bias; Integration; Segregation
diversified curricula and, 142–143, 148
mental measurement movement and, 164–165
scientific surveys and, 162–164
social studies and, 158–162
Social reform
Great Depression and, 190–194, 201–208
Hispanic education and, 201–203
Native American education and, 203–207
organized curriculum and, 199–201
reorganization of schools and, 190–194
Social studies education, 146, 147, 158–162, 181–190
Solomon, Patrick, 323
Southern Christian Leadership Conference (SCLC), 272
Soviet Union, former
Red Scare, 175
and Sputnik crisis in U.S., 246, 260
Spencer, Herbert, 93–94
Spring, Joel, 211–212, 214, 238
Sputnik, 246, 260
Standardized tests
achievement, 362–373
intelligence, 164–165, 234, 312
Starr, Ellen, 127
Stowe, Calvin, 60–61, 62, 64–65, 69–70
Strayer, George, 163–164
Student Nonviolent Coordinating Committee (SNCC), 279
Stuyvesant, Peter, 9
Sumner, Charles, 86
Superintendents, 200–201
Swint, Henry Lee, 82

Taba, Hilda, 305–307
Talbot, Marion, 152
Taylor, Frederick W., 150, 200–201
Teachers
ability grouping and, 266–267
bilingual, 163–164
culture of poverty and, 300–301, 306–307
in the Great Depression, 179–182, 207–208
school segregation and, 244–245
training of, 58–63, 64–65, 69, 70, 76–77, 99, 219
Textbooks
five fields of knowledge and, 92–95
history, 186–187
and Kanawha County, West Virginia textbook controversy, 271, 281–293
kindergarten movement and, 95–98
manual training method and, 98–102
multicultural studies and, 287–294
role of, 90–93
science, 253
social problems and, 181–182
Thayer, V. T., 195–196
Third Plenary Council (1884), 104–106, 172–173
Thompson, Eleanor Wolf, 59
Thorndike, Edward Lee, 139–143, 157, 165
Thurmond, Strom, 243, 247
Tocqueville, Alexis de, 48–49
Toliver, James, 287
Tracking, 164–165, 261, 262–268, 299–300
Trimmer, Sarah, 36
Truman, Harry, 225
Trybom, J. H., 101
Tugwell, Rexford Guy, 222–223
Tuition tax credits, 375
Turner, Frederick Jackson, 18
Tuskegee Institute, 124–127
Tyler, Ralph, 258–260

U.S. Bureau of Indian Affairs, 339, 340, 342
U.S. Commission on Civil Rights, 273–274, 277, 309–310, 342–344, 346

U.S. Constitution, 22, 23–24, 37
U.S. Department of Education, 284, 347, 364, 365, 368
U.S. Department of Health, Education, and Welfare (HEW), 245, 247, 270–271, 273, 274, 275–277, 280, 304, 312, 330, 335, 341, 342. *See also* U.S. Office of Education
U.S. Department of Housing and Urban Development (HUD), 280, 324
U.S. Office of Education (USOE), 226, 227, 228, 230, 236, 248, 273, 304–305, 324, 331, 344–345, 378
U.S. Supreme Court
  bilingual education and, 342, 345
  integration of schools and, 242–245, 246, 270–271, 272, 275, 277, 278–279, 281, 295
University of Chicago, 128
University of Illinois Committee on School Mathematics (UICSM), 250–251, 254
University of Virginia, 40–41, 44
Urbanization, 54–55, 115
Ursuline Sisters, 7–8

Valentine, Charles, 322–323
Values
  clarification of, 289–290
  conflict of, 288–289
  public schools and, 107–108
Vinovskis, Maris, 74–75
Violas, Paul, 132
Vitz, Paul C., 292
Vocational education, 135–136, 141–143, 236. *See also* Industrial training
  American Youth Commission (AYC) and, 214, 222, 226, 238–239
  Educational Policies Commission (EPC) and, 213
  in Hawaiian schools, 218
  in high schools, 264, 266
  home economics, 151–154, 157
von Braun, Wernher, 246–247
Vouchers, 375

Walker, Lawrence, 354–355
Wallerstein, Nina, 354
War on Poverty, 274, 298, 302–309, 311, 315–316, 324–325
Wartime Handbook for Education (NEA), 227–228, 230
Washburne, Carlton, 195
Washington, Booker T., xiv, 111, 123–127
Washington, George, 42, 55
Weber, Max, 28–29
Webster, Noah, 22, 23, 30–34, 45–46, 49–50
Weller, Jack, 321
Western Literary Institute and College of Professional Teachers, 57–58, 62, 64–65, 69, 70, 76–77
West India Company, 8–9
What the High Schools Ought to Teach, 226–227
What Works, 364–365
Whipple, Guy, 199–200
Wiley, Calvin, 57
Willard, Emma Hart, 22, 46–48, 66
Willis, Paul, 267, 323
Winthrop, John, 10
Women. *See also* Gender; Gender bias
  advocacy groups for, 348–356
  attitudes toward education of, 45–49
  common schools and, 58–63, 66–70
  employment of, 115, 151, 153–154
  as missionaries, 62–63
  training as teachers, 58–63
Women's seminaries, 22, 47–48, 66–67
Woodward, C. Vann, 85
Woodward, Calvin M., 99–100, 102
Woodworth, R. S., 139–140
World War II
  Chinese Americans and, 215
  curriculum improvements following, 245–262
  democracy following, 230–232
  federal government influence on education and, 229–230
  Hawaii and, 217, 219–222
  influence on U.S. schools, 226–232

Yale College, 22, 32, 42–45
Yezeirska, Anzia, xiii
Young, Ella Flagg, 180

Zacharias, Jerrold R., 249–250, 254
Zachry, Caroline, 195–196
Zakrsewska, Marie E., 118